OXFORD **READERS**

Classical Philosophy

Edited by Terence Irwin

OXFORD
UNIVERSITY PRESS

OXFORD
UNIVERSITY PRESS

Great Clarendon Street, Oxford OX2 6DP

Oxford University Press is a department of the University of Oxford.
It furthers the University's objective of excellence in research, scholarship,
and education by publishing worldwide in

Oxford New York

Athens Auckland Bangkok Bogotá Buenos Aires Calcutta
Cape Town Chennai Dar es Salaam Delhi Florence Hong Kong Istanbul
Karachi Kuala Lumpur Madrid Melbourne Mexico City Mumbai
Nairobi Paris São Paulo Singapore Taipei Tokyo Toronto Warsaw

with associated companies in Berlin Ibadan

Oxford is a registered trade mark of Oxford University Press
in the UK and in certain other countries

Published in the United States
by Oxford University Press Inc., New York

British Library Cataloguing in Publication Data

Data available

Library of Congress Cataloging in Publication Data

Data available

ISBN 0–19–289253–3

10 9 8 7 6 5 4 3 2 1

Typeset in Dante
by Cambrian Typesetters, Frimley, Surrey

Printed in Great Britain
on acid-free paper by
Biddles Ltd.
Guildford and King's Lynn

Contents

Classical Philosophy

I: Introduction

The purpose of this book

[1] This book seeks to introduce some of the main philosophical questions raised by the Greek philosophers. Since it is intended for readers who are at an early stage of their acquaintance with philosophy, I try, both in texts and in comments, to explain the questions, and to connect them with questions raised by philosophers in other historical periods, including our own.

In speaking of 'Greek philosophy', or 'ancient philosophy', I refer to the philosophy of Classical (Greek and Roman) antiquity, expressed primarily in the Greek language, from about 550 BC to about AD 550. 'Greek' is not used in an ethnic or geographical sense. Though many of the writers quoted wrote in Latin, almost all of them were familiar with Greek, and for all of them philosophical thinking was conducted in Greek or in a Latin philosophical vocabulary derived from Greek philosophy.[1]

The history of philosophy in Classical antiquity covers over 1100 years. A short selection from the large body of philosophical literature that survives from this period is bound to leave out important philosophical developments. This book tries to introduce ancient philosophy through some of the issues that are most likely to interest readers who are new to this fundamental period in the history of thought.

The chapters of this book present the major questions and their treatment by different philosophers. The organization is primarily topical, rather than historical. There are already several anthologies and accounts of ancient philosophy presented in historical order; it may be useful to offer an alternative.

Within each chapter, the organization is mainly, but not exclusively, historical. In some cases, it is helpful to study history backwards. Later Greek philosophers reflect on their predecessors, and some of the questions that they raise may also help us to ask the right questions about earlier philosophers. In studying the Presocratic philosophers, for instance, we need some grasp of the philosophical presuppositions that underlie Plato's and Aristotle's attitude to their predecessors.

Central questions in philosophy are not always clearly recognized by the philosophers who raise them. Aristotle often remarks that the Presocratics have not clearly set out a problem that needs a full discussion. Moreover, some questions that we recognize as central—about the foundations of knowledge,

---

[1] The one person who did not know Greek well is Augustine; the extent of his knowledge of Greek is disputed.

or about free will, for instance—are first clearly identified and discussed by the Hellenistic philosophers. (See **108**, **351**.) This does not mean earlier philosophers have nothing relevant to say about them; but we often need to approach what they say in the light of questions that are explicitly asked only by their successors.

No one way of presenting a short selection of texts is ideal. To gain the most benefit from the texts presented in this book, the reader ought to reflect on them in both topical and historical order. This introduction should make it easier to follow the historical sequence, especially if one uses it in conjunction with the Index of Authors and Texts. Readers will gain far more from this book if they pursue the cross-references, and especially if they use the Index of Authors and Texts to read through the extracts from each of the philosophers represented here. Though the extracts from Plato's *Republic* (for instance) are scattered through several chapters, readers can read them in Plato's order if they turn to the Index of Texts.

This book is not a history of ancient philosophy, and it does not give the proper historical context for all the texts quoted in the following chapters. Even a brief historical introduction to all these writers would be too long to fit into this book.

According to the divisions of philosophy usually recognized now, Chapters 2–7 cover some connected issues in natural philosophy, metaphysics, and epistemology. Chapters 8–9 discuss questions about the soul and free will; answers to these questions partly depend on answers to the more general questions discussed in the previous chapters. Chapters 10–13 deal with moral philosophy, and Chapter 14 with political philosophy. Chapter 15 discusses some connections between philosophy and theological and religious belief, and returns to many of the questions raised in the previous chapters.

This is not the order that any of the Greek philosophers follow (as far as we know) in their exposition of their positions.[2] In particular, one ought not to suppose that Greek philosophers derive their moral and political views entirely from their views in metaphysics and epistemology, with no influence in the reverse direction. But it may be useful to see how issues in natural philosophy and metaphysics raise epistemological questions, how both metaphysics and epistemology affect discussions of mind, action, ethics, and society, and how all these questions are connected to conceptions of the nature of divine being. If one reads the following chapters in order, the earlier chapters will prepare for the later ones.

I have tried to choose topics and texts that are philosophically central, but accessible to novice readers. For this reason I have largely omitted some topics (including mathematics, formal logic, and philosophy of language) to which the

---

[2] The order of Aristotle's works: **19–20**. The Stoic division of philosophy: **30**.

Greek philosophers made important contributions. Moreover, I have given very little space to the philosophers of late antiquity, since their writings often presuppose knowledge of (especially) Plato and Aristotle. For similar reasons, the treatment of some topics—especially political philosophy—is biased towards Plato and Aristotle. I have included a few extracts from non-philosophical writers—such as dramatists, historians, and medical writers—since these often throw light on philosophical issues.

Occasionally I have included brief extracts from modern philosophers, either commenting on a Greek philosopher or expounding a specific philosophical issue without reference to any Greek source. I have included them when they seemed to me to offer an especially clear or forceful statement of an issue, argument, or objection. I could certainly have multiplied such extracts; the ones that appear will give the reader no more than an idea of some connections between ancient and modern philosophy.

My own introductory comments are intended to help readers to understand the texts and to notice some of the questions that can be raised about them. I try to give some idea of various disputes about interpretation and evaluation, but this is not a complete or unbiased survey. Moreover, when I raise objections that I do not answer, this is not necessarily because I think they cannot be answered. Sometimes it seems better to introduce readers to some appropriate questions than to set out answers (which often could not be defended without using more space than is available).

Why read a book of selections, instead of some of the complete texts? A book of selections offers an opportunity to read texts that an elementary student could not reasonably be expected to read in their entirety. The reader will find a much wider range of texts than in most introductory courses on Greek philosophy. I do not believe, however, that reading selections from, say, Plato's *Republic* is an acceptable substitute for reading the whole *Republic*; on the contrary, I hope that readers who have read some of the extracts in this book will want to read the relevant works in full.

In the rest of this chapter, I describe the main periods and schools of Greek philosophy, and mention some general questions that should be kept in mind in reading the texts presented in later chapters. Readers may want to refer back to sections of this chapter as they proceed.

Philosophy in the history of the ancient world

2 In the 1100 years of the Greek philosophical tradition, Greek philosophy spread from Asia Minor to the territories of the Roman Empire (centred on the Mediterranean, but stretching from Britain southwards to North Africa and eastwards as far as Iran). Philosophers worked in changing social, political, and cultural environments. They came from different parts of the Greek and

Roman world. Many of the Presocratics and the early Stoics came from western Asia; Plato and Epicurus were Athenians; Aristotle was a Macedonian; Lucretius and Cicero were Roman; Seneca came from Spain, Plotinus from Egypt, and Augustine from North Africa. They came from different social classes; at one extreme, Marcus Aurelius was a Roman Emperor, and at the other extreme, Epictetus was a slave.

Philosophy began in the independent Greek city-states of western Asia and Sicily in the sixth and fifth centuries BC. It spread to Athens, one of the largest of the Greek states. In the fourth century, Plato and Aristotle established Athens as the major centre of philosophical activity.

In the 330s and 320s Alexander's Macedonian army conquered Egypt and a large area in western Asia (roughly the present 'middle East'). His successors divided this area into different monarchies, which eventually came under the control of Rome; this process of Roman domination was more or less complete by the reign of the Roman Emperor Augustus (31 BC–AD 14). The Macedonian monarchies established Greek cities in their territories, and thereby encouraged the spread of Greek culture and institutions. During this period, Athens retained a leading position as a philosophical centre; both the Stoic and the Epicurean schools established themselves there. Alexandria, a new city founded by Alexander in Egypt, became a scientific and cultural centre, and eventually produced its own philosophical movements as well.

When the Romans gradually absorbed the Macedonian kingdoms, by diplomacy or conquest, they also absorbed Greek culture. Roman literature, architecture, and sculpture followed Greek models (not slavishly), and educated Romans learnt Greek; many of them went to Athens for their higher education. From the middle of the second century BC, we hear of Greek philosophers at Rome and of Romans taking an interest in Greek philosophy. In the first century BC Lucretius (a committed Epicurean) and Cicero (an undogmatic student of the different schools) used Latin to present the philosophy of the Greek schools. Under the Roman Empire, philosophy was written in Greek (e.g. Epictetus, Marcus Aurelius, Plotinus) and in Latin (e.g. Seneca, Augustine).

From the reign of Augustus until its gradual collapse in the west during the fifth century AD, the Roman Empire had a central government that covered a larger area of Europe, Asia, and Africa than has lived under a single central government in any later period. From the political and social point of view, this compared unfavourably in many ways with the city-states familiar to Socrates and Plato. The citizens of Socrates' Athens had a considerable degree of control over the political decisions that affected their lives, since Athens was both democratic and free of domination by other states. (It was not a typical Greek city, especially in the second respect.) Citizens of the Roman Empire—in Italy, Germany, Spain, Algeria, Turkey, or Egypt—had relatively little influence or control over the central government and imperial court, or even over the provincial governments. None the less, Greek and Latin were widely understood (by the educated classes) throughout the empire, and Greek literature and philosophy became parts of the higher education of people from diverse backgrounds.

This diffusion of Greek philosophy under the Roman Empire helps to explain two aspects of the later history of Greek philosophy. (1) It provided the philosophical basis of some aspects of Jewish thought under the Roman Empire, and of Christian theology in its formative period. Even when Greek learning and culture collapsed in western Europe, Greek thought remained an element in Christian thought. (2) Greek philosophy was taken up by the Asian peoples who gradually conquered the Roman Empire in the east. It was translated into Arabic, and in this form it gradually became known again in western Europe.

This book does not go far into the history of Greek philosophy in the Roman Empire, still less into later periods. But for this very reason readers ought to realize that Greek philosophy was not limited, in space or in time, by the limits of the Greek world, the Greek language, or the Roman Empire, or 'western' culture. The conventional divisions in the history of philosophy should not be allowed to conceal the important elements of continuity.

The Presocratics

3 Plato and Aristotle regarded themselves as successors of a sequence of philosophers going back to Anaximander (c.610–540 BC), or perhaps to Thales (c.625–c.545 BC). In the time of Socrates (469–399), philosophy took a new turn. Hence, it is conventional to refer to these philosophers as 'Presocratics'; though the term itself is modern, it corresponds to a division marked by Plato and Aristotle themselves. It is misleading, however, since the later Presocratics— Anaxagoras, Zeno, Democritus—are contemporaries of Socrates. Indeed, the lifetime of Democritus (d. c.360 BC?) may have extended well into the lifetime of Plato (d. 347 BC).

As Plato and Aristotle recognize, the Presocratic philosophers are closely connected to a tradition that extends back to the beginning of Greek literature, as we know it, in the eighth century.[3] The epic poets Homer and Hesiod (both c.750 BC?) consider questions such as 'How did the world begin?', 'Why is it wet in the winter and dry in the summer?', 'Why does the sea sometimes flood the land?'. Their answers normally involve the plans of one or another of a number of gods and goddesses, often conflicting and competing. Particularly striking floods or earthquakes, for instance, may show the anger of the sea-god Poseidon; the plague that begins the *Iliad* is the result of the wrath of Apollo, and so on. Conflicts among the gods are the ultimate source of the conflicts among

---

[3] Aristotle on naturalists and traditional beliefs in gods: **100**.

Greeks and Trojans in the *Iliad*, and of the wanderings of Odysseus in the *Odyssey*. In Hesiod's *Theogony* (*theogonia*, 'origins of the gods') and *Works and Days*, features of the natural world as we know it are explained by past conflicts among the gods (**574–5, 577**).

Though the Presocratics are concerned with some of Homer's and Hesiod's questions, their answers are different. They do not simply tell a story asserting that this is how things are, or how things happened. Nor do they appeal to the choices and whims of anthropomorphic gods. They try to explain what happens, and why things are as they are, by appeal to laws involving natural stuffs, events, and processes, apart from the anger of Poseidon or Apollo. In Aristotle's view, the theories of the Presocratics are crucially different from stories about conflicts among the gods, because they offer rational arguments and attempt proofs.

This approach to understanding the world is sometimes described as an inquiry into 'nature' (*phusis*). Our sources attribute treatises 'On Nature' to different Presocratic philosophers (**69–70**), though we do not know how many of them used this title. The first one who certainly spoke of nature is Heracleitus; he remarks that 'nature tends to hide' (**39**), because it is not easy to discover, and does not lie open to a superficial view.

This description of the interests of the Presocratics suggests that they belong to the early stages of the history of natural science. While their speculations clearly lack some of the characteristics that we might attribute to scientific inquiry (attention to experimental evidence, use of mathematical and quantitative formulations), their search for rational explanations and general laws marks an important aspect of continuity in scientific thinking.

Their inquiries also count as philosophy, as Plato and his successors conceived it, in so far as they try to understand the foundations and presuppositions of their inquiries into nature. They ask, for instance, not only how the world came to be, or what causes what sorts of changes, but also what the nature of becoming is, or what counts as an adequate cause, or how we can come to know that the world is as we say it is.

Interest in the foundations and presuppositions of inquiry into the world appears in Xenophanes, Heracleitus, and Parmenides. Parmenides' reflections on the nature of change lead him to the conclusion that no talk of change can possibly be true, or even significant. His arguments, supported by those of Zeno and Melissus, contest the assumptions of cosmologists. Equally important, they raise questions about the conceptions of language, meaning, change, time, and reality on which Parmenides' own arguments rest.

The later cosmologists—especially Empedocles, Anaxagoras, and the Atomists Leucippus and Democritus—show the influence of Parmenides' criticism; they seek to construct theories that do not imply the sort of change that Parmenides has declared to be impossible.

Among these later Presocratics, the Atomists are the most influential. The early Atomists are Leucippus and Democritus; their different contributions cannot be distinguished, given the character of our sources. Since most of the fragments are attributed to Democritus, modern writers tend to use his name in discussions of early Atomism. The Atomists' views are discussed at length by Aristotle, and they are later revived, in a modified form, by Epicurus.

Sources for the Presocratics

4 The works of the Presocratic naturalists did not survive beyond late antiquity; even then, as Simplicius remarks (**69**), copies of some of their works were hard to find. The surviving evidence is all derived from writers of various periods in antiquity. It consists of (*a*) reports and paraphrases, and (*b*) purported quotations, usually referred to as 'fragments'.

Some of the main points that any reader ought to bear in mind in reading these sources are these:

1. The distinction between paraphrase and quotation is not always clearly observed. Sometimes—especially when the original is written in verse (as Xenophanes, Parmenides, and Empedocles are)—we can be confident that a source gives us a verbatim quotation. But we cannot always be so confident. Ancient writers (notably Aristotle) often quote from memory, and hence not always exactly; nor are they always careful to distinguish quotation from paraphrase.

2. Much of our evidence comes from histories or historical surveys of ancient philosophy that were written in late antiquity. Authors of these historical works include Eusebius, the major historian of the early Church; Hippolytus, bishop of Rome; and Aetius, the presumed author of a history excerpted in a spurious work of Plutarch. These authors used sources probably derived from Aristotle's student Theophrastus (**21**).

This means that most of our evidence on the Presocratics has reached us through Theophrastus, and hence through Aristotle. Often we lack the independent evidence that would allow us to confirm or reject their account. We should not suppose that Aristotle or Theophrastus describes the Presocratics in terms that the Presocratics themselves would use or understand. Aristotle tries to make clear what the naturalists were trying to say, and how close they came to expressing distinctions that are clear from the Aristotelian point of view. This approach may be illuminating for us, provided that we do not regard it as an attempt to see the issues through the Presocratics' own eyes.

Passages from or about the Presocratics are normally cited by the source, followed by a reference to the collection of fragments and other evidence gathered by Diels and Kranz, in *Die Fragmente der Vorsokratiker* (DK). To each Presocratic writer, DK assigns a numbered chapter divided into two sections—A for indirect evidence ('testimonia') and B for (supposed) direct quotations. Hence the reference 'DK 22 B 123' refers to fragment 123 in section B of chapter 22. Since DK references are standard in other collections of evidence on the Presocratics and in books about them, they allow the reader to find other discussions of a passage easily.

The medical writers

5 Though the fragments of the naturalists are our evidence for the thought of those whom Aristotle recognizes as philosophers, they are not our only sources for early Greek philosophical thought. From the middle of the fifth century onwards, Greek medical writers reveal both the development of medical theory and practice in Greece and its relations with philosophical thought. Many of the medical writings are attributed to the celebrated physician Hippocrates of Cos (from *c.*460?). Plato's reference to Hippocrates shows that he recognizes him as a medical authority; but the dates and authors of individual Hippocratic treatises are difficult to determine.

Some of the medical writers are openly hostile to philosophical theory, and to the speculative principles that they attribute to the Presocratics. Their tendency is (broadly speaking) empirical, refraining from speculation on the unobserved causes of observed symptoms. Others are more receptive to philosophical speculations, and some of their works show how the theories of some of the Presocratics might be used and applied to medical practice.

Medicine also influences philosophy, by providing a model of a systematic rational discipline constituting what Plato and Aristotle regard as a body of 'knowledge' (*epistêmê*). When Plato and Aristotle seek to describe a science, with proper explanatory principles, in contrast to a mere empirical knack or technique, they sometimes turn to mathematics, and sometimes to medicine (**106, 179**). Moral philosophers find it useful to compare their aims and methods with those of medicine; sometimes they claim to be concerned with the health of the soul, just as medicine is concerned with the health of the body (**444, 470, 529**).

The conflict between empirical and theoretical medicine continues in later Greek medical writers. It is represented especially in Galen and in Sextus Empiricus, both of whom see a close connection between issues about medical theory and practice and more general epistemological issues.

....

6 PLATO, *Phaedrus* 270 C SOCRATES: Then do you think it is possible to have any worthwhile understanding of the nature of the soul without the nature of the whole <universe>? PHAEDRUS: If we are to believe Hippocrates of

the Asclepiads[4] about anything, we can't even understand the body without following this line of inquiry.—Yes, my friend, he's quite right. But we mustn't only appeal to Hippocrates; we must also examine the account itself, to see whether it is in accord <with the truth>.—I agree.—Then consider what Hippocrates and the true account say about nature.[5]

Poets and historians

7 According to Aristotle, philosophy took a new turn in the time of Socrates, by beginning to discuss moral questions (**99**, **197**). Aristotle means not that no one before Socrates discussed moral questions, but that those who discussed them were not philosophers. Reflections on questions of right and wrong action, and good and bad character, are as old as Greek literature itself. In Homer, the rights and wrongs of the dispute between the Greeks and the Trojans, between Achilles and Agamemnon, and between Odysseus and the suitors, are central themes. In fifth-century literature, these moral issues are discussed at a more theoretical level. Some plays of the Athenian tragedians reflect conflicting conceptions of right and good, and suggest how each conception might be defended. Sophocles' *Philoctetes* and *Oedipus Coloneus*, and Euripides' *Medea* and *Hippolytus*, provide especially clear examples.

The two fifth-century historians whose works survive, Herodotus and Thucydides, share some of the aims of the natural philosophers and the medical writers; they seek systematic and detailed descriptions and explanations of the character of different societies, and of conflicts within and between societies. In Herodotus the major theme is the conflict between the Greek cities and the Persian Empire. Thucydides' subject is the war between Athens and Sparta, involving many of the other cities in the Greek world. Some of their analysis and explanation relies on their presentation of moral and political issues. Herodotus often uses stories or debates to present questions and disputes about human well-being, the relation of human freedom to external circumstances and divine action, and the best form of political organization (**350**, **388**, **532**). In Thucydides, moral and political comment is generally conveyed in the speeches by different military and political leaders (**461**, **534–5**); but sometimes Thucydides presents his analysis of the relevant moral and political issues in his own voice (**536–45**).

The relations between philosophy, poetry, historical writing, and rhetoric, are important throughout the history of Greek and Latin literature. Only a few

---

[4] A medical guild, followers of Asclepius.

[5] Socrates goes on to describe a procedure, but it is not clear how far it reflects Hippocrates and how far 'the truth', as Plato conceives it. The remark has proved difficult to connect with any specific passage in the Hippocratic corpus.

examples are offered in this book, almost all of them from Greek literature of the fifth century.

Sophists

8 Plato and Aristotle regard themselves as participants in philosophical debates not only with previous philosophers, but also with contemporary writers on philosophical topics. The most important of these are collectively known as 'sophists'. Plato mentions Protagoras, Prodicus, and Hippias as leading sophists, and discusses their views. He gives special attention to Protagoras.

The sophists provided higher education, going beyond the traditional education in gymnastics and 'music' (*mousikê*, including Homer and other Greek poets, as well as what we call music). Some of them gave lectures on the topics discussed by the Presocratic naturalists. In particular, they discussed moral and political questions, and techniques of persuasive argument, so that they taught people to speak persuasively on these questions in political gatherings. In the Athenian democracy, public speaking—either in the sovereign assembly of all the citizens, or in the large jury-courts—was an important source of political influence. For rich young Athenians ambitious for a career in public life in a democracy, the abilities that could be learnt from a sophist promised a competitive advantage in public debate and deliberation. The sophists charged fees—often large—for their instruction, so that their pupils were restricted to young men who could afford them.[6]

Plato does not suggest that the sophists' views were all mistaken or pernicious. He criticizes above all the people who go to the sophists in the expectation of finding the key to worldly success. The sophists are at fault, because they simply try to satisfy this expectation. They do not examine moral and political questions in order to explore their basic difficulties or to find their true principles. They simply present popular views with a veneer of understanding that conceals some of their basic confusions (**551**).

Whether or not Plato's picture of the sophists is completely fair, it provides an important point of contrast for his presentation of Socrates. Socrates does not teach for pay; he does not restrict his instruction to private pupils; he does not claim the status of a teacher; most important, he seeks to explore real difficulties, and to discover true principles of morality.

The historical Socrates

9 As far as we know, Socrates wrote no philosophical works himself. But our evidence on his life and activity is quite plentiful. Indeed, some difficulties arise

---

[6] Sophists as educators; **139**. Protagoras as a sophist: **156**, **160**, **429**.

from the task of assessing the testimony of the four primary sources of information on Socrates.

Aristophanes (?c.450-c.385), an Athenian comic dramatist, makes Socrates the main character in the *Clouds* (**581**). Some features of Socrates may be comic inventions: he is represented as being dirty, avaricious, and deceptive. Other features are philosophically interesting.

(1) Socrates teaches natural philosophy, and investigates the questions pursued by the Presocratics.

(2) He is an atheist.

(3) The arguments that young men learn from Socrates are responsible for their rejection of conventional moral standards; they learn slick defences for cowardice, theft, disloyalty to parents, and every other recognized vice.[7]

Xenophon (c.428–c.354) was a politically conservative soldier, with intellectual interests and limited philosophical acumen. He wrote several Socratic conversations, in which Socrates gives conventionally respectable moral and political advice, and expresses conventional religious views. One of Xenophon's main aims was apparently to reject the picture of Socrates that we find in the *Clouds* (whether or not Xenophon actually has Aristophanes in mind).

The most extensive source for Socrates' life and work is the dialogues of Plato. It is fairly widely agreed that the early group of dialogues (see **18**) purports to represent the personality and philosophical outlook of the historical Socrates. Many of the Platonic Socrates' views are somewhat similar to those of the Xenophontic Socrates, but the Platonic Socrates displays an inquiring outlook and a degree of philosophical depth that are absent in Xenophon. From reading Plato, it is easier to understand why Socrates affected people as strongly as he did.

Aristotle makes a number of important, though brief, remarks about Socrates (**99**, **141**, **197**). They support the view that Socrates is accurately portrayed in Plato's earlier dialogues. In particular, Aristotle mentions Socrates' disavowal of knowledge and his interrogative method of inquiry—found in Plato, but not in Xenophon.

Study of this evidence on Socrates tends (in many people's view, not everyone's) to vindicate the reliability of Plato's early dialogues as sources for the personality and outlook of Socrates. According to Plato, Socrates' intellectual interests changed sharply. In his youth, he may have shared the Presocratics' interest in natural philosophy (so that Aristophanes' presentation of him is not entirely baseless: **96**, **583**). His later philosophical activity was exclusively ethical and primarily interrogative. He cross-examined other people, searching for understanding of basic ethical principles. He did not teach for pay; indeed, he

---

[7] Aristophanes and Socrates; see **581**.

claimed, in contrast to the sophists, to have nothing to teach (**139**). None the less, he attracted the attention of upper-class young men, many of whom were involved in the political struggles of the late fifth century in Athens, in opposition to the democracy (Critias, Charmides), or in defence of it (Chaerephon), or firmly attached to neither side (Alcibiades).[8]

Socrates claims to be a loyal citizen of Athens, who distinguished himself in his military service and performed his civic duties with the appropriate respect for law and justice (**540**), even when this resulted in unpopularity or danger for him. He did not, however, go into public life as a professional politician. None the less, he became unpopular. After the fall of the regime of the Thirty Tyrants and the restoration of democracy, he was tried for impiety—specifically for not recognizing the gods of the city, but introducing new supernatural beings, and for corrupting the young men (**583**, **585**). He was convicted, by a small majority of the jury (**10**), and sentenced to death. The trial and death of Socrates are discussed or alluded to in many passages of Plato's dialogues. Both Plato and Xenophon wrote an 'Apology' (*apologia*, i.e. defence), purporting to represent Socrates' speech on his behalf at his trial. Plato's *Crito* and *Phaedo* deal with Socrates' imprisonment and death.

....

10   PLATO, *Apology* 36 A[9]   What has happened was not unexpected; I am much more surprised by the number of votes cast on each side. For I thought the margin would be large, not as small as it actually was. As it is, it would seem, if only thirty had changed their votes, I would have been acquitted.

11   CICERO, *Tusculan Disputations* v. 10   Early philosophy, as far as Socrates, who had attended lectures of Archelaus, a pupil of Anaxagoras, treated numbers and motions, and the origin from which everything arises and to which everything returns; they eagerly inquired into the size of the stars, the distances between them, and their motions, and into everything in the heavens. But Socrates was the first[10] who called philosophy down from the sky, placed it in cities, even brought it into people's homes, and forced it to examine life and conduct, and good and bad things.

12   PLATO, *Laches* 181 AB LACHES: I've seen Socrates elsewhere upholding the honour of both his father and his fatherland. He retreated with me after the defeat at Delium, and I can tell you that if others had been willing to be as

---

[8] Critias: **584**. Chaerephon: **139**. Alcibiades: **462**.

[9] Speech by Socrates at his trial. He has just heard the jury's vote convicting him. We have no clear evidence of the number of jurors; there may have been 500, so that the vote would have been 280:220.

[10] Cicero does not take account of the sophists here. On the change of philosophical direction in the time of Socrates see **99**.

he was, the honour of our city would have been upheld, and it would never have fallen to such defeat.

13 PLATO, *Symposium* 221 A–C [ALCIBIADES]   Socrates was a sight worth seeing when the army was retreating in defeat from Delium. I happened to be there on horseback, and he was in armour on foot. He was retreating together with Laches. ... The first thing I noticed was how much calmer Socrates was than Laches. Moreover, he seemed to me to be going along there, just as he does in Athens, 'swaggering and glaring from side to side', calmly surveying both friend and foe. It was clear to everyone, even from a distance, that if you laid a hand on him, he would fight back strongly. That's why both he and his companion got away safely; for practically no one ever lays a hand in a battle on people with that attitude—the ones they pursue are those who run away headlong.

14 AUGUSTINE, *City of God* viii. 3   So remarkable, then, were the life and death of Socrates that he left behind many followers of his philosophy, who competed in their eagerness to discuss moral questions, where the topic is the highest good, by which a human being can become blessed. But in Socrates' discussions, where he introduced, put forward, and destroyed every position, this highest good was not made clear. And so everyone took what he agreed with from Socrates, and each set up whatever he thought best as the highest good ... So various were the views that the Socratics held about this end that—though it seems hard to believe about followers of one teacher—some, such as Aristippus, said that the highest good is pleasure, and others, such as Antisthenes, that it is virtue.

Plato and his dialogues

15 Plato's (alleged) Seventh Letter (**538**) mentions his early interest in politics, his disillusionment with the tyrannical regime of the Thirty, his disappointment in the democracy that succeeded them, his rejection of politics for philosophy, and his later attempts to intervene in political struggles in Syracuse. He was one of the young associates of Socrates. Sometime after the death of Socrates, he founded a philosophical school in the precincts of the hero Academius (hence called the 'Academy'); Aristotle was a member of the school in Plato's later years.

As far as we know, Plato's whole literary output has survived; we have no evidence of any written work that does not survive. This situation (unusual among classical Greek authors) probably results from the fact that Plato's philosophical school, the Academy, survived continuously until late antiquity, and took special care to preserve his writings.

His written works consist almost entirely of dialogues.[11] Plato himself is a speaker in none of them. In most of them Socrates is the main speaker. These facts raise some important preliminary questions for students of Plato's philosophy.

Why did Plato write dialogues? Some answers worth considering are these:

(1) The dialogue form is an attractive literary device, recalling the debates commonly found in tragedies, and in historical writing (**461**, **532**). It allows Plato to characterize the setting and the personalities of the speakers.

(2) It allows Plato to avoid commitment to the positions taken by Socrates or by any other speaker.

(3) It represents the distinctive character of Socrates' inquiries. Plato takes this, rather than a systematic treatise, to be an appropriate way to present the essentially interrogative character of philosophical thinking.

The third answer is supported by some ancient critics (**189–91**), and it is the answer of greatest philosophical interest. If it is right, the first and second answers may still be right. To decide how far the second answer is right, we must consider how plausible it is to attribute positive doctrines to Plato on the strength of the dialogues.

The dialogues differ sharply in length, in degree of difficulty, and in literary form and structure. Some are 'direct' dialogues, in which the characters speak (as in a play) without any narrator. Others are 'reported' dialogues, in which a narrator gives a (supposedly) verbatim report of a dialogue. Some of the reports are by Socrates himself; he introduces his own reported remarks with 'I said', and sometimes comments, as reporter, on the character or behaviour of himself or his interlocutors (see **18**). Sometimes the reporter is not himself a participant in the reported conversation. These third-person reports give the reporter an opportunity to comment on Socrates as well as on his interlocutors. Some of the reporters claim to recall a conversation from many years ago; some even claim to report a conversation reported to them by an intermediary (**80**). Sometimes Plato finds these layers of reporting cumbersome, and warns the reader that he will not keep mentioning them.

In the selections in this book from direct dialogues, the names of the speakers occur without brackets. In the selections from reported dialogues, the names of the speakers are introduced in square brackets. After the first introduction of the speaker, changes of speaker (or reported speaker) are introduced simply by a dash.

According to one story (which may go back to a dialogue of Aristotle's), a Corinthian farmer who encountered the *Gorgias* was converted to Plato's philosophy (**16**). This story presupposes a fairly wide circulation for some dialogues

---

[11] The exceptions are the Letters (probably spurious) and the *Apology*, Socrates' speech at his trial. The *Menexenus* consists largely of a speech.

among the general public. This would not be surprising, since some of the dialogues do not seem to presuppose extensive acquaintance with philosophical issues. Some of the dialogues, however, seem to be directed to more specialized readers (or hearers); it reasonable to suppose that they aimed primarily at Plato's own students in the Academy.

Not all the works that we find in manuscripts of the Platonic Corpus are genuine. Critics in antiquity regarded some of them as spurious. Modern readers have doubted the genuineness of some of the others. The spurious and dubious works are not to be neglected simply because Plato did not write them. They are often interesting for (among other things) the light they shed on the use of Platonic doctrines by later philosophical schools, including later Platonism. I have occasionally quoted from them (**321**, **424**).

....

16 THEMISTIUS, *Orations* xxxii. 90. 25–91. 2 A Corinthian farmer, after coming into contact with Gorgias—not Gorgias himself, but the dialogue Plato wrote to refute the sophist—at once gave up his farm and his vines, mortgaged his soul to Plato, and sowed and planted Plato's views there. This is the man whom Aristotle honours in his Corinthian[12] dialogue.

Plato's dialogues and Plato's thought

17 Plato's dialogues contain his philosophy, in the minimal sense that characters in them discuss philosophical issues and put forward original (as far as we know) philosophical positions. These are probably positions that Plato takes to be worth discussing. It is more difficult, however, to decide whether the dialogues present Plato's philosophy, in the sense that they present a relatively systematic body of philosophical doctrine that Plato himself believes at the time when he writes a given dialogue. Even if we take the controversial step of assuming that the character Socrates presents Plato's own views, we face difficulties. Socrates seems to defend different views in different dialogues; moreover, in some dialogues he expresses doubt and puzzlement on questions that in other dialogues he seems to answer firmly.

These facts have led to different ways of interpreting Plato's dialogues. Three main lines of interpretation are worth considering. According to one view, the dialogues are primarily critical and exploratory, and do not contain a systematic philosophical position. There is no reason to suppose that one dialogue will reach conclusions consistent with those of another, or that any of their conclusions state Plato's views. This approach to the dialogues was favoured in antiquity by those (including some of Plato's successors in the Academy) who took Plato to be sympathetic to Scepticism (**170**, **202**).

---

[12] Otherwise unknown. Some editors suggest 'Nerinthus', the title of a dialogue of Aristotle.

The second view begins from the observation that the dialogues share more positive conclusions than a purely critical interpretation can explain. Some readers find a positive systematic view present in the dialogues, and they explain the differences between the dialogues in ways that fit this general systematic interpretation. For expository and didactic purposes, some dialogues refrain from going into some details given in others, or they confine themselves to raising puzzles that are answered in other dialogues. In general, any apparent philosophical differences between dialogues should be taken to be expository, not doctrinal. This was the general attitude to the dialogues among the Platonists of late antiquity.

A third line of interpretation agrees with the systematic view in taking the dialogues to express Plato's positive doctrines; but it rejects some of the devices adapted by systematic interpreters to explain away apparent conflicts between different dialogues. According to this line of interpretation, the dialogues express Plato's views as they change and develop during fifty years of philosophical thinking. In particular, the early dialogues are intended to represent the views of the historical Socrates (probably Plato's own views), but the middle and late dialogues present Plato's own views, which are not necessarily those of the historical Socrates.

This third, 'developmental' line of interpretation appeals to two main considerations: (a) the most plausible criteria for ordering the dialogues confirm the division between the 'Socratic' stage of Plato's philosophical development and the later stages in which Plato's reflections are more independent of Socrates; (b) Aristotle supports the view that Plato's views develop, and that they depart from Socrates' views (**197**). He attributes different views to Socrates and to Plato. The views he attributes to Socrates can be found in the early dialogues, and those he attributes to Plato can be found in the middle and later dialogues. The assessment of these supposed doctrinal differences is especially important for the understanding of Plato's Theory of Forms and for central aspects of his moral theory.

Some of the issues on which one might see a development from the Socratic to the Platonic position are as follows. (i) Some dialogues (the *Euthyphro* and the *Laches*, for instance) are mostly engaged in cross-examination. Others (the *Phaedo* and the *Republic*, for instance) contain longer expositions of positive doctrine (**205-7, 326-30, 554-6**). (ii) The Theory of Forms seems different in the *Phaedo* and *Republic* from the claims found in the shorter and (supposedly) earlier dialogues (**194**). (iii) The theory of recollection appears in the *Meno* and *Phaedo*, but not in the short, 'early' dialogues (**183-6**). (iv) The *Phaedo* offers an elaborate defence of the immortality of the soul, on which the 'early' dialogues have much less to say (**324-30**). (v) The *Republic* seems to challenge the views of the *Protagoras* on the relation of knowledge and desire (**437-9**). (vi) The political theory of the *Republic* seems to go beyond the principles accepted in the 'early' dialogues (**549-56**). In all these cases, readers who are sceptical about any explanation that appeals to developments in Plato's thought will want to consider other ways of explaining the apparent difference between one dialogue and another.

Readers should also keep in mind a feature of the dialogues that distinguishes them from Aristotle's works and from many other philosophical texts. Though different Platonic dialogues emphasize different areas of philosophy, many of them combine (for instance) ethical, epistemological, and metaphysical discussion. The Theory of Forms, in particular, is relevant to several aspects of Plato's thought. The *Republic* and *Laws* are Plato's two major works on political philosophy, but (as the extracts in this book show) they also contain discussions of several other topics. To gain an impression of the range of topics treated in Plato's major dialogues, readers should be especially careful to look at the extracts that are dispersed among different chapters of this book.

Plato's dialogues

18 For the reader's convenience, I list below the Platonic dialogues that are excerpted in this book. The list follows a reasonably plausible, but by no means certain, chronological order. It mentions the form of a given dialogue (direct or indirect), and gives a very rough indication of the contents and connections with other dialogues.

(1) *Socratic dialogues*

Apology (*apologia*, i.e. 'defence'). Speech by Socrates addressing the jury at his trial.
Crito. Direct dialogue. Socrates and Crito consider whether Socrates should try to escape from prison after he has been found guilty at his trial and is awaiting execution. The laws of Athens are represented as arguing against escape.
Euthyphro. Direct. Euthyphro is on trial for impiety. Socrates and Euthyphro discuss the nature of piety and its relation to justice.
Laches. Direct. Socrates and the two generals Laches and Nicias discuss bravery and its relation to knowledge of good.

(2) *Later (?) Socratic dialogues*

Euthydemus. Mostly reported by Socrates, with a 'framing' conversation (introducing the main discussion) between Socrates and Crito. The dialogue mostly discusses the method and arguments of the two sophists, Euthydemus and Dionysodorus. In two ethical sections, Socrates contrasts his method with theirs.

Protagoras. Reported by Socrates. In a gathering of several eminent sophists, Protagoras and Socrates discuss whether virtue can be taught, and hence consider the nature of virtue, its relation to knowledge of good, the nature of the good, and its relation to pleasure.

Gorgias. Direct. Socrates examines the rhetoricians Gorgias and Polus about whether rhetoric is a genuine craft, and about the value of rhetoric. He examines Polus and Callicles on the related question about whether it is in one's interest to acquire wealth and power for oneself (the alleged benefit of rhetoric) or to be just.

(3) *Middle dialogues*

Meno. Direct. After an inconclusive discussion of the nature of virtue, Meno expresses doubts about the value of Socrates' method of cross-examination. Socrates answers by defending an account of knowledge as recollection. He clarifies this account by introducing a distinction between knowledge and belief.

Cratylus. Direct. Socrates, Hermogenes (sympathetic to Protagoras), and Cratylus (a Heracleitean) discuss whether and how language can give a correct or incorrect account of reality. Socrates examines the Protagorean and Heracleitean accounts of reality.

Phaedo. Indirect, reported by Phaedo. Just before Socrates takes a lethal dose of poison (the Athenian form of death sentence), he discusses the immortality of the soul with Simmias and Cebes. He introduces the Forms as objects of definition and knowledge. The dialogue ends with a description of Socrates' death.

Symposium (i.e. 'banquet'). Indirect, reported by Apollodorus, after a framing conversation. In the setting of a banquet, several speakers make after-dinner speeches on different aspects of love. The last of these is by Socrates; in the course of his speech, he reports a further speech, by a prophetess Diotima. Alcibiades interrupts the party, and makes a speech about Socrates.

Republic (*Politeia*, i.e. 'constitution'). Indirect, reported by Socrates. This and the *Laws* are the longest Platonic dialogues. An introductory discussion in Book I, mainly with Thrasymachus, examines justice. In Book II Glaucon and Adeimantus (Plato's brothers) ask Socrates to defend his claim that it is always better for a person to be just rather than unjust. Socrates' exploration of the nature of justice leads him to describe a just city, and the philosophers who rule it. The dialogue covers many questions in moral and political philosophy, metaphysics and epistemology, psychology, and philosophy of art.

(4) *Later dialogues*

Parmenides. Reported (Cephalus reports Adeimantus reporting Antiphon reporting Pythodorus reporting a conversation between Parmenides, Zeno, and Socrates). In the first part of the dialogue, Parmenides confronts Socrates with a series of difficulties in the Theory of Forms (cf. *Phaedo*). In the second part, he presents a series of puzzles about one and many.

Phaedrus. Direct. Socrates and Phaedrus discuss both rhetoric and the nature of love (taking up themes from the *Gorgias* and *Symposium*). Further discussion of the immortality of the soul, recollection, and the Forms (cf. *Phaedo*).

Theaetetus. Direct. Taken (according to a framing conversation) from notes by Eucleides of a conversation reported by Socrates, which Eucleides recast in the form of direct dialogue. Socrates examines Theodorus, and Theaetetus (mathematicians) on the nature of knowledge. They discuss the positions of Protagoras and Heracleitus (cf. *Cratylus*), and consider some suggestions about the relation of knowledge to belief (cf. *Meno*).

Sophist. Direct. An 'Eleatic Visitor' (the main speaker) and Socrates try to understand the nature of a sophist (cf. *Euthydemus*). The discussion requires an answer to Parmenides' questions about how it is possible to speak of what is not, and to speak falsely. The nature and relations of the Forms (cf. *Parmenides*) are discussed.

Timaeus. Direct. A framing conversation presents the dialogue as a sequel to the *Republic*. Timaeus the natural philosopher (the main speaker) gives an account of the creation of the natural world by a designer who tries to embody the Forms in the world.

Philebus. Direct. Socrates, Protarchus, and Philebus (two hedonists) discuss the nature of pleasure and its relation to the good (cf. *Protagoras*). They discuss the nature of the Forms (cf. *Parmenides*, *Sophist*).

Laws. Direct. The longest dialogue. In a conversation with a Cretan and a Spartan, an 'Athenian Visitor' (the main speaker; Socrates does not appear) describes an ideal state (cf. *Republic*), with a detailed description and explanation of its laws. The dialogue includes a defence of the immortality of the soul (cf. *Phaedrus*), and an account of god and the world (cf. *Timaeus*).

(5) Doubtful or spurious works

First Alcibiades. Direct. Its authenticity is disputed; no internal evidence requires a date later than Plato's lifetime. Socrates and Alcibiades (cf. *Symposium*) discuss several moral questions, leading to a division between body and soul.

Axiochus. Direct. Its inauthenticity is generally acknowledged; it seems to show Epicurean influence. Socrates and Axiochus discuss the fear of death.

Letters. Some are generally regarded as spurious. The authenticity of the long, purportedly autobiographical, Seventh Letter, is disputed.

Aristotle

19 Aristotle was born in 384 BC, in the Macedonian city of Stagira (now part of northern Greece). In his lifetime the kingdom of Macedon, first under Philip

and then under Philip's son Alexander, conquered the Greek cities of Europe and Asia, and then the Persian Empire. Though Aristotle spent much of his adult life in Athens, he was not an Athenian citizen. He was closely linked to the kings of Macedon; his father was Nicomachus, a doctor attached to the Macedonian court. Many Greeks regarded the Macedonians as foreign invaders; Aristotle's own life in Athens was affected by this suspicion of Macedon.

In 367 Aristotle came to Athens. He belonged to Plato's Academy until 347. During these years Plato wrote his important later dialogues (including the *Sophist, Timaeus, Philebus, Statesman,* and *Laws*). In 347 Plato died, and his nephew Speusippus (apparently not Aristotle's favourite philosopher) became head of the Academy. Aristotle left Athens (we do not know why) for Assos in Asia Minor. Later he moved to Lesbos, in the eastern Aegean. He went on to Macedon, where he was a tutor of Alexander. In 334 he returned to Athens and founded his own school, the Lyceum. In 323 Alexander died; in the resulting outbreak of anti-Macedonian feeling in Athens Aristotle left for Chalcis, on the island of Euboea, where he died in 322.

Aristotle married Pythias, a niece of Hermeias, the ruler of Assos. They had a daughter, also called Pythias. After the death of his wife, Aristotle formed an attachment to Herpyllis, and they had a son Nicomachus (who may have edited the ethical work of Aristotle that bears his name).

The reader of Plato's dialogues who turns to Aristotle can hardly fail to notice the different character of the two philosophers' works. Aristotle's lack the conversational form and vivid characterization of almost all the Platonic dialogues. This does not mean he was a less skilful writer than Plato. Aristotle also wrote dialogues; these are among the large number of his works that have not survived, and all we know of them is whatever is quoted or paraphrased by other authors.[13] These short fragments do not allow a comparison with the Platonic dialogues.

The works of Aristotle that have survived appear to be closely related to his lectures in the Lyceum. They show considerable stylistic variation; while some passages are quite finished and ready for publication, others seem rough and compressed, and to be close to Aristotle's notes for lectures. They might be compared to files, arranged by topic, in which Aristotle kept both notes and more finished essays.

We lack any clear indication of the order of Aristotle's works. Critics have tried to place different works in Aristotle's period in Plato's Academy, in the years he spent in the eastern Aegean (after 347), and in his years as head of the Lyceum (after 334). Some evidence suggests that some of his biological works (including the *Parts of Animals,* often quoted in this book) are based on research carried out during his years in the eastern Aegean. Arguments from content suggest that the treatment of form and matter in the *Metaphysics* is probably

---

[13] Extracts from or references to lost works: **86, 116, 143, 222, 306**.

later than the treatment in the *Categories*, *Physics*, and *Generation and Corruption*. It is reasonable, but not certainly correct, to place *On the Soul*, the *Nicomachean Ethics*, and the *Politics* among the later works.

Aristotle's works

20 In contrast to Plato's dialogues, Aristotle's works are divided by subject-matter. This is how they are arranged in the manuscripts of Aristotle. The standard English titles (some, but not all, of which clearly go back to Aristotle himself) are translations or Anglicizations of the traditional Latin titles, which are not always very informative. The reader may find it useful to have a brief description of Aristotle's surviving works, arranged according to the standard order.

1. *Logic* (Categories, Interpretation, Prior and Posterior Analytics, Topics)

These works are traditionally referred to as the *Organon* (i.e. 'instrument'), on the ground that logic is an instrument of philosophical thinking in all areas. 'Logic', as Aristotle conceives it, also includes the study of language, meaning, and their relation to non-linguistic reality; hence it includes many topics that might now be assigned to philosophy of language or philosophical logic. This is true of the *Categories* (i.e. 'Predications'), *Interpretation* (from the use of 'interpret' for understanding a language, hence referring to the relation of thought to language and reality), and *Topics* (dealing with *topoi*, ('places'), common patterns of philosophical argument). The *Organon* also includes formal 'logic' in the narrower sense; the *Prior Analytics* constitutes the first attempt to formulate a system of deductive formal logic, based on the theory of the 'syllogism'. The *Posterior Analytics* uses this system to formulate an account of scientific knowledge; it is concerned with metaphysics, epistemology, and philosophy of science (as they are understood in contemporary philosophy).

2. *Natural Philosophy*

This long series of works includes philosophical examinations of the principles of natural science. The *Physics* ('works on nature (*phusis*)') covers the general principles of inquiry into nature, and also discusses change, time, place, and the first mover of the natural world. *On the Heavens* (*De Caelo*) is concerned with cosmological topics, and with the universe beyond the natural organisms found in the sublunary world; the topics are often those discussed by the Presocratics. *Generation and Corruption* (more accurately 'coming into existence and going out of existence') discusses two specific types of natural change characteristic of organisms in this world. The *Meteorology* is a survey and discussion of evidence on (especially) winds and tides. The series of biological treatises begins with *On the Soul* (*De Anima*). Aristotle uses his doctrine of form and matter to explain the relation of soul and body, and the different types of soul found in different types of living creatures. His discussion ranges over topics in philosophy of mind, psychology, physiology, epistemology, and theory of action. The treatises on animals include the *Parts of Animals*, which draws on the long survey of empirical evidence in the *History of Animals*. A short selection of philosophical texts inevitably fails to represent the quantity of detailed description and analysis in Aristotle's biological works. This book includes part of his general introduction to biology, and some descriptive passages.

3. *Metaphysics*

In his reflections on the foundations and presuppositions of other disciplines, Aristotle describes a universal 'science of being qua being', or 'first philosophy'. This is the main subject of the work called (not by Aristotle) the *Metaphysics*. (The Greek *ta meta ta phusika* means 'the things after nature'; 'after' probably includes both 'going beyond', hence theology, and 'reflecting on the basis of', as in 'meta-historical' or 'meta-mathematical'.) Four parts are excerpted in this book.

(1) Aristotle discusses his predecessors in this inquiry; in doing so, he gives a valuable account of the Presocratics and of Plato, organized around his doctrine of the four causes (**34**, **43**, **85**).

(2) Part of this universal science examines basic principles of thought and knowledge, and hence discusses some aspects of scepticism (**168**, **277**).

(3) Another part explores questions about substance, form and matter (**253-9**).

(4) The last part gives an account of divine substance, the ultimate principle of the cosmic order (**601-3**).

4. *Ethics and politics*

Aristotle regards the *Nicomachean Ethics*[14] (one of three ethical treatises in the Aristotelean corpus) and *Politics* as part of a single inquiry into the human good and the conditions of its realization. The *Ethics* and *Politics*, taken together, cover most of the topics of Plato's *Republic* and *Laws*, which Aristotle sometimes discusses or has in mind. The *Ethics* discusses the human good, and the virtues that achieve it. The *Politics* considers how a society might embody these virtues in individual and social life. It discusses the successes and

---

[14] The traditional title of this book may reflect the view that the treatise was edited after Aristotle's death by his son Nicomachus.

failures of actual states, and the character of a state that would embody the virtues.

5. *Literary criticism and rhetorical theory* (Poetics, Rhetoric)

These works are closely connected both to Aristotle's logic and to his ethical and political theory. They take up some of the topics of Plato's *Gorgias* and *Phaedrus*.

Though Aristotle's works are divided by subject-matter, some of his major philosophical ideas both influence and are influenced by his more specific inquiries. The conceptions of form, matter, substance, and nature introduced at the beginning of the *Physics* are applied to very general questions about identity and change, to the study of nature, and to the relation of soul and body. His views about souls and natures, in turn, are fundamental in his moral and political theory. This is especially clear in the passages from the *Ethics* and *Politics* that discuss human nature and the human function.

As we have already seen, Aristotle is important in the history of Greek philosophy not only because of his own philosophical views, but also because he is the first historian of philosophy. His study and criticism of his predecessors is part of his argument for his own views, since he argues both (i) that his predecessors have gone wrong by neglecting some distinction that he has made clear, and (ii) that his own views are often simply clearer formulations of points that his predecessors have already grasped incompletely and inarticulately. He makes both claims in the elaborate examination of his predecessors that begins the *Metaphysics* (**34**, **43**, **85**).

Theophrastus

21 Aristotle designated Theophrastus as his successor as head of the Lyceum. A very small proportion of Theophrastus' writings has survived, but we can gather that he shared Aristotle's wide-ranging philosophical and scientific interests. He followed him in detailed biological inquiries. He also wrote on natural philosophy, metaphysics, and ethics. He may have been partly responsible for the tendency of the later Lyceum to concentrate on biology, to the comparative neglect of more general philosophical issues.

Theophrastus was by no means a slavish follower of Aristotle. We can see this in the extract from his *Metaphysics* (**247**), where he reflects critically on Aristotle's defence of teleological explanation. By applying Aristotle's doctrine to specific examples, he suggests that it needs more restriction and qualification than Aristotle recognizes.[15]

---

[15] Theophrastus on ethics: **513**.

Apart from the importance of his own philosophical views, Theophrastus is indirectly a crucially important source for the history of early Greek philosophy (**4**). Following Aristotle's lead (in, for instance, the beginning of the *Metaphysics*), he wrote a systematic history, from an Aristotelian point of view, of Presocratic philosophy. The character of his discussion may be gathered from passages of one work, *The Senses*, of which a substantial part survives (**130**, **133**). We know of the rest of Theophrastus' history only indirectly, through other histories that rely on it.

Hellenistic Philosophy

22 The Hellenistic period of Greek history (a division marked by modern historians, not by the ancients) begins with the deaths of Alexander the Great (323 BC) and Aristotle (322). In political and social history, the accession of Octavian (later Augustus) as emperor (31 BC) marks the end of the Hellenistic period. In the history of philosophy, the main Hellenistic schools eclipsed the Platonic and Aristotelian positions during the third and second centuries BC. The later revival of Platonic and Aristotelian philosophy (first century BC) after a period of decline marks the end of the Hellenistic period. Some of our main sources for Stoicism (Epictetus, Seneca) and for Scepticism (Sextus Empiricus) actually belong to the first century AD, and hence to the post-Hellenistic period. It is convenient, however, to discuss them as part of Hellenistic philosophy.

The main Hellenistic schools are these:

(1) The Cynics and Cyrenaics appear to be inspired by conflicting interpretations of the point of Socratic ethics. The Cyrenaics are extreme hedonists and empiricists. The Cynics maintain the sufficiency of virtue for happiness, and (apparently) attach no importance at all to non-moral goods. The Cyrenaics maintain that the pleasure of the moment is the only good (**489**), and they connect this position with an extreme empiricist claim that the only objects of knowledge are our sensations. The Cynics and Cyrenaics, respectively, present the extreme positions that Stoics and Epicureans try to avoid.

(2) A Sceptical[16] position was first formulated by Pyrrhon, and later elaborated by Aenesidemus and Agrippa. 'Academic' Scepticism was developed by some of Plato's successors in the Academy, especially by Arcesilaus and Carneades.[17]

(3) Epicurus revives the Atomism of Democritus.

---

[16] I use 'Sceptic' (etc.) to refer to the ancient school and its doctrines, and 'sceptic' to refer to the holder of sceptical doctrines in the broader sense that includes modern sceptics. See 108.
[17] Carneades on Chrysippus: **292**. Cf. **487**.

(4) The Stoics formulate their system, partly inspired by Heracleitus, and partly by Plato.

The Hellenistic period is marked by vigorous discussion between members of these different schools; this discussion seems to have contributed to the development of the schools themselves. The philosophical outlooks of Plato and Aristotle are comparatively neglected, though not entirely ignored. The explanation for this neglect seems to differ in the two cases.

Plato's constructive philosophical views were developed into a highly speculative metaphysical position by Speusippus (**19**). Some of Speusippus' views appear to influence (directly or indirectly) the much later Platonism of Plotinus. But soon the Academy turned away from this outlook, and adopted Scepticism. In taking this line, the Academy emphasized one aspect of the Platonic dialogues, turning from Speusippus to the opposite extreme. It is safe to assume that the dialogues were widely available and familiar; they are especially important for the development of Academic Scepticism and of Stoicism.

The position of Aristotle's works is less clear. They were certainly less influential than we might have expected. Both Strabo and Plutarch tell a curious story that purports to explain this lack of influence. They describe the loss and rediscovery of some copies of Aristotle's works, and they suggest that before the rediscovery (early in the first century BC) his works had been largely unavailable (**23-4**).

This suggestion is probably an exaggeration. Aristotle's views probably influence Hellenistic philosophers,[18] but it is difficult to say in particular cases how far Hellenistic theories and arguments were formulated in the light of direct knowledge of his major works. This difficulty itself suggests that Aristotle's works may not have been widely studied and quoted; and that may be the grain of truth in Plutarch's and Strabo's story.

23 STRABO xiii. 55[19] Aristotle left his books to Theophrastus, to whom he also left his school. He was the first person we know of who made a collection of books, and taught the kings of Egypt how to organize a library. Theophrastus left them to Neleus, who took them to Scepsis, and left them to his heirs, people uninterested in philosophy, who stored the books carelessly and kept them locked up. ... Later, when the books had been damaged by damp and worms, the descendants of Neleus' heirs sold the books of Aristotle and Theophrastus to Apellicon of Teos at a high price. He was more of a book-lover than a philosopher; and so, seeking to restore the worm-eaten parts, he made new copies, but did not complete them well, and published the books full of errors. And so it came about that the earlier Peripatetics,

[18] Aristotle and the Stoics: see **260**.
[19] The section of Strabo's work geography on the eastern Mediterranean describes Scepsis.

those who came after Theophrastus, had none of the books at all, except a few, mainly popular works; and so they could not engage seriously in philosophy, but just made a song and dance about commonplaces. The later Peripatetics, from the time the books appeared, were better as philosophers and as Aristotelians, but were compelled to present <mere> likelihoods,[20] because of the number of errors <in the copies>.

24 PLUTARCH, *Sulla* xxvi.1–2 Sulla secured for himself the library of Apellicon of Teos, which included most of the works of Aristotle and Theophrastus, not yet well known at that time to most people. It is said that when the library was brought to Rome, Tyrannion the grammarian arranged most of it, and that when Andronicus of Rhodes had been supplied with copies by him, he published them, and drew up the current list of works. The earlier Peripatetics were evidently cultivated and learned, but they knew few of the works of Aristotle and Theophrastus, and did not know them well, because the estate of Neleus of Scepsis, to whom Theophrastus had left his books, had fallen into the hands of people with no ambition or interest in philosophy.

Scepticism

25 The ancient Sceptics are literally 'inquirers' or 'examiners' (*skeptikoi*), who examine the different justifications that different people give for accepting one belief over another. When the Sceptics find these justifications unsatisfactory, they reach a sceptical (in the modern sense) conclusion; they refrain from accepting various sets of beliefs as justified.

One major source of Sceptical arguments is Sextus Empiricus. Sextus regards himself as a 'Pyrrhonian', a follower of Pyrrhon. Our information about Pyrrhon is rather scanty and inconsistent. Some of it suggests that he was an extreme Sceptic who took himself to have undermined justifications for all beliefs, including the elementary beliefs that guide action; he saw no reason to believe that it would be bad for him to step over a precipice, or that there was a precipice in front of him; and so he no longer guided his actions by these beliefs. Pyrrhon survived only because his friends (apparently less Sceptical) looked after him.

Whatever truth there may be in these stories, they suggest a question that Sceptics needed to answer. The version of Pyrrhonian Scepticism that Sextus accepts is the one formulated by Aenesidemus, who tries to set out clearly the general principles that underlie the Sceptic's examination of other positions, and to explain the sense in which the Sceptic does or does not have convictions of his own.

[20] Text uncertain.

Sextus contrasts this Pyrrhonian outlook with the outlook of the 'Academics'. These are the Sceptics, including Arcesilaus and Carneades, who took over Plato's Academy in the Hellenistic period. Their dominance in the Academy marks the acceptance of a one-sided view of Plato that emphasizes the critical and aporetic character of some of the Socratic dialogues, and claims that this represents the true Socratic and Platonic spirit. The Academics examine other philosophical positions, without committing themselves to the truth of the premisses they rely on in these examinations; we know most about Carneades' discussions of the Stoicism of Chrysippus. Apparently he argued that the Stoics, according to their own principles, had no escape from a Sceptical conclusion (**292**). His criticism may have contributed to the reformulation of Stoic doctrine.

The exact differences between Pyrrhonian and Academic Sceptics are not completely clear. Aenesidemus and Sextus, at any rate, represent the Academics as less thoroughly sceptical. Sometimes they are said to claim to have discovered that nothing can be known, whereas the Pyrrhonians simply report that they have found no knowledge. Sometimes the Academics are said not to maintain complete suspension of judgement, but to discriminate more plausible (or 'persuasive') from less plausible views, and to rely on the more plausible. Most of the passages on Scepticism in the following chapters are from Sextus, and describe the Pyrrhonian version of Scepticism.

26 PHOTIUS, *Library* 169^{b}18–170^{a}2   I read Aenesidemus' eight Pyrrhonian discourses. The general purpose of the book is to confirm that there is nothing firm to be grasped, either through sense-perception or through thought. That is why neither the Pyrrhonians nor the others know the truth about reality, but the philosophers of other schools are ignorant of everything else, wearing themselves out pointlessly and wasting themselves in ceaseless tortures, and are also ignorant of this very thing, that they have apprehended none of the things they think they have grasped. … In the first discourse he introduces the disagreement between the Pyrrhonians and the Academics, and says this, almost word for word, that the Academics are dogmatic, and set some things down without hesitation and reject some without ambiguity. The Pyrrhonians, however, are at a loss, and released from all dogma, and none of them has ever said that everything can be apprehended, or that nothing can be; rather, they say that things are no more this way than that …

27 SEXTUS, *Pyrrhonian Outlines* i. 226 The Academics do not say that something is good or bad in the way that we Pyrrhonians do. They say it with the persuasion that it is more plausible that what they say is good is really good than that the contrary is good, and similarly with bad. But when we say something is good or bad, we never say this with the thought that what we say is plausible; rather, we follow <common> life, in order to avoid being inert.

Epicureanism

28 Epicurus is inspired by the Atomism of Democritus. He defends it against some of Aristotle's criticisms of Atomist materialism. But he revises some central Democritean doctrines. (1) He uses empiricism to defeat Scepticism. To avoid Democritus' Sceptical tendencies, he argues that Atomism is supported by the evidence of the senses and does not conflict with it. (2) He affirms indeterminism in the area of human choice and action, whereas Democritus seems to have been a determinist. (3) These two changes may be connected with the announced motive for Epicurus' inquiries. He presents Atomism as a view of the world that releases us from the fear of death, and from the moral errors that result from this fear. (4) In focusing on fear and anxiety as overriding evils, Epicurus relies on his hedonism, which he seeks to distinguish from any doctrine that advocates excess or self-indulgence.

The different branches of Epicurean philosophy appear to form an impressively integrated system. He defends his hedonism in ethics by appeal to the senses, arguing that these reveal pleasure as the primary good. Epicurean hedonism shows us that we ought above all to avoid anxiety. Fear of the gods and of punishment after death is our primary source of anxiety. We remove this fear of the gods by developing a world view that has no room for punishment after death. Atomism gives us the right sort of world view. Epicurus does not suggest, however, that we ought to try to talk ourselves into Atomism simply to relieve us from anxiety; for any such attempt would leave us with the anxious fear that our theory might be false. Only empiricism, in his view, can remove such anxiety; we can be free of doubt and fear only if we are sure that we are following the evidence of the senses. Hence, we must argue that the senses support the atomic theory.

The systematic character and practical aim of Epicurus' philosophy may help to explain why it was maintained largely unaltered by his successors.[21] Rejection of any part of the system would undermine the practical significance of the whole. The doctrinal rigidity of Epicureans was in some ways fortunate, from our point of view, since only a few of Epicurus' own writings have survived. The most extensive are three letters and a collection of short remarks, all preserved in Diogenes Laertius. For some details of his position we depend on later writers. One of the most important of these is the Roman poet Lucretius, who wrote a long epic poem *De Rerum Natura* ('On the Nature of Things'), presenting Epicurean natural philosophy as the means of release from the fear of death.

Stoicism

29 The Stoic[22] school regarded itself as having three founders: Zeno, Cleanthes, and Chrysippus. While it is sometimes possible to distinguish their contributions,

---

[21] Later Epicureans seem to take different views on friendship (**491**).
[22] They met in the Stoa Poikilê (painted porch) in Athens.

the task is often too conjectural to be appropriate for an introductory presentation; hence, this book makes no effort to assign specific Stoic doctrines to individual Stoics.

Stoic doctrines lack the tight connections and explicitly ethical motivation of Epicureanism. None the less, they are intended to constitute a philosophical system. The Stoics distinguish three areas of philosophy:

(1) Logic, including epistemology, philosophy of language, dialectic, and rhetoric, as well as formal logic.

(2) Physics, including natural philosophy, psychology, cosmology, and theology.

(3) Ethics, including political theory.

Different Stoics have different views about which of these areas should be studied first. The different reasons they give indicate different, but compatible, views about the structure of Stoic philosophy. Indeed, the fact that different approaches can be defended may indicate that Stoic doctrines do not form a hierarchy in which some principles are taken to be altogether basic and independent of all the others.

Our sources for Stoicism are quite plentiful, but not necessarily the ones we would most like. No complete work by any of the three founders of the school has survived; we have to rely on paraphrases or quotations by later writers, many of whom oppose the Stoic doctrines they are reporting (Plutarch, Galen, and Sextus, for instance), and some of whom (Cicero, for instance) may not fully understand these doctrines. The Stoic writers whose works survive— Epictetus, Seneca, Marcus Aurelius—are much later than the founders of the school. They are more interested in the practical applications of Stoicism, and devote less space to the arguments and theories that support these practical applications.

In quoting from the sources, I have sometimes added a reference to two modern collections of texts: Von Arnim's *Stoicorum Veterum Fragmenta* (cited as SVF; Greek and Latin texts only), and Long and Sedley's *Hellenistic Philosophers* (cited as LS; Greek and Latin texts with translation and commentary). These references are given in cases where the original source may be difficult to find. Most of the other passages I quote will also be found in one or both of these collections.

....

30 DIOGENES LAERTIUS vii. 40   They compare philosophy to an animal, likening the logical part to the bones and sinews, the ethical part to the fleshier parts, and the natural part to the soul. Or again they compare it to an egg. For the outer parts are the logical part, the next part is the ethical, and the inmost part is the natural. Or they compare it to a productive field, of which the surrounding wall is the logical part, the fruit is the ethical part, and the land or trees the natural part. Or they compare it to a city that is excellently fortified and governed in accord with reason. Some Stoics say that no part is separate from another, but the parts are mixed. And they taught <the three parts> mixed together. Others put the logical part first, the natural part second, and the ethical part third. Zeno (in his *On Rational Discourse*) and Chrysippus and Archedemus and Eudromus are in this group. Diogenes of Ptolemais, though, begins with the ethical part, and Apollodorus puts the ethical part second. Panaetius and Poseidonius start with the natural part.

Later Aristotelianism and Platonism

31 Limitations of space prevent proper coverage of Greek philosophy in the Roman Empire. But the importance of some of these writers for earlier philosophy makes it necessary to comment on them briefly, without attempting to give any idea of their intrinsic interest.

From the first century BC onwards, Aristotle's works began to be more widely available, and a long series of commentaries was begun. These commentaries, some of which were written from a Platonist point of view, are important in these ways:

(1) They discuss the interpretation of Aristotle in some detail.

(2) Sometimes they examine Aristotle's position in comparison with other philosophers, especially the Stoics. Some of the comparative essays of Alexander of Aphrodisias are especially important.

(3) They are an important source for Presocratic philosophy, especially in the commentaries on Aristotle's historical surveys.

(4) Their interest in issues about Aristotle sometimes leads them to develop their own answers to questions raised by reflection on Aristotle.

In the first century BC, Plato's Academy took a new turn. Some of its members abandoned Scepticism, and began a revival of constructive Platonism. Antiochus' version of Plato's position includes some Aristotelian and Stoic elements. This tendency to combine elements of different philosophical positions becomes especially clear in the 'middle' Platonism of the first and second centuries AD. No long continuous works survive from this period, but we can form some idea of this side of Platonism from Alcinous' summary of Plato's doctrines. Middle Platonism is also a major philosophical inspiration for the medical writer Galen, for the Jewish theologian Philo, and for some early Christian writers, including Justin Martyr, Clement of Alexandria, and Origen.

The outlook that modern writers describe as 'Neoplatonism' is contained primarily in the works of Plotinus and his successors. They regard themselves as students and defenders of Plato, not as innovators. Their conception of Plato's philosophy, however, is highly selective. They place relatively little emphasis on the Socratic, exploratory side of Plato, and on his moral and political philosophy. They place most emphasis on his metaphysics, which they take to affirm the unreality of the material world, the unreliability of the senses, and the exclusive reality of the non-sensible, non-material, non-temporal world of Forms.

Translations

32 The translations from Greek and Latin are my own, but I have consulted published versions throughout. When I have departed from published versions, this is not necessarily because I thought they were defective; often it is because I wanted the translations to be suitable for a volume of this sort. No one approach to translation is best for every purpose and for every sort of reader.

Translators differ, quite understandably, about (i) how much of the information available to a reader of Greek and Latin should be made available to the reader of the translation; (ii) how far the original should be recast so as to make reasonably natural English; (iii) how far the original should be expanded, supplemented, or paraphrased to make it intelligible to the reader without a detailed commentary.

Decisions about these questions may lead the translator in different directions. The price of conveying to the English reader all the stylistic nuances and shades of meaning of the Greek or Latin may be rather awkward English. Greek and Latin syntax is different from modern English syntax, especially in its preference for hypotactic constructions (creating a long sentence with many subordinate clauses), rather than the paratactic constructions favoured by modern English. Moreover, some of the ancient writers are obscure, compressed, or awkward; the translator has to decide how far these features of the original should be made evident to the English reader.

Different answers to these questions may be appropriate for different purposes. If one were translating a single text for the use of readers who propose to study it in detail, one might well decide that one ought to put the reader, as far as possible, in the position of someone who knows the Greek or Latin original, and that one ought not to smooth out the style or syntax, or to amplify or clarify the thought. Such a version, however, is likely to be initially frustrating to the reader. In an introductory selection of texts, one may claim some freedom to make the texts more accessible to the reader who is not intending to puzzle over each sentence with the help of detailed commentaries.

I have claimed this freedom, but I have tried not to abuse it. In some cases—in Parmenides and Heracleitus, for instance—no version that is reasonably close to the original can hope to avoid being obscure and puzzling. When it is important for the reader to know exactly how the ancient author expresses himself, I have tried to convey this, even by sacrificing natural English. I cannot pretend, then, to have made the ancient texts easy to read, but I hope I have removed some obstacles that can be removed without serious distortion of the originals.

A translation ought to follow a reasonably consistent policy in rendering specific Greek and Latin words, in cases where it is philosophically relevant to know that the same word, or a grammatical variant, occurs in different contexts. Greek moralists, for instance, argue over several centuries about the nature of virtue, *aretê*. They suppose their disputes are about the nature of one and the same thing. It is difficult to follow their disputes if one does not recognize occurrences of the word *aretê*; if one is to recognize these occurrences without knowing Greek, they need to be translated uniformly, or, at least, without so much variation that one cannot identify them as occurrences of the same Greek word. This apparently reasonable constraint often raises difficulties for the translator, since no one English rendering is clearly appropriate for all contexts. Similar questions arise with Aristotle's claim that one of the oldest questions in Greek philosophy is the question 'What is being (*on*)?', and that this question is equivalent to the question 'What is substance (*ousia*)?'. Unless one can trace occurrences of the verb 'to be' (*einai*) and of *ousia* in the right places, one will not know what Aristotle is talking about. In such cases, I have tried to help the reader by sticking to a small number of variant renderings of crucial terms, and by making it clear when they translate a specific Greek term.

Since I have tried to make the texts intelligible by expanding and clarifying, I have resolved ambiguities present in the original, and have therefore assumed a specific interpretation of some difficult passages. In some important cases, I have tried to indicate where I have done this, by giving alternative renderings. In some cases, these alternatives rest on different views about the probable text of the Greek or Latin manuscript itself; in others, they reflect some ambiguity resulting from grammar or syntax, or from the meaning of specific words. Readers who attend to the footnotes will have some idea of some of the more controversial decisions I have made.

I have marked insertions with angle brackets <...>. I have used these only in cases where the original is not clear and some philosophically significant point turns on our decision about what to insert. Square brackets at the beginning of a passage are used to indicate the philosopher who is being quoted or paraphrased. I have marked omissions in the usual way, with dots. The passages omitted are often quite long and important; they add complications, qualifications, illustrations, or side issues that did not seem vital for understanding the main point. Though I have tried to select passages that are reasonably intelligible by themselves, I cannot pretend that they are all easy to understand, or that this book provides all the resources for understanding them. Readers who are puzzled ought to turn to the original sources, and to the more detailed commentaries and discussions by modern students; the list of Further Reading suggests where one might turn for help.

II: Nature, Change, and Cause

Natural philosophy before Plato

Change and nature

33 Aristotle calls the early philosophers 'naturalists' (*phusiologoi*), in contrast to the mythological and theological thinkers who preceded them, because they seek a rational understanding of nature (*phusis*). (See **101**.) He sees that in describing their inquiry into the world as an inquiry into nature, the early philosophers assumed some general principles about the scope and form of their inquiry.

We speak of x's nature both in saying what x comes to be from and in saying what x is made of. These two ways of speaking of nature often pick out the same thing: a house is built from bricks and mortar, and it consists of bricks and mortar. Hence, the naturalists seek to discover what things come from and what they consist in. They seek to understand the observed processes and changes in the natural world, by tracing them to their underlying constituents. An underlying constituent is a 'principle' (*archê*; or 'beginning') (**43-4**). Hence the naturalists inquire into principles.

This inquiry leads naturalists to look for laws and explanations underlying the variety of changes that we observe. When Herodotus describes the 'nature' of the crocodile, and the Hippocratic writer describes the 'nature' of the so-called 'sacred disease' (epilepsy), they describe the regular and permanent traits manifested in the behaviour of the animal or the disease. A search for the permanent traits leads the naturalists to the underlying constitution of things. This underlying constitution is hard to find; Heracleitus warns the investigator that nature tends to hide (**39**).

To look for explanations involving nature is to assume that something's behaviour can be explained by laws and regularities in its own constitution. This assumption did not seem obviously correct to the contemporaries of the naturalists. They were used to explanations that referred to interventions by capricious gods which caused things to behave in unexpected ways. The naturalists implicitly reject such views in confining their explanations to nature (**40, 351–3, 574**).

34 ARISTOTLE, *Metaphysics* 1014^{b}16–35 What is called nature is[1] ... the first thing that any natural object consists of or comes to be from, this being

---

[1] Aristotle mentions other uses of 'nature' (*phusis*) before he comes to the one most relevant to the Presocratics.

previously shapeless and unchanged from its own capacity. Thus, for instance, bronze is said to be the nature of a statue and of bronze utensils, and wood the nature of wooden things. The same is true in all other cases; for each product consists of these things, with the first matter being preserved throughout. This is what people mean in calling the elements of natural objects their nature. Some say this about fire, others about earth, or air, or water, or something else of this sort; some say this about more than one of these, and others about all of them.

35 HERODOTUS, ii. 68   The nature of crocodiles is this: For the four winter months, it eats nothing. It has four feet, and it lives both on land and in the water. For it lays eggs and hatches them out on land and spends most of the day on dry land, but it spends the whole night in the river, since the water is warmer than the air and dew. Of all the mortal creatures we know, this one grows from the smallest beginnings to the greatest length; for its eggs are not much bigger than goose eggs, and the young crocodile is in proportion to the egg, but when it grows, it reaches twenty-eight feet and more.

36 HIPPOCRATES, *Sacred Disease* 1[2]   About what is called the sacred disease the facts are these: It seems to me to be not at all more divine or more sacred than other diseases. On the contrary, it has a nature and an explanation. Human beings, however, have conventionally regarded it,[3] as divine because of their inexperience and their amazement, since it is not at all like other diseases. Its reputation for being divine is maintained by people's puzzlement,[4] resulting from their ignorance, but it is exploded by the ease of curing it—for people are cured of it by purifications and incantations. But if it is to be regarded as divine because it is amazing, there will turn out to be many sacred diseases, not just one; for, as I will show, there are others no less amazing and prodigious that no one regards as sacred. ... It seems to me that the first to sanctify this disease were people such as the magicians, purifiers, charlatans and quacks who are around now, who actually make a show of great piety and superior knowledge. When these people, then, were at a loss, they put forward the divine to cover their incompetence, since they had no treatment that could be applied to relieve it; and to prevent their ignorance from being exposed, they regarded this illness as sacred.

37 HIPPOCRATES, *Sacred Disease* 5   But this disease seems to me to be no more divine than the rest. On the contrary, it has a nature, as the other diseases have, and an explanation of how a given aspect of it comes to be.[5] And

[2] On the theological significance of this passage see **574**.
[3] *nomizein*, cognate with *nomos*. See **125**.
[4] aporia. See **142**.
[5] Text uncertain.

it is curable no less than others, unless from length of time it is so ingrained as to be too severe for the remedies that are applied.

38 HIPPOCRATES, *Sacred Disease* 20   This disease called sacred comes to be from the same explanations from which the others arise too: from the things that enter and leave the body, from cold, sun, and winds, which are always changing and never at rest. Since these things are divine, one ought not to separate this disease and regard it as more divine than the rest. On the contrary, all are divine, and all human. Each has its own proper nature and power; none is insoluble or beyond treatment.

39 THEMISTIUS, *Orations* 5, 101. 13 = DK 22 B 123   Nature,[6] according to Heracleitus, tends[7] to hide.

40 GREGORY VLASTOS, *Plato's Universe*,[8] p. 10   ... the failure of ... observable regularity implies no disturbance of the more massive constancies which constitute the order of nature, and, if known, would yield the ultimate explanation of every natural phenomenon, no matter how unusual or surprising. On this point Heracleitus, Anaximander, and all the *physiologoi* would stand united—a handful of intellectuals against the world. Everyone else, Greek and barbarian alike, would take it for granted that any regularity you care to mention could fail, and for a reason which ruled out a priori a natural explanation of the failure: because it was caused by divine intervention.

Explaining change: Aristotle on the naturalists

41 In Aristotle's view, the naturalists had an intuitive sense of some of the questions that needed to be asked, but they did not ask exactly the right questions, because they did not fully understand the assumptions underlying some of their questions. He believes they were wrong to confine questions about nature to questions about origin and constitution (**99, 235–7**).

While the naturalists (according to Aristotle) all assume that we understand natural objects and processes by deriving them from their basic underlying constituent ('subject'; **227**) or constituents, they disagree about the character of the basic constituents. Anaximander, for instance, decided that no ordinary material element—such as water (favoured by Thales) or earth—could be suitably basic, since each is destroyed by its opposite (cold by hot, dry by wet, and so on). To find a persisting subject more basic than the elements, Anaximander introduced 'the Unlimited' (*apeiron*). The Greek term might be rendered 'boundless', 'infinite',

[6] Or 'the nature of a thing'.
[7] Or 'loves'.
[8] Seattle: University of Washington Press, 1975.

or 'indeterminate', and each rendering may convey part of what Anaximander intended. According to Simplicius, the Unlimited is the basic persisting subject, and every apparent coming-to-be and perishing is really just a change in the Unlimited (**44**).

....

42 ARISTOTLE, *Parts of Animals* 640^{b}4–17   The early thinkers, the first to engage in philosophical inquiry into nature, investigated the material principle and cause, to see what it is and of what sort, how the whole universe comes into being from it, and what initiates the process. In their view, strife, for instance, or love, or mind, or chance initiates the process, and the matter that is the subject necessarily has a certain sort of nature; fire, for instance, has a hot and light nature, earth a cold and heavy nature. This, indeed, is how they bring the world-order into being. They give the same sort of account of how animals and plants come into being. They say, for example, that the flowing of water in the body brings into being the stomach and every receptacle for food and waste, and the flow of air results in the breaking open of the nostrils. Air and water are the matter of bodies, since all these philosophers constitute nature from elementary bodies of this sort.

43 ARISTOTLE, *Metaphysics* 983^{b}1–984^{a}27   Let us ... enlist those who previously took up the investigation of existing things and pursued philosophical study about the truth; for it is clear that they also mention causes and principles of some sort.[9] A discussion of their views, then, will advance our present line of inquiry; for either we shall find some other kind of cause or we shall have more confidence in those we have just mentioned.

Most of the first philosophers thought the only principles of everything were material. For, they say, there is some subject that all existing things come from. This is the first thing they come to be from and the last thing they perish into; this substance remains throughout and changes by being affected in different ways. This is the elementary basis and the origin of beings. For this reason they think nothing either comes to be or perishes, since they assume that in every change this nature persists. For we say Socrates does not come to be unqualifiedly whenever he becomes good or musical, and does not perish unqualifiedly whenever he loses these states—for the subject, Socrates himself, remains. In the same way, then, they say, nothing else either comes to be or perishes unqualifiedly, since there must be some nature, either one or more than one, that persists while the other things come to be from it.

But they do not all agree about the number or type of this material

[9] Aristotle has just listed the four types of causes he recognizes; see **98**. A 'principle', *archê* (also translated 'origin' and 'beginning'), is not linguistic or conceptual, but, as the following discussion shows, a basic reality.

principle. Thales, the originator of this sort of philosophy, says it is water (that is why he also declared that the earth rests on water). Presumably he reached this view from seeing that what nourishes all things is wet and that the hot itself comes from the wet and is kept alive by it (and what all things come to be from is their principle). Another reason he reached this view was that he thought that the seeds of all things have a wet nature (and water is the principle of the nature of wet things). ... Anaximenes and Diogenes take air to be both prior to water and also the most basic principle of all the simple bodies, while Hippasus of Metapontium and Heracleitus of Ephesus say this about fire. Empedocles takes the four bodies to be principles, adding earth as a fourth to the ones mentioned. These, he says, always remain, and do not come to be, except in so far as they come to be more or fewer things, by being combined into one and dispersed from one into many. Anaxagoras[10] of Clazomenae, who was older than Empedocles but wrote later, says that the principles are unlimited; for he says that practically all the uniform[11] things (for instance, water or fire) come to be and perish only in the ways we have mentioned, by being combined and dispersed; they do not come to be or perish in any other way, but always remain.

If one went by these views, one might suppose that the material cause is the only sort of cause. But as people thus progressed, reality itself made a path for them and compelled them to inquire. For however true it might be that all coming to be and perishing is from one (or more than one) thing, still, why does this happen, and what is the cause? For surely the subject does not produce change in itself; neither the wood, for instance, nor the bronze causes itself to change, nor does the wood itself produce a bed, or the bronze a statue, but something else is the cause of the change. And an inquiry into this is (in our view) an inquiry into the second principle—the source of the principle of change.

44 SIMPLICIUS, *Commentary on the Physics* 24. 13–25 Of those who hold that the principle is one, moving, and unbounded, Anaximander, son of Praxiades, a Milesian, who became a successor and student of Thales, says that the unbounded is principle and element of existing things. He was the first to use this name of the principle.[12] He says that it is neither water nor any other of the things called elements, but some different and unbounded nature, from which (he says) all the heavens and the world-orders in them come into being. And the things from which existing things come into being are also the things into which they are destroyed, in accordance with what must be. For

[10] Anaxagoras; **96**, **242**, **588**.

[11] Uniform things; **252**.

[12] Or 'the first to use this word "principle" '. It is not clear whether Theophrastus (reported here by Simplicius) means that Anaximander was the first to use *archê* or that he was the first to use *apeiron*.

(he says) they pay justice and reparation to one another for their injustice, in accordance with the ordering of time—this is how he speaks of them in rather poetical words.[13] It is clear that he observed the change of the four elements into one another, and so thought that none of them, but something else apart from them, should be the subject.[14] He brings about coming into being not by the alteration of the element, but by the separating off of the contraries through the everlasting motion.

Heracleitus: change over time

45 Heracleitus rejects Anaximander's Unlimited; he believes (according to Aristotle) no basic continuing subject is needed. In his view, fire is the basic constituent, and all changes are really modifications of fire. Aristotle attributes to Heracleitus an argument beginning from a general preoccupation with change and stability (**54**).

Heracleitus begins with ordinary ways (which he gradually questions) of speaking and thinking about change. When we say Socrates was thin and is now fat, we assume that one and the same subject, Socrates, existed when Socrates was thin and exists now when Socrates is fat. Heracleitus questions this assumption. He asks about the criterion of identity that we presuppose, and argues that no satisfactory criterion can support our belief in one and the same persisting Socrates.

He raises different issues about identity (perhaps without explicitly distinguishing them).

(1) We seek a criterion of unity at a time, if we ask what makes it true that (for instance) this book is one book and not simply a collection of pages, or that this dog is one dog and not simply a collection of flesh and bones.

(2) We seek a criterion of distinctness at a time, if we ask what makes it true that these two pennies are two and not one, or that Socrates and Plato are two and not one.

(3) We seek a criterion of continuity over time, if we ask what makes it true that the tall tree today is the same tree as the short tree of fifty years ago or the seventy-year-old Socrates of 399 BC was the same person as the twenty-year-old Socrates of 449 BC.

Some of Heracleitus' views about change seem to rely on a compositional criterion of continuity. This criterion is explained by Locke, who applies it to bodies composed of atoms (**49**). According to Locke, the same thing exists at two

[13] This makes it clear that Simplicius has been quoting Anaximander; but it is not clear where the quotation began. On cosmic justice see **574**.
[14] Subject; **227**.

different times if and only if a collection of exactly the same components exists at these two times. If, for instance, I have a collection of six coins in a box, and I keep the very same coins together (in the same or in a different container), I have exactly the same collection of coins. If, however, I lose one coin, I no longer have the same collection; I have a collection of five coins. If I replace my lost coin with a different coin, I have a different collection with the same number of coins.[15]

Heracleitus relies on this compositional criterion of continuity (identity through time) in claiming that the sun does not really persist from one day to the next (because it is a new mass of fire each day), and that we cannot step into the same river twice. The water constituting a river is always flowing away and being replaced; since loss of constituents means destruction, each river is always being destroyed and being replaced by a different river. Hence, no continuous subject that is the same river exists at any two times; there is simply a process (**48**, **50**-**2**).

This argument applies not only to things with evidently transitory components, such as rivers, but also to apparently stable things such as ships (§55), trees, and animals. Each of these things grows and decays and interacts with other things; its composition changes, and, since identity is determined by composition, it is passing out of existence all the time, to be replaced by something else. Since human beings constantly change in some way, no one is strictly the same person from one time to another (**53**, **56**).

Heracleitus infers that 'everything flows' and nothing remains stable. We are wrong to believe that ordinary subjects such as Socrates persist through change. The naive belief in persisting subjects with opposite properties at different times turns out to be confused. For though we accept this naive belief, we also accept the compositional criterion of continuity, and therefore we must admit that ordinary things are not stable.

....

46 DIOGENES LAERTIUS ix. 5–6   The book attributed to Heracleitus is a work on nature, from its connecting theme, but it is divided into three discourses, one on the universe, one on politics, and one on the gods. He deposited it in the temple of Artemis, and, according to some, he deliberately made it more obscure, so that only capable[16] readers would approach it, and it would be less subject to the contempt of the masses ... Theophrastus says that his fluctuating moods made him leave some parts of the book half-finished, and other parts disorganized.

47 EUSEBIUS, *Preparation for the Gospel* xv. 20 = DK 22 B 12   On those who step into the same rivers, different waters flow at different times.

[15] The compositional criterion; **238**, **250**.
[16] Or perhaps 'powerful'.

48 PLATO, *Cratylus* 402 A   Heracleitus says somewhere[17] that everything passes away and nothing remains. In likening beings to the flow of a river, he says that you could not step into the same river twice.

49 LOCKE, *Essay* ii. 27. 3   … if two or more atoms be joined together into the same mass, … whilst they exist united together, the mass, consisting of the same atoms, must be the same mass, or the same body, let the parts be ever so differently jumbled. But if one of these atoms be taken away, or any new one added, it is no longer the same mass or the same body.

50 PLUTARCH, *The E at Delphi* 392b–393a = DK 22 B 91   For it is not possible to step twice into the same river, according to Heracleitus, nor to touch mortal substance[18] twice that is the same in its condition. By the swiftness and speed of its change, it scatters and gathers together again—or rather, it is not again and later but simultaneously that it comes together and departs, approaches and re-treats. … [392e] For time is something changeable, and appears together with changing matter, and it flows always and keeps nothing, like a bucket of per-ishing and coming to be—of which in fact the 'next', the 'before', the 'will be', and the 'has come to be' simply by being uttered are an immediate admission of not being. … And if the nature that is measured by time undergoes the same things as what measures it, then none of it persists, or even is.

51 ARISTOTLE, *On the Heavens* 298^{b}25–33[19]   There are some who say that nothing is ungenerated, but everything in the world comes into being, but after coming into being some things remain without destruction, while the rest are again destroyed. This has been asserted most of all by Hesiod and his followers, and then outside his circle by the earliest students of nature. These people say that everything else comes into being and flows, and nothing firmly is, except one single thing that persists, from which all these result by transformation. This is what Heracleitus of Ephesus and many others would seem to mean.

52 ARISTOTLE, *Physics* 253^{b}9–12   Moreover, the view is actually held by some that not merely some things but all things in the world are in change and always in change, though we do not notice this with our senses … The supporters of this theory do not state clearly what kind of change they mean, or whether they mean all kinds.

53 DIOGENES LAERTIUS iii. 9–11   Plato evidently often borrows from Epicharmus. Consider: Plato says that what is perceptible is what never persists

---

[17] Or 'I presume'.
[18] *ousia*; **227**.
[19] This follows **71**.

in quality or quantity, but is always in flux and change.[20] The assumption is that the things from which you take away some number are no longer equal nor the same things, nor have the same quantity or quality. These are the things that always have becoming and never have being. But the object of thought is what has nothing subtracted or added. This is the nature of the eternal things, the attribute of which is to be always alike and the same.

And indeed Epicharmus speaks plainly about what is perceived and what is thought: ... 'A: Suppose someone chooses to add a single pebble to a heap containing either an odd or an even number, whichever you like, or to take away one of those already there; do you think the number of pebbles would remain the same? B: I don't think so. A: Nor yet, if one chooses to add to a yard measure another length, or cut off some of what was there already, would the original measure still exist? B: Of course not. A: Now consider human beings in the same way: One person grows, and another shrinks; they are all in course of change the whole time. But a thing that naturally changes and never remains in the same state must always be different from what has changed. In the same way, you and I were one pair yesterday, are another today, and again will be another tomorrow, and will never remain the same people, according to this argument.'

54 ARISTOTLE, *Meteorology* 354[b]34–355[a]14   Hence those earlier thinkers who supposed that the sun was nourished by moisture are ridiculous. Some go on to say that this is why the solstices happen, because the same places cannot always supply the sun with nourishment, but it needs nourishment if it is not to perish; for the fire we observe lives as long as it is fed, and the only food for fire is moisture. This account assumes that the moisture that rises can reach the sun, and that this rising is really like the way flames rise when they come into being; they drew the analogy from this, and applied it to the sun. But it is not at all similar. For a flame comes into being through a constant interchange of moist and dry; it is not nourished,[21] since it remains the same for hardly any time at all. This cannot be true of the sun; for if it were nourished in this way, as those thinkers say it is, clearly there would not only be a new sun every day, as Heracleitus says, but a new sun every moment.

55 PLUTARCH, *Theseus* 23   The Athenians preserved this ship—the thirty-oared ship on which Theseus sailed with the youths and returned in safety—down to the time of Demetrius of Phaleron. They preserved it by removing old timbers, inserting new and firm ones, and fastening them together. And so the ship became an example for the philosophers in the disputed 'growing argument'; for some said that it remained the same, others that it did not.

[20] Plato on change; **200–1**.
[21] Aristotle on nutrition and growth; **252**.

56 PLATO, *Theaetetus* 158 E–159 B   SOCRATES: This is the question they[22] ask, I take it: 'Theaetetus, when one thing is altogether different from another, it cannot in any way have any capacity the same as the other's, can it? Let us not suppose that the thing we are asking about is in some way the same and in other ways different, but that it is altogether different.' THEAETETUS: If so, it can have nothing the same, either in capacity or in anything else, whenever it is completely different.—Must we not also admit, then, that such a thing is unlike the other?—I agree.—If it happens, then, that one thing comes to be like or unlike either itself or something else, we'll say that when it is made like it becomes the same, when unlike different.—Necessarily. ... [159 B]— Now let's take you and me and the other things in accordance with the same account: healthy Socrates and sick Socrates, for instance. Are we to say that one of these is like or unlike the other?—You mean, is sick Socrates as a whole like healthy Socrates as a whole?—You've understand me perfectly; that's just what I mean.—Then of course I say he is unlike.—Then in so far as he is un-like, he is different?—Necessarily.—And will you say the same of Socrates asleep or in any of the other conditions we mentioned?—Yes.

Heracleitus: the unity of opposites

57 When our sources report Heracleitus' belief in change and flux, they some-times include in it his belief in the 'unity of opposites' (**50**). The road up and the road down, he says, are one and the same. The same water is both good (for fish) and bad (for human beings). The strung bow is held together in being pulled apart. God is both day and night, summer and winter, war and peace, satiety and hunger. 'War is the father and king of all', because everything depends on a ceaseless struggle between opposites (**58–60**).

These cases raise a question about our criterion of unity at a time. We are in-clined to assume that though the railway goes east (from Moscow to Vladivos-tok) and the railway goes west (from Vladivostok to Moscow), these are simply two aspects of one and the same railway, which can be described (as the Trans-Siberian Railway) without reference to its easterly or westerly direction. Simi-larly, the water that is healthy and unhealthy can be described as sea water, without reference to its healthy or unhealthy character. This way of thinking about the railway or the water takes it for granted that there is some subject dis-tinct from the pair of opposite properties. If, however, a purely compositional criterion of unity is correct, there is no such subject apart from a particular col-lection of component properties, and hence there is no subject beyond the op-posites that make it up.

Heracleitus infers there are no persistent objects of the sort we normally

---

[22] Heracleiteans.

suppose there are. The world is, in this respect, less stable than we suppose. But he also argues for the underlying stability of the processes that explain the flux in ordinary things. The stable aspects of the universe are not the rocks, trees, and other ordinary objects that appear to common sense, but the processes of change that these ordinary objects undergo.

This conclusion is summarized in Heracleitus' comparison of the universe to a fire (**61, 64**). A bonfire may be made of wood, grass, paper, leaves, or any other suitable material, in the right proportions, and it keeps burning as long as more fuel is added, and the same physical laws hold. None of the fuel survives, but there is one process, since the fire still burns. Constant change and destruction is just the manifestation of the continuous process that is the world-order as a whole (**66**).

....

58 HIPPOLYTUS, *Refutation* ix. 10. 4 = DK 22 B 60–1   Heracleitus says: 'The road up and down are one and the same.' And he says the filthy and the pure, and the drinkable and the undrinkable, are one and the same: 'The sea is both the purest and the foulest water. For fish it is drinkable and healthy, for human beings it is undrinkable and ruinous.'[23]

59 HIPPOLYTUS, *Refutation* ix. 9. 4 = DK 22 B 53   War is the father of all and king of all, and showed some as gods, and others as human beings, made some slaves, and others free.

60 HIPPOLYTUS, *Refutation* ix. 10. 8 = DK 22 B 67   The god is day and night, winter and summer, war and peace, plenty and hunger. He alters in the way in which <oil>, whenever it is mixed with spices, takes the name of the fragrance of each one.

61 CLEMENT, *Miscellanies* v. 14. 104. 2 = DK 22 B 30   This world order,[24] the same for all, was made by no god or man, but always was and is and will be an ever-living fire, being kindled in measures and quenched in measures.[25]

62 CLEMENT, *Miscellanies* vi. 2. 17. 2 = DK 22 B 36   For souls, it is death to become water, and for water it is death to become earth. But from earth water comes into being, and from water soul comes into being.[26]

63 CLEMENT, *Miscellanies* v. 14. 104. 3 = DK 22 B 31   Turnings of fire: first sea; of sea half is earth, half burning.[27]

[23] See also **118**.
[24] *kosmos*; see **113**.
[25] Soul and fire; **310–11**.
[26] It is not clear whether this passage deals with physiology or cosmology.
[27] Translation uncertain.

64 PLUTARCH, *The E at Delphi* 388e = DK 22 B 90   The first principle by changing produces the world order from itself, and, again, ends by producing itself out of the world order, as Heracleitus says: 'All things are an exchange for fire, and fire for all things, as goods are for gold, and gold for goods.'

65 ORIGEN, *Against Celsus* vi. 42 = DK 22 B 80   Celsus says the ancient writers alluded obscurely to some war among the gods, Heracleitus writing as follows: 'It is necessary to know that war is common, justice is conflict, and that all things come into being in accordance with how things must be.'

66 HIPPOLYTUS, *Refutation* ix. 9. 5 = DK 22 B 54   That God is unapparent, unseen, and unknown to human beings he says in these words: 'Unapparent order is superior[28] to apparent.'

67 LUCRETIUS i. 690–700   To say, as Heracleitus does, that all things are fire, and nothing can be counted among genuine things except fire, seems totally crazy. For, setting out from the senses, he attacks and undermines the senses; but on them all beliefs rest, and from them he himself has come to know the thing he calls fire. For he believes that the senses really come to know fire, but he does not believe the other things that are no less clear. This seems to me both pointless and crazy. For what else can we appeal to? What can be a surer basis for marking true things off from false than the senses themselves?[29]

Parmenides on speaking and thinking

68 Heracleitus wants a rational account of change and stability to make cosmology intelligible. Parmenides believes cosmology is unintelligible; it seeks to understand and to explain change, but change is unintelligible. He argues for this conclusion about change in his long philosophical poem. According to Simplicius (**69–70**), this was called 'On Nature', recalling the naturalists' claim to inquire into nature (see **3**, **33**); but it departs from naturalist assumptions by denying the very possibility of discovering any truth about nature.

The first part of the poem is called 'The Way of Truth'; it argues that change is unreal, because change involves not-being, which must be rejected. The second part of the poem, 'The Way of Belief', presents an elaborate cosmology, giving an account of the natural world and its various processes. But this whole cosmology is based on the false assumption that change is real, and so the account itself is false (**121–4**).

Parmenides asserts that we must choose between 'is' and 'is not', and that we

---

[28] Either 'better' or 'stronger' or both.
[29] Epicurus on reliance on the senses; **278–81**.

cannot choose 'is not' (**72–3**). Why must we make this choice? Why not choose both 'is' and 'is not'? Parmenides answers:

(1) Anything that can be spoken of or thought must be.

(2) Nothing cannot be.

(3) Hence, nothing cannot be spoken of or thought.

(4) What is not is nothing.

(5) Hence, what is not cannot be spoken of or thought.

This conclusion requires us to reject any alleged speaking or thinking that presupposes speaking or thinking of what is not. Parmenides' argument continues:

(6) We can speak and think of change only if we can speak or think of what is not.

(7) Hence (by (5)) we cannot speak or think of change.

Why does Parmenides insist on his first premiss? Plato offers a possible explanation, in an argument (which he rejects) to show that false belief is impossible (**74**). This argument rests on an analogy between believing and seeing or touching; just as touching what is not is touching nothing, which is not touching at all, so false belief (believing what is not) is believing nothing, which is not believing at all. Speaking may be understood in the same way, as direct contact with an object (**75**). We give a name to something by pointing to it and uttering the name. If we point at nothing, we are naming nothing, and just utter empty noise. Hence, speaking of what is not is not really speaking at all.

....

69 SIMPLICIUS, *Commentary on the Physics* 144. 25–8 = DK 28 A 21   If it does not strike anyone as too elaborate, I would like to transcribe in this commentary Parmenides' verses concerning the one being—in fact there are not many of them—both because it gives credibility to my comments and because of the rarity of Parmenides' treatise.

70 SIMPLICIUS, *Commentary on On the Heavens* 556. 25–30 ... both Melissus and Parmenides entitled their books *On Nature* ... and indeed in these books they discussed not only things beyond the realm of nature, but also natural things. And perhaps that is why they did not hesitate to entitle them *On Nature*.

71 ARISTOTLE, *On the Heavens* 298^{b}11–24   This is presumably the first question to be considered: is there coming to be or not? The earlier philosophers who inquired into the truth disagreed both with one another and with what we say now. For some of them did away with coming to be and destruction altogether; for, they say, nothing comes to be or is destroyed, but it only seems[30]

....

[30] *dokein*. An allusion to Parmenides' 'Way of Belief' (*doxa*).

so to us. This was the view of the school of Melissus and Parmenides. But, even if everything else they say is right, we still cannot count them as speaking as students of nature; for the existence of things without any sort of coming to be or change is a question for another form of inquiry,[31] prior to the study of nature. They, however, supposed that there was nothing apart from the substance of perceptible things; and, since they were the first to think of changeless things as conditions for knowledge and understanding,[32] they transferred what was true of them to perceptible things.[33]

72 PROCLUS, *Commentary on the Timaeus* i. 345. 18 = DK 28 B 2–3 [PARMENIDES:] But come, I will tell you—and pass the story on when you hear it—the only roads of inquiry that are there to be thought of. One road—that it[34] is and it is not <possible> for it not to be—is the path of persuasion; for it attends on truth. Another—that it is not and must not be—this, I tell you, is an altogether undiscoverable track. For you could neither know nor speak of what is not; for the same thing is for thinking and for being.[35]

73 SIMPLICIUS, *Commentary on the Physics* 86. 27, 117. 4–13 = DK 28 B 6 [PARMENIDES:] What is for speaking of and for thinking must be; for it is for being, and nothing is not. These things I bid you say. From this first road of inquiry <I restrain> you. And then <I restrain you> from that road where ignorant mortals wander, two-headed; for confusion directs the wandering thought in their breast. They are borne along, deaf and blind at once, gaping, undiscerning masses, who count[36] being and not-being as the same and not the same, and who all follow a backward-turning path.

74 PLATO, *Theaetetus* 188 D–189 B[37]   SOCRATES: Then what will we say, Theaetetus, if someone asks us: 'But ... can anyone believe what is not, either about something that is or all by itself?'? It would seem we will answer to that, 'Yes, when he thinks things that are not true, but thinks they are true.' Or what are we going to say? THEAETETUS: We must say that.—Then does this sort of thing happen in any other case?—What sort of thing?—That someone sees something, but sees nothing.—No. How could that be?—Surely if he sees one thing, he sees something that is. Or do you suppose that *one* can ever be included among things that are not?—No, I don't.—Then, if he sees one thing, he sees a thing that is.—Apparently.—And if he hears something, he hears one thing and

---

[31] i.e. for metaphysics (**20**, 601).

[32] Conditions for knowledge; **194**.

[33] Aristotle continues with **51**.

[34] Subject supplied.

[35] The 'for . . .' clause appears by itself in an ancient source; modern editors have argued that it belongs with the preceding sentence.

[36] *nomizein*; **125**.

[37] False belief; **160**.

hears a thing that is.—Yes.—And if he touches something, he touches one thing, and if one, a thing that is.—That is also true.—And if he believes, he believes some one thing, doesn't he?—Necessarily.—And when he believes some one thing, he believes a thing that is?—I agree.—So if he believes what is not, he believes nothing.—Apparently.—But surely if he believes nothing, he does not believe at all.—That seems plain.—Then it is impossible to believe what is not, either about anything that is, or all by itself.—Apparently.

75 PLATO, *Sophist* 236 D–237 E   ELEATIC VISITOR: My dear friend, we are engaged in a very difficult investigation; for something's appearing and seeming, but not being, or saying things, but not true things—these have always been, and still are, full of puzzles. For how is one to say or believe that false things really are, and, having said this, not be caught in a contradiction? Indeed, Theaetetus, the task is a difficult one. THEAETETUS: Why?—This claim dares to assume that not-being is; for otherwise no falsehood would come about. But, my boy, in the days when I was a boy, the great Parmenides protested from beginning to end against this view, on every occasion, both in prose and in verse, saying this: 'For this will never be proved, that things that are not are. But in inquiring keep your thought from this path.'[38] That is his protest; and the assertion itself, if examined a little, makes the same point clear. Would you mind beginning with this point?—As far as I'm concerned, proceed as you please; consider how best to advance the argument, and lead me with you on that road.—That's what we must do. Now tell me: I presume we dare to utter 'what is not'?[39]—Certainly we do.—Let's be serious then, and consider the question neither for the sake of contention[40] nor for amusement. Suppose that one of our hearers had to think about it and answer the question what this name 'not-being' is to be applied to. What sort of thing do we think he would appeal to and point out to the questioner?—That's a difficult question, and altogether puzzling for someone like me to answer.—Well, this much is clear, that 'not-being' can't be applied to any being.—Yes, that's clear.—And if not to being, then it is not correctly applied to something.—Of course not.—It is also clear that in saying 'something' we apply it to being on each occasion; for to speak of it alone, as though naked and isolated from all beings, is impossible.—Yes, impossible.—By this investigation you agree that one who says something must speak of[41] some one thing?—Yes.—Then the one who does not speak of something, it would seem, must say nothing at all.—He certainly must.—Then surely we can't admit that such a person speaks, but says nothing. The one who undertakes to utter 'not-being' does not speak at all.— That's the greatest puzzle in the argument.

[38] Cf. **123**. Plato's text is slightly different.
[39] No quotation marks in the Greek.
[40] Contentious argument; **182**.
[41] Or 'say'.

Parmenides against change

76 This conception of thinking and speaking explains why we cannot speak of change and time. To speak of change is to speak of Socrates being different now from how he previously was or later will be. How he was or will be is a state of affairs that does not exist now; if it exists now, there is no change. But if it does not exist now, we cannot point to it; hence we cannot speak of it. This is what Parmenides means by saying that we cannot speak of anything as having come to be from what is not (i.e. from a condition that it no longer has, and therefore a state of affairs that no longer exists; **77**).

If we cannot speak of what is not, we cannot speak of past and future time. Past and future time do not now exist. If they do not exist now, we cannot point to them, and hence we cannot really speak of them. Hence Parmenides concludes that any genuine being—anything we can speak of or point to—must be wholly present.

Parmenides' argument raises important questions about the nature of thinking and speaking. We may protest that if Parmenides' conception of thinking and speaking implies all the conclusions he draws, his conception must be wrong. But if we are to justify our protest, we must say where he is wrong. What is it about speaking and thinking that allows us to speak and think about something, so that we do not simply make empty noise? Parmenides maintains that unless we speak and think of what exists now, we are making empty noise, and are not speaking or thinking about anything. If we reject his position, we must give some other account of what is required for speaking and thinking about something, and we must show that our account avoids Parmenides' conclusions. Plato sees the importance of Parmenides' questions (**78**; cf. **75**).

....

77 SIMPLICIUS, *Commentary on the Physics* 145. 1–146. 23 = DK 28 B 8.   [PAR-MENIDES:] Only one story of a road remains to be told—that it is. On this road there are very many signs that, being without coming-to-be, it[42] is also without destruction—whole, of one kind, unwavering, and complete.[43] Nor was it ever, nor will it ever be, since it is now all together, one, continuous. For what coming-to-be will you seek for it? How, and from what, had it grown <when it came to be>? Nor will I allow you to say or to think <that it came> from what is not; for that it is not cannot be said or thought. And what need brought it to be later or earlier, having begun from nothing? Hence, it must either altogether be or not be. Nor will the strength of belief allow that from what is not[44] it can become anything besides itself. Therefore justice[45] has not

---

[42] 'It', the subject of this argument, probably is what can be spoken of or thought.
[43] Text uncertain.
[44] Text uncertain.
[45] Cosmic justice; cf. **574**.

loosened its fetters to allow it to come to be or to perish, but holds it fast. The discrimination about these things lies in this: it is or it is not. Well, the discrimination is already made, as it must necessarily be made: that one road must be left unthought and nameless (for it is no true road), but that the other is and is genuine. And how could what is then be destroyed?[46] How could it ever come into being? For if it came into being, it is not; nor <is it> if it is ever going to be in the future. Thus coming to be is extinguished, and perishing unheard of.

Nor is it divided, since it is all alike; nor is it more here and less there, which would prevent it from holding together, but it is all full of being. Hence, it is all continuous; for what is draws near to what is. But changeless within the limits of great bonds it is without beginning or ceasing, since coming to be and perishing have wandered very far away, and true conviction has expelled them. Remaining the same and in the same <place> it lies on its own and thus fixed it will remain. For strong necessity holds it within the bonds of a limit, which keeps it all around. Therefore it is right that what is should not be imperfect; for it is not deficient—if it were, it would be deficient in everything.

What is there to be thought is the same as the thought that it is.[47] For you will not find thinking without what is, in which it has been expressed. For there neither is nor will be anything else besides what is, since fate[48] fettered it to be whole and changeless. It has been named all the things that mortals have laid down, persuaded that they are true—coming to be and perishing, being and not being, changing place, and altering in bright colour. But since there is a furthest limit, it is perfected, like the bulk of a ball well-rounded on every side, equally balanced in every direction from the centre. For it cannot be more or less here or there. For, since it is, it is neither a not-being, which would stop it from reaching its like, nor, since it is, can there be more being here, less there, since it is all inviolate; for, being equal to itself on every side, it lies uniformly within limits.[49]

78 PLATO, *Theaetetus* 180 DE, 183 E–184 A   SOCRATES: Theodorus, I had almost forgotten that others have put forward the contrary view: 'Alone what is remains unmoved, to which all are a name', and the other things that Parmenides, Melissus, and their followers say, who oppose all those people[50] and maintain that all things are one, and this one remains stable and in the same place, having no place to move to. ... [183 E] I would be ashamed to be too

[46] Text uncertain.

[47] i.e. the only thought that is possible is the thought that something is. The thought that something is not is a thought of not-being, and hence not a thought at all.

[48] Fate; **574**.

[49] Continued at **124**.

[50] The believers in flux.

crass in examining Melissus and the others, who say that all is one and at rest—but less ashamed before them than before Parmenides above all, venerable and formidable, to use Homer's words. I met him when he was quite old and I was quite young, and he appeared to me to have an altogether noble depth. So I am afraid that we may not understand his words, and may be still further from understanding his meaning ...

Zeno against plurality

79 Zeno was (according to Plato's report) a disciple of Parmenides (**80**). To defend Parmenides' rejection of change, he argues that common views about motion are inconsistent. Aristotle reports several of Zeno's arguments, with his own replies. It is often difficult to work out the exact structure of Zeno's arguments, and to identify the assumptions that he relies on. But some of his objections seem to rest on objections to assumptions about continuity and infinity.

Zeno's strategy is easiest to grasp from the argument that Aristotle calls the 'bisection' (**82**). Zeno argues that we cannot consistently believe that Achilles can overtake the Tortoise, because overtaking it would require him to carry out a task—covering an infinite distance in a finite time—that we admit is impossible.[51]

He seems to argue as follows:

(1) Suppose that distance D_1 separates Achilles from the Tortoise. If Achilles overtakes the Tortoise, he must cover D_1. If he covers D_1, he must cover D_2 ($= $ half of D_1). If he covers D_2, he must cover D_3 ($=$ half of D_2)... and so on to infinity.

(2) An infinite number of lengths, however small each length may be, adds up to an infinite length.

(3) Hence the distances $D_1, D_2, D_3. ...$, that Achilles must cover adds up to an infinite length.

(4) Even Achilles cannot cover an infinite length in a finite time.

(5) Hence he will never overtake the Tortoise.

(6) Hence nothing ever moves, since the same argument can be used to show that nothing can cover any distance, however small.

Zeno's other arguments seem to rest on further claims about the contradictory character of the ordinary concepts involved in assertions about motion. The argument about the arrow (**82**) raises a difficulty about time parallel to the one about motion. It seems to be this:

---

[51] The argument that Aristotle calls the 'Achilles' (the second in **82**) proceeds on different assumptions, but, as Aristotle says, it makes the same point as the 'bisection'.

(1) Suppose that a train leaves Waterloo at 9.00 and arrives in Clapham Junction at 9.10.

(2) At 9.00 precisely it travels no distance. Similarly, at any instant between 9.00 precisely and 9.10 precisely—e.g. at 9.05 precisely—it travels no distance. Similarly at any instance between 9.00 and 9.05—e.g. at 9.01, 9.02, etc.—it travels no distance. Similarly, at any instant between 9.00 and 9.01 it travels no distance.

(3) But the time between 9.00 and 9.05 (and between 9.04 and 9.05, etc.) is exhausted by these instants.

(4) Hence, if the train is not travelling any distance at any of these instants, it cannot travel any distance in the whole time between 9.00 and 9.10.

If Zeno is right, our belief that things can move over a distance through time is inconsistent, once we recognize that things cannot move any distance at any instant. His objections to motion stimulate Aristotle to work out an account of motion, and especially of its continuity, that will dispel the appearance of incoherence that leads Zeno to endorse Parmenides' conclusion. Questions about motion lead into questions about time (as the arrow shows), and these questions require some consideration of the relation between instants of time and parts of time.

....

80 PLATO, *Parmenides* 127 B–128 D[52] [ADEIMANTUS:] Antiphon told us that Pythodorus had told him that Parmenides and Zeno once came to the great Panathenaea. Parmenides was quite old, about 65, with very white hair, but still cut a fine figure. Zeno was nearly 40, tall and handsome in appearance; he was reported to have previously been Parmenides' boy friend. They lodged with Pythodorus in the Ceramicus, outside the wall. Socrates came to see them, and many others with him; they were eager to hear the writings of Zeno—for that was the first time they came to Athens, when these two brought them. Socrates was then a very young man. Zeno himself read his work to them in the absence of Parmenides, and had very little left to read when Pythodorus himself entered (he said), together with Parmenides and Aristoteles who was afterwards one of the Thirty.[53] They heard the little that remained of Zeno's work; Pythodorus had heard it from Zeno before.

When Socrates had heard it, he asked Zeno to read the first assumption of the first argument over again, and when it had been read, he said: What do you mean by this, Zeno? Do you maintain that if the beings are many, they must be both like and unlike, and that this is impossible, since neither can the like be unlike, nor the unlike like? Is that what you say? [ZENO:] That's right, said Zeno.—And if the unlike cannot be like, or the like unlike, then according to you, beings

[52] A later passage from the *Parmenides* is at **220**.
[53] The Thirty; **533**, 537–40.

could not be many; for if they were, impossible things would apply to them. In all that are you contending precisely that beings are not many? And don't you think each argument in your work proves this, so that there are as many proofs of the not-being of the many as the arguments you have constructed? Is that what you mean or have I misunderstood you?—No, said Zeno, you have correctly understood the sense of my work.—I see, Parmenides, said Socrates, that Zeno would like to be not only close to you in the rest of friendship, but your ally in his writings too. He varies what you say, and tries to deceive us into believing that he is saying something different from you. For you, in your poems, say that all is one, and provide excellent proofs of this. He in turn says there are no many, and presents many cogent proofs of this. You say that all is one; he denies that it is many. And so you seem to say different things when really you are saying practically the same. This seems to be above the heads of most of us.

— Yes, Socrates, said Zeno, but you haven't completely discerned the truth about the book. You're as keen as Spartan hounds in pursuing the track, but you don't realize that it is not quite as solemn a work as you suppose. ... This work of mine was meant to support the argument of Parmenides against those who make fun of him and seek to show that if there is one, many ridiculous and contradictory results follow. My work is aimed at the supporters of the many. I repay them with interest, aiming to show that their assumption that there are many has even more ridiculous results, if you trace them properly, than those that follow from the assumption that there is one.

81 ARISTOTLE, *Physics* 233ᵃ21–8   ... Zeno's argument makes a false assumption in saying that it is impossible for something to traverse infinitely many things or to touch each of infinitely many things one by one in a finite time. For both length and time, and in general everything continuous, are said to be infinite in two ways—either infinitely divisible or infinitely long. If, then, they are infinite in quantity, it is impossible to touch them in a finite time; but if they are only infinitely divisible, it is possible to touch them—and in fact this is the way in which time itself is infinite. ...

82 ARISTOTLE, *Physics* 239ᵇ5–240ᵃ18   Zeno argues fallaciously. If, he says, in every case a thing is at rest when it occupies a space equal <to itself>, and in every case what is travelling is in the now, it follows that the travelling arrow is not in motion. This is false; for time is not composed of indivisible nows, any more than any other magnitude is. Zeno has four arguments about motion, and they cause trouble to someone trying to solve them. (1) According to the first argument, nothing is in motion, because the travelling object must first reach the half way mark before it reaches the end. We have examined this argument in our previous discussion.[54] (2) The second argument is

---

[54] i.e. in **81**.

the one called the Achilles. According to this, the slowest runner will never be caught, as long as it is running, by the fastest; for the pursuer must first reach the place that the leader has left, so that the slower must always be some distance ahead. This argument is the same as the bisection; the only difference is that it divides, instead of bisecting, whatever magnitude you care to take. The conclusion that the slower runner is not overtaken results from the argument by the same method as in the bisection. In both arguments the result is failure to arrive at the end because the magnitude is divided in some way. But in the Achilles it is added that even the fastest runner (this is the dramatic element added) will not reach the end in its pursuit of the slowest. And so the solution must be the same as that of the bisection. To claim that the leader is not overtaken is false; for certainly it is not overtaken while it is in the lead, but it is overtaken none the less, if you grant that it is possible to traverse a finite distance. These, then, are the first two arguments. (3) The third is the one we have mentioned, that the arrow is at rest while it travels. This conclusion results from supposing that time is composed of nows; for if this is not conceded, the conclusion will not follow. (4) In the fourth argument, blocks of equal size are moving past each other in a stadium, from opposite ends, one lot beginning from the starting line of the stadium, the other lot from the far end, moving at equal speed. The conclusion, according to Zeno, is that half the time is equal to double the time. The error in this argument is the assumption that equal magnitudes moving at equal speeds, one past a moving object, the other past a stationary object, travel by in an equal time. This assumption is false. Zeno argues: Suppose, for instance, that AA are the stationary equal blocks; that BB are the blocks, equal in number and size to AA, beginning from the middle; and that CC are the ones, equal in number and size to the preceding, and travelling at equal speed to BB, beginning from the end. The result, then, is that <as the Bs and Cs> move past each other, the first B reaches the last <C>, and the first C <reaches the last B>. But a further result is that the <first> C has passed all the Bs, while the <first> B has passed half <the As>; hence the time taken <by the first B> must be half <the time taken by the first C>, since each takes an equal <time> to pass each block. Further, at this same time the first B will have passed all the Cs; for the first C and the first B will reach the opposite extremes of the stadium at the same time, because both take equal time to pass the As. This, then, is the argument. The false move in it is the one we have mentioned.

Atomism and change

83 Parmenides' main successors—Empedocles, Anaxagoras, and the Atomists, Leucippus and Democritus—agree that he has shown the impossibility of a certain kind of change. But they argue that we can allow other types of change that do not violate legitimate Parmenidean conditions. Hence they defend cosmology.

A distinction drawn by Aristotle makes it easier to see what these successors of Parmenides have in mind. Aristotle marks two sorts of coming to be, by saying that the first sort is 'coming to be something' (e.g. pale, dark, musical), whereas the second is 'coming to be without qualification', which happens when a statue, plant, or animal comes to be. We can speak of perishing in the same two ways. Only unqualified coming to be is coming into existence, and only unqualified perishing is going out of existence (**224 6**).

The Atomists argue that if we recognize atomic bodies, we can explain all natural processes without believing in unqualified becoming or perishing. The basic subjects of change are the atoms, which change only by moving around in the void, and so changing their place.[55] Aristotle recognizes their basic status in the Atomist theory by applying his terms 'substance' and 'matter' to them. Macroscopic objects are just temporary collections of atoms. The atoms (Greek *atomon*, 'uncut' or 'uncuttable') are indivisible. Democritus argues that unless some components of compound bodies are indivisible, no compounds of finite size can exist. If there are no indivisible parts, compounds will consist of an infinite number of parts that are either extended or unextended. If they are extended, the compound will be infinitely extended; if they are unextended, the compound will also be unextended.

Atomism (both in its original form and in Epicurus' version[56]) expresses clearly a conviction shared by several opponents of Parmenides. At the most basic level (in their view) nothing really comes into existence or goes out of existence. The changes we normally regard as unqualified becomings do not involve any genuine thing coming into existence or going out of existence; they are simply rearrangements of the basic things.

This reply presupposes that Parmenides is right to rule out unqualified becoming. Unqualified becoming involves non-existence at one time of the subject that exists at another time. This seems to imply 'coming to be from non-existence' and 'perishing into non-existence', and hence 'coming to be from not-being' and 'perishing into not-being'. Since not-being is nothing, unqualified becoming seems to involve coming to be from nothing and perishing into nothing. The Atomists apparently agree with Parmenides that this sort of change is unintelligible.

Qualified becoming, however, seems not to involve any necessary reference to the non-existent. If it can all be resolved into the motions of atoms, it simply involves the basic subjects changing place, which is not a real change in them, but simply a change in their relation to one another. Hence, the Atomists may suppose that Parmenides' objections do not affect movement in place by the atoms.

---

[55] Atoms; cf. **125**, **130–3**.

[56] Epicurus also disagrees with Democritus on some issues; see **282**, **360**, **366**.

84 SIMPLICIUS, *Commentary on the Physics* 161. 13–20   That [Empedocles] also assumed that coming to be happens in accordance with some association and dissociation is shown by the first passage I set down: 'At one time they increased to be just one from many; at another they grew apart to be many from one.' See also his remark that coming to be and perishing are nothing other than this: 'but mixing and interchange of the things mixed', and ordered combination and dissolution.

85 ARISTOTLE, *Metaphysics* 985^{b}4–20   According to Leucippus and his colleague Democritus, the elements are the full and the empty; the full and solid is what is, and the empty is what is not—that is why they also say that what is is no more of a being than what is not, because body is no more of a being than the empty is.[57] They take these to be the material causes of beings. Those who take the substance that is the subject to be one bring everything else into being by the ways in which the subject is affected, taking the rare and the dense to be the principles of the various ways it is affected. In the same way Leucippus and Democritus take the differentiae of the atoms to be the causes of the other things. They say, however, that there are three of these differentiae—shape, order, and position. For they say that what is is differentiated only by rhythm, touching, and turning. Of these rhythm is shape, touching is order, and turning is position; for A differs from N in shape, AN from NA in order, and Z from N in position. Like the other people, however, they were too lazy to take up the question about change and to ask from what source and in what way it is to belong to beings.

86 SIMPLICIUS, *Commentary on On the Heavens* 294. 33–295. 22 = DK 68 A 37   A short quotation from Aristotle's work *On Democritus* will show what the view of these <Atomists> was: 'Democritus thinks that the nature of everlasting things consists in infinitely numerous small substances[58] and for them he assumes a place other than them and infinitely extended. He calls place by the names 'void', 'nothing', and 'infinite'; and each of the substances he calls 'this',[59] 'solid', and 'being'. He thinks the substances are so small that they escape our senses, and that they have all sorts of shapes, figures, and differences in size. From these, then, as from elements, he knew[60] how to generate and constitute masses that appear to sight and are sensible. …' He speaks of coming to be and of its contrary, perishing, not only about animals, but also about plants and worlds, and, speaking generally, about all sensible bodies.

---

[57] Atoms and void; cf. **159**.

[58] Aristotle on substance; **227**.

[59] Text uncertain.

[60] Text uncertain.

87 EPICURUS = DIOGENES LAERTIUS X. 39–41   The totality is bodies and void; for in all cases perception itself testifies that bodies exist, and in accordance with perception we must judge by reasoning what is non-evident ... And if there did not exist what we call by the names of void and space and intangible nature, bodies would have no place to be in or to move through, as they evidently do move. ... Further, among bodies, some are compounds, and some are those things from which compounds have been made. The latter are indivisible and unchangeable, as they must be if not everything is to be destroyed into not-being, but some things are to be strong enough to survive in the dissolution of compounds. These are full by nature and indissoluble in every respect and in every way. And so the principles must be indivisible natures of bodies.

88 ARISTOTLE, *Generation and Corruption* 316ª13–34   Democritus would appear to have been convinced of the impossibility of infinitely divisible bodies by appropriate arguments drawn from facts about nature. ... For to suppose that a body and magnitude is divisible throughout, and that this division is possible, raises a puzzle. For what will there be that survives the division? If it is divisible throughout, and if this division is possible, then it might be, at one and the same time, divided throughout, even if it has not been divided at one and the same time; and if this were to happen, there would be no impossibility. Therefore, if it is divided by bisection, or in any way, if it is by nature divisible throughout, nothing impossible will result; for if it has been divided into innumerable parts, themselves divided innumerable times, there is no impossibility, though perhaps no one would divide it. Since, therefore, the body is divisible throughout, suppose it has been divided. What, then, will be left? A magnitude? No; that is impossible, since in that case there will be something not divided, whereas the body was assumed to be divisible through and through.

But if there will be no body and no magnitude, and yet there is to be division, then either the body will consist of points and its constituents will have no magnitude, or it will be absolutely nothing. If the latter, then it would come to be out of nothing and be composed of nothing; and so the whole body will turn out to be nothing but an appearance. But, similarly, if it consists of points, it will have no magnitude. For when the points were touching and were one magnitude and together, they did not make the whole any bigger; for, when the body was divided into two or more parts, the whole was neither smaller nor bigger than it was before. Hence, even if all the points are put together, they will not make any magnitude.

89 EPICURUS = DIOGENES LAERTIUS X. 56   ... We must not believe that there can be infinitely many masses, however small, in any finite body. And so, not only must we do away with infinite division into ever smaller pieces, so that we do not make everything weak, and are not compelled in our conceptions of compounds to wear out existing things by throwing them away into non-existence; but we must also not believe that there is infinite movement, even by ever smaller stages, in finite bodies.

Atoms, compounds, and becoming

90 Though the Atomists reject unqualified becoming at the most basic level, they also agree with Heracleitus' suggestion that at one level there are many more unqualified becomings than we ordinarily recognize. A tree or a horse is a collection of atoms, and so (by the compositional criterion of identity, **45**) it ceases to exist whenever it loses any of its atoms. Every change in a compound implies its destruction (**93–4**). Among compounds we find many more unqualified becomings than common sense recognizes. But among atoms no new substance at all comes into being, since atoms undergo only qualified becoming. From an Atomist point of view, the unqualified coming to be (as we normally describe it) of a tree or a horse is simply a rearrangement of the underlying matter.

This claim about compounds and their atoms raises a general question about the implications of Atomism for common-sense beliefs in macroscopic objects and their properties. If only atoms and void are real, are compounds of atoms unreal? Are we wrong to suppose that trees come into being, grow for many years, decay for many years, and perish after many years of life? If there are really no such things as trees, we must be wrong in attributing any properties to trees; the Atomists must hold an eliminative view of the objects recognized by common sense.[61]

We might reject this inference. We might argue, on behalf of the Atomists, that trees are real in so far as they are composed of atoms and void. If they are real, at least some of what we normally believe about them may be true. If the Atomists hold this view, then, apparently, they need not reject most of our common-sense beliefs about macroscopic objects and their properties. Such a view is reductive. It reduces trees and tables to collections of atoms, since it claims that they are nothing more than this. But it offers a vindicating reduction of ordinary beliefs about trees, in so far as it claims that most of our ordinary beliefs turn out to be true of the relevant collections of atoms.

This reductive vindication of ordinary beliefs, however, is difficult for Atomists to defend. If the compositional criterion of identity is right, ordinary objects do not really persist when common sense supposes they do. Atomists must say that a tree perishes when it loses a single leaf. Trees, understood as short-lived collections that exist only until they undergo some change, clearly lack many of

---

[61] Eliminative atomism: **235, 312, 331, 351**.

the properties (growth, decay, losing leaves, etc.) that we ordinarily attribute to trees. Apparently, then, the Atomists cannot say that trees (objects that sometimes grow for many years and perish after many years of life) exist and are composed of atoms; they must say that atoms exist and trees do not.[62] In that case, the Atomist position is eliminative, and not merely reductive; it does vindicate our beliefs about trees, but undermines them. The choice between reductive and eliminative conclusions from Atomism confronts us on several issues.[63]

....

91 SIMPLICIUS, *Commentary on the Physics* 163. 18–24 = DK 59 B 17   In the first book of his work on natural things Anaxagoras clearly says that coming to be and perishing are combination and dissolution. He writes as follows: 'The Greeks recognize[64] coming to be and perishing incorrectly. For nothing comes to be or perishes, but things are mixed together and dissolved from existing things. And thus they would correctly call coming to be mixing together and perishing dissolution.'

92 EPICURUS = DIOGENES LAERTIUS X. 68–9   The shapes, colours, sizes, and weights and all the other things that are predicated of body as coincidents (either coincidents of all bodies or coincidents of those seen and known[65] by perception) must be thought of neither as natures in their own right (for it is impossible to conceive these), nor as altogether non-existent, nor as some other incorporeal things added to the body, nor as parts of it. Rather, we should think that the whole body throughout has its own permanent nature from all these—though not in such a way as to be composed out of them (as when a larger aggregate is constituted from the masses themselves, whether the primary ones or those smaller than a given whole), but only, as I say, deriving its own permanent nature from all of these.

93 LUCRETIUS ii. 747–56   ... Now I will teach you that the primary bodies lack colour. For any colour at all is changed, and every body that changes colour changes;[66] but the primary bodies must not do this at all. For something unchangeable must persist, so that all things are not brought back completely to nothing. For whatever by changing departs from its limits, that is at once the death of the thing that was before. Be careful, then, not to tint the seeds of things with colour, so that you do not find things returning completely to nothing.

94 LUCRETIUS iii. 510–19   And since we see that the mind is cured, just as a sick body is, and can be changed by medicine, this also foretells that it lives a

---

[62] Aristotle's reply; **250–2**.
[63] Reduction and elimination; **312**, **351**, **355**.
[64] *nomizein*, cognate with *nomos*. See **125**.
[65] Text uncertain.
[66] Conjectural supplement for a gap in the text.

mortal life. For if someone undertakes and sets out to change the mind or to modify any other nature, that is the same as adding parts or moving them from their order or taking some bit or other from the total. But what is immortal refuses to have its parts moved or to have parts added or to have them removed. For whatever by changing departs from its limits, that is at once the death of the thing that was before.

Plato: criticism of naturalist views on causes

95 The Atomists offer the most elaborate attempt to carry out the naturalists' primary aim of explaining the observed variety of things and events by laws that refer to their constitution—to what Aristotle calls the 'material cause'. Both Plato and Aristotle criticize this exclusive focus on the material cause.

Plato's *Phaedo* presents an ostensibly autobiographical sketch by Socrates.[67] Socrates was once interested in the questions pursued by the naturalists, but was disappointed by the naturalists' answers. He raises these objections:

(1) The naturalists say too little attention about mind as a cause.

(2) They do not try to explain how things are by showing that it is best for them to be this way.

(3) They do not offer a plausible way of explaining intelligent goal-directed action by human agents.

Plato implies that these objections are closely connected. He assumes that if we consider mind as a cause, we will explain things by showing how mind designs them for the best result. Moreover, he seems to assume that if we explain human actions as aimed at the best result, we must also try to explain the world as a whole, and the different events and processes in it, as the product of mind aiming at the best. Even though Plato does not sharply distinguish his different objections to the naturalists, we might want to distinguish them. For we might well suppose that his claims about human action are more immediately plausible than his claims about the universe as a whole.[68]

Plato does not entirely reject the naturalists' appeal to material constituents and to processes involving them.[69] Such processes are necessary conditions of rational action, but they do not explain why Socrates did that action when he did it. The real explanation of his staying in prison must include the fact that the Athenians thought it best to put Socrates to death, and the fact that he thought it best to obey their sentence by staying in prison.

[67] The historical Socrates; **9**.
[68] Plato on explanation and goodness; **215**, **590–2**.
[69] Plato on non-teleological explanation; **591–2**.

96 PLATO, *Phaedo* 96 A–99 D [SOCRATES:] When I was young, Cebes, I had a strong desire to know the area of wisdom that is called inquiry into nature. This appeared to me to have lofty aims, knowing the causes of a thing, why it comes to be, perishes, and remains in being. I often agitated myself by asking questions such as these: 'Do animals grow whenever heat and cold produce some decay, as some people used to say? Is it by blood, or air, or fire, that we think? Or is it none of these, but the brain that provides the senses of hearing and sight and smell? Do memory and belief come from them, and does knowledge result from memory and belief when it has come to rest?' Then I went on to examine their decay, and then what happens in heaven and earth. At last I concluded that I was wholly incapable of these inquiries, as I will adequately prove to you. For I was so fascinated by them that they blinded me to things that I had seemed to myself, and also to others, to know quite well. I unlearned what I used to think obvious, about why a human being grows, for instance; for I had previously thought it obvious that this was because of eating and drinking. ... Wasn't that a reasonable view? [CEBES:] Yes, said Cebes, I think so. ...

[97 B]—But I once heard someone reading from a book, as he said, by Anaxagoras.[70] He said that it is actually mind that sets everything in order and causes everything. This explanation pleased me. Somehow it seemed good[71] that mind should be the cause of everything. I reflected: 'If this is so, then mind, in setting all things in order, also arranges each individual thing however it is best. And so, if anyone wants to discover the explanation of how any given thing comes to be, or perishes, or remains in being, he must find out how it is best for that thing to be, or to act or be acted on in any other way ...' Thinking along these lines, I was delighted with the thought that I had found in Anaxagoras a teacher to expound the explanation of beings— an explanation that suited my mind. I imagined that he would tell me first whether the earth is flat or round; and then he would further expound the explanation and the necessity of this, by saying what is better, and that it is better for the earth to have this shape. And if he said the earth is in the centre, he would further expound how this position was the best. If this could be shown, I was ready to forgo any other sort of explanation.... I had hopes that I would not have sold even at a high price. I seized the books and read them as fast as I could, so that I would know the better and the worse as quickly as possible.

What an amazing hope, and how far short of it I fell. As I read on, I found that Anaxagoras made no use at all of mind or any other explanation for setting things in order, but he treated air, ether, water, and many other absurd things, as causes. I thought he was very like someone who began by saying

---

[70] Anaxagoras; **91, 242, 588**.
[71] As Socrates goes on to explain, this is characteristic of mind.

that everything Socrates does he does by mind, but, when he tried to give the explanation of each of my actions, went on to say, first, that I'm sitting here because my body is made up of bones and muscles; and the bones, as he would say, are hard and have ligaments that divide them, and the muscles are elastic, and they cover the bones, which have also a covering or environment of flesh and skin that contains them; and as the bones are lifted at their joints by the contraction or relaxation of the muscles, I am able to bend my limbs, and this is why I am sitting here in a curved posture. And for my conversing[72] with you, he would give similar explanations, treating sound, air, hearing, and ten thousand other such things, as causes.

In all this, he would neglect the true causes—namely that the Athenians have thought it better to condemn me, and that is why I in turn have thought it better to sit here and more just to undergo my punishment. For, by the dog, I think these muscles and bones of mine would have been off long ago to Megara or Boeotia, carried off by a belief about what was best, if I had not thought it more just and finer not to flee and run away, but instead to submit to punishment, whatever the city imposes. But it is totally absurd to call these other things causes. If one were to say that without bones and muscles and the other parts of the body I would not be able to do what had seemed best to me, that would be true. But to say that I do as I do because of them, and that I do these things by mind, but not from the choice of the best—that is a long drawn-out waste of words.

I'm amazed that they can't see the difference between the real cause and that without which the cause would not be the cause—this is what the many, feeling about in the dark, are always mistaking and misnaming. That's why one man makes a vortex all round the earth and makes the earth stay still because of the heaven; another gives the air as a support to the earth, which is a sort of flat lid. They never look for any power that in disposing them as they are disposes them in the best possible way; nor do they imagine that there is any superhuman strength in that. Instead, they expect to find another Atlas of the world who is stronger and more immortal and more all-embracing than the good is; clearly they think there is no such thing as the binding[73] and embracing power of the good.

This, then, is the explanation that I would most gladly learn about. But, since I have failed either to discover it myself or to learn about it from anyone else, I will exhibit to you, if you like, what I have found to be the second route[74] in the search for an explanation.[75]

[72] *dialegesthai*; cf. **214**, **220**.
[73] *deon* might be translated 'binding' or 'obligatory'; Socrates plays on the two senses.
[74] Or 'second-best route'.
[75] Continued at **207**.

Aristotle: the four causes

97 Aristotle agrees with Plato in believing that the naturalists were not looking for all the right sorts of causes. He distinguishes four different types of causes that mark four ways we can answer the question 'Why?'. If, for instance, we ask why a chair is as it is, we can explain its different features by giving four types of explanations:

(1) The material cause (it is made of wood).

(2) The formal cause (it is a chair).[76]

(3) The efficient cause[77] (this carpenter made it).

(4) The final cause,[78] specifying the goal or end of the thing or event (it is for sitting on).

The four causes are not meant to be rival explanations. Indeed, we must often appeal to more than one of them to explain the same event or object. We might say that a plane crashed because its sides were not strong enough to resist the pressure exerted on them, or because a bomb exploded on board, or because the terrorists had chosen this plane in the belief that the president was on board. None of these explanations is false simply because the others are true.

Not every event, object, or state of affairs has all four causes; triangles, for instance, have no final cause. But the student of nature ought to keep all four causes in mind, to see how many of them apply to a given natural process or event.

This brief introduction to Plato's and Aristotle's views on causes and explanation shows that they both advocate explanations referring to the good and to forms. To understand what they mean, we must pause, and consider some of the other tendencies in early Greek philosophy; these will help us to understand Plato's reasons for introducing forms, and Aristotle's reasons for agreeing with Plato on some points and disagreeing on others.

Aristotle's historical comments (**99**) suggest that a new approach to philosophy began in Socrates' time. Socrates' autobiographical sketch in the *Phaedo* also suggests an important change of direction. The reasons for the change of direction will become clearer if we examine some of the epistemological implications of the naturalists' inquiries.

....

98   ARISTOTLE, *Physics* 194^{b}16–195^{a}8   We should consider how many and what sorts of causes there are. For our inquiry aims at knowledge; and we think we know something only when we find the reason why it is so, i.e.

---

[76] Matter and form; **224**.

[77] Aristotle calls it 'the moving cause', or 'the source of motion'.

[78] Aristotle calls it 'for something', or 'what something is for'. This is sometimes called 'teleological' explanation. See **240**.

when we find its primary cause. Clearly, then, we must also find the reason why in the case of coming to be, perishing, and every sort of natural change, so that, when we know their principles, we can try to refer whatever we are inquiring into back to these principles. (1) In one way, then, that from which, as a constituent present in it, a thing comes to be is said to be that thing's cause—for instance, the bronze and silver, and their genera, are causes of the statue and the bowl. (2) In another way, the form—i.e. the pattern—is a cause. The form is the account (and the genera of the account) of the essence (for instance, the cause of an octave is the ratio two to one, and in general number), and the parts that are in the account. (3) Again, the source of the primary origin[79] of change or stability is a cause. For instance, the one who advised a course of action is its cause, and a father is a cause of his child; and in general the producer is a cause of the product, and the initiator of the change is a cause of what is changed. (4) Again, something's end—i.e. what it is for—is its cause, as health is of walking. For why does he walk? We say, 'To be healthy'; and in saying this we think we have provided the cause.... Since causes are spoken of in many ways, there are many non-coincidental causes of the same thing. Both the sculpting craft and the bronze, for instance, are causes of the statue—not in so far as it is something else, but in so far as it is a statue—but not causes in the same way: the bronze is a cause as matter, the sculpting craft as the source of the change.

99 ARISTOTLE, *Parts of Animals* 642ᵃ1–32   There are, then, these two causes—what something is for and what is of necessity (since many things come to be because it is necessary). ... We speak of food as necessary ... because an organism cannot exist without it. One might call this conditional necessity. For instance, since an axe is needed for splitting wood, it is necessary for it to be hard; and, if it is to be hard, it is necessary for it to be made of iron. In the same way, the body is also an instrument, since each of its parts, and the whole likewise, is for something; it is necessary, then, for it to be of this sort and to have constituents of this sort, if what it is for is to result.

It is clear, then, that there are two types of cause and that in what we say we must either find both of them or at least try to make it clear that we cannot find both. It is also clear that people who do not do this might be said to tell us nothing about nature; for nature is a principle more than matter is. Sometimes, indeed, Empedocles is led by the truth itself, and stumbles on the right sort of cause, and is compelled to say that the form is a thing's substance and nature. When, for instance, he expounds what bone is, he does not say that it is one, two, three, or all of its elements, but that it is the form of their mixture. It is clear, then, that flesh and every other part of that sort have this character. The reason our predecessors did not discover this character is that

---

[79] *archê*, also translated 'principle'.

they had no grasp of essence, or of how to define substance. Democritus was the first to touch on them, but that was all he did—and not because he supposed it to be necessary for the study of nature, but because the facts themselves carried him away from his own views. In the time of Socrates, this concern with essence and definition grew, but investigation into nature stopped; philosophers turned away to study the virtue that concerns the conduct of life, and to political study.[80]

[80] Continued in **244**.

III: Origins of Scepticism

Knowledge and belief in early Greek philosophy

Questions about knowledge

100 According to Aristotle, the early naturalists differ from the 'theologians' (*theologoi*) who preceded them, because they offer rational proofs for their claims, instead of simply relying on the traditional stories (*muthoi*) about the gods. This is why he thinks it is worth examining what they have to say (**101**). Aristotle's contrast is supported by the naturalists' own attacks on tradition. Both Xenophanes and Heracleitus attack Homer's and Hesiod's conception of the gods (**575-80**).

The poems of Homer and Hesiod contain an implicit defence of their own reliability. They assume that a story about the origins of the world is worthy of acceptance if and only if it has been revealed by the gods. Homer and Hesiod's stories are credible—so the poems tell us—because they have been revealed to the poets by their memory of tradition and by the goddesses who inspire poets (the Muses); and so they ultimately rest on revelation from the gods.

Since the naturalists reject many of the traditional stories, they undermine this defence, and must defend their own position. Xenophanes argues that human beings can discover things by inquiry, without recourse to divine revelation mediated by tradition. Moreover, he argues that Homer and Hesiod are unreliable witnesses to divine revelation, because what they tell us is false.

101 ARISTOTLE, *Metaphysics* 1000ª5-22   One difficulty which is as great as any has been neglected both by modern philosophers and by their predecessors—whether the principles of perishable and those of imperishable things are the same or different. If they are the same, how are some things perishable and others imperishable, and for what reason? The school of Hesiod and all the theologians thought only of what was plausible to themselves, and had no regard for us. For, asserting the first principles to be gods and born of gods, they say that the beings which did not taste of nectar and ambrosia became mortal. Clearly they understand what they are talking about, but what they have said about the very application of these causes is beyond our grasp. For if the gods taste of nectar and ambrosia for their pleasure, these cannot be the causes of their existence; but if they taste them to maintain their existence, how can gods who need food be eternal? But it is not worth our while to inquire seriously into the subtleties of the mythologists. The people we must cross-examine are those who speak of proofs. We must ask them why it is that, among things consisting of the same elements, some are everlasting in nature, while others perish.

102 HIPPOLYTUS, *Refutation* ix. 10. 2 = DK 22 B 57 [HERACLEITUS] Most people's teacher is Hesiod. They are sure he has most knowledge—the same Hesiod who did not recognize day and night! For they are one.

103 PLUTARCH, *Camillus* 183a = DK 22 B 106 Should we suppose that certain days are unlucky, or was Heracleitus right? He attacked Hesiod's view that some days are good and others bad, on the ground that Hesiod did not recognize that the nature of every day is the same.

Belief versus knowledge: Plato's division

104 The attacks on traditional stories lead the Greek philosophers into questions of epistemology (from Greek *epistêmê*, 'knowledge')—questions about the nature and sources of knowledge. The earliest philosophers do not formulate the issues in precisely these terms, but they implicitly rely on a distinction that is clearly formulated by Plato. It is useful, then, to begin with a brief statement of Plato's distinction between knowledge and belief, so that we can see more clearly what Plato's predecessors take for granted.

In the *Meno* Plato distinguishes true from false beliefs, and then draws a further distinction among true beliefs, counting some but not others as knowledge. He disapproves of the indiscriminate use of 'know' for all true beliefs, and defends a distinction between knowledge (*epistêmê*) and belief (*doxa*).

We implicitly accept a distinction between knowledge and true belief whenever we admit that people get something right by luck, or guesswork, or habit, without really knowing. In Plato's example, someone has been told the way to Larisa, but has never been there himself and does not really know that this is the best way to go. In such cases, we may happen to get the right answer, but something more than simply getting the right answer is needed for knowledge. What more is needed?

Plato is the first to formulate this question about knowledge and belief, but he does not invent the whole issue. The Hippocratic writer distinguishes 'craft' (or 'expertise'; *technê*) from random success in medical treatment. A craft is systematic, reliable, and rational; this is why Aristotle distinguishes it from mere 'experience' that happens to have been successful (**105-6**). In Plato's view, knowledge is the mark of genuine craft (**175**, **179**).

Plato suggests that we have knowledge, rather than mere true belief, if we give the appropriate account of the 'reason why'. In that case, we have given a reason for accepting the belief that is supported by this account, and for preferring it over beliefs that conflict with it. If we cannot give an appropriate account, we cannot say why we should hold our current belief rather than its contrary. An account and a 'reason why' gives us a belief that is not merely true, but also justified. In the previous example, if I have been to Larisa, I can justify my belief that this way, rather than some other way, is the right way to go.

Plato's account of knowledge leads to two questions. (1) What sort of account is the mark of knowledge, as opposed to mere true belief? (2) Are we ever in a position to give the right sort of account, so that we are justified in preferring one belief over another? These questions occupy the Presocratics. Though they do not formulate the questions in Plato's terms, they are often concerned to distinguish one favoured cognitive state from the unreflective, or superficial, or irrational cognitive state of most people.

105 HIPPOCRATES, *Ancient Medicine* 1   Among those who have undertaken to speak or write on the medical craft, some have first assumed for themselves some assumption underlying their argument, such as hot, or cold, or moist, or dry, or whatever else they choose. In doing so, they narrow down the origin of the cause for diseases or death among human beings; they make the causes the same in all cases, by assuming just one or two things as causes. These people are all clearly mistaken even in much that they say. Their policy is especially blameworthy since it is about a craft which all use on the most important occasions, and in which they give the highest honours to the good craftsmen and practitioners. Some practitioners are inferior and some far superior, but this would not have been true if there had been no medical craft, and if nothing had been investigated or found out in it; rather, all would have been equally inexperienced and without knowledge, and everything to do with the sick would have been ruled by chance. But in fact it is not so. For, just as in the other crafts those who practise them differ widely in manual dexterity and in knowledge, the same is true of the medical craft. That is why I did not think it needed any empty assumption of the sort that we need in those subjects that are obscure and puzzling. If one undertook to handle these, it would be necessary to use some assumption, as, for example, in the case of things above us and things below the earth; if anyone were to treat of these and undertake to find out how they are constituted, it would not be clear to the reader or hearer whether what he says is true or false, since there is nothing we can refer to in order to know the clear truth.

106 ARISTOTLE, *Metaphysics* 980^{b}25–981^{b}10   Other animals live by appearances and memories but have very little experience,[1] whereas human beings

---

[1] Aristotle uses 'experience' (*empeiria*) to refer not to what we call a single experience ('I had a frightening experience yesterday'), but to the experience that builds up over time ('My experience came in handy').

also live by craft and reasoning. In human beings experience results from memory, since many memories of the same thing produce the capacity for a single body of experience. Experience seems to be quite like science and craft, and indeed human beings attain science and craft through experience ... Craft comes into being when many thoughts that arise from experience result in one universal view about similar things. For the view that in this illness this treatment benefited Callias, Socrates, and others, in many particular cases, is characteristic of experience, but the view that it benefits everyone of a certain sort (marked out by a single kind) suffering from a certain disease (for instance, phlegmatic or bilious people when burning with fever) is characteristic of craft... . We attribute knowledge and comprehension to craft more than to experience, and we suppose that craftsmen are wiser than experienced people, on the assumption that in every case wisdom follows from knowledge, rather than from experience. This is because craftsmen know the cause, but merely experienced people do not; for experienced people know the fact that something is so but not the reason why it is so, whereas craftsmen know the reason why, i.e. the cause.... And in general, a sign that distinguishes those who know from those who do not is their ability to teach. Hence we think craft, rather than experience, is knowledge, since craftsmen can teach, while merely experienced people cannot.

107   PLATO, *Meno* 97 A–98 A   SOCRATES: ... Suppose that someone knows the way to Larisa, or anywhere else you like; when he goes there, and guides others, won't he guide well and correctly? MENO: Of course.—Now what if someone has a correct belief about which is the road, without having been there and without knowing? Won't he also guide others correctly?—Yes, he will.—And, presumably, as long as he has a correct belief on the points the other knows, he will be just as good a guide, thinking true things, but without wisdom?—Just as good.—Then true belief is as good a guide as wisdom to correctness in action. ... —In that case, I wonder why knowledge should be so much more honoured than correct belief, and indeed what distinguishes them.—That's because you haven't attended to the statues of Daedalus. ... If no one ties them down, they run away and escape. If tied, they stay where they are put. ... Similarly, true beliefs are a fine thing and do all sorts of good so long as they stay in their place, but they are not in the habit of staying long. They run away from a human soul; and so they are not worth much until you tie them by reasoning out the explanation.[2] That, Meno my friend, is recollection, as we agreed earlier. Once they are tied, they become, first of all, knowledge and, secondly, stable. That is why knowledge is more honoured than true belief. What distinguishes one from the other is the tie, and knowledge is better than[3] correct belief in being tied.

[2] Or 'reasoning about the explanation'. On knowledge and recollection see **183–6**.
[3] Or 'different from'.

Knowledge and scepticism: Xenophanes

108 Once we distinguish knowledge from true belief, we make it possible to raise doubts about whether anyone has achieved or can achieve knowledge. Such doubts express different degrees of scepticism. A sceptic expresses doubt or disbelief about whether anyone has found any reliable justification that entitles us to regard any of our beliefs as true; some sceptics go on to maintain that no such justification can be found.

Scepticism as a relatively systematic body of destructive arguments and techniques challenging different claims to knowledge is a part of Hellenistic philosophy (**25–7**). Sceptical questions and doubts, however, are present in Greek philosophy nearly from the beginning. As Sextus sees, some of the Presocratics formulate some of the lines of argument that lead to Scepticism. Debates in later Greek philosophy about knowledge and Scepticism cite the Presocratics, Plato, and Aristotle on different sides of one or another issue. If we look at these philosophers in the light of epistemological questions that they do not self-consciously ask, we can see how they raise many of the issues that are explicit topics of later debate.

Xenophanes' critique of the traditional picture of the world expresses his concern with knowledge. This concern seems to leave an opportunity for Sceptical argument.[4] One of his attacks on Homer and Hesiod may be represented in this way:

(1) Homer and Hesiod present the gods behaving immorally.

(2) But the gods do not behave immorally.

(3) Therefore Homer's and Hesiod's presentation is mistaken.

This argument does not support Scepticism; if we believe the first two claims are both true, we can rely on them to reject Homer's and Hesiod's views. If, however, we think the two premises are just as credible as Homer's and Hesiod's views of the gods, we will conclude that we cannot tell whether or not the Homeric and Hesiodic presentation is correct. We will find we have conflicting beliefs about the gods, and no way of resolving the conflict.

Homer and Hesiod are also open to criticism, according to Xenophanes, for making the gods resemble Greeks. His objection—explicit or implicit—is this:

(1) According to the Greek tradition, the gods are like Greeks.

(2) According to the Ethiopian tradition, the gods are like Ethiopians.

(3) There is no reason to prefer the Greek picture of the gods over the Ethiopian picture.

(4) The gods cannot be both like Greeks and like Ethiopians.

(5) Therefore we cannot accept either tradition about the gods.

[4] Xenophanes on traditional views; **575–9**.

Xenophanes himself is cautious about the prospects of replacing the traditional picture with assured knowledge. He recognizes that even if we stumble on the truth, we cannot necessarily claim to know that we have found it. He relies on a distinction very close to the Platonic distinction between knowledge and mere true belief. Sextus (**575**) takes Xenophanes' outlook to be implicitly Sceptical, claiming that we cannot expect to find anything better than mere 'seeming' and that we lack adequate justification for any alternative to the traditional picture. This is not Xenophanes' intention; he affirms a confident belief of his own about a single supreme god (**576, 578**). But we may wonder how he can avoid a Sceptical conclusion.

....

109 SEXTUS, *Against the Professors* vii. 89–90 The students of nature, beginning with Thales, are thought to have been the first to introduce the inquiry about a criterion.[5] For when they had condemned sense-perception in many cases as untrustworthy, they set up reason as judge of the truth in beings. Starting from this, they set out their doctrines of principles, elements, and so on; the grasp of these is acquired through the capacity of reason. Hence the foremost student of nature, Anaxagoras, denounces the senses as weak. He says: 'Because of their infirmity, we are incapable of judging what is true.' To confirm belief in their untrustworthiness, he cites the gradual change in colours. For if we were to take two colours, black and white, and pour some of the one into the other a drop at a time, our sight will be incapable of discriminating the gradual alterations, though they are present in the underlying nature of things.

110 STOBAEUS, *Anthology* i. 94. 1–3 = DK 21 B 18 [XENOPHANES:] The gods did not disclose everything to mortals from the beginning. But in time mortals find something better by searching.

111 PLUTARCH, *Table Talk* ix. 7. 746b = DK 21 B 35 [XENOPHANES:] Let these things be believed as similar to the truth.

112 SEXTUS, *Against the Professors* vii. 46–52 Let us next consider the division in views that has arisen among the dogmatists about the criterion; for while we are investigating its existence, we must also consider at the same time what it is. ... Some have abolished the criterion, and others have retained it. Among those who have retained it, the three main views are these: some have retained it in reason, others in non-rational evident appearances, others in both. It has been rejected by Xenophanes of Colophon ... According to some,[6] Xenophanes takes this position, saying that nothing can be grasped. He writes: 'And no man has seen what is clear, nor will anyone

[5] Criterion; **169**.
[6] A different view of Xenophanes; **122**.

know concerning the gods and about all the things of which I speak. For even if he were to succeed in saying what is the case, nevertheless he himself does not know it; but belief is found over all things.' For here he seems to mean by 'clear' what is true and known … By 'man' he seems to mean 'human being', using the specific term instead of the generic; for man is a species of human being. … Hence, his statement, when simplified, amounts to this—'Yet the true and known—at least in non-evident things—no human being knows; for even if by chance one were to hit upon it, still one does not know that one has hit upon it,[7] but thinks and believes it.' For suppose that certain people are looking for gold in a dark room containing many treasures; it will turn out that each of them, whenever he gets hold of one of the treasures lying in the room, will think he has grasped the gold, but none of them will be convinced that he has lighted on the gold, however true it may be that he has in fact lighted on it. Similarly, then, a host of philosophers has arrived in this universe, as in a great house, bent on searching for truth; it is quite likely that the one who has got hold of the truth does not believe that he has hit the target.

Heracleitus: sense, reason, and the common world

__113__ Heracleitus takes up Xenophanes' aim of applying critical reflection to improve ordinary, traditional beliefs about the world. He articulates the standards for criticism of traditional beliefs. Heracleitus' argument turns on three related contrasts:

(1) He opposes dreaming, in which each person has his own 'private world', to waking, in which we all recognize a common world.

(2) He opposes the 'private understanding', that most people rely on, to the common 'reason' or 'account' (logos)[8] that we ought to rely on.

(3) He opposes the everyday picture of the world as a collection of relatively stable objects undergoing changes to his own picture of the world as a collection of processes rather than objects (**45**).

According to Heracleitus, these three contrasts are connected. We see that we must prefer the common, waking world; then we see we must prefer the conclusions of the 'common account' over the assumptions of our 'private understanding'. If we follow the common account, we must agree with the Heracleitean conception of the world.

The connection that Heracleitus sees between the three contrasts is clearest

---

[7] Cf. Meno's paradox in **182**.

[8] 'Account' = logos, cognate with logismos in **107**. In some contexts one might render logos by 'word', 'speech', or 'reason'. If you speak and I understand you, you use your logos to produce a logos, and I use my logos to understand you. Cf. **558**.

in his remarks on the senses. If we consider possible sources of belief and knowledge, it is natural to examine the senses, since some of our beliefs come to us as a result of seeing, hearing, and so on. We have to ask whether the senses are sources of knowledge, and whether they are the only ones.

Sometimes Heracleitus expresses confidence in the senses. At other times, however, he warns us that they are sometimes 'bad witnesses': they mislead me if I rely on them uncritically. To avoid being misled, I must criticize the senses by rational reflection on them.

To show that uncritical reliance on the senses is mistaken, Heracleitus appeals to the difference between sleeping and waking (**114**, **119**). If I trust my senses without any attempt at rational discrimination, I must accept all my immediate appearances uncritically. In that case, I must also take the appearances in my dreams at face value; for only rational discrimination assures me that these are not genuine experiences of an objective world. But if I trust the appearances in my dreams, I must conclude that (i) I live in a world that is as disorderly as the appearances in my dreams, and (ii) I live in a world that differs from the world in which other people live as much as my dream-world differs from other people's dream-worlds.

We all reject these two conclusions; for we believe that we live in a common world and that this common world is more orderly than the appearances in our dreams. Since we reject the conclusions that follow from an uncritical attitude to the senses, we must also reject the uncritical attitude to the senses. Hence we must agree that the senses are not to be trusted uncritically.

To discover the errors resulting from uncritical reliance on the senses, we must use critical reason (*logos*). Critical reason is 'common', accessible to everyone (**120**), and it offers a shared rational standard for evaluating beliefs; but not everyone grasps or accepts it at first. The correct 'common account' shows us that the world is an order (*kosmos*), not the unpredictable, disorderly world that we would have to believe in if we relied uncritically on the senses. In saying that the senses will mislead people who have the souls of 'foreigners' (*barbaroi*; i.e. those who do not speak or understand Greek), Heracleitus implies that we will not understand what the senses tell us unless we interpret them correctly (**114**). This is why the mere accumulation of information is not sufficient for knowledge (**116**); to acquire knowledge, we must interpret the senses correctly.

Heracleitean cosmology claims to rely on the same critical reason that underlies our common-sense contrast between the objective world and our dreams. Cosmology seeks to discover regularity, law, and order in the world. We cannot, in Heracleitus' view, reject this demand for regularity unless we also reject our common-sense conception of an external objective world. Some claims of naturalist cosmology appear to conflict with experience and observation; as Heracleitus says, the order of nature is an 'unapparent order' (**66**) and 'nature tends to hide' (**39**). But the appearance of conflict is misleading, and deceives only those who refuse to apply critical intelligence to their experience.

Heracleitus maintains that we are justified in accepting his cosmology if and only if we are justified in believing that a critical attitude to the senses sometimes gives us knowledge. According to Heracleitus, we are justified in believing this because a critical attitude to the senses gives us knowledge of a common, orderly world. Uncritical reliance on the senses both overestimates and underestimates the degree of stability in the world, since we do not always recognize the implications of the compositional criteria of unity and continuity that we implicitly accept (see **45**).

He does not argue, however, that we know we live in a common, orderly world. He assumes that we know this, and argues from it to the conclusion that the right critical attitude to the senses yields knowledge. To this extent, his epistemological support for his metaphysical principles is incomplete. If we doubt whether we know we live in a common, orderly world, we raise a sceptical doubt about Heracleitus' system as a whole.

....

114   SEXTUS, *Against the Professors* vii. 126–34   Heracleitus also supposed that human beings are equipped with two instruments for gaining knowledge of truth, namely sense-perception and reason. And so he held, similarly to the students of nature mentioned above, that one of these instruments, sense-perception, is untrustworthy, and he assumes reason as criterion. He refutes sense-perception in these words: [B107] 'Bad witnesses for human beings are the eyes and ears of those who have the souls of foreigners'.[9] This is equivalent to saying 'To trust in the non-rational senses is characteristic of foreign souls.' The reason that he declares to be the judge of truth is not just any kind of reason, but the reason that is common and divine. ... [131] Heracleitus, then, says that this common and divine reason, participation in which makes us rational, is a[10] criterion of truth. Hence, what appears to everyone in common is (in his view) trustworthy—for it is grasped by the common and divine reason—whereas what affects one person alone is, for the contrary reason, untrustworthy. Thus, at the beginning[11] of his work on nature ... he says: [B1] 'Of this account which holds invariably[12] human beings turn out to be uncomprehending, both before they hear it and when they first hear it. For although everything comes about in accordance with this account, they would seem to be untried novices when they make trial of the words and the actions I expound as I divide each thing according to its nature and say how it is. Other people[13] fail to notice what they do when they are awake, just as they forget what they do when asleep.' For, after arguing in these words that we do and think everything through participation in the divine reason, he adds, a little further on: 'Therefore one must follow the

[9] Heracleitus on the soul and the senses; **305–11**.
[10] The Greek has no article.
[11] These are the first words of Heracleitus' work (as we learn from other evidence).
[12] The clause is ambiguous, since 'invariably' might go with 'holds' or 'turn out'.
[13] i.e. people other than Heracleitus.

comprehensive', that is 'the common' (for 'comprehensive' means 'common'); 'and though reason is comprehensive, most people live as though they had their own private intelligence.' Therefore, in so far as we share in the memory of that reason we say what is true, but whenever we express our own private thoughts, we speak falsely. Here, then, and in these words he most expressly declares that the common reason is a criterion, and that the things that appear in common are trustworthy, as being judged by the common reason, whereas the things that appear privately to a given person are false.

115 HIPPOLYTUS, *Refutation* ix. 9. 5 = DK 22 B 55   [HERACLEITUS:] I honour more those things which are learned by sight and hearing.

116 DIOGENES LAERTIUS ix. 1 = DK 22 B 40   [HERACLEITUS:] Much learning does not teach understanding.[14]

117 HIPPOLYTUS, *Refutation* ix. 9. 1 = DK 22 B 50.   [HERACLEITUS:] Listening not to me but to the account, it is wise to agree that all things are one.

118 HIPPOLYTUS, *Refutation* ix. 9. 2 = DK 22 B 51   [HERACLEITUS:] They do not comprehend how, in differing, it agrees with itself—a backward-turning connection, like that of a bow and a lyre.[15]

119 PLUTARCH, *Superstition* 166c   Heracleitus says that for those awake the world is one and common, but when anyone goes to sleep, he lives in a private world.[16] But for the superstitious person there is no common world. For he neither uses his intelligence when he is awake, nor frees himself from his agitation when he goes to sleep, but his reason is dreaming, his fear is awake, and he has neither escape nor relief.

120 STOBAEUS, *Anthology* iii. 129. 14–130. 3 = DK 22 B 114.   Those who speak with understanding must rely strongly on what is common[17] to all, just as a city relies on its law, and indeed much more strongly. For all human laws are nourished by the one divine law; for it controls as much as it wills, and is sufficient for all, and overcomes.

Parmenides and Zeno: sense and reason

121 Parmenides exploits both Xenophanes' contrast between mere belief and knowledge and Heracleitus' contrast between sense and reason. In his view, the

---

[14] *nous;* cf. **214–15**, **274**.

[15] Unity of opposites; **57**.

[16] The quotation or paraphrase of Heracleitus probably ends here. Waking and sleeping; **277**.

[17] 'With understanding' = *xun nô(i)*. 'Common' = *xunô(i)*. One might capture the pun by paraphrasing: 'Common-sense advice must rest on the common sense'.

unreflective, uncritical beliefs of mortals are based on the senses, and are false. He urges us to reject these beliefs in favour of conclusions that have a better claim to our acceptance. He believes Heracleitus does not go far enough. According to Heracleitus, we must criticize the senses and recognize that they mislead us about the extent and types of changes that really happen; they are bad witnesses if we interpret them badly, but good witnesses if we interpret them intelligently. Parmenides, by contrast, believes that the senses are misleading in principle; they suggest the reality of change, but rational argument proves that change is unreal.

Parmenides describes his argument as a 'refutation' (*elenchos*), since it refutes those who assume the reality of change. He does not believe he is simply asserting some eccentric view of his own about change; he seeks to clarify our implicit beliefs and to expose a conflict in them. His argument seems to be this:

(1) Change is real (according to common sense).

(2) If change is real, we can speak and think of what is not.

(3) But we cannot speak or think of what is not.

(4) Therefore change is not real.

Parmenides appeals to the evident truth of (2) and (3) to undermine our belief in (1).

Zeno's arguments against motions are also attempted refutations that clarify our assumptions about motion and infinity. He argues that these assumptions cannot all be maintained. We might dismiss Parmenides and Zeno if they simply presented counter-intuitive doctrines about not being and about change; but we cannot dismiss them so easily if we are implicitly committed to self-contradictory views that they revise.[18]

If Parmenides is right, we cannot know anything about any world of changing objects, since we must agree that it is illusory. While we may still follow Parmenides' 'Way of Belief', and construct theories about the natural world, we must acknowledge that these theories, in contrast to the 'Way of Truth', are simply fictions.

Parmenides' attack on the senses does not lead him to universal scepticism, since he is firmly anti-sceptical about reason. Since he takes steps (2) and (3) of his argument to be evidently true, he takes his argument to show that change is unreal, not simply that we do not know whether or not change is real. But his strategy invites sceptical questions. Why should we trust rational argument, if it leads us to the apparently absurd result that there is no change?

---

[18] Cf. Socrates' cross-examinations, **142**.

122 SEXTUS, *Against the Professors* vii. 110–14   Xenophanes, according to those who expound him differently,[19] ' … ',[20] appears not to abolish every sort of grasp, but the sort that involves knowledge and is free of error, and to leave standing the sort involving belief, so that, in his view, the reason that involves belief turns out to be a criterion; this is the sort that holds on to what is likely but not on to what is firm. But his friend Parmenides condemned the reason that involves belief—I mean the kind that has weak suppositions—and laid down the reason involving knowledge, i.e. inerrant reason, as criterion of truth, having abandoned trust in the senses. At any rate, he writes as follows at the beginning of his work on nature: … [21] [114] Intellect … promises to teach him two things—'the unwavering heart of persuasive truth', which is the im-movable seat of knowledge, and, secondly, 'the beliefs of mortals, in which there is no true conviction'—that is to say, everything that depends on belief, because it is insecure. And at the end, he also makes it clear that one must not pay attention to the senses, but to reason; for he says 'Do not let custom …' This man himself, then, as is plain from what he says, announced the reason involving knowledge as standard of truth in beings, and gave up reliance on the senses.

123 PLATO, *Sophist* 237 A and Sextus, *Against the Professors* vii. 111 = DK 28 B 7[22]   For this will never prevail, that what is not is. Rather, restrain your thought from this road of inquiry.[23] Do not let custom force you along this fa-miliar road,[24] diverting unobservant eye and echoing ear and speech.[25] No; judge by reason the much-contested refutation[26] that I have spoken.

124 SIMPLICIUS, *Commentary on the Physics* 30. 14–19   Parmenides passes from objects of thought to objects of sense, or from truth, as he himself puts it, to belief, when he writes: 'Here I cease for you my trustworthy argument and thought about the truth. Henceforward learn mortal beliefs, listening to the deceitful ordering of my words…. [39. 8–12] I tell you this whole suitable ordering, so that no opinion of mortals will ever outstrip you.' He describes this discourse as a matter of belief and as deceptive, not as being unquali-fiedly false, but as having fallen away from the truth grasped by understand-ing to the object of sense that appears and seems.[27]

---

[19] Sceptical interpretation of Xenophanes; **112**.

[20] The quotation omitted here is in **112**.

[21] Here Sextus offers an interpretation of the prologue to Parmenides' poem.

[22] This follows **73**.

[23] Quoted by Plato in **75**.

[24] Or 'Do not let custom, based on much experience, force you along this road.'

[25] Literally, 'tongue'. It might refer to the organ of taste, rather than to speech.

[26] Or 'much-contesting'. On refutation (*elenchos*) cf. **142**.

[27] 'Seems' = *dokein*, cognate with 'belief' (*doxa*). Simplicius' remark on Parmenides is influenced by Plato's account of knowledge and belief (**212–13**).

Democritus: the senses and convention

125 Democritus follows Heracleitus and Parmenides in connecting the division between ungrounded belief and knowledge with the division between sense and reason. He agrees with Parmenides in arguing that the senses are misleading about some features of reality, but he does not believe they are as radically misleading as Parmenides takes them to be; he agrees with Heracleitus in supposing that a critical use of sensory evidence will tell us about the character of reality.

To show that the senses cannot be accepted uncritically, Democritus seems to appeal to 'conflicting appearances'—more precisely, to ostensibly conflicting appearances.[28] He argues (according to Aristotle, in **126**) that if something appears to different perceivers to have incompatible properties, and there is no way to tell which of these apparently conflicting appearances is right, we ought to conclude that the thing itself has neither property.

The argument is this:

(1) The water appears hot to you, cold to me.

(2) Either (a) one of us is right, one wrong, or (b) both of us are right, or (c) both of us are wrong.

(3) The appearances are equipollent (i.e. we have no reason to prefer one over the other).

(4) So we must reject (a).

(5) But it is impossible for the same thing to have contradictory properties at the same time.

(6) So we must reject (b).

(7) So we must accept (c).

This argument applies to every perceptible quality that allows conflicting and equipollent appearances. Democritus concludes that all such qualities are simply matters of 'convention' (*nomos*) rather than reality. If it is a matter of convention to drive on the right in the USA, then it depends on agreement; if there were no agreement, there would be no reason to drive on the right rather than the left. Similarly, then, according to Democritus, when we say that something is red, we are saying how people take it to be, not how it really in its own right.[29] In Democritus' view the senses offer a 'bastard' form of judgement; only reason offers genuine knowledge. How, then, can we reach the 'genuine' form of knowledge, and how can reason correct the senses? Democritus believes reason can discover the hidden order that is inaccessible to the senses. Rational argument, independent of sensory appearances, shows us that reality must allow

[28] Protagoras (see **156**) argues that the conflict is only apparent.
[29] On convention and nature see **36**, **149–51**, **458**.

the possibility of change. For even if our appearances are misleading, they change; their changes must have some cause; hence reality must include some cause of change. In his view, the basic realities are permanent, indivisible atoms; these have size, shape, and weight, but no other perceptible qualities, and are always in motion. Their temporary combinations form the apparently solid objects that appear to us. The apparent perceptible qualities—colour, taste, smell—of tables and cabbages appear to us to belong to external bodies, but are really only our appearances, resulting from the interaction between us and the atoms.

To show how the atoms might cause these appearances, Democritus uses analogies from observation; he gives credit to Anaxagoras for this policy (**131**). Just as pins make a sharper impression on us than blunt objects, so also, we may assume, atoms of different shapes cause sweet or sharp sensations on the tongue. Bitter tastes, for instance, come from sharp atoms (as we speak of a 'sharp' taste).

....

126 ARISTOTLE, *Metaphysics* 1009^{b}1–1010^{a}1 Some people have been led to believe in the truth of appearances because of perceptible things. In their view, one ought not to judge the truth of something by the large or small number of people who believe it. But the same thing seems sweet to some who taste it, bitter to others, so that if all were sick or all insane except for two or three healthy or sane people, these two or three, not the majority, would seem to be sick or insane. Further, many of the other animals have appearances contrary to ours about the same thing, and even for each one of us in relation to himself things do not always seem the same as far as perception goes. It is unclear, then, which appearances are true or false; for one lot are no more true than another lot, but all are on the same footing. This is why Democritus says that either nothing is true or to us, at any rate, it is unclear... . [1009^{b}33] If those who more than anyone else have seen such truth as it is possible to see—those who more than anyone else search for it and love it—if they believe and affirm such views about truth, how can we expect beginners in philosophy not to lose heart? For inquiry into the truth would be a wild goose chase.

127 SEXTUS, *Pyrrhonian Outlines* ii. 63 The only remaining possibility is judgement by means of both senses and thought. But this again is impossible; for not only do the senses not guide thought to a grasp of truth; they are even contrary to it. For it is certain, at any rate, that from the fact that honey appears bitter to some and sweet to others, Democritus said it is neither sweet nor bitter, but Heracleitus said it is both. The same account may be given in the case of all the other senses and their objects. And so, when thought sets out from the senses, it is compelled to make statements that are at variance and in conflict; and this is foreign to a criterion for grasping truth.

128 SEXTUS, *Pyrrhonian Outlines* i. 8–10 The Sceptical ability is the ability to oppose things appearing to things thought in any way at all. From this ability we proceed through the equipollence in the opposed objects and arguments, and arrive, first, at suspension of judgement, and, after that, at freedom from disturbance.... By 'things appearing' we now understand those things that appear to the senses.... [10] By 'equipollence' we mean equality in credibility and the lack of it, so that neither of the conflicting arguments[30] stands out as more credible than the other. 'Suspension of judgement' is the repose of thought, because of which we neither deny nor affirm something.

129 SEXTUS, *Pyrrhonian Outlines* i. 203. And so, when I say 'To every argument an equal argument is opposed', I mean this: 'every argument that I have examined and that establishes something dogmatically appears to me to be opposed by a second argument that establishes something dogmatically and is equal to the first argument in credibility and lack of it'. Hence, the utterance of this statement is not dogmatic; it merely reports a human affection, which is a thing appearing to the subject affected.

130 THEOPHRASTUS, *Senses* 69–70 Altogether, the greatest contrariety, one common to every case of sense-perception, is the fact that Democritus makes flavours affections of the sense, but at the same time differentiates them by the shapes of the atoms and says the same <shape>[31] appears bitter to some and sweet to others, and still another way to others. This is self-contradictory, because it is not possible for the shape to be an affection; nor is it possible for the same shape to be round for some perceivers and differently shaped for others—but this would presumably be necessary, if the same shape were sweet for some and bitter for others; nor can the shapes of atoms change in accordance with our own states. The shape is, without qualification, something in its own right, whereas the sweet, and the perceptible in general, is relative to something else and is in other things, according to him.

131 SEXTUS, *Against the Professors* vii. 135–40 Democritus sometimes undermines the things appearing to the senses, and says that none of them appears in accordance with the truth, but only in accordance with belief, and the truth in beings is that there are atoms and void. For he says: 'By convention sweet, bitter, hot, cold, colour, but in reality atoms and void'. He means: objects of perception are conventionally supposed and believed to exist, but in truth none of them exists, but only atoms and void exist. And in his Confrontations, although he had promised to ascribe the strength of credibility to the senses, none the less he is found condemning them. For he says: 'But in reality we understand nothing true, but only what fluctuates in accordance

---

[30] Or 'statements' (*logoi*).
[31] Or 'the same flavour'.

with the condition of our body and of the things that come into it and the things that oppose it.' And again he says: 'Now in truth it has been made clear in many ways that we do not understand what the character of anything is.' In his book On Forms he says: 'A human being must recognize by this standard that he is separated from truth'. Again, 'This argument also makes it clear that we know nothing in truth about anything, but each person's belief is an influx <of atoms>'. Yet again, 'It will, however, be plain that it is a puzzle to find out what the character of anything is in truth.' Now in these passages he rejects practically every sort of grasp of reality, even though he fastens especially on just the senses. But in his 'Standards', he says there are two kinds of knowledge, one through the senses, and the other through thought. He calls the knowledge that comes through thought 'genuine', testifying to its credibility for discriminating truth. The knowledge that comes through the senses he calls 'bastard', denying it inerrancy in the distinguishing of what is true. He says in so many words: 'Of knowledge there are two sorts, the genuine and the bastard. The bastard form includes all these—sight, hearing, smell, taste, touch. The other sort is genuine, and separated from the first sort.' Then, while giving precedence to the genuine over the bastard, he proceeds: 'Whenever the bastard kind is unable any longer to see anything smaller, or to hear or smell or taste or perceive it by the touch, we must turn to something more subtle.' Hence, according to this man also, reason is the criterion; he calls it genuine knowledge. But Diotimus used to say that according to Democritus there are three criteria. The criterion of the grasp of non-evident things is the things that appear; for things are the sight of things that are not clear, as Anaxagoras says—and Democritus praised him for this. The criterion of investigation is the conception: 'For in every case, my son, the one starting-point is to know what the investigation is about.' The criterion of choice and aversion is the affections; for what is congenial to us is choiceworthy, but what we are alienated from is to be avoided.

132 GALEN, *Elements* i. 2. 12 'For colour is by convention, sweet by convention, bitter by convention, but in truth atoms and void', says Democritus. He supposes that all the sensible qualities come into being from the coming together of atoms, in relation to us who perceive them, and that by nature nothing is white or black or yellow or red or bitter or sweet. For 'by convention' means something like 'conventionally' and 'relatively to us', 'not in accordance with the nature of the things themselves'.... So the sense of his statement as a whole will be this: Human beings conventionally suppose that something is white, black, sweet, bitter, and so on, but in truth the totality of things is one <i.e. atoms>[32] and nothing <i.e. void>.

---

[32] Text uncertain.

133 THEOPHRASTUS, *Senses* 65–7 According to Democritus, sharp flavour is whatever has these shapes: angular, crinkled, small and fine. For because of its asperity it spreads quickly and all around, and being rough and angular, it gathers and holds things together.... Sweet flavour is composed of round shapes that are not too small. That is why it relaxes the body completely, but not violently, and does not spread quickly through all of it. ... [67] He treats the other capacities of each thing in the same way, deriving them from the shapes.... The preponderant shape has the greatest effect in relation to our perception and its own capacity. Moreover, the state we are in when it reaches us makes no little difference. That is why sometimes the same thing produces contrary affections, and contrary things produce the same affection when they are present in a perceived object.

Scepticism in Democritus?

134 In describing atoms and their relation to our perceptions, Democritus relies on analogies with observable situations. If these analogies are to be any guide to the character of the atoms, the observations that give us the basis for the analogies must themselves be reliable. We must be right, for instance, to believe, on the basis of sensory evidence, that sharp things tear the surfaces of bodies they touch, whereas smooth things do not. Such beliefs support Democritus' view about the different sorts of atoms that interact with our sense-organs to produce different sorts of perceptions.

It is difficult, however, to reconcile this argument with Democritus' use of the argument from conflicting appearances. He relies on conflicting appearances to reach his conclusion that sensory observation is always wrong about the real nature of things. And he relies on this conclusion for the further conclusion that atoms have none of the qualities (colour, sound, etc.) about which the senses mislead us.

Apparently, he must accept this argument:

(1) If the argument from conflicting appearances is sound, the senses are unreliable about the nature of reality.

(2) We have reason to believe the atomic theory because of examples drawn from sensory observation.

(3) So, if we have reason to believe the atomic theory, sensory observation must be reliable.

(4) But the argument from conflicting appearances is sound.

(5) Hence the senses are unreliable.

(6) Hence we have no reason to believe the atomic theory.

If this argument is sound, neither sense-perception nor reason has reached any justified belief about the nature of reality. Democritus sees the danger of this sceptical conclusion. He presents a dialogue between the senses and the intellect. The senses allege that when the intellect undermines their credibility, it also undermines its own credibility, since it draws its evidence from the senses (**137**).

Democritus reaches this sceptical conclusion by trying to combine elements of Heracleitus' and Parmenides' attitudes to the senses. He agrees with Heracleitus' aim of using the senses, critically interpreted, to acquire knowledge. But his attack on the senses seems to undermine his attempts to use them. He follows Parmenides in presenting a general argument against the reliability of the senses. Unlike Parmenides, however, he relies on the senses even in his 'way of truth'. Hence he defeats his own position.

He clearly does not intend to be a sceptic; for he affirms the truth of the atomic theory. But he seems to commit himself to scepticism. For if neither the senses nor reason can lead us to the truth, Democritus must admit that we have no access to how things really are—that 'either there is no truth or to us at least it is not evident' (**126**). If we cannot undermine this conclusion, we must admit that Democritus' arguments leave us 'puzzled' or 'at a loss' (*aporein*; cf. **142**, **171**) about what to believe, so that the only option open to us is to 'suspend judgement' (*epechein*; cf. **174–5**) about which view is right.

....

135   DIOGENES LAERTIUS ix. 72   According to some, Xenophanes, Zeno of Elea and Democritus were Sceptics ... Democritus ... does away with qualities where he says: 'By convention hot, by convention cold; in reality atoms and void.' And again: 'In reality we know nothing; for truth is in the depths.'

136   DIOGENES OF OENOANDA, fr. 6, ii. 2–13   Democritus also made a mistake unworthy of him, when he said that only the atoms really exist among beings, and everything else is by convention. For according to your argument, Democritus, quite apart from not finding the truth, we will not even be able to live, since we will not avoid fire, or a wound, or ...[33]

137   GALEN, *Medical Experience* 15. 7–8 = DK 68 B 125   Everyone knows that the most serious charge against any argument is that it conflicts with what is immediately evident. For arguments cannot even start without the immediately evident; how then can they be credible if they are foolhardy enough to attack the immediately evident from which they took their beginnings? Democritus knew this also. After denouncing the senses,[34] ... he presented

---

[33] A gap in the inscription follows. For this argument about practical results see **297**.
[34] See **135**.

the senses replying to thought: 'Poor mind, after taking your sources of credibility from us, are you now trying to overthrow us? That overthrow is a downfall for you.' And so you should condemn reason for being incredible since it is so depraved that when it is most persuasive it conflicts with the appearances from which it began.

IV: Knowledge and Belief

From Socrates to Scepticism

Socrates' ignorance

138 None of the philosophers we have considered so far intends to be a sceptic. They all set out to defend some claims to knowledge, even if their views invite sceptical questions. Socrates, however, refuses to claim knowledge about the questions he investigates (**141**). His disavowal of knowledge may suggest sceptical doubt about the possibility of knowledge and of justified belief. Even if we eventually reject this interpretation of Socrates (see **177**), we ought to consider why it might appear plausible.

Socrates examines other people about moral questions, and especially about the virtues. People think they know about the virtues, since they think it important to decide whether they themselves and other people are brave, just, honest, and so on. Socrates' questions, however, show that his interlocutors do not know what they thought they knew about the different virtues. Nor does he claim to know the answers to questions that they cannot answer. He claims only that he is wiser than they are.

When one of Socrates' associates asked the Delphic Oracle whether anyone was wiser than Socrates, the oracle said No. Socrates could not see how the oracle could be right in any obvious sense; but he followed Heracleitus' suggestion (**140**; cf. **582**), and looked for the less obvious significance of the answer. To see what it meant, he tried to find someone wiser than himself. But he found that people who might have been expected to know about morality, and thought they knew about it, could not answer his questions, showing that they lacked the knowledge they claimed. Socrates concluded he had found what the oracle meant, and that what it said was true; no one was wiser than Socrates, because, unlike his interlocutors, he recognized his lack of knowledge.

139 PLATO, *Apology* 19 C–23 B[1]   [SOCRATES:] The fact is that there is nothing in any of these charges, and if you have heard anyone say that I undertake to educate people and that I make money from it, that is not true either. Mind you, I think it is a fine thing if someone is able to educate people—someone like Gorgias of Leontini, Prodicus of Ceos, and Hippias of Elis. For each of them is able to go into any city and to persuade the young men who are free to associate with any fellow citizen they like at no charge—they persuade

---
[1] This follows **583**.

these young men to abandon the company of their fellow citizens, and to associate with him, not only paying him fees but even being grateful for it.[2] ... [20 D] I have gained this reputation, gentlemen, just because of a sort of wisdom. What kind of wisdom is this? Human wisdom, I suppose; for it looks as though I really am wise in this sort of wisdom, whereas the people I mentioned just now are perhaps wise in a greater wisdom than human wisdom. I don't know what else to say. For I certainly have no knowledge of such wisdom; anyone who says I have is a liar and says it to slander me.

Now, gentlemen, please do not interrupt me if I seem to make some grand claim; for what I am going to tell you is not my own account; I am going to refer you to a weighty authority for it. I will call as witness to my wisdom, if it is any, the god of Delphi. You know Chaerephon, of course. He was a friend of mine from boyhood, and a good friend of the people, who shared in the recent expulsion and came back with you.[3] And you know what sort of person he was—how intense he was about whatever he had undertaken. Well, one day, he actually went to Delphi and asked this question of the god—as I said before, gentlemen, please do not interrupt—he asked whether there was anyone wiser than I am. The priestess replied that there was no one... .

When I heard about the oracle's answer, I said to myself: 'What does the god mean? Why does he speak in riddles? For I am aware that I am wise in nothing, great or small.[4] What, then, does he mean by asserting that I am the wisest? He cannot be telling a lie; that would not be right for him.' I puzzled about this for a long time. Then at last I set out, with great difficulty, to inquire into it in this way: I went to someone thought to be wise, on the assumption that here if anywhere I would refute the oracle and point out to my divine authority, 'This man is wiser than I am, but you said I was wisest.'

Well, I gave a thorough examination to this person—I needn't mention his name, but it was one of our politicians whom I was examining. And here's what happened to me, men of Athens: in conversation with him it seemed to me that this man seemed wise to many people, and especially to himself, but he was not... . I reflected as I walked away: 'I'm wiser than this man. For it looks as though neither of us knows anything fine and good, but he thinks he knows something when he does not know, whereas I neither know nor think I know. At any rate, it seems to me that I am wiser than he is to this small extent, that I don't think I know the things I don't know... .

[22 E] The effect of this investigation of mine, gentlemen, has been to arouse many people's hostility—hostility of a particularly bitter and serious kind—which has resulted in many slanders, including the description of me as wise.

---

[2] Sophists; **8**.
[3] The Thirty Tyrants and the restoration of democracy; **537–8, 540**.
[4] Arcesilaus' interpretation of this remark; **170**.

For whenever I refute someone else, the bystanders assume that I am wise in that subject myself. But in fact, gentlemen, it looks as though the god is really wise, and in this oracle he tells us that human wisdom is worth little or nothing. He appears to speak of Socrates, but to have used my name to serve as an example, as if to say: 'The wisest of you human beings is the one who has recognized, as Socrates has, that, as far as wisdom is concerned, he is really worthless.'

140   PLUTARCH, *Decay of the Oracles* 404de = DK 22 B93   I think you know Heracleitus' remark that the king whose oracle is in Delphi neither speaks nor hides, but gives a sign.

141   ARISTOTLE, *Sophistical Refutations* 183ᵃ37–ᵇ8⁵   … Our plan was to find some technique for forming deductions from the most commonly accepted beliefs available on any question proposed to us. For this is the task both of dialectic in its own right and of testing. We must also, however, prepare ourselves in advance⁶ for it because of its closeness to sophistry, so that we shall be able not only to test dialectically, but also to argue as people who know. This was why we laid down not only the previously mentioned task for our discussion—to be able to get someone else to give an account—but also the task of defending a position dialectically, as far as possible, through the most commonly accepted beliefs … Indeed, this was why Socrates used to ask questions, but did not answer; for he acknowledged that he did not know.

Socrates' inquiries

142   When Socrates examines people, he just asks them questions. They supply the answers, and they see for themselves that their answers are inconsistent. If Laches believes p, q, and r, and he discovers that q and r imply not-p, he must give up at least one of p, q, and r. This pattern of refutation (*elenchos*)⁷ recalls Parmenides' attempted refutation of the belief in change and Zeno's attempted refutation of the belief in motion. Aristotle recognizes this continuity, by saying that Parmenides and Zeno were early practitioners of 'dialectic',⁸ the systematic question-and-answer method characteristic of the Platonic dialogues (**143**). Like Parmenides and Zeno, Socrates claims to expose conflicts in our beliefs. We have not noticed these conflicts, because we have not examined the various implications, sometimes surprising, of our beliefs.

---

⁵ This comes at the end of Aristotle's account of dialectic. He connects the role of dialectic in testing other people's beliefs with Socrates' procedure. Though some of the passage is obscure, it provides clear evidence of Socrates' disavowal of knowledge.

⁶ Text and sense uncertain.

⁷ The verb *elenchein* means both 'cross-examine' and 'refute'. Cf. **187**.

⁸ *dialektikê*, from the verb *dialegesthai*, 'converse'. Cf. **214–15**, **220**. Dialectic and dialogue; **189–90**.

In contrast to his predecessors in dialectic, however, Socrates does not focus on metaphysical and cosmological questions, on which ordinary people might expect to find themselves confused. He considers moral questions; these are apparently more familiar and intelligible than the questions that concern the Presocratics. The *Euthyphro* is about holiness (piety),[9] the *Laches* is about bravery, and the *Charmides* is about temperance. These are some of the major virtues of character; people appeal to them in assessing themselves and other people. Hence, they are surprised and annoyed when they cannot answer Socrates' questions.

Socrates asks 'What is the F?' (the pious, the brave, etc.). The interlocutor answers briskly, supposing the question is easy to answer (**181**, **463**). Socrates asks further questions, eliciting the interlocutor's other beliefs, and shows that these other beliefs imply the falsity of the initial answer to the 'What is the F?' question.

This result tends to undermine a claim to knowledge. If we first claim to know something, but then find that our other beliefs conflict with our original belief, we come to doubt what we initially claimed to know. But if we are in doubt about whether to believe p or not-p, we can hardly claim to know that p is true. Parmenides uses this form of argument against our belief in change. Democritus uses it against our belief that things really have colours. Socrates uses it against moral beliefs.

Socrates' question 'What is the F?' is unexpectedly difficult to answer because Socrates presupposes that F things have a common property that makes it correct to apply the same name to them; this property must be shared by all and only brave (for instance) actions and people (cf. **180**). Neither Socrates nor his interlocutor questions this presupposition; it determines Socrates' conception of an acceptable answer. The apparent difficulty of finding an acceptable answer may lead us to question Socrates' presupposition (**146**).

These dialogues about the virtues end with no answer to Socrates' questions. He admits that he, no less than his interlocutors, is 'puzzled', or 'at a loss' (*aporein*; **36**, **169**, **182**, **188**). Some readers in antiquity attribute scepticism to Socrates, and take Plato to have written these dialogues in support of a sceptical position (**25**, **170**, **202**).

....

143 SEXTUS, *Against the Professors* vii. 6–7   Aristotle[10] says Empedocles was the first to take up rhetoric … And it would seem that Parmenides was not unpractised in dialectic, since Aristotle, again, took his familiar companion Zeno to be the originator of dialectic.

---

[9] Socrates uses not only the abstract noun ('holiness'), but also the adjective ('the holy' and 'the holy itself') to describe what he is looking for; **144**.

[10] Other sources attribute this remark to a lost work of Aristotle, the *Sophist*.

144   PLATO, *Euthyphro* 5 C–6 E   SOCRATES: ... Tell me now about the matter you just now claimed to know clearly. What sort of thing do you say the pious and the impious are, with reference to murder and all other cases? Isn't the holy always the same as itself in every action, and, again, isn't the unholy always opposite to all <that is> holy, and similar to itself? If anything is to be unholy, mustn't it have some one character in accordance with <its> unholiness? EUTHYPHRO: Yes, surely, Socrates.—Then tell me: what do you say the holy and the unholy are?—Well, then, I say that the holy is what I am doing now, prosecuting the one who does injustice, who offends by committing murder, or sacrilegious robbery, or something else of that sort, whether the offender is one's father or mother, or whoever it may be. And I say that not to prosecute is unholy. ... —[6 D] You didn't teach me adequately before, when I asked what the holy is. You merely said that what you are doing now is holy—prosecuting <your>[11] father for murder.—And what I said was true, Socrates.—Presumably. But, Euthyphro, there are many other things that you say are holy.—Indeed there are.—Well, bear in mind that what I asked of you was not to teach me one or two of the many holies, but to teach me that very form[12] by which all the holies are holy. For, I take it, you said that there is one character by which the unholies are all unholy, and <one> by which all the holies are holy. Do you remember that?—I do.—Well, then, teach me what this very character is, so that I can focus on it and use it as a pattern,[13] to say that any action done by you or anyone else is holy if it is of this sort, or, if it is not, to deny that it is holy.[14]

145   PLATO, *Laches* 190 A–193 D   SOCRATES: Suppose we know that the presence of sight makes better the eyes in which it's present, and we are also able to make sight present in the eyes. Clearly, in that case, we know what sight itself is, and we could advise about how one might best and most easily acquire it. For if we knew neither what sight is, nor what hearing is, we would hardly be worth taking seriously as advisers or physicians for the eyes or the ears, on how best to acquire hearing or sight. LACHES: That's true, Socrates.—And aren't our two friends, Laches, at this very moment urging us to advise them on how virtue might make the souls of their sons better by its presence?— Very true.—Then mustn't we first know what virtue is? For if we didn't know at all what virtue is, how could we advise anyone about the best way to acquire virtue?—I don't think we could, Socrates.—Then, Laches, we say that we know what virtue is.—Yes.—And if we know it, we can presumably say what it is.—Certainly. ...

---

[11] Or '<one's> father'.
[12] Forms; **192**.
[13] *paradeigma*. Cf. **219–20**.
[14] The discussion continues at **148**. On piety cf. **457**.

[190 D]—Then, Laches, let's first set about saying what bravery is. Then we'll inquire how it might come to be present in the young men, to the extent that it's possible for it to be present from pursuits and studies. Try to tell me what I'm asking about, what bravery is.—Indeed, Socrates, that's not hard to say. For if someone were willing to remain at his post and to fight against the enemy, and did not run away, be assured that he would be brave.[15]—Very good, Laches. But no doubt it's my fault, because I didn't express myself clearly, that you haven't answered the question I had in mind when I asked, but a different one. ... [191 C] For I meant to ask you not only about those who are brave as heavy infantry, but also about those who are brave as cavalry, and in every other sort of warfare; and not only about those who are brave in war, but also about those who are brave in perils by sea, and those who are brave in face of disease, or poverty, or again in politics; and not only about those who are brave in the face of pains or fears, but also about those who are formidable fighters against desires and pleasures, whether fixed in their rank or turning upon their enemy. There are people who are brave in these cases too, aren't there, Laches?—There certainly are, Socrates.—And all these are brave, but some possess bravery in pleasures, and some in pains, some in desires, and some in fears; and some are cowards under the same conditions, I suppose. ... So try again to say, first of all, what bravery is, the same in all these cases. ...

[192 B]—It seems to me that bravery is a sort of endurance of the soul, if I am to speak of what is naturally present throughout all these cases.—Yes, that's what we must do if we are to answer our question. Now this appears to me: not every kind of endurance appears to me, in my opinion,[16] to be bravery. I infer it from this: I pretty well know, Laches, that you consider bravery to be a very fine[17] thing.—One of the finest, you can be sure.—And you would say that endurance with wisdom is also fine and good?—Certainly.—But what would you say about endurance with foolishness? Doesn't that, on the contrary, do evil and harm?—True.—And will you say anything is fine that does evil and harm?—It would be wrong to say that, Socrates.—Then you won't agree that such endurance is bravery, since it is not fine, whereas bravery is fine?—You're right.

— Then, according to your account, wise endurance is bravery?—True.— Then let's see: wise in what? ... [193 A] Take a man who endures in war, and is willing to fight, and wisely calculates and knows that others will help him, and that there will be fewer and inferior men against him than there are with him; and suppose that he also has a stronger position. Would you say that a man who endures with all this wisdom and preparation is braver than someone in

[15] Remaining at one's post; **445**.
[16] Socrates' excessive tentativeness may be intended as politeness.
[17] Fine (*kalon*); **449**.

the opposing army who is willing to stand firm and endure?—I'd say the second man was the braver, Socrates.—But, surely, this one's endurance is more foolish than the other's? ... [193 D] Didn't foolish daring and endurance appear to us before to be shameful and harmful to us?—Quite true.—Whereas bravery was agreed to be something fine.—It was indeed agreed.—And now, on the contrary, we are saying that that shameful thing, foolish endurance, is bravery.—It looks like it.—And are we right in saying so?—Indeed, Socrates, I'm sure we're wrong.

146 WITTGENSTEIN, *The Blue and Brown Books*,[18] p. 19 The idea that in order to get clear about the meaning of a general term one had to find the common element in all its applications has shackled philosophical investigation; for it has not only led to no result, but also made the philosopher dismiss as irrelevant the concrete cases, which alone could have helped him to understand the usage of the general term. When Socrates asks the question, 'what is knowledge?', he does not even regard it as a *preliminary* answer to enumerate cases of knowledge.[19]

The extension of scepticism

147 Socrates' questions confront his interlocutors with puzzles about their moral beliefs. Democritean arguments from conflicting appearances can also be applied to moral beliefs, to show that they are merely matters of convention that correspond to no further reality (cf. **150-1**, **153-4**). Socrates notices that different people in a given society may disagree about what is just and right, with no prospect of resolving their disagreements (**148**). Similarly, Greeks, Persians, and Egyptians hold incompatible outlooks and practices, and reject the outlooks and practices of other societies as immoral.

Differences between societies may suggest that a moral norm is similar to a law or convention.[20] Just as Athenian law is normally followed in Athens, Athenian morality is prevalent there too; and just as laws represent a collective agreement with no further basis in reality, moral norms might equally be taken to be relative to social agreement (**154**, **193**).

Parallel sceptical doubts might affect religious belief. Xenophanes suggests a sceptical argument about the gods of Greek mythology, when he remarks that Greeks make their gods Greek, Scythians make them Scythian, and so on (**108**, **577**). Xenophanes does not infer that all belief in gods is subject to an argument from conflicting appearances. Herodotus' story about different attitudes towards

[18] Oxford: Blackwell, 1958.
[19] Wittgenstein refers to *Tht.* 146–7. The fairness of his general criticism may be judged from **144–5**, **181**, **457**.
[20] Greek uses *nomos* for both.

the disposal of the dead bodies of one's parents makes a similar point about the variety of beliefs in different societies (**149**). Herodotus does not draw any sceptical conclusion from the observed variety in religious practices; he argues that one ought to respect the customs of one's own society and other societies (cf. Heracleitus, **120**). One might infer, however, that religious beliefs and practices are merely matters of convention, not to be taken seriously as true. Critias, indeed, concludes that belief in gods is entirely a fiction (**584**).

Plato suggests that if we are exposed to sceptical arguments about morality, and lack the intellectual resources to answer them, the result will be scepticism, indifference, and immorality (**152**; cf. **462**). If it appears to us that the moral views we had taken seriously are simply matters of convention that happen to be shared in our society, why should we take them seriously any more (apart from any punishment that may result from openly flouting them)?

148 PLATO, *Euthyphro* 7 A–8 A   SOCRATES: Come now, let's examine what we are saying. What is god-beloved,[21] and the god-beloved man, are holy; what is god-hated, and the god-hated man, unholy. For the holy and the unholy are not the same; the holy is most contrary to the unholy. Isn't it so? EUTHYPHRO: It is.—And the matter appears to have been well stated?—I accept it, Socrates; that was stated.—Was it not also stated, Euthyphro, that the gods form factions, and dispute with one another, and that hatreds come between them?—That was stated.—Hatred and wrath, my friend, arise from disputes about what sorts of things? Let's look at it this way: If you and I were to dispute about which of two numbers is the greater, would a dispute about that make us hostile, and angry at each other? Wouldn't we resort to calculation, and so be quickly reconciled on any such point?—Yes, certainly.—Similarly, if we disputed about greater or lesser length, we would resort to measurement, and quickly end the dispute?—Just that.—And in the same way, I think, we would resort to scales and settle any question about a lighter or a heavier weight?—Of course.—What sort of thing, then, do we dispute about until we are unable to reach a decision, and might be hostile, and angry at one another? Perhaps you have no answer ready, but listen to me. Aren't they these things: just and unjust, fine and shameful, good and bad? Aren't these the things we dispute about without being able to reach a decision, so that we sometimes grow hostile to one another, you and I and all other human beings?— Yes, Socrates, those are the things we dispute about.—What about the gods, then, Euthyphro? If indeed they have disputes, mustn't it be about these things?—Quite necessarily.—Accordingly, my noble Euthyphro, by your account some gods take one thing to be just and others take another, and similarly with the fine and shameful, and good and bad. They would hardly form factions against one another if they didn't dispute about these

---

[21] We need this awkward adjective to grasp some of Plato's points.

questions, would they?—You're right.—And the things each party thinks fine, good, and just are what it loves, and the contrary things are what it hates?—Yes, certainly.—But it is the same things, so you say, that some of them think just, and others unjust, and as a result of controversy about these they form factions, and make war on one another. Isn't it so?—It is.—Accordingly, so it would seem, the same things will be hated by the gods and loved by them, and the same things will be both god-hated and god-loved.—It would seem so.—And so, by this argument, the same things, Euthyphro, will he holy and unholy.[22]

149 HERODOTUS iii. 38   … It is clear to me, in every way, that Cambyses[23] was raving mad. Otherwise he would not have set out to ridicule holy rites and customary[24] practices. For if one offered human beings a choice among all the customs in the world, and instructed them to choose those that seemed to them the best, they would examine them all, and each group would choose its own established custom. That is how firmly they count their own customs as by far the finest. And so unless someone was mad, it is not likely that he would ridicule such things. That all humanity regard their own customs in this way may be recognized by very many proofs, including this one: When Darius had established his rule, he called into his presence some Greeks who were at hand, and asked them what price it would take to make them want to eat their fathers when they died. To this they answered that they would not do it for any price. He then sent for some Indians, of the tribe called Callatians, people who eat their fathers. While the Greeks stood by and knew by the help of an interpreter all that was being said, he asked the Indians what price it would take to make them agree to burn their fathers after their death. The Indians exclaimed aloud, and told him not to speak the unspeakable. Such is people's custom in these matters; and it seems to me that Pindar's poem was right when he said, 'Custom is king of all'.

150 SEXTUS, *Pyrrhonian Outlines* i. 145–68   The tenth mode,[25] which is especially connected with ethics, is the one that depends on patterns of conduct, and on habits, laws, mythic beliefs, and dogmatic suppositions. A pattern of conduct is the choice of a way of life, or of some action, referring to one person or many—for example, to Diogenes or the Spartans. A law is a written convention among the participants in political life, the violator of which is punished. A habit or custom (for there is no difference) is the common acceptance by a number of people of a type of action, where the violator is not invariably punished.

---

[22] The discussion continues at **586**. Cf. **575**.

[23] Cambyses and Darius were both kings of Persia.

[24] This subscript indicates *nomos* or a cognate.

[25] The 'modes' (or 'tropes' or 'ways', *tropoi*) are the different lines of argument that lead to puzzlement (*aporia*) and hence to suspension (*epochē*) of judgement. Cf. **171–2**.

For instance, it is a law that no one is to commit adultery, but it is our habit not to have intercourse with a woman in public. A mythic belief is the acceptance of things that did not happen and are fictional—such as, among others, the myths about Cronus; for these induce belief in many people. A dogmatic supposition is the acceptance of something that seems to be supported by analogy or by some kind of demonstration, such as that there are atomic elements of things, or uniform parts, or least parts, or other things. We oppose each of these things sometimes to itself and sometimes to each of the others. ... [163] Since so much discrepancy in things has been shown by this mode also, we will be unable to say how a given subject[26] is in its nature; we will only be able to say how it appears relative to a pattern of conduct, or law, or habit, and so forth. And so this mode also must lead us to suspend judgement about the nature of the external subjects.

151   DIOGENES LAERTIUS ix. 83–4   This mode includes questions about fine and shameful things, true and false, and good and bad things; about gods, and about the coming to be and destruction of all the things that are apparent. For instance, the same thing is just among some people and unjust among others, to some good and to others bad. For Persians do not regard it as strange to have intercourse with their daughters, whereas Greeks regard it as prohibited. The Massagetae, according to Eudoxus in Book I of his *Journey around the World*, have their wives in common; Greeks do not. The Cilicians used to take pleasure in being pirates; but not the Greeks. Different people believe in different gods; some believe the gods have foreknowledge, and others do not. The Egyptians dispose of their dead by embalming, the Romans by cremation, the Paeonians by throwing them into lakes. Hence the suspension of judgement about what is true.

152   PLATO, *Republic* 538 c–539 c   ... [SOCRATES] You know that some beliefs about just and fine things were taught us in childhood, and we've been brought up under them as parents, obeying and honouring them. [GLAUCON] That's true. ... [538 D]—Now, suppose someone is in this condition, and some questioner comes and asks what the fine is, and in answer he says what he has heard from the legislator, and then the argument refutes him in many and various ways, until it drives him into believing that nothing is fine any more than it is shameful, or just and good any more than the reverse, and so on for all the things he most honoured. Do you think he will still honour and obey them as before?—Impossible.—And when he ceases to think they are honourable and appropriate to him as he did before, and he doesn't discover true answers, is he likely to resort to any life other than the one that flatters[27]

---

[26] Subjects; **227**. 'Subject' is also used for the external subject corresponding (or believed to correspond) to appearances; **277**.

[27] Flattery; **179**.

him?—He cannot.—And from being a keeper of the law he is converted into a breaker of it?—He is bound to be.... [539 B]—And when they have refuted many people, and been refuted by many, they violently and speedily get into the habit of not believing anything they believed before, so that not only they, but philosophy and all that relates to it have been slandered to the rest of the world.—All too true, he said.

153   ARISTOTLE, *Nicomachean Ethics* 1094^{b}11–27   Our discussion will be adequate if it is clear enough for the subject-matter; for we would not seek the same degree of exactness in all sorts of arguments alike, any more than in the products of different crafts. Moreover, fine and just things, the topics of inquiry in political science, differ and vary so much that they seem to rest on convention only, not on nature. Goods, however, also vary in the same way, since they cause harm to many people; for it has happened that some people have been destroyed because of their wealth, others because of their bravery. Since these, then, are the sorts of things we argue from and about, it will be satisfactory if we can indicate the truth roughly and in outline; since we argue from and about what holds good usually, it will be satisfactory if we can draw conclusions of the same sort. Each of our claims, then, ought to be accepted in the same way, since the educated person seeks exactness in each area to the extent that the nature of the subject allows; for apparently it is no less mistaken to demand demonstrations from a rhetorician than to accept merely persuasive arguments from a mathematician.

154   ARISTOTLE, *Nicomachean Ethics* 1134^{b}18–1135^{a}5   One part of what is politically just is natural, and the other part legal. What is natural is what is equally valid everywhere alike, independent of its seeming so or not. What is legal is what originally makes no difference one way or another, but makes a difference whenever people have laid down the rule—that a mina is the price of a ransom, for instance, or that a goat rather than two sheep should be sacrificed ... Now some people think that everything just is merely legal, since what is natural is unchangeable and equally valid everywhere—fire, for instance, burns both here and in Persia—while they see that what is just changes. This is not so, though in a way it is so. With us, though presumably not at all with the gods, there is such a thing as what is natural, even though all is changeable; despite the change there is such a thing as what is natural and what is not. What sort of thing that admits of being otherwise is natural, and what sort is not natural, but legal and conventional, if both natural and legal are changeable? It is clear in this and in other cases, and the same distinction will apply to them all; for the right hand, for instance, is naturally superior, even though it is possible for everyone to become ambidextrous.

The sorts of things that are just by convention and expediency are like measures. For measures for wine and for corn are not of equal size everywhere, but in wholesale markets they are bigger, and in retail smaller. Similarly, the things that are just by human enactment, not by nature, differ from place to place, since political systems also differ; still, only one system is by nature the best everywhere.[28]

Scepticism and realism

155 According to Parmenides and Democritus, arguments to show that colours, or justice, or the gods, are matters of convention rather than nature support a nihilist conclusion; if they are sound, they prove that there are no real colours (etc.) and no genuine truths about them. This nihilist conclusion about reality and truth presupposes a realist and objectivist conception of truth; truths about the world must apply to some objective reality whose properties are not wholly constituted by our beliefs about it.

If we accept this realist conception of truth, then, according to Parmenides, we are left with very little that we can claim to be true. We may be able to formulate plausible views, but these are simply 'mortal beliefs' (**124**). Even views that 'no opinion of mortals can outstrip' (**124**) are not truths about the world, since we believe they do not apply to anything existing independently of our conventions.

Similar views about truth seem to force Democritus into Scepticism. Apparently equipollent conflicting appearances convince him that things are white, sweet, and so on, only 'by convention', not 'in reality' (**125**). He assumes that how things really are is how they are objectively—independently of how they appear to any perceiver or thinker. Similarly, he assumes that what is true is what is true objectively—apart from how it may appear to anyone. When he claims that human beings are cut off from reality, that truth is 'in the depths' (**135**), and that it is 'unclear to us' (**126**), he assumes this realist conception of truth. He would have given no reason for drawing this Sceptical conclusion if he intended it to apply to our beliefs about things that are matters of convention.

This same point applies equally to Sceptical arguments from variations in moral beliefs. We may agree that if Greeks and Persians have conflicting moral beliefs, we cannot claim to know whose beliefs are objectively true, and we cannot claim any access to objective facts about right and wrong. If knowledge of truths about right and wrong must be knowledge of objective facts, then we have no knowledge about right and wrong.

If, then, Sceptics rely on these apparently conflicting appearances to reach a Sceptical conclusion, they rely, at least for the sake of argument, on a realist conception of truth. They differ from their opponents only in their view of the prospects for finding any beliefs that we can reasonably regard as true. Both

[28] The best political system; **563**. Disputes about justice; **458**, **461–3**.

sides assume that any claim to truth for our beliefs about the physical world or about morality must assert that our beliefs are true of some objective world that is not wholly constituted by the beliefs themselves.

Protagoras, Scepticism, and subjectivism

156 These assumptions about truth and knowledge help to explain Protagoras' position. He proposes:

(1) We ought to accept arguments from conflicting appearances.

(2) Hence, if we accept a realist assumption, we ought to agree with the Sceptic that we have no knowledge of truths about the world.

(3) But we ought to reject this realist assumption.

(4) Hence, we ought to claim knowledge of truths about the world as it appears to us, while recognizing that other people have knowledge of quite different truths about the world as it appears to them; we have no reason to believe in any world beyond the world as it appears to us and the world as it appears to others.

In his third claim, Protagoras maintains a subjectivist standard of truth and reality. In his view, a human being is the 'measure' of how things are. By this he means, first, that how things appear to a particular perceiver is how they are for that perceiver: if the wind is blowing on me and on you, and it appears warm to me but cold to you, then it is really hot for me and really cold for you. Secondly, what is true is nothing beyond how things are for this or that perceiver; hence it is true both that the wind is hot and that the wind is cold. Similarly, moral truths depend on the outlook of a given society. We (Greeks) know that killing an innocent person is wrong, since it is prohibited by the conventions of our society. But it is equally true that killing an innocent person is right, if it conforms to the appearances of some other society. Truth and reality depend on convention.

Protagoras is a sophist (**8**). He claims that his teaching is both socially useful and useful for success in one's own life (**429**). He believes that some Sceptical arguments lead to suspension of judgement about any objective truth, but not about the sorts of truths that he allows. Sceptics do not believe they know whether the traffic light is now red or green, or that the fire will be hot when they put their hands into it, or that murder is wrong (**159**). We might infer that the results of Scepticism are both paralysing (depriving us of the elementary beliefs that we need in everyday life) and socially dangerous (depriving us of the shared moral convictions that support social life). Protagoras, however, is confident that the fire is hot (for him), murder is wrong (for the Athenians), and so on; he shares the convictions of his society. This is how he defends himself in Plato's *Theaetetus* (**160**).[29]

---

[29] Protagoras' subjectivism also affects beliefs about the gods; **584**.

157 SEXTUS, *Against the Professors* vii. 60–4   Some have also enrolled Protagoras of Abdera among the philosophers who abolish the criterion, since he asserts that all appearances and beliefs are true, and that truth is relative, because everything that has appeared or seemed to someone is thereby the case relative to him. Certainly, at the start of his book *The Overthrowers*[30] he proclaimed that ' ... '.[31] To this statement even the opposite statement appears to bear witness.[32] For if anyone asserts that the human being is not the criterion of all things, he will strengthen the statement that the human being is the criterion of all things; for the one who says this is himself a human being, and in affirming what appears relative to himself he admits that this is one of the things appearing relative to himself. Hence also the madman is a trustworthy criterion of the things appearing in madness ... [62] Nor is it appropriate to disqualify one set of circumstances because of a different set of circumstances—that is to say, to disqualify the things appearing in the state of madness because of those that occur in sanity.... . For, just as the latter things do not appear to the former people, so also conversely the things appearing to these do not occur in those... . [64] And Protagoras, as some have supposed, removes the criterion, since this is meant to test subjects[33] that are in their own right, and to discriminate the true from the false, whereas he has left nothing that either is the case or is false in its own right.

158 PLATO, *Theaetetus* 151 E–152 E   THEAETETUS: ... It seems to me that one who knows something perceives the thing he knows, and it appears to me at present that knowledge is nothing but perception. SOCRATES: ... The account you gave of knowledge looks most impressive—the very one that was given by Protagoras. He said the same things in a somewhat different way. He says, doesn't he,[34] that a human being is the measure of all things—of things that are, how they are, and of things that are not, how they are not?[35] I suppose you've read that?[36]—Yes, often.—And doesn't he mean something like this[37]—that any given lot of things are to me such as they appear to me, and are to you such as they appear to you, you and I being human beings?—Yes, that's what he means.[38]—Well, what a wise man says is not likely to be nonsense. So let's follow him up. Sometimes, when the same wind is blowing,

---

[30] This is apparently an alternative title of the work Plato calls 'Truth'; see **158**, 162.

[31] Here Sextus quotes the Measure doctrine, quoted at the beginning of **158**.

[32] Protagoras (as represented by Sextus) claims that the denial of the Measure doctrine is self-refuting. Contrast Plato's argument to show that the Measure doctrine itself is self-refuting; see **161–2**.

[33] i.e. external realities as distinct from appearances. See **150** n.

[34] Or 'somewhere'.

[35] Or 'Man is the measure of all things, of things that are, that they are, and of things that are not, that they are not.' This is Protagoras' 'Measure Doctrine'.

[36] Or 'you've read that somewhere?'

[37] Or 'He puts it in this sort of way, doesn't he, ... '

[38] Or 'Yes, that is how he puts it.'

one of us shivers, the other does not, or one shivers a bit, the other a lot.—Certainly.—Well, in that case are we to say that the wind in itself is cold or not cold? Or are we to agree with Protagoras that it is cold for[39] the one who shivers, and not for the other?—That seems more reasonable.—And further that it so appears to each of us?—Yes.—And 'it appears' means 'he perceives it'?—True.—Appearing, then, is the same thing as perceiving, in the case of hot things or any other things of that kind. It looks as though they are for each person such as he perceives them.—So it seems.—Perception, then, is always of something that is, and, as being knowledge, is infallible.—That is clear.[40]—In the name of the Graces, what a completely wise man Protagoras was! He said these things in a riddle to the common herd, such as you and me, but told the truth, his Truth,[41] in secret to his own disciples.—What do you mean, Socrates?—I'm about to speak of a most impressive argument, in which nothing is in its own right, nor can you rightly call anything something[42] or attribute any character to it, such as great or small, heavy or light. If you call it great, it will also appear small, and if you call it heavy, it will appear light, and so on for everything, since nothing either is anything nor has any character. Rather, out of motion and change and admixture all things are becoming relatively to one another, all the things to which we ascribe being, ascribing it incorrectly—for nothing ever is, but all things are becoming. Summon all philosophers—Protagoras, Heracleitus, Empedocles, and the rest of them, one after another—and, except for Parmenides, they will all agree with you in this.[43]

159   PLUTARCH, *Against Colotes* 1108f–1109b = DK 68 B 156[44]   Colotes first charges Democritus with saying that each thing is no more of one sort than of another, and so confusing our life. But Democritus is so far from thinking that each thing is no more of one sort than of another that when the sophist Protagoras said this, Democritus opposed him and wrote down many persuasive arguments against him. But Colotes has no idea of what Democritus said, and so has misunderstood his form of expression in which he determines that thing is no more than nothing is. What he calls 'thing' is body, and what he calls 'nothing' is the void, claiming that void has a nature and subsistence of its own.[45] But, in any case, anyone who has believed that nothing is any more of one sort than of another has relied on an Epicurean belief, that

---

[39] Or 'to'.

[40] Another statement of a Protagorean position; **183**.

[41] 'Truth' is the title of the book of Protagoras that Socrates has been quoting.

[42] e.g. a wall, or a stick.

[43] For a comment on this passage see **201**.

[44] Democritus and Scepticism; **136**. Plutarch argues against the Epicureans that their own position leads to Scepticism.

[45] Void; **86**.

all the appearances through sense are true.[46] For if one of two people says that the wine is dry and the other that it is sweet, and neither is mistaken in his sense-perception, in what way is the wine dry any more than sweet?

160 PLATO, *Theaetetus* 166 D–167 B[47]   Each one of us is a measure of things that are and are not, but there is all the difference in the world between one of us and another, in the very fact that the things that are and appear for one are different from those that are and appear for the other. As for wisdom and the wise person, I am very far from saying that they do not exist. On the contrary, by a wise person I mean precisely one who can change any of us, when bad things appear and are for us, so as to make good things appear and be for us.... For the sick person, food appears sour and is so; for the healthy person, it is and appears the opposite. Now there is no need to represent either of the two as wiser—that cannot be—nor is the sick person to be pronounced unwise because of believing such things, or the healthy person wise because of believing different things. What is needed is a change to the opposite condition, because that is the better condition. So too in education, one needs to make a change from the worse condition to the better; but whereas the physician produces a change by drugs, the sophist does it by discourse. It is not that someone takes another who believes false things and makes him believe true things; for it is not possible either to believe things that are not,[48] or to believe anything but the things one undergoes, all of which are true. Rather, in my view, when someone because of a bad state of soul believes things corresponding to it, one makes him acquire a sound state, and so believe things that are sound instead of unsound. These appearances some people ignorantly call true, whereas I call one lot of thoughts better than the other, but not in any way truer.

Protagoras on truth

161 In the *Theaetetus* Plato argues against (i) Protagoras' conception of truth; (ii) his claims about moral and political knowledge; and (iii) his claims about the physical world. This and the following sections (**162–8**) present Plato's argument on each of the three points.

Protagoras' claims about truth depend on the Measure doctrine, which says that whatever appears to me is true for me, and what appears to you is true for you. If the Measure doctrine is true, it must hold, without restriction, of all beliefs held by everyone. 'All beliefs' must include the Measure doctrine itself.

[46] Epicurus on the senses; **278–81**.

[47] Socrates is speaking, putting the case for Protagoras. The first person singular refers to Protagoras.

[48] False belief; **74**.

Hence it is true for those to whom it appears true, and false for those to whom it appears false. 'Everyone' must include Protagoras. Hence what appears true to him is true for him, and what appears false to him is false for him.

Once this is made clear, the Measure doctrine, applied to Protagoras and his belief in it, turns out to refute itself. For if Protagoras agrees that everyone's appearances are true,[49] then he must agree that the appearances of those who take the Measure doctrine to be false are also true. Since their appearances appear true to him, the Measure doctrine appears false to him, and so he must agree that it is false for him. Hence, if he takes the Measure doctrine to be true, he must also take it to be false. Hence, if the Measure doctrine is true, it is false.

....

162 PLATO, *Theaetetus* 170 A–171 A   SOCRATES: He says, doesn't he, that what seems to anyone is for the one to whom it seems? THEODORUS: He does.— Well now, Protagoras, we are expressing the beliefs of a human being, or rather of all humanity, when we say that everyone without exception holds that in some respects he is wiser than other people and in other respects they are wiser than he is. For instance, in moments of great danger and distress, whether in war or in sickness or at sea, people regard as gods those who can take control of the situation, and they look to such people as saviours, when they are superior precisely in knowledge.... [170 B] In all these cases mustn't we say that people think wisdom and ignorance exist among them?—We must say that.—And don't they think wisdom is thinking truly and ignorance is false belief?—Of course.—In that case, Protagoras, what are we to do with your claim?[50] Are we to say that people always believe true things, or that sometimes they believe true things and sometimes false things? For in either case it follows that they do not always believe true things, but both true and false. For consider, Theodorus. Are you, or is any Protagorean, prepared to maintain that no one regards anyone else as ignorant and believing false things?—That's incredible, Socrates.—But it's the inevitable consequence of the doctrine that makes a human being a measure of all things.—How's that?—When you've formed a judgement on some matter in your own mind and you express a belief about it to me, let's grant that, as Protagoras' theory says, it is true for you. But are we to understand that the rest of us can't make any judgement about your judgement? Or, if we can make a judgement, do we always judge that you believe true things? Don't you find, on the contrary, thousands of opponents who believe counter to you on every occasion, holding that you judge and believe false things?—I certainly think so, Socrates— thousands and tens of thousands, as Homer says, and they give me all the

---

[49] It is disputed whether 'for him (them)' ought to be inserted in the different steps of this argument, or Plato is entitled to omit this qualification. If his argument is to be valid, the omission must be legitimate.

[50] Or 'argument' (*logos*).

troubles of humanity.—And what then? Are we to say that in such a case you believe things true for yourself and false for these tens of thousands?—His claim certainly seems to imply that.—And what follows for Protagoras himself? Isn't it this? Suppose that not even he thought that a human being is a measure and the world in general didn't think so either—as indeed they don't. In that case, this Truth which he wrote would not be <true> for anyone. If, on the other hand, he thought so, but the majority don't agree with him, then, you see, it is more false than true by just so much as the unbelievers outnumber the believers.—That follows, if its truth or falsity varies with each person's belief.

Protagoras on experts

163 In his self-defence (**160**) Protagoras affirms the truth of his moral beliefs relative to his own appearances; hence he affirms that theft is wrong, and agrees with the prevalent appearances of the Athenians which he shares. If some Athenians think theft is right, their belief is also true—according to Protagoras' conception of truth—in their subgroup of Athens. Still, Protagoras claims that his appearances are preferable to other people's. The views of the medical expert, he claims, are no truer than those of anyone else, but they are preferable; for we prefer the consequences of following the expert's advice to the consequences of following someone else's advice. Similarly, we can prefer one set of moral beliefs over another for its social benefits, without supposing that it is truer.

Plato answers that this defence of Protagoras presupposes objective reality and truth, and hence conflicts with Protagoras' subjectivism. We prefer the views of medical experts because we suppose that their predictions about the effects of this medicine will turn out to be true. Our preference, therefore, presupposes that experts hold true beliefs about an objective reality. Protagoras' recommendation of his subjectivist position over a Sceptical position relies on assumptions that conflict with subjectivism.

164 PLATO, *Theaetetus* 177 C–179 B   SOCRATES: Hadn't we reached the point in the argument where the partisans of unstable being, who say that what seems to each one also is for him to whom it seems, were confidently maintaining this especially about just things? They said that the things that have seemed good to a city and that it has laid down, are just for the city that has laid them down, for as long as they remain laid down. But about good things, none of them was bold enough to contend that whatever things a city has thought beneficial and has laid down are indeed beneficial for a city, as long as they remain laid down.... . [177 E] The city aims at the good in legislation, and as far it has an opinion and is able, the city lays down all the laws so as to be most beneficial for it. Has its legislation got any other aim?—Certainly not.—But does

it always achieve its aim? Doesn't each city often fail?—Yes, I think they sometimes fail.—Their failure will be more readily agreed, if we consider the
whole kind to which the beneficial belongs. Presumably it has to do with the
future. For when laws are passed, we assume that they will be useful in a later
time, which is correctly called future.—Very true.—Now suppose we ask
Protagoras, or one of his disciples, a question: 'Protagoras', we will say to
him, 'a human being is, as you declare, the measure of all things—white,
heavy, light, and all such things. For he has the standard[51] of them in himself,
and when he thinks that things are such as he undergoes, he thinks things that
are true for himself. Is it not so?'—Yes.—'Then' (we will say) 'has he also got
within himself the standard of things that are going to be? Whatever way he
thinks they will be, do they turn out that way, for the one who has thought so?
For example, take the case of heat. When an ordinary man thinks that he is
going to have a fever, and that this kind of heat is coming on, and another person, who is a physician, thinks the contrary, whose opinion is likely to prove
right?[52] … [178 E] And wouldn't you, Protagoras, be better than a layman at
predicting the arguments in a court that would convince anyone among
us?'—Certainly, Socrates, he used to assure us in the strongest manner that
he was superior to everyone in this respect…. [179 A]—Aren't legislation and
benefit concerned with the future, and won't everyone admit that a city, in
laying down laws, must often fail to get what is most beneficial?—Quite
true.—Then we may fairly argue against your teacher, that he must agree
that one person is wiser than another, and that the wiser is a measure, and
that it is not at all necessary for me, who know nothing, to turn out to be a
measure, which the argument on behalf of Protagoras was just now com-
pelling me to be, whether I wanted to or not.

Protagoras and Heracleitus on change

165 Plato argues that since Protagoras accepts the truth of all appearances, he
must also give some account of the sort of world in which all appearances are
true. According to Protagoras, there is no world beyond the world as it appears
to me, and the world as it appears to you; but this world as it appears to me and
to you is not a figment of our imagination. Hence Protagoras must say what it
is like. Apparently, the extent of change in the world must be radical enough to
accommodate the truth of all appearances. If something appears hot to me and
cold to you, it must change from being hot to being cold. To cope with all possible appearances, it must be possible for things to change in all respects all the
time.

[51] *kritêrion*; **169–72**.
[52] Aristotle comments in **277**.

Plato argues that this extreme Heracleitean flux is impossible. Aristotle agrees, and presents some of the argument more clearly.[53] Belief in extreme flux makes it impossible to give an account of change. If there is change, there must be at least one subject that changes; and if there is any subject that changes, something about this subject must be stable. There cannot be an extreme Heracleitean world, since there cannot be any subject of change that changes in all respects all the time.[54] Since Protagoras' Measure doctrine implies that such a world is possible, it must be rejected.

....

166 PLATO, *Theaetetus* 156 A–157 C   Their starting-point is that all is motion ... which has two forms, one active and the other passive, both in endless number. Out of their association and friction infinitely numerous offspring are born, having two forms, the object of sense and the sense, which invariably emerges and comes to be with its object.... This motion is of two kinds, a slower and a quicker. The slower things have their motions in the same place and in relation to things near them, and so they generate; the offspring are quicker, since they are carried to and fro, and their natural motion is from place to place. And so, the eye and its correlative sensory object meet and generate whiteness and the sense naturally correlated with it, which could not have come into being if either of them had been elsewhere. When this happens, the sight flows from the eye and whiteness proceeds from the object that co-operates with the eye in producing the colour. And so the eye is filled with sight, and now sees, and becomes, not sight, but a seeing eye. Similarly, the object that combined to produce the colour is filled with whiteness, and becomes not whiteness, but a white thing—wood or stone or whatever the object may be that gets coloured white.... [157 A] No firm conception, they say, can be formed of the agent or patient, as being by itself. For the agent is nothing until it meets the patient, and the patient is nothing until it meets the agent.... Nothing is one thing itself by itself, but everything is becoming and relative to something. Being must be altogether abolished, even though from habit and ignorance we are compelled even in this discussion to retain the use of the term.... And this should be the way of speaking, not only of particular colours, sounds, etc., but of many aggregates—those we call a man or a stone, or any animal or kind of thing.

167 PLATO, *Theaetetus* 181 C–183 A   SOCRATES: What do they mean when they say that all things change? I mean: are they speaking of one kind of change, or, as it appears to me, two? I would like your view on this point as well as my own, so that you'll be a partner in whatever happens to me, if it must happen. Tell me, then: when a thing passes from one place to another,

[53] Aristotle on change and its subject: **224–6**.
[54] Plato on flux: **198–211**.

or goes round in the same place, do you call that change? THEODORUS: Yes.—
Here, then, we have one kind of change. But when a thing, remaining on the
same spot, grows old, or becomes black from being white, or hard from
being soft, or undergoes any other alteration, can't we properly call this a
change of another kind?—I think so.—Indeed, it must be so. Change, then,
has these two kinds, alteration and movement in place.—You are right.—
And now, having made this distinction, let's address those who say that everything changes. Let's ask them: do all things, according to them, have the two
kinds of change, and are they altered as well as moving in place, or is one
thing changed in both ways, and another in one only?—Indeed, I don't know
what to answer; but I think they would say all things are moved in both
ways.—Yes, my friend. For otherwise they would have to say that the same
things change and are at rest, and it would be no more true to say that everything changes than that everything is at rest.—That's right.—And if they are
to change, and nothing is to lack change, all things must always have every
sort of change?—Quite true... . [182 c]—If they only moved in place, and
were not altered, we could say what the character is of the things that change
and flow?—Exactly.—But as things are, not even this endures, that the flowing thing flows white; and so there is a flowing of this very thing, the whiteness, and a passing into another colour, so that it can't be caught enduring. In
that case, is it possible to say correctly that anything is any colour?—How is
that possible, Socrates, either in this case or any other case of the same sort,
if while we are using the word the thing is escaping in flux?—And what
would you say about any perception, such as seeing or hearing, or any other
kind? Does it ever endure in the act of seeing and hearing?—Certainly not, if
everything changes.—Then we mustn't say anything is seeing any more than
not-seeing, or any other perception more than non-perception, if all things
change in every respect?—Certainly not.—Yet perception is knowledge; so
Theaetetus and I were saying.—Very true.—And so when we were asked
what knowledge is, we no more answered with what is knowledge than with
what is not knowledge?—I suppose not.

168 ARISTOTLE, *Metaphysics* 1010ª7–ᵇ1   Further, since they saw that all of
this nature around us is in motion and that nothing true can be said about
what is changing, they said it is impossible to say anything true about what
undergoes every sort of change in every respect. From this view there blos-
somed the most extreme of the views we have mentioned, that of the self-
styled Heracleitizers. This was the sort of view held by Cratylus, who ended
up thinking he must say nothing, and only moved his finger.[55] He criticized
Heracleitus for saying one could not step into the same river twice; for Cratylus thought one could not do it even once. We also reply to this argument as

---

[55] Cratylus and Plato: **197, 210**.

follows. Though they do have some argument for their view that what is changing, when it is changing, is not, still this is at any rate disputable. For what is losing something has some of what is being lost, and some of what is coming to be must already be. And in general, if something is perishing, there must be something that it is; and if something is coming to be, there must be something from which it comes to be and something that generates it, and this does not go on without limit. But let us leave these arguments aside and insist that a change in quantity is not the same as a change in the sort of thing the subject is. Hence, even if we concede that something is unstable in quantity, still we know each thing by its form. Further, those who suppose that everything changes should also be criticized for something else. The things that they saw constantly changing are a minority even of perceptible things, but they declared that the same constant change was true of the whole universe. In fact it is only the area of the perceptible universe around us that is in constant destruction and generation, and this is an insignificant part of the whole universe. And so it would be more just to acquit this part of the world from constant change because of the other part than to condemn the other part for constant change because of these things. Again, clearly we shall also say in response to these people what we said before; for they should be shown and persuaded that there is some unmoved nature. In any case, to say that things simultaneously are and are not is to imply that they are at rest rather than that they are moving; for there is nothing for anything to change into, since everything belongs to everything.

The criterion

169 Protagoras accepts some Sceptical arguments, but rejects Scepticism; his subjectivism professes to preserve truth without objectivity (156). If, however, his position collapses in the face of Plato's objections, the Sceptical conclusion is more difficult to avoid. Later Sceptics claim that reflection on the history of philosophy makes Scepticism irresistible. Democritean arguments seem to undermine the initially plausible suggestion that the senses provide a reliable basis for claims about the world. Socratic arguments seem to remove any reliable basis for our moral beliefs; for any moral belief seems to be shaken by Socratic cross-examination and refutation. This is why Arcesilaus and Cicero suggest that Socrates and Plato come close to Scepticism themselves (170); reflecton on Socratic and Platonic arguments seems to support a Sceptical conclusion.

According to Sextus, the general problem raised by conflicting appearances is a problem about the existence of any 'criterion' (or 'standard'; Greek *kritêrion*, from *krinein*, 'judge' or 'discriminate').[56] Appearances conflict; different things

---

[56] Criterion; **109, 112**.

appear true to different people, and so we look for a criterion that we can use to discriminate true appearances or beliefs from false ones, or justified from un-justified. But we have no such criterion. Since we cannot dismiss the appear-ances on either side, the appearances are equipollent. Hence, we are puzzled and at a loss (*aporein*; **142**), as Socrates' interlocutors are, about how to resolve conflicts among appearances.

If, however, we suggest a criterion, it is open to a similar argument. Suppose we suggest a criterion to answer an objection to a claim to knowledge, but then we discover that the criterion itself is subject to an objection. In that case, we need to answer the objection to the suggested criterion before we can use the suggested criterion to answer an objection to our initial claim to knowledge. If objections to the suggested criterion require answers, but these answers pro-voke further objections that need answers, we can never use the suggested cri-terion. Hence it will not be a genuine criterion.

In some cases dogmatists (*dogmatikoi*; i.e. those who hold some *dogma*, a be-lief about how things really are, not simply about how they appear) might reject the objection raised by conflicting appearances. They might insist that, in some cases, conflicting appearances are not equipollent, because we can resolve the conflict by appeal to some further principle—let us call it P1—that supports one side of the dispute rather than the other. If appearances about something's colour conflict, the appearances of the normal perceiver might be preferred. If moral appearances conflict, the appearances of more experienced people might be preferred.

This dogmatist answer invites further Sceptical objections. Even if P1 is not challenged by a conflicting appearance that appears equipollent, why we should accept P1? Once we ask this, we offer a further opening to the Sceptic. Apparently, we are justified in treating P1 as a criterion only if we know that P1 gives us true answers; but apparently we cannot know that without appealing to some further principle P2 to serve as a criterion for deciding whether P1 is a criterion; but P2 raises the very question that we asked about P1; we must resort to a further principle P3; and now we face an infinite regress, giving us no an-swer to our original question. We can break the infinite regress if we appeal over again to one of our earlier principles—to P1, say—in support of P3; but then we are arguing in a circle, since we are apparently trying to prove P1 by appeal to P1 itself.

To avoid a circle, the dogmatist might simply claim that P3 deserves accep-tance without reference to any further criterion. But why should we accord this status to P3 rather than to P2 or P1? If the dogmatist refuses to answer this ques-tion, he treats P3 as an unproved assumption. But there are many other unproved assumptions that we might choose to accept, and some of these would under-mine P2 and P1; why should we prefer P3 to one of these other unproved as-sumptions? If we cannot answer this question about P3, then we do not seem to have found a criterion that supports P2 and P1 after all. To answer the question, we must show why P3 is especially reliable; hence we must apparently look for a further criterion, leading us to an infinite regress or to a circle.

This trilemma—infinite regress, circle, or unproved assumption—is formulated by the Sceptic Agrippa.[57] It is a powerful weapon in the hands of a Sceptic. Moreover, it raises large questions in epistemology. If this trilemma exhausts the possibilities for any attempted justification, and all three options are as unacceptable as they seem, Scepticism becomes attractive. If we reject Scepticism, and we take the trilemma to be exhaustive, at least one of the three options must be more acceptable than it seems, and we must show why it is acceptable.

....

170 CICERO, *Academica* i. 44–6 ... Arcesilaus began his whole dispute not from obstinacy or from eagerness for victory (so it seems to me anyhow), but because of the obscurity of those things that had led Socrates to an avowal of ignorance, and already before Socrates, Democritus, Anaxagoras, Empedocles, practically all the old philosophers. They said nothing could be apprehended, nothing grasped, nothing known, and that the senses were limited, minds were weak, the course of life was short, and, as Democritus said, truth is sunk in the depths, everything is subject to opinions and customs, no room is left for truth, and everything in succession is shrouded in shadows. That was why Arcesilaus used to say that there is nothing that can be known—not even that very thing, the piece of knowledge that Socrates had left himself[58] ... [45] [Arcesilaus] ... led many people to agree with him by arguing against everyone's beliefs, so that when on a given issue equal weight of reasons was found on opposite sides, assent was more easily withheld from both sides. This they call the New Academy, though to me it seems old, at any rate if we count Plato as part of that old Academy; for nothing in his books is asserted, many arguments are offered on each side of a question, everything is inquired into, but nothing firm is said.

171 SEXTUS, *Pyrrhonian Outlines* ii. 15–20 In the most specific sense, a criterion is any technical measure for the apprehension of a non-evident thing. ... [18] Of those who have considered the criterion, some ... have asserted that there is one; others ... have asserted that there is not; while we have suspended judgement about whether there is one or not. This dispute, then, they will either declare to be decidable or to be undecidable. If they say it is undecidable, they will thereby grant that we must suspend judgement. If they say it is decidable, let them say what it is to be decided by; for we have no agreed criterion and do not know that there is one at all, but are inquiring about this. In any case, if we are to decide the dispute about the criterion, we

[57] Agrippa's trilemma; **214, 272, 276**.

[58] Arcesilaus maintains that Socrates claims to know (not merely to believe) that he does not know anything. Contrast **139**.

must have an agreed criterion through which we will be able to decide it; and to have an agreed criterion, we must first have decided the dispute about the criterion. And so, since the argument falls into the circular mode,[59] we are at a loss about finding a criterion. For if we do not allow them to adopt a criterion on an assumption, and if they want to decide about the criterion by means of a criterion, we push them into an infinite regress. Further, since proof requires a criterion that has been proved, while the criterion needs a proof that has been decided to be a proof, they are pushed into the circular mode.

172 SEXTUS, *Pyrrhonian Outlines* i. 165–72   The mode based on disagreement is the one in which we find that about the matter proposed an unsettled disagreement has arisen both in ordinary life and among philosophers. Because of this disagreement we can neither accept nor reject anything, and so we end up in suspension of judgement.

The mode based on infinite regress is the one in which we say that the thing brought forward to give credibility to the matter proposed needs some other source of credibility, and this again another, and so on to infinity, so that, when we have no starting-point for establishing an argument, suspension follows.

The mode from the relative ... is the one in which the subject appears one way or another in relation to the one judging and to the things observed with it, but we suspend judgement about how it is in relation to its own nature.

The mode from assumption is whenever the dogmatists are being pushed into an infinite regress, and then begin from a starting-point that they do not establish, but think it appropriate to take as conceded, baldly and without demonstration.

The circular mode arises whenever what ought to be firmer than the thing inquired into itself needs to be made credible from the thing inquired into; when that happens, we are unable to take either as a basis for establishing the other, and so we suspend judgement about both.... .

[171] If they say a controversy is settled by an object of sense, then, since our initial inquiry is about objects of sense, the one we appeal to will need a second one to make it credible. And if the second one is sensible, it will also need another to make it credible, and so on to infinity. If the object of sense needs to be settled by an object of understanding, then, since objects of understanding are also matters of disagreement, this object of understanding also will need to be judged and found credible. What then will make it credible? If an object of understanding makes it credible, we fall into an infinite regress in the same way as before. If an object of sense makes it credible, then, since an object of understanding was brought in to make an object of

---

[59] Modes; **150** n.

sense credible, and an object of sense to make an object of understanding credible, the circular mode is introduced.

Living as a Sceptic

|173| Is the Sceptic's conclusion disturbing? According to the Sceptic, we resist Scepticism because we misunderstand its consequences. When we confront Sceptical arguments, we are anxious about abandoning our cherished views. If, however, we become convinced of the equipollence of conflicting appearances, we will give up the anxious search for a way of choosing between them. We will suspend judgement about their truth. This suspension of judgement (*epochê*) is not a deliberate decision; it is just the result of inability to endorse either set of conflicting beliefs.[60]

According to the Sceptic, this suspension of judgement leads to 'tranquillity' (or 'absence of disturbance', *ataraxia*), since we no longer inquire anxiously about which of the conflicting appearances is correct. This tranquillity is preferable to the dogmatist's anxiety. Once a Sceptic has reached a condition of suspension of belief, he does not want to leave it, since he recognizes it as the source of his tranquillity.

Does Sceptical inquiry make us chronically indecisive? Will we not be unable to make up our minds about whether the senses are reliable, or striking a match causes a fire, or we ought to inflict pain on innocent victims? And is this not an unwelcome result? Ought we, therefore, to avoid Sceptical questions in the first place? The Sceptic can hardly reply that we ought to ask Sceptical questions, whatever the result; for that claim is itself subject to arguments from conflicting appearances.

The Sceptics agree that they can find no proof for either one of a pair of conflicting appearances; to this extent they are undecided. But they deny that they are chronically indecisive in any practical sense; for they are in no doubt about what to do. Some of their appearances are more forceful than others, though not thereby more reasonable; and these forceful appearances incline us strongly to one course of action over another. Even if I cannot prove that this fire will burn me if I put my hand in it, or that it is wrong to torture this innocent person, I will still be strongly inclined to avoid the fire and to refrain from torturing this person.

This is why Sextus rejects Plato's suggestion (**152**) that Scepticism leads to indifference and immorality. He assures us that the Sceptic conforms to the conventional morality of his society, will practise a profession, and will live normally in other ways. We should not cling to dogmatism out of fear that Scepticism will subvert our way of life; for this fear is groundless.

---

[60] This is the point of the story of Apelles in **175**.

Sextus' defence of the Sceptical outlook (**174–5**) is worth comparing with Hume's defence (**176**). In contrast to Sextus, Hume agrees that if Sceptical suspension of judgement were taken seriously, it would indeed prevent us from living in the normal way. Despite this, we need not fear Scepticism, because we cannot actually take suspension of judgement seriously in the ordinary course of life, and so we ignore the implications of Sceptical arguments. These different views on the implications of Scepticism will concern us again when we consider replies to Scepticism (**297–9**).

174 SEXTUS, *Pyrrhonian Outlines* i. 12   We say that the starting-point that leads to the Sceptic way is the hope of achieving tranquillity. For some naturally able people were disturbed by the discrepancy in things, and were at a loss about which they should assent to. And so they turned to inquiry into what is true and what is false in things: they assumed that by deciding this they would achieve tranquillity. But the main starting-point of the Sceptic system is the opposing to each argument an equal argument; for from doing this we seem to end up no longer dogmatizing.

175 SEXTUS, *Pyrrhonian Outlines* i. 23–30   Sticking to the appearances, then, we live without beliefs but in accordance with the observance that belongs to ordinary life, since we are unable to be wholly inactive. This observance belonging to ordinary life would seem to have four parts. One part consists in the guidance of nature, one in the necessity of affections,[61] one in the tradition of laws and customs, and the fourth in the teaching of crafts. The guidance of nature is what makes us naturally capable of sense and thought. The necessity of affections is what makes hunger lead us to food and thirst to drink. Tradition of customs and laws is what makes us take over, as part of ordinary life,[62] that pious action is good and impious action bad. The teaching of crafts is what makes us not inactive in whichever of these we take over. Now we say all these things without belief.…

[25] The end of the Sceptic is tranquillity in matters of belief, and moderate affection[63] in things that are necessitated. For the Sceptic began to philosophize with the aim of reaching a judgement about the appearances and of grasping which ones are true and which false, so as to achieve tranquillity in that way. But he fell into the disagreement among beliefs of equal weight, on which he was unable to reach a judgement, and so he suspended judgement. Once he had suspended judgement tranquillity in matters of belief followed by chance. For anyone who believes that something is fine or bad by nature is disturbed all the time. And when he cannot get the things that he believes to

---

[61] Or 'feelings' or 'passions' (*pathê*); cf. **526**.
[62] Translation uncertain.
[63] Moderate passions; **528**.

be fine, he supposes he is tormented by things that are bad by nature, and he pursues the goods, as he supposes. But when he has got them, he falls into more disturbances because of his unreasonable and immoderate elation. Fearing a change of circumstances, he goes to all lengths to avoid losing the things that he believes to be goods. But the one who determines nothing about things fine or bad by nature neither avoids nor pursues anything intensely; that is why he is tranquil.

And so what is said to have happened to Apelles the painter is what happened to the Sceptic. For the story goes that Apelles was painting a horse and wanted to represent in the painting the horse's foam; but he was so unsuccessful that he gave up and threw at the painting the sponge he was using to wipe the colours off the paintbrush. When the sponge hit the painting, it produced a likeness of the horse's foam. Well, the Sceptics also began by hoping that they would achieve tranquillity through reaching a judgement on the discrepancy of things appearing and things thought. When they were unable to do this, they suspended judgement; and once they had suspended judgement, they found that tranquillity followed by chance (one might say), as a shadow follows a body.

Mind you, we do not suppose that the Sceptic is untroubled in every respect. We say he is troubled by necessitated things; for certainly we concede that he is sometimes cold and thirsty and has all sorts of other affections of this sort. But in these cases ordinary people are beset by two sorts of circumstances—by the affections themselves, and no less by the fact that they believe these circumstances to be bad by nature. The Sceptic, by contrast, gets rid of the added belief that each of these things is bad by nature, and so escapes even here with a more moderate suffering. That, then, is why we say that in matters of belief the Sceptic's end is tranquillity, but in necessitated things it is moderate affection.

176   HUME, *Inquiry concerning Human Understanding* xii. 1   But a Pyrrhonian[64] cannot expect that his philosophy will have any constant influence on the mind: or if it had, that its influence would be beneficial to society. On the contrary, he must acknowledge, if he will acknowledge anything, that all human life must perish were his principles universally and steadily to prevail. All discourse, all action would immediately cease; and men remain in a total lethargy, till the necessities of nature, unsatisfied, put an end to their miserable existence. It is true; so fatal an event is very little to be dreaded. Nature is always too strong for principle.

---

[64] Pyrrhon; **25–7**.

V: Knowledge, Belief, and Forms

Socrates and Plato

Socrates' convictions

177 In Chapter 4 we saw that one interpretation of Socrates makes him a Sceptic, or at least argues that his inquiries ought to lead him to a sceptical conclusion. We may now turn to the anti-sceptical aspects of Socrates.

Socrates believes he ought to act justly, and that (for instance) it would be unjust to co-operate in the arrest of an innocent person (**540**). He also claims to have reasons for these moral convictions (**453–4**). His discussions with Laches, Euthyphro, and Meno give him these reasons. Discussions about the virtues do not simply undermine the interlocutor's view; they also support positive claims about the virtue under discussion. The participants in the discussion agree, for instance, that bravery is displayed in a wider range of circumstances than Laches allows; that piety is not the same as what the gods love; and that virtue is the same in everyone, and requires justice and temperance (**144–5, 148, 181, 586**).

Not all of Socrates' conclusions are immediately plausible. In the *Protagoras* he defends the paradoxical view that we cannot believe that one course of action is better than another and choose the one we believe to be worse (**435–6**). Moreover, some of his convictions strike most people as both paradoxical and offensive. He defends these convictions with arguments; he believes, for instance, that most people wrongly assume that it is right to return evil for evil, and he argues against this position (**454**).

These attitudes separate Socrates from Scepticism. He does not claim that conflicting appearances are equipollent. Different people's views about justice conflict, but Socrates claims to give us good reasons for accepting his conception of justice even when most people would disagree with it (**540**). Nor does he suspend judgement about the truth of moral claims; he affirms the truth of the convictions that he acts on.

Do these expressions of positive views simply show that Socrates is not a consistent sceptic? We might object that they are inconsistent with his disavowal of knowledge and that his disavowal of knowledge on a given question implies the Sceptical suspension of judgement on that question. Socrates disagrees; he explains why his disavowal of knowledge does not lead to suspension of judgement. He tells Callicles (**178**) that he has proved his conclusion by arguments as firm as iron, and that he does not know that it is true. He implies that his convictions rest on some degree of justification, but that the degree does not constitute knowledge.

What is the knowledge that Socrates disavows? He distinguishes knowledge from true belief by reference to the various crafts. Rhetoric, he claims, is not a genuine 'craft' (or 'expertise', *technê*), because it cannot give an account of what it is doing, and cannot explain why it is best to do what it does. In assuming that a craft displays articulate understanding and grasp of explanations, Socrates relies on a traditional distinction between crafts and mere empirical knacks or techniques (**105–6**); he applies this distinction to moral and political knowledge.

178 PLATO, *Gorgias* 508 E–509 B[1]   These things already appeared in the previous discussion to be as I say they are. And now they are fixed and tied down, if I may use a brash expression, by iron and adamantine arguments, so it would now seem. And unless you or someone still bolder unravels them, it's impossible to disagree with me and be right. For what I say is always the same, that I myself don't know how these things are, but I have never met anyone who could say otherwise, any more than you can, without being ridiculous. These things, then, I lay down as being so. If they are so, injustice is the greatest of evils for the one who commits it, and moreover, there is even a greater evil—if that is possible—than this greatest of evils: namely, to commit injustice and not to pay the just penalty. In that case, what defence does someone need to avoid being truly ridiculous? Mustn't it be the defence that will avert the greatest harm?

179 PLATO, *Gorgias* 464 B–465 A   The soul and body, being two, have two crafts corresponding to them. The craft assigned to the soul I call the political craft.[2] For the one craft assigned to the body I don't know any single name. While this craft caring for the body is one, I say it has two parts, one the gymnastic craft, and the other the medical craft. The political craft has one part that is the legislative craft, corresponding to the gymnastic craft, as justice[3] corresponds to the medical craft. ... Now, given these four crafts, two of them assigned to the body and two to the soul, providing care with a view to what is best, flattery,[4] knowing this, or rather guessing it, has divided itself into four shams or simulations of them. It puts on the likeness of some one or other of them, and pretends to be what it simulates. It has no concern for the best, but deceives its foolish victims with what is pleasant at any time, and seems to have the highest value. Cookery disguises itself as the medical craft, and pretends to know the best foods for the body; so that if the physician and the cook had to compete before children, or before men who had no more understanding than children, about which of them best understands good or

[1] This follows **496**.
[2] The political craft; **434**, **547–8**.
[3] i.e. the judicial craft.
[4] Flattery; **152**, **399**.

bad foods, the physician would starve to death. I call this a type of flattery, and a shameful sort of thing ... because it guesses at the pleasant without the best. I don't call it a craft, but a knack, because it can't give an account of the things it applies to a given subject.[5] I don't call any irrational thing a craft.[6]

A puzzle about inquiry

180 Socrates maintains that he has reasons to justify confidence in his positive conclusions, such as those he reaches in the *Crito* or the *Gorgias*. We might well doubt, however, whether his method of cross-examination can provide such reasons. The *Meno* voices some of these doubts, and tries to answer them.

The dialogue begins with Meno asking Socrates whether virtue can be taught. Socrates replies that we cannot know the answer to that question unless we know what virtue is; and so he raises his familiar 'What is it?' question. He elicits from Meno some assumptions about virtue that undermine Meno's proposed accounts. Meno is surprised that it is difficult to answer Socrates' question.

The difficulty results from Socrates' standards for an acceptable answer. He wants more than a description that is true of all virtues. He also wants to identify the property that explains their being virtues; this is the sort of explanation that Aristotle describes as a formal cause (**98**). In the *Euthyphro* Socrates criticizes an account of piety as what the gods love, on the ground that it does not capture the property that really explains why pious things are pious (**586**). Similarly, he asks Meno for the feature that makes all virtues virtues, or 'that because of which' they are all virtues.

Once we understand Socrates' goal, we may wonder how he can advance towards it by his method. He refutes Meno's proposals by showing that they conflict with other assumptions that Meno accepts. But if Socrates does not know that these assumptions are true, how does reliance on them ensure progress towards finding what virtue is? If Socrates is really as ignorant as he claims to be, is there any point in his looking for answers to his questions? After repeated and apparently fruitless efforts to answer Socrates' questions, Meno protests that Socrates can always attack other people's views, but has nothing to put in their place. It is pointless for him to inquire into virtue when he admits he has no knowledge about virtue to start from (**182**). Socrates agrees that Meno has raised a legitimate puzzle about inquiry (often called 'Meno's Paradox'). If we do not know what we are inquiring into, inquiry seems to be impossible; if we do know, it seems to be pointless.

---

[5] e.g. a patient.
[6] Continued at **546**.

181 PLATO, *Meno* 70 A–72 D MENO: Can you tell me, Socrates—is virtue teachable? Or is it not teachable, but acquired by practice? Or is it neither acquired by practice nor learnt, but do people attain it in some other way? ... [71 B] SOCRATES: ... I blame myself for not knowing at all about virtue. And when I don't know what something is, how can I know what sort of thing it is? Or do you suppose that someone who doesn't know at all who Meno is knows whether he is handsome and rich and well-born or the reverse? Is that possible, do you think?—No. But is this really true about you, Socrates, that you don't even know what virtue is? Is this the report that we are to take home about you?—Not only that; you can also tell people that, to the best of my belief, I have never yet met anyone who did know. ... [71 E]—It's simple to answer your question, Socrates.[7] Take first the virtue of a man. His virtue is to know how to administer the state, and in the administration of it to benefit his friends and harm his enemies, while making sure he comes to no harm himself. A woman's virtue, if you want to know about that, is also easily described. She must order her household, take care of what is in it, and obey her husband. There is a different virtue for a child, male and female, and for an older man, and indeed, I tell you, one for a free person and one for a slave. And there are many other virtues, so that it's no puzzle to say what virtue is; a different virtue corresponds to the actions and ages of each of us in all that we do. And the same is true, I presume, of vice, Socrates.—How lucky I am, Meno! When I ask you for one virtue, you present me with a swarm of them that you keep. Let's carry on the comparison with the swarm. I ask you what it is to be a bee,[8] and you answer that they are many and various. Then I reply: 'Are you saying that bees are many and various and different from one another, in being bees? Or don't they differ at all in this respect, but only in some other respect, such as beauty, size, or something else of that sort?' How would you answer me?—I would answer that bees don't differ from one another, as bees.—And suppose I went on to say: 'Then tell me this, Meno: That in respect of which they don't differ, but are all the same—what do you say that is?' Would you be able to answer?—Yes, I would.—Similarly, then, the virtues, however many and different they may be, all have one and the same form because of which they are virtues. Anyone who is answering the question, 'What is virtue?' would clearly do well to fix his attention on that.

182 PLATO, *Meno* 79 E–80 E SOCRATES: ... Go back to the beginning, and answer my question. What do you ... say virtue is? MENO: Socrates, even before I met you, they told me that in plain truth you are puzzled[9] yourself and make others puzzled. And at this moment, it seems to me, you're practising

---

[7] Meno's confidence; cf. **463**.

[8] Literally, 'about the essence (*ousia*) of a bee'. On *ousia* see **193** n., **227**.

[9] *aporein*; **36**, **142**, **169**, **188**.

magic and witchcraft on me, and positively laying me under your spell, until I'm full of puzzlement. If it's all right to make a joke about it, I think you not only look like the flat sting-ray in the sea, but you're just like it in other ways too. Whenever anyone comes close and touches it, it numbs him; and that's just what you seem to have done to me now. For my mind and my lips are simply numb, and I can't give you any answers. And yet I've spoken about virtue hundreds of times, and often held forth on the subject in front of large audiences, and very well too, or so I thought. But now I can't even say what it is at all. It seems to me you're quite right not to leave Athens and live abroad. If you behaved like this as a foreigner in another country, you would most likely be arrested as a wizard.— ... [80 c] SOCRATES: If the sting-ray numbs others only by being numb itself, then I'm like it, but not otherwise. It isn't that I'm free of puzzlement and make others puzzled. The fact is that I make them puzzled in the way I'm puzzled. The same is true with virtue now; I don't know what it is. Perhaps you knew before your contact with me, but now it looks as though you don't. Nevertheless I'm ready to carry out together with you a joint investigation and inquiry into what it is.—But how will you inquire into something, Socrates, when you don't know what it is at all? What sort of thing among those you don't know are you going to propose for inquiry? Even if you encounter it, how will you know that this is the thing you didn't know?—I know what you mean. Do you realize that what you are bringing up is the contentious[10] argument that a man can't inquire either into what he knows or into what he does not know? He wouldn't inquire into what he knows—for, since he knows it, he doesn't need to inquire—or into what he doesn't know—for in that case he doesn't even know what he is to inquire into.[11]

Recollection and inquiry

183 Socrates replies to Meno's Paradox in three stages:

1. According to a story told to him by 'priests and priestesses', our souls are immortal and had knowledge when they existed without bodies. All learning is simply a process of recollection of what we knew in our previous existence.

2. Socrates puts a series of geometrical questions to a slave who has never been taught geometry. He presents the slave with a square, and asks him the length of a side of a second square with an area double the area of the first square. At first the slave answers that the second square must have a

---

[10] *eristikos*; cf. **75**, **184**.
[11] Continued at **184**.

side twice as long as a side of the first square. But he gradually comes to see that this answer is wrong; he realizes that the second square must have a side equal to the diagonal of the first square.

3. From the slave's answers Socrates infers that we can inquire constructively and make progress in our beliefs, even if we lack knowledge, and even if we are not told the answers, but have to work them out for ourselves.

At the second stage, Socrates puts the geometrical questions to a slave who has not previously been taught geometry, in order to show that we have the capacity to inquire and to discover the truth for ourselves. Hence he wants to exclude the obvious possibility that he is simply telling the slave the answers. He claims that he does not 'teach' the slave; meaning that he does not impart new information. We need new information if we are to learn, for instance, the capital cities of Asia, or the names and dates of the Stuart or Capetian kings and queens. The slave, however, does not need to be given new information in order to reach the right answers in the geometry lesson.

The three stages of Socrates' answer to Meno are connected. The hypothesis of pre-natal knowledge (in the first stage) is meant to explain our success when we inquire without being given new information; we make progress without being given new information only because Socratic questioning leads us to recollect what we once knew and have forgotten. But even though Socrates maintains this connection between the three stages, he is cautious. For he suggests that he has more confidence in his defence of the possibility of successful inquiry than in his explanation of success that refers to recollection.

If the discussion with the slave is meant to answer Meno's objections to inquiry, it ought to show or suggest how Socrates can reach credible positive conclusions, as he claims to do (**187**). Though Socrates asks leading questions and makes suggestions, the slave does not simply repeat what he is told; he works out what seems reasonable to him in the light of his other beliefs. Socrates assumes that he and his other interlocutors can do the same; we all have enough plausible beliefs about the subject of inquiry to give us somewhere to start, and, when we must choose some of our previous beliefs over others, we can sort out the beliefs that matter more. The discovery that we have conflicting beliefs is unwelcome and uncomfortable (**188**), but it helps us to improve our beliefs by further reflection.

Socrates' inquiries make clear to us things that—in a way—we have believed all along. He tells Polus that Polus agrees with the controversial Socratic position that Polus rejects (**187**). Polus implicitly accepts the premises from which Socrates' conclusion follows, but does not yet realize that he is committed to Socrates' conclusion. Similarly, when Euthyphro reflects, he realizes that he has believed all along that it is more important to recognize that the gods love the pious because it is pious than it is to maintain his view of the pious as what the gods love (**586**). When Callicles reflects, he realizes that he has believed all along that he cares most about presenting the superior person as brave and resolute; he would rather maintain this than maintain his hedonist position (**389**, **392–3**). Socrates' interlocutor thinks about the implications of something he has believed all along, until he can decide whether he still accepts it.

Some ancient writers even suggest that Plato chooses the dialogue form because it best represents the progress of Socratic inquiry and dialectic (**189–91**). Socratic questioning causes the interlocutor to turn into himself and work out the answer for himself (**191**). It is not surprising, then, that Plato compares inquiry to the recollection of something that we previously knew. Even if we do not agree with Plato's further claim that inquiry actually is recollection, we may find this comparison instructive.

In the *Meno* Plato does not develop his claim that inquiry is recollection of pre-natal knowledge. He does not take this claim to be necessary for the resolution of Meno's Paradox; the paradox is resolved by showing that we have the capacity for constructive inquiry, whether or not this capacity is explained by pre-natal knowledge. In other dialogues, however, he appeals to the reality of pre-natal knowledge to support his belief in the immortality of the soul (**205**, **329**).

The slave's discussion with Socrates in the *Meno* does not result in knowledge, but only in true belief. Plato suggests that the continuation of this same process of inquiry is a route to knowledge. Socratic inquiry should eventually result in the stability and 'reasoning about the explanation' that are characteristic of knowledge (**104**, **107**).

....

184   PLATO, *Meno* 81 A–E[12]   MENO: Well, do you think it is a good argument?[13] SOCRATES: No.—Can you say how it fails?—I can. Here's what I have heard from men and women who are wise about divine things—What account did they give?—A true and fine account, I thought … I'll tell you what they say; see whether you think they are speaking the truth. They say that the human soul is immortal. At one time it reaches an end, called death, and at another it is born again, but it is never destroyed. … And so the soul, since it is immortal, and has been born many times, and has seen all things both here and in the other world, has learned everything that is. So we need not be surprised that it can recollect about virtue or anything else that it previously knew. For all nature is akin, and the soul has learned everything, so that when someone has recalled only one thing—what people call learning—there is nothing to prevent him from finding all the rest, if he is brave and doesn't weary in the search; for inquiry and learning are in fact nothing but recollection. We ought not, then, to be led astray by that

[12] This immediately follows **182**.
[13] The argument against the possibility of inquiry.

contentious argument;[14] for it would make us lazy, and is pleasant to weaklings. But the present argument makes us active and eager to inquire. Since I'm convinced of its truth, I'm ready, with your help, to inquire into what virtue is.

185 PLATO, *Meno* 84 A–D SOCRATES: Do you notice, Meno, how far he has gone on the path of recollection? To begin with, he didn't know the side of the square of eight feet. Nor indeed does he know it now. But then he thought he knew it, and he answered confidently, on the assumption that he knew; he didn't think he was puzzled. Now, however, he thinks he is puzzled. Not only does he not know, but he doesn't think he knows either.—Quite true.—Isn't he better off now in relation to the thing he didn't know?—I admit that too.—So in perplexing him and numbing him like the sting-ray, have we done him any harm?—I don't think so.—In fact we have helped him to some extent towards finding how things are. For now, since he doesn't know, he will be pleased to inquire. In the past, he thought he could speak readily and well on many occasions and before large audiences, on the subject of a square double <the size of a given square>, maintaining that it must have a side of double the length.—No doubt.—Do you suppose, then, that he would have tried to inquire into, or learn, what he thought he knew, though he didn't know it, before he was thrown into puzzlement by recognizing his ignorance, and first longed to know?—No.—Then the numbing was good for him?—I agree.—Now notice what he will actually discover if he starts from this puzzlement, and inquires together with me, while I simply ask him questions without teaching him. Watch out to see whether I teach or expound, instead of simply interrogating him about his own beliefs.

186 PLATO, *Meno* 85 B–86 C SOCRATES: What do you think, Meno? Has he answered with any belief that was not his own?—MENO: No, they were all his.—Still, he didn't know, as we agreed a little earlier.—True.—But these beliefs were in him, weren't they?—Yes. So the one who doesn't know has in him true beliefs about the things that he doesn't know?—So it appears.—At present, these beliefs, being newly aroused, are like a dream. But if someone asks him the same questions on many occasions and in many different ways, you can see that in the end he will have knowledge about these things that is as exact as anyone's.—So it would seem.—This knowledge will not come from teaching, but from questioning. He will recover it from himself.— Yes.—And this recovery of knowledge in himself by himself is recollection, isn't it?—Yes.—Either, then, he has at some time acquired the knowledge that he has at this time[15] <when he has recollected>, or he always had it. If he always had it, he was always in the condition of knowing. If, however, he

---

[14] sc. the argument against the possibility of inquiry. 'Contentious'; **182** n.
[15] Or 'now'.

acquired it at some previous time, it cannot have been in this life, unless someone taught him geometry. He will do the same with all geometrical knowledge and with every other subject. Has anyone taught him all these? You ought to know, especially since he was born and brought up in your household.—Yes, I know that no one has ever taught him.—And has he these beliefs or hasn't he?—It seems we can't deny it.—Then if he didn't acquire them in this life, isn't it immediately clear that he had them and had learned them during some other period?—It seems so.—When he was not a human being?—Yes.—If, then, there turn out to be in him, both while he is and while he is not a human being, true beliefs that are aroused by questioning and become pieces of knowledge, may we say that his soul has always been in a condition of having learned? Clearly, for all of time he always either is or is not a man.—Clearly.—And if the truth about reality is always in the soul, the soul must be immortal, and you must be confident, and undertake to inquire into and recollect what you don't actually know or, in other words, remember at the moment.—Somehow or other I believe you are right, Socrates.—I think so, Meno. I don't insist that my argument is right on all other points, but I'll contend at all costs, both in word and in deed, as far as I can, that we will be better and braver and less idle, if we think we must inquire into the things we don't know, than if we believe that we can't discover the things we don't know and that we ought not to inquire into them.[16]

187   PLATO, *Gorgias* 473 E–474 B   SOCRATES: What's this? You're laughing, Polus? Well, this is a new kind of refutation;[17] whenever any one says anything, you don't refute it, but laugh at him. POLUS: But, Socrates, don't you think, you've been adequately refuted, when you say things that not a single person would say? Ask the company.—Polus, I'm not one of the politicians. Indeed, last year, I was elected by lot to the Council, and my tribe were serving as presidents,[18] and I had to put a question to a vote. I raised a laugh when I didn't know how to do it. So don't ask me now to put the question to a vote of the present company. No; if, as I was saying, you have no better refutation than numbers, then do as I suggested now. Let me have a turn; make trial of the sort of refutation that I think is required. For I know how to produce one witness only to the truth of what I say—the person I'm arguing with, whoever he is; but I forget about the many. I know how to put the question to this one person's vote, but I don't even have a discussion with the many. See, then, whether you are willing to undergo examination in turn, and answer my questions. For I certainly think that I and you and everyone else really believe that doing injustice is worse than suffering it, and that not being punished is

[16] Aristotle comments on recollection at **274**.
[17] *elenchos*; **142** n.
[18] Presidents; **531**, **540**.

worse than being punished.—And I think neither I nor anyone else believes it. For would you yourself, for example, choose to suffer rather than do injustice?—Yes, and so would you and everyone else.—Quite the reverse; neither you nor I nor anyone else.[19]

188 PLATO, *Sophist* 230 B–D   ELEATIC VISITOR: They[20] interrogate someone who thinks he is saying something, but is really saying nothing. They find it easy to examine his beliefs, since they are so confused. They collect his beliefs by the questions they ask, and place them side by side. Then they show that the beliefs contradict one another about the same things, in relation to the same things, and in the same respect.[21] Those who see this are harsh to themselves, but grow gentle towards others, and in this way are entirely freed from great errors and rigid beliefs, in a way that most pleases the hearer, and produces the most lasting benefit for the person examined. The physician considers that the body will receive no benefit from taking food until someone gets rid of the obstacles inside the patient. Similarly, the purifiers of the soul recognize that the soul will receive no benefit from the application of any branch of learning until someone refutes the person, and, when he is refuted, makes him ashamed, and, by removing the beliefs that are obstacles to learning, purges him and leads him to think that he knows only what he knows, and no more.

189 ANON., *Prolegomena to Plato* v. 209. 29–36   Plato adopted the dialogue form because it imitates dialectic.[22] For just as dialectic proceeds by question and answer, so the dialogue is composed of characters questioning and answering. Now dialectic compels the soul to reveal the labours it undergoes; for, according to Plato, the soul is like a writing tablet with nothing written on it. Similarly, then, so that the dialogue would compel the reader to assent to the things being said, Plato used this type of composition.

190 DIOGENES LAERTIUS iii. 48   A dialogue is a discourse[23] composed of question and answer, about some philosophical or political issues, with appropriate representation of the characters of the people being depicted, and appropriate forms of expression. Dialectic is a craft of discourse, through which we refute or establish something by questions and answers of the participants in the discussion.

---

[19] Continued at **493, 455**.

[20] 'They' are the 'noble sophists'. This dialogue is concerned with identifying the sophist (see **8**).· In the course of the discussion the Eleatic Visitor describes people who might easily be confused with sophists, but really are quite different. These are the 'noble' sophists; they practise a recognizably Socratic method.

[21] This leads to the condition of 'puzzlement', *aporia*; **182** n.

[22] Dialectic: **142**.

[23] *logos*; **113** n.

191 PROCLUS, *Commentary on the Alcibiades* 170. 11–171. 1[24]   Dialectical questioning is most stimulating to one's investigative capacity, since it persuades the hearer himself to search out the appropriate answers, by focusing him on the questions and turning him into himself.[25] It contributes considerably to recollection; for the fact that one discovers the truth in oneself, asserts it oneself, turns to oneself, and views in oneself what is known, truly reveals that acts of learning are acts of recollecting.

Language and reality

192 The demand in the *Meno* for an 'explanation' or a 'reason why' (*aitia*) is related to Socrates' inquiries into the virtues. He demands a single 'form' (*eidos*) or 'character' (*idea*) of justice, piety, and so on, that is present in all its instances. An account of this form will give us knowledge, not mere belief, because we can use it as a 'pattern' (*paradeigma*) to explain why a particular action or person is, say, just or pious (**144**, **181**). The *Meno* defends the possibility of constructive inquiry without antecedent knowledge; but the inquiry may still be misguided, if there are no explanatory forms of the sort that Socrates seeks.

Plato argues that the belief in forms avoids a Protagorean view (cf. **156**) of the relation between our beliefs and the reality they are about. The *Cratylus* discusses a Protagorean view on the 'correctness of names'. Hermogenes, the defender of Protagoras, connects questions about the correctness of names with issues about nature and convention (cf. **125**). He maintains that only convention determines the correctness of our names for things; nothing about the nature of things themselves makes it correct to apply one name rather than another.

The argument from variation makes a conventionalist account of the correctness of names seem plausible, since different people obviously use different names that seem equally correct. It seems to be a matter of convention that we use the words we use in English, say, or German, to refer to one thing rather than another. Nothing about 'dog', for instance, rather than 'Hund', makes it the right word to apply to dogs; it is correct in English and incorrect in German only because of the conventions of English and German.

In Plato's view, however, this claim about convention does not support Protagoras' broader conventionalist conclusion. Though it may be a matter of convention whether 'dog' or 'Hund' is the name for dogs, and neither may be more correct than another, it is not a matter of convention (Socrates claims) whether or not 'dog' (or 'Hund') names a genuine kind. 'Dog' is a correct name, in

---

[24] This is an excerpt from a series of points on the advantages of Plato's question-and-answer method. On the *First Alcibiades* see **321**.

[25] Turning into oneself; **217**.

Plato's view, if the things we call 'dogs' constitute a genuine kind whose nature is marked out by the answer to the Socratic question 'What is a dog?'. The objective truth of such answers and the objective reality of the kinds that they refer to excludes the Protagorean view of truth and reality.

193 PLATO, *Cratylus* 385 D–386 E HERMOGENES: ... I can't find any correctness of names other than this, Socrates, that I call a thing by one name I have laid down, and you call it by another name that you have laid down. Similarly, I see that in different cities the same things have different names; Greeks differ from foreigners in their use of names, and Greeks from Greeks. SOCRATES: But would you say, Hermogenes, that the things differ as the names differ? Is their nature[26] private to each individual, as Protagoras used to say? For he said that a human being is the measure of all things, and that things are for me such as they appear to me, and are for you such as they appear to you. Does it seem[27] so to you, or do things seem to you to have some stability of being?— There have been times, Socrates, when I've been so puzzled that I went in Protagoras' direction, though it doesn't altogether seem right to me.—Well, have you ever gone so far that not a single human being seemed to you to be bad?—No, indeed; it has often happened that it seemed to me that there are very bad people, and a good many of them.—And did it ever seem to you that there were any very good ones?—Not many.—Still, they seemed so?—Yes.— What do you mean by affirming this? Don't you mean that the very good were the very wise, and the very bad very foolish?—It seems so to me.—But if what Protagoras said is true, and the truth is that things are such as they appear to anyone, is it possible for some of us to be wise and others foolish?— Impossible.—And I think it seems to you that if there are such things as wisdom and folly, it can't be altogether possible for Protagoras to speak the truth. For if what seems to each person is true, one person can't truly be wiser than another.—No, he can't.—But if ... things are not private to each individual, they clearly have some stable nature of their own. They are not relative to us, dragged this way and that by us, according to our appearance; they are naturally related, themselves in their own right, to their own nature.—It seems so to me, Socrates.[28]

Forms and the senses

194 This argument in the *Cratylus* shows that we cannot be Protagoreans if we accept the common belief that some people are better and wiser than others. In

---

[26] Or 'essence', *ousia*. See **181** n., **227**.

[27] Since Hermogenes inclines to a Protagorean position, Socrates refutes him by appeal not to what is the case, but to what seems to Hermogenes to be the case.

[28] A further argument from the *Cratylus* is in **210**.

rejecting Protagoras' position, we implicitly recognize that things have objective forms and natures. But what are these forms, and what reason have we—apart from our reluctance to be Protagoreans—to believe they exist?

One major theme of Plato's middle dialogues is his discussion of Forms.[29] He agrees with Socrates in recognizing forms that are the objects of definition, but (it is usually supposed) he goes beyond Socrates by believing in Forms that are different from sensible objects and properties. These Forms cannot be grasped by the senses, because of the instability of sensible things; they must be grasped by thought. Unlike sensibles, they are free of change and imperfection.

This account of Plato's position reflects Aristotle's comparison of Socrates and Plato (**197**). He takes Plato to have been influenced by Cratylus, an extreme disciple of Heracleitus. The extreme instability of sensibles persuades Plato that, if knowledge is possible, there must be stable objects of knowledge, and hence there must be non-sensible Forms.

Aristotle's account is supported by the contrasts that Plato draws between Forms and sensible things. Plato claims that sensible things are always changing and are not stable; this is why the Forms must be outside the sensible world. But what does he mean by his claim about change in sensibles, and why does he take this change to imply the existence of unchanging objects of knowledge? We must consider some different ways of understanding the position set out in the middle dialogues.

....

195 PLATO, *Phaedo* 65 A–C [SOCRATES:] What again are we to say about acquiring wisdom? If the body is admitted as a partner in the inquiry, is it a hindrance or not? For instance, have sight and hearing any truth for human beings? Or is what the poets are always telling us right, that we neither hear nor see anything accurate? But if these bodily senses are neither accurate nor clear, the other senses hardly will be, since they are inferior to them. Or don't you think so? [SIMMIAS:] I do think so, he replied.—Then when does the soul reach truth? For if it undertakes to examine anything in company with the body, clearly it is deceived by the body.—True.—Then isn't it reasoning, if anything, that makes any being clear to the soul?—Yes.—And I suppose the soul reasons best when none of these things, namely sight, hearing, pain or pleasure, distresses it, but it is as far as possible by itself, lets the body go, and as far as possible has no dealings or contact with it, but aims at being?—Certainly.

196 PLATO, *Phaedo* 66 B–E [SOCRATES:] So long as we have the body, and our soul is contaminated with this sort of evil, we will surely never reach

---

[29] Middle dialogues; **17–18**. It is conventional to use the initial capital in 'Forms' to distinguish 'Platonic' Forms (with the distinctive features attributed to them in the middle dialogues) from 'Socratic' forms.

what we desire, namely the truth. For the body presents us with innumerable distractions because of the need to sustain it. Further, any diseases that attack us impede our search for being. Besides, the body fills us with loves, appetites, fears, all sorts of images, and a great deal of nonsense, so that we can never exercise intelligence on anything. For indeed wars, conflicts, and battles result precisely from the body and its appetites. For wars aim at gaining wealth, and we are compelled to acquire wealth because of the body, if we are slaves to its service. ... We have shown that if we are ever to have pure knowledge of anything, we must free ourselves of the body and look at things themselves with the soul itself.

197 ARISTOTLE, *Metaphysics* 987ᵃ32–ᵇ10   In his youth Plato first became familiar with Cratylus and with the Heracleitean beliefs that all perceptible things are always flowing and that there is no knowledge of them; he held these views later too. Socrates, however, was concerned with ethics and not at all with nature as a whole; he was inquiring into the universal in ethics and was the first to turn his thought to definitions. Plato agreed with Socrates, but because of this <Heracleitean view> he took these definitions to apply not to perceptible things but to other things; for, he thought, the common definition could not be of any of the perceptible things, given that these are always changing. Beings of the sort that definitions apply to, then, he called Ideas, and he said that perceptible things are apart from these, and are all called after them, since the things with the same names as the Forms are what they are by participation in them.

Change and the sensible world

198   To evaluate Aristotle's summary of Plato's argument, we must ask whether Plato commits himself to a Heracleitean belief in radical flux in the sensible world. Many of his remarks about change (**199–200**) fall short of this position; for they do not commit him to the extreme view (**165–8**) that sensibles are always changing in every respect.

The *Theaetetus*, however, puts forward a doctrine of radical Heracleitean flux (**166**). If this is Plato's own view, he may intend to argue for Forms, in this way:

(1) The extreme Heracleitean view, that everything is constantly changing in every respect, is incoherent.

(2) Everything in the sensible world constantly undergoes change in every respect.

(3) If the sensible world suffers this sort of change, it cannot be known.

(4) Hence, if knowledge is possible, there must be unchanging objects of knowledge, the Forms.

(5) Knowledge is possible.

(6) Hence the Forms must exist outside the sensible world (**203**).

We might infer that Plato believes in two separate worlds. One of them (the physical world) is mutable, sensible, and unknowable; the other (the world of Forms) is immutable, non-sensible, and knowable. According to this 'Two Worlds' doctrine, Heracleitus is right, but only about the sensible world. Moreover, Parmenides is right, but only about the existence of a non-sensible world of unchanging objects of knowledge (cf. **58**).

If Plato accepted this Two Worlds doctrine, would he hold a coherent position? We might doubt, for instance, whether it is reasonable to accept both (1) and (2). Some ancient critics took (1) and (2) to betray Plato's acceptance of a Sceptical position (**202**). If Plato is to hold (2), he must show that the reasons for rejecting the unrestricted extreme Heracleiteanism in (1) do not also undermine the restricted version of Heracleiteanism in (2). We might also doubt the inference from (3) and (4); for why should the fact that something completely unstable cannot be known require us to believe in objects of knowledge that are completely stable? Why not consider objects that are neither completely unstable nor entirely unchanging?

----

199 PLATO, *Timaeus* 49 B–E[30] TIMAEUS: … we see that what we just now called water condenses, as it seems to us, to become stone and earth, and this same water melts and disperses to become vapour and air. We see air inflamed, to become fire, and again fire condensed and extinguished, to pass once more into the form of air, and once more air collected and condensed, to turn into cloud and mist; and from these, when still more compressed, we see flowing water come, and from water earth and stones once more. In this way they pass on becoming, as it appears, from one to another in a circle. Thus, since these things never appear the same, how can anyone insist firmly that any of them, whatever it may be, is one thing rather than another, without putting himself to shame? No one can. By far the safest plan is to lay this down about them. Whatever we see to be continually changing, as, for example, fire, we must not call it 'that'. Instead, we must say that fire is 'what is of such a nature at a given time'. Nor must we call water 'that' but 'what is such at a given time'. Nor must we speak of any other one as having the stability that we take ourselves to indicate by using 'this' and 'that'; for they escape, and do not wait for any such expressions as 'this' or 'that' or 'here' or any other way of speaking that represents them as being stable.

200 PLATO, *Symposium* 207 D–208 B[31] For a time an animal is said to be alive and to be the same so that, for instance, he is called the same from

----

[30] This is part of the long speech by Timaeus that takes up most of the dialogue.
[31] This is part of a reported speech by Socrates. He reports a discourse by a prophetess Diotima.

childhood to old age. But for all this time he never has the same things in him, but is still called the same. He is always becoming new[32] and always losing something—hair, flesh, bones, blood, and the whole body. This is true not only of the body, but also of the soul and of its habits, traits, beliefs, desires, pleasures, pains, fears; none of these remains the same for any one of us, but some come to be and others perish. And it is still more surprising that not only do different types of knowledge come to be and perish in us at different times, so that in respect of them we are never the same, but the same is also true of a particular type of knowledge. For what we call practice implies the departure of knowledge; for forgetting is the departure of knowledge, and practice produces a new memory in place of what departs, and so preserves knowledge, so that it seems to be the same. For this is the way in which everything mortal is preserved, not by being the same in all respects, as the divine is, but by what grows old and departs leaving behind a new thing of the same sort as the old.[33]

201 ANON., *Commentary on the Theaetetus* 70. 5–26[34] The argument about what grows was first put forward by Pythagoras. Plato also put it forward, as we remarked in our commentary on the *Symposium*.

202 ANON., *Prolegomena to Plato* x. 205. 3–206. 43 Some people try to push Plato into the camp of those who suspend judgement and of the Academics, claiming that he induces inapprehensibility[35] ... [205. 26] Their fourth argument is this. He thinks there are two sorts of cognition, one arising through sense and the other through intellect, and he says that each of these makes errors; hence he clearly favours inapprehensibility. For, he says, we neither hear nor see anything accurately, but our senses are in error. And again about intelligible things he says that our soul, caught up in this evil, the body, grasps nothing by intellect. To these people we will reply that when he says the senses do not grasp sensible objects, he means that they have no cognition of the essence[36] of sensibles; for they grasp the affection that comes to them from the sensible objects themselves, but, left to themselves, they do not grasp the essence—sight, for instance, penetrated by the white, perceives it, but, left to itself, it does not know what white is, but discerns this when caught up with imagination.[37] Similarly, belief left to itself does not know

---

[32] One Greek word means both 'new' and 'young'.

[33] **201** and **53** show that some ancient interpreters took this passage to assert that sensible objects do not persist through any change in their composition.

[34] See LS 28B. The passage comments on *Theaetetus* 152 CD (**158**). A little later the author also ascribes the argument about growth to Epicharmus; see **53**.

[35] Suspension of judgement; **173**. The author goes on to state and to rebut five arguments for regarding Plato as a Sceptic.

[36] *ousia*; **181** n., **193**, **227**.

[37] Or 'appearance' (*phantasia*).

what it knows when combined with thought. Again, when he says the soul cannot grasp anything by intellect when it is together with this evil, he is not referring to all human beings, but only to those who live immersed in matter; for they have their soul subdued by the body ... But those who are pure—whom he elsewhere calls citizens of heaven—these have knowledge through intellect.

203 F. M. CORNFORD, *Plato's Theory of Knowledge*, p. 97[38]   Plato stands by his analysis of sense-perception, which is now recalled. It is still attributed to those more refined thinkers who have been alleged to hold the doctrine of flux. That doctrine was originally stated without any reservation as applying to 'all things'. Plato has now to point out that, if the objects of perception (to which it does, in his opinion, apply) are taken to be 'all things', there can be no such thing as knowledge at all, since no statement we make about these perpetually changing things can remain true for two moments together. All discourse will be impossible, since there will be no fixed and stable things for words to refer to.

Change, explanation, and Forms

204 Does Plato actually hold the Two Worlds doctrine? One objection to this interpretation arises from the *Theaetetus* itself. Nothing suggests that in this dialogue the Platonic Socrates endorses the Heracleitean doctrine of flux. On the contrary, he introduces it only to make clear the Heracleitean doctrines that follow from acceptance of the Protagorean position. Moreover, he argues against the Heracleitean, and hence the Protagorean, position by arguing that belief in extreme flux results in a self-refuting description of the sensible world (**167–8**; cf. **210**).[39]

We may, therefore, set aside the *Theaetetus*, and turn to the arguments offered for Forms in the middle dialogues, to see whether they really rely on extreme flux, or defend a Two Worlds doctrine. In considering these arguments, we ought to ask what kind of 'change' or 'flux' Plato ascribes to sensibles. In Heracleitus, and in the *Theaetetus*, a Heracleitean doctrine about change might refer (*a*) to temporal succession in either qualified or unqualified becoming; or (*b*) to the compresence of opposite properties at the same time (**50, 57**). The facts that things lose a little of their matter all the time and that the same water is healthy for some and poisonous for others are both taken as examples of change.

When Plato argues in the middle dialogues from flux in sensibles to the existence of non-sensible Forms, he seems to appeal to compresence, not to

---

[38] London: Routledge, 1935. Cornford is commenting on **167**.
[39] Contrast Owen's account in **211** with Cornford's in **203**.

temporal succession. In his account of how recollection begins (**205**), he argues that we are reminded of the Form of equality by seeing sensible equals, which are unlike the Form in so far as they are both equal and unequal. By this Plato means that they are equal and unequal in different respects, not that at one time they are equal and at a later time they change to being unequal. He infers that we cannot identify the equal itself with any sensible equal; for the equal itself, unlike sensible equals, cannot be both equal and unequal.

Plato's remarks about adequate explanations may clarify this argument. Forms are introduced as properties that provide definitions by explaining why different just things (for instance) are just; the Form of justice is what makes all just things just (**180–1**). Some properties cannot be Forms because they cannot provide the right sort of explanation. Plato rejects explanations that say (for instance) that A is taller than B 'by a head'; for 'by a head' explains A's being taller than B no more than it explains B's being shorter than A. To say what makes A taller rather than shorter, we must say that A exceeds B. Similarly, to say what makes A equal to B, we cannot refer to any specific quantity (for instance, being a foot long or weighing a pound), since this makes things equal no more than it makes them unequal.

Plato uses this simple point to make a more important point. For he also rejects explanations that say (for instance) that this picture is beautiful because of its bright colour, or that this statue is beautiful because of its symmetrical shape, or that this person's action was just because he was paying back what he borrowed. 'By a head' explains being taller no more than it explains being shorter, and so cannot be an adequate explanation of being taller; equally, having bright colour sometimes makes something beautiful, but sometimes makes something ugly. Hence bright colour no more explains beauty than it explains ugliness; it cannot be an adequate answer to the question 'What is the beautiful?'.

These objections to sensible properties seem to explain Plato's complaints about variability in sensibles (**206**, **208–9**). His remarks about flux and change need not express a radical Heracleitean belief in constant change in every respect in sensible objects.

....

205 PLATO, *Phaedo* 72 E–74 D   [CEBES:] Besides, Socrates, rejoined Cebes, according to that view you regularly mention—that learning for us is actually recollection—it necessarily follows that what we recollect now we must have learned at some previous time. We couldn't do that unless our souls existed somewhere before they entered this human shape; and so, by that argument also, the soul would seem to be immortal. [SIMMIAS:] What were the proofs of that view, Cebes? broke in Simmias. Remind me, because at the moment I can't quite remember.—One very good argument, said Cebes, is that when people are asked questions in the right way, they answer them quite correctly, which they could not do unless some knowledge and correct

reason had been present in them. And then if you present them with a dia-
gram or anything like that, they give the right answer most clearly.
[SOCRATES:] And if you don't find that convincing, Simmias, said Socrates,
see whether you agree with this when you consider it. ... We are agreed, I
suppose, that if someone is to be reminded of something, he must first
have known it at some previous time?—Quite right.—And are we also
agreed in calling it recollection when knowledge arises in a particular way?
I will explain what I mean. Suppose that when someone sees or hears or
otherwise perceives one thing, he not only recognizes that thing, but also
thinks of another thing known by a different sort of knowledge. Isn't it
right to say that he was reminded of the object that he formed the thought
of? ... For instance, is it possible for someone who sees a picture of a horse
or a musical instrument to be reminded of a human being, or for someone
who sees a picture of Simmias to be reminded of Cebes?—Perfectly possible.—And is it possible for someone who sees a portrait of Simmias to be
reminded of Simmias himself?—Yes it is.—Doesn't it follow from all this
that recollection may be from either similar or dissimilar things?—Yes, it
does.—When you are reminded by similarity, surely you must also have in
mind whether what reminds you does or doesn't fall short, in respect of
similarity, of what it reminds you of?—Yes, you must.—Then consider
whether this is so, said Socrates. I suppose we say that there is such a thing
as equal—not stick equal to stick or stone to stone, and so on, but something different, apart from all these—the equal itself. Are we to say there is
such a thing, or no such thing?—Indeed we must say so, said Simmias, most
emphatically.—And do we know what it is?—Certainly.—Where did we get
our knowledge of it? Was it not from the things we mentioned just now?
Was it not from seeing equal sticks or stones or other equals that we
thought of it, it being different from them? Or doesn't it seem to you
different? Then look at it in this way also. Don't equal sticks and stones
sometimes, being the same, appear equal to one, and not to another?—Certainly.—But have the equals themselves ever appeared unequal to you, or
equality inequality?—No, never, Socrates.—Then these equals are not the
same as the equal itself.—They don't appear so to me, Socrates.—And
yet it is from these equal things, being different from that equal itself, that
you have thought of and acquired knowledge of it?—Perfectly true.—
Whether it is similar to them or dissimilar?—Certainly.—It doesn't matter,
said Socrates. So long as from seeing one thing you think of another,
whether similar or dissimilar, it must have been recollection.—Quite so.—
Well now, he said, what do we find in the case of the equal sticks and other
things we were speaking of just now? Do they appear to us to be equals in
the same way as what equal is itself, or do they fall short of it in being such
as the equal is? Or don't they fall short at all?—They do, said Simmias, a
long way.

206 PLATO, *Phaedo* 78 C–79 A [SOCRATES:] Then let us now return to the things we were considering in the previous discussion. Is that being of whose nature we give an account in asking and answering questions—is it always in the same condition, or is it in different conditions at different times? The equal itself, the beautiful itself, each nature itself,[40] does it allow the least variation? Or is each nature itself, by itself as a single form, always in the same condition, never admitting any alteration in any way or at any time? CEBES: They must be always in the same condition, Socrates, replied Cebes.—And what would you say of the many[41]—human beings, horses, clothes, or anything else of that sort—the many equals, or beautifuls, and all that have the same names as those <Forms>? Are they the same always, or, contrary to those, are they practically never at all in the same condition as themselves or as one another?—The latter, replied Cebes; they are never in the same condition.—And these you can touch and see and perceive with the other senses, but the things that are always in the same condition you can grasp only with the reasoning of thought—they are invisible and are not seen?—That is very true, he said.[42]

207 PLATO, *Phaedo* 100 B–102 D[43] Well, said Socrates, what I mean is this, and there is nothing new about it. I have always said it, and in fact I have never stopped saying it, especially in the earlier part of this discussion. ... I am assuming that there is some beautiful by itself, and good, and large, and all the rest of them. ... It appears to me that whatever else is beautiful apart from the beautiful itself is beautiful precisely because it partakes of that beautiful itself; and I deal with them all in the same way. Do you accept this kind of explanation?—Yes, I do.—Well, when I come to those other sophisticated causes, I don't understand or grasp them. If someone tells me that a thing is beautiful because it has a bright colour or shape or any other such thing, I ignore these other things, since I get confused among them. I cling simply, straightforwardly, and perhaps naively, to the explanation that the one thing that makes that object beautiful is the presence to it or association with it of that beautiful <itself>, in whatever way it comes to be in it[44]—for when I come to this question <about the precise account of its presence> I do not insist on any definite view, but I simply maintain that all beautiful things are beautiful by the beautiful. This seems to me to be the safest answer for me or for anyone else to give, and I believe that while I stick to this I will never fail; it's safe for me or for anyone else to answer that it is by beauty that beautiful things are beautiful. Don't you agree?—Yes, I do. ... [102 B] If you hold this

[40] Literally, 'each what-it-is itself'. The same phrase is rendered by 'nature' below.
[41] Text uncertain.
[42] Continued in **329**.
[43] Follows **96**.
[44] Text and sense uncertain.

view, I suppose that when you say that Simmias is taller than Socrates but shorter than Phaedo, you mean that at that time both tallness and shortness are in Simmias?—Yes, I do.—But do you agree that the statement that Simmias exceeds Socrates is not true in the way it is stated? For presumably Simmias exceeds not by being Simmias, but by the tallness he actually has. Again, he exceeds Socrates not because Socrates is Socrates, but because Socrates has shortness in comparison with Simmias' tallness.—True.—And again, Simmias is exceeded by Phaedo not by Phaedo's being Phaedo, but because Phaedo has tallness in comparison with Simmias' shortness.—Quite so.—So that is how Simmias is called both short and tall, because he is intermediate between the two of them, and presents his shortness to be exceeded by the tallness of the one, and his tallness exceeding the smallness of the other. He added with a smile, I seem to be talking like a book, but the facts are surely as I say.—Simmias agreed.[45]

208   PLATO, *Republic* 485 AB   [SOCRATES:] Let us take this to be agreed about the nature of philosophers, that they always love the kind of knowledge that reveals to them something of the being that always is, and does not wander because of coming to be and perishing.

209   PLATO, *Republic* 508 D   [SOCRATES:] When the soul turns to where truth and being shine, it thinks of them and knows them, and appears to have intelligence. But when it turns to what is mixed with darkness, what comes to be and perishes, it has beliefs and becomes dull, and it shifts its beliefs this way and that, and now seems as though it lacked intelligence.

210   PLATO, *Cratylus* 439 C–440 B   SOCRATES: Consider this view, Cratylus, that I often dream about.[46] Are we to say there is some beautiful itself, good itself, and each of the beings[47] of this sort, or not? CRATYLUS: Certainly, Socrates, I think so.—Then let's consider this very question, not whether a face, or anything of that sort, is beautiful, and whether all such things appear to be in flux. Are we not to say that the beautiful itself is always such as it is?—Certainly.—Then is it possible to speak of it correctly either as being this or as being such, if it is always slipping away? Mustn't it be becoming something different immediately while we are speaking, and pass away and no longer be in this state that we ascribed to it?—It certainly must.—Then how can it be anything, if it is never in the same state? For if it is ever in the same state, in that time it clearly does not change, and if it is always the same and in the same state, and never departs from its character, how could it change or be

---

[45] Continued in **330**.

[46] Socrates seems to speak of dreaming when he sets out a view that he does not think he can prove, or does not want to defend on this particular occasion.

[47] Or 'things that are', a common way of referring to forms.

moved?—Certainly it could not.—Nor yet could it be known by anyone: for at the moment when the prospective knower approaches, it becomes different and of a different character, so that you cannot get any further in knowing its nature or state, since no knowledge knows something that it knows as not being in any state.—True.—Nor can we reasonably say, Cratylus, that there is knowledge at all, if everything is changing and nothing remains. For if this very thing, knowledge, does not change from being knowledge, then knowledge would always remain and would be knowledge; but if the very form of knowledge changes, it will at the same time <as being knowledge> be changing into some other form than knowledge, and will not be knowledge, and if it always changes, it will always not be knowledge, and, according to this argument, there will be no one to know and nothing to be known. But if there is always the knower and the known, and the beautiful, the good, and each one of the beings, these things we are speaking of now evidently are not, to my mind, like flux or movement.[48]

211 G. E. L. OWEN, 'The Place of the *Timaeus* in Plato's Dialogues', p. 323[49] … the *Theaetetus* states and explodes the thesis that *becoming* excludes *being* … Plato eliminates *be* in favour of *become* in all contexts (*Tht.* 157 A 7–C 2; cf. *Tht.* 152 E I with *Tim.* 27 D 6–28 A I). And then by using the distinction between change of quality and change of place he shows that this convention produces absurdities. Some have wanted to believe that Plato is at this point trying to establish … that, although *becomes* alone is appropriate to contingent statements, there must be some entities (viz. the Forms) to whose description only *is* is appropriate. If Plato had drawn this conclusion from his argument, it would have been a sheer blunder. But he does not draw it. … What he plainly points out is that if anything (and anything in this world, not the next) were perpetually changing in all respects, so that at no time could it be described as being so-and-so, then nothing could be said of it at all—and, inter alia, it could not be said to be changing. … Notice that Plato does not say … that knowledge is not perception because the objects of perception are always in flux. … His instances are drawn from the everyday world, not from the world of Forms.

Belief, knowledge, and the Forms

212 Plato's discussion of 'flux' in sensible things concludes that if we are to know the answers to Socratic questions ('what is the just?', 'what is virtue?', and

---

[48] Cf. and contrast this passage with **167**.

[49] In R. E. Allen (ed.), *Studies in Plato's Metaphysics* (London: Routledge, 1965), 313–38. From *Classical Quarterly*, 3 (1953), 79–95. For Greek words used by Owen I have substituted English translations in italics.

so on), we cannot mention only the properties that are accessible to the senses (colour, shape, and so on). If we confine ourselves to such properties, we will have to say that, for instance, justice is both giving back what we have borrowed and not giving it back (because it is sometimes unjust to give it back), and so on.

To see what is wrong with these answers, we should remember that Socrates' 'What is it?' question seeks an explanatory account. We suppose we can explain why justice sometimes requires us to return what we have borrowed and sometimes requires us not to return it (if, for instance, our friend has lent us his knife, and wants it back when he is in a suicidal mood; **457**). This further explanation ought to appear in our account of what justice is.

Plato argues that the 'lovers of sights and sounds', those who think beauty is to be identified with many different sensible properties, cannot give the right explanatory account of beauty. Mention of 'the many beautifuls' does not explain why these properties sometimes make a thing beautiful and sometimes make it ugly. Since knowledge requires an account and an explanation (**107**), those who recognize only the many beautifuls cannot acquire knowledge of what beauty is; they have only belief about it.

....

213 PLATO, *Republic* 476 B–479 E[50]   [SOCRATES:] The lovers of sounds and sights, I said, delight in beautiful sounds, colours, and shapes, and in everything manufactured out of these, but their thought is incapable of seeing and taking delight in the nature of the beautiful itself. [GLAUCON:] Why yes, he said, that is so.—And on the other hand, won't there be few who would be able to approach the beautiful itself and see it in itself?—Few indeed.—And so if someone recognizes[51] beautiful things, but neither recognizes beauty itself nor is able to follow when someone tries to guide him to the knowledge of it, do you think his life is a dream or a waking? Just consider. Isn't dreaming, whether asleep or awake, just this: thinking that what is similar to something else is not <merely> similar, but is the very thing it is similar to?[52]—I would certainly say such a person was dreaming, he said.—Well, then, take the opposite case, one who thinks there is some beautiful itself and is able to discern both it and the things that participate in it, and neither supposes the participants in it to be it nor supposes it to be the participants. Do you think his life is a case of waking or of dreaming?—He's very much awake, he replied.—Then wouldn't we be right to call the mental state of the one knowledge, since he knows, and the state of the other belief, since he believes?—Certainly.—But suppose the person we take to have belief but not knowledge quarrels with us, and disputes our statement; can we win him over gently and persuade him, while concealing his unhealthy condition

[50] This follows the claim in **554** that philosophers should be rulers.
[51] *nomizein*, cognate with *nomos*. See **125**.
[52] Similarity; **205**.

from him?—We must certainly do this, he replied.—Come, then, and consider what we are to say to him. ... Does the one who has knowledge know something or nothing? (You must answer for him.)—I answer that he knows something.—Something that is or something that is not?—Something that is; for how could something that is not be known?—And do we adequately grasp, after considering it from many points of view, that what altogether is is altogether knowable,[53] and what is not at all is altogether unknowable?—Quite adequately.—Good. But if anything is such as to be and not to be, that will lie between what completely is and what in no way is?—Yes, between them.—And knowledge belongs to what is, ignorance of necessity to what is not; and for what is intermediate between what is and what is not we must look for an intermediate between ignorance and knowledge, if there is one?—Certainly.—Do we say there is such a thing as belief?—Undoubtedly.—Do we regard it as the same capacity as knowledge, or another capacity?—Another capacity.—Then belief and knowledge are assigned to different kinds of things, in accordance with their different capacities?—Yes. ... [478 c] Of necessity we assigned ignorance to what is not, and knowledge to what is.—True, he said.—Then one believes neither what is nor what is not?—Neither.—Then belief is neither ignorance nor knowledge?—So it would seem. ... —Then belief is between them?—No question.—But weren't we saying before that, if anything appears to be of a sort that is and is not at the same time, that sort of thing would appear also to lie between what completely is and what altogether is not, and that what belongs to it will be neither knowledge nor ignorance, but what has turned out to be between them?—True.—And now what we call belief has turned out to be between them?—It has.—Then what remains to be discovered, it would seem, is what shares in both, in what is and in what is not, and cannot rightly be called either what is or what is not altogether. And if we find this, we can truly say that this is what is believed, assigning the extreme states to the extremes and the intermediate state to the intermediate. Isn't that so?—Yes.—Now that we've laid this down, I will say, let him answer me, that worthy person who doesn't think there is any beautiful itself or any character of beauty itself always remaining in the same condition, but who regards the beautifuls as many—the lover of sights, who can't stand it if anyone says that the beautiful is one and the just is one, and so on for other things. We'll ask him this: My friend, is there any of those many beautifuls that will not appear ugly, or any of the justs that will not appear unjust, or any of the piouses that will not appear impious?—No, he said; they are bound to appear to be both beautiful in a way and ugly, and so with all the other things you asked about.—What about the many doubles? Do they appear any less halves than doubles?—No less so.—And similarly for the larges and smalls, the lights and heavies—will they be

---

[53] Or 'known' (and elsewhere in this passage).

called these things any more than their contraries?—No, he said, each of them will always partake of both. ...—Do you know what to do with them, then, I said, or can you find a better position for them than the one between being and not-being? For we surely won't find a darker place than not-being in the direction of being still less, or one brighter than being in the direction of being still more.—Quite true, he said.—We seem to have found, then, that the many things conventionally recognized[54] by the many about the beautiful and the other things roll around somewhere between what is not and what fully is.—That's what we have found.—Now we agreed in advance that if anything of that sort appeared, it must be called a matter of belief, not of knowledge; since it wanders between <being and not being>, it belongs to the intermediate capacity.—Yes, we agreed on that.—And so we'll affirm that those who view many beautifuls, but do not see the beautiful itself and cannot follow someone else leading them to it, and who view many justs, but not the just itself, and so on—we'll say that such people have beliefs about everything, but know none of the things they have beliefs about.—That must be so.—And, on the other hand, what about those who in each case view the things themselves that are always in the same condition? Won't we say that they know and don't believe?—That must also be so.

The growth of knowledge

214 Even if Plato has shown that knowledge about virtue, justice, and so on, requires knowledge of non-sensible Forms, he has not yet shown that this knowledge is possible. His further discussion of knowledge and belief argues that we can progress from uncritical acceptance of observational beliefs to reasoned and justified claims to knowledge. He distinguishes two levels of belief and two levels of knowledge, assigning them to four segments of the 'Divided Line' (**215**). He sketches the steps in a progress from a lower stage of the Line to a higher one.

We begin with 'imagination' (*eikasia*), uncritical acceptance of conventional beliefs. We advance to 'confidence' (*pistis*) as we recognize that beliefs based on simple observation, and the moral rules based on these beliefs, are inadequate. We may initially believe (as some of Socrates' interlocutors do) that standing firm is bravery or that returning what we have borrowed is justice; but Socratic inquiry shows that these rules do not fully specify the relevant virtues.

We reach the third stage of the Line, 'thought' (*dianoia*), through the use of 'assumptions' (from *hupothesis*, 'laying down'), to reach a reasonable, though incomplete, answer to Socrates' demand for definitions. In the *Phaedo* (**216**) Plato advises us to rely on the assumption that appears on examination to be the

[54] *nomima*, cognate with *nomos*. See note earlier in this section.

strongest; some Socratic inquiries suggest how we might find this assumption. It is reasonable to assume that (for instance) justice always seeks the benefit of the people affected. This may conflict with our initial belief that it is always just to give back what we borrow, but we must reject that belief if it conflicts with still further beliefs that, on reflection, seem more reasonable. In that case, the assumption is to that extent vindicated. We now have a type of knowledge, because we have an account that justifies our well-founded beliefs; we are better off than Socrates and his interlocutors were.

These assumptions do not yet count as complete knowledge. At the fourth stage of the Line, 'intelligence' (noêsis), we reach knowledge of the Good through dialectic (i.e. Socratic cross-examination);[55] knowledge of the Form of the good is the source and basic principle of knowledge of other Forms. Questions about the virtues suggest why Plato introduces the good. The different virtues should all contribute to some good; if an allegedly just action turns out to have consequences that we would regard as worse on the whole, it is not (in Plato's view) a just action after all. Adequate accounts of the virtues must relate them to an adequate conception of the good that they promote.[56]

According to Plato, discovery of this good reveals an adequate first principle that explains and justifies our assumptions. If we have reached the third stage of the Line, we have only examined the consequences of the assumptions, and the consistency of our views; we have not yet considered whether the assumptions support each other. If they turn out to support each other, they are not mere assumptions; each gives us further reason to accept the others, and we are justified in accepting them all. We find this mutual support in reaching the fourth stage of the Line.

In describing this progress through the stages of the Line, Plato implies that if we trust some of our beliefs and reflect on them, we can acquire a coherent, mutually supporting structure of reasoned beliefs. This is the aim of Socratic inquiry, as Plato interprets it in his theory of recollection. Contrary to the suggestion of the Sceptics, examination of our initial beliefs allows us to remove apparent conflicts, and to find an explanation of and justification for some of our initial beliefs. Plato seems to assume that coherence is a source of justification; this is his implicit answer to Agrippa's trilemma (cf. **169, 171**).

Some readers do not agree that Plato regards coherence as a source of justification.[57] They argue that the highest stage of the Line implies a different answer to Agrippa; it is meant to reach a self-evident starting-point, and this is why Plato claims that the first principle is not an assumption. If, however, this is Plato's view, it becomes difficult to see why he lays such emphasis on Socratic

---

[55] Dialectic and dialegesthai; **96, 142, 189–90, 220, 317, 321.**

[56] Plato's concern with goodness is not confined to questions about morality. It is also relevant in his view, to the understanding of the universe as a whole; **96, 590–2.**

[57] These readers rely especially on **218.**

dialectic as a route to knowledge; for this appears to be a method for securing coherence and mutual support, not for discovering a self-evident principle.

215   PLATO, *Republic* 509 D–511 E   [SOCRATES:] ... take a line divided into two unequal sections, and cut each section again in the same ratio—the section, that is, of the visible kind and the section of the intelligible kind, to express their comparative perspicuity and the lack of it. In the visible area, one section will be images. By images I mean, first, shadows, and then reflections in water and on surfaces of dense, smooth, and bright texture, and everything of that kind, if you follow. [GLAUCON:] I do.—As the second section assume what the first is a likeness of—that is, the animals about us and all plants and the whole class of manufactured things.—I assume it, he said.—Would you be willing to say, I said, that the division in respect of truth or the opposite is this: as the believed is to the known, so the likeness is to what it is a likeness of?—I certainly would.—Now consider in turn how we are to divide the intelligible section.—How?—So that there is one section that the soul is compelled to investigate by treating as images the things imitated in the former division, investigating from assumptions, not going to a principle, but to a conclusion. In the other section it reaches a principle that is not assumed, advancing from an assumption, without the images used in the other section, relying on Forms themselves and carrying out its line of inquiry through Forms.—I don't fully understand what you mean by this, he said.—Then I'll try again, I said; for you'll understand better after these preliminaries. For I think you are aware that students of geometry, arithmetic, and such subjects assume the odd, the even, the various figures, three kinds of angles, and other things related to these in each line of inquiry. They regard them as known, and make them assumptions; they don't think it appropriate to give any further account of them to themselves or others, regarding them as evident to everyone. They begin from these, pursue the inquiry from this point, and reach a conclusion in agreement with their starting-points.—Certainly, he said, I know that.—And don't you also know that, in addition, they use visible forms and make their arguments about them, though they are not thinking of them, but of those things of which they are a likeness, making their arguments for the sake of the square itself and the diagonal itself, and not for the sake of the diagonal that they draw? And so in all cases. The very things that they mould and draw, which have shadows and images of themselves in water, these things they treat in their turn as images. They seek to see those things that can be seen only by thought. ...—I understand, he said, that you're referring to what falls under geometry and the crafts related to it.— Understand, then, I said, that by the other section of the intelligible I mean the one that reason itself grasps by the power of dialectic, treating assumptions not as principles, but as truly assumptions, like starting-points and springboards, so that it can proceed to what is not an assumption, to the principle of everything, and after grasping that can again take hold of the things that come next to it, and so proceed downward to the end, using nothing perceptible, but using Forms themselves, proceeding from Forms to Forms, and ending with Forms.—I understand, he said, not adequately—for you seem to be describing a long task—but I do understand that you mean to distinguish the part of being and the intelligible that is studied by dialectical knowledge, as more perspicuous than what is studied by the disciplines called crafts. In these crafts assumptions are principles, and those who view them are compelled to view them by thought, not by the senses; but because they don't go up to the principle in their examination, but examine from assumptions, you don't think they have intelligence about them, though the things themselves are intelligible when understood with a principle. And I think you call the state of geometers and so on thought, but not intelligence, because you regard thought as something intermediate between belief and intelligence.—You've expounded it quite adequately, I said. And now, answering to these four sections, assume these four conditions in the soul: intelligence for the highest, thought for the second, confidence for the third, and for the last imagination. Arrange these in a proportion, considering that they partake in perspicuity to the same degree as what they are about partakes of truth.

216 PLATO, *Phaedo* 100 A–101 E [SOCRATES:] I assume on each occasion whatever account I judge to be the strongest; the things that seem to me to agree with this I take to be true ... [101 D] And if someone attacks the assumption itself, you will pay no attention to him, and will not answer, until you have examined the consequences of the assumption, to see whether they agree or disagree with each other. And when you need to give an account of the assumption itself, you will give it in the same way, by assuming in turn whichever higher assumption seems best to you, until you come to something adequate. But you won't mix things up, as the controversialists do, discussing at the same time both the principle and its consequences. You will avoid what they do, if you want to find anything out about beings.

217 PLATO, *Republic* 518 D [SOCRATES:] ... there must be some craft for turning the soul round, for changing its direction as easily and effectively as possible. The aim is not to produce sight in us; rather, we assume that sight is already present, but has been turned the wrong way round and is not looking where it should. Our aim is to put this right.[58]

218 PLATO, *Republic* 533 B–D [SOCRATES:] This, at any rate, I said, no one will maintain in dispute against us, that there is any other line of inquiry besides dialectic that undertakes systematically and in all cases to grasp what a

[58] Turning the soul; **191**.

given thing is. All the other crafts are directed either to human beliefs and desires, or to coming-to-be and composition, or to the care of the things that come to be and are put together. Those we described as having some grasp on being—geometry and the studies that follow it—are, as we see, dreaming about being, but cannot have a waking sight of it, as long as they use assumptions and leave them undisturbed, <because> they cannot give an account of them. For if one does not know the principle, and the end and the intermediate stages are composed of what one doesn't know, how can this sort of agreement <between premises and conclusion> turn out to be knowledge? [GLAUCON:] It can't, he said.—Then, I said, isn't dialectical inquiry the only one that advances in this way, doing away with assumptions, as far as the principle itself, to confirm <them>? ... It gently draws the eye of the soul, and leads it up with the help of the studies and sciences we mentioned, using them as helpers and co-workers in turning it around.

Objections to the Theory of Forms

219 Though Plato takes knowledge to require knowledge of Forms, his conception of Forms fails to answer some important questions. We might, for instance, suppose that the Form (e.g. the just itself) and the property or universal (justice) are the very same thing; this is what Socrates seemed to be looking for in his search for an account of the 'one pious' and so on. Some of Plato's remarks, however, suggest to many readers (including Aristotle) that he cannot consistently identify the Form with the property. For when he opposes the Form of F to sensible Fs that are both F and not-F, he does not say that the Form is neither F nor not-F, but that it is perfectly F. On this view, the Form of justice is perfectly just, not also unjust, the Form of large perfectly large, the Form of equal perfectly equal, and so on. In that case, apparently, the Form must be an instance of the property it corresponds to, not the property itself.

This feature of the Forms has been described (by modern critics) as 'self-predication'. More exactly, it rests on the assumption that every Form bears the predicate that it corresponds to. A reason for believing that Plato takes self-predication seriously is the fact that he speaks of sensible things as 'sharing' or 'participating' in Forms by being similar to them to some degree (**205**). Forms are said to be 'paradigms' (i.e. patterns; **144**) that sensibles resemble to some degree.

Though some of Plato's remarks suggest that he accepts self-predication, perhaps he ought not to accept it. It seems difficult to apply to every Form: how large must the Form of large be, and what is the Form of equal equal to? The fact that such questions arise suggests that self-predication rests on a mistake.

In the *Parmenides* Plato himself seems to recognize the plausibility of some objections to his position. Parmenides presents a series of objections to a theory of Forms; several objections seem to focus on the difficulties of self-predication as a feature of all the Forms under discussion.

One striking objection to Forms appears in the argument usually known as the 'Third Man' (the name is due to Aristotle; see **221–2**). Its exact interpretation and significance have been disputed. One formulation is this:

(1) Since Socrates and Plato are both large, there is a Form, the Large, by participation in which they are both large.

(2) Since Socrates, Plato, and the Large are all large, there is a further Form, the Large-2, by participation in which they are all large.

(3) Since Socrates, Plato, the Large, and the Large-2 are all large, there is a further Form, the Large-3 … and so on ad infinitum.

The conclusion implies that infinitely many Forms correspond to each property; and so, to understand what makes Socrates and Plato large, we must understand an infinite number of Forms. Since we cannot perform this infinite task, we cannot understand what makes anything large.

The argument as it stands is clearly incomplete. Step (1) is supposed to be justified by the reasoning that (according to Parmenides) leads Socrates to believe in a Form for any property. Steps (2) and (3) are supposed to be warranted by the very same reasoning. Several steps need to be added to make a valid argument; and then we need to ask whether Plato's claims about Forms (in other dialogues) commit him to the acceptance of these steps.

According to Aristotle, the Third Man argument identifies one of Plato's basic mistakes. The acceptance of self-predication requires Plato to treat properties as though they were further particulars (as though tallness were a tall thing, white had some colour, and so on). This claim about Platonic Forms provides Aristotle with a point of comparison for his own theory of universals and forms. Though Aristotle rejects Plato's conception of Forms, he believes Plato is right to insist on the reality of something beyond material particulars (**223**). In defending some aspects of Plato and rejecting other aspects, Aristotle develops his own metaphysical position, which we will consider in the next chapter.

....

220 PLATO, *Parmenides* 130 A–135 C [PARMENIDES:] Socrates, he said, your eagerness for arguments is quite admirable. Tell me now: do you, as you say, separate, on the one side, certain Forms themselves, and, on the other side, the things partaking in them? And do you think that there is likeness itself, separate from the likeness we have, and that there is one <itself> and many, and the other things Zeno[59] mentioned? [SOCRATES:] I think so, said Socrates.—Parmenides said: And would you also say there is a Form itself of, for instance, just, fine, and good, and of everything of that sort?—Yes, he said.—Well, is there a Form of man separately from us and the sort we are, or

[59] Zeno; **80**.

of fire or water?—I'm often puzzled, Parmenides, about whether I ought to say the same about these as about the other cases, or not.—And what about these things, Socrates, that might seem ludicrous—for instance, hair, mud, dirt, or anything else contemptible and paltry? Are you puzzled about whether to say that each of these has a Form in separation, different from the things we encounter, or not?—Certainly not, said Socrates; these are just the things we see. I fear it would be absurd to think there is a Form of them. Still I'm sometimes disturbed, and begin to think that in all cases there is some <Form that is> one and the same. But then again, when I've taken up this position, I run away, because I'm afraid I may fall into a bottomless pit of nonsense, and perish. And so I return to the things we just now said had Forms, and I occupy myself with them.—Yes, Socrates, said Parmenides; that's because you are still young. Philosophy hasn't yet gripped you as firmly as it will, I believe; then you won't despise even the meanest things. At your age, you are too easily impressed by people's prejudices. But tell me this: Does it seem to you, as you say, that there are Forms of which all these other things partake, and thereby have the names of the Forms? Do similar things, for example, turn out to be similar by partaking of similarity, and large things to be large by partaking of largeness, and just and fine things to be just and fine by partaking of fineness and justice? Yes, certainly, said Socrates. ... [132 A]—I suppose your ground for thinking each Form is one is this. Whenever it seems to you that a number of things are large, presumably there seems to be some one idea[60] that is the same when you have looked at them all, so that you think the large is one.—True, he replied.—But now take the large itself and the other large things. Suppose you look at all these in the same way in your mind; won't some one large appear in turn, by which all these appear large?—So it would seem.—If so, a second Form of largeness will appear, in addition to largeness itself and the things that partake of it, and again, over all these, yet another, by which all of them are large. And so you will find that each Form is no longer one, but unlimited in number.—But Parmenides, said Socrates, may not the Forms be thoughts only, so that they cannot be anywhere except in minds? For in that case each Form may still be one, and the result that you mentioned would not happen.—Well, is each thought one, but a thought of nothing?—Impossible, he said.—Then it is a thought of something?—Yes.—Of something that is or of something that is not?—Of something that is.—Mustn't it be of some one thing, which that thought thinks as being over all, being some one idea?—Yes.—And won't that thing thought to be one be a Form, since it is always the same over all?—That also appears necessary.—In that case, said Parmenides, if you say that everything else participates in the Forms, mustn't you say either that everything is made up of thoughts, so that everything thinks, or that everything is thoughts, but

[60] Or 'character'.

thoughtless?—The latter view, Parmenides, is no more rational than the previous one. It seems most plausible to me that these Forms are as patterns fixed in nature, and other things are similar to them, and likenesses of them. Other things' partaking of the Forms turns out, then, to be being made similar to them.—But, he said, if something is similar to the Form, mustn't the Form also be like it, in so far as it has been made like the Form? Or is it possible for one thing to be like a second thing without the second thing being like the first?—Impossible.—And when two things are alike, mustn't they partake of the same thing?—They must.—And will not that of which the two partake, by which they are alike, be the Form itself?—Certainly.—Then nothing can be like the Form, nor can the Form be like anything else; for if they are alike, some further Form, in addition to the <first> Form, will invariably appear; and if that is like anything else, another Form in turn; and new Forms will be always arising, if the Form turns out to be like what partakes of it.— Quite true.—Then other things do not partake of the Forms by likeness, and we must search for some other way they partake of Forms.—It would seem so.—Do you see then, Socrates, how great the puzzle is, if one distinguishes the Forms themselves by themselves?—Yes, indeed. ...—[135 B] And yet, Socrates, said Parmenides, if someone focuses so much on these and similar difficulties that he refuses to allow Forms of things that are, and does not recognize one Form of each <sort of> thing, he will have nowhere to turn his mind, if he refuses to allow that there is one idea, always the same, for each thing that is; and so he will utterly destroy the capacity for dialectic.[61] You seem to me to have noticed this even more clearly.—Very true, he said.—But, then, what will you do about philosophy? Where will you turn, if the Forms are unknown?—I don't think I see clearly at the moment.

221 ARISTOTLE, *Metaphysics* 990ª34–ᵇ17 ... As for those who posited Ideas, the first objection is that in seeking to grasp the causes of the beings in this world, they introduced different things, equal in number to them. It is as though someone wanted to count things and thought he could not do it if there were fewer of them, but could do it if he added more. For the Forms they resorted to in their search for the causes of things in this world are practically equal in number to—or at any rate are no fewer than—the things in this world. For take each <kind of> thing that has a one over many, both substances and non-substances, both things in this world and everlasting things; in each case there is some <one over many> that has the same name <as the many>. Further, none of the proofs we[62] offer to show that there are Forms appears to succeed; for some of them are invalid, and others yield Forms of things that we think have no Forms. For the arguments from the sciences

[61] Dialectic; **214**.
[62] Aristotle thinks of himself as one of the Platonic school, though he does not endorse their position.

yield Forms of all the things of which there are sciences; the one over many yields Forms even of negations; and the argument from thinking about something that has perished yields Forms of things that perish, since there is an appearance of these. Further, among the more accurate arguments, some produce Ideas of relatives,[63] whereas we deny that these are a kind of things that are in their own right; others introduce the third man.

222 ALEXANDER, *Commentary on the Metaphysics* 84. 21–85. 3[64] The third man is … proved in this way. Suppose that what is predicated truly of some plurality of things is also something other than and apart from the things of which it is predicated, being separated from them; for this is what those who posit the Ideas think they prove—this is why, according to them, there is such a thing as man-itself, because the man is predicated truly of the particular men, these being a plurality, and it is other than the particular men. Now, if this is so, there will be a third man. For if the <man> being predicated is other than the things of which it is predicated and subsists on its own, and the man is predicated both of the particulars and of the Idea, it follows that there will be a third man apart from the particular and the Idea. In the same way, there will also be a fourth <man> predicated of this <third man>, of the Idea, and of the particulars, and similarly also a fifth, and so on to infinity.

223 ARISTOTLE, *Metaphysics* 1040[b]25–34 Moreover, one thing would not be in many places at once, but what is common exists in many places at once. Hence clearly no universal exists separately apart from particulars. But those who say there are Forms are right in one way, in separating them, if they are indeed substances; but in another way they are wrong, because they say that the one over many is a Form. The reason is that they cannot describe these imperishable substances apart from particular and perceptible substances, and so they make them the same in kind as perishable things (since these are the substances we know); they speak of man itself and horse itself, <merely> adding to perceptible things the word 'itself'.

---

[63] Relatives include large, small, equal.
[64] Alexander's commentary (on the passage just quoted) contains fragments (paraphrased) from Aristotle's lost work *On Ideas*, criticizing Plato's theory of Forms.

VI: Form and Matter

Aristotle and Stoicism

Changes and subjects

$\boxed{224}$ Like Plato, Aristotle criticizes the Presocratic naturalists for their exclusive attention to the material cause and for their neglect of form. He disagrees, however, with Plato's conception of forms as self-predicative paradigms separated from ordinary particular material objects. In his view, both the Presocratics (especially Heracleitus and the Atomists) and Plato ignore or misunderstand what we normally say and assume about change and continuing subjects. The Presocratics ignore the role of form as a stable element in change, and so they consider only composition.[1] Plato ignores the role of matter, and so introduces forms that purport to be both universal properties and non-material subjects (**223**).

Aristotle criticizes the Presocratic and the Platonic conception of change from simple examples of qualified becoming (Socrates becomes fat or thin, pale or dark) and unqualified becoming (Socrates comes into being or perishes). These simple examples introduce Aristotle's basic claims about substance, form, and matter; they reveal the principles that, in his view, his predecessors have missed.

According to Aristotle, every change requires a persisting subject and two non-persisting contraries, the privation and the form. A particular man Socrates, for instance, changes from being unmusical (i.e. ignorant of music) to being musical (when he learns music). In this case the man is the subject, unmusical is the privation, and musical is the form. The subject, the individual man, exists both before and after the change, whereas the two contraries do not persist; the privation perishes, and the form comes into being.

Both types of becoming require subject, privation, and form. In qualified becoming, the subject that remains throughout the change is an ordinary substance—a man, horse, etc. In unqualified becoming, the subject that remains through the change is its matter (*hulê*)[2]—the flour from which we make the loaf of bread, the bronze from which we make the statue, and so on. But in this case a new substance (the loaf, the statue) comes into being when the matter acquires the form.

According to Aristotle, the Presocratics implicitly grasp part of this analysis

---

[1] Aristotle on Heracleiteanism; **168**.

[2] *Hulê* is originally used for timber. Aristotle generalizes its use to apply to other kinds of raw material.

of change (**83**). Some of them recognize qualified becoming, since they recognize matter as a continuing subject that changes its qualities. But they wrongly treat matter as the only genuine continuing subject, and assume that a change of form does not mark a new subject. Their assumption is reasonable in the case of qualified becoming. In this case, 'musical' or 'pale' simply designates a feature of the very same subject that existed all along; no new subject has come into being. Their assumption is false, however, for unqualified becoming; in this case what comes into being is a new subject—the loaf of bread or the statue—defined by its form.

Aristotle, therefore, recognizes two sorts of subject. Both the statue and the bronze are subjects, but the bronze is the subject of the statue, and the converse is not true. Moreover, the statue has both a formal and a material aspect, whereas the bronze lacks the formal aspect (since it is not, in its own right, a statue). The statue is coincidental to the bronze (since the bronze existed before the statue was made, and still exists after the statue is melted down again), but it is not merely a feature of the bronze; it is also a subject in its own right.

....

225 ARISTOTLE, *Physics* 188ᵃ31–ᵇ8   We must first of all grasp the fact that nothing that exists is naturally such as to act or be affected in a random way by the agency of a random thing; nor does something come to be a random thing from a random thing, except coincidentally. For how could something come to be pale from being musical, unless the musical were a coincident of the not-pale or the dark? Rather, something comes to be pale from being not-pale—and not from every way of being not-pale, but from being dark or something between dark and pale. Similarly, something becomes musical from being not-musical, and not from every way of being not-musical but from being unmusical or from being something (if there is anything) between musical and unmusical. Nor, on the other hand, does anything perish primarily into a random thing. The pale thing, for instance, does not perish into the musical thing (except coincidentally), but into the not-pale thing, and not into a random not-pale thing, but into the dark thing or into something between pale and dark. In the same way the musical thing perishes into the not-musical thing, and not into a random not-musical thing, but into the unmusical thing or into something between musical and unmusical.

226 ARISTOTLE, *Physics* 189ᵇ30–191ᵃ12   Let us, then, give our own account of coming to be, in the following way. ... When we say that something comes to be one thing from being another, and a different thing from being a different thing, we refer either to simple or to compound things. What I mean is this: it is possible that a man comes to be musical, that the not-musical thing comes to be musical, and that the not-musical man comes to be a musical man. By 'simple thing coming to be' I mean the man and the not-musical thing; and by 'simple thing that comes into being' I mean the musical thing.

By 'compound' I mean both the thing that comes into being and what comes to be that thing, whenever we say that the not-musical man comes to be a musical man. In one type of case we say not only that something comes to be, but also that it comes to be one thing from being another—for instance, musical from being not-musical. But we do not say this about everything; for the man did not come to be musical from being a man, but rather the man came to be musical. When something comes to be something (in the sense in which we say a simple thing comes to be something), in some cases it remains when it comes to be something, and in other cases it does not remain. The man, for instance, remains a man and is still a man when he comes to be musical, whereas the not-musical or unmusical thing, either simple or compound, does not remain.

Now that we have made these distinctions, here is something we can grasp from every case of coming to be, if we look at them all in the way described. In every case there must be some subject that comes to be something; even if it is one in number, it is not one in form (by 'in form' I mean the same as 'in account')—for being a man is not the same as being an unmusical thing. One thing that comes to be remains, and one does not remain. The thing that is not opposite remains, since the man remains; but the not-musical thing, or the unmusical thing, does not remain. Nor does the thing compounded from both (for instance, the unmusical man) remain. We say that something comes to be one thing from being another (as opposed to saying that one thing comes to be another) more often in cases where something does not remain; for instance, we say that a man comes to be musical from being unmusical, but not that the unmusical comes to be musical from a man. Still, sometimes we speak in the same way in cases where a thing remains; we say, for instance, that a statue comes to be from bronze, not that the bronze comes to be a statue. ...

Things are said to come to be in many ways, and some things are said not to come to be, but to come to be something; only substances are said to come to be unqualifiedly. In the other cases it is evident that there must be some subject that comes to be something; for in fact, when something comes to be of some quantity or quality, or relative to another, or somewhere, something is the subject, because a substance is the only thing that is never said of any other subject, whereas everything else is said of a substance. However, substances—the things that are without qualification—also come to be from some subject. This will become evident if we examine it; for in every case there is something that is a subject from which the thing that comes to be comes to be, as plants and animals come to be from seed. ... And so it is clear from what has been said that, in every case, what comes to be is composite: there is something that comes into being and something that comes to be this. And this latter thing is of two sorts: either the subject or the opposite. I mean, for instance, that the unmusical is opposite, and the man is subject;

and that the lack of figure, shape, and order is the opposite, and the bronze, stone, or gold is the subject. ... The nature that is subject is knowable by analogy. For as bronze is to a statue, or wood is to a bed, or as the shapeless before it acquires a shape is to anything that has a shape, so the nature that is subject is to a substance, a this, and a being.

Substance and non-substance

227 The capacity to persist through change makes an individual man a primary 'substance' (*ousia*; **232**); he is the subject of the contraries and they are not his subject.[3] The contraries are assigned to one or another non-substance 'category'[4]—quality, quantity, and so on (**228**). In calling something an *ousia* Aristotle implies that it is in some way a basic reality. The primary substances are the subjects presupposed by the possibility of change.

Other people agree with Aristotle in recognizing some things as *ousiai*, but disagree about which things these are. Aristotle takes Democritus to have claimed that the atoms are *ousiai* (**84**). Plato calls forms *ousiai*, implying that they are basic realities, explaining the features of other things. Aristotle regards individual men, horses, and so on as primary *ousiai*, because they are basic elements in change; changes happen to them, and so any account of change must presuppose them. On this point he disagrees with Plato about which things are basic realities; in treating material subjects as basic realities, he is closer to the Atomist position.

He also, however, uses *ousia*, as Plato does, for essence, which we mention in answering the Socratic question 'What is it?' (**142**). This use of *ousia* is also intelligible as picking out the basic reality. If we ask what the basic reality of a triangle is, the definition of a triangle answers our question. In Aristotle's terms, this definition tells us the 'essence' (*ti esti*, *ti ên einai*) of a triangle, and he often uses 'essence' and *ousia* interchangeably.

Aristotle's conception of *ousia*, therefore, includes both the idea of a subject and the idea of essence. Questions about the relation between these two elements are among the most difficult questions about Aristotle's view of *ousia*. These questions may be easier if we consider some of the different tasks for which Aristotle uses his conception of *ousia*, and examine the relation of *ousia* to matter and form.

To express the basic status of a primary substance, Aristotle claims that it is a 'subject' (or 'underlying thing', *hupokeimenon*). We can roughly grasp this

---

[3] *Ousia* is an abstract noun formed from the verb 'to be'; the best translation might be 'being' or 'reality', but 'substance' or 'essence' ('the *ousia* of *x*') has become traditional in discussions of Aristotle. *Ousia* in Plato; **181** n., **193**, **202**, **586**.

[4] *katêgoria*, literally 'predication'.

conception of a subject by recalling three different, but connected, uses of 'subject':

(1) The subject of a sentence is the noun to which verbs and adjectives are attached.

(2) The subject of a speech is the topic that the speech is primarily about and seeks to expound.

(3) The subject of a change is what the change happens to, what undergoes the change.

This general idea of the basic thing that other things are about helps to explain why Aristotle identifies primary substance with a subject. The subject is what the various properties and characteristics are about, or attributed to. This man is the subject both of the species man and the genus animal (which belong to him essentially) and of paleness and a weight of 80 kilos (which belong to him coincidentally, non-essentially).

Primary substances are not only subjects, but basic subjects. As Aristotle puts it, they are neither 'said of' a subject nor 'in' a subject, whereas other things are either said of them as subjects or in them as subjects (**229**). 'Other things' are of two sorts:

(a) The species horse and the genus animal are what we mention to say what an individual horse is; they are therefore secondary substances, said of the individual horse.

(b) Properties such as pale, or frisky, or six feet tall are all in an individual horse as subject, but are not said of it. These properties do not tell us what the individual is, since they do not place it into its species; but they describe it. They belong to the various non-substance categories (**231**).

These things that are said of primary substances are universals (*katholou*; or 'general') rather than particulars; they exist in many places at once, whereas a particular is in only one place (**230**).[5] Aristotle, then, affirms the reality of universals that are not reducible to particulars, or to words or concepts. In his view, Plato was right to recognize the reality of universals, but wrong to treat them as though they were independent of the particulars that they are said of or in (**221, 223**).

The division between what is said of a primary substance and what is in it corresponds roughly to the division between 'essential' (or 'intrinsic') and 'coincidental' (or 'accidental') properties (**233–4**);[6] hence Aristotle sometimes says that being a horse is an essential property of this horse, whereas being pale or dark is one of its coincidental properties.

---

[5] Most interpreters believe that particulars as well as universals in non-substance categories are in primary substances.

[6] The correspondence is not exact, since 'distinctive properties' (**233**) are necessary, but not part of the essence.

Both these divisions (said of–in; essential–coincidental) reflect facts about change: Socrates could not cease to be a man without ceasing to exist; hence a change from being a man would not be a change of which Socrates is the subject, since he would not remain after the change. That is why being a man is an essential property of Socrates, so that man is said of him. He could, however, cease to be pale without ceasing to exist; hence a change from being pale to being dark would be a change of which he is the subject. That is why being pale is a coincidental property of Socrates, so that pale is 'in' rather than 'said of' primary substance.

....

228 ARISTOTLE, *Categories* 1^b25–2^a11 Of things said without combination, each signifies either substance, or quantity, or quality, or relative, or where, or when, or being in a position, or having, or acting on, or being affected. To describe these in outline, here are some examples. Substance: man, horse. Quantity: two feet long, three feet long. Quality: white, grammatical. Relative: double, half, larger. Where: in the Lyceum, in the market-place. When: yesterday, last year. Being in a position: is lying, is sitting. Having: has shoes on, has armour on. Acting on: cutting, burning. Being affected: being cut, being burnt. None of the things just mentioned is said all by itself in any affirmation, but an affirmation results from the combination of these things with one another. For every affirmation seems to be either true or false, whereas nothing said without combination—for instance, man, white, runs, wins—is either true or false.

229 ARISTOTLE, *Categories* 2^a11–19 What is called substance most strictly, primarily, and most of all, is what is neither said of any subject nor in any subject—for instance, an individual man or horse. Secondary substances are both the species in which the things primarily called substances belong and the genera of these species. An individual man, for instance, belongs in the species man, and animal is the genus of the species; these things, then (for instance, man and animal), are called secondary substances.

230 ARISTOTLE, *On Interpretation* 17^a38–$^b1$ Some things are universals, others are particulars. By universal I mean what is naturally such as to be predicated of more than one thing; by particular, what is not such. Man, for instance, is a universal, whereas Callias is a particular.

231 ARISTOTLE, *Categories* 2^b29–36 It is not surprising that, after the primary substances, only their species and genera are said to be secondary substances; for they are the only things predicated that reveal the primary substance. For if one says what an individual man is, it will be appropriate to mention either the species or the genus, though it will be more informative to mention man than animal. But it would be inappropriate to mention anything else—for instance, white or runs or any other such thing.

232 ARISTOTLE, *Categories* 4ᵃ10–21 It seems most distinctive of substance that numerically one and the same thing is able to receive contraries. ... An individual man, for instance, being one and the same, becomes at one time pale, at another time dark, and hot and cold, and bad and good.

233 ARISTOTLE, *Topics* 101ᵇ37–102ᵇ14 We must say, then, what a definition, a distinctive property, a genus, and a coincident are. A definition is an account that signifies the essence.[7] One provides either an account to replace a name or an account to replace an account—for it is also possible to define some of the things signified by an account. ... if we are able to argue dialectically that things are the same and that they are different, we will in the same way be well supplied to take on definitions; for once we have shown that two things are not the same, we will have undermined the definition. The converse, however, is not true; showing that two things are the same is not enough to establish a definition, whereas showing that two things are not the same is enough to destroy a definition. A distinctive[8] property is one that does not reveal the essence, but belongs only to that subject and is reciprocally predicated of it. It is distinctive of man, for instance, to be receptive of grammatical knowledge; for if someone is a man, he is receptive of grammatical knowledge, and if someone is receptive of grammatical knowledge, he is a man. ... A genus is what is essentially predicated of a plurality of things differing in species. Let us count as essentially predicated whatever it is appropriate to mention if we are asked what a given thing is; when we are asked what man is, for instance, it is appropriate to say that it is an animal. ... A coincident is whatever, while being none of these things—neither a definition nor a distinctive property nor a genus—belongs to the subject. Again, it is whatever admits both of belonging and of not belonging to one and the same subject. Being seated, for instance, admits both of belonging and of not belonging to one and the same subject, and so does being pale, since the same subject may easily be pale at one time and not pale at another. The second of these two definitions of coincident is better. For if the first is stated, we will understand it only if we first know what a definition, a distinctive property, and a genus are; the second, however, is sufficient in its own right for our knowing what is spoken of in its own right. ...

234 ARISTOTLE, *Metaphysics* 1025ᵃ14–24 We call a coincident whatever belongs to something and can be truly said of it, but neither of necessity nor usually ... A musician might be white, but since this does not happen of necessity nor usually, we call it a coincident. Therefore, since these belong to a subject, and some of them belong to it in a particular place and at a particu-

---

[7] Or 'what <the subject> is'.

[8] Or 'peculiar'. Cf. **236, 246, 409, 558** (but in these passages distinctive properties are not contrasted with the essence).

lar time, whatever belongs to a subject—but not because it is this subject—at this time or in this place, will be a coincident.

How many substances?

235 If Aristotle's analysis of change is right, our views about the sorts of change that happen will be connected with our views about the sorts of substances there are. Aristotle believes that when Socrates becomes pale or dark, no new substance comes into being, and hence this change is a qualified becoming. If we disagree with him, we will recognize more unqualified becomings than he recognizes; we will count Socrates' ceasing to be pale and becoming dark as the perishing of the pale-Socrates and the unqualified coming to be of the dark-Socrates. In that case, we will reject the distinction Aristotle draws between genuine subjects and merely coincidental compounds (such as pale-Socrates, composed of a genuine subject and one of its coincidents).

When Socrates dies, this is a case of perishing, according to Aristotle, not simply of qualified becoming. If we disagree with him, we will recognize fewer unqualified becomings, and hence fewer genuine subjects, than he recognizes. We will say Socrates is not a genuine subject; the only genuine subject is the one that persists from the time before his coming into being until the time after his perishing.

Aristotle's predecessors sometimes (in his view) recognize too many unqualified becomings, sometimes too few. Acceptance of a compositional criterion of persistence requires belief in unqualified becomings where Aristotle sees only qualified becomings. This is Heracleitus' view (**45**). It is also the Atomists' view, in so far as they treat collections of matter such as tables, trees, and so on, as subjects of change.

Other Presocratic naturalists allow many fewer unqualified becomings than Aristotle allows, because they do not regard individual men, horses, and so on as (in Aristotle's terms) primary substances. Aristotle illustrates this position with an example of Antiphon's (**236**). When we consider apparent cases of unqualified becoming, we notice that there is some underlying matter that persists throughout the change; hence we may conclude that what we thought was an unqualified becoming was really no more than a qualified becoming in the more basic subject.

The Atomists also accept this eliminative view,[9] in so far as they believe that the processes we ordinarily regard as unqualified becomings and perishings of trees, dogs, and so on, are not really unqualified becomings, since they are nothing more than local rearrangements of the atoms. They believe (in Aristotle's terms) that the conventionally recognized subjects of common sense are not

---

[9] Eliminative Atomism: **90**, **312**, **351**.

real subjects, and that only the atoms are genuine subjects and substances; hence they treat matter as the only substance, and deny that there are any genuine substances whose form—in contrast to their components—is essential to them.

In Aristotle's view, the Atomists have both an overgenerous view of unqualified becoming (by the first criterion Aristotle ascribes to them, which makes any change of components an unqualified becoming) and an over-restrictive view (by the second criterion, which treats all change as a mere rearrangement of atoms). Hence he takes their position to be both internally inconsistent and incapable of marking the appropriate distinctions between qualified and unqualified becoming.

An Atomist might reply that the choice between the more and less generous criterion is arbitrary. Perhaps they are just two ways of describing the same facts; if so, their failure to capture our ordinary distinction between types of becoming is unimportant, because this distinction captures no genuine feature of reality. To see Aristotle's answer to this defence of the Atomist position, we must consider his views on form more closely.

----

236 ARISTOTLE, *Physics* 193ᵃ9–28[10]   Some people think the nature and substance of a natural thing is the primary constituent present in it, having no order in its own right, so that the nature of a bed, for instance, is the wood, and the nature of a statue is the bronze. A sign of this, according to Antiphon, is the fact that if you were to bury a bed and the rotting residue were to become able to sprout, what would come into being would be wood, not a bed. He thinks that this is because the conventional[11] arrangement, i.e. the result of craft, is a coincident of the wood, whereas the substance is what remains continuously while it is affected in these ways. And if each of these things is related to some further thing in the same way (bronze and gold, for instance, to water; bones and wood to earth; and so on with anything else), that further thing is also their nature and substance. This is why different people say that fire or earth or air or water, or some of these, or all of them, is the nature of existing things. For whenever any of these people supposes one, or more than one, of these things to be the primary constituent, he takes this or these to be all the substance there is, and he takes everything else to be attributes, states, and conditions of these things; and each of these is held to be everlasting (since they do not change from themselves), but the other things come to be and are destroyed an unlimited number of times.

237 ARISTOTLE, *Generation and Corruption* 314ᵃ6–ᵇ8   Some of the early thinkers say that what is called unqualified coming to be is alteration, while

----

[10] Aristotle on the naturalists; cf. **43**.
[11] *Nomos*; **125**.

others say that alteration is different from coming to be. For those who say that the whole universe is some one thing, and make everything come to be from one thing, have to say that coming to be is alteration, and that what <allegedly> comes to be in the strict sense is <really only> altered. Those who say, by contrast, that matter is more than one thing—for instance, Empedocles, Anaxagoras, Leucippus—have to say that coming to be and alteration are different. Anaxagoras, however, misunderstood his own statements. At any rate, he says that coming to be and perishing are the same as alteration, even though, like others, he says that there are many elements. ... [314ᵇ1] Those, then, who constitute everything out of some one thing must say that coming to be and perishing are alteration. For in their view, in every change the subject remains one and the same; and that is the sort of thing that we say is altered. Those, however, who recognize more than one kind of thing must distinguish alteration from coming to be; for when things are combined there is coming to be, and when they are dissolved there is perishing. That is why Empedocles also speaks in this way, when he says 'There is no birth of anything, but only mixture and the dissolution of things that have been mixed.'

Form as cause

238 To answer the Atomists, Aristotle needs to explain why the perishing of Socrates or of this dog is really an unqualified perishing, and why Socrates' becoming dark after being pale, or the dog's becoming fat after being thin, is not the unqualified perishing of the pale-Socrates or the thin-dog, but only an alteration. To answer these questions, Aristotle must explain why Socrates and the dog are substances, but the pale-Socrates and the thin-dog are not.

According to Aristotle, we should reject a strong compositional criterion of identity and continuity that makes every change in a subject count as its destruction; this is how he differs from Heracleitus (**45**). But he also rejects the other Presocratic view, that if anything survives a change, no genuine subject has gone out of existence. Even though the dog's matter survives after the death of the dog, Aristotle believes that a substance has gone out of existence. According to this criterion of continuity, this dog is a substance persisting from its birth to its death. Continuity requires the persistence of the same form, not of the same matter.

Why does the persistence of the same form mark an important type of continuing subject? Common sense, admittedly, relies on form; but why should we accept common sense? According to some Presocratic views, the nature of things—their underlying reality—is their matter (**41–4**). Aristotle denies that the nature of things is purely material. Form as well as matter is nature, because form explains the characteristic properties and behaviour of the subject whose form it is. Hence some substances essentially have the forms they have.

This claim about form rests on Aristotle's conception of a thing's nature as its internal 'origin' or 'principle' (*archê*) of change and stability. Since a thing's form explains why the thing changes in some respects, but is stable in other respects, its form is its nature. The explanatory aspect of the form makes it one of Aristotle's four causes (**97–9**).

To show how form is a cause, Aristotle appeals to the production of artefacts and to intentional action in general. Suppose we ask why all the legs of this chair are of the same length, or why there is padding on only one side of the solid vertical and horizontal parts of the chair, but none on the legs. We could answer this question by describing how the chair was made, and pointing out that one part of the process involved making the legs of equal length, etc. But this answer would not satisfy us; we still might ask 'But why was it made this way, given that it could easily have been made some other way?' To answer that question, we must mention the fact that a chair is for sitting in, and it is usually better for sitting in if it has these features.

Here, then, we refer to the form, since we assume that a chair is for sitting in. We refer to the definition of a chair, giving an essential property. This essential property is formal rather than material. It does not refer to the matter—wood, metal, or plastic—that the chair is made of, but to the arrangement of the matter. We can write the syllable 'CAT' by writing the right letters in the right order, whether we write them in ink or in mud; but writing 'TCA' or 'ATC' is not forming the syllable 'CAT' (cf. **259**).

In the case of artefacts, the formal cause also specifies the final cause; the designer was aiming at the end of making something for sitting in, and this end guided the manufacture of the chair. Moreover, we could give the same explanation for chairs that were manufactured in quite different ways from different materials; if we want to understand why all of them are made the way they are, we have to mention the formal and the final cause; it is not enough to mention the material components.

....

239 ARISTOTLE, *Physics* 192^{b}8–193^{a}1 Some existing things are natural, while others are due to other causes. Those that are natural are animals and their parts, plants, and the simple bodies (earth, fire, air and water); for we say that these things and things of this sort are natural. All these things evidently differ from those that are not naturally constituted, since each of them has within itself an origin of change and stability—for some things, in change and stability in place; for others, in growth and shrinking; for others, in alteration. In contrast to these, a bed, a cloak, or any other artefact, in so far as this is true of it and it is a product of a craft, has no innate impulse to change; but in so far as it is coincidentally made of stone or earth or a mixture of these, it has an innate impulse to change, and just to that extent. This is because a nature is a type of

origin and cause of change and stability within those things to which it primarily belongs in their own right and not coincidentally. (By 'not coincidentally' I mean this: someone who is a doctor might cause himself to be healthy,
but it is not in so far as he is being healed that he has the medical science; on
the contrary, it is coincidental that the same person is a doctor and is being
healed, and that is why the two characteristics are sometimes separated from
each other.) ... A nature, then, is what we have said; and the things that have
a nature are those that have this sort of origin. All these things are substances;
for <a substance> is a sort of subject, and a nature is invariably in a subject.
The things that are in accordance with nature include both these and whatever belongs to them in their own right, as travelling upwards belongs to
fire—for this neither is nor has a nature, but is natural and in accordance with
nature.

Causes in nature

240 It is fairly easy, then, to show that the form is a cause of artefacts. Aristotle
sees that it is more difficult to show that it is a cause of natural organisms. Artefacts are produced by the intentional actions of designers, but—in Aristotle's
view—no intelligent designer intends or produces natural organisms with their
goal-directed features. He denies, however, that this difference affects the truth
of claims about formal and final causes in nature.

He defends final causes (teleology, from *telos*, 'end' or 'goal') in nature by
denying that all natural processes happen only 'by necessity'. He mentions
Empedocles as a believer in necessity, but his remarks also apply to the Atomists, who explain every substance and event as the result of combinations of
atoms in accordance with laws that necessarily determine their behaviour (**351**,
353).

In Aristotle's view, the function of an organ in a plant or animal is its final
cause. Organs perform functions that benefit the whole organism; he claims
that they exist in order to carry out these beneficial functions. We must refer to
the benefit of the whole organism if we are to understand the different
processes in the parts. These processes happen as they do because they fit together for the benefit of the whole organism.

The form, then, has the same final-causal role in organisms as in artefacts; it
explains their change and stability by reference to ends and functions. The functions that belong to the form of an organism explain why this organism changes
and is stable in its characteristic ways (why, for instance, the heart pumps blood
as it does, why the digestive organs work as they do). To this extent, artefacts
and organisms should be understood in the same way, except that no design or
intention is required in organisms. Processes and activities of natural organisms
are to be explained functionally, by reference to their contribution to the good

of the organism as a whole. The organism as a whole is something organized for living a certain way. The functional organization of the matter is the form; hence the form explains why the organism is constructed in the way it is and behaves as it does. The form is the nature of the organism.[12]

These claims about final causation and form raise further issues. When Aristotle claims that a heart is for pumping blood to benefit the organism, he implies that there is some causal connection between the benefit to the organism and the heart's pumping blood. But he does not say exactly what makes this causal claim true. On the one hand, he does not say that organisms are the products of intelligent design (as Plato and the Stoics believe).[13] On the other hand, he does not believe that organisms result from any process of evolution.

How, then, should we understand the relation between final causes and other sorts of causes? Two answers have been defended:

(1) An 'incompatibilist' view (**248**). Every goal-directed process requires some material process (nutrition, for instance, requires the various processes involved in digesting food), but the goal-directed process cannot be wholly constituted by any material process or processes. If it were wholly constituted by such processes, it would be fully explicable by material and efficient causes, and therefore would have no final cause.

(2) A 'compatibilist' view: Even if every goal-directed process were wholly constituted by material processes, each of them explicable by material-efficient causes, the final-causal explanation would still be the only adequate explanation of the process as a whole. Final causes are irreducible to material-efficient causes, because the explanations given by final causes cannot be replaced by equally good explanations referring only to these other causes. Sometimes there is a systematic causal connection between benefit to the organism and the structure or working of a particular organ or process; the organ or process works differently in different circumstances to maintain the benefit to the organism (it takes longer, for instance, to digest fats than to digest carbohydrates). In such cases the organ or process is as it is for the sake of the benefit to the organism.

The difference between these two views of final causation may be illustrated from Empedocles' account of apparent teleology (**242–3**). According to Empedocles, animals acquire teeth of all kinds—both suitable and unsuitable—because of random processes not directed to any goal. The animals we encounter have suitable teeth only because those with unsuitable teeth have died out. This

---

[12] Aristotle's arguments concern the benefits of specific processes for specific organisms, not the benefits of one organism to another. However, he also affirms his belief in the latter sort of teleology in the natural world. See **596–8**.

[13] Design; **589**, **591–3**, **614–15**. The independence of teleology from claims about intelligent design is important in understanding the 'function argument' in the *Ethics*. See **407**.

account gives a non-teleological account of the apparent basis of goal-directed processes; hence, from an incompatibilist view, it excludes any true teleological explanation.

From a compatibilist point of view, however, this account suggests a causal basis for teleology. If later generations have the sort of teeth they have because these teeth had survival value for members of earlier generations, these later generations have them because of their survival value. Hence, in these later generations, the animals have the teeth they have because they are beneficial, and so belief in final causation is vindicated.

The question about these accounts of Aristotle on final causation raises more general questions about whether his claims about form conflict with different versions of materialism, and about where he basically disagrees with the Presocratics. One version of materialism claims simply that everything that exists is made out of matter, and that all events consist in interactions of matter (**249**). Aristotle's claims about formal and final causes do not assert or imply the falsity of this claim, if they allow a compatibilist interpretation. In that case, he disagrees fundamentally with Atomism not because of the truth or falsity of materialism, but because Atomism seeks to eliminate, and not to vindicate, explanations that essentially refer to the form rather than to the material composition.[14]

Aristotle's teleological claims influence his detailed investigation of plants and animals; his discussion of the elephant's trunk provides one vivid example (**246**). In this case, as in many others, he offers both teleological and non-teleological explanations of various aspects of an animal. He does not claim that every aspect of the structure and behaviour of natural organisms can be explained teleologically; some material and efficient causes operate without formal and final causes.

The limits of teleological explanation are emphasized by Theophrastus, Aristotle's successor as head of the Lyceum (**21**). Theophrastus mentions some of the difficulties and apparent exceptions (**247**) that encourage the Epicureans to abandon appeal to final causes altogether. But he does not endorse the Epicurean reaction.

....

241 ARISTOTLE, *Parts of Animals* 639^{b}14–21   The primary cause is apparently the one that we say is for something. For this is the form, and the form is the origin, in the products of craft and in naturally constituted things alike. For the doctor or the builder begins by fixing, in thought or perception, the definition of health or a house, and goes on to provide the forms and the causes of each thing he produces, and why it should be produced in this way. And, moreover, what something is for—i.e. the fine—is present in the products of nature more than in the products of craft.

[14] Vindication and elimination in Atomism; **90**.

242 ARISTOTLE, *Physics* 198ᵇ10–199ᵃ30 We must first say why nature is among the causes that are for something, and then how necessity applies to natural things. For everyone refers things to necessity, saying that since the hot, the cold, and each element have a certain nature, certain other things are and come to be necessarily. For if they mention any cause other than necessity (as one thinker[15] mentions love or strife, and another[16] mentions mind), they just touch on it, then let it go. ...

Why not suppose that nature acts not for something or because it is better, but of necessity, as Zeus rains[17] not to make the grain grow, but of necessity? For it is necessary that what has been drawn up is cooled, and that what has been cooled and become water comes down, and it is coincidental that the grain grows when this has happened. Similarly, if someone's grain is spoiled on the threshing-floor, it does not rain in order to spoil the grain, but this result is coincidental. Why not suppose, then, that the same is true of the parts of natural organisms? On this view, it is by necessity that, for example, the front teeth grow sharp and well adapted for biting, and the back ones broad and useful for chewing food, since this was coincidental, not what they were for. The same will be true of all the other parts that seem to be for something. On this view, then, whenever all the parts came about coincidentally as though they were for something, these animals survived, since their constitution, though coming about by chance, made them suitable. Other animals, however, were differently constituted and so were destroyed; indeed they are still being destroyed, as Empedocles says of the man-headed calves.[18]

This argument, then, and others like it, might puzzle someone. In fact, however, it is impossible for things to be like this. For these and all natural things come to be as they do either always or usually, whereas no result of luck or chance comes to be either always or usually. (For we do not regard frequent winter rain or a summer heat wave, but only summer rain or a winter heat wave, as a result of luck or coincidence.) If, then, these seem either to be coincidental results or to be for something, and they cannot be coincidental or chance results, they are for something. ...

[199ᵃ17] If ... the products of a craft are for something, clearly the products of nature are also for something; for there is the same relation of later stages to earlier in productions of a craft and in productions of nature. This is most evident in the case of animals other than man, since they use neither craft nor inquiry nor deliberation in producing things—indeed this is why some people are puzzled about whether spiders, ants, and other such things operate by understanding or in some other way. If we advance little by little along the

---

[15] Empedocles.
[16] Anaxagoras. See **91, 96, 588**.
[17] Rain; cf. **581**.
[18] Empedocles; **243**.

same lines, it is evident that even in plants things come to be that promote the end—leaves, for instance, grow for the protection of the fruit. If, then, a swallow makes its nest and a spider its web both naturally and for some end, and if plants grow leaves for the sake of the fruit, and send roots down rather than up for the sake of nourishment, it evidently follows that this sort of cause is found in things that come to be and are by nature.

243 AELIAN, *Nature of Animals* xvi. 29 = DK 33 B 61   Empedocles the naturalist, who also speaks of the distinctive character of some animals, says that some hybrids are generated, different in the blending of the form but connected by the unification of the body. These are his words: 'Many grew double-faced, double-chested—man-fronted oxen arose, and again ox-headed men—creatures mixed partly from male partly from female form, fitted with dark limbs.'

244 ARISTOTLE, *Parts of Animals* 642^{a}31–^{b}2[19]   Our proof should be on these lines: respiration, for instance, is for this, but this comes about because of these things of necessity. Necessity sometimes signifies that if that end is to result, it is necessary for these things to be. Sometimes it signifies that things are so by nature. It is necessary, for instance, for the hot to go out and to come back in when it meets resistance, and for the air to flow in. This is all necessary; and when the hot that is inside resists as cooling goes on, the air outside enters or leaves.

245 ARISTOTLE, *Parts of Animals* 658^{b}2–10   No animal has so much hair on the head as man. This, in the first place, is by necessity, because of the fluidity of his brain, and the many sutures in his skull; for wherever there is the most fluid and the most heat, it is necessary for the outgrowth to be largest. But it is also for the sake of protection, to shelter against excessive heat or cold. And since the human brain is larger and more fluid than that of any other animal, it also needs more protection. For the most fluid is also most prone to be heated or chilled, while something in the contrary state is affected less.

246 ARISTOTLE, *Parts of Animals* 658^{b}33–659^{a}23   The elephant has the most distinctive[20] nose, since it is remarkably large and strong. Its nose is used as though it were a hand, to bring food, both fluid and solid, to its mouth. It also uses its nose to uproot trees by coiling it round them, and uses it just as if it were a hand. For the elephant has the nature of a land animal and is a swamp dweller. It gets its food from the water, but it needs to breathe, since it is a land animal and has blood; moreover, because of its excessive weight it cannot move quickly from water to land, as some other sanguineous vivipara that

[19] This follows **99**.
[20] Distinctive properties; **233**.

breathe can do. And so it is necessary for it to deal with the water and dry land in the same way. It is like divers, who are sometimes provided with an instrument for breathing, so that they can stay under the sea a long time, by drawing air from outside the water through the instrument. This is the character of the long nose that nature has given elephants. That is why, whenever they have to make their way through water, they lift their nose above the surface and breathe through it; for the elephant's trunk, as already said, is its nose. Now it would have been impossible for this nose to have done all this if it had been hard and rigid. For its length would then have impeded the animal from getting food from outside, just as the horns of the 'backward-grazing' oxen are said to do—for these are said to walk backwards to graze. It is therefore soft and flexible; and so nature, in its usual way, uses it for an additional task, to serve instead of the fore-feet. …

247 THEOPHRASTUS, *Metaphysics* 10ª21–11ª15   About the view that all things are for something, and that nothing is pointless—the determining of ends is in general not easy, as it is often stated to be. (Where are we to begin, and where are we to set the terminus?) In particular, some things do not seem to be for anything, but to occur, some of them, by coincidence, and others by some sort of necessity, as in the case both of celestial and of most terrestrial phenomena. … [10ᵇ21] In the case of plants and still more of inanimate things that have some definite nature, as it seems, in their shapes and forms and powers, one might ask what these are for … If they are not for anything, we must set limits to what is for something and to the tendency towards the best, and not assume it in all cases without qualification. For even statements of the following kind give rise to some doubt, whether they are made without qualification or with reference to particular cases; when, for instance, it is said without qualification that it is to be expected that nature in all cases aims at the best and, whenever possible, gives things a share in what is everlasting and ordered. The same is true when a similar statement is made about animals; for we are told that where the better is possible, it is never absent, so that, for instance, the windpipe is in front of the gullet because this is more honourable, and the mixture of the blood is best in the middle ventricle of the heart because the middle is most honourable; and similarly with the parts that are for the sake of ornament. For even if this is the aim of nature, still the facts make this at least evident, that there is much that does not serve or receive the good …

248 JONATHAN LEAR, *Aristotle: The Desire to Understand*,[21] p. 36   In the twentieth century much work has been done by philosophers to show that teleological explanations are compatible with mechanical explanations. For

---

[21] Cambridge: CUP, 1988.

example, one can say that the spider builds its web in order to secure nourishment, but one can also explain its orderly activity via its neuro-physiolog-
ical makeup and genetic inheritance. That is, actual physical structure
grounds teleological behaviour. It is important to realize that Aristotle does
not believe in any such compatibility. For Aristotle, the reason one has to cite
the form in its final, realized state is that it is only by reference to that form
that one can understand teleological behaviour.

249 RICHARD BOYD, 'Materialism without Reductionism',[22] p. 85   The materialist asserts that all natural phenomena, all events, processes, objects, and
so forth, are in fact physical: all objects are composed solely of matter and all
events and processes consist solely in interactions between material things.
Mental events, states, and processes, in particular, differ from uncontrover-
sially physical events, states, and processes only in the particular arrangements or configurations of matter and material forces that realize them.
Pains are quite different from, for instance, earthquakes, but the difference is
configurational, not constitutional. They are made of the same sorts of stuff.

Form and identity

250 Aristotle's reasons for regarding form as nature also support his objections
to naturalist views about the extent of unqualified becoming (**90**). An artefact
survives through change even if the same collection of matter does not survive.
A chair could be repainted, or damaged, or repaired, without ceasing to exist
(contrast **55**). The functional organization of the matter remains in being; so
the form remains in being; hence the chair remains in being. Aristotle points out
that simple and apparently uncontroversial judgements about change and becoming presuppose the general views that he sums up in his claims about form.

For artefacts, then, Aristotle has a good objection to a purely compositional
criterion of identity. If the form is stable, even though the composition changes,
the same thing remains in existence. If form is the nature of natural organisms,
they also persist as long as their form persists, even if they change in other ways.
The formal properties are the essential properties of a natural organism; if they
persist, the organism persists through changes in its coincidental properties.

Hence there must be more unqualified becomings than the Atomists supposed. The Atomists are wrong about the extent of unqualified becoming because they have the wrong conception of causes. If a particular subject of
change persists as long as its form persists, the same formal-causal and final-
causal principles explain the behaviour of this matter. The subject has the same

---

[22] In *Readings in Philosophical Psychology*, ed. N. J. Block (Cambridge, Mass.: Harvard UP, 1980),
67–106.

goal-directed structure even if its composition is not exactly the same (cf. **334**). The Atomists must be wrong, then, to suppose that bits of matter are the only genuine substances (**84**), and the only genuinely persistent subjects of change. If ordinary substances were simply collections, a compositional criterion of persistence would apply to them; but since their persistence does not depend on composition, they are not simply collections.

The importance of form for the understanding of persistence is clear in the case of nutrition and growth. Aristotle points out that the organism grows and persists, even if no individual material part of it persists. In a comparison that recalls Heracleitus on the river, he maintains that even if the matter is always changing like water flowing in and out of the same measure, the persistence of the same measure implies a persistent subject (**252**). This comparison helps us to understand the persistence of an organism with constantly changing matter.

....

251 ARISTOTLE, *Parts of Animals* 640^{b}22–641^{a}14   For it is not enough to say what each of these parts is made of—of fire or earth, for instance. If we were speaking of a bed or any other artefact, we would try to define its form rather than its matter (for instance, bronze or wood), or at any rate we would define the matter as the matter of the compound. For a bed is this form in this matter, or this matter of this sort. And so we ought to speak of the thing's form and the sort of character it has as well as its matter, since the nature corresponding to the form is more important than the material nature. If, then, an animal and its parts have their being by having their figure and colour, Democritus will prove to be right, since this is what he seems to suppose.[23] At any rate he says it is clear to everyone what the human form is, assuming that man is known by his visible figure and his colour. This is false, however; a dead man also has the same visible shape and figure that the living man has, but still it is not a man. Further, it is impossible for something to be a hand if it is not in the right condition—if, for instance, it is a bronze or wooden hand; in that case it can be a hand only homonymously,[24] just as the doctor in a picture is a doctor only homonymously. For it will be unable to perform the function of a hand, just as a doctor in a picture or a stone flute is unable to perform the function of a doctor or flute. Similarly, none of the parts of a dead man is any longer the relevant sort of part—an eye or a hand, for instance. Hence Democritus' claim lacks the appropriate qualifications; it is no better than a carpenter claiming that a wooden hand is a hand. For that is how

[23] Democritus' materialism; **312**.
[24] Aristotle takes banks (for instance) to be homonymous because 'bank' has a different definition in 'The bank is open for business' and 'The bank burst because of the flood'. Here he claims (roughly speaking) that we use 'doctor' in a different sense when we say that the doctor in the painting is carrying a medicine chest; we simply apply 'doctor' to a likeness of a doctor. For the same reasons, a dead hand is no longer a hand in the strict sense, but only in a derivative sense, since it is merely a likeness of a hand. Cf. **252**, **257**, **336**, **558**.

the naturalists describe the coming to be and the causes of something's figure. For suppose we ask, 'What capacities produced this?'. Presumably the carpenter will mention an axe or an auger, whereas the naturalist will mention air and earth. The carpenter, however, gives the better answer. For he will not suppose that it is enough to say that when his tool struck the wood, this part became hollow and this part plane. He will also mention the cause that explains why and for what end he struck this sort of blow—that is to say, in order to produce this or that sort of shape. It is clear, then, that the naturalists are wrong, and that we must say an animal has the character we have described. We must say, both about the animal itself and about each of its parts, what it is and what sort of thing, just as we also speak of the form of the bed.

252 ARISTOTLE, *Generation and Corruption* 321^{b}16–32   To grasp the cause of growth we must draw some distinctions. First, a non-uniform part grows by the growth of uniform parts, since it is composed of them. Second, flesh and bone and each of these uniform parts, like the other things that have form in matter, have two aspects, since both matter and form are called flesh or bone. It is possible, then, for something, in so far as it is form, to grow in every part by the addition of something; but in so far as it is matter, this is not possible. For we must take it to be similar to measuring water with the same measure, where what comes to be is always one thing after another. Similarly, the matter of flesh grows and not every single part of it is added to, but rather one flows out and another is added; every part of the shape and the form, however, is added to. It is still clearer in the case of the non-uniform parts—a hand, for instance—that it has grown in proportion; for the fact that the matter is different from the form is clearer in this case than in the case of flesh and other uniform parts. That is why, when an animal has died, we are more inclined to think flesh or bone still exists than that a hand or arm does.[25]

Form as substance

253 Aristotle sums up and develops some of his reflections on substance and related questions, in the complex and often obscure argument of *Metaphysics* vii. His discussion is too complex to be adequately represented by a few extracts. Moreover, disagreements about the interpretation of his position make even the choice of extracts controversial; it may omit what some people regard as the crucial parts of Aristotle's solution (if, indeed, he offers one). But it is worth mentioning some points in his discussion, to see how they are connected with the issues already raised.

Aristotle discusses the claim of matter to be substance (**256**). The claim is ambiguous, and he recognizes three claims that it might express:

[25] Dead organisms and their parts; **257, 336**.

(i)   Matter is the only sort of substance there is.

(ii) It is the primary type of substance.

(iii) It is one type of substance, or substance to some degree.

Aristotle rejects the first two claims, but accepts the third.

Aristotle's favoured candidate for substance is form. He argues for it by claiming that natural organisms are essentially formal, and cannot be identified simply with their matter (**257**). This claim can be understood partly from the contrast between mere heaps of matter and genuine substances, which are unified by their form (**258**). The form, including the organism's vital functions, is the criterion of persistence through time because it is the criterion of unity at a time. It makes a heap of material constituents—a collection of flesh and bones, for instance—a single living organism. The vital functions are the final cause of the movements of the different parts. The organism remains in being through changes of matter, as long as it retains its formal, functional properties.

We might give two different accounts of how Aristotle develops these observations into an account of form and matter and their relation to substance:

1. He takes the form to be the universal essence that all members of a species share, and the matter to be the source of their particularity. Socrates and Plato share one form, since each is a human being. Each is what he is because of his form, since he remains in being as long as he is human. But they are two different human beings in so far as the specific property (being human) occurs in two different pieces of matter. The one form is the substance, i.e. the essence (**227**), of the two particulars.

2. He recognizes not only universal forms, but also particular forms that are particular substances. The particular form is a subject in its own right, not simply a coincident of matter. Since it is a mark of a substance to persist through change, and since the form of an organism persists through change, the form is itself a persisting subject. According to one view, Aristotle takes an organic substance—this particular dog or horse, for instance—to be identical to its form, not to the material constituents that embody the form at different times. According to another view, he regards the form as one particular and the dog as a further particular, the compound of the form and the matter.

It is difficult to decide between these two interpretations (and variants of them) of Aristotle's views. Each interpretation expresses something that Aristotle might reasonably infer from the claims we have discussed about form and matter; each raises various difficulties about the understanding of different passages, and about the coherence of Aristotle's general position.[26]

The discussion of form as substance is closely connected with Aristotle's

---

[26] See esp. **257**, **259**.

treatment of questions about the relation of body and soul. Since he identifies the form with the soul, he believes—according to one conception of form—that an organic substance is properly identified with its soul (**334–7**). Our explanation of the connection between an organism and its soul will depend on our view about the way in which form is substance.

A further application of Aristotle's claims about substance is his conception of divine substances. These are pure form, because form is actuality. We can see what Aristotle means by considering ordinary substances. The form of an artefact or organism consists in the functions that are the states and activities actualizing the capacities of the constituent matter (iron can be sharpened to cut, and a knife is the actualization of this capacity in the iron). Hence Aristotle identifies matter with capacity and form with actuality (cf. **334–5**). Divine beings are permanently active, and hence do not include any element of capacity or potentiality; hence they are form without matter (**601–3**). In their case, as in artefacts and organisms, form is substance.

....

254   ARISTOTLE, *Metaphysics* 1017^{b}10–26   The things called substance are, first, the simple bodies (earth, fire, water, and everything of that sort) and in general bodies and the things composed from them (animals and divine things and their parts). All these things are said to be substance because they are not said of a subject, but the other things are said of them. In another way, whatever is the cause of the being of the things that are not said of a subject, by being present in them—for instance, the soul for an animal—is called substance. Further, the parts present in such things, defining them and signifying a this, the things with whose destruction the whole is destroyed, are called substance; for instance, the body is destroyed with the destruction of the plane (as some people say), and the plane with the destruction of the line. And in general it seems to some people that number is this sort of thing, since if it is destroyed nothing exists, and it defines all things. Further, the essence, whose account is a definition, is also said to be the substance of a thing. It turns out, then, that substance is spoken of in two ways. It is both the ultimate subject, said of nothing further, and whatever, being a this, is also separable—this is true of the shape, i.e. the form, of a thing.

255   ARISTOTLE, *Metaphysics* 1028^{a}10–^{b}7   Being is spoken of in many ways ... for it signifies either what-it-is and a this, or quality, or quantity, or any of the other things predicated in this way.[27] But while being is spoken of in this many ways, it is evident that among these the primary being is the what-it-is, which signifies substance. For whenever we say what quality this has, we call it good or bad, not six feet long or a man, whereas whenever we say what it is, we call it a man or a god, not pale or hot or six feet long; and the other things

[27] The categories; **288**.

are called beings by belonging to this type of being—some as quantities, some as qualities, some as affections, some in some other such way. ... Clearly, then, it is because of substance that each of those other things is also a being, so that what is in the primary way—what is not something, but is without qualification a being—is substance. Now the primary is so spoken of in many ways, but still, substance is primary in every way: in nature, in account, and in knowledge.[28] For none of the other things predicated is separable, but only substance. Substance is also primary in account, since its account is necessarily present in the account of a given thing. Moreover, we think we know a thing most of all whenever we know what man or fire, for instance, is, rather than when we know its quality or quantity or place; for indeed we know each of these only when we know *what* the quantity or the quality *is*. Indeed, the old question—always pursued from long ago till now, and always raising puzzles—'What is being?' is just the question 'What is substance?' For substance is what some say is one and others say is more than one, some saying that it is limited in number, others that it is unlimited. And so we too must make it our main, our primary, indeed (we may say) our only, task to study what it is that is in this way.

256 ARISTOTLE, *Metaphysics* 1028[b]36–1029[a]33 ... The subject is that of which the other things are said, but which is not itself said of anything further; hence we must first determine what it is, since the primary subject seems to be substance most of all. What is so spoken of is in one way the matter, in another way the form, and in a third way the thing composed of these. (By the matter I mean, for example, the bronze; by the form I mean the configuration of the shape; and by the thing composed of them I mean the statue, i.e. the compound.) And so if the form is prior to the matter, and more of a being, it will also, by the same account, be prior to the thing composed of both. We have now said in outline, then, what substance is: it is what is not said of a subject but has the other things said of it.

We must not leave it at that, however, since it is inadequate: first, it is itself unclear, and, further, the matter turns out to be substance. For if the matter is not substance, it is hard to see what other substance there is; for when the other things are removed, nothing evidently remains. For the other things are affections, products, and capacities of bodies; and length, breadth, and depth are kinds of quantities but not substances (for quantity is not substance), but the primary <subject> to which these belong is more of a substance than they are. But when length, breadth, and depth are abstracted, we see that nothing is left, except whatever is determined by these. And so, if we examine it in this way, the matter necessarily appears as the only substance. By matter I mean what, in its own right, is spoken of neither as something, nor

---

[28] Text doubtful.

as of some quantity, nor as any of the other things by which being is determined.[29] For there is something of which each of these is predicated, something whose being is different from that of each of the things predicated; for the other things are predicated of the substance, and the substance is predicated of the matter. And so the last thing, in its own right, is neither something nor of some quantity nor any other <of the things mentioned>; nor <in its own right> is it the negations of these, since the negations as well <as the positive properties> will belong to it <only> coincidentally.

And so, if we study it from this point of view, it turns out that the matter is substance; but that is impossible. For being separable and being a this seem to belong to substance most of all; that is why the form and the compound of both matter and form would seem to be substance more than the matter is. And so the substance composed of both—I mean composed of the matter and the form—should be set aside, since it is posterior to the other two, and clear. The matter is also evident in a way. We must, then, consider the third type of substance, since it is the most puzzling.

257   ARISTOTLE, *Metaphysics* 1035^{a}1–^{b}27   If, then, … matter, form, and the compound of them are all substance, it follows that in one way matter is also called a part of something, but in another way it is not, and in this second way only the components of the account of the form are parts. Flesh, for instance, is not a part of concavity (since it is the matter in which concavity comes to be), but it is a part of snubness. Again, bronze is a part of the compound statue, but not a part of the statue spoken of as form. For it is the form of the statue—i.e. the statue in so far as it has form—and never the material aspect in its own right, that should be spoken of as the statue. This is why the account of a circle does not include that of the segments, whereas the account of a syllable does include that of the letters; for the letters are not matter, but parts of the account of the form, while the segments are material parts in which the form comes to be. … [1035^{b}11] And so all the material parts—i.e. those into which the whole is divided as its matter—are posterior to it, but the parts that are parts of the account and of the substance corresponding to the account are, either all or some of them, prior to the whole.

Now an animal's soul—the substance of what is ensouled—is the substance corresponding to the account; it is the form and essence of the right sort of body. At any rate, a proper definition of each part requires reference to its function, and this function requires perception. Hence the parts of the soul, either all or some of them, are prior to the compound animal, and the same applies to the particular. The body and its parts are posterior to this substance <i.e. the soul>, and its parts are the matter into which the compound, but not this substance, is divided. In a way they are prior to the compound,

[29] The categories; **255**.

but in a way they are not, since they cannot exist when they are separated; for a finger is not an animal's finger in all conditions, but when it is dead, it is only homonymously[30] a finger. <The compound and> some of these parts are mutually dependent, if they are the controlling parts, those on which the account and the substance primarily depend—the heart or the brain, for instance (for it does not matter which of the two it is).

258 ARISTOTLE, *Metaphysics* 1040^{b}5–14   It is evident that even among the generally recognized substances most are capacities. These include the parts of animals (for none of them is separated <as long as they remain parts of animals>; whenever they are separated, they all exist as matter), and also earth, fire, and air. For none of these is one, but each is a sort of heap, until they are worked up and some one thing comes to be from them. One would be most inclined to suppose that the parts of ensouled things that are closely <associated with> the soul are beings both in actuality and in capacity; for they have origins of change from some source in their joints, which is why some animals keep on living when they are divided. But none the less, all these things exist <only> in capacity.

259 ARISTOTLE, *Metaphysics* 1041^{a}9–^{b}33   ... Since, then, substance is some sort of origin and cause, we should proceed from here. In every case, we inquire into the reason why, by asking why one thing belongs to another. ... We might, ... ask why a man is this sort of animal. Here, then, we are clearly not asking why something that is a man is a man. We are inquiring, then, into why one thing belongs to another; that it does belong must already be clear, since otherwise we are inquiring into nothing. For instance, when we inquire into why it thunders, we are asking why there is a noise in the clouds; here we inquire into why one thing belongs to another. Similarly, we ask why these things—for instance, bricks and stones—are a house. Evidently, then, we are inquiring into the cause; and this is the essence (speaking from a logical point of view). In some cases—for instance, presumably, a house or a bed—the cause is what something is for; sometimes it is what first initiated the change, since this is also a cause. We inquire into the latter type of cause in the case of coming to be and perishing; in the case of being as well as in the case of coming to be we inquire into the former type of cause. ... Clearly, we inquire into why the matter is something. We ask, for instance, 'Why are these things a house?' Because the essence of house belongs to them. Similarly, a man is this, or rather is this body having this. Hence we inquire into the cause on account of which the matter is something, i.e. into the form; and this cause is the substance. ...

Now a composite is composed of something in such a way that the whole

---

[30] For this doctrine of homonymy cf. **252**, **336**, **407**, **558**.

thing is one, not as a heap is, but as a syllable is. A syllable is not the letters—
for instance, B and A are not the same thing as BA, nor is flesh fire and earth.
For when the components are dispersed, the flesh or syllable no longer exists,
though the letters or the fire and earth still do. Hence the syllable is something—not only the vowel and the consonant, but also some further thing;
and similarly, flesh is not only fire and earth, or the hot and cold, but also
some further thing. Now suppose that this further thing must be either an element or composed of elements. If it is an element, there will be the same argument over again; for flesh will be composed of this new element, plus fire
and earth, plus some further thing, so that it will go on without limit. If the
further thing is composed of an element, it is clearly not composed of just
one (otherwise it would itself be this one), but of more than one; and then we
will repeat the same argument about it as about flesh or a syllable. It would
seem, however, that this further thing is something other than an element,
and that it is the cause of one thing's being flesh and another thing's being a
syllable, and similarly in the other cases. Now this is the substance of a given
thing; for this is the primary cause of the thing's being <what it is>. Some
things are not substances, but the things that are substances are naturally
constituted; hence this nature—the one that is not an element but an origin—will apparently be substance. An element is what the thing is divided
into, being present in the thing as matter—for instance, the A and the B in the
syllable.

The Stoics on persisting subjects

260 The Stoics seem to develop some aspects of the second interpretation
(**253**) of Aristotle's views about form, subject, and substance.[31] For they agree
with Aristotle's claim (according to that second interpretation) that something's formal properties mark a distinct subject with its own conditions for persistence and perishing. In their view, the existence of an organism requires the
existence of two subjects in the same place at the same time. The 'first' subject
is a purely material subject, whereas the 'second' subject is a formal subject. We
must recognize these two subjects if we are to capture the facts about growth
and persistence. Only a formal subject is capable of growth. A purely material
subject is incapable of growth, because it is incapable of remaining in existence
through any quantitative change.

The Stoic theory of two subjects articulates Heracleitus' reasons for believing we cannot step into the same river twice, and Aristotle's reasons for believing, against Heracleitus, that the same subject persists because the same formal

[31] It is not certain that the Stoics knew the works that we know as the Aristotelian corpus. See
22.

properties persist through change in matter. In the Stoic view, Heracleitus is right about some subjects, and wrong about others, and Aristotle is right about the subjects about which Heracleitus is wrong.

The 'first' subject is also called 'matter'. The Stoics, opposing Aristotle, reserve 'substance' for this purely material subject. Its criterion of continuity is purely compositional; it persists only as long as it consists of precisely the same components composed in exactly the same way. This is how Heracleitus thinks of ordinary objects.

The second subject, which they call a 'qualified thing' (*poion*),[32] persists through time even with a different composition, because it retains the same quality. The Stoic conception of quality corresponds to the Aristotelian conception of form; the Stoics claim that the name 'Socrates' is really the name not of a particular piece of matter, but of a 'peculiar quality', the quality peculiar to him. This peculiar quality is a persisting subject that retains the distinctive properties of Socrates through the replacement of bits of his matter. Though this second subject cannot exist without a first subject existing at every time the second subject exists (since Socrates always needs some matter), it does not require the existence of one and the same first subject throughout all the times the second subject exists (since Socrates can remain in being while replacing his matter); it survives the perishing of many first subjects that constitute it at different times.

....

261 PLUTARCH, *Common Conceptions* 1083cd = LS 28 A   What do the Stoics maintain, these defenders of what is evident, who claim to define standards of common conceptions? They say ... that each of us is two subjects. One is substance, the other is qualified.[33] The first is always in flux and being carried off, neither increased nor decreased nor remaining such as it is at all; the second remains and increases and decreases, and is affected in every way opposite to the first subject, though it is coalesced and conjoined and commingled with it, and never allows perception to grasp the difference.

262 STOBAEUS, *Anthology* i. 178. 10–179. 5 = Poseidonius, fr. 96 = LS 28 D   Substance is neither increased nor decreased by addition or subtraction, but is only altered, as happens with numbers and measures. But with the peculiarly qualified, such as Dion and Theon, increase and decrease happens. Hence the quality of each remains from coming to be until destruction, as in the case of animals and plants and things like them that admit destruction. In the case of peculiarly qualified things there are two receptive parts, the one corresponding to the subsistence of substance, the other corresponding to the subsistence of the peculiarly qualified thing. For the latter, as we have

[32] Quality in Aristotle; **228**.
[33] Text uncertain.

often said, admits growth and shrinking. The peculiarly qualified thing is not the same as the substance it is composed of; nor, however, are they different, but only not the same. For the substance is a part of the peculiarly qualified thing and has the same place; but if one thing is said to be different from another, it must be both separated in place from the other, and not viewed as a part of it.

The Stoics on form and matter

263 The Stoics not only recognize formal subjects distinct from subjects with a purely compositional criterion of continuity; they also try to say how the formal properties of formal subjects are materially realized. In their view, Aristotle is right, against the Atomists, to believe in the reality of form as well as matter. The Atomists, in turn, are right to be materialists, since everything that is real is a material body. The Stoics believe there are stable, unified, coherent bodies whose properties and behaviour are explained by their natures as wholes, not by mere reference to the stuff that constitutes them. Pools of water, rocks, blocks of wood, all have some degree of unity and stability; and the Stoics analyse all these into form and matter. Bodies that have a form are held in some 'condition',[34] by having their matter in the right sort of 'tension'.[35] Even the most elementary bodies can be analysed into unqualified matter and the form that gives the matter its qualities.

The Stoics therefore reject the Atomist position that denies any fundamental explanatory role to the properties of complexes and wholes, and so they accept Aristotle's reasons for recognizing the reality of form. Aristotelian substances—artefacts and organisms—are among the essentially formal things that the Stoics recognize.

Being materialists, however, the Stoics argue that since form is real, and only bodies are real, form must be a body. Their argument is this:

(1) Something is real if and only if it can act or be acted on.

(2) Something can act or be acted on if and only if it is a body.

(3) Therefore something is real if and only if it is a body.

(4) Form is real.

(5) Therefore form is a body.

This argument shows that the Stoics emphasize the role of form as formal cause. They agree with Plato and Aristotle in taking a purely material-causal account of natural processes to be inadequate. But since they believe that only

---

[34] Or 'state'; literally 'holding', *hexis*.
[35] Or 'balance' (*tonos*, hence 'tone').

bodies can act on anything, and that only what acts on something can be a cause, they infer that a form must be a body.

How effective is the Stoic argument for taking reality to consist in bodily existence? Their premiss (1) is widely accepted; but non-materialists will reject (2), if, for instance, they believe (as Plato believes) that non-material minds cause movements in material bodies.[36] Perhaps such a belief is false; but we need to be convinced that it is false before we have reason to accept (2); by itself (2) is not a strong argument against it.

The Stoics identify form with *pneuma* ('breath', 'wind'), a very fine and subtle body, whose movements in different directions keep the matter in the right unity and tension. This *pneuma* explains the cohesion of the particles in a rock, and, at a more complex level, the growth of a plant, the behaviour of an animal, and the rational action of a human being; soul and reason are simply particular manifestations of *pneuma*.

Doubts about the general argument for materialism do not refute the identification of form with *pneuma*; but one of Aristotle's arguments for form seems to challenge it implicitly. He argues that the form cannot be a bodily element. We do not suppose we could make letters into a syllable by simply adding a further letter to them; something else would be needed to unify this collection of the old letters plus the new letter. If the form is one of the elements that constitute the unified whole, it cannot explain the unity of the whole (**259**). If Aristotle is right, the Stoics seem to conceive the form as the wrong sort of thing. The organization of the body is not the same as its ordinary material components plus its *pneuma*, since this collection (even including *pneuma*) must be suitably organized if it is to constitute an organism. Alexander criticizes the Stoic position from this Aristotelian point of view, arguing that the Stoics cannot account for the role of form as the principle of unity in a body (**345**).

To reject Stoic materialism about form is not necessarily to believe that the form is an immaterial component of anything. Aristotle identifies soul with form, but he does not conceive the soul as an immaterial component, added to the material body, to make the complex of soul and body that is a human being (**334–7**). He does not deny that living organisms and their forms are wholly constituted by their matter, in the way the house is composed of bricks and a seal is composed of wax. The Stoics are more clearly committed than Aristotle is to a version of materialism. But the specific version of non-reductive materialism that they defend seems to obscure some plausible aspects of Aristotle's view of form.

....

264 DIOGENES LAERTIUS vii. 134–9 They believe that there are two principles of the universe, the active and the passive. The passive, then, is unqualified substance, i.e. matter, while the active is the reason in matter, i.e. god; for

[36] Plato; **329**.

this, being eternal and penetrating all of matter, fashions all things. ... [138] The cosmos is the peculiarly qualified <subject> belonging to the substance of the universe ... The cosmos is administered by mind and providence, ... since mind penetrates every part of it just as soul penetrates us. But it penetrates some things more than others. For it penetrates some things as a condition, for example, bones and sinews, and other things as mind, for example, the leading part of the soul. In this way the whole cosmos too, being an animal, ensouled, and rational, has aether as its leading part.[37]

265 PLUTARCH, *Stoic Contradictions* 1053f–1054b.   In the books *On States* Chrysippus says states are nothing but bits of air. For bodies are held together by these, and it is air that holds together and is responsible for each of the things held together by a state. They call this air hardness in iron, denseness in stone, whiteness in silver.

266 [GALEN], *Introduction* 697. 6 = SVF 2. 716 = LS 47N   According to the early writers, there are two sorts of pneuma, that of nature and that of soul. The Stoics add a third, that of state. ... [726. 8] The pneuma that holds things in a state is what makes stones cohere, while that of nature is what nourishes animals and plants, and that of the soul is what in ensouled things makes animals capable of perception and of every kind of movement. It is seated in animals; for animals are constituted of the three kinds of pneuma.

267 PLATO, *Sophist* 246 A–247 D   ELEATIC VISITOR: Indeed there seems to be a sort of battle among them of gods and giants, because of their dispute about being. THEAETETUS: How is that?—One side is trying to drag everything down to earth out of heaven and the unseen. They insist that what is is only what can be struck and touched ... They define being as the same thing as body, and as soon as someone on the opposite side asserts that anything without a body is a being, they despise him altogether, and refuse to listen to anything more. ... And so their opponents are very wary in defending their position somewhere up above in the unseen. They insist forcefully that real being consists in certain intelligible and incorporeal forms. ... [247 D] I suggest that whatever has any sort of power either to act on anything else or to be acted on ... is really a being. ... I am proposing as a mark to distinguish beings that they are nothing but power.

268 CICERO, *Academica* i. 39   Zeno disagreed with [Academics and Peripatetics] in so far as he thought it totally impossible for anything to be produced by what lacks body; ... and indeed he held that whatever produces something or is produced by something must be body.

---

[37] The cosmos as an animal; **615–16**.

The Stoics on causes

269 The Stoics' corporeal conception of form rests on the claim that form must be a cause and that causes must in some way act on things. This claim about how a form is a cause relies in turn on the Stoics' doctrine of causes.

They believe in a 'containing' or 'complete', or 'perfect and principal' cause, which they distinguish from the other things that might contribute to the explanation of an event. To illustrate the different explanatory roles of the different causes, the Stoics consider a cylinder pushed so that it rolls down a slope. If we ask what started the cylinder moving, the answer is that I pushed it. If we ask what made it move in the particular way it moved, we must refer to its own nature and shape. The nature and shape is the principal cause, and my pushing it is simply the antecedent cause. Similarly, when we say that arson was the cause of a brush fire, we implicitly distinguish the antecedents and circumstances (the wind blowing at a particular speed, the area being heavily wooded, the wood being dry, the match being dry, etc.) from the principal cause (someone's decision to set the brush alight). It would be deceptive for someone who had deliberately set the fire to claim that he was not to blame, because the fire would not have started if the match had not been dry, and would not have spread if the wood had not been dry and the wind had not been blowing. We might say that some causes provide the conditions for the agent's decision, but the decision itself is the principal cause.

The normal request for 'the' cause of an event, then, is a request for the principal cause. The Stoics recognize other causes, since the principal cause alone does not answer all the relevant questions. If we want to explain an event fully, the antecedent cause, for instance, must also be mentioned. Often we mention only the principal cause, because we take the others for granted.

Aristotle does not say, as the Stoics do, that one type of cause is a principal cause. But perhaps he implies this, given the central place of the efficient cause.[38] The Stoics make this implicit claim explicit; the principal cause corresponds closely to the Aristotelian efficient cause. From the Stoic point of view, if Aristotle's formal cause is really a cause, it must be a principal cause, and therefore an efficient and active cause; and so—given their views about action—it must be a body.

This doctrine of causes is an important part of the Stoics' belief in cosmic determinism and fate, and an equally important part of their explanation of how their determinist views are compatible with human freedom and responsibility. We will turn to these aspects of their position later (**375–7**). According to the Stoics, the doctrine of causes is plausible independently of these applications to other parts of their position; its independent plausibility is an important defence of these other parts of their position.

---

[38] Aristotle on causes; **97–9**, **238–46**.

270 CLEMENT, *Miscellanies* viii. 9. 25. 1–33. 9   Among causes some are antecedent, some containing, some cooperative, some necessary conditions. The antecedent are those that first provide a starting-point for something to come to be, as beauty provides a starting-point for desire in intemperate people (for when it is seen it produces a desiring condition, but not necessarily). Containing causes are those that are synonymously called self-complete, since they are productive of the effect self-sufficiently through themselves. All the causes in order are to be shown in the case of a learner. For the father is the antecedent cause of the learning, the teacher the containing, the nature of the learner the cooperative, and time counts as a necessary condition. A cause, primarily so called, is what is actively productive of something. For we say that iron is a cutter, not only while it is cutting but also when it is not. So also, then, the productive signifies both what is now acting and what is not yet acting but possesses the capacity to act. … [97. 8] … The producer is indicative of activity. The producer is not of one thing, and the cause of another. Rather, they are of the same thing, a cloak or a house, for instance; for in so far as someone is the cause of something's coming to be, in the same way he is the producer of its coming to be. And so the same thing is cause and producer. And if something is cause and producer, that is always also that because of which; but if something is that because of which, it is not always also the cause. For many things concur towards one end and because of them the end comes about, but they are not all causes. For Medea would not have killed her children if she had not been angry; nor would she have been angry if she had not become jealous; nor this if she had not fallen in love; nor this if Jason had not sailed to Colchis; nor this if the Argo had not been fitted out; nor this if the logs had not been cut down from Mount Pelion. For in all these cases the because of which is found, but they are not all found to be causes of the child-killing; only Medea is the cause. … (101. 17) When antecedent causes are removed, the result remains. A cause is a containing cause, just in case (i) if it is present, the result remains, and (ii) if it is removed, the result is removed. They call the containing cause self-complete, synonymously, since it is productive of the result self-sufficiently through itself. If the self-complete cause is indicative of a self-complete activity, the cooperative signifies service and aid with something else, and so if it provides nothing it is not called cooperative either; if it does provide something, it is always the cause of what it provides, i.e. of what comes to be through it. The cooperative is that in the presence of which the result came to be … The co-cause is in the genus of causes, just as a fellow-soldier is a soldier, and a fellow-cadet[39] a cadet. The co-operative cause aids the containing towards the intensification of what comes to be by it, but the co-cause is not conceived in the same way; for the co-cause is capable of being present even if there is no containing cause.

---

[39] A young man in military training.

271 CICERO, *Topics* 58 There are two sorts of cause. One is the sort that by its own force certainly produces what is subject to that force; for instance, fire burns. Another is the sort that does not have the nature of producing, but without which something cannot be produced—if, for instance, someone wanted to call the bronze a cause of the statue, because the statue could not be produced without it. Among causes of this sort, without which something is not produced, some are quiet, inactive, inert, so to speak—for instance, place, time, matter, instruments, and other things of this sort; some, however, provide some preparation for producing something and bring some things that themselves help, though they are not necessary—for instance, a meeting had provided a cause for love, and love for crime. From causes of this sort, forming a series from eternity, the Stoics weave fate. And just as I have distinguished the types of cause without which something cannot be produced, so also the kinds of producing causes can be distinguished. For there are some that plainly produce with nothing helping, and others that need to be helped. Wisdom, for instance, produces wise people by itself through itself; but there is a question about whether or not it produces happy people by itself.[40] Hence, when a cause producing something necessarily comes into an argument, you can without doubt infer the existence of what is produced by that cause. But when there is a cause such that there is no necessity of producing the effect, no necessary inference follows.

[40] Virtue; **508–15**.

VII: Knowledge and Belief

Answers to Scepticism

Aristotle: knowledge of principles

|272| Plato's reflections on inquiry, belief, and knowledge constitute an elaborate, but largely implicit, reply to Scepticism. In some dialogues his argument relies on his claims about Forms (**212–18**); in others—notably in the *Theaetetus*—his epistemological argument does not mention Forms (**161–7**). In all these dialogues, he answers attacks on the possibility of knowledge. His discussion of Scepticism is largely implicit, because the Sceptical position had not been formulated in detail—though we have found some elements of it in Democritus (**134–7**).

Aristotle's contribution to the discussion of issues raised by Scepticism is also partly implicit. He does not mention an elaborate Sceptical position of the sort we find in Sextus (**108**, **169**), but he considers some of the assumptions that make Scepticism seem attractive and argues against these assumptions. In different works he offers different anti-Sceptical arguments. His arguments suggest anti-Sceptical strategies that are developed in Hellenistic debates.

In the *Posterior Analytics*, Aristotle discusses the structure of a scientific theory, and the standards that it must meet in order to count as genuine scientific knowledge. He argues that it must be expressible in demonstrations—deductive inferences in which the conclusion is shown to be necessarily true because it follows necessarily from premises that are themselves necessarily true. Though Aristotle does not claim that we must arrive at scientific truths by demonstration, he believes that the truths we arrive at must be capable of being presented in this way if they achieve genuine knowledge.

In considering how we know the basic principles that underlie demonstration in a science, Aristotle considers the three options that are later incorporated into Agrippa's trilemma (**169**, **171–2**, **214**). He insists that the basic principles cannot themselves be proved by a demonstration. If a proof of p requires a proof of q, a proof of q requires a proof of r, and so on, so that at each stage we can always ask for a further proof of any principle that we invoke to prove something else, then—in Aristotle's view—we can never find any proof, because we set ourselves an infinite task.[1] He also argues that if any alleged proof of p appeals to q to prove p, to r to prove q, and to p to prove r, this argument in a circle will never yield a genuine proof of p (**273**).

[1] Arguments about infinite tasks; **79**, **219**.

Aristotle, therefore, seems to rule out two of the three possible strategies of proof discussed by Agrippa, since he rejects both circular argument and an infinite regress. He seems to embrace Agrippa's third option, the appeal to an 'assumption', some principle that is not proved from anything else. According to Agrippa, this resort to unproved assumptions is arbitrary, if we give no reason for adopting this unproved assumption rather than its contrary; if we give a reason, we face a circle or infinite regress.

Aristotle does not believe that the adoption of a first principle is arbitrary. In his view, we grasp basic principles by 'understanding' (*nous*, **274**[2]); we recognize them as basic without deriving them from more basic principles (hence we avoid an infinite regress). But we accept these principles rather than others as a result of experience and induction from more specific beliefs. It is open to question whether this account of principles avoids Agrippa's objections. If we take 'as a result of' to refer to a purely causal relation, not involving justification, no circle of justification is present. But it still seems appropriate to ask why this causal relation should lead us to trust the principles that emerge from experience. Any answer to this question may well appear to invite Agrippa's questions.

....

273 ARISTOTLE, *Posterior Analytics* 71^{b}9–73^{a}6   We think we have unqualified scientific knowledge of a thing ... whenever we think we know the explanation because of which the thing is <so>, know that it is the explanation of that thing, and know that it does not admit of being otherwise. Clearly, then, scientific knowledge is something of this sort; for both those who lack it and those who have it think they are in this condition, but those who have such knowledge are really in it. And so whatever is known scientifically without qualification cannot be otherwise.

We shall say later whether there is also some other form of scientific knowledge; but we certainly say that we have it through demonstration. By 'demonstration' I mean a deduction expressing scientific knowledge; by this I mean that having the deduction constitutes having the knowledge. If, then, having scientific knowledge is the sort of thing we assumed it is, demonstrative knowledge must also be derived from things that are true, primary, immediate, better known than, prior to, and explanatory of the conclusion; for in that case the principles are proper to what is being proved. For these conditions are not necessary for a deduction, but they are necessary for a demonstration, since without them a deduction will not produce scientific knowledge. The conclusions must be true, then, because we cannot know what is not <true> (for example, that the diagonal is commensurate). They must be derived from premises that are primary and indemonstrable, because otherwise we will have no knowledge unless we have a demonstration

---

[2] *nous*; cf. Plato's use of the cognate *noêsis*, **119**. Heracleitus on *nous*, **116**.

of them—for to have non-coincidental knowledge of something demonstrable is to have a demonstration of it. They must be explanatory, better known, and prior. They must be explanatory, because we have scientific knowledge whenever we know[3] the explanation. They must be prior if they are indeed explanatory. And they must be previously known not only in the sense that we comprehend them, but also in the sense that we know they are <true>. Things are prior and better known in two ways; for what is prior by nature is not the same as what is prior to us, nor is what is better known <by nature> the same as what is better known to us. By 'prior and better known to us' I mean what is closer to perception, and by 'prior and better known without qualification' I mean what is further from perception. What is most universal is furthest from perception, and particulars are closest to it; particular and universal are opposite to each other. Derivation from primary things is derivation from proper principles. (I mean the same by 'primary things' as I mean by 'principles'.) A principle of demonstration is an immediate premiss, and a premiss is immediate if no others are prior to it. ...

[72ᵃ25] Since our conviction and knowledge about a thing must be based on our having the sort of deduction we call a demonstration, and since we have this sort of deduction when its premisses obtain, not only must we have previous knowledge about all or some of the primary things, but we must also know them better. For if x makes y F, x is more F than y; if, for instance, we love y because of x, x is loved more than y.[4] Hence if the primary things produce knowledge and conviction, we must have more knowledge and conviction about them, since they also produce it about subordinate things. Now if we know q, we cannot have greater conviction about p than about q unless we either know p or are in some condition better than knowledge about p. This will result, however, unless previous knowledge <of the principles> is the basis of conviction produced by demonstration; for we must have greater conviction about all or some of the principles than about the conclusion. If we are to have scientific knowledge through demonstration, then not only must we know the principles better and have greater conviction about them than about what is proved, but we must also not find anything more convincing or better known that is opposed to the principles and allows us to deduce a mistaken conclusion contrary to the correct one. For no one who has unqualified scientific knowledge can be persuaded out of it.

Some people think that because demonstration requires scientific knowledge of the primary things, there is no scientific knowledge; others think that there is scientific knowledge, and that everything <scientifically knowable> is demonstrable. Neither of these views is either true or necessary. The first

---

[3] *eidenai*, not the same verb as in 'scientific knowledge' (*epistasthai*).

[4] The dummy letters in this paragraph are not Aristotle's. In the last paragraph of this passage, the dummy letters are his.

party—those who assume that there is no knowledge at all—claim that we face an infinite regress. They assume that we can have no scientific knowledge of posterior things because of prior things, if there are no primary things; and their assumption is correct, since it is impossible to go through an infinite series. If, on the other hand, the regress stops, and there are principles, these are, in their view, unknowable, since these principles cannot be demonstrated, and, in these people's view, demonstration is the only form of scientific knowledge. But if we cannot know the primary things, then neither can we have scientific knowledge, in the unqualified and strict sense, of the things derived from them; we can know them only conditionally, on the assumption that we can know the primary things. The other party agree that scientific knowledge results only from demonstration, but they claim that it is possible to demonstrate everything, since they take circular and reciprocal demonstration to be possible.

We reply that not all scientific knowledge is demonstrative,[5] and in fact knowledge of the immediate premisses is indemonstrable. Indeed, it is evident that this must be so; for if we must know the prior things (i.e. those from which the demonstration is derived), and if eventually the regress stops, these immediate premisses must be indemonstrable. Besides this, we also say that there is not only scientific knowledge, but also some principle of it, by which we know the definitions.

Unqualified demonstration clearly cannot be circular, given that it must be derived from prior and better-known things. For the same things cannot be both prior and posterior to the same things at the same time, except in different ways (so that, for example, some things are prior relative to us, and others are prior without qualification—this is the way induction makes something known). If this is so, our definition of unqualified knowledge will be faulty, and there will be two sorts of knowledge; or <rather> perhaps the second sort of demonstration is not unqualified demonstration, since it is derived from what is <merely> better known to us. Those who allow circular demonstration must concede not only the previous point, but also that they are simply saying that something is if it is; and on this basis it is easy to prove anything. This is clear if we consider three terms—for it does not matter whether we say the demonstration turns back through many or few terms, or through few or two. For suppose that if A is, necessarily B is, and that if B is, necessarily C is; it follows that if A is, C will be. Suppose, then, that if A is, B necessarily is, and if B is, A is (since this is what circular argument is), and let A be C. In that case, to say that if B is, A is is to say that <if B is,> C is; this <is to say> that if A is, C is. But since C is the same as A, it follows that those who allow circular demonstration simply say that if A is, A is. On these terms it is easy to prove anything.

---

[5] Here Aristotle uses 'scientific knowledge' (*epistêmê*) more broadly than usual. In **274** he expresses the same claim by saying that understanding (*nous*) is not *epistêmê*.

274   ARISTOTLE, *Posterior Analytics* 99^{b}17–100^{b}17   … But how do we come to know principles, and what state knows them? This will be clear from the following argument, if we first state the puzzles. We said before that we cannot have scientific knowledge through demonstration without knowing the first and immediate principles. But one might be puzzled about whether knowledge of the immediate principles is or is not the same as knowledge of truths derived from them; whether there is scientific knowledge of each, or scientific knowledge of one but something else of the other; and whether the states are acquired rather than <innately> present or are <innately> present in us without our noticing them.[6]

Now, it would be absurd if we had the principles <innately>; for in that case we would possess knowledge that is more exact than demonstration, but without noticing it. If, however, we acquire the principles and do not previously possess them, how could we know and learn them from no prior knowledge? That is impossible, as we also said in the case of demonstration. Evidently, then, we can neither possess the principles <innately> nor acquire them if we are ignorant and possess no state <of knowledge>. Hence we must have some suitable capacity, but not one that is at a higher level of exactness than the things we acquire.

All animals evidently have such a capacity, since they have the innate discriminative capacity called perception. Some animals that have perception (though not all of them) also retain in memory what they perceive; those that do not retain it have no knowledge outside perception (either none at all or none about what is not retained), but those that do retain it keep in their souls what they have perceived. When this has happened many times, a difference arises: in some but not all cases, a rational account arises from the retention of perceptions.

From perception, then, as we say, memory arises, and from repeated memory of the same thing experience arises; for a number of memories make up one experience. From experience, or from the whole universal that has settled in the soul—the one apart from the many, whatever is present as one and the same in all of them—arises a principle of craft (if it is about what comes to be) or of science (if it is about what is). Hence the relevant states are not <innate> in us in any determinate character and do not arise from states with a better title to knowledge; rather, they arise from perception. It is like what happens in a battle when there is a retreat: first one soldier makes a stand, then a second, then another, until they reach a starting-point.[7] The soul has a capacity to be affected in this way.

Let us state again, then, what we stated, but not perspicuously, before. When one of the undifferentiated things makes a stand, that is the first

---

[6] Innate grasp of principles; Aristotle alludes to Plato's *Meno*. Cf. **183–6**.

[7] *archê*, also translated 'principle'.

universal in the soul; for though one perceives the particular, perception is of the universal—of man, for instance, not of Callias the man. Again in these something makes a stand, until what has no parts and is universal makes a stand—first, for example, a certain sort of animal makes a stand, until animal does, and in this something else makes a stand in the same way. Clearly, then, we must come to know the first things by induction; for that is also how perception implants the universal.[8]

Among our intellectual states that grasp the truth, some—scientific knowledge and understanding[9]—are always true, whereas others—for example, belief and reasoning—allow falsity; and understanding is the only sort of state that is more exact than scientific knowledge. Since the principles of demonstration are better known than the conclusions derived from them, and since all scientific knowledge requires an account, we can have no scientific knowledge of the principles. Since only understanding can be truer than scientific knowledge, we must have understanding of the principles. The same conclusion follows from the further point that since the principle of a demonstration is not a demonstration, the principle of scientific knowledge is not scientific knowledge. If, then, the only sort of state apart from scientific knowledge that is <always> true is understanding, understanding must be the principle of scientific knowledge. The principle, then, will grasp the principle, and, similarly, all <scientific knowledge> will grasp its object.

275 ARISTOTLE, *Nicomachean Ethics* 1140^{b}30–1141^{a}8   Scientific knowledge is apprehension of universals, things that are by necessity. Further, everything demonstrable and every science has principles, since scientific knowledge involves reason. Hence there can be neither scientific knowledge nor craft-knowledge nor intelligence about the principles of what is scientifically known. For what is scientifically known is demonstrable, and craft and intelligence are about what admits of being otherwise. ... The remaining possibility, then, is that we have understanding about principles.

Aristotle: defence of the senses

276 In the *Metaphysics*, Aristotle takes up a different issue raised by the Sceptics, about the reliability of the senses. Here he is not concerned primarily with the highly theoretical statements of a science, but with ordinary observations. Once again, however, he has in mind those Sceptical doubts about justification that are summarized in Agrippa's trilemma. His answer to these doubts seems to be different from his answer in the *Analytics*.

[8] On the growth of knowledge cf. **106**.
[9] *nous*; see **272** n.

Against the argument from conflicting appearances (**125**), Aristotle maintains that, in the relevant cases, the conflicting appearances are not equipollent (**277**). We rely on a close view against a distant view, and on the appearances of the healthy person or the expert against the appearances that conflict with them. The Sceptic will reply that we need some way to identify the healthy person, and some way of knowing we are awake rather than asleep, so that we know which appearances are trustworthy. Aristotle does not take this reply seriously. He suggests that we do not face any serious difficulty in identifying the trustworthy appearances, and that we need not appeal to some criterion that would, in turn, require defence by appeal to a further criterion.

Aristotle's reply to doubts about justification is similar to the reply he offers in the *Analytics*, in so far as he rejects the Sceptical demand to have everything 'demonstrated', i.e. proved from some more basic principle; in his view, this demand betrays a basic mistake about justification. In defending the senses, however, he does not appeal explicitly to 'assumptions', as he does in defending the principles of scientific knowledge.

We might wonder, indeed, whether his defence of the reliability of ordinary perceptual judgements does not implicitly appeal to coherence. If we assume that our senses normally give us reliable information, and that our dreams (say) do not, we can predict many aspects of stability and change in our experiences that we would otherwise be unable to predict; as Heracleitus says, we take ourselves to be in a 'common' world that conforms to constant laws (**114**, **119**). But this reply to the Sceptic assumes that we can justify one set of beliefs by showing that they help to explain and justify other beliefs that are themselves ultimately explained and justified by the first set of beliefs (if I suppose that I am really seeing a chair, I am justified in believing that it will offer resistance if I try to sit in it; if it seems to me that the chair offers resistance when I try to sit in it, that justifies my belief that I am really seeing a chair). In that case, we deny the Sceptical claim—apparently accepted by Aristotle in the *Analytics*—that circular argument cannot justify.

....

277 ARISTOTLE, *Metaphysics* 1010ᵇ1–1011ᵃ13 … We say that not everything that appears is true. First, even if perception, at least of its proper objects, is not false, still, appearance is not the same as perception. Further, one may justifiably be surprised if they are puzzled by such questions as these: 'Are magnitudes and colours such as they appear to observers from a distance or such as they appear to observers close at hand? Are they such as they appear to be to healthy people or such as they appear to be to sick people? Are things heavier if they appear so to feeble people or if they appear so to vigorous people? Are things true if they appear so to people asleep or if they appear so to people awake?'[10] For it is evident that at any rate they do not really think the

[10] Waking and sleeping; **119**.

appearances of the dreamer are true—certainly no one who is in Libya and one night supposes in a dream that he is in Athens goes off towards the Odeion. Further, as for the future, as Plato says,[11] the belief of a doctor and of an ignorant person surely do not have equal authority about, for instance, whether someone is or is not going to be healthy. ...

If there is only what is perceptible, nothing would exist unless animate things existed, since without them there would be no perception. Now presumably it is true that <without animate things> there would be neither perceptible things nor perceivings, since this is a way in which a perceiver is affected; still, there must be subjects[12] that cause perception and that exist whether or not they are perceived. For perception is certainly not of itself; on the contrary, there is also something else apart from the perception, which is necessarily prior to perception. For what initiates a change is naturally prior to what is changed, and this is no less true even if what initiates the change and what is changed are spoken of in relation to each other.

Some people, however, including some who are genuinely persuaded by these puzzles about the senses, as well as some who merely put forward these arguments, are puzzled. For they ask who is to discriminate which people are healthy and, in general, who is to discriminate correctly about anything. But being puzzled about these sorts of questions is like being puzzled about whether we are now awake or asleep. All such puzzles have the same force. For those who raise them demand to be given an argument for everything, since they seek a principle, and seek to reach it through demonstration; for it is evident in their actions that at any rate they are not really persuaded by their puzzles. But as we said, this is what happens to them; they search for an argument for things for which there is no argument. For the starting-point[13] of demonstration is not a demonstration.

Epicurus' reply to Scepticism

278 Epicurus agrees with the Sceptical goal of tranquillity (**173–4**, **414**), and he agrees that Democritus' critical attitude to the senses leads to Scepticism. But he rejects Scepticism as a means to securing tranquillity. The Sceptic leaves us unable to decide between two views that are supported by equipollent appearances, claiming that this indecision and suspension of judgement leads to tranquillity. In Epicurus' view, however, indecision leaves us worried and agitated; tranquillity results only if we have some basis for judgement and decision.

---

[11] Plato; **164**.
[12] Subjects, i.e. things external to perception: cf. **150**.
[13] Or 'principle', *archê*.

To avoid indecision, Epicurus defends the reliability of the senses, as Aristotle does. But he rejects Aristotle's selective defence of the senses, and offers an 'all or nothing' argument about their status. He appears to argue as follows:

(1) If we believe the senses are sometimes mistaken, we are not justified in believing they are ever reliable.

(2) If we recognize that we are not justified in believing the senses are ever reliable, we are Sceptics about the senses.

(3) Hence, if we reject Scepticism about the senses, we must believe the senses are always correct.

We may be surprised by the first step. Why should we not believe (as we normally do believe) that the senses are sometimes mistaken, but usually reliable? Epicurus might answer that if we are to distinguish the occasions on which the senses are mistaken from those in which they are reliable, we will need to appeal to some further criterion, and (for reasons suggested by Sextus, **171**) this appeal will lead us into an infinite regress or a circle.

To avoid this path to Scepticism, Epicurus defends the correctness of the senses. We normally believe that when we put a straight stick into water and it looks bent, it is not really bent. We believe this because we assume that the stick will still be straight when we take it out, and that sticks do not change their shape when they are immersed in liquid. Epicurus argues that, since these assumptions rest on the senses, we cannot rely on any of these assumptions unless we can always rely on the senses (cf. **67**).

To show that we need never reject the senses, he distinguishes the appearance of the stick's being bent now from the false assumption that it will continue to be bent. We mistakenly reject the appearance because we reject the false assumption. Since the appearance itself does not contain that assumption, our tendency to make the assumption is no reason for rejecting the appearance.

To explain how the present appearance could be true, Epicurus appeals to the Atomic theory. The appearance of the bent stick is true, in so far as it corresponds to a bent configuration of atoms thrown off by the stick and eventually hitting the eyes. The later appearance of the straight stick is also true, because it corresponds to a straight configuration of atoms. We are usually wrong if we expect the bent-stick-in-water appearance to be followed by a bent-stick-out-of-water appearance. But the error lies in us and our hasty inferences and false beliefs, not in the senses themselves.

We can therefore rely on the senses, according to Epicurus, without being liable to the argument from conflicting appearances (**125**). This argument cannot get started; for the apparently conflicting appearances are indeed equipollent, but do not conflict, since they are both true. On this point Epicurus agrees with Protagoras (**158**), but he rejects Protagoras' inference to a subjectivist conclusion.

Does Epicurus pay too high a price for preserving the truth of appearances? If we are to accept the truth of the appearance that the stick in water is bent, then we must not assume that our true appearances are fairly stable; we cannot assume that a stick that looks bent now will continue to look bent. Must we not also, therefore, reject our normal assumption that a stick out of water that looks straight will continue to look straight when it is out of water, since this assumption is also (according to Epicurus) strictly unwarranted by the senses? If we must doubt the stability of our true perceptual appearances, we must apparently be Sceptics (**159**).

Epicurus might answer that we can rely on our senses because Atomic theory is true and it says our senses are usually reliable. Since the Atomic theory itself relies on the accuracy of the senses, Epicurus seems to avoid the argument from conflicting appearances by an argument that is open to Agrippa's objections to circular argument. If he replies that circular arguments are sometimes legitimate, he raises doubts about his initial objection to selective reliance on the senses.

....

279 EPICURUS = DIOGENES LAERTIUS X. 146–7   If you fight all your sense-perceptions, you will have no standard to refer to in judging even those sense-perceptions that you say are false. If you reject unqualifiedly any sense-perception, and do not distinguish the belief and what awaits confirmation from what is now present in the sense-perception, in the affections, and in every application of thought to appearance, you will also disturb the rest of your sense-perceptions with your empty belief, so that you will reject every standard. If, on the other hand, in your conceptions formed by belief, you affirm everything that awaits confirmation and what has no confirmation,[14] you will not escape error, so that you will have maintained every disputable point in every judgement about what is correct or incorrect.

280 SEXTUS, *Against the Professors* vii. 205–6   [EPICURUS:] And so all the appearances turn out to be true. ... But some people are deceived by the difference between the appearances that seem to come from the object of sense, for example, a visible thing. This difference makes the object appear to vary in colour, or shape, or in some other respect. For they have supposed that when appearances differ and conflict in this way, one of them must be true and the one on the contrary side must be false. This is foolish; it is the position of men who do not take a comprehensive view of the nature of things.

281 SEXTUS, *Against the Professors* vii. 208–9   [EPICURUS:] I would not say that sight is mistaken because from a long distance it sees the tower as small and round, but from closer at hand it sees it as larger and square. Rather, I would

[14] Text uncertain.

say that sight is truthful. When the object of sense appears to it as small and of such a shape, it is really small and of such a shape, because the edges of the images are broken off by the movement through the air. But when it appears large and of a different shape, then, similarly, it is large and of a different shape, but it is not the same thing with both of the sizes and shapes. For it is left to misguided belief to suppose that it was the same thing that appeared both close at hand and at a distance.

Atomism and the senses

282 Apart from these questions about circularity, Epicurus faces a more general question: does an appeal to the senses support the Atomic theory, and the Atomic theory vindicate the senses? He derives the main ideas of his Atomic theory from Democritus, but his defence of it is quite different, since he tries to avoid a Sceptical conclusion that seems to follow from Democritus' arguments.

Democritus notices that the Atomic theory seems to rely on two incompatible claims about the senses. He defends the Atomic theory as the product of reason superseding the senses; reflection on the conflicting appearances of sense shows that reality cannot consist of things with colour, taste, and so on, but must consist of indestructible atoms. But when Democritus tries to say how the atoms interact so as to produce compound bodies, he uses comparisons with ordinary observable situations; if these comparisons give a true account of the atoms, the senses must be reliable in telling us that (for instance) sharp things tend to tear soft bodies. The Atomic theory, therefore, seems to depend both on the rejection and on the acceptance of the senses (**134–7**).

To resolve this conflict in Democritus, Epicurus discards the first type of argument and relies exclusively on the second type. We need not reject the senses at all, in his view, since they support the Atomic theory. His treatment of colour illustrates his strategy. We can see, even from macroscopic examples, that change of colour must be explained by something about the body other than colour; for the colour that disappears when another colour comes into being cannot explain the change. Hence the senses themselves assure us that the basic elements underlying changes of colour cannot be coloured (**284–7**). This was the conclusion that Democritus believed to be contrary to the senses. Epicurus concludes, against Democritus, that Atomists need not reject the senses.

283 EPICURUS = DIOGENES LAERTIUS X. 46–7   Further there are outlines similar in shape to solids, but much finer than things that appear. For it is not impossible for such effluences to come into being in the surrounding environment, nor that there should be suitable circumstances for the production of hollow and thin films, nor that effluences should retain the place and the order that they had in the solid objects. These outlines we call 'images'. ...

None of the appearances testifies against the view that the images have an unsurpassed fineness; that is why they have unsurpassed speed too. ...

284 EPICURUS = DIOGENES LAERTIUS X. 54–5 Further, one must suppose that the atoms bring with them none of the qualities of the things that appear, except shape, weight, size, and whatever necessarily accompanies shape. ... Even in the case of things observed to change shape by the removal <of matter>, we grasp the shape as inherent in the thing that changes, whereas colours do not inhere in it ... And so the things left behind after a change are sufficient to produce the differences in compounds, since it is necessary for some things to be left behind so that things are not destroyed into what is not.

285 LUCRETIUS ii. 112–24 An image and likeness of this movement of the atoms ... continually moves and passes before our eyes. For observe what happens when sunbeams enter a building and pour sunlight into its dark places. You will see many tiny particles mixing in many ways through the empty space within the light of the sunbeams, as though fighting in ceaseless war, one troop rushing into battle against another without a pause, pressed by rapid combinations and dissolutions. From this you may picture what it is for the beginnings of things to be perpetually tossed about in the great void. To some extent a small thing may give us an illustration of great things, and traces of a conception of them.

286 LUCRETIUS ii. 308–22 In this matter, you should not be surprised that, even though all the beginnings of things are in motion, the whole appears to stand wholly motionless, except when something starts a movement with its own body. This is because the whole nature of the first bodies lies far below our senses. And so, since you cannot see them, their movements must also escape you, especially since even things we can see often hide their movements when they are separated by distance. For often on a hillside fleecy sheep, as they crop their lush pastures, creep slowly onward to wherever each one is called and invited by grass sparkling with fresh dew, while the lambs that have been fed frisk and butt playfully. But all this is blurred when it appears to us looking from a distance; it appears to us as a white patch lying still on the green hill.

287 LUCRETIUS ii. 731–833 Do not suppose that the white objects you see shining before your eyes are made of white elements, or that black objects come from black seeds. And in general do not believe that anything dyed with any other colour wears its colour because the bodies composing matter are tinted with the same colour. For the bodies composing matter have no colour at all, neither the same colour as the objects they compose nor a different one. If you think the mind cannot grasp such bodies, you are quite wrong ... [15] [826] The more anything is divided into tiny parts, the more you can see the colour gradually fading and being quenched. When red cloth, for instance, is pulled to pieces thread by thread, its crimson or scarlet colour, the brightest of colours by far, is all destroyed. From this you can recognize that, even before its particles are divided into the seeds of things, they shed all their colour.

Empirical equivalence

288 Epicurus makes two claims about the Atomic theory:

(1) Sensory evidence is consistent with the truth of the Atomic theory.

(2) Sensory evidence supports the truth of the Atomic theory against other theories that seek to explain the same phenomena. In his view, some questions allow several answers that are consistent with such evidence of the senses, whereas the Atomic theory is the only account of the universe that is consistent with this evidence.

Questions of the first type (including astronomical questions, about the size of the sun, for instance, **289**) arise because the relevant observations are not available. In such cases the phenomena have many different explanations that are equally consistent with the evidence of the senses, and we ought not to try to choose between 'empirically equivalent' theories and explanations. The Atomic theory, however, is not meant to be one of a number of empirically equivalent theories. It is intended to free us from anxiety about the world and about death; it would not do this if (say) belief in punishments after death was equally compatible with observation.

Epicurus' arguments, however, seem to show only that Atomism is consistent with observation, not that it is the only theory of this sort. For instance, the principle that the atoms must be indestructible is supposed to rest on the more basic principle that destruction into nothing and coming to be from nothing are both impossible. Democritus probably regards this as a principle that is accessible to reason, but not to the senses, but Epicurus claims to prove it by appeal to the senses alone. It is difficult to agree with him. Whether or not this basic principle is true or false, it does not seem to be the only one that is consistent with the evidence of the senses.

In that case, the Atomic theory seems to be only one of a number of empirically equivalent theories, so that Epicurus' own principles forbid us to prefer it over rival theories that are equally consistent with observations. Even if we take the senses to be reliable, they do not seem to support belief in the Atomic theory in particular (cf. **338**).

....

[15] Lucretius presents a series of arguments and illustrations, one of which is quoted here.

289 EPICURUS = DIOGENES LAERTIUS X. 91 The size of sun <and moon> and the other stars in relation to us is such as it appears to be. ... In itself it is either <slightly> greater than what we see or slightly smaller or the same size; for the same is true of the fires on earth, when they are viewed from a distance by the senses. And every objection to this point will easily be dissolved if we attend to obvious things.

290 EPICURUS = DIOGENES LAERTIUS X. 85–7 ... Do not suppose any other goal can be reached from knowledge of things in the heavens—whether they are discussed in conjunction with physics in general or by themselves—than tranquillity and firm conviction, as in the other sciences. We do not snatch at what is impossible, or seek a view that is in every way similar either to our discussions on the ways of life or to our clarification of other questions about nature—for instance, that everything is body and intangible nature, and that the elements are atomic, and all the things that agree with the appearances in only one way. For this is not so with the things above us; they admit of more than one cause of coming into being, and more than one way of clarifying their nature in agreement with our perceptions. For we must inquire into nature not by means of empty assumptions and stipulations, but in the way called for by appearances. For now our life has no need of irrationality and empty belief, but we must live free from trouble. Now all goes on without disturbance in the case of each of these things that can be clarified in more than one way in agreement with the appearances, whenever one leaves standing, as one must, plausible accounts of them. But when one accepts one theory and rejects another that agrees no less well with the appearances, it is clear that one abandons inquiry into nature and relapses into myth.

Selective defences of the senses: Stoicism

291 The Stoics agree with Epicurus in defending the reliability of the senses against Sceptical challenge, but they reject his extreme empiricism. They argue that we can distinguish reliable from unreliable appearances, and so they reject the 'all or nothing' argument accepted by both Epicurus and the Sceptics. Sceptical criticism focuses on Stoic attempts to mark reliable appearances. According to Carneades, the Stoics' own principles force them into a Sceptical position (cf. **292**).

The Stoics begin their account of rationally justifiable belief by distinguishing mere appearance from belief. They insist that a sensory appearance derived from an external object is not enough for a belief about the object. If I have an appearance of, say, a red wall, but I have other reasons for believing that the wall is white and a red light is shining on it, I will not believe I see a red wall. To believe that the wall is red, I must also 'assent' to the appearance; and this assent is an act of thought and reason, not merely a product of sense.[16]

For the Stoic, then, the problem of the criterion is the question: 'What sorts of appearances justify us in assenting to them?' They answer that the criterion of truth is the 'grasping' or 'apprehending' (*katalêptikê*) appearance, the one that grasps reality.[17] This is the sort of appearance that presents a real object as it is, would not come from an unreal object, and compels our assent.

It follows from the definition of such an appearance that it is reliable. But how can we tell that a particular appearance does or does not count as grasping reality? The Stoics cannot say that if just anyone feels compelled to assent to an appearance, that appearance grasps reality; for many people mistakenly feel compelled to assent to an appearance that turns out to be false. The person who, in the Stoic view, reliably identifies the appearances that grasp reality is the 'sage' (*sophos*)— the experienced, fully informed Stoic who has complete knowledge of the world.

But if we must turn to the sage for a reliable source of appearances that grasp reality, the Stoic answer to the problem of the criterion seems to be open to further Sceptical objections. Since the sage is the one with reliably true beliefs on the questions at issue, we can identify her only if we can identify the true beliefs. But we were looking for a sage as a criterion to identify the true beliefs. If we must first identify true beliefs before we can find a sage, we have no criterion.

This Sceptical objection assumes that the Stoics want a wholly self-sufficient criterion that allows us, all by itself and without any further information or inference, to see that a given belief is true, and therefore supplies a self-evident foundation for claims to knowledge. The Stoics supply no such criterion.

Ought they even to try to supply the sort of criterion that the Sceptic wants? The Sceptical demand for a self-sufficient criterion does not itself seem self-evidently correct; and it is not clear what further argument should persuade us to accept it. If we do not demand a self-sufficient criterion, the Stoic appeal to the appearances that grasp reality, and to the sage as the reliable source of such appearances, seems more reasonable. The Stoics assume that for the interpretation and understanding of the senses we must rely on the rest of the theory that seeks to explain appearances as a whole.

....

292 DIOGENES LAERTIUS iv. 62   Carneades ... read the writings of the Stoics carefully, and especially those of Chrysippus. By arguing well against them he became so famous that he would often say, 'If there had been no Chrysippus, I would be nothing.'

293 CICERO, *Academica* i. 40   Zeno ... said some new things about the senses themselves, which he said were composed of a sort of impact presented from

---

[16] Stoic views on assent: cf. **375–9**, **526–30**.
[17] Assent and grasping the truth; cf. **514–15**, **519**.

outside. He called this *phantasia*; let us call it appearance ... To these things that appear and are, so to speak, received by the senses he adds assent of our minds, which he wants to be placed in our power and voluntary. He did not attach trust to all appearances, but only to those that had some manifestation, peculiar to themselves, of the things that appeared. ... When it had been received and approved, he called this a grasping, similar to those things that are grasped by the hand.

294 CICERO, *Academica* ii. 145   First Zeno showed his open hand with the fingers stretched out, and said 'Appearance is this way.' Then he tightened his fingers a little and said 'Assent is this way.' Then he tightened them fully to make a fist, and said that this was grasping—and from that similarity he even gave that thing the name *katalêpsis*[18] which it had not had before. But then he moved his left hand to grasp the right fist closely and vigorously, and said that this is what knowledge[19] is like, which no one possessed but the wise man— but who the wise man is or has been not even the Stoics themselves will say.

295 SEXTUS, *Against the Professors* vii. 151–2   For the Stoics say three things are linked[20]—knowledge, opinion, and, set between them, apprehension.[21] Of these knowledge is the unerring and firm apprehension that is unalterable by reason; opinion is a weak and false assent; and apprehension is intermediate between these, being assent belonging to an apprehensive appearance. An apprehensive appearance, according to them, is one that is true and of such a kind that it would not turn out false. Of these, they say, knowledge is found only in sages, and opinion only in inferior people, whereas apprehension is common to both sages and inferior people, and this is the standard of truth.

296 SEXTUS, *Against the Professors* vii. 257   The apprehensive appearance is not the standard of truth unconditionally, but when it has no obstacle. For this appearance, being obvious and striking, practically grabs us by the hair, as they say, and draws us towards assent, needing nothing else to make it strike us as such or to mark it as superior to all others. This is also why everyone who is eager to apprehend anything exactly appears to seek, on his own initiative, this sort of appearance. This happens, for instance, in the case of things we see, whenever we get a dim appearance of the object. For one looks more intently and goes close to the object ... until one gets a clear and striking appearance of what one is trying to decide about, as taking the credibility of apprehension to depend on this sort of appearance.

---

[18] i.e. 'grasping' or 'apprehension'.
[19] Or 'science'.
[20] They are linked because they all involve assent.
[21] Or 'grasping' (*katalêpsis*).

Scepticism, belief, and action

297 Even if these positive defences of a criterion do not convince a Sceptic, we might argue that the Sceptical conclusion is unacceptable, and hence we ought not to suspend judgement. We have seen why the Sceptic tries to answer objections to the Sceptic's way of life (**173–5**); we must now consider whether those answers are satisfactory.

First, we might question the Sceptic's goal. Since the Sceptic claims to have found tranquillity, Sceptical inquiry ought to appeal to us if we are certain that tranquillity is more desirable than any result we could achieve if we avoided Scepticism. But to be certain of this, we must apparently be convinced that the ultimate good, happiness, is simply tranquillity (**174**). Perhaps an Epicurean may be expected to agree with the Sceptic on this point, while disagreeing on the means to tranquillity (**414**). But others—Plato, Aristotle, and the Stoics— clearly disagree (**495–6, 499–500, 508–15**). Hence, the claim that happiness is tranquillity is itself subject to the argument from conflicting appearances. If we must suspend judgement about its truth, then apparently we do not know whether or not we ought to engage in Sceptical inquiry.

Even if we do not endorse one of the conceptions of happiness that conflict with the Sceptic's preference for tranquillity, we might be dissatisfied with the Sceptic's claim to lead a normal life (minus the anxieties that result from dogmatic belief). Some critics argue that, once the Sceptic has suspended judgement, he cannot act at all. This is the 'inaction' (*apraxia*) argument. Sextus replies that the Sceptic has strong inclinations even when he has suspended judgement on questions that bother the dogmatist.

To see whether this reply is satisfactory, we must examine the Sceptic's inclinations more closely. They might be understood in either of two ways:

(1) They are still beliefs, which we hold even though we recognize that we cannot prove them by appeal to a criterion that is beyond objection.

(2) We must distinguish genuine belief, based on evidence and reason, from an appearance that may influence action without reference to reason and belief.

Though Sceptics have no beliefs, they still have appearances. This is the answer that Plutarch offers, from the Sceptic's point of view, to defeat the inaction argument (**298**).

It is difficult to understand the first account of the Sceptic's inclinations without taking his suspension of judgement to be more restricted than he claims it is. If we hold beliefs that rest on no unquestionable criterion, must we not recognize that they may be open to objections, or at least recognize that it is possible they are open to objections? In either case, we do not seem to be entirely free from anxiety.

The second account avoids this objection. When we see a snake, we may not believe it is dangerous, but it may none the less strike us as dangerous and we may be moved to avoid it. If we bring our hand close to the fire, we may have a vivid appearance of danger, even if we have no beliefs; this vivid appearance may cause us to remove our hand. Similarly, Sceptics find that the generally recognized morality of their society is vividly apparent to them, whether or not they believe it. These vivid appearances will make them act as dogmatists act.

This account of the Sceptic's inclinations leaves some unanswered questions. Even if Sceptics act in response to appearances, can they act, as other people do, on the basis of discrimination among appearances? The Sceptic has no reason to say that the oar in the water is really straight when it appears bent, and has no explanation for his acting on that judgement rather than on the judgement that it is bent. If it strikes the Sceptic that he is thirsty, why does he refrain from drinking the contents of the bottle in front of him when he realizes that it is vodka and that he has to drive home? The Sceptic may answer that he has further appearances and acts on the later ones rather than the earlier ones. But can he explain how this happens, unless he regards some considerations as better reasons for acting than others?

Another way to see what the Sceptic loses in abandoning belief is to notice that his 'undogmatic' attitude does not make him more open-minded, or more disposed to take other views seriously, or more inclined to revise his own views in the light of other people's reasonable objections. All these attitudes rest on the assumption that we can improve our grasp of the truth by forming beliefs that rest on better reasons; but the Sceptic rejects this assumption. He does not believe that other people's views deserve to be taken seriously or that he can learn anything from them.

....

298   PLUTARCH, *Against Colotes* 1122a–f Suspension of judgement about everything was not shaken even by those who worked hard and drew out their treatises and arguments against it. Finally these people[22] brought out the 'inaction' argument like a Gorgon from the Stoa against it, and then stopped.[23] For though they tried and twisted everything, impulse did not submit to them to become assent, nor did it accept sense-perception[24] as the origin of inclination. It clearly led to actions all by itself, needing no addition. ... For those who attend and follow the argument,[25] it is this: there are three movements of the soul—appearance, impulse and assent. We cannot remove the movement of appearance even if we want to; it is necessary when we encounter things to be imprinted and affected by them. The movement of

[22] Epicureans, whom Plutarch is discussing here.

[23] The Gorgon turned people to stone; the inaction argument is supposed to do the same to the Sceptics, by showing that suspension precludes action.

[24] The Stoics define sense-perception (*aisthêsis*) as including assent.

[25] i.e. the argument to show that (contrary to the Stoic inaction argument) we can suspend judgement and still act.

impulse aroused by the movement of appearance moves us actively towards suitable things, when its weight tilts[26] the leading part of the soul. And so those who suspend judgement about everything do not remove this movement either; they follow an impulse leading them naturally to what is apparently suitable.

Then what is the only movement the Sceptics avoid? The only one in which falsity and deception grow up—believing, and assent falling on us, a yielding to appearances because of weakness, having nothing useful. For action needs two things, the appearance of the suitable, and impulse towards what has appeared suitable, neither of which conflicts with suspension; for the argument for suspension removes us from belief, not from impulse or from appearance. And so whenever something suitable appears, we have no need of belief to be moved and carried off towards it; impulse comes at once, being a movement and carrying off of the soul. ...

'But how is it that the one who suspends judgement doesn't run off to a mountain, but to the bath, and doesn't stand up and walk to the wall, but to the door, when he wants to go to the market-place?'[27] How can you ask that, given that you say the sense-organs are accurate and the appearances true? Presumably because it is not the mountain but the bath that appears a bath to him, and it is not the wall but the door that appears a door, and similarly for each of the other things. For the argument for suspension does not pervert sense, nor does it produce in the non-rational affections and movements themselves any alteration disturbing the movement of appearances; it only removes beliefs, but follows the others in the natural way.

299 CICERO, *Academica* ii. 37–9   For while we were explaining the power present in the senses, this point was also made clear, that many things are grasped and perceived by the senses, which cannot happen without assent. And then, since this is the greatest difference between an animal and something inanimate, that an animal does something—for an animal doing nothing cannot even be thought of—either we must deny sense to it or we must attribute the assent that is in our power to it. But indeed mind is in a way removed from those who are unwilling either to sense or to assent; for just as it is necessary for the pan of a balance to be pushed down when weights are placed into it, so it is necessary for the mind to give way to clear things. ... Without assent neither memory nor conceptions of things nor crafts can arise; and, the most important point, nothing will be in the power of someone who will assent to nothing. ... Therefore, whoever removes either appearance or assent removes all action from life.

---

[26] As in a balance: cf. **299**.
[27] This question is asked by the opponent of Scepticism; cf. **277**.

VIII: Soul and Body

Homer: soul and life

300 In Homer, human beings have souls as long as they are alive, and their souls leave them when they die. The soul (*psuchê*) is closely connected with breath; at death it departs like a puff of smoke. From this we might infer that the soul perishes when a human being is killed, but this is not Homer's view. He presents the souls of dead heroes returning to warn their friends. He even depicts Odysseus in conversation with souls of the dead in Hades. The souls have some sort of shadowy existence, but they need to drink blood before they can communicate with Odysseus.

From these few Homeric remarks on the soul, we can gather some of the background to Greek philosophical thought.

(1) The belief in souls is not taken to be controversial; it is as obvious that human beings have souls as it is that they are alive.

(2) The soul is the principle of life; it marks the difference between the living and the non-living.

(3) The soul is closely connected with the person whose soul it is. When Odysseus addresses the soul of Achilles in Hades, he calls it 'Achilles', and it carries the memories and attitudes of Achilles.

(4) Though a belief in souls is not necessarily a belief in anything immortal, belief in an after-life is naturally expressed as a belief in the survival of souls after death. Since the soul is the bearer of life and personality, it is the appropriate bearer of immortality.

These assumptions about the soul help to explain why Thales, according to Aristotle, took souls to be present in all sorts of things, including those that we would not normally count as alive. In a human being or animal, a soul is an 'origin of change',[1] since human beings and animals are capable of change as long as they are alive and have souls. Thales generalizes this view still further, suggesting that we should speak of a soul wherever we have an origin of change in a body. According to this suggestion, magnets as well as human beings and animals should have souls.

We do not know how far Thales develops this suggestion. It suggests that the division between organisms, on the one hand, and inorganic bodies such as magnets, on the other, is not a fundamentally important division. None of his successors goes as far in extending the range of souls.

---

[1] *archê kinêseôs.* This is Aristotle's term for the efficient cause; **98**.

301   HOMER, *Odyssey* xi. 36–564   Then the souls of the dead gathered around me from Erebus—brides, young bachelors, old men worn out with toil, tender young women disappointed in love, with grief still fresh in their spirit, brave men pierced by bronze-tipped spears, with their armour still bloody. They came from every side and fluttered around … with a strange screaming; and pale fear seized me. … [152] I sat still where I was until my mother came up and tasted the dark blood. Then she knew me at once and spoke to me, lamenting: 'My son, how did you come down below the fog and darkness while you are still alive? It is difficult for the living to see these places; for between us and them there are great rivers and terrible waters, first of all Oceanus, which no one can cross on foot, but travellers need a well-built ship to take them. Are you wandering on your journey home from Troy for so long a time, with your ship and your companions? Have you never yet got back to Ithaca nor seen your wife in your own house?' … As for my own death—Artemis did not take me quickly with her gentle shafts in my own house, nor was I attacked by any illness such as those that generally wear people out and kill them. It was my longing to know what you were doing and my affection for you—this took my sweet spirit away.' So she spoke; and as I took it in, I tried to embrace the soul of my dead mother. Three times I tried, and my spirit urged me to take hold. Three times it flew from my arms, like a shadow or a dream, and piercing sorrow kept rising in my heart. I said, 'Mother, why do you not stay still when I try to embrace you, so that by embracing we might delight in cold lamentation, even in the house of Hades? Has proud Persephone sent me an image, to make me lament and grieve still more?' 'My son,' she answered, 'most unfortunate of all mankind, it is not Persephone who forbids it; this is the way of mortals when they are dead. The sinews no longer keep the flesh and bones; these perish in the strength of consuming fire as soon as the spirit has left the body, and the soul flutters out and flies off as though it were a dream. But now go back to the light of day as soon as you can, and take note of all these things so that you can tell them to your wife later.' … [471] The soul of swift Achilles knew me and spoke words of grief: 'Odysseus, noble son of Laertes, what next? What greater action than this can you be planning in your heart? How could you dare to come down to the house of Hades where the witless dead stay, the images of toiling mortals?' And I said, '… As for you, Achilles, no one was ever yet so blessed as you have been, nor ever will be; for when you were alive, all we Greeks gave you honour equal to a god's, and now that you are here you are a mighty ruler among the dead. And so, do not grieve at being dead, Achilles.' He answered: 'Do not say a word in death's favour. I would prefer to be a menial labourer in the household of a man with little property, with little to live on, if I could only be on earth, rather than be king over all the dead souls.' … [541] The souls of other dead men stood near me and each told me his own cares; but the soul of Ajax son of Telamon alone held aloof—still angry with

me for having won the cause in our dispute about the armour of Achilles. ...
When I saw him, I spoke with gentle words: 'Ajax, will you not forget even in
death your anger at me over that hateful armour? It was a curse the gods sent
on the Greeks, since we lost such a tower of strength as you. We mourned
you as much as we mourned Achilles son of Peleus himself. No one is the
cause except Zeus, who bitterly hated the army of the Greeks, and laid this
fate on you.[2] Come, then, king Ajax, and hear what I have to say; subdue your
might and your proud spirit.' He made no reply, but went off after the other
souls to Erebus, the house of the dead.

302 ARISTOTLE, *Soul* 405[a]19–21 To judge from what is recorded about him,
Thales also seems to have held soul to have been some sort of originator of
change, given that he said the magnet had a soul, because it moves iron.[3]

303 ARISTOTLE, *Soul* 411[a]7–8 Some say that soul is mixed into the whole
world, which is presumably why Thales also thought that everything was full
of gods.

304 ARISTOTLE, *Soul* 403[b]20–9 In our examination of the soul, we must
both set out the puzzles that are to be solved as we advance, and enlist the
views of all the previous thinkers who have expressed views on the soul, so
that we can accept whatever is correct in their views and avoid whatever is
mistaken. The right starting-point for our investigation is to set out the features that most commonly seem to belong to the soul by nature. What has a
soul, then, seems to differ from what lacks a soul in these two most characteristic ways—change and perception. These are also roughly the two features of the soul that have been handed down by our predecessors; for some
say that the soul is what most characteristically and primarily originates
change.

Heracleitus

305 Heracleitus differs from Thales in attending to features of the soul beyond
its being an originator of change. He takes up the traditional connection between the existence of Achilles and the presence of soul in Achilles' body. But
he exploits this connection more extensively than Homer ever exploits it. He
identifies the soul with the person whose soul it is; that is why his inquiry into
his soul is his inquiry into himself (**306**).

Heracleitus believes that inquiry into himself is difficult. Though the soul is
familiar to us, we easily misunderstand its character, partly because we confuse

[2] The responsibility of the gods; **346–8**.
[3] 'Because' may indicate an explanation supplied by Aristotle.

the soul with the senses. To identify ourselves simply with our senses is to make the mistake of those who have 'foreign' souls, and therefore cannot interpret correctly what the senses tell them (**114**).

Inquiry into his soul is not simply Heracleitus' inquiry into himself; it is also inquiry into the cosmos. For he identifies the soul with the cosmic reason (*logos*; **113** n.) that guides the universe. That is why he regards the soul as fire and makes fire a primary component of the universe. Soul is a basic element of the cosmos that Heracleitus identifies with an orderly process of change and flux (**61–4**).

The surviving evidence on Heracleitus does not allow us to say precisely what he takes to be the relation between individual reason, the basic laws of the physical universe, and the intelligence that guides the physical universe. He may not have worked out their connection precisely. But his views suggest a line of argument that is pursued in more detail by the Stoics (**342**, **616**, **618**).

306 PLUTARCH, *Against Colotes* 1118c We pass to the place where Colotes ridicules and talks nonsense about Socrates, for asking what a human being is and for boasting, as Colotes alleges, that he did not even know himself. It is clear that Colotes has never paid any attention to this question. Heracleitus says, as though he had achieved something great and impressive, 'I inquired into myself'. And of the things written in Delphi, the most divine was thought to be 'Know yourself'. This was what led Socrates to begin being puzzled and to inquire, as Aristotle says in his Platonic writings.[4]

307 DIOGENES LAERTIUS ix. 7 = DK 22 B B45 [HERACLEITUS:] If you travel every road, still you will not find the limits of the soul; so deep is its account.

308 CLEMENT, *Miscellanies* ii. 2. 8. 1 = DK 22 B 17 [HERACLEITUS:] Most people do not understand the things they encounter; nor, when they have learned, do they know; but they seem to themselves to know.

309 HISDOSUS SCHOLASTICUS[5] = DK 22 B 67A Heracleitus gives an excellent comparison of the soul to a spider and the body to the spider's web. As the spider, he says, waiting in the middle of the web, notices as soon as a fly breaks any of the threads and then quickly runs to the spot, as if she were distressed by the breaking of the thread; just so, when any part of a human body is harmed, the soul hastens there, as if disturbed by the wound of the body, to which it is firmly and fittingly linked.

---

[4] The soul and the self in Plato; **316**, **321–3**. Plutarch refers to one of Aristotle's lost works (see **19** n.).

[5] This report is sometimes regarded as a mistaken attribution of Stoic views to Heracleitus; cf. **342**.

310 CLEMENT, *Miscellanies* vi. 17. 2 = DK 22 B 36   [HERACLEITUS:] For souls it is death to become water, and for water it is death to become earth. From earth water comes into being, and from water soul.

311 STOBAEUS, *Anthology* iii. 5. 8 = DK 22 B 118   [HERACLEITUS:] A dry soul is wisest and best.

Democritus

312 Like Heracleitus, Democritus identifies the soul with some appropriate material constituent of the body. Since the soul initiates change without any obvious external stimulant, and with no noticeable disturbance in the body, Democritus suggests that it is composed of especially fine spherical atoms in constant motion. Because of their small size and smooth shape, their own constant motion and their initiation of bodily motion easily escapes notice.

This identification of the soul with a collection of atoms of a specific type implies that when we explain bodily motion as a result of perception or thought or desire, our explanation is logically parallel to our explanation of the ripples on a lake by reference to a stone thrown into the middle. In both cases, we refer to the initial impact, and the diffusion of the motion caused by this impact.

Aristotle objects that this way of understanding explanations that refer to the soul is misguided, because the soul moves the body through decision and thought, not in the way that Democritus describes (**313**). He may assume that Democritus' Atomism commits him to an eliminative conception of atomic compounds.[6] According to this conception, nothing except the movements of atoms is strictly real, and no explanation that does not refer exclusively to movements of atoms can be correct.

This eliminative Atomist position implies the unreality of form, and the falsity of explanations that refer to the formal and final causes. Since thought and decision are mentioned in explanations referring to formal and final causes, they have no place in explanation if formal and final causes are unreal. Hence— Aristotle may infer—Democritus cannot avoid denying that we really act in ways that are correctly explained by thought and decision.

The soul also has a central place in Democritus' ethical theory. He suggests that happiness is to be identified with a temperate and undisturbed condition; here he anticipates some of the later theories that identify happiness with tranquillity (cf. **173**). Democritus may have taken this undisturbed condition of the soul to be a specific condition of the atoms constituting the soul; the appropriately tranquil soul is not moved 'over large intervals'. If this is what Democritus

[6] Eliminative atomism; **90**, **234**, **331**, **351**.

intends, it shows how seriously he takes the task of giving an atomic translation of truths about the soul.[7]

....

313 ARISTOTLE, *Soul* 406^{b}15–25 Some people say that the soul moves the body that it belongs to, with the same motion that it has itself. This is what Democritus says, in terms rather similar to those used by Philippus the comic poet, who says that Daedalus set the wooden statue of Aphrodite in motion, by pouring in quicksilver. Democritus says the same sort of thing; he says the indivisible spheres are in motion, because by nature they are never at rest, and that they drag along and move the whole body. In reply we will ask whether the same thing causes the body to come to rest; it is difficult, or even impossible, to say how it will do this. In general, the soul appears to move the animal not in this way, but through some sort of decision and thought.

314 STOBAEUS, *Anthology* iii. 1. 210 = DK 68 B 191 [DEMOCRITUS:] For human beings acquire good spirits through moderation of enjoyment and a measured life. Excesses and deficiencies tend to change into their opposites and to produce large disturbances in the soul. But souls that suffer motion over large intervals[8] are neither well balanced nor in good spirits.

Socrates on the soul

315 Socrates agrees with Democritus' emphasis on the moral importance of the condition of one's soul, but he has no theory or hypothesis about the composition of the soul. He neither says nor denies that it is made of any of the material stuffs that appear in Presocratic speculation. Indeed, he suggests that such questions about the soul are irrelevant to his claims about the nature and importance of the soul. The soul is important to ethics, because ethics is about making ourselves good or bad, and the self who is made good or bad is identical to the soul. Socrates urges the Athenians to care about themselves and the welfare of their real selves, not about their external possessions. To care about ourselves we must care about our souls, to make them as virtuous as possible; no other benefit can possibly compensate for the harm we do ourselves by having vicious souls, and our welfare is secured if and only if our souls are virtuous (**316**).

In these remarks Socrates assumes that his soul is himself. He contrasts virtue, understood as the health of the soul, with the health of the body, and he argues that the soul is more important than the body, because I myself am more important than what belongs to me. He assumes without explanation that my

---

[7] Pleasure and psychic movement; **392**, **415–17**.
[8] i.e. motion of the atoms constituting the soul.

beliefs, choices, aims, and character are parts of myself more properly than my heart, arms, or weight are.

Socrates' special concern with the soul is intelligible in the light of Heracleitus' remarks about the soul. Socrates might reasonably claim, as Heracleitus does, to be inquiring into himself. But Socrates goes further in maintaining the superior value of the soul, and especially its moral aspects, in comparison with anything else about us (cf. **453**). Since his soul is himself, he secures his own welfare by securing the welfare of his soul, and he secures the welfare of his soul by acquiring the virtues (**492**). Poverty, imprisonment, sickness, and so on happen to Socrates' body, not to his soul. To suppose that his happiness required anything more than his virtue would be to have a mistaken conception of himself.

In the *Apology* Socrates is non-committal about immortality (**317**), but in the *Crito* he affirms it (**318**). He assumes that after death he will be called to account for how he has lived. This judgement after death is assumed in the 'myth' that ends the *Gorgias* (**319**). Socrates does not commit himself to belief in the details of the myth, which are drawn from traditional Greek religion. But he seems to accept the central claim about immortality and responsibility.

316 PLATO, *Crito* 47 C–48 A   SOCRATES: When we are concerned with just and unjust, shameful and fine, good and evil, as we are now, ought we to follow the belief of the many and to fear it? Or the belief of the one person, if there is any such person, who understands these things? He is the one we ought to fear and reverence more than all the others, and the price of deserting him will be ruin and injury to what is improved by justice and destroyed by injustice. Or is there no such thing? CRITO: Certainly there is, Socrates.— Well, if we destroy what is improved by health and ruined by disease, because we have followed the belief of those with no understanding, is life worth living with that destroyed? And isn't that the body?—Yes.—Then is life worth living with a bad and ruined body?—Certainly not.—And is life worth living if what is improved by justice and ruined by injustice is ruined? Do we suppose that this, whatever it may be in us that has to do with justice and injustice, is inferior to the body?—Certainly not.—More valuable, then?—Far more valuable.[9]

317 PLATO, *Apology* 40 C–41 C   Let us grasp in this way that there is much ground for hope that death is good. For being dead is one of two things. Either to be dead is to be nothing and to have no awareness of anything, or, as people say, it is in fact a change and migration of the soul from here to another place. Now if you suppose that there is no awareness, but the sort of sleep that someone sleeps when he sees nothing even in dreams, death will be an amazing gain. For if someone had to pick the night in which he slept so soundly that he

[9] The health of the soul; **470**.

saw nothing even in a dream, and had to compare it with the other days and nights of his life, and tell us how many days and nights he had passed in the course of his life better and more pleasantly than this one, I believe no one— never mind an ordinary person, but even the Great King[10]—will find many such days or nights, when compared with the others. Now if death is like this, I say that to die is gain; for all of time then appears no more than a single night.

But if death is a sort of journey from here to another place, and what people say is true, that all the dead are there, what good can be greater than this, members of the jury? If indeed someone arrives in Hades, and is freed from those who claim to be judges here on earth, and finds the true judges who are said to give judgement there, Minos, Rhadamanthys, Aeacus, and Triptolemus, and other demigods who proved just in their own life, that journey will be worth making. What would any of us not give to converse with Orpheus, Musaeus, Hesiod, and Homer? If this is true, I'm ready to die many times over. I, too, will have a wonderful stay there, where I can meet Palamedes, Ajax the son of Telamon, and any other people of old who have been unjustly condemned to death; there will be no small pleasure, I think, in comparing what has happened to me and to them.

Above all, I will pass my time examining and interrogating people there, as I do with people here, about who among them is wise, and who thinks he is wise, and is not. And what would one not give, members of the jury, to be able to examine the leader of the great Trojan expedition; or Odysseus or Sisyphus, or numberless others, both men and women? What amazing happiness it would be to meet them, to converse[11] with them and examine them. For presumably there they don't put someone to death for doing this; for, besides being happier there than here, they will be immortal for the rest of time, if what is said is true.

Then you too, members of the jury, must have good hope about death, and must think this one thing to be true, that nothing is bad for a good man, either in life or after death. His affairs are not neglected by the gods; nor has what has happened to me happened by mere chance. No; it is clear to me that to die now and to be released is better for me; that is why the sign[12] at no point turned me away. For the same reason I am not altogether angry with my accusers, or my condemners. However this good was not what they had in mind for me in condemning or in accusing me; they thought they were harming me, and for this it is right to blame them.

318 PLATO, *Crito* 54 BC[13] Listen, then, Socrates, to us the laws, who have brought you up. Do not value children, or life, or anything else, above what

---

[10] The king of Persia.

[11] *dialegesthai*, used for a Socratic cross-examination. Cf. **96**, **142**, **189–90**, **220**, **321**, **583**.

[12] Socrates' sign; **540**, **582**.

[13] This is part of the speech that Socrates attributes to the laws of Athens, dissuading him from escaping. See also **454**, **542**.

is just, so that when you go to Hades, you will have a defence to present to the rulers there. For neither for you nor for any that belong to you will it be better, or holier, or more just, in this life, or better when you arrive there, if you do these things that Crito urges on you. As it is, you go, if you go, as a victim of injustice, not at our hands, but at the hands of human beings. But if you escape, and so return evil for evil, and wrong for wrong, violating your covenants and agreements with us, and wronging those who least deserve it—yourself, your friends, your country, and us—we shall be angry with you while you live, and our brothers, the laws there in Hades, will not receive you with goodwill, since they will know that you undertook to destroy us, as far as lay in you. Listen, then, to us, not to Crito.

319 PLATO, *Gorgias* 522 E–527 C   For anyone who is not an utter fool and coward is not afraid of death itself, but he is afraid of doing wrong. For to go to the world below having one's soul full of unjust actions is the ultimate and worst of all evils. ... [524 B] Death, it seems to me, is nothing other than the separation of two things, soul and body. And after they are separated each keeps almost the condition it had when the human being was alive. ... When the soul is stripped of the body, all its natural or acquired conditions are open to view. And when they come to the judge, as those from Asia come to Rhadamanthys,[14] he places them near him and inspects each person's soul, not knowing whose it is. Often he has taken hold of the soul of the Great King, or of some other king or ruler, and noticed that nothing in the soul is healthy, but it is entirely disfigured and full of the scars of perjuries and injustice with which each action has stained his soul, and he is all crooked with falsehood and boasting, and has no straightness, because he has lived without truth. Rhadamanthys saw his soul full of all deformity and shamefulness, caused by power, luxury, insolence, and incontinence, and sent him off without honour straight to prison, to undergo the full measure of appropriate treatment. Everyone who is correctly punished by another ought either to become better and benefit from it, or to be made an example to others, so that when they see what he suffers, they will be afraid and become better. Those who are improved when they are punished by gods and human beings are those whose errors are curable. Still, their benefit comes through pain and suffering, both in this world and in Hades; for there is no other way to free them from injustice. But those who have done the worst injustices, and because of them become incurable, are made examples. Since they are incurable, they can no longer benefit themselves, but others benefit when they see them undergoing for ever the most terrible, painful, and fearful sufferings because of their errors. ... [527 A] Now perhaps you[15] think all this is only an old wives' tale, and you

---

[14] On the function of Rhadamanthys see **317**.
[15] 'You' = Callicles.

will disdain it. Your disdain would not be surprising, if our inquiries had led us to anything better or truer. But in fact, as you see, you and Polus and Gorgias, the wisest of the Greeks of our day, cannot prove that we ought to live any life other than this one, which evidently benefits us in the next world as well as in this one. And in our discussions everything else has been refuted, and only this claim stands firm: that doing injustice is more to be avoided than suffering injustice; that a man should above all practise being good rather than appearing good, both in private and in public life; that when anyone has become bad in any way, he is to be corrected; and that the next best thing to being just is becoming just by being corrected through punishment.

From Socrates to Plato

320 In these claims about the soul, the self, and immortality, Socrates leaves some metaphysical questions unanswered. He does not say, for instance, whether the soul is a sort of material stuff (as Democritus supposed), what aspects of Socrates are immortal (his physical characteristics? his character? his emotions? his reason?), or how something immortal can survive the dissolution of his body. These are questions that Plato tries to answer. He argues that each person is identical to her reason and capacity for thought, and that since the rational intellect is immortal, each person is immortal.

The *First Alcibiades* is probably not by Plato, but it gives a good idea of how these Platonic views of the soul emerge from Socrates' concern with ethics.[16] It argues that the soul, as Socrates understood it (the subject of virtue and vice), must be non-bodily. As the later Platonist Proclus says, the dialogue is concerned especially with Socrates' search for self-knowledge; this search leads to recognition of a soul distinct from the body (**322**).

In the *Phaedo*, Plato makes his most serious effort to argue for a conception of the soul that both justifies Socrates' moral claims about the importance of the soul and explains how the immortality of the soul is possible. At the end of the dialogue Socrates tells Crito that the corpse he will bury will not be Socrates. Socrates himself survives his death, even though his body decays. He identifies himself with an immortal soul that is capable of existing without any body. The rest of the dialogue seeks to describe more fully the soul for which one can reasonably claim immortality.

....

321 [PLATO], *First Alcibiades* 129 A–130 C SOCRATES: Come now, tell me who is your partner in conversation?[17] Surely it's me?—ALCIBIADES: Yes.—And

---

[16] The *First Alcibiades* may have been written as an introduction to the study of Platonic philosophy. At any rate, it was used for this purpose by later Platonists.

[17] *dialegesthai*; **317**.

I'm your partner?—Yes.—Then Socrates is conversing?—Yes.—And Alcibiades is the hearer?—Yes.—And doesn't Socrates converse in speech?[18]—Certainly.—And you take conversing and using speech to be the same?—To be sure.—And isn't the user different from what he uses? ... —Yes.— ... And doesn't a human being use the whole body?—Certainly.—And we agreed that the user is different from what is used?—True.—Then a human being is not the same as his body?—It would seem so.—What is he then?—I can't say.—Surely you can say that he is the user of the body.—Yes.—And the user of the body is the soul?—Yes, the soul.—And the soul rules?—Yes.—And here is something else that no one will disagree with.—What is it?—That a human being is one of three things.—What are they?—Soul, or body, or both together as a whole.—Certainly.—But did we not say that the very thing that rules the body is the human being?—Yes, we did.—Now does the body rule itself?—Certainly not.—For it is ruled, as we were saying?—Yes.—Then it isn't what we are looking for?—It would seem not.—But does the combination of the two rule the body, and is this the human being?—Perhaps—No indeed—least of all; for if one of them is not a joint ruler, the combination cannot possibly rule.—True.—But since neither the body nor the combination of the two is the human being, all that remains is that either the human being is nothing, or, if he is something, it turns out that the human being is nothing other than the soul.—Just so.

322 PROCLUS, *Commentary on the Alcibiades* 4. 21–5. 12   We regard this as the most appropriate starting-point both for all philosophy and for Plato's doctrine ... the pure and unalloyed knowledge of ourselves, defined in terms expressing scientific knowledge, and bound firmly by 'reasonings about the explanation'.[19] For where else is it proper to begin the purification and perfection of ourselves than at the point where the God of Delphi urged us to begin? For just as the notice told those entering the temple at Eleusis not to go inside the shrine if they were not initiated and perfected, so also the notice 'Know yourself' in front of the temple at Delphi indicated the way to ascend to the divine and the most effective way to purification, practically saying straight out, to those able to understand, that the one who has gained knowledge of himself has begun at the right beginning, and so is able to be joined to the god who reveals the whole truth and guides us in the life that purifies us.

323 PLATO, *Phaedo* 115 C–116 A [CRITO:] ... And in what way are we to bury you? [SOCRATES:] In any way you like, if you catch me, and I don't escape from you. Then he turned to us, and added with a smile: I haven't persuaded Crito that I am the same Socrates who is conversing now, and

[18] *logos*; see **113**n.
[19] Quoted from the *Meno*, **107**.

conducting the argument. He thinks I am that corpse he will soon see, and he asks how he is to bury me. I have constructed a long argument to show you that as soon as I have drunk the poison, I will be waiting around for you no longer, but I'll leave you and go to the various kinds of happiness enjoyed by the blessed. But in saying all this, encouraging both you and myself, I seem to have had no success with Crito. The rest of you must be my surety to him … that I won't stay around, but go away and depart. Then he will bear my death more easily, and when he sees my body being burned or buried, he will not grieve over any supposed suffering of mine. Nor will he say at the burial that he is laying out Socrates, or following Socrates to the grave, or burying Socrates. For you can be sure, excellent Crito, that speaking wrongly is not only inappropriate in itself, but also inflicts harm on the soul. You must have confidence, and say that you are burying my body only; do it however you like, and in the way you think most lawful.[20]

Aspects of the soul

324 Plato's belief in the distinctness and separability of body and soul rests on several contrasts between their capacities, functions, and activities. We need to ask what contrasts does Plato assert? Are these genuine contrasts? Are they contrasts between body and soul? Do they support Plato's view that the soul is capable of existing without the body?

1. In the *Meno* Plato argues that inquiry is a process of 'recollection', which is complete when we have achieved knowledge (**183–6**). If this is literal recollection of what we knew before our birth, Plato commits himself to the existence of our souls before they are connected to our bodies. In the *Phaedo* he reaffirms his belief in recollection, and presents it as an argument for the immortality of the soul (**205**).

2. Plato considers the role of mind in the explanation of a person's actions (**96**). According to Socrates, the reason he stayed where he was rather than leaving was his belief that it would be best. States of mind explain human action; they explain what Socrates does rather than simply what happens to his body. The mind is the source of the rational, goal-directed action that is characteristic of a human being.[21]

3. This claim refers to mind, and specifically to rational mind, not to soul. But Plato sometimes seems to identify soul with rational mind. He contrasts the soul with the senses, attributing the senses to the body, and identifying the soul with the rational, reflective, intellect. The senses

---

[20] *nomos*; **125**.
[21] Soul as cause of motion; **594**.

distract the soul, and hence distract us, from grasping the truth (**195–6**). The soul, as Plato conceives it in the *Phaedo*, does not seem to include all those states that we would call 'mental' or 'conscious'. Irrational desires and sense-impressions are conscious and mental; but Plato attributes them to the body, not to the soul. He develops a suggestion of Heracleitus (**114**), and identifies the soul with our capacity to reflect on and examine our sensory input; in discovering this capacity we also discover ourselves (**306**).

4. Plato returns to this question in a practical context. He considers the view that the soul is to be identified with a 'harmony' or 'adjustment' of the various elements that make up the body (**325**; cf. **333**). Socrates objects that if the harmony theory were right, we would never find the soul ruling the body or opposing the affections of the body; but we find the soul doing exactly these things. Socrates appeals to a passage in Homer where Odysseus speaks to himself, when he is facing a difficult situation; he tells his spirit (*thumos*) not to give way but to 'endure'. Plato cites this passage in *Republic* iv to support the division of the soul into three parts (**438**). In the *Phaedo* (**326**) he cites it to support a division between body and soul. Here also, just as in the contrast between the soul and the senses, Plato identifies the soul—the critical, reflective capacity—with the self. If I ask 'What do I really want?' or 'What do I really believe?', I do not simply rely on my first impressions or my first reactions; I try to form a view as a result of critical reflection about the best conclusion. This is another reason why Plato's account of the causation and explanation of human actions focuses especially on the good. He connects mind with the good because he takes us to be identified with the critical, reflective capacity that allows us to distinguish what we really think best from what we find immediately attractive.

5. In coming to know the Forms and in cultivating the virtues, we reduce our concern for the body. Some people do brave or temperate or just actions only when they see some further material advantage and sensory pleasure coming from them; these people have a mere 'facade' of virtue (**327**). The philosopher, however, is unreservedly committed to the virtues, because he does not care about any worldly loss they may involve. Plato does not suggest that the philosopher's indifference to ordinary worldly considerations will also make him indifferent to the virtues of ordinary social life. This suggestion, however, appears in Plotinus' account of the philosopher's renunciation of worldly concerns (**607**).

....

325 PLATO, *Phaedo* 85 E–86 D   [SIMMIAS:] You might say … that the attunement is something invisible, incorporeal, splendid, and divine in the tuned lyre, and the lyre itself and its strings are bodies and have a bodily character, and are composite, earthly, and mortal in kind. Now suppose someone breaks the lyre, or cuts or tears out its strings. If someone were to insist on your argument, that attunement must still exist unbroken; for it would be impossible, when the strings are torn out, for the lyre and the strings themselves, which have a mortal nature, to remain in being, while the attunement, which has the nature and character of the divine and immortal, has been destroyed and has perished before the mortal part. He would say that the attunement must still exist somewhere just as it was, and that the wood and the strings will rot before anything happens to it. I say this, Socrates, because, as I think you yourself are aware, we[22] hold that the soul is more or less of this kind. Our body is stretched out and held together by hot, cold, dry, wet, and so on, and our soul is a mixture and attunement of these same things, when they are mixed in the right proportion. Well, if the soul is really some sort of attunement, obviously, as soon as our body becomes too slack or too tight because of diseases and other ills, the soul must at once be destroyed, however divine it is, like any other attunement, either in music or in any manufactured product; in each case the remains of the body last a long time until they are burned or they rot. Consider what we are to say to this argument, if someone claims that the soul, since it is a mixture of the elements in the body, is the first thing to be destroyed in what is called death.

326 PLATO, *Phaedo* 94 B–E [SOCRATES:] Of everything in a human being, can you mention anything that rules, except for the soul, especially a wise soul?—[SIMMIAS:] No, I can't.—Does it rule by giving in to the affections of the body or by opposing them? I mean, for example that when heat and thirst are present, the soul draws in the opposite direction, not to drink, and when hunger is present, not to eat, and presumably in thousands of other ways we see the soul opposing what is in the body, don't we?—Certainly.—Didn't we also agree a little while ago that if it is an attunement, it can never sound a note that conflicts with the tension or relaxation or vibration or anything else that happens to its constituents, but must always follow them and never lead?—Yes, we did of course.—Well, surely we can now see that the soul produces just the opposite effects. It directs all the elements of which it is said to be composed, opposing them in almost everything all through life, and dominating them in every way. Sometimes it corrects by severe and unpleasant means, such as gymnastics and medicine, and sometimes by gentler means, sometimes with threats, sometimes with instruction; it converses with the appetites and impulses and fears as though it were one thing conversing with a different thing. That is the sort of thing Homer portrayed in the *Odyssey*, where he says that Odysseus 'then struck his breast, and reproved his heart: Endure, my heart; still worse you have endured.' Do you suppose that when

[22] Simmias speaks as a Pythagorean.

he wrote that he thought the soul was an attunement, the sort of thing that is swayed by affections of the body? Surely he regarded it as the sort of thing that leads and dominates them, as something much too divine to rank with an attunement?—That is certainly how it seems to me, Socrates.

327 PLATO, *Phaedo* 68 B–69 C [SOCRATES:] And so if you see anyone distressed at the prospect of dying, said Socrates, it will be proof enough that he is not a lover of wisdom[23] but a lover of the body. Presumably he is in fact also a lover of wealth and reputation—one or the other or both. [SIMMIAS:] Yes, you are quite right.—Doesn't it follow, Simmias, he went on, that what is called bravery is proper most of all to the lover of wisdom?—Yes, no doubt it does, he said.—Temperance too—what even the many call temperance, which is being calm in the face of appetites, and keeping an orderly disposition that attaches little importance to them—isn't this proper only to those who more than anyone else attach little importance to the body, and spend their lives in philosophy?—Certainly. ... —You know, don't you, that everyone except the philosopher regards death as a great evil?—Yes indeed.—Don't the brave among non-philosophers face death from fear of greater evils, when they face it?—Yes, it is true.—So all except the philosophers are brave because they are afraid, though it is unreasonable for someone to count as brave because of some sort of fear and cowardice?—Quite right.—What about temperate people among non-philosophers? Doesn't the same thing happen to them, that they are temperate by a sort of intemperance? ... They are afraid of losing other pleasures that they have an appetite for, and so they refrain from one kind because they are overcome by the other. ... —Yes, that seems to be true.—Blessed Simmias. surely this is not the correct sort of exchange in relation to <the standard of> virtue—exchanging smaller pleasures or pains or fear for greater, like coins. Surely the only correct currency, for which all these should be exchanged, is wisdom. ... When <pleasures, pains, and fear> are exchanged for one another, in separation from wisdom, that sort of virtue is an illusion, a truly slavish virtue that has nothing sound or true in it. Temperance, justice, and bravery are really a kind of purification from all these things, and wisdom itself is a means of purification.

Plato's argument for dualism

328 In attributing these different features to Socrates' soul and in identifying Socrates' soul with Socrates, Plato argues that we are right to identify ourselves with our critical, reflective capacities rather than with our immediate impressions. He infers that the soul that is the subject of these capacities is capable of

---

[23] *philosophos*, translated 'philosopher' in what follows; cf. **388**.

existing without any body, and hence without the other capacities that result from our having a body. He also claims that when the soul exists without these other capacities, it is still to be identified with the person whose soul it is. This claim must be true if Plato is to prove that the immortality of our souls constitutes our immortality.

In defence of his belief in the immortality of the soul, Plato argues for a dualist doctrine; body and soul are two different things, and the soul is immaterial, imperceptible, and immortal, while the body is material, perceptible, and mortal. The soul can know the Forms without the senses, and, like the Forms, it is imperceptible and indestructible; it survives any and all of the bodies that ever belong to it.

These arguments for immortality are intended to support the philosopher's way of life. In Plato's view, genuine virtue requires us to cultivate independence from the needs and impulses of the body. This demand of virtue determines the philosopher's way of life; he concentrates, as Socrates advised, on concern for the soul. To explain why virtue imposes this demand, and why the demand is reasonable, Plato appeals to the belief in dualism and immortality. It is reasonable for us to be indifferent to the needs of the body, if the body is no part of us and if its condition does not affect our vital interests. If the body is no part of us, then we must be capable of existing without a body. Hence the philosopher's practice of virtue is to be understood as preparation for death, when he will be free of the distractions that result from association with a body.

Plato claims (1) that we identify ourselves with our critical, reflective capacities that go beyond immediate impressions of the senses and the body. But he also claims (2) that we identify ourselves with these same critical, reflective capacities, even if they exist without immediate impressions of the senses and the body. Even if we think the first claim is reasonable, we might hesitate about the second. I might well agree that I am something beyond my particular feelings and impressions; but I do not thereby agree that I would still be what I am without them. Readers of Plato's arguments need to ask whether he gives any good reason for accepting his second claim.

329　PLATO, *Phaedo* 79 A–80 B[24]　[SOCRATES:] Well then, added Socrates, are we to suppose there are two sorts of beings[25]—one seen, the other unseen.[26] [CEBES:] Let us suppose so.—The unseen is always in the same condition, and the seen is never in the same condition?—We can also suppose that.—And, further, isn't one <part> of us body, another <part> soul?—To be sure.— And to which would we say the body is more similar and akin?—Clearly to the seen—no one can doubt that.—And what about the soul? Seen or un-

---

[24] This follows **206**.

[25] Plato often confines 'being' to Forms, but here uses it to include sensible things.

[26] Or 'visible … invisible'.

seen?—Not seen by human sight, anyhow, Socrates.—And when we spoke of what is or is not seen, we referred to human sight?—Yes, human sight.—Then what do we say about the soul? Is it seen or unseen?—Not seen.—Unseen, then?—Yes.—Then the soul is more similar than the body to the unseen, and the body is more similar to the seen?—That follows necessarily, Socrates.—And were we not saying earlier that when the soul uses the body to examine something, through sight or hearing or some other sense (since examining through the body is examining through sense), it is dragged by the body to things that are never in the same condition, so that it wanders in confusion, and gets dizzy like a drunkard, since it has contact with such things?—Very true.—But when it examines by itself, it passes to what is pure, what always is, immortal, in the same condition; being akin to this, the soul always remains in the same condition, as long as it is by itself and is not hindered, but stops wandering, and is always in the same condition, since this is the sort of reality it has grasped. And this state of the soul is called wisdom?—Well said and quite true, Socrates, he replied. ... —When the soul and the body are together, nature orders the soul to rule and dominate, and the body to be ruled as a slave. Now in these respects, which seems to you similar to the divine, and which to the mortal? Doesn't the divine seem to you to be such as to rule and lead by nature, and the mortal to be such as to be ruled as a slave?—True.—And which is the soul like?—Clearly, Socrates, the soul is like the divine, and the body is like the mortal.—Then consider, Cebes, whether it follows for us, from everything that has been said, that the soul is most similar to what is divine, immortal, intelligible, uniform, indissoluble, always in the same condition; and that the body is most similar to the human, mortal, multiform, unintelligible, dissoluble, never in the same condition as itself. Can this be denied, my dear Cebes?—No, it can't.—But if it is true, then isn't it proper to the body to be soon dissolved, and proper to the soul to be altogether indissoluble or nearly so?—Certainly.

330 PLATO, *Phaedo* 104 E–107 B[27] [SOCRATES:] Let us return, then, to the cases where one thing is not contrary to another, but still does not admit the other, as ... three, though not contrary to the even, still does not admit the even, since three always imports the contrary to the even, just as two imports the contrary to the odd, and fire imports the contrary to the cold, and the same is true in many other cases. See whether you now agree that not only does the one contrary not admit the other, but also whatever imports one contrary does not admit the other contrary ... [CEBES:] Yes, he said, I entirely agree, and go along with you in that.— ... If you ask me 'What is it whose presence makes the body hot?', I will mention not heat ... but fire ... Or if you ask me what it is whose presence makes a body diseased, I will not say that it

---

[27] This follows **207**.

is disease, but that it is fever … —Yes, he said, I quite understand you.—Tell me, then, what is it whose presence makes the body alive?—The soul, he replied.—And is this always the case?—Yes, he said, of course.—Then whatever the soul possesses, it always imports life to it?—Yes, certainly.—And is there any contrary to life, or not?—There is, he said.—And what is that?—Death.—Then the soul will never admit the contrary that is contrary to the one it imports, as we agreed before.—Quite right, replied Cebes.—And now, he said, what did we just now call what does not admit the even?—The odd.—And what is it that does not admit the musical or the just?—The unmusical, he said, or the unjust.—And what do we call what does not admit death?—The immortal,[28] he said.—And does the soul admit death?—No.—Then the soul is immortal?—Yes, he said.—And may we say that this has been proved?—Yes, abundantly proved, Socrates, he replied.

—Well, Cebes, if it were necessary for the odd to be imperishable,[29] wouldn't three be imperishable?—Of course.—And if it were necessary for the heatless to be imperishable, then whenever someone brought heat to snow, wouldn't the snow depart whole and unmelted, since it could not have perished, nor have remained and admitted the heat?—True, he said. … — Then surely it's necessary also to say this about the immortal: if the immortal is also imperishable, it is impossible for the soul to perish when death comes to it; for, by the previous argument, the soul will not admit death, or ever be dead, any more than three or the odd will admit the even, or fire, or the heat in the fire, will admit the cold. But someone might say: 'Granted that, as we agreed, the odd will not become even when the even approaches, why may not the odd perish and the even take the place of the odd?' If someone could said this, we could not counter by maintaining that the odd does not perish; for the odd is not imperishable. But if it had been agreed that the odd is imperishable, we could easily have countered by maintaining that at the approach of the even the odd and three depart; and the same argument would apply to fire and heat and anything else.—Very true.—And isn't the same true of the immortal? If the immortal is also imperishable, the soul will be imperishable as well as immortal. But if not, some other proof will have to be given.—No other proof is needed, as far as this question is concerned, he said; for if the immortal, being eternal, admits perishing, nothing else could be imperishable.—Yes, replied Socrates, and I think all human beings would agree that God, and the form itself of life, and anything else immortal never perishes.—Yes, human beings would agree, he said; and, what is more, gods also, I think.

—Since, then, the soul is indestructible, must not the soul, if it is in fact

---

[28] As the following argument shows, the sense Socrates attaches to 'immortal' or 'deathless' here implies only that if x is immortal, then it is impossible for x to exist and be dead.

[29] Or 'unperishing'.

immortal, be also imperishable?—Most certainly.—Then when death comes to a human being, the mortal <part> of him, it would seem, dies, but the immortal departs at the approach of death and is preserved safe and sound?—True.—Then, Cebes, beyond question, soul is immortal and imperishable, and our souls will truly exist in Hades?—I have no further doubt, Socrates, said Cebes, and have nothing more to say. ... —I have no point of doubt either, said Simmias, as far as this argument goes. But when I recognize how great a subject the arguments have discussed, and take proper account of human weakness, I am bound to have some doubt about what has been said.—Yes, Simmias, replied Socrates, you're right. Moreover, our basic assumptions, even if we have confidence in them, must be examined more perspicuously. If we articulate them adequately, you will follow the argument, as far as it is possible for a human being; and if this becomes perspicuous, you will inquire no further.—You are right, he said.

Aristotle: the problem of soul and body

331 Aristotle regards his account of the soul as a special case of his general claim that a thing's form is its nature (**239**); in his view, the soul is the form of the living body. It is easiest to understand this account if we see what questions it is meant to answer, and, in particular, what errors it is meant to correct. At the beginning of his work 'On the Soul' (*De Anima*), Aristotle opposes a one-sided emphasis on form, to the exclusion of matter; he attributes this emphasis to a 'dialectician'. He also opposes a one-sided emphasis on matter, which he attributes to a 'student of nature' (**332**). In the rest of book i of the *De Anima*, Aristotle opposes different one-sided views, in preparation for his statement of his own view.

Among the people who concentrate on the matter to the exclusion of the form, he attacks Democritus. Just as he criticizes Democritus elsewhere for insufficient recognition of form, so also he argues against Democritus' purely materialist account of the soul. In Democritus' view, common sense tries to explain the behaviour of living creatures by reference to the soul, but we can find a correct explanation of this behaviour only by identifying the soul with highly mobile atoms. Aristotle suggests that this attempted explanation is too simple.

To show that Democritus over-simplifies, Aristotle argues that we cannot explain why the agent starts and stops a deliberate action if we simply refer to the movement of the constituent atoms; reference to the atoms does not show us the point of the action (**99, 241–2, 245**). Aristotle seems to agree with Plato's claim in the *Phaedo* that explanation of our goal-directed action requires reference to thoughts and beliefs, and that material states are just necessary conditions (**96**). He also agrees with Plato in denying that the soul is simply an attunement of the bodily parts (**333**).

Aristotle criticizes Plato, however, for over-reaction to Democritus' error; Plato focuses on the form, and neglects the matter. From his arguments against materialism Plato infers (**326**) that the soul is a completely immaterial substance that can exist independently of any body. Aristotle objects that this dualist position fails to explain the close connection between a specific type of body and the corresponding soul. If the soul can exist without any suitable matter, why, he asks, do we not find a specific type of soul in many different sorts of bodies? Why do we not find a cat's soul in a mouse's body (**333**)?

An example that Aristotle offers to illustrate the relation of matter to form also illustrates the error that he sees in both dualism and materialism. He points out that a syllable is neither simply the sum of its component letters nor some further component besides the letters. The syllable CAT is the first syllable of 'catastrophe', but the sum of the letters, irrespective of their arrangement (TAC, TCA, ACT), is not the first syllable of 'catastrophe'. Hence the syllable is not identical to the sum of the letters. Still, the syllable is not a further letter besides the original ones; no letter needs to be added to the letters TCA in order to produce the syllable CAT (**259**).

Similarly, Aristotle's belief in formal and final causes does not imply that there is anything non-physical about the processes that are explained by them. He does not mean that, for instance, some non-physical soul is involved in the production of chairs, simply because a material-causal explanation is insufficient. The point is simply that the various physical processes fit together in a systematic and regular way; this is what we capture in speaking of the form. His account of how forms are causes (**240-6**) should also explain how souls are causes.

332 ARISTOTLE, *Soul* 403ᵃ28–ᵇ9   The student of nature and the dialectician would give different definitions of each of these affections—of anger, for instance. The dialectician would define it as a desire to inflict pain in return for pain, or something of that sort, whereas the student of nature would define it as a boiling of the blood and the hot element around the heart. Of these two, the student of nature describes the matter, whereas the dialectician describes the form and the account: desire, for instance, is the form[30] of the thing, but if it is to exist, it must be in this sort of matter. Similarly, the account of a house is of this sort: a shelter preventing destruction by wind, rain, or heat. Someone else will say that a house is stones, bricks, and timber; someone else again will say that it is the form in these stones, etc., for the sake of this end. Which one of these, then, is the student of nature? Is he the one who considers the matter but is ignorant of the account, or the one who considers only the account? Or is he more properly the one who mentions both form and matter?

---

[30] Both 'form' here and 'account' in the previous clause translate *logos*.

333 ARISTOTLE, *Soul* 407^{b}13–408^{a}5   This account[31] and most accounts of the soul have an absurd result, since they attach the soul to a body and place it there, with no further specification of why this happens and in what bodily condition. But further specification would seem to be needed, since it is because of this association that one acts and the other is affected, and one initiates change and the other is changed; none of these interactions happens between a random soul and body. These people, however, confine themselves to an attempt to say what sort of thing the soul is, and they specify nothing further about the sort of body that is to receive it. They speak as though it were possible, as in the Pythagorean stories, for a random soul to be inserted into a random body, whereas in fact each body seems to have its own distinctive form and shape. What they say is as absurd as saying that carpentry gets inserted into flutes; for a craft must use suitable instruments, and equally the soul must use a suitable body.

There is also another view about the soul that has been handed down ... People say that it is some sort of attunement; for, they say, an attunement is a blending and combination of contraries, and the body is composed of contraries. An attunement, however, is some sort of ratio or combination of the things mixed together, and the soul cannot be either of these. Further, an attunement does not initiate change, whereas practically everyone ascribes this most of all to the soul. It is more in tune with the facts to speak of attunement in the case of health and of bodily excellences in general than in the case of the soul. This would be most evident if one tried to assign the actions and affections of the soul to some sort of attunement; for it is difficult to attune them to it.

The definition of soul

334 Aristotle's criticism of materialism and of Platonic dualism suggests that mistaken views about the soul result from misunderstanding the character of form and matter and the relation between them. His own account of the soul clarifies this suggestion. His main argument is this:

(1) The soul is what makes a body alive.

(2) What makes something alive is not its matter but its form.

(3) What is made alive by the form is the matter.

(4) Hence the soul is the form and the body is the matter.

(5) The soul is substance.

(6) Hence the soul is the substance that is the form of the living body.

---

[31] Aristotle has just been discussing Plato's account in the *Timaeus*.

In (1) Aristotle indicates that he intends his account of the soul to extend to all living things, including plants. We have found a connection between soul and life in Homer and in Plato, who argues that Socrates' body ceases to be alive as soon as Socrates' soul leaves it. Aristotle generalizes and extends this traditional connection, attributing soul to everything that has life.

Aristotle explains (2) by saying that by 'life' he means especially nutrition and growth through oneself. These sorts of changes depend on the form rather than the matter. If a young tree grows into a mature tree, or a young child into an adult, the matter, shape, and size are changed. The only thing that is continuous is the form. The activities characteristic of being alive are continuous through the changes in the matter; these activities belong essentially to the form. The heart, for instance, continues in its role of pumping blood even though the matter of the heart changes. We remain in existence even though our matter changes, because the form is continuous (**252**; cf. **260–2**).

And so Aristotle concludes in (5) that, since form constitutes the continuity and identity of a living organism, the form is what makes the organism alive, and therefore soul is form. He identifies the form with the actuality, and the matter with the potentiality or capacity that is actualized by the form (**253**). The matter has the potentiality for various activities, and the form is the way in which the matter is organized to carry out those activities. The activities themselves (eating, breathing, walking, seeing, etc.) are what Aristotle calls 'second' actuality. If something has its matter organized for these activities, it has a soul; that is why Aristotle calls the soul a 'first' actuality (cf. **408**).

Aristotle believes that his account of the soul as form explains the truth in Plato's view, but without Plato's dualism. He thinks Plato is right to reject a strong version of materialism; we cannot understand a person's behaviour if we regard him simply as a collection of his matter (**96**). Plato is also right to claim that (in Aristotelian terms) the soul is a substance. According to Aristotle, the soul is a substance because it does not depend on any material body that is independent of it; that is why the soul is not simply an 'attunement' of material constituents (**333**). The body of an organism is not an independent substance; it is the living body that is alive because of its soul and cannot survive the loss of the soul (**336**).

Plato is wrong, however (according to Aristotle), to argue that, since Socrates is a substance irreducible to his matter, he is therefore an immaterial substance that can exist independently of his body. In saying that the soul is form, Aristotle insists that it is not simply matter. In saying that it is the form of the body, he insists that it is not some essentially immaterial form.

....

335 ARISTOTLE, *Soul* 412ª11–28 Bodies most of all seem to be substances, and, among these, natural bodies most of all, since they are the principles of the others. Some natural bodies are alive, some are not; by 'life' I mean nutrition, growth, and shrinking through oneself. And so every natural body sharing in life is a substance—more precisely, substance as compound. But since this is also this specific sort of body—that is, the sort that is alive—the soul cannot be a body, since the body <is substance> as subject and matter, and is not said of a subject. The soul, then, must be substance as the form of a natural body potentially living. Now substance is actuality; hence the soul will be the actuality of this specific sort of body. Actuality is spoken of in two ways—one corresponding to the state of knowing, and the other to attending to what one knows. Evidently, then, the soul is the same sort of actuality that knowing is; for both being asleep and being awake require the presence of the soul—being awake corresponds to attending, and being asleep to the state of inactive knowing. Moreover, in the same subject the state of knowing precedes the activity. Hence the soul is the first actuality of a natural body potentially living.

336 ARISTOTLE, *Soul* 412^{b}10–27   We have said in general, then, what the soul is: it is the substance that corresponds to the account,[32] and this sort of substance is the essence of this sort of body. It is as if some instrument—an axe, for instance—were a natural body; for in that case being an axe would be its substance and its soul; if this were separated from it, it would no longer be an axe, except homonymously. In fact, however, it is an axe; for the soul is not the essence and form of this sort of body, but of the specific sort of natural body that has in itself an origin of change and rest. We must also study this point by applying it to parts.[33] If the eye, for instance, were an animal, sight would be its soul. For sight is the eye's substance that corresponds to the account, while the eye is the matter of sight; if the sight departs, it is no longer an eye, except homonymously, as a stone eye or a painted eye is.[34] We must apply this point about the part to the whole living body; for what holds for the relation of part <of the faculty of perception> to part <of the body> holds equally for the relation of the whole <faculty of> perception to the whole perceptive body, in so far as it is perceptive. The sort of body that is potentially living is not the one that has lost its soul but the one that has it; the seed or the fruit is potentially this sort of body.

337 ARISTOTLE, *Soul* 414^{a}28–^{b}6   ... some things have all the capacities of the soul that were previously mentioned; other things have some of them, and others have only one. The capacities we mentioned were the nutritive, perceptive, desiring, locomotive, and understanding parts.[35] Plants have only the nutritive part. Other things have the nutritive and the perceptive parts, and if they have this, they also have the desiring part. For desire includes appetite,

---

[32] *logos*; i.e. the definition describing the form.

[33] With the argument from artefacts and organs to organisms, cf. **408**.

[34] With this claim about homonymy, cf. **252**, **257**.

[35] Or 'aspects': see **438**n.

spirit, and wish; but all animals have at least one sense, the sense of touch, and whatever has any perception has pleasure and pain and finds things pleasant or painful. Whatever finds things pleasant and painful also has appetite, since this is desire for the pleasant.[36]

Atomism and the soul

338 Epicurus wants to show that the soul is a collection of atoms, just as trees and chairs are, and therefore will certainly dissolve into its constituents. If Epicurus is right, Plato must be wrong to believe in an immaterial and immortal soul. If we do not believe in immortality, we will not believe that we can suffer harm after death, and therefore, Epicurus thinks, we have no reason to fear death. If we see we have no reason to fear death, we will not (according to Epicurean psychology) fear death (**421–6**).

To support this conclusion, Lucretius collects twenty-nine arguments for the mortality of the soul. These arguments raise some of the questions that arise for Epicurus' attempts to defend Atomism by appeal to the senses. According to Epicurus, we should accept the Atomic theory because it is the only possible explanation of experience; but all he seems to show is that it is one among a number of possible explanations of experience (**288–90**). Similarly, Lucretius finds abundant evidence to show that the soul is affected by what happens to the body: a blow on the head causes me pain, my mind decays with my body, and so on. One possible explanation of these facts will say that the soul is material and destructible, and depends on the body for its existence. But that is only one possible explanation, and someone who agrees with Plato that the soul is immaterial and immortal can offer other explanations.

To rule out these other explanations, a materialist might claim that only material bodies can be affected by material bodies (cf. **263**). If this claim is true, the soul cannot be immaterial; but how do we know it is true? Epicurus will hardly convince us that no other view is consistent with the evidence of the senses; to justify his materialism he must rely on a claim that is not warranted on empiricist grounds (as he understands them). Since he believes that a claim about reality is illegitimate unless it is warranted on empiricist grounds, his argument faces grave objections, even from an Epicurean point of view.

Epicurus' treatment of the soul raises a broader question about the extent of his disagreement with Aristotle. He wants to show not only that the soul is mortal, but also that it is simply a collection of atoms. He therefore rejects the claims of form (and therefore of soul) to be anything distinct from the collection of atoms.

[36] Types of soul; **408**.

339 LUCRETIUS iii. 161–76   This same reasoning shows that the nature of mind and soul is bodily. For we see that it pushes on the limbs, rouses the body from sleep, changes the expression on one's face, and guides and turns the whole man. But we see that none of these things can happen without touch, and that touch, in its turn, cannot happen without body. Surely, then, we must admit that mind and soul are formed of bodily nature? Moreover, you see that our mind suffers along with the body, and is equally affected in the body. If the shuddering force of a weapon, thrust into the body and laying bare bones and sinews, does not reach the life, even so it leads to faintness, a pleasant collapsing on the ground, a turmoil of mind that follows the collapse, and sometimes a sort of uncertain will to get up again. Therefore the nature of the mind must be bodily, since it suffers from the blow of bodily weapons.

Now what kind of body is this mind, and what parts is it made of? I will go on to give an account of this in what I say. First of all, I say that it is very fine in texture, and is made of very tiny bodies. You can learn that this is so, if you pay attention, from what follows. We see that nothing happens as quickly as what the mind proposes to itself and starts to do itself. Therefore the mind arouses itself more quickly than any of the things whose nature is obvious before our eyes. But because it is so very mobile, it must be made of extremely round and tiny seeds, so that they can move when a light blow strikes them.

340 LUCRETIUS iii. 417–58   Come now, I will show you that the minds and light souls of animate things have birth and death. ... First of all, I have shown that the soul is of fine texture, made of tiny bodies, of elements far smaller than the liquid moisture of cloud or smoke ... When jars are shattered, you see the water flowing away on every side, and the liquid parting this way and that; similarly, cloud and smoke dissipate into air. Hence, you must believe that the soul is also scattered and perishes far more quickly, and is dissolved sooner into its first bodies, as soon as it leaves a man's limbs and departs. ... [445] Moreover, we are aware that the mind comes into being along with the body, grows together with it, and grows old along with it. ... When the body is shattered by the strong forces of time, and the frame has sagged with its force dulled, then the reason is maimed, the tongue raves, the mind stumbles, everything collapses and fails at once. And so it is appropriate that all the nature of the mind is scattered like smoke into the high breezes of the air, since we see that it comes into being along with the body, grows along with it, and, as I have shown, becomes weary and worn with age at the same time as the body.[37]

---

[37] Lucretius adds further arguments. He takes the opportunity to stress the gloomy and painful aspects of life, from which Epicureanism is supposed to give us some relief (**503**). The conclusion of this series of 'proofs' is in **425**.

Stoic materialism and the soul

341 Like Aristotle, the Stoics associate soul very closely with form and the organization of matter. Unlike Aristotle, they identify form with a certain kind of body; they also hold a corporeal conception of the soul. They identify it with a certain condition of the sustaining 'breath' (*pneuma*) in an organism (**263–8**).

They restrict the extent of soul more narrowly than Aristotle does. Aristotle allows soul, but no sensation or desire, to plants. The Stoics, however, accept the traditional association of soul with perception, and therefore deny soul to plants. Plants have a 'nature' that makes them capable of self-nourishment and growth, but they have no soul (**266**).

To defend their corporeal conception of the soul, the Stoics appeal to claims about the soul that Plato and Aristotle accept; but they argue from these claims to conclusions that Plato and Aristotle reject. Like Plato, they regard death as the separation of soul and body; but they assume that nothing incorporeal is separated from a body, and so they infer that the soul must be a body. Perhaps they assume that separation must result in two separated entities in two different places, and that only a body can occupy a place; if they are separated, they were in contact, and only bodies can be in contact with each other.

The Stoics also argue from a common Aristotelian way of speaking. Aristotle often says that an organism is composed of form and matter, and that form and matter are its parts. If soul and body are form and matter, the soul is also a part of the animal. Since the animal is a body, the soul is a part of a body; but whatever is part of a body is a body; therefore the soul is a body.

As Alexander points out (**345**), the Stoics apply Aristotle's terms contrary to Aristotle's intentions, showing where their philosophical assumptions differ most clearly from his. Though Aristotle speaks of the form as a part of the compound, he does not intend it to be a physically separable proper part, still less to be a material part; if he thought of the form that way, his argument about letters and syllables would be inept and unintelligible.

The sort of body that, within the Stoic system, comes nearest to fulfilling Aristotle's criteria for form is the *pneuma* ('breath' or 'spirit'; **264–6**). By regarding the soul as the *pneuma* diffused throughout the body the Stoics meet Aristotle's objections to placing the soul exclusively in one place in the body, as though the body were just its container. The soul is not just some stuff mixed in with the bodily stuff, but totally interpenetrates all the bodily stuff.

....

342 CALCIDIUS, *Commentary on the Timaeus* 220 = SVF ii. 879   The Stoics indeed argue that the heart is the seat of the leading part of the soul. ... For Zeno argues that the soul is breath,[38] in this way: If when something leaves the body, the animal dies, this is certainly the soul; when the natural breath

---

[38] *spiritus*, i.e. *pneuma*. Cf. **300**.

leaves, the animal dies; therefore the natural breath is the soul. In the same way Chrysippus says: Certainly, by one and the same thing we breathe and live; we breathe by the natural breath; therefore we also live by the natural breath; we live by the soul; therefore the natural breath is found to be the soul. This, he says, is found to be divided into eight parts. For it is composed of the leading part and the five senses, and also of the voice-producing substance and the power of sowing and procreating. Now the parts of the soul flowing from their seat in the heart, as though from a fountain-head, are spread through the entire body, fill all the limbs everywhere with vital breath, and rule and guide by innumerable different powers—they nourish, foster, move, order with local movements, compel to act by the senses. The whole soul spreads out the senses that are its functions, as though they were branches from that leading part, as though it were the trunk, to be messengers of what they sense; and the leading part, like a king, judges about the messages they bring. Now the things sensed are composite, such as bodies, and each of the single senses senses only one thing—this sense discerns colours, another sounds, a third the taste of juices, this the breath of odours, this discerns roughness and smoothness by touch. And these all apply to the present; for a single sense neither remembers things past nor anticipates the future. It belongs to internal deliberation and reflection to understand how each sense is affected, to collect from the messages they bring what that thing is—to take hold of the present thing, to remember what is absent and to foresee what is future. Chrysippus defines that internal deliberation of the mind this way: the internal movement of the mind is the rational power. For even mute animals have a leading part of the soul by which they discern food, imagine, avoid traps, leap over high and steep obstacles, recognize necessity; but yet this part is not rational, but rather natural. Human beings are the only mortal creatures who use this leading good of the mind, that is reason.

The same Chrysippus says: Just as a spider[39] in the middle of its web holds all the beginnings of the threads in its feet, so that whenever any small beast falls into the traps, it senses it at first hand—so also the leading part of the soul, placed in the middle seat that is the heart, holds on to the beginnings of the senses, so that when they bring any message it recognizes it at first hand. The Stoics also say that the voice is sent from the depths of the breast, that is from the heart. The breath presses against the bosom of the heart; the heart covered with muscles is a boundary separating the breath from the lungs on each side and from the other vital organs; and from this, when the tongue and other organs of the voice batter the narrow passages of the throat to form them, articulated sounds are produced, the elements of discourse; with this discourse as interpreter, the hidden movements of the mind are revealed. This he calls the leading part of the soul.

[39] Cf. **309**.

343 NEMESIUS, *Human Nature* 2, 22. 3–6 = SVF ii. 790 Chrysippus says: Death is the separation of soul from body. Now nothing incorporeal is separated from a body; for neither does an incorporeal touch a body. But the soul both touches and is separated from the body. Therefore the soul is not incorporeal.

344 ALEXANDER, *Appendix on the Soul* 117. 1–118. 2 = SVF ii. 792[40] The fact that similarity is predicated of the soul does not imply that it is a body; for similarity does not belong to bodies alone <as the Stoics believe> ... [9] Further, the argument is false that says: 'The incorporeal does not suffer something together with a body, so that the soul is not incorporeal.' ... [30] Nor is it true to say: 'That by which we breathe, by that we are embreathed, and by the soul we are ensouled.' And even if animals cannot exist without the inborn *pneuma*, it does not follow that this is the soul.

345 ALEXANDER, *Soul* 18. 10–19. 6 = SVF ii. 793 <The Stoics say>: 'It is necessary for the parts of a body to be bodies, since the parts of a line are lines, of a surface surfaces, of time times; the parts of an animal, which is a body, are form and matter; and so form and matter are bodies.' This argument is mistaken. For these are not parts of a body in such a way that the body is cut into them. For those parts of the body into which it is cut contribute to the quantity of the body, and subsist and remain when cut off. But form and matter are not parts of the body in this way, but as the bronze and the shape are parts of a statue. The statue is not divided into these, as it is divided into head and chest and legs; and yet the composite of matter and form is also composed of form and matter as parts, though not in the same way. For the shape is a part of the statue not as contributing something to its quantity, but as contributing to its quality, and not as being capable of being preserved in separation from the matter. ...

Nor does the argument saying 'That of which a part is a body is itself a body; but sense, being a part of the soul, is a body; hence the soul itself is also a body' prove anything. For if sense is understood to be the sense organ, then, so understood, it is a body, but it is not part of the soul. If, on the other hand, it is understood as the sensory capacity, then, so understood, it is not a body. For indeed if the soul is body, and body not as matter is, it will be composed of matter and form, since, according to the Stoics, every body is such because of something apart from matter.[41] But if that is so, then the form in that body will be soul.

---

[40] Alexander comments on Stoic arguments for the corporeality of the soul.
[41] Text doubtful.

IX: Free Will

Action, responsibility, and fate

346 From the beginning, Greek thought recognizes that human beings are open to praise and blame for their actions. It is reasonable to advise, warn, punish and reward them, and to express gratitude and resentment to them. It would be inappropriate and pointless to take these attitudes to rocks, trees, or storms, however destructive they might be; all or most of these attitudes would be inappropriate towards cats and horses. In Homer, people do not get angry at the sea, but at the sea-god Poseidon, understood as an intelligent agent. These attitudes presuppose that in some way human beings are in control of their actions, that it is up to them to do what they do, and that advice, warning, praise, and blame can give them reasons that influence their actions.

These presuppositions do not cover all human behaviour. When a Homeric hero is knocked over by a god, he cannot avoid it, just as he cannot avoid being knocked over by a strong wind. Generally speaking, we believe that if our behaviour results entirely from some process that we do not control, we are not responsible for it, and are not open to praise or blame for it.

Homer shows how we might extend the area we do not control until it includes many actions that we might have thought we did control. Homer's characters believe that the gods not only intervene with irresistible physical force, but also influence an agent's actions by intervening in his thoughts, beliefs, and plans. The gods put it in someone's mind to act in a specific way; to that extent, we might say, the specific action is attributable to the god and not to the agent.

Agamemnon takes advantage of this belief in 'inner' divine intervention, to disclaim responsibility for the quarrel with Achilles. Early in the *Iliad*, he seems to admit that he is responsible for beginning the quarrel. Later on, however, he alleges that he is not the cause; the cause is 'Zeus and fate and the Fury that walks in darkness' (**347**).

Agamemnon's audience neither clearly accept nor clearly reject his excuse. Its implications for the assessment of human actions might be radical; how many actions might be excused on the plea that 'a god made me do it'? This plea does not seem to be confined to actions that are surprising, or unusual, or out of character; it seems equally appropriate in any case in which our actions are the result of some process whose origins we do not control. How do we know that the origins of all our actions are not controlled by the gods?

Though Homer's examples raise this possibility, Homer and his characters do not pursue it. The role of the gods, and especially of the supreme god Zeus, is left obscure. Sometimes human beings and gods seem to thwart the will of

Zeus. Sometimes Homer suggests that the will of Zeus is eventually fulfilled. Sometimes Zeus himself appears to be powerless in the face of the fates.[1] He weighs the fates of different individuals, and the one whose fate weighs more heavily in the balance is the one who has to die—independently (it seems) of anyone's will. An individual's life and death seem to be determined by some inevitable process independent of divine and human wills. But if Hector's death today, for instance, is inevitable, how can Achilles be held responsible for killing Hector? Homer does not say how many events are subject to fate, or how subjection to fate affects human responsibility for them.

Some of these questions are faced more openly by later Greek writers. In Aeschylus' *Agamemnon*, a discussion between the Chorus and Clytaemnestra reveals different views about Clytaemnestra's responsibility for killing Agamemnon. First, Clytaemnestra tries to shift responsibility to a hereditary curse laid on Agamemnon's father. The Chorus answer that this explanation does not remove responsibility from her; but they admit that they are puzzled about how she can really be responsible, if Zeus causes everything.

Questions about fate and inevitability arise in Herodotus' story of Polycrates. He fears that his prosperity may be dangerous for him, since he believes, as other people in Herodotus believe, that the gods envy and destroy human prosperity (**388**; cf. **591**). He takes pre-emptive action to avoid his fate; but it catches up with him anyhow. The bad end that he cannot avoid seems to be the result of his prosperity, not of any fault of his. It is prosperity itself that arouses divine envy, irrespective of whatever else he tries to do; it seems that he can neither help being prosperous nor avoid suffering for it.

This, at any rate, is how Polycrates and his friend Amasis understand the action of the gods. They seem to misunderstand it, however. The sequel in Herodotus shows that, even though Polycrates is willing to sacrifice one of his possessions, he does not give up his reckless behaviour; his risky foreign policy eventually ruins him.

....

347 HOMER, *Iliad* xix. 85–138   The Achaeans have often said this to me, and criticized me. But I am not the cause, but Zeus, and fate, and the Fury that walks in darkness.[2] They brought a wild delusion on my heart in the assembly, on the day when I myself took Achilles' duly-awarded prize from him. But what was I to do? A god brings everything to fulfilment; cursed Delusion, the eldest daughter of Zeus, deludes everyone. She walks delicately, not on the solid earth, but moving over the heads of men to ruin them. Indeed, she has overcome others before me. Yes, once she even deluded Zeus himself, who, they say, is greatest among gods and men; for Hera, being a woman, deceived him by guile on the day when Alcmene was to give birth to mighty

[1] A Stoic view on Zeus and fate; **617**.
[2] The responsibility of Zeus; **301**.

Heracles in the fortified city of Thebes.[3] ... Zeus was stung to the quick. In his anger he caught Delusion by her shining hair, and swore a great oath that never again would Delusion, who deludes everyone, enter the starry heavens and Olympus. Then he whirled her around, and threw her down from the starry heavens, and soon she reached the homes of mortals; and always he was angry with her when he saw his son suffering the harsh labours that Eurystheus laid upon him. And I, too, all the time when great Hector with the shining helmet was killing the Argives at the sterns of their ships, could not forget the delusion that first deluded me. But since I was deluded, and Zeus took away my wits, now I am ready to make amends, and to give abundant gifts in reparation.

348 HOMER, *Iliad* xvi. 431–61   When Zeus, the son of scheming Cronus, saw them, he pitied them, and said to Hera his wife and sister, 'Alas for me, that it is fate for Sarpedon, the dearest of men, to be killed by the hand of Patroclus. My heart in my breast is equally balanced, as I consider whether to snatch him up alive out of the battle that brings mourning, and set him down safe and sound in the fertile land of Lycia, or to crush him under the hands of the son of Menoetius.' Wide-eyed Hera answered, 'Most terrible son of Cronus, what are you saying? Do you really want to snatch a mortal man, long marked by destiny, out of clamorous death? Do it then as you will, but all we other gods will not approve. And I tell you this to lay in your heart: if you send Sarpedon safely to his own home, take care, in case some other god will also want to send his dear son out of the mighty battle; for there are many sons of gods fighting round the city of Troy, and you will arouse a fierce grievance. ... ' The father of gods and men assented, but he shed a rain of blood upon the earth, honouring his dear son whom Patroclus was going to kill on the rich plain of Troy far from his home.

349 AESCHYLUS, *Agamemnon* 1498–1512   CLYTAEMNESTRA: You are sure that this is my doing. But do not imagine I am Agamemnon's wife. No; the ancient fierce avenger punishing Atreus, the cruel provider of the feast, has appeared in the likeness of this corpse's wife, and offered this full-grown victim on top of the young ones.[4] ... [1505] CHORUS: That you are innocent of this murder—who will bear you witness? How could anyone do so? And yet the avenging spirit might have cooperated with you. Amid streams of kindred blood dark war presses violently on, until it provides just retribution for the

---

[3] Agamemnon recounts how Hera's trick caused Zeus to impose twelve arduous labours on his son Heracles.

[4] Clytaemnestra has just killed Agamemnon, her husband. She alludes to the crime of Agamemnon's father Atreus, who killed the children of his brother Thyestes, and served them to Thyestes to eat. Clytaemnestra suggests that the 'avenging spirit' punishing Agamemnon for the crimes of Atreus has been at work through her.

clotted blood of devoured children. ... [1465–8] CHORUS: Alas, all because of Zeus, who causes all, who brings all about. For what is fulfilled for mortals without Zeus? Which of these events is not god-ordained?

350 HERODOTUS iii. 40–3   Amasis noticed the great good fortune of Polycrates, and he was concerned about it. When Polycrates had even more good fortune, Amasis wrote him this letter, and sent it to Samos: 'Amasis to Polycrates. It is a pleasure to hear of a friend and ally doing well. But your great good fortune gives me no pleasure, since I know that the divine is envious. ... Think of whatever it is that you value most—whatever you would most regret the loss of—and throw it away.' ... And so Polycrates began to look around among his treasures for what he thought he would be most grieved to lose. Finally he thought of this: he had a signet-ring he used to wear, an emerald set in gold. ... Having decided that this was the thing to get rid of, he manned a fifty-oared ship, went aboard, and gave orders to put to sea. When the vessel was a long way from shore, he took the ring from his finger, in full view of everyone on board, and threw it into the water. Then he rowed back to the island, returned to his house, and lamented what had happened. Five or six days later, this is what happened. A fisherman caught a fine big fish, and thought it would make a suitable present for Polycrates. He took it to the door and asked for an audience; this being granted, he offered the fish ... Polycrates' servants cut up the fish, and found the signet-ring in its belly. The moment they saw it, they picked it up, and, taking it to Polycrates with delight, told him how it had been found. But when it struck him that this was a divine event, Polycrates wrote to Amasis in Egypt, and told him everything he had done and how it had turned out. Amasis read the letter, and at once replied that it was impossible for one human being to save another from what was going to happen, and that Polycrates was not going to end his life well, given that he had such good fortune in everything that he even found what he had thrown away.

Atomism and necessity

351 The questions about freedom and fate raised by Aeschylus and Herodotus are not discussed explicitly in the surviving texts of the Presocratics. Indeed, they are not thoroughly and consciously discussed until Epicurus and the Stoics take them up; that is why this chapter is mostly concerned with Hellenistic philosophy. Still, some of the relevant questions arise earlier, especially in the Atomists and in Aristotle; their remarks raise some of the problems that provoke the Hellenistic debates about freedom.[5]

---

[5] Plato's rather scattered remarks on questions about responsibility are omitted here. His fullest treatment is in *Laws* ix.

A belief in necessity may appear to follow from naturalist assumptions about explanation (**33**). If we suppose that all explanations of something's behaviour come from its nature and basic constitution, as the Presocratic naturalists suppose, we seem to imply that from basic laws about something's constituents, all its behaviour necessarily follows.[6] For this reason the naturalists reject explanations that involve divine intervention, and so they reject one of the forces that, in Homer's view, can interfere with human choice (**40, 352**). But if they make everything the result of something's basic constitution, do they not make everything necessary, and thereby exclude human freedom?

This question about human freedom is not raised by most of the Presocratics. But it seems to be suggested by the Atomists, who accept the line of argument we have just described, leading from naturalism to necessity. The Atomists recognize that a doctrine of necessity follows from their account of the basic realities and of the laws governing their movements. When they insist that everything happens by necessity, they mean:

(1) The movements of the atoms are determined simply by their properties and by their previous movements. No other causal force, and no interruption of the regular causal forces moving the atoms, is present in the universe.

(2) Everything that happens is simply the movement of atoms in the void, since nothing else really exists besides atoms and void.

The first of these claims implies 'determinism'—the view that every event is the inevitable result of prior events that are its sufficient conditions. On this view, there are no chance or random events, and there are no new causal sequences that are wholly independent of any prior causal sequence. The second of these claims is eliminative (**90**); it implies that only the properties of atoms and void explain the causal sequences that happen in the world. According to an eliminative position, claims about freedom and responsibility require the existence of goal-directed choices for which Atomism leaves no room.

The view that everything happens by necessity appears to imply that we are never responsible for our actions (**366**). If everything that happens is the inevitable result of causal forces determining the movements of the atoms, everything seems to be subject to laws independent of human choices. Homer's suggestion that the fates control events, independently of any divine or human will, seems to be true of the laws of an Atomist universe.

The view that the Atomist doctrine of necessity undermines responsibility perhaps underlies the later stories about Democritus that present him as the laughing philosopher, laughing at the meaninglessness and pointlessness of human lives. Our lives may seem, from the Atomist point of view, to lack the significance we normally attach to them, if what happens to us is not really influenced by choices

---

[6] Cf. references to 'what must be' and fate, **44, 65, 77**.

and actions that we control. If we make no difference, there seems to be no point in our trying to do one thing rather than another.

Among later philosophers, different people fasten on these different features of the Atomist position, and hence on different lines of argument against the Atomists' implicit denial of responsibility.

....

352   PLUTARCH, *Exile* 604a = DK 22 B94   [HERACLEITUS:] The sun will not overstep its measures; otherwise the Furies, helpers of justice, will find it out.

353   STOBAEUS, *Anthology* i. 4. 7 = DK 67 B2   Leucippus says that everything happens by necessity, and that necessity is the same as fate. For he says in *On Mind*: 'Nothing happens at random,[7] but everything happens for a reason and by necessity'.

354   LUCIAN, *Sale of Lives* 13   [DEMOCRITUS:] There is nothing in them to be taken seriously, but they are all vain and empty, a movement of atoms and infinity.

Aristotle on necessity

355 Aristotle sometimes seems to assume that Atomism implies an eliminative treatment of organisms and their properties (**90**). He suggests that Democritus recognizes only the material cause, and hence does not recognize substances that are defined by formal properties and capable of goal-directed behaviour (**99, 242, 251**). Moreover, Democritus' Atomist account of the soul implies (according to Aristotle) the rejection of our ordinary view that thought, desire, and decision move us to action (**313**). If this is a fair estimate of Democritus' position, Democritus apparently cannot find any place for choice and responsibility.

Aristotle's attitude to Democritus' belief in necessity is less clear. He certainly takes a doctrine of necessity, under one interpretation, to undermine belief in our freedom and control over our actions. A 'fatalist' position (this is a modern term, not Aristotle's) goes beyond the mere belief in fate (which commits us only to determinism) to the further conclusion that our actions are predetermined in a way that excludes our being able to do anything about them. Aristotle's discussion of the 'sea-battle' (**356**) first presents an argument for fatalism, and then rejects fatalism.

The fatalist argues from the truth of statements about what I will do to the conclusion that my actions are necessary, in the sense that I cannot do otherwise than I will actually do. The argument is this:

....

[7] Or 'in vain'.

(1) It is true that I will post a letter this evening.

(2) Hence it was true in the past (both yesterday and a thousand years ago) that I would post a letter this evening.

(3) If it was true in the past that I would post a letter this evening, then, necessarily, I will post a letter this evening.

(4) Hence, necessarily, I will post a letter this evening.

(5) Hence I cannot avoid posting a letter this evening.

The fatalist suggests that we are committed to fatalism whether or not we accept Democritus' Atomism, because some very simple facts about truth and time imply fatalism. Since it was true in the past that I will do what I will actually do, everything that I actually do is necessitated by the past, and so I can do nothing about it. Aristotle claims that if the fatalist conclusion is true, it is pointless to deliberate about what to do.

Since Aristotle rejects fatalism, he must reject some part of this argument for fatalism. But what does he reject? Two answers have been offered.

(i) He rejects premiss (1), so that he denies that there are any future-tense truths about particular human actions. Until I post a letter this evening, it is not true that I will post a letter, but, after I have posted it, it becomes true that I did post a letter. Before I post the letter, it is true that either I will post a letter or I will not; but neither part of this disjunction is true.

(ii) Aristotle accepts (1), but claims that (3) is ambiguous. It might mean: (3a) necessarily, if (2) is true, I will post a letter this evening; or (3b) if (2) is true, then it is necessary that I will post a letter this evening.

This ambiguity undermines the argument for fatalism; for only (3a) follows from (1) and (2), but (3b) is needed for (4) and (5).

It is difficult to decide which answer Aristotle intends. Indeed, some of the crucial passages in his solution to the puzzle raised by fatalism might be taken to express either answer.[8] If the text requires no more than the plausible claims in the second answer, some further reason is needed to warrant us in ascribing to him the more controversial claims in the first answer.

....

356 ARISTOTLE, *On Interpretation* 17^{b}26–19^{b}4   Of contradictory universal statements about a universal, one or the other must be true or false; similarly if they are about particulars—for instance, 'Socrates is pale' and 'Socrates is not pale'. But if they are about universals, but are not universal statements, it is not always the case that one is true, the other false. For it is true to say at the same time that a man is pale and that a man is not pale, and that a man is handsome and that a man is not handsome; for if ugly, then not handsome.

[8] See notes to **356**.

And if something is becoming F, it is also not F. This might seem strange at first sight, since 'A man is not pale' might appear to signify at the same time that no man is pale; but it does not signify the same, nor does it necessarily hold at the same time. ...

[18ᵃ28]–19ᵇ4 In the case of what is and what has been, then, it is necessary that the affirmation or negation be true or false. And in the case of universal statements about universals, it is always necessary for one to be true and the other false; and the same is true in the case of particulars, as we have said. But in the case of universals not spoken of universally, this is not necessary; we have also discussed this.[9] But in the case of particulars that are going to be, it is not the same.

For if every affirmation or negation is true or false, it is also necessary that everything either is the case or is not the case. And so if someone says that something will be and another denies the same thing, clearly it is necessary for one of them to speak truly, if every affirmation is true or false. For both will not be the case at the same time in such cases. For if it is true to say that something is pale or not pale, it is necessary for it to be pale or not pale; and if it is pale or not pale, it was true to affirm or deny this. And if it is not the case, one speaks falsely; and if one speaks falsely, it is not the case. Hence it is necessary for the affirmation or the negation to be true or false.[10] Therefore nothing either is or happens by chance or as chance has it; nor will it be or not be thus. Rather, everything happens from necessity and not as chance has it, since either the affirmer or the denier speaks truly. For otherwise, it might equally well happen or not happen; for what happens as chance has it neither is nor will be any more this way than that.

Further, if something is pale now, it was true to say previously that it would be pale, so that it was always true to say of any thing that has happened that it would be. But if it was always true to say that it was or would be, it could not not be, or not be going to be. But if something cannot not happen, it is impossible for it not to happen; and what cannot not happen necessarily happens. Everything, then, that will be will be necessarily. Therefore, nothing will be as chance has it or by chance; for if it is by chance it is not from necessity.

But it is not possible to say that neither is true—that, for example, it neither will be nor will not be. For, first, if this is possible, then though the affirmation is false, the negation is not true; and though the negation is false, it turns out on this view that the affirmation is not true. Moreover, if it is true to say that it is pale and dark, both must be the case; and if both will be the case tomorrow, both must be the case tomorrow. But if it neither will nor will

---

[9] See the previous paragraph.

[10] The preceding passage (and some of the later argument) might be taken in either of two ways. (1) It is necessary that if p is true, then the state of affairs described by p obtains. (2) If p is true, then the state of affairs described by p is necessary.

not be tomorrow, even so, the sea-battle, for instance, will not happen as chance has it; for in this case, the sea-battle would necessarily neither happen nor not happen.

These and others like them are the absurd consequences if in every affirmation and negation (either about universals spoken of universally or about particulars) it is necessary that one of the opposites is true and the other false, and nothing happens as chance has it, but all things are and happen from necessity. Hence there would be no need to deliberate or to take trouble, thinking that if we do this, that will be, and if we do not, it will not be; for it might well be that ten thousand years ago one person said that this would be and another denied it, so that whichever it was true to affirm at that time will be so from necessity. Nor does it matter whether or not anyone made the contradictory statements; for clearly things are thus even if one person does not affirm it and another deny it. For it is not because of the affirming or denying that it will be or will not be the case, nor is this any more so for ten thousand years ago than for any other time. Hence if in the whole of time things were such that one or the other statement was true, it was necessary for this to happen, and each thing that happened was always such as to happen from necessity. For if someone has said truly that something will happen, it cannot not happen; and it was always true to say of something that has happened that it would be.

But surely this is impossible. For we see that both deliberation and action originate things that will be; and, in general, we see what is possible to be and not to be, among things that are not always in actuality; in these cases, both being and not being, and hence both happening and not happening, are possible. We find that this is clearly true of many things. It is possible, for instance, for this cloak to be cut up, though in fact it will not be cut up but will wear out first instead. Similarly, its not being cut up is also possible; for its wearing out first would not have been the case unless its not being cut up were possible. Hence the same is true for other things that happen, however many result from this sort of capacity. Evidently, then, not everything is or happens from necessity. Rather, some things happen as chance has it, and the affirmation is no more true than the negation. In other cases, one alternative happens more than the other, and happens usually, but none the less it is possible for the other to happen and for the first not to happen.

It is necessary for what is, whenever it is, to be, and for what is not, whenever it is not, not to be. But not everything that is necessarily is; and not everything that is not necessarily is not. For everything's being from necessity when it is is not the same as everything's being from necessity without qualification; and the same is true of what is not.[11] The same argument also applies

---

[11] The previous two sentences might be understood in either of two ways. (1) It is true to say that necessarily (when *x* is, *x* is); but it does not follow that when *x* is, *x* necessarily is. (2) When *x* is (i.e. is present), then *x* necessarily is.

to contradictories. It is necessary for everything either to be or not to be, and indeed to be going to be or not to be going to be. But one cannot divide the contradictories and say that one or the other is necessary. I mean that, for instance, it is necessary for there to be or not to be a sea-battle tomorrow, but it is not necessary for a sea-battle to happen tomorrow, nor for one not to happen. It is necessary, however, for it either to happen or not to happen. And so, since the truth of statements corresponds to how things are, it is clear that, for however many things are as chance has it and are such as to admit contraries, it is necessary for the same to be true of the contradictories. This is just what happens with things that neither always are nor always are not. For in these cases it is necessary for one of the contradictories to be true and the other false, but not this or that one. Rather, it is as chance has it, or else one is more true than the other, but not thereby true or false. Clearly, then, it is not necessary that of every affirmation and negation of opposites, one is true and one false. For what holds for things that are does not also hold for things that are not but are capable of being and of not being; in these cases it is as we have said.

Aristotle on responsibility

357 Aristotle's discussion of responsibility confirms his rejection of any doctrine of necessity that removes our actions from our control. Normal human beings (he claims) control their actions and are appropriately held responsible (praised, blamed, etc.) for what they do. When we act voluntarily—on our own beliefs and desires, without external compulsion, and knowing what we are doing—we are justly open to praise and blame.[12]

In Aristotle's view, our responsibility extends beyond our actions. He rejects the suggestion that we cannot help being the sorts of people we are, and therefore (since the sorts of people we are determines what we do) cannot help doing what we do. He answers that we form and maintain our characters by voluntary actions, and therefore we are also justly praised and blamed for being virtuous or vicious. Both our actions and our character are in our control and up to us.

In arguing that our beliefs and desires are the proper basis for praising, blaming, and holding responsible, Aristotle implies that they are part of the sequence of causes leading to our actions and characters. He does not ask whether, as Democritus implies, all the members of this sequence of causes are themselves necessitated—that is to say, whether they inevitably result from some previous events. He is silent, therefore, about the truth or falsity of Democritus' determinism (in the sense explained in **351**).

We might explain Aristotle's silence on this question in different ways:

[12] Blameworthy action; **400**, **402**.

(1) He does not notice that Democritus' determinist claims threaten responsibility.

(2) Democritus' determinist claims are irrelevant to responsibility, and so
Aristotle does not need to mention them.

The first of these answers supports Epicurus' account of responsibility; the second supports the Stoics' account.

....

358 ARISTOTLE, *Nicomachean Ethics* 1109^{b}30–1111^{a}24   Virtue, then, is about
feelings and actions. These receive praise or blame when they are voluntary,
but pardon, sometimes even pity, when they are involuntary. Hence, presumably, in examining virtue we must define the voluntary and the involuntary. This is also useful to legislators, both for honours and for corrective
treatments.

What comes about by force or because of ignorance seems to be involuntary. What is forced has an external principle, the sort of principle in which
the agent, or rather the victim, contributes nothing, if, for instance, a wind or
people who have overpowered him were to carry him off. Some actions,
however, are done because of fear of greater evils, or because of something
fine, if, for instance, a tyrant tells you to do something shameful, when he has
control over your parents and children, and if you do it, they will live, but if
not, they will die. These cases raise dispute about whether they are voluntary
or involuntary. However, the same sort of thing also happens with throwing
cargo overboard in storms; for no one willingly throws cargo overboard,
without qualification, but anyone with any sense throws it overboard to save
himself and the others. These sorts of actions, then, are mixed, but they
would seem to be more like voluntary actions. For when they are done they
are choiceworthy, and the goal of an action corresponds to the occasion;
hence we should also call the action voluntary or involuntary with reference
to the time when he does it. Now in fact he does it willingly; for in these sorts
of actions he has within him the principle of the movement of the limbs that
are the instruments of the action, and in cases where the principle of the actions is in him, it is also up to him to do them or not to do them. Hence actions of this sort are voluntary, though presumably the actions considered
without qualification are involuntary, since no one would choose any action
of this sort in itself. ...

[1110^{b}25] Action caused by ignorance would seem to be different from action
done in ignorance. For if the agent is drunk or angry, his action seems to be
caused by drunkenness or anger, not by ignorance, though it is done in ignorance, not in knowledge. Now certainly every vicious person is ignorant of the
actions he must do or avoid, and this sort of error makes people unjust, and in
general bad. But talk of involuntary action is not meant to apply to ignorance
of what is beneficial. For the cause of involuntary action is not ignorance in the

decision, which causes vice; it is not ignorance of the universal, since that is a cause for blame. Rather, the cause is ignorance of the particulars which the action consists in and is concerned with; for these allow both pity and pardon, since an agent acts involuntarily if he is ignorant of one of these particulars. ... [1111ᵃ22] Since, then, what is involuntary is what is forced or is caused by ignorance, what is voluntary seems to be what has its principle in the agent himself, knowing the particulars that the action consists in.

359   ARISTOTLE, *Nicomachean Ethics* 1113ᵇ3–1114ᵇ25   We have found that we wish for the end, and deliberate and decide about what promotes it; hence the actions concerned with what promotes the end will be in accordance with decision and will be voluntary. Now the activities of the virtues are concerned with these things <that promote the end>; hence virtue is also up to us, and so is vice. For when acting is up to us, so is not acting, and when No is up to us, so is Yes. Hence if acting, when it is fine, is up to us, then not acting, when it is shameful, is also up to us; and if not acting, when it is fine, is up to us, then acting, when it is shameful, is also up to us. Hence if doing, and likewise not doing, the fine or shameful actions is up to us, and if, as we saw, this is being a good or bad person, it follows that being good or bad is up to us.

The claim that no one is willingly bad or unwillingly blessed would seem to be partly true but partly false. For certainly no one is unwillingly blessed, but vice is voluntary. If it is not, we must dispute the conclusion just reached, that a human being originates and fathers his own actions as he fathers his children. But if our conclusion appears true, and we cannot refer actions back to other principles beyond those in ourselves, it follows that whatever has its principle in us is itself up to us and voluntary. There would seem to be testimony in favour of our view not only in what each of us does as a private citizen, but also in what legislators themselves do. For they impose corrective treatments and penalties on anyone who does vicious actions, unless his action is forced or is caused by ignorance that he is not responsible for; and they honour anyone who does fine actions; they assume that they will encourage the one and restrain the other. But no one encourages us to do anything that is not up to us and voluntary; people assume it is pointless to persuade us not to get hot or distressed or hungry or anything else of that sort, since persuasion will not stop it happening to us. ...

[1114ᵃ31] But someone may say, 'Everyone aims at the apparent good, and does not control how it appears, but rather his character controls how the end appears to him.' First, then, if each person is in some way responsible for his own state of character, he is also himself in some way responsible for how the end appears. Suppose, on the other hand, that no one is responsible for acting badly, but one does so because one is ignorant of the end, and thinks this is the way to gain what is best for oneself. One's aiming at the end will not be one's own choice, but one needs a sort of natural, inborn sense of sight, to judge finely and to choose what is really good. Whoever by nature has this sense in a fine condition has a good nature. For this sense is the greatest and finest thing, and one cannot acquire it or learn it from another; rather, its natural character determines one's later condition, and when it is naturally good and fine, that is true and complete good nature. If all this is true, how will virtue be any more voluntary than vice? For how the end appears is laid down, by nature or in whatever way, for the good and the bad person alike, and they refer all the other things back to the end in doing all their actions.

Suppose, then, that it is not nature that makes the end appear however it appears to each person, but something also depends on oneself; or, alternatively, suppose that the end is natural, but virtue is voluntary because the virtuous person does the other things voluntarily. In either case vice will be no less voluntary than virtue; for the bad person, no less than the good, is responsible for his own actions, even if not for the end. Now the virtues, as we say, are voluntary, since in fact we ourselves are in a way jointly responsible for our states of character, and by having the sort of character we have we lay down the sort of end we do. Hence the vices will also be voluntary, since the same is true of them.

Epicurus: the conflict between necessity and freedom

$\boxed{360}$ Epicurus, like Aristotle, considers and rejects fatalism; but, in contrast to Aristotle, he explicitly argues that if we are to reject fatalism, we must reject determinism. The specific doctrine that he attacks is determinism, the view that every event is necessitated by earlier events and the laws of nature. The earlier Atomists accept determinism because they take all natural processes to be the necessary results of atomic processes that are immune from interference by the gods and subject to no laws except the uniform laws of atomic motion. The same patterns are repeated in nature because the same atomic forces operate, and their operations necessarily produce the same results.

Epicurus believes that determinism is incompatible with responsibility. If determinism is true, then, given the fixed laws of nature, our choices and decisions are determined by events that are themselves determined by previous events, and so on. Since earlier events necessitate the later events, our actions are necessitated by processes whose earlier stages we cannot control. Hence, it appears, we have no real control over our actions, and so we cannot be responsible for them. His argument is this:

(1) Whatever happens is wholly determined by the distant past and the laws of nature.

(2) I do not control the laws of nature.

(3) I do not control what happened in the distant past.

(4) Hence I do not control what determines my action.

(5) If I do not control what determines my action, I do not control my action.

(6) Hence, I do not control my action.

Since Epicurus believes the Democritean Atomist must accept this argument, he believes Democritean Atomism excludes freedom and responsibility (**366**). The argument is similar to the first interpretation of Aristotle's argument about future truths. Both Epicurus and Aristotle (on this interpretation) believe that if a sufficient condition for my action exists before I choose to do it, it is not in my control and I am not responsible for it. Epicurus infers that belief in determinism amounts to belief in the sort of fate that caught up with Polycrates, which no human action could affect.

Indeed, he suggests it is more disastrous for freedom if everything is subject to inexorable fate than if there are interfering gods, whom we can at least influence (**361**). Just as Polycrates could do nothing about what was fated independently of his control, we can do nothing about what is fated because of what has happened in the distant past according to immutable laws of nature (**362**). If I am a part of nature, it seems to follow that Aristotle is wrong to claim that anything is really up to me or in my control. For if I am a part of nature, and my behaviour is wholly governed by laws of nature, events that happened even before I was born cause me to do what I do.

We might expect Epicurus to conclude that, since we ought to believe Atomism, and since Atomism is committed to determinism, which excludes freedom, we ought to deny freedom. He rejects this conclusion, however. For he urges us to believe the Atomic theory only because he assumes it is in our power to acquire the virtues appropriate to people who do not fear death. In giving us this advice, he assumes that we control our choices and actions.

If Epicurus' Atomism commits him to determinism, his position seems inconsistent. The Epicurean presupposes a real choice about how to live our lives. Epicurus argues for Atomism on the ground that if we believe it, we can choose to relieve our lives from anxiety. But Atomism—as understood by Democritus—seems to imply determinism, which excludes freedom. Epicurus, therefore, must both affirm and deny freedom; Atomism relieves our fear of interfering gods, but confronts us with the equally dispiriting fear that we cannot do anything about our lives.

....

361 EPICURUS = DIOGENES LAERTIUS X. 134   For it would be better to follow the stories told about the gods than to be a slave to the fate of the natural philosophers. For the former suggest a hope of success in praying to escape bad things, by means of honouring the gods, but the latter involves a necessity that cannot be swayed by prayer.

362 CICERO, *Fate* 21   ... If I here preferred to agree with Epicurus and to deny that every proposition is either true or false, I would rather accept that blow than agree that everything happens by fate. For the former claim is at least open to discussion, but the latter claim is intolerable. ... Epicurus fears that if he should concede this <claim that every proposition is either true or false>, he must also concede that whatever happens happens by fate. For, in his view, if either the assertion or the denial of a given proposition is true from eternity, it is also certain, and if certain, then also necessary; that is how he takes necessity and fate to be confirmed.

Epicurus' solution

363 Since Epicurus is convinced both that we are responsible for our actions, and that Democritean Atomism cannot acknowledge this fact, he has to modify Democritean Atomism. If he abandons the main principles of Atomism, however, he undermines his own natural philosophy and the ethical argument that demands the truth of Atomism. Hence, the modification that ensures freedom must be small enough to leave the main principles of Atomism intact.

The right way to modify Atomism, in Epicurus' view, is to reject Democritus' determinism. Epicurus claims that the atoms 'swerve' from the course that they normally follow, and that the occasions of the swerves are undetermined by any laws of nature (**364–5**). Since these swerves happen, events are not determined wholly by the distant past and the laws of nature. We can still hold that Atomism is the true account of the basic substances and of the laws that they normally conform to; Democritus wrongly believes that they always conform to these laws. Hence Atomism does not require determinism.

Belief in an atomic swerve does not, in Epicurus' view, violate the principle of reliance on the senses (cf. **278–81**). Since it is evident to us that we act freely and responsibly, we must attribute to the atoms whatever properties and motions are needed to explain freedom. To show that freedom is evident to us, Epicurus argues that even if you argue that you are not free, you presuppose that you are free; for in trying to convince yourself and your opponents of the truth of your position, you must assume that it is up to you and up to them to accept one argument rather than another. Hence you cannot argue against freedom without undermining your argument (**366**).

Since determinism is false, future-tense statements about particular human actions are, according to Epicurus, neither true nor false. He seems to assume that if we allow such statements to be true or false, then we imply that the future is fixed independently of our choice. His attitude to future-tense statements agrees with the first interpretation of Aristotle's solution to the argument about the sea-battle (**362**).

---

364 CICERO, *Fate* 22–3 Epicurus thinks that the necessity of fate is avoided by the swerve of an atom, so that a certain third movement arises, in addition to weight and collision, when the atom swerves by a smallest distance (what he calls a 'minimum'[13]). He is forced to concede, by the facts themselves if not by his words, that this swerve happens without a cause. For an atom does not swerve as a result of being struck by another atom; for how can one be struck by another if indivisible bodies are borne downwards by their weight in straight lines, as Epicurus believes? For if one is never pushed to one side by another, it follows that one never even touches another. Hence it results that, even if there is an atom and it swerves, it swerves without a cause. Epicurus introduced this line of reasoning because he was afraid that if an atom always moved by natural and necessary weight, nothing would be free for us, since the mind would be moved in such a way that it would be compelled by the motion of atoms. Democritus, the originator of the atoms, preferred to accept this result, that everything happens by necessity, rather than remove the natural motion from indivisible bodies. Carneades spoke more acutely, in teaching that the Epicureans could defend their view without this imaginary swerve. For since Epicurus taught that there could be some voluntary movement of the mind, it would have been better to defend that than to introduce the swerve, especially given that they cannot find a cause for it.

365 LUCRETIUS ii. 251–93 ... Suppose that every motion is always linked, and the new arises from the old motion in a fixed order, and the primary bodies do not swerve to make some beginning of movement to break the decrees of fate, so that one cause may not follow another from infinite time. In that case, what is the source of this free will for living things all over the earth? What is the source, I ask, of this will wrested from fate, this will through which we move forward wherever our pleasure leads each one of us, and, similarly, through which we swerve in our motions, neither at a fixed time nor at a fixed place, but just where our mind has carried us? For certainly a person's own will gives him a start for this movement, and from the will the motions pass, flooding through the limbs. And don't you see how, when the starting-gates are flung open, still for an instant of time the eager strength of the horses cannot burst out as suddenly as their mind itself desires? ... Don't you now see, then, that, even though a force outside pushes many people, and often forces them to go forward against their will and to be hurried away headlong, still there is something in our breast that can fight against it and resist it? ... And so you must allow that the seeds also contain another cause of motion besides blows and weights, and that this is the source of the innate power in us, since we see that nothing can come to be from nothing. For weight prevents all things happening by blows, as by some outside force. But that the mind itself has no internal necessity in all it does, and is not forced, like a passive victim, to bear and undergo—this results from the tiny swerve of the elements, at no fixed place and at no fixed time.

[13] Cicero uses the Greek term.

366 EPICURUS, *On Nature* = Arr. 34. 26–30 = LS 20C   From the beginning, we always have seeds directing us some towards these, some towards those, some towards these and those—seeds of actions and thoughts and characters, in greater and smaller numbers. And so, this or that result at first depends on us without qualification, and the things that necessarily flow in through our passages from surrounding things depend, at one stage, on us and on beliefs that come from us. ...

We rebuke, oppose, and reform one another on the assumption that we have the cause in ourselves also, not merely in our initial constitution and in the random necessity of things that surround and enter us. For suppose that someone were to claim that rebuking and being rebuked themselves have the very same random necessity of whatever happens to be present to oneself at a time. ... still, he would be leaving intact this very behaviour that, in our own case, produces the preconception of the cause. ... And even if he goes on to infinity saying that this action of his is in turn necessitated, always appealing to arguments, he does not draw the further conclusion[14] that he still leaves in himself the cause of having argued correctly, and in his opponent the cause of having argued incorrectly. ...

The first men to give a satisfactory account of causes were not only much greater than their predecessors, but also many times greater than their successors. And yet—even though in many things they had relieved us from great evils—they overlooked themselves <in looking for causes>, so as to make necessity and the random the causes of everything. Indeed, the account expounding this view collapsed, when the great man[15] overlooked the conflict between his actions and his belief. <For he did not notice> that if in his actions he had not forgotten about his belief, he would have constantly perplexed himself; in any case where the belief controlled him, he would have fallen into desperate calamities, and in any case where it did not control him, he would be filled with conflict because of the contradiction between his actions and his belief.

367 EPICURUS = DIOGENES LAERTIUS X. 134–5   The sage does not think that anything good or bad that bears on living blessedly is given to human beings by fortune, though he thinks it supplies the starting-points of great good and bad things. He thinks it is better to act reasonably and suffer misfortune than to act reasonably and be fortunate.

368 EPICURUS = DIOGENES LAERTIUS X. 144   Fortune has a slight impact on the sage. Reasoning has directed, and for the whole course of his life directs and will direct, the greatest and most important things.

---

[14] Sense uncertain.
[15] Democritus.

Objections to Epicurus

369 Even if Epicurus' indeterminism is consistent with the main principles of Atomism, does his appeal to the swerve make it reasonable to believe in freedom and responsibility? How often do atomic swerves happen? If the only ones that affect S happen before S's lifetime, they do not seem to guarantee that S's actions are in S's control. If the last swerve was in 1900, but S was born in 1901, S's actions are determined (according to Epicurus' principles) by what happened before S was born, and hence S is not responsible for them. Moreover, if a further swerve happened in 1930, and none happened thereafter in S's lifetime, what S did in 1929 or 1960 was not in S's control. Apparently, then, Epicurus needs to say that swerves happen often, indeed that a swerve happens in S whenever S does an action that S is responsible for.

However often a swerve happens, does it explain why S should be held responsible for S's actions? We normally think our actions are the result of our characters and of the plans, intentions, and dispositions we have formed in the past. This is how Aristotle understands them. But if a free action results from an uncaused choice (as Epicurus maintains), it cannot be caused by my past choices and my states of character. Actions that are unconnected to my past and my character are not the ones we think we are responsible for; indeed, we are more likely to regard them as aberrations. If we are convinced that a person's action was entirely 'out of character' and was not at all caused by her past choices and decisions, then we may well doubt whether she is responsible for that action at all.[16]

Epicurus' solution seems to overlook a different source of objection to Atomism. He assumes that Democritean Atomism threatens responsibility only if it accepts determinism. He does not seem to consider Aristotle's objection that, since Democritus denies the reality of formal and final causes, he cannot even recognize the causal role of thoughts and decisions in actions. If thoughts and decisions do not affect my actions, they cannot make me responsible for them; but it is difficult to see how random atomic events that are not thoughts and decisions could make me responsible for my actions. If this objection is fair, Epicurus' introduction of indeterminism does not make Atomism compatible with responsibility.

....

370 D. J. FURLEY, *Two Studies in the Greek Atomists*,[17] p. 232   Aristotle's criterion of the voluntary was a *negative* one; the source of the voluntary action is in the agent himself, in the sense that it cannot be traced back beyond or outside the agent himself.[18] Lucretius says that *voluntas*[19] must be saved from a

---

[16] Defence of Epicurus against such objections; **370**.
[17] Princeton: Princeton UP, 1967.
[18] This claim about Aristotle may be compared with **358–9**.
[19] i.e. will.

succession of causes which can be traced back to infinity.[20] All he needs to satisfy the Aristotelian criterion is *a break in the succession of causes*, so that the source of an action cannot be traced back to something occurring before the birth of the agent. A single swerve of a single atom in the individual's *psyche* would be enough for this purpose. ... The swerve, then, ... saves *voluntas* from necessity, as Lucretius says it does, but it does not feature in every act of *voluntas*. ... [p. 234] The motions of the *psyche* ... are not determined *ab initio*, because a discontinuity is brought about by the atomic swerve. The swerve of an atom or atoms in the *psyche* means that the inherited motions are disturbed, and this allows new patterns of motion to be established which cannot be explained by the initial constitution of the swerve.

The Stoics on fate and determinism

371 The Stoics accept determinism, because of their natural philosophy and theology. They believe in a single, teleologically organized, cosmic order that follows unchanging laws (**372, 614, 620**). Hence, they believe that every event is caused by a previous event according to laws necessitating each event. They accept and reinterpret one aspect of the traditional Greek belief in fate, and they refer to Zeus and fate without distinction; they clear up an obscurity that we noticed in Homer's remarks about Zeus and the fates (**617**).

According to Epicurus, this belief in fate is worse than the traditional belief in the gods, because it destroys freedom and responsibility (**361**). Epicurus assumes that belief in fate, as the Stoics understand it, amounts to a 'fatalist' belief (see **355**) in the fixed and unalterable order that confronted Polycrates; no matter what we do, the future seems to be fixed independently of our choice.

The Stoics reject Epicurus' inference from fate (as they understand it) to this fatalist conclusion. In their view, it is possible to maintain fate while escaping necessity. Their belief in fate is simply a belief in determinism. By 'necessity' they mean the sort of necessity that Aristotle takes to be incompatible with freedom, because it makes me unable to influence my actions by my choices and decisions. The Stoics deny that determinism implies this sort of inability. Following the second interpretation of Aristotle on the sea-battle (**355-6**), they believe that the prior truth of future-tense statements about my action does not remove my freedom.

The Stoics believe that the argument from determinism to the denial of freedom rests on the claim that (1) If my action is fated, I cannot do anything about it. In their view, (1) is true only if it is also true that (2) If my action is fated, it will happen whatever I choose to do. Since they reject (2), they reject (1).

To refute (2), the Stoics consider the 'Lazy Argument':

[20] See **365**.

(a) Either it is fated that I will pass the examination tomorrow or it is fated that I will fail it.

(b) If it is fated that I will pass (fail), then I will pass (fail) whether I study or not.

(c) Hence there is no point in my studying, since it will make no difference whether I study or not.

If this Lazy Argument were sound, then fate would imply fatalism; it would follow that if something is fated, then it will happen no matter what I do, and so I cannot do anything about it. The Stoics, however, reject the argument because (b) is false. In saying that something is fated, the Stoics simply mean that there is a series of causes, each of which is sufficient (because of the unchanging laws of nature) for its effect; this series stretches back into the distant past and continues without interruption into the future. But this sequence of causes does not make the different links on the causal chain unnecessary.

We can see the Stoics' point without reference to questions about fate. Suppose, for instance, we are bowling at a row of ten pins, and we hit the middle two pins hard enough so that they hit the next two, these two hit the two next to them, and so on, until all ten fall over; it does not follow that by hitting the middle pins we would make the pins at the outer ends fall over even if the intermediate ones were not hit. Similarly, even if some sequence of causes will inevitably result either in our passing or in our failing the examination, it does not follow that our action of studying or failing to study is unnecessary for one or the other result.

This is why the Stoics say some events are 'co-fated'. They mean that if the laws of nature and the past are what they are, then certain intermediate events are fated if the outcome is fated. If, for instance, it is fated that you will drive from London to Glasgow tomorrow, it is also fated that there will be fuel in your car tomorrow.

Once we see the flaw in the Lazy Argument, we also see, according to the Stoics, the flaw in the inference from the fact that our actions are fated to the conclusion that we lack freedom. If my choice to study affects whether I pass the examination, then, if it is fated that I will pass the examination, it is also fated that I will choose to study and pass the examination as a result of studying. Hence, my choice makes a difference to whether I pass or fail.

....

372 THEODORET, *Remedy for Greek Diseases* vi. 14 = Diels, *DG* 332–4
Chrysippus the Stoic said that what is necessitated is nothing other than what is fated, and that fate is an everlasting, continuous, and ordered motion. Zeno of Citium called fate a power that moves matter, and called it providence and nature. His successors said that fate was a rational account[21]

---

[21] *logos.*

of the things ordered in the universe by providence. Again, in other treatises they called fate a chain of causes.

373   CICERO, *Fate* 27–30   There is an argument that philosophers call the 'lazy argument';[22] if we followed it, we would do nothing at all in our lives. They argue: 'If it is fate for you to recover from this illness, you will recover whether or not you bring a doctor. Similarly, if it is fate for you not to recover from this illness, you will not recover, whether or not you bring a doctor. But one or the other is fate. Hence there is no point in bringing a doctor.' This sort of argument is rightly called lazy and inactive, because by the same reasoning all action is removed from life. We can even change it so as not to attach the name of fate and still retain the same opinion, as follows: 'If this was true from eternity,[23] "You will recover from this illness", you will recover whether or not you bring a doctor. Similarly if this was false from eternity, "You will recover from this illness", you will not recover whether or not you bring a doctor.' And then the rest as before.

Chrysippus attacks this argument. Some things, he says, are simple, some compound. 'Socrates will die on that day' is simple; for him the day of his death is determined whether he does something or does not do it. But if it is fated 'Oedipus will be born to Laius',[24] it cannot be said 'whether Laius has been with a woman or not'. Here the thing is complex and confatal—for that is what he calls it because it is fated thus both that Laius will lie with a woman and that by her he will beget Oedipus. Likewise if it were said 'Milo will wrestle in the Olympics', and someone answered, 'And so he'll wrestle whether he has an opponent or not', he would be wrong. For 'will wrestle' is complex, since there is no wrestling without an opponent. And so all captious arguments of that sort are refuted in the same way. 'Whether you bring a doctor or not you will recover' is captious; for it is just as much fated that you bring a doctor as that you recover. These things, as I said, he calls confatals.

374   ALEXANDER, *Fate* xxii. 191. 30–192. 28 = SVF ii. 945   The Stoics say that this universe is one. It includes in it all existing things. It is governed by living, rational and understanding nature, so that it has the everlasting government of beings, proceeding in a certain chain and order. The first things become the causes of things that come to be after them, and in this way all things are bound to one another. And so nothing comes to be in the universe in such a way that something else does not in any case follow on it, bound to it as to its cause. Nor again can any of the things following be detached from the things preceding so as not to follow one of them as being bound to it. Rather, on everything that has come to be something else follows, depending on it as on

---

[22] Cicero gives the Greek, *argos logos*.

[23] True from eternity; **356**.

[24] Oedipus; **400–2**.

its cause by necessity; and everything that happens has something before it, on which it depends as on its cause.

For nothing in the universe either is or comes to be without a cause, because nothing in it is detached and separated from all the things that have come before. For the universe would be torn apart and divided and no longer remain always one, directed according to one order and government, if uncaused change were introduced. And uncaused change would be introduced if all the things that are and come to be did not have causes that previously have come to be, on which they follow by necessity. They say that something's coming to be without a cause is similar to something's coming to be from nothing, and similarly impossible. ...

But there is a difference between causes that they set out. For they list a whole swarm of causes—some originative, some joint causes, some containing, others something else[25] ... With these many causes they say it is equally impossible with all of them—if all the circumstances are the same about the cause and about the thing it causes—for it to happen not this way one time and this way another time. For if it happened this way, there would be some uncaused change. But they say that fate, and nature and the reason according to which everything is guided is God; it is in all things that are and come to be, and uses the nature proper to all beings for the government of the whole.

Fate and causation

375 This argument about co-fated events shows that even if everything is fated, I can still do something about what happens, and therefore I have some ability to affect the future. But is this the ability I need for freedom and responsibility? The Stoics show that my choice is needed if the fated event is to occur. But it is equally true that I need paper to write on if I am to pass the exam; and we do not attribute free will to the paper simply because it plays some essential role in the causal process. We might say that the paper itself does not control its place in the causal process. We normally suppose that I can do something about whether or not I write on the paper, whereas the paper cannot do anything about whether or not it is written on.

The Stoics claim to justify this distinction between my ability and the inability of the paper. They argue that I not only contribute to what happens, but also contribute as a free agent. They rely on their doctrine of different types of causes (**269–71**). As we have seen, this doctrine is supposed to be independently plausible, apart from any issues about determinism and freedom. In the Stoics' view, we can resolve these issues about freedom once we see what kinds of

[25] Causes; **269–71**.

causes are involved; the kinds of causation that we can rightly attribute to ourselves are the kinds that preserve our freedom. The causal role of our assent and choice implies that we are responsible for the actions that they cause.

....

376 AULUS GELLIUS, *Attic Nights* vii. 2. 6 = SVF ii. 1000   Although, Chrysippus said, it is true that by fate all things are constrained and linked by a necessary and primary reason, still the character of our minds is subject to fate in a way that accords with their proper quality. For if our minds were originally formed by nature soundly and beneficially, they accept all the externally imposed force of fate quite easily and without any obstacle. If, however, they are rough, ignorant, and uncouth, not built up by any good training, then, even if the impact of any fated disadvantage is little or nothing, these people, because of their own ineptitude and voluntary impulse, will plunge themselves into constant wrongdoings and errors. But the very fact that it happens this way is itself the result of that natural and necessary sequence of things that is called fate. For it is by its own nature a fated result that bad characters are not free of misdeeds and errors.

Chrysippus then offers a remarkably appropriate and clever example of this situation. If, he says, you throw a cylindrical stone down a steep slope, you are indeed the cause and origin of its downward movement. Soon, however, it keeps rolling down, not because you are still throwing it, but because its nature and its form's capacity to roll are as they are. Similarly, then, the order and reason and necessity of fate sets in motion the general types and beginnings of the causes, but each person's own will and the character of his mind direct the impulses of our deliberations and minds and our actions themselves.

377 CICERO, *Fate* 41–3   Chrysippus, however, both rejects necessity and wants nothing to happen without previous causes. And so he distinguishes kinds of causes, so that he can both escape necessity and hold on to fate. 'For', he says, 'among causes some are perfect and principal, others auxiliary and proximate. Hence we say that all things happen by fate by antecedent causes, but by this we mean not perfect and principal causes, but auxiliary and proximate causes.' Hence he answers the argument I presented a little earlier by saying: If all things happen by fate, it follows indeed that they all happen by previous causes—not, however, by principal and perfect causes, but by auxiliary and proximate. And so, granted that the auxiliary and proximate causes are not in our power, it does not follow that the desire is also not in our power. But if we were to say that all things happen by perfect and principal causes, it would follow that, given that these causes are not in our power, desire would not be in our power either.

Hence, for those who introduce fate in such a way that they attach necessity, this conclusion will apply; but for those who do not say that antecedent causes are perfect and principal causes it will not apply at all. For the Stoics think they can easily explain the remark that assents happen from previous causes. For admittedly assent cannot happen unless provoked by an appearance, but when it has this appearance as its proximate cause, not its principal cause, it is explained in the way Chrysippus wants—the way we have just described. It does not mean that assent could happen without being stimulated by any external force—for assent must be provoked by appearance.

He turns to the roller and the spinning-top, which cannot begin to move unless struck; but when this happens, he thinks that for the rest the roller rolls and the top spins by its own nature. He says: 'Someone who has pushed a roller gives it an origin of motion, but he has not given it the capacity to roll. So also an appearance, when it strikes us, will indeed imprint and, so to speak, seal its character in the mind; but our assent will be in our power, and, as we said about the roller, once it is struck from outside, for the rest it will be moved by its own force and nature. Hence, if something were effected without an antecedent cause, it would be false that all things happened by fate. But if it is likely that there is an antecedent cause for all things that happen, what can be adduced to show why we do not have to admit that all things happen by fate? We need only understand what is the distinction and difference of causes.'

Assent and freedom

378 When I act, the principal cause is my assent and choice. What I do depends on my choice, and my choice depends on appearance and assent. The Stoics claim that since my action is caused by my assent, my action is up to me, and I am responsible for it. The appearance may not be up to me: whether it appears to me that I see a tomato or not may depend on whether there is a tomato-like object in the environment. But whether or not I assent to the appearance and judge that there is a tomato, depends on me and on my rational estimate of the appearance. Since the action is caused by the assent, the action is up to me; I am fairly held responsible for it, and praise and blame are fairly applied to me, since they influence my assent and rational judgement, and these determine my action.[26]

In claiming that assent is the basis of freedom, the Stoics do not mean that assent is undetermined. Assent matters for freedom because it depends on our assessment of the situation, on what we think we have better reason to believe or to do. The Stoics claim not simply that something or other about us causes our reaction to an external situation, but that our assessment of a situation causes our choice of one or another response to it.

---

[26] Assent and action, **291–6**; assent and passions, **526–30**.

Why is this assessment relevant to responsibility? As Aristotle and Epicurus agree, we are right to hold people responsible for their actions if we are right to praise and blame them for what they have done. The point of praising and blaming is to lead people to see things differently, or to confirm them in seeing things the way they do. This practice would be unreasonable and futile if how I see things and how I interpret situations makes no difference to what I do. But if it does make a difference, then it is reasonable to praise me for what I do well and criticize me for what I do badly.

According to the Stoics, praise and criticism are reasonable if assent plays a decisive role. If they show that assent plays a decisive causal role, they explain why praise and criticism are appropriate. If they explain this, they show that we are responsible for our actions.

....

379   STOBAEUS, *Anthology* ii. 349. 23 = SVF ii. 74   The Stoics did not place perception in appearance alone. They made its being depend on assent; for perception is assent to a perceptual appearance, and the assent is in accord with one's impulse.

380   EPICTETUS, *Manual* 53   On all occasions we ought to have these thoughts ready at hand: 'Lead me, Zeus, and lead me, Fate, to wherever you have assigned to me. For I will follow without shrinking; and if I am unwilling, and turn out vicious, none the less I will follow.'[27] 'Whoever has given way rightly to necessity is counted wise among us and knows the way of the gods.'[28] 'Well, Crito, if this is what pleases the gods, let it come about this way.'[29] 'Anytus and Meletus are able to kill me, but not to harm me.'[30]

[27] Quoted from a poem of Cleanthes.
[28] A fragment of Euripides.
[29] Plato, *Crito* 43 D.
[30] Plato, *Apology*. Socrates explains his view of death in **317**.

X: Good, Pleasure, and Happiness

The final good

381 According to Socrates, the starting-point for ethical thought is the universal human desire to 'fare well'. In his view, we all aim at 'welfare' (*eu prattein*) or 'happiness' (*eudaimonia*). Most other Greek moralists agree with this starting-point. Aristotle, for instance, begins his discussion of common views about ethics by listing some general descriptions of *eudaimonia* (**384**). In the light of these, he sums up popular views about the 'parts' of *eudaimonia*—the various states and activities that are generally supposed to produce *eudaimonia*. Ethical inquiry consists in a search for the genuine parts and constituents of happiness, so that we can aim at these and avoid the actions and pursuits that divert us from our real welfare. Happiness or welfare is the ultimate end that makes it reasonable to care about our more specific ends.

Aristotle explicates the role of happiness in ethical inquiry by arguing that we must recognize an ultimate end, something that we pursue for its own sake (**385-6**). His argument is this:

(1) A particular action is rational in so far as we can answer the question 'Why are you doing that?' or 'What's the point of that?'. The answer to this question tells us the end or aim of our action.

(2) Our aims form chains: I open the front door to walk down the street to go to the shop to buy food to cook dinner ... etc. In such cases our more immediate ends are means to our further ends, and if we did not care about the further ends, it would be foolish to try to get the more immediate ends.

(3) If, however, we were always pursuing one thing for the sake of another, our concern for these further ends would be inexplicable, and so concern for these further ends would never explain our more immediate ends. Hence there must be some end that we pursue as an end in itself, not for the sake of anything further.

We identify our single ultimate end by seeing how we try to reconcile our more immediate aims. If we simply had a list of things that we care about for their own sakes, but had no idea of their relative importance to us, we could not make reasonable decisions about how far to pursue any one of them, or about what we ought to do if we must sacrifice one to achieve another. If we decide not to buy a new car because the cost of it would leave us with nothing to pay the rent, we care more about having somewhere to live than about driving a new car. If we decide not to buy a new car because we could not afford it unless we swindled our friends, we care more about our friends than about a new car. In Aristotle's view, these decisions show that we implicitly believe that friendship counts for more than a new car in our conception of happiness.

This very general description does not tell us what happiness actually consists in, or how to achieve happiness, but it helps us to understand the nature of disputes about happiness. We reveal our conception of happiness in so far as we articulate what we ultimately aim at in our lives, and which aims make it worth while to aim at the other things we aim at. Different people dispute about whether we are well off by enjoying ourselves, by devoting ourselves to the good of others, or by pursuing our own intellectual or artistic development. These disputes are disputes about the character and constituents of happiness.

Herodotus' story of a meeting between the Lydian (non-Greek) king Croesus and the Athenian poet and legislator Solon discusses some of the different elements of happiness (**388**; cf. **409**, **531**). Croesus assumes that his wealth and power guarantee his happiness, but Solon warns him not to overlook the other elements of human well-being. He mentions people who have lacked the wealth of Croesus, but none the less have had good lives that ended well. It turns out later that Croesus' life does not end well; Herodotus implies that Croesus has overlooked some essential elements in a good life.

382 JOHN STUART MILL, *Utilitarianism*, ch. 1   From the dawn of philosophy, the question concerning the summum bonum, or, what is the same thing, concerning the foundations of morality, has been accounted the main problem in speculative thought, has occupied the most gifted intellects and divided them into sects and schools carrying on a vigorous warfare against one another. And after more than two thousand years the same discussions continue, philosophers are still ranged under the same contending banners, and neither thinkers nor mankind at large seem nearer to being unanimous on the subject than when the youth Socrates listened to the old Protagoras and asserted (if Plato's dialogue be based on a real conversation) the theory of utilitarianism against the popular morality of the old sophist.

383 PLATO, *Euthydemus* 278 E–279 C   [SOCRATES:] Do all we human beings want to fare well? ... Surely it's foolish to ask questions like that; for what human being doesn't want to fare well? ... Since we all wish to do well, how could we do well? Perhaps if we had plenty of good things? Or is that an even sillier question than the first one? For it's clear, I suppose, that this is true?—[CLEINIAS:] He agreed.—Very well, what sorts of things, among all the things there are, are in fact good for us? Isn't this an easy question that needs no great man to supply an answer? For everyone would tell us that to be rich is good. What do you say?—Yes indeed, he said.—Also to be healthy and to be handsome, and to have enough of all the other bodily goods?—He thought so too.—Again, good birth and power and honour in one's own city, aren't these clearly good?—He agreed.—Then what other good things do we find? What about being temperate and just and brave?[1] What do you think, in heaven's name, Cleinias? If we count these as goods, will we be right, or not? For perhaps someone might quarrel with this. What do you think?—I think they are goods, said Cleinias.[2]

384   ARISTOTLE, *Rhetoric* 1360ᵇ4–29   For practically every individual and all people in common, there is a target that they aim at in their choice and avoidance. This target, to state it in summary, is happiness and its parts. Let us then grasp, in order to have an example, without going into details, what happiness is, and what things compose its parts … Let us, then, take happiness to be doing well combined with virtue; or self-sufficiency of life; or the pleasantest life combined with safety;[3] or prosperity of possessions and slaves combined with the capacity to keep them and to use them in action. For everyone more or less agrees that happiness is one or more of these. If, then, happiness is this sort of thing, its parts must be good birth, many friends, good friends, wealth, good children, many children, prosperous old age. They must also include bodily excellences[4] (for instance, health, beauty, strength, size, athletic ability), reputation, honour, good fortune, and virtue. For this is the way for someone to be most self-sufficient, by having both the goods internal to himself and the external goods, since there are no other goods besides these. The internal goods are those in the soul and body, and the external are good birth, friends, money, and honour; and we also think it suitable to have power and good fortune, since in that way one's life is safest.

385   ARISTOTLE, *Nicomachean Ethics* 1094ᵃ1–22   Every craft and every investigation, and likewise every action and decision, seems to aim at some good; hence some have rightly declared that the good is what all things aim at. However, there is an apparent difference among ends. For some are activities, and others are products apart from the activities; and in cases where there are ends apart from the actions, the products are by nature better than the activities. Since there are many actions, crafts and sciences, the ends turn out to be many as well; for health is the end of medicine, a boat of boat-building, victory of generalship, and wealth of household management. In some cases some of these sciences are subordinate to some one capacity; for instance, bridle-making and every other science producing equipment for horses are subordinate to horsemanship, while this and every action in warfare are in turn subordinate to generalship, and in the same way other sciences are subordinate to further ones. In all these cases the ends of the ruling sciences are

---

[1] For this list of virtues cf. **430–2**.
[2] This discussion is continued in **497**.
[3] Pleasure; **389**.
[4] *aretê*, translated 'virtue' just below.

more choiceworthy than all the ends subordinate to them, since the superordinate ends are those for which the subordinate ends are also pursued. Here it does not matter whether the ends of the actions are the activities themselves, or something apart from them, as in the sciences we have mentioned.

If then, there is some end of the things achievable by action, which we wish for because of itself, and because of which we wish for the other things, and we do not choose everything because of something else—since, if we do, it will go on without limit, making desire empty and futile—clearly this end will be the good, i.e. the best good.[5]

386 ARISTOTLE, *Nicomachean Ethics* 1095ª14–30 Since every sort of knowledge and decision pursues some good, what is that good that we take to be the aim of political science? What is the highest of all the goods achievable in action? As far as its name goes, most people virtually agree; for both the many and the cultivated call it happiness, and suppose that living well and doing well are the same as being happy. But they disagree about what happiness is, and the many do not give the same answer as the wise. For the many think it is something obvious and evident—for instance, pleasure, wealth or honour—some thinking one thing, others another. Indeed, the same person keeps changing his mind, since in sickness he thinks it is health, in poverty wealth. And when they are conscious of their own ignorance, they admire anyone who speaks of something grand and beyond them. Some people, however, used to think that besides these many goods there is some other good that is something in itself, and also causes all these goods to be goods.[6] Presumably, then, it is rather futile to examine all these beliefs, and it is enough to examine those that are most current or seem to have some argument for them.

387 MILL, *Utilitarianism*, ch. 4 The ingredients of happiness are very various, and each of them is desirable in itself, and not merely when considered as swelling an aggregate. The principle of utility does not mean that any given pleasure, as music, for instance, or any given exemption from pain, as for example health, is to be looked upon as means to a collective something termed happiness, and to be desired on that account. They are desired and desirable in and for themselves; besides being means, they are a part of the end.[7] ... What was once desired as an instrument for the attainment of happiness has come to be desired for its own sake. In being desired for its own sake it is, however, desired as *part* of happiness. The person is made, or thinks he would be made, happy by its mere possession; and is made unhappy by failure to obtain it. The desire of it is not a different thing from the desire of

[5] Continued at **405**.
[6] The Platonic Form of the good. See **214–15**.
[7] Means versus parts of the end; **407**.

happiness any more than the love of music or the desire of health. They are included in happiness. They are some of the elements of which the desire of happiness is made up. Happiness is not an abstract idea but a concrete whole; and these are some of its parts.

388 HERODOTUS i. 30–2   When Solon came to Sardis, he was entertained by Croesus in his palace, and on the third or fourth day after his arrival the servants, on Croesus' orders, took Solon round the treasuries and displayed to him how prosperous and rich they were. When he had seen and examined them all, Croesus took the opportunity to ask Solon: 'My friend from Athens, much talk of you has reached me, about your wisdom and your travelling; they say your love of wisdom[8] has led you to travel over much of the earth to observe it. And so now I'm filled with longing to ask you whether, among all the people you have seen, anyone is the most prosperous of all.' He asked this in the expectation that he would turn out to be the most prosperous of humanity.

But Solon did not flatter him at all, but kept to the truth in his answer. He said: 'Yes, your majesty. It was Tellus the Athenian.' Croesus was amazed at this, and pursued his question insistently. 'And what do you think makes Tellus the most prosperous?' Solon said: 'His city was in a good condition when he had fine and good sons, and he saw children born to all of them, and all surviving. Moreover, after his life had gone well—as we count it—it came to a most glorious end; for in a battle between the Athenians and their neighbours in Eleusis, he came to the aid of his comrades, routed the enemy, and died most finely. The Athenians gave him a public funeral where he had fallen, and honoured him greatly.'[9] ...

[32] Croesus was provoked, and said: 'My Athenian friend, do you despise my happiness so much that you don't think I even reach the level of mere private individuals?' Solon answered: 'Croesus, you are asking me about human fortunes, and I know that the divine is altogether envious[10] and prone to trouble us. In the whole length of time one can see many things one would rather not see, and suffer many things one would rather not suffer. ... And so, Croesus, a human being is altogether a creature of his circumstances. To me you appear to be very rich, and to be king over many people; but I can't answer the question you asked me, until I hear that your life has ended finely. For the very rich man is no more prosperous than one who has enough for daily needs, unless fortune follows him and he ends his life well, having everything fine. ... If ... he ends his life well, he is the one you are looking for, the one who deserves to be called prosperous. But before he is dead, wait; don't call him prosperous, but fortunate.'

---

[8] *philosophia;* cf. **327**.
[9] Solon adds a second example of people who are happy without great wealth or power.
[10] Or 'everything divine is envious'. On envy (*phthonos*) cf. **350**, **532**, **536**, **591**.

Happiness as pleasure

389 It is standard practice to use 'happiness' to translate *eudaimonia*. This is reasonable, but it may be misleading. We tend to suppose that happiness is to be identified with feeling happy, hence with feeling pleased, and hence with pleasure. This tendency, however, gives us a false impression of *eudaimonia*. It is not an obvious truth (as we might take it to be if we think of the English word 'happiness') that *eudaimonia* is simply pleasure; such a conception has to be argued for. Indeed, one major dispute in Greek ethics is about the relation of pleasure to *eudaimonia*, or (equivalently) about its relation to the ultimate human good. The arguments for and against the identification of pleasure with the good reveal some of the main questions about *eudaimonia*.

Arguments for the hedonist[11] view that happiness consists wholly in pleasure have a secure basis in common beliefs; Aristotle, indeed, mentions 'the pleasantest life combined with safety' (**384**) as one widely accepted description of happiness. According to a hedonist view, any means to happiness promotes it only by promoting pleasure.

Some of the arguments for and against a hedonist conception of happiness appear in different dialogues of Plato.[12] In the *Protagoras*, Socrates seems to identify happiness with pleasure, and to identify the different virtues with means to pleasure. We may find some reason to question the degree of Socrates' or Plato's commitment to the arguments for hedonism. But the arguments themselves show why hedonism might appear to be a plausible account of the good.

Socrates defends hedonism by an analysis of our choice between goods. He argues that when we apparently forgo some pleasure because we think the more painful course of action is better, we are really forgoing a lesser pleasure for the sake of a greater pleasure. Socrates infers that if it is rational to forgo some pleasure or to accept some painful course of action, the less immediately pleasant course must yield more pleasure in the longer term. Hence, brave people who accept danger and hardship do not forgo pleasure for some good other than pleasure; they simply forgo a smaller pleasure now for the sake of a greater pleasure later.

In the *Gorgias*, Callicles affirms the hedonist thesis that happiness consists in maximum pleasure. Since, in his view, we get greater pleasure from satisfying a larger appetite, happiness requires us to form large and demanding appetites and then to find the resources to satisfy them. These large and demanding appetites include bodily appetites for food, drink, and sex, since these are especially powerful and insistent. Such appetites are also expensive; they require large material resources. To acquire such resources, we often need to compete

---

[11] From Greek *hêdonê*, 'pleasure'.
[12] The order of the dialogues, and the relation of Socrates and Plato; **17–18**.

with others for scarce resources, so that the pursuit of satisfaction for these appetites forces us to violate the accepted standards of morality.

Callicles infers that if the accepted standards of morality restrain our pursuit of our own pleasure and happiness, they are simply a matter of convention. They belong to convention rather than nature, because they do not express the genuine interests and needs of the individual human beings who are required to obey them, but simply express the demands of the people who impose these rules of behaviour.[13] According to Callicles, we have no reason to take this conventional morality seriously.

Callicles' presentation of hedonism conflicts sharply with Socrates' presentation in the *Protagoras*. The *Protagoras* suggests that a hedonist conception of the ultimate end supports the virtues that are encouraged by ordinary morality. The *Gorgias*, however, implies that hedonism precludes any respect for the recognized virtues.

This conflict between the pursuit of pleasure and the recognized virtues is the basis of Socrates' answer to Callicles. Even though he denounces temperance and justice as mere convention, Callicles admires bravery, since it is the virtue that makes someone resolute in pursuing his own aims without being diverted by fear. Socrates argues that bravery and resolution are not always the best means to securing pleasure, because sometimes we can secure more pleasure by cowardice than by bravery. Hence, Callicles' hedonism conflicts with his admiration for the rational planning and resolution that belong to bravery.

We might explain Socrates' different attitudes to hedonism in the *Protagoras* and *Gorgias* in different ways:

(1) Perhaps Socrates or Plato changes his mind.

(2) Perhaps he accepts hedonism in the *Protagoras* only for the sake of argument.

(3) Perhaps the hedonist thesis he accepts in the *Protagoras* is different from the one he rejects in the *Gorgias*.

At any rate, Plato's two accounts in these dialogues of pleasure and the good define the two main positions that Greek moralists take towards hedonism. Plato (in later dialogues) and Aristotle are closer to the position of the *Gorgias*, whereas Epicurus revives the position of the *Protagoras*.

....

390 PLATO, *Protagoras* 353 C–355 A[14] [SOCRATES:] We take you to say ... that, for instance, you are often overcome by food or drink or sex, which are pleasant things, and that, though you recognize that they are bad, nevertheless you act in these ways. ... In what respect do you call them bad? Is it because

---

[13] This is the view that Alcibiades expresses to Pericles in **463**. Nature and convention; **125**.

[14] Socrates and Protagoras are discussing the views of 'the many'. Protagoras' assents on behalf of the many are omitted from the selection.

for the moment each of them provides this pleasure and is pleasant, or because in the future they produce disease or hold suchlike things in store? If they held none of these things in store, but produced nothing but enjoyment, would they none the less be bad, no matter why or how they give enjoyment? Can we expect any other answer than this, Protagoras, that they are not bad on account of the immediate production of pleasure, but on account of their consequences, disease and the rest? ... In causing disease and poverty, don't they cause pain? ... So the only reason why these pleasures seem to you to be evil is ... that they result in pains and deprive us of further pleasures. ...

You say also that pains may be good. You mean, I take it, such things as physical training, military campaigns, doctors' treatment involving cautery or the knife or drugs or a starvation diet. These, you say, are good but painful? ... Do you call them good in this respect, that in the present they cause extreme pain and agony, or because in the future they result in health, bodily well-being, the safety of one's city, rule over others, wealth? ... Are they good for any other reason than because they result in pleasures and the cessation or prevention of pains? Can you say that you attend to any other end in calling them good, than pleasures or pains? ... So you pursue pleasure as being good, and avoid pain as bad? ...

This, then, namely pain, you take to be bad, and pleasure you take to be good. ... [355 A] You can still retract what you have said, if you can find any way to say that anything other than pleasure is the good, or that anything other than pain is the bad. Or are you satisfied if you live out your life pleasantly without pains? If you are satisfied, and you can't say that anything else is good or bad that doesn't lead to this, then hear what comes next.[15]

391 PLATO, *Protagoras* 359 D–360 A[16] [SOCRATES:] What is it that brave men go eagerly to meet? Do they go eagerly to meet what is terrible, knowing that it is terrible? [PROTAGORAS:] Your own argument has shown that to be impossible.[17] ... —But as for what inspires confidence, everyone makes for that, cowards and brave men alike, and in this respect cowards and brave men make for the same things.—But, on the contrary, Socrates, what the coward makes for is precisely the opposite of what the brave man makes for. For instance, the brave are willing to go into battle, but the cowards refuse.—Is this going into battle fine or shameful?—Fine.—If, then, it's fine, we agreed earlier that it's good, since we agreed that all fine actions are good. ... But which people did you say refuse to enter battle even though that is a fine and good thing to do?—The cowards ... —Well, if it's fine and good, it's also pleasant.—We certainly agreed to that.—And so, when the cowards refuse to go into battle,

---

[15] What comes next is Socrates' argument against incontinence. See **436**.
[16] This follows **436**.
[17] Protagoras refers to the argument against incontinence, **436**.

do they do that in the knowledge that going into battle is finer and better and pleasanter?—If we say so, … we'll confound our previous conclusions.

392   PLATO, *Gorgias* 491 D–495 C[18]   SOCRATES: Is there no need to rule one-self? Do we only need to rule others? CALLICLES: What do you mean, 'rule oneself'?—Nothing subtle, but just what the many say: to be temperate and master of oneself, and ruler of one's own pleasures and appetites.—How charming! By 'temperate people' you mean fools.[19]—Certainly not; anyone can tell that that isn't what I mean.—But it is what you mean, Socrates. How could a human being become happy while being enslaved to anything at all? On the contrary, what is naturally fine and just is what I'm telling you now quite frankly: anyone who is to live correctly must allow his appetites to grow as large as possible and not restrain them, and when they are as large as possible, he must have the power to serve them, because of his bravery and wisdom, and to fill them with whatever he has an appetite for at any time. But I think this isn't in the power of the many. That's why they blame such people; they are moved by shame, and want to conceal their own powerlessness; and so they say that intemperance is actually shameful, … They enslave the people who are naturally best, and when they lack the power to find ways to fulfil their pleasures, they praise temperance and justice, because of their own cowardice … [492 C] But in truth, Socrates, … this is how it is: luxury, in-temperance, and freedom, if it is well supplied, is virtue and happiness; and those other things, those decorations, those human agreements contrary to nature, those are worthless rubbish.

—You speak with noble frankness, Callicles, in developing your position; for what you say is what other people think, but aren't willing to say. And so I ask you: by all means continue, so that it may become clear how we should live our lives. Tell me, then: you say, don't you, that if someone is to be as he ought, he must not restrain his appetites, but must let them grow as large as possible and satisfy them from somewhere or other, and that this is virtue?— Yes; that's what I say.—Then people are wrong to say that those who want for[20] nothing are happy?—Quite wrong; for if they were right, stones and corpses would be the happiest of all. … [493 D]—Now see whether you say this about the lives of the temperate and the uncontrolled person. There are two people, and both have a number of jars. The first person has his jars sound and full, one of wine, another of honey, and a third of milk, besides others filled with other liquids. The sources that fill them are few and difficult to find, and he can draw from them only with a great deal of toil and diffi-culty; but as soon as his jars are filled, he has no need to supply them any

---

[18] This follows Callicles' attack on justice (**458**) and his claim that the strong should rule the weak, which provokes Socrates' first question here.

[19] Temperance; **445**.

[20] Or 'need' or 'lack'. On this conception of happiness see **501**.

more, and has no anxiety about them, but, as far as they are concerned, he is at rest. The other person, in the same way, can find sources of supply, though with difficulty, but his jars are leaky and unsound. Night and day he is compelled to keep filling them, or else to suffer the most extreme pains. These, then, are their lives; and do you say that the life of the uncontrolled person is happier than the life of the orderly person? Do I convince you at all by this to agree that the orderly person's life is better than the uncontrolled person's, or don't I convince you?—You don't convince me, Socrates. For the one who has filled himself has no longer any pleasure left; but this, as I was just saying, is the life of a stone, whenever he is filled, with no more enjoyment or distress. But living pleasantly depends on this: having as much as possible flowing in.—But if so much flows in, mustn't much flow out, and mustn't the holes be large to take the outflow?[21]—Certainly.—Then you're describing the life of a stone-curlew,[22] not the life of a corpse or a stone. Tell me this: you mean being hungry and eating when hungry?—Yes.—And being thirsty and drinking when thirsty?—Yes, that's what I mean; and having all one's other appetites, and being able to fill them up with enjoyment, and so living happily. ...

[495 A]—Now tell me again, do you say that pleasant and good are the same, or that there is something pleasant that isn't good? ... Consider whether enjoyment, from whatever source, is the good; for if this is true, many shameful consequences, just now alluded to, evidently follow, and many others.—So you think, Socrates.—Then do you, Callicles, really maintain these things?—Indeed I do.—Then are we to proceed with the argument, on the assumption that you're serious?—Yes, certainly.[23]

393   PLATO, *Gorgias* 497 E–499 B   SOCRATES: Don't you call good men good by the presence of goods, just as you call beautiful those to whom beauty is present? CALLICLES: I do.—Well then, do you call fools and cowards good men? You didn't just now, anyway; you were saying that the brave and wise are good. Aren't these the ones you call good?—Quite.—Now did you ever see a foolish child enjoying himself?—I did.—And did you ever see a foolish man enjoying himself.—I think I did. What of it?—Nothing at all. Just answer.—I did see one.—Well, did you see an intelligent man in distress and enjoyment?—I did.—Which ones have more distress and enjoyment, the wise or the foolish?—I don't think they differ all that much.—Well, that's enough. Now did you ever see a cowardly man in war?—Of course.—Now when the enemy withdrew, who did you think enjoyed it more? The cowards or the brave men?—I thought they both enjoyed it; perhaps the cowards enjoyed it more, or if not, about the same.[24]—It doesn't matter. At any rate, the cowards

---

[21] Pleasure and psychic disturbance; **314**, **415–17**.
[22] A bird that excretes as fast as it eats.
[23] **393** gives the conclusion of Socrates' argument against Callicles' hedonist position.
[24] Text uncertain.

also enjoy it?—Very much so. ... [498 B]—But now the wise and brave are good, the cowardly and foolish bad.—Yes.—Then the good and the bad have about the same enjoyment and distress?—I agree.—Then are the good and the bad about equally good and bad, or are the bad even better? ... [499 B] Doesn't this follow, with those previous things, if someone says that the same things are pleasant and good?

Pleasure as a part of happiness

394 In his later dialogues, the *Republic* and *Philebus*, Plato argues, as Socrates does in the *Gorgias*, that some pleasures are good in themselves, and others are bad in themselves (not simply because they yield a smaller quantity of later pleasure). He infers that happiness cannot be defined as maximum pleasure. Some pleasures—those that are taken in the right objects—are necessary parts of happiness, but pleasure alone is insufficient for happiness. Happiness must be the right combination of pleasure and rational understanding (or 'intelligence', *phronêsis*).

Plato considers a hedonist objection to the argument of the *Gorgias*. Different people take pleasure in different things; brave people take pleasure in one thing and cowards in another. This variation, however, does not (in the hedonist view) refute hedonism. All it shows is that different people find their happiness in different ways, virtuous people in virtuous action and vicious people in vicious action (**395**).

In Plato's view, this objection misses a basic feature of *eudaimonia* (**396**). In saying that someone is *eudaimon*, we imply that his condition is a matter for congratulation and imitation. But someone who takes pleasure in foolish or vicious activities and cares about nothing else for its own sake is to be pitied, not congratulated or imitated. Such a person cannot be well off or happy; whether we are or are not well off depends not only on how we feel about what we are doing, but on what we are doing.

Aristotle agrees with Plato's claim that pleasure is insufficient for happiness. If we care only about pleasure and gratification, and not about the source of the pleasure, we cannot (according to Aristotle) achieve the good. We pursue the pleasures that really contribute to our good only if we pursue good rather than bad pleasures. The goodness of these pleasures must be measured by standards other than pleasure and pain. Pleasure alone is incomplete, because we can add further goods to it to make a better good (**398-9**).

If pleasures differ in kind, and the goodness of a given pleasure depends on the goodness of the object that we take the pleasure in, something else besides pleasure (namely, the object we take the pleasure in) must be good. Hence, Aristotle infers, a 'mixed' life (to use Plato's term in the *Philebus*) that contains this further good together with pleasure is better than one that contains pleasure alone (**398**).

....

395 PLATO, *Philebus* 12 C–E SOCRATES: Pleasure, if one goes by the mere word, is one thing; but surely it has all sorts of different types that are in some respect unlike one another. For consider: we say that someone acting intemperately takes pleasure, but we also say that someone acting temperately takes pleasure in acting temperately itself. Again, we say that someone who is being foolish and is full of foolish beliefs and hopes takes pleasure, but we also say that someone who is exercising intelligence takes pleasure in that exercise itself. Now if anyone says that each member of these pairs of pleasures is like the other, surely he will deserve to be thought foolish? PROTARCHUS: These pleasures are certainly from contrary things, Socrates, but they are not themselves contrary to each other. For how could pleasure not be most similar of all things to pleasure, being similar to itself?

396 PLATO, *Philebus* 21 A–D SOCRATES: Would you accept, Protarchus, a life spent entirely in the enjoyment of the greatest pleasures? PROTARCHUS: Certainly.—Then do you think you would need anything else added, if you had enjoyment in the fullest measure?—I'm sure I wouldn't.—Now consider: what about intelligence, thought, reasoning about what ought <to be done>, and so on? Wouldn't you need these at all?—Why? If I had my enjoyment, I would have everything.—Then if you lived your whole life long like that, you would be enjoying the greatest pleasures, would you?—Of course.—But if you were without thought, memory, knowledge, and true belief, wouldn't you necessarily be unaware even whether you were or were not enjoying yourself, since you would be empty of all intelligence?—Necessarily.—Similarly, if you had no memory, you would necessarily, I imagine, not even remember that you had been enjoying yourself; the pleasure occurring at the moment would leave no memory at all. Again, if you had no true belief, you couldn't believe that you were enjoying yourself when you were; if you lacked the power of reasoning, you couldn't even reason that you would enjoy yourself later on. You would be living the life not of a human being, but of some sort of sea lung, or one of those animate creatures of the ocean whose bodies are encased in shells. Am I right, or can we think of it any differently?—No, we can't.—Then is that sort of life choiceworthy?—Your argument, Socrates, has reduced me now to complete speechlessness.

397 ARISTOTLE, *Nicomachean Ethics* 1095^{b}14–22 For, it would seem, people quite reasonably reach their conception of the good, i.e. of happiness, from their lives; for there are roughly three most favoured lives—the lives of gratification, of political activity, and, third, of study. The many, the most vulgar, would seem to regard the good and happiness as pleasure, and hence they also like the life of gratification. Here they appear completely slavish, since the life they decide on is a life for grazing animals. And yet they have some argument in their defence, since many in positions of power react in the same way as Sardanapallus did.[25]

398 ARISTOTLE, *Nicomachean Ethics* 1172^{b}9–34   Eudoxus thought that pleasure is the good. This was because he saw that all animals, both rational and non-rational, seek it. In everything, he says, what is choiceworthy is good, and what is most choiceworthy is supreme. Moreover, each thing finds its own good, just as it finds its own nourishment. Hence, when all are drawn to the same thing, this indicates that it is best for all; and what is good for all, what all aim at, is the good. Eudoxus' arguments were found credible because of his virtuous character, rather than on their own merits. For since he seemed to be outstandingly temperate, he did not seem to be saying this because he was a friend of pleasure; rather, it seemed what he said was how it really was.

He thought it was no less evident from consideration of the contrary. Pain in itself is to be avoided for all; similarly, then, its contrary is choiceworthy. Now, what is most choiceworthy is what we choose not because of, or for the sake of, anything else; and it is agreed that this is the character of pleasure, since we never ask anyone what his end is in being pleased—we assume that pleasure is choiceworthy in itself. Moreover, when pleasure is added to any other good—to just or temperate action, for instance—it makes that good more choiceworthy; and good is increased by the addition of itself.

This argument, at any rate, would seem to represent pleasure as one good among others, no more a good than any other. For the addition of any other good makes a good more choiceworthy than it is all by itself. Indeed Plato[26] uses this sort of argument when he undermines the claim of pleasure to be the good. For, he argues, the pleasant life is more choiceworthy when combined with intelligence than it is without it; and if the mixed good is better, pleasure is not the good, since nothing can be added to the good to make it more choiceworthy. Nor, clearly, could anything else be the good if it is made more choiceworthy by the addition of anything that is good in itself.

399 ARISTOTLE, *Nicomachean Ethics* 1173^{b}31–1174^{a}11   The difference between a friend and a flatterer[27] seems to indicate that pleasure is not a good, or else that pleasures differ in kind. For in dealings with us the friend seems to aim at what is good, but the flatterer at what is pleasant; and the flatterer is reproached, whereas the friend is praised, on the assumption that in their dealings they have different aims. Further, no one would choose to live with a

[25] Sardanapallus was a king known for his extravagant way of life. Aristotle continues at **403**.
[26] Plato; **396**.
[27] Flattery; **179**, **546–8**.

child's level of thought for his whole life, taking as much pleasure as possible in what pleases children, or to enjoy himself while doing some utterly shameful action, even if he were never going to suffer pain for it. Moreover, there are many things that we would be eager for even if they brought no pleasure—for instance, seeing, remembering, knowing, having the virtues. Even if pleasures necessarily follow on them, that does not matter, since we would choose them even if no pleasure resulted from them. It would seem to be clear, then, that pleasure is not the good, that not every pleasure is choiceworthy, and that some are choiceworthy in themselves, differing in their kind or in their sources.

Beyond pleasure

400 If happiness is not simply pleasure, what are its other components? The examples mentioned by Herodotus and Aristotle (**384**, **388**) suggest that our happiness depends not only on how we feel about our lives, but also on what we have actually achieved. Wealth, power, fame, honour, or some combination of them are different aspects of success. Since they often mark success in worthwhile and difficult endeavours, they are often appropriate objects of admiration, and therefore appropriate measures of welfare. Aristotle calls these 'external' goods or 'goods of fortune', because they mark some achievement external to our choosing and acting. Our success in achieving these goods makes us fortunate in our lives.

This conception of happiness makes a happy person's condition unstable, always liable to a reversal of fortune. This danger is illustrated by Herodotus' stories of Croesus (**388**) and Polycrates (**350**), and by many Greek tragedies, especially Sophocles' *Oedipus Tyrannus* and Euripides' *Heracles* and *Hecuba*. The Chorus in the *Oedipus Tyrannus* treat the sharp reversal in the fortune of Oedipus as a reason for counting no human being happy until he is dead, beyond the shifting fortunes of life.

In the *Poetics* Aristotle comments on this preoccupation of tragedy with reversals of fortune. Oedipus and Agamemnon[28] (among others) suffer misfortunes out of proportion to their moral character. Though they are not wholly blameless, the consequences of their actions are worse than they could reasonably have expected. Their disproportionate sufferings are proper objects of pity and fear. Hence, the best sort of tragedy, arousing the appropriate sort of pity and fear, presents the misfortunes of fairly good people—those who are neither especially bad nor outstandingly good. To present a good person

---

[28] Agamemnon; **347**, **349**. Shakespeare's Othello and Macbeth show the same disproportion between a genuine fault and the bad results.

suffering a reversal of fortune is, in Aristotle's view, simply 'abhorrent', not the most appropriate subject for a tragedy.[29]

The instability of external goods may suggest that happiness itself is unstable, since it consists in the achievement of these goods. Plato and Aristotle draw a different conclusion: happiness cannot consist in these goods, since it cannot be as unstable as they are. They have two main reasons:

(1) Our conception of happiness is supposed to give us a basis for our aims and plans in our life as a whole; but it is unreasonable to devote all our plans to achieving something that is easily lost.

(2) In saying that someone is happy, we imply that something about the person himself deserves congratulation and imitation. But if happiness consists in the goods of fortune, calling someone happy simply says something about his circumstances, not about the person himself.

These two arguments imply that if we conceive happiness simply as the achievement of goods subject to fortune, we give too little weight to agency. Since we are agents, and we can control some aspects of what happens to us by our rational agency, a true conception of happiness ought to take account of the fact that it is the welfare of rational agents who act, and not of mere victims of circumstances.

This emphasis on agency has to be balanced by the appropriate emphasis on external success. Aristotle takes it to be absurdly paradoxical to claim that external success does not matter at all for happiness (**403**). He wants to show not only that both agency and external success matter, but also how much they matter and why. His view needs to be compared with the views of Socrates and the Stoics, who take him to underestimate the place of agency. We will be able to understand this dispute when we have gone further into Aristotle's own view of happiness (**498–500**).

....

401 SOPHOCLES, *Oedipus Tyrannus* 1186–1204[30]   Alas, generations of mortals; I count your lives as close to nothing. For what man gains any more of happiness than enough to make him seem happy, and after seeming to fall away? Taking your fortune as my pattern, wretched Oedipus, I count nothing belonging to mortals as blessed. You succeeded beyond expectation and hit the target, and gained prosperity that turned out to be not entirely happy.[31] You destroyed the prophetess with crooked talons,[32] and stood up as a tower for my land to ward off death. For that you are called my king, and were

---

[29] Plato on tragedy; **439**.

[30] The chorus sings this ode just after hearing that Oedipus, king of Thebes, has killed his father and married his mother. Cf. **373**.

[31] Text uncertain.

[32] The Sphinx.

given the greatest honours, reigning in great Thebes. But now whose story is more wretched?

402 ARISTOTLE, *Poetics* 1452^{b}34–1453^{a}17 Virtuous men must not appear passing from good to bad fortune; for this is not an object of fear or pity, but of abhorrence. Nor must vicious people appear passing from bad fortune to good. For this process is the most untragic of all; it has none of the features needed in a tragedy, since it arouses neither our feeling for humanity nor our pity nor our fear. Nor must an extremely vicious person appear passing from good fortune to bad. For though this construction appeals to our feeling for humanity, it arouses neither pity nor fear. For pity is felt for someone suffering ill fortune who does not deserve it, and fear for someone like <ourselves>; hence the result arouses neither pity nor fear. The remaining case is the person between these. He is a person who is not superior in virtue and justice, but passes into ill fortune, not because he is bad and vicious, but because he makes some error[33]—someone in high esteem and good fortune, such as Oedipus, Thyestes, and the other illustrious men of such noble families. And so a story that is well constructed must ... must involve passing from good fortune to bad, not the other way round, and this must happen because of some great error by an agent who is either the sort of person we have described or better than that rather than worse.

403 ARISTOTLE, *Nicomachean Ethics* 1095^{b}22–1096^{a}2[34] The cultivated people, those active in politics, conceive the good as honour, since this is more or less the end of the political life. This, however, appears to be too superficial to be what we are looking for; for it seems to depend more on those who honour than on the one honoured, whereas we intuitively believe that the good is something of our own and hard to take from us.[35] Further, it would seem, they pursue honour to convince themselves that they are good; at any rate, they seek to be honoured by intelligent people, among people who know them, and for virtue. It is clear, then, that in the view of active people at least, virtue is superior to honour. Perhaps, indeed, one might take virtue more than honour to be the end of the political life. However, this also is apparently too incomplete. For, it seems, someone might possess virtue but be asleep or inactive throughout his life, or, worse than that, he might suffer the worst evils and misfortunes; and if this is the life he leads, no one would count him happy, except as a philosophical exercise.[36]

---

[33] An error may be blameworthy, though it is not necessarily the result of vice. On blameworthiness see **358–9**.

[34] This follows **397**.

[35] Happiness as 'our own'; **518–19**.

[36] See also **499**.

Aristotle: criteria for happiness

404 Aristotle's objections to one-sided emphasis on pleasure and external goods suggests a different approach. The one-sided views fail because happiness must be a complete and self-sufficient good, and it must be the good for a human being as a rational agent. He defends and clarifies these demands on happiness.

The demand for completeness rules out one-sided conceptions of happiness. If our conception of a good human life lacks something that deserves to be chosen, we have not described a happy life. A life that is complete (**406** n.) must include all the goods that are worth including in a person's life. We rely on our beliefs about what makes a person's life better in order to decide whether a particular conception of happiness describes a complete good; if we find that it leaves out some kind of thing that we take to make a person's life better, then it has not described a complete good. Aristotle tests pleasure and honour by the criterion of completeness, and argues that they fail. Each lacks some feature that makes a human life better.

If this were all we could say about completeness, we might have a plausible negative criterion, but we would have no positive criterion to identify elements of happiness. To find a positive criterion, Aristotle argues that happiness is a complete good for human beings as rational agents. To see how he understands this criterion, we must examine his account of human nature and rational agency.

......

405 ARISTOTLE, *Nicomachean Ethics* 1094^{a}22–^{b}11[37] Then surely knowledge of this good is also extremely important for the conduct of our lives, and if, like archers, we have a target to aim at, we are more likely to hit the right mark. If so, we should try to grasp, in outline at any rate, what the good is, and which science or capacity is concerned with it. It seems to concern the most controlling science, the one that, more than any other, is the ruling science. And political science apparently has this character. For it is the one that prescribes which of the sciences ought to be studied in cities, and which ones each class in the city should learn, and how far; again, we see that even the most honoured capacities—generalship, household management and rhetoric, for instance—are subordinate to it; further, it uses the other sciences concerned with action, and moreover legislates what must be done and what avoided. And so its end will include the ends of the other sciences, and therefore will be the human good. For, granted that the good is the same for a city as for an individual, still the good of the city is apparently a greater and more complete good to acquire and preserve; for while it is satisfactory to acquire and preserve the good even for an individual, it

[37] Continues **385**.

is finer and more divine to acquire and preserve it for a people and for cities. And so, since our investigation aims at these goods, it is a sort of political science.[38]

406 ARISTOTLE, *Nicomachean Ethics* 1097ᵃ28–ᵇ21 The best good is apparently something complete.[39] And so if only one end is complete, this will be what we are looking for; and if more than one are complete, the most complete of these will be what we are looking for. An end pursued in itself, we say, is more complete than an end pursued because of something else; and an end that is never choiceworthy because of something else is more complete than ends that are choiceworthy both in themselves and because of this end; and hence an end that is always choiceworthy in itself, never because of something else, is unqualifiedly complete. Now happiness more than anything else seems unqualifiedly complete, since we choose it always because of itself, never because of something else. Honour, pleasure, understanding and every virtue we certainly choose because of themselves—for we would choose each of them even if it had no further result; but we also choose them for the sake of happiness, supposing that through them we shall be happy. Happiness, however, no one ever chooses for their sake, or because of anything else at all.

The same conclusion also appears to follow from self-sufficiency, since the complete good seems to be self-sufficient.[40] What we count as self-sufficient is not what suffices for a solitary person by himself, living an isolated life, but what suffices also for parents, children, wife, and in general for friends and fellow-citizens, since a human being is a naturally political <animal>. Here, however, we must mark some limit; for if we extend the good to parents' parents and children's children and to friends of friends, we shall go on without limit; but we must examine this another time. Anyhow, we take what is self-sufficient to be whatever, all by itself, makes a life choiceworthy and lacking nothing; and that is what we think happiness does. Moreover, we think happiness is most choiceworthy of all goods, not counted as one good among many.[41] If it were counted as one among many, then, clearly, it would be more choiceworthy with the smallest of goods added; for what is added becomes an extra quantity of goods, and the larger of two goods is always more choiceworthy. Happiness, then, is apparently something complete and self-sufficient, since it is the end of the things achievable by action.

---

[38] The city and the human good; **558**.

[39] The word translated 'complete' (*teleion*) may also be translated by 'perfect' or 'final'. These different renderings may affect our interpretation. Complete life; **423**.

[40] Self-sufficiency; **606**.

[41] This clause might mean 'since it is not …' or 'if it is not …'. Similarly, in the next sentence, for 'If it were …' we might substitute 'If it is …' and for 'it would be …' we might substitute 'it is …'.

Happiness and the human function

407 To explain the claims about human nature that bear on claims about happiness, Aristotle introduces the human 'function' (or 'work' or 'characteristic activity': *ergon;* cf. **428**). He clarifies his notion of function through examples of craftsmen, artefacts, and organs (cf. **336**). The function of each of these things is the goal-directed activity that makes it the kind of thing it is—the activity that is essential to it as that kind of thing. Something is an axe in so far as it has the function of cutting; when it no longer cuts, it is no longer an axe.[42] Aristotle does not mean that everything that has a function has been designed to serve that function.[43] He means that it has some goal-directed organization that defines its form and its essence. That is why he extends his claim about functions from craftsmen and organs to natural organisms.

The human function, according to Aristotle, is a specific kind of life, distinct from plant and animal life. This function is the activity of the soul expressing reason. In *On the Soul* Aristotle argues that the soul is the form of the living body, so that it is what makes the living body alive. In finding a living organism's form and function, we find its soul. Different kinds of life correspond to the different kinds of soul that are described in *On the Soul* (**337**). The human good is determined by the human function in so far as it is determined by the human form— the pattern of life and activity that is characteristic of human beings in contrast to other things.

Aristotle has been attacked for focusing arbitrarily on reason as the unique attribute of human beings. Why (critics ask) should we focus on reason rather than on other features that might distinguish human beings from other animals? Why suppose that what is unique must be especially important? It is difficult to see why the fact (if it is one) that we differ from other animals in our capacity for thought shows that we ought to spend as much time as possible on thinking (**410**).

To see how far these objections are warranted, we should bear in mind that, according to Aristotle, human reason is not a feature that merely happens to be unique to human beings. He is looking for a feature that is essential to human beings. He claims that it is essential to human beings, in contrast to other animals, that they guide their actions by reason. When he says that the human good must consist in some life that 'expresses reason', he primarily has in mind practical rather than theoretical reason. He does not mean that the human good consists primarily in thinking or reasoning, but that it consists in a life that expresses reason in controlling and guiding our lives.[44]

He clarifies 'controlling and guiding' in saying what is involved in having a

---

[42] Cf. Aristotle's comments on homonymy, **252**, **257**, **336**, **558**.
[43] On the independence of teleology from claims about intelligent design see **240**.
[44] Theoretical reason, however, has an important place in happiness. See **606**.

conception of happiness. When we care about several things for their own sakes, we can form some view of how much each of them matters to us. In doing this we exercise practical reason. In taking this rational activity to be essential to human agency, Aristotle does not deny the importance of other human activities besides reasoning; he simply emphasizes the importance of guiding these other activities by rational reflection.

The human good cannot consist merely in the exercise of rational agency without any further condition on how it is exercised; for we can exercise reason badly or perversely, in ways that clearly harm the agent. To rule out such cases, Aristotle claims that the good consists in the good exercise of reason; that is why happiness must consist in activity in accordance with virtue.

In claiming that happiness is activity in accordance with virtue Aristotle does not simply mean that virtuous activity promotes happiness by causing some further state—pleasure, for instance—that is happiness. He means that happiness is to be identified with the virtuous activity itself; virtuous activity is a component of happiness, and not merely instrumental to it (cf. **387**). This is because virtuous activity in itself exercises rational agency. The next question must be: which forms of rational agency constitute the best exercise of reason? The answer to this question gives us an account of the virtues (**440**).

....

408   ARISTOTLE, *Nicomachean Ethics* 1097^{b}22–1098^{a}20[45]   But presumably the remark that the best good is happiness is apparently something generally agreed, and we still want a clearer statement of what the best good is. Well, perhaps we shall find the best good if we first find the function of a human being. For a flautist, a sculptor, and every craftsman, and, in general, for whatever has a function and action, the good, i.e. doing well, seems to depend on its function. The same, then, seems to be true of a human being, if a human being has some function. Then do the carpenter and the leather-worker have their functions and actions, while a human being has none, and is by nature idle, with no function? Or, just as eye, hand, foot and, in general, every part apparently has its function, may we likewise ascribe to a human being some function besides all of theirs? What, then, would this be? Living is apparently shared with plants, but what we are looking for is the distinctive[46] function of a human being; hence we should set aside the life of nutrition and growth. The life next in order is some sort of life of sense-perception; but this too is apparently shared, with horse, ox and every animal. The remaining possibility, then, is some sort of life of action of what has reason. Now one part of this obeys reason, while the other part itself has reason and thinks.[47] Moreover, life is also spoken of in two ways, and we must

---

[45] Continued from **406**.
[46] *idion*; cf. **233**, **246**, **558**.
[47] Both ways of having reason are included in the human function. See **441**.

take the human function to be life as activity, since this seems to be called life to a fuller extent.[48] We have found, then, that the human function is the soul's activity that expresses reason or requires reason. Now the function of a harpist, for instance, is the same in kind, so we say, as the function of an excellent harpist, and the same is true without qualification in every case, when we add to the function the superior achievement that expresses the virtue; for a harpist's function is to play the harp, and a good harpist's is to do it well. Now we take the human function to be a certain kind of life, and take this life to be the soul's activity and actions that require reason; hence the excellent man's function is to do this finely and well. Since each function is completed well when its completion expresses the proper virtue, the human good turns out to be the soul's activity that expresses virtue; if there are more virtues than one, the good will express the best and most complete virtue. Moreover, it will be in a complete life. For one swallow does not make a spring, nor does one day; nor, similarly, does one day or a short time make us blessed and happy.

409 ARISTOTLE, *Nicomachean Ethics* 1100^{a}5–^{b}22   As we said, happiness needs both complete virtue and a complete life. For life includes many changes and all sorts of fortune, and it is possible for the most prosperous person to fall into a terrible disaster in old age, as the Trojan stories tell us about Priam. If someone has suffered these sorts of misfortunes and has come to a miserable end, no one counts him happy. Then should we also count no other human being happy during his lifetime, but follow Solon's[49] advice to wait to see the end? ... If we must wait to see the end, and must then count someone blessed, not as being blessed then, but because he previously was blessed, surely it is absurd if at the time when he is happy we will not truly ascribe to him the happiness he has. We hesitate out of reluctance to call him happy during his lifetime, because of the changes in life, and because we suppose happiness is enduring and definitely not prone to fluctuate, whereas the same person's fortunes often turn to and fro. For clearly, if we are guided by his fortunes, we will say the same person is often happy and then miserable again, so that we will represent the happy person as a kind of chameleon, with no firm foundation. But surely it is quite wrong to be guided by someone's fortunes. For his doing well or badly does not rest on them; though a human life, as we said, needs these added, it is the activities expressing virtue that control happiness, and the contrary activities that control its contrary. ... For no human achievement has the stability that belongs to activities that express virtue, since these seem to be more enduring even than our knowledge of the sciences; and the most honourable of the virtues

---

[48] Capacity and activity; **335–6**.
[49] Solon: **388**.

themselves are more enduring, because blessed people devote their lives to them more fully and more continually than to anything else—for this would seem to be the reason we do not forget them. It follows, then, that the happy person has what we are looking for and keeps the character he has throughout his life. For always, or more than anything else, he will study what expresses virtue, and will bear fortunes most finely, in every way and in all conditions appropriately, since he is truly 'good, foursquare and blameless'.[50]

410 BERNARD WILLIAMS, *Morality*,[51] pp. 75–7 There are more general objections to the procedure of trying to elicit unquestionable moral ends or ideals from distinguishing marks of man's nature. We may mention three. First, a palpable degree of evaluation has already gone into the selection of the distinguishing mark which is given this role, such as rationality or creativity. If one approached without preconceptions the question of finding characteristics which differentiate men from other animals, one could as well, on these principles, end up with a morality which exhorted men to spend as much time as possible in making fire; or developing peculiarly human physical characteristics; or having sexual intercourse without regard to season; or despoiling the environment and upsetting the balance of nature; or killing things for fun. Second, and very basically, this approach bears out the moral *ambiguity* of distinctive human characteristics (though Aristotle paid some attention, not totally successfully, to this point). For if it is a mark of a man to employ intelligence and tools in modifying his environment, it is equally a mark of him to employ intelligence in getting his own way and tools in destroying others ... Third, if we revert to that particular case of the *rational* as the distinguishing mark of man; there is a tendency for this approach to ... emphasize virtues of rational self-control at the expense of all else. ... If rationality and consistent thought are the preferred distinguishing marks of man, then, even if it is admitted that man, as a whole, also has passions, the supremacy of rational thought over them may well seem an unquestionable idea. This is all the more so, since it is quite obvious that gaining some such control is a basic condition of growing up, and even, at the extreme, of sanity. But to move from that into making such control into the ideal, rules out a priori most forms of spontaneity. And this seems to be absurd.

Epicurus' defence of hedonism

411 Epicurus revives hedonism. He accepts Aristotle's criteria, requiring happiness to be complete and self-sufficient, but he claims that these criteria show

---

[50] Continued at **500**.
[51] Cambridge: CUP, 1976.

that pleasure is the good. Even if happiness requires rational activity in accordance with virtue, the role of this activity is strictly instrumental. Virtue is no part of happiness itself, as Epicurus conceives it; but he argues that maximizing pleasure requires the exercise of reason and virtue.

To show that pleasure is happiness, Epicurus reminds us that happiness is the ultimate end, and therefore something chosen purely for its own sake, for the sake of no further end. The question 'But why do you pursue that?' is not supposed to arise when we come to the ultimate end. Pleasure seems to meet this condition. If you answer my question 'Why are you doing that?' with 'Because I enjoy it', it does not seem appropriate to ask 'But why are you doing what you enjoy?' My pursuit of enjoyment seems self-explanatory.

Eudoxus (**398**) and Epicurus seem to rely on this self-explanatory character of pleasure. They argue from the fact that pleasure is the original, basic, and natural aim of a sentient creature. All animals immediately recognize that pleasure is good, and pursue it as their end; children pursue it spontaneously before they have acquired any other beliefs about what is good. Epicurus infers that pleasure is the ultimate end; it is the common end of all the actions of sentient creatures, the end that makes all their actions intelligible.

....

412 EPICURUS = DIOGENES LAERTIUS X. 128–9 ... We say pleasure is the origin[52] and end of living blessedly. For we recognized this as our first and innate good, and from this we begin every choice and avoidance, and we arrive at this by judging every good by our feeling as a standard.

413 CICERO, *Ends* i. 30 As soon as each animal is born, it seeks pleasure, and rejoices in it as the highest good, and rejects pain as the greatest evil ... It does this while it is not yet ruined, while nature herself judges without corruption or damage. Therefore, Epicurus says, we need no reason or discussion about why pleasure is to be pursued and pain to be avoided. He thinks that these things are perceived, just as we perceive that fire is hot, snow is white, and honey is sweet. None of these things has to be supported by elaborate reasons, but it is enough to draw attention to them; ... this is what indicates evident and obvious things.

Varieties of hedonism

414 Though Epicurus defends hedonism on these grounds, he rejects Callicles' views (**392**) about its implications. He denies that maximum pleasure requires more and more demanding desires that require ever larger material resources for their unrestrained satisfaction. Callicles' way of life makes us

---

[52] Or 'beginning' or 'principle' (*archê*).

depend on abundant material resources, but nature—according to Epicurus—does not require the satisfaction of ever more demanding appetites. On the contrary, dependence on external resources beyond our control creates anxiety that a clear-headed hedonist must avoid. Callicles' way of life increases fears and anxieties, and fails to remove some of those that, in Epicurus' view, we need to remove. Contrary to Callicles, Epicurus advocates 'static' over 'kinetic' pleasures. He claims that an enlightened hedonist prefers the static pleasures of satisfied desire and tranquillity over the kinetic pleasure involved in the process of satisfying desire and removing pain. Hence the enlightened hedonist cannot be accused of advocating gross sensual pleasures, or the immorality that results from the pursuit of them (**420**).

This specific version of hedonism is closely connected with Epicurus' view about what is wrong in most people's lives and how philosophy can put it right; indeed, his conception of the good as freedom from anxiety is the starting-point for philosophical inquiry itself (**290**). He believes that the source of our worst fears and anxieties is the groundless fear of death; and so he tries to persuade us that death is nothing to be afraid of. The aim of Epicurean philosophy—natural philosophy as well as moral philosophy—is to free us from fear and anxiety, and especially from the fear of death. In valuing this freedom from disturbance, or 'tranquillity' (*ataraxia*) as the ultimate good, Epicurus agrees with Democritus and the Sceptics (**174**, **278**, **297**, **314**). Whereas the Sceptics take anxiety about the truth of dogmatic convictions to be the source of disturbance, Epicurus traces disturbance to a specific sort of anxiety, about death and what follows it.

Once we see that the ultimate good is freedom from anxiety, we will see that we can reach the ultimate good without pursuing more and more pleasure (**290**, **339–40**). Similarly, once we see that death does not lead to post-mortem punishments, we see that it does not threaten any disturbance; hence we should not cling to life, and should not regard the ending of life as bad for us. According to Epicurus, there is nothing worse about the life of someone who dies at the age of 20 than about the life of someone who has lived a life of good actions until the age of 80.

Since Epicurus' natural philosophy is intended to secure our good by removing anxiety, he must show that our good consists simply in freedom from anxiety. He must therefore justify, on purely hedonist grounds, his preference for tranquillity and freedom from disturbance. If he must introduce some non-hedonistic reasons for preferring some pleasures to others, pleasure alone cannot be the good. If, however, Epicurus sticks to purely hedonistic reasons, he also leaves room for hedonist objections. Callicles might grant that the 'kinetic' pleasures he cares about produce more pain and anxiety than he would have if he had more moderate pleasures. But if these pleasures give him more enjoyment, why is the enjoyment not worth the extra anxiety?

It is difficult to see how some hedonistic calculation, not already committed to valuing the Calliclean or the Epicurean pleasures, could settle this dispute.

Epicurus does not completely answer the criticisms of hedonism made in the *Gorgias* and by Aristotle (**394**, **399**). He may have reasons for rejecting the Calliclean position, and for arguing that the Epicurean life of moderate desire is preferable. But if these reasons are not adequately supported by appeal to maximum pleasure, he avoids the Calliclean position only by abandoning hedonism.

Even if Epicurus is right to prefer freedom from disturbance over Calliclean pleasures, has he found a satisfactory conception of happiness? Plato and Aristotle object that we can secure pleasure even from foolish and vicious activities. Can we not also secure tranquillity in this way? If we can, our life still lacks something of value; tranquillity alone, irrespective of its source, cannot constitute happiness.

Epicurus might try either of two replies:

(1) He might insist that tranquillity, however achieved, is all there is to happiness.

(2) He might agree that not every sort of tranquillity counts as happiness, and restrict his claims to the sort of tranquillity that results from the appropriate exercise of rational agency.

The first answer implies that if (for instance) Sceptics also achieve tranquillity, we have no better reason for being Epicureans than for being Sceptics. In that case happiness does not require us to accept Epicurus' outlook. Epicurus might answer that the Sceptic does not in fact achieve tranquillity.

Alternatively, he might turn to his second reply, claiming that when he seems to identify happiness with tranquillity, he only means to identify it with the tranquillity that results from a true rational understanding of the world and of the good. But if this is his answer, he is no longer a hedonist, since he does not take pleasure itself to be the end.

....

415 EPICURUS = DIOGENES LAERTIUS X. 128 We must derive every choice and avoidance from the health of the body and the tranquillity of the soul, since this is the end of a blessed life. For we do everything for the sake of this, so that we will suffer neither pain nor terror.[53]

416 PLUTARCH, *Against Epicurean Happiness* 1088c Epicurus has assigned a common limit to pleasures, namely the removal of everything painful. In his view, nature has increased the pleasant to the point where it removes the painful, but nature allows pleasure no further increase in size; pleasure simply admits of some non-necessary variations once it reaches a point of no distress.

---

[53] Continued at **502**. On the happy person as the one who is in need of nothing cf. **392**.

417 PLUTARCH, *Against Epicurean Happiness* 1089d   The stable condition of the flesh and the trustworthy expectation of <the continuation of> this <stability> contains the highest and most secure joy, for those who are capable of reasoning about it.[54]

418 EPICURUS, *Vatican Sayings* 33 = Arrighetti, p. 147   The cry of the flesh is not to be hungry or thirsty or cold. For if someone avoids these things, and expects to avoid them in the future, he might rival even Zeus for happiness.

419 CICERO, *Ends* i. 37–8   For we do not pursue only the pleasure that moves our nature itself with a kind of agreeableness, and is perceived by the senses with a sort of delight. Rather, we take the greatest pleasure to be the one we perceive when all pain is removed. For since, when pain is removed, we rejoice in the very release, and in the absence of annoyance, and since everything we rejoice in is pleasure, ... the removal of all pain is rightly called pleasure.

420 MILL, *Utilitarianism*, ch. 2   Now such a theory of life excites in many minds ... inveterate dislike. To suppose that life has (as they express it) no higher end than pleasure—no better and nobler object of desire and pursuit—they designate as utterly mean and grovelling, as a doctrine worthy only of swine, to whom the followers of Epicurus were, at a very early period, contemptuously likened ... When thus attacked, the Epicureans have always answered that it is not they, but their accusers, who represent human nature in a degrading light, since the accusation supposes human beings to be capable of no pleasures except those of which swine are capable ... The comparison of the Epicurean life to that of beasts is felt as degrading, precisely because a beast's pleasures do not satisfy a human being's conception of happiness.

Death and evil

421 These questions about the relation between good, pleasure, and freedom from anxiety will affect our views about the connection between Epicurus' moral philosophy and his natural philosophy. He assumes that we can remove anxiety from our lives only by removing the fear of death. He argues that we need not fear death, because we will feel no pain when we are dead, and the only evil is pain.

It is difficult to see why, on purely hedonist grounds, we should regard Epicurus' philosophy as the only route to tranquillity. Why should we not reach tranquillity by Sceptical suspension of judgement about death?

---

[54] *epilogismos*; cf. **424**.

If Epicurus argues that Sceptical tranquillity is not the best kind, and that some non-hedonic value belongs to tranquillity that is based on correct beliefs, he opens his position to another objection. We seem to have non-hedonistic grounds for denying his claim that a longer life is never preferable to a shorter one, and that therefore death is never bad for us. If a painter is working with enthusiasm on a great painting, and he dies before he finishes it, something bad seems to have happened to him, because he was prevented from completing his project.

If this is a good objection, Epicurus' view that nothing bad happens in death rests on a weak point in his moral theory. We can agree that death is not an evil only if we agree that freedom from anxiety is the whole of our good. If this claim about our good is wrong, he gives us no sufficient reason not to be afraid of death.

....

422 EPICURUS = DIOGENES LAERTIUS X. 124   Get into the habit of thinking that death is nothing to us, since every good and evil is in sense-perception, and death is deprivation of sense-perception. Hence correct recognition that death is nothing to us makes the mortality of life enjoyable—not by adding unlimited time, but by having removed the longing for immortality.

423 EPICURUS = DIOGENES LAERTIUS X. 145   The flesh regarded the limits of pleasure as boundless; <only> an unlimited time would have provided it. But the intellect grasped a reasoned account of the end and limit of the flesh, and it dissolved fears of everlasting <life>. And so it provided us with the complete life,[55] and had no further need of unlimited time.

424 [PLATO], *Axiochus* 365 C–E[56]   AXIOCHUS: … A kind of fear resists <my beliefs about death>. It stings my mind in various ways that I am to lose this light and these goods, that unseen and forgotten I will lie somewhere rotting, and changing into worms and wild beasts. SOCRATES: Axiochus, that's because you are so distracted by grief that you combine sensation and the absence of it, without reasoning about it. What you're doing and saying is self-contradictory, because you don't reason and see that at one and the same time you're lamenting the absence of sensation and suffering pain at the thought of decay and loss of pleasure—as though you died into another life, and didn't change into the same insensibility that you had before you were born. In the administration of Dracon and Cleisthenes nothing bad involved you, since you weren't even there to be involved. Similarly, nothing bad will involve you after you are dead; for you won't be there to be involved.

[55] Completeness; **406**.

[56] This is a spurious dialogue in the Platonic corpus, of uncertain date. Socrates is consoling Axiochus, who is facing death with fear and sorrow. The dialogue combines themes from Plato's *Apology* (see **317**) with Epicurean themes.

425 LUCRETIUS iii. 830–903[57]   Death, then, is nothing to us, nor does it concern us at all, since the nature of the mind is regarded as mortal. In the past we suffered nothing when the Carthaginians came from all sides in the shock of battle,[58] when all the world, shaken by the trembling turmoil of war, shuddered and quaked beneath the lofty breezes of heaven, in doubt about who would be master over all humanity by land and sea. So also in the future, when we are no more, when body and soul, from which we are constituted into one, come apart, certainly nothing at all will be able to affect us, who then will be no more, or stir our feeling, not even if earth mixes with sea, and sea with sky. ... For if someone is to suffer grief and pain in the future, he must also exist at that time to undergo the evil. Since death removes this, and prevents the being of him in whom these misfortunes might gather, we may know that we have nothing to fear in death, and that he who is no more cannot be wretched, and that it would be no different if he had never at any time been born, when once immortal death has taken away his mortal life. ... [894] [59] 'Now no more (they say) will your glad home and good wife welcome you, nor will your sweet children run up to snatch the first kisses, and touch your heart with silent joy. Nor more will you have power to prosper in your ways, or to protect your loved ones. Pitiful you are, and pitifully indeed has one hostile day taken from you all the many rewards of life.' But to this they do not add: 'And you no longer miss any of these things in the least.' But if they saw this clearly in their mind, and expressed it in their words, they would free themselves from great anguish and fear of mind.

426 EPICURUS = DIOGENES LAERTIUS X. 142   If the things that produce the pleasures of profligate people also dissolved the fears of the intellect about heavenly things and about death and pains <after death>, and if, moreover, they taught the limit of appetites, we would have nothing to reproach them for ...

---

[57] This follows Lucretius' attempted proofs of the mortality of the soul; see **340**.

[58] Lucretius refers to the Second Punic War, when Hannibal invaded Italy, about 150 years before his time.

[59] Lucretius quotes the conventional laments of mourners, and then (in 'But to this ...') answers them.

XI: Knowledge and Desire in Virtue

Why virtue?

427 Aristotle argues that a correct account of happiness must give virtue a prominent place (**407-8**). We can describe the virtues in very general terms as those features of a person herself—rather than the ways other people or external circumstances affect her—that are elements of her well-being. But we should try to say more precisely what the virtues are.

Concern with virtues is not a peculiarity of Greek ethics; it is also a familiar part of our own description and evaluation of people. If we ask how children should be brought up, or what sort of people we want for our friends or colleagues or co-workers, we often say that (for instance) we want them to be considerate, dependable, honest, sympathetic, and so on. These are the sorts of traits that we refer to collectively as virtues.

Greek moral philosophers ask two main question about the virtues:

(1) What sort of thing is a virtue?

(2) What are the virtues?

In asking the first question, we are asking what conditions a state (trait, characteristic) must satisfy in order to be a virtue. In asking the second question, we are asking what actual states (etc.) satisfy the conditions that answer the first question. Once we have answered these two questions, we have a description of a good person.

To answer the first question, we must notice two aspects of a virtue. The first is virtue as doing: we expect a generous person, for instance, to act in a specific way. If you never give to any charitable causes, though you have ample means, and you believe these are good causes and your money will be well spent, that is a reason for doubting whether you are a generous person. Someone who does the actions of the different virtues does what is expected of a good person. The second aspect is virtue as being: simply doing the right actions does not seem to be enough for virtue. If someone gives the right amount to the right charitable causes, but only because he can do it conspicuously and can gain some further advantage by it, he does some of the actions of a generous person, but he is not a generous person; he lacks the generous person's motives, aims, concerns, and outlook.

Socrates' question 'What is bravery (temperance, etc.)' and his more general question 'What is virtue?' seek an account of virtue that includes the right outlook as well as the right actions. He makes it clear to his interlocutors that a virtue cannot be defined simply by listing the actions expected of a virtuous person (**142**, **144-5**, **181**, **457**). An account of the virtues ought to describe both the first ('doing') and the second ('being') aspect of the virtues. Greek moralists dispute especially over the second aspect—over the kinds of beliefs and motives that ought to be ascribed to a good person. In particular, they differ over the role of cognitive states (knowledge, belief, etc.) and affective states (desires, feelings, emotions) in a virtue.

To find how many virtues there are, and which states are virtues, we might try a functional account of goodness (**428**; cf. **407-8**, **443**). In general, if x is good, x is good for something; a good knife is good for cutting. We may think of some kinds of goodness in a person in the same way; a good soldier or a good policeman is good for the tasks of a soldier or a policeman. But when we step outside these specialized roles, and ask about the character of a good person, not of a good carpenter or good soldier, does the functional account still work? Can we say what a good person is good for?

Greek philosophers consider two answers to this question:

(1) A good person is good for other people or for society as a whole; hence we might say that a good person is a good member of a community or association (**558**).

(2) A good person is good for herself; she has the traits that are needed to secure her own good.

The first, 'other-directed', answer seems quite plausible. Kindness, generosity, and trustworthiness benefit their recipients; these traits seek to benefit other people, not to benefit the virtuous agent himself. Greek philosophers recognize a number of other-directed virtues. They count justice as a primary virtue precisely because it is concerned especially with the good of others (**451**, **478**).

The second, 'self-directed', answer is also prominent in Greek philosophy. This conception of virtue explains why virtue is a necessary component of happiness. Greek philosophers generally agree that all rational action has to focus on the agent's ultimate good, identified with happiness (**381**). To show that a trait of character is a virtue that we have good reason to cultivate, we must show (according to a theorist who begins from happiness) that such a trait promotes the agent's happiness.

The other-directed and the self-directed conceptions may well appear to conflict. It is not obvious that the other-directed virtues promote the good of the virtuous agent. Indeed, the whole point of some other-directed virtues seems to be to restrain the pursuit of one's own interest when it conflicts with the interests of other people. If, however, one's other-directed virtues cannot be shown to promote one's own interest, they cannot be rationally justified to a rational agent concerned above all with her own happiness. Hence the moralist must show how virtue, including other-directed virtue, promotes the agent's happiness (**456**).

Greek moralists generally agree about some of the traits or states that count as virtues. Even if they recognize many virtues, they tend to give a special place to four virtues: wisdom, bravery, temperance, and justice. These are sometimes called 'cardinal' virtues. These four (together with piety) are the focus of the *Protagoras*; they are the central virtues recognized in the *Republic*. They are also prominent in Aristotle. The Stoics recognize them as the generic virtues, of which other virtues are species (**433**). We must see, then, how these cardinal virtues, in particular, meet the general conditions for a virtue, and how far each of them can be defended with reference to other people's interest and with reference to the agent's own interest.

428 PLATO, *Republic* 352 E–353 C [SOCRATES:] Tell me, then—do you think a horse has a function? [THRASYMACHUS:] I do—Then would you take the function of a horse or of anything else as to be what one can do only with it or do best with it?—I don't understand, he replied.—Well, consider it this way. Could you see with anything but eyes?—Certainly not.—And could you hear with anything but ears?—Not at all.—Aren't we right to say that these are the functions of these things?—By all means.—Well, then, you could use a dagger, or a knife, or many other things to trim the branches of a vine?—Certainly.—But, I take it, nothing would trim them as well as a pruning knife made for this?—That's true.—Then won't we take this to be its function?—We must.—Now, then, I suppose, you'll understand better what I meant just now when I asked whether the function of a thing is what that thing alone can perform, or what it can perform better than anything else can perform it.—Yes, he said, I understand, and I think this is a thing's function.

—Very good, I said. Don't you also think that whatever has a function assigned to it also has a virtue? Let's return to the same things. The eyes, we say, have a function?—They have.—Is there also a virtue of the eyes?—There is.—And wasn't there a function of the ears?—Yes.—And so also a virtue?—Also a virtue.—And what about all other things? Isn't the same true?—It is.—Take note now. Could the eyes possibly perform their function well if they lacked their own proper virtue and had a vice[1] instead?—How could they?, he said. For I presume you meant blindness instead of sight.—Whatever, I said, the virtue may be. For I haven't yet come to that question. I'm only asking whether the things that perform a function won't perform it well by their own virtue, and perform it badly by vice.—That much, he said, is certainly true.

429 PLATO, *Protagoras* 318 D–319 A[2] [SOCRATES:] When Protagoras heard me, he said: ... When Hippocrates comes to me, I won't subject him to the same things that another sophist would. For the others mistreat the young

---

[1] Or 'badness' or 'defect' (*kakia*).

[2] Socrates and the young man Hippocrates are wondering what Hippocrates will learn if he becomes the pupil of a sophist (cf. **8**, **551**). Protagoras; **156–60**.

men. The young men have avoided crafts,[3] but the sophists lead them, against their will, back into crafts, by teaching them arithmetic, astronomy, geometry, and music (here he glanced at Hippias[4]). As my student, however, he will learn only the subject he has come to learn. That subject is good deliberation—both about his household affairs, so that he can best manage his own household, and also about the city's affairs, so that he will be most capable[5] in the city, both in speaking and in action.—Do I follow what you've said? I asked. I take you to speak of the political craft, and to promise to make men good citizens.—Yes, Socrates, he said. That's exactly what I profess to do.[6]

430 PLATO, *Protagoras* 324 D–325 A [PROTAGORAS:] Is there or is there not some one thing that all citizens must share in if there is to be a city? Here, if anywhere, lies the solution of your puzzle.[7] ... This one thing is not the craft of building or forging or pottery, but justice, temperance, piety, and, in sum, I call it this one thing, the virtue of a man. This is what all must share in, and this is how every man must act, whatever else he wants to learn or to do.

431 PLATO, *Protagoras* 329 C–330 A [SOCRATES:] You[8] said that Zeus bestowed on human beings justice and shame;[9] again, at several points in your discourse, you mentioned justice, temperance, piety, and the rest, saying that in sum they are one thing, virtue. Now go over these more exactly for me in your account. Is virtue some one thing, and are justice, temperance, and piety all parts of it? Or are these latter all names of one and the same thing? That is what I'm still anxious to know. [PROTAGORAS:] Well, that's easy to answer, he said. Virtue is one, and the things you ask about are parts of it. ... — [329 E] Then do people share in these parts of virtue in such a way that some have one and some another part? Or is it necessary that, if someone acquires one, he has them all?—Not at all, he said. For many people are brave but unjust, and others are just but not wise.—Then are these also parts of virtue? I said. Wisdom, I mean, and bravery?—Absolutely; and indeed wisdom is the greatest of the parts.

432 ARISTOTLE, *Rhetoric* 1366[a]23–[b]22 We have now to consider virtue and vice, the fine and the shameful, since these are the objects of praise and blame. ... The fine is that which is both choiceworthy for its own sake and also praiseworthy. If this is the fine, it follows that virtue must be fine, since it

---

[3] Or 'expertises', *technai*; cf. **179**. The following examples show what contrast Protagoras has in mind.

[4] Another sophist taking part in the dialogue.

[5] Or 'most powerful'.

[6] Continued at **541**.

[7] Socrates raises this puzzle in **541**.

[8] Protagoras, in the long speech that includes **430**.

[9] i.e. shame at acting contrary to the virtues. Cf. **512**, **534**.

is both a good thing and also praiseworthy. Virtue is, according to the usual view, a capacity to provide and preserve good things, or a capacity to confer many great benefits, and benefits of all kinds on all occasions. The parts of virtue are justice, bravery, temperance, magnificence, magnanimity, liberality, gentleness, prudence, wisdom.

If virtue is a capacity for beneficence, the highest kinds of it must be those that are most useful to others, and for this reason people honour most the just and the brave, since bravery is useful to others in war, justice both in war and in peace. Next comes liberality; liberal people let their money go instead of fighting for it, whereas other people care for money more than for anything else. Justice is the virtue through which everyone has his own[10] in accordance with the law; its contrary is injustice, through which people have what belongs to others in defiance of the law. Bravery is the virtue that disposes people to do fine actions in situations of danger, in accordance with the law and in obedience to its commands; cowardice is the contrary. Temperance is the virtue that disposes us to obey the law where physical pleasures are concerned; intemperance is the contrary. Liberality disposes us to spend money for the good of others; illiberality is the contrary. Magnanimity is the virtue that disposes us to do good to others on a large scale; its contrary is meanness of spirit. Magnificence is the virtue productive of greatness in matters involving the spending of money. The contraries of these two are smallness of spirit and meanness respectively.[11] Prudence is the virtue of the understanding that enables people to come to wise decisions about the relation to happiness of the goods and evils that have previously been mentioned.

433　STOBAEUS, *Anthology* ii. 59. 4 = LS 61H　[The Stoic view:] Some virtues are primary, and others are subordinate to them. The primary virtues are four: prudence, temperance, bravery, justice … To prudence are subordinated good deliberation, good reasoning, quick-wittedness, discretion, resourcefulness. To temperance, good discipline, good order, proper shame, continence. To bravery, endurance, confidence, magnanimity, cheerfulness, industriousness. To justice, piety, honesty, equity, fair dealing.[12]

Virtue and knowledge

434　Socrates examines other people's attempts to find definitions of the virtues, and exposes their inadequacy. But he also offers his own suggestion

---

[10] On this conception of justice see **469**.

[11] Text uncertain.

[12] For the four main virtues see also **383**.

about the character of a virtue, comparing it systematically with a *technê*, a productive craft or form of expertise (**105-6**, **177**, **179**, **547-8**). Whether or not Socrates actually identifies a virtue with a craft, the comparison is useful in understanding some of the difficulties he faces and some of the solutions he offers.[13]

The comparison between a virtue and a craft seems plausible if we try to understand virtue by reference to function. A good carpenter is good at making furniture because she knows about making furniture; what makes a carpenter a good carpenter is the carpenter's craft. Socrates suggests that, similarly, what makes a person a good person is the craft that is relevant to living one's life.

This craft, according to Socrates, is knowledge of what promotes one's ultimate good, happiness. His general conception of a virtue is self-directed. Once we know what happiness is, we can define virtue as the craft that is the knowledge of how to achieve happiness. To become virtuous, we need to learn the relevant body of knowledge about how to achieve happiness.

An objection to this conception of virtue arises from the apparent gap between knowledge and action. Someone could be a skilled carpenter without wanting to use his knowledge to make furniture. Similarly, someone could apparently know what virtue requires of him, but not care about acting virtuously. This seems to be true even if virtue aims at one's own good; apparently we could know what promotes our good, and still not care enough to do anything about it. It seems that we can know that x is better, all things considered, than y, and still choose y over x. To choose y (the apparently less good option) in these circumstances is to display the condition often called weakness of will; in Greek philosophy it is called 'incontinence' or 'lack of control' (*akrasia*), while the opposite condition is called 'continence' (*enkrateia*). If incontinence is possible, then simply knowing what is good does not ensure action.

Virtue seems to differ from knowledge on exactly this point. For we do not suppose we can be virtuous if we do not care about doing the virtuous action. Since knowledge alone does not ensure action, virtue must apparently include a distinctive affective element. Hence it cannot be simply knowledge. According to Socrates, the virtuous and the non-virtuous person share the desire for happiness, and differ only in their knowledge. But the possibility of incontinence seems to show that virtue must include a distinctive affective element as well.

Socrates answers this objection by denying the possibility of incontinence, as ordinarily understood.[14] He offers a different explanation of actions that appear to display incontinence. According to Socrates, such actions simply result from ignorance about comparative benefits. Since the short-term benefit of y will

---

[13] These claims about Socrates refer to the 'Socrates' of Plato's early dialogues, often identified with the historical Socrates. See **17-18**.

[14] At any rate, this is how Aristotle interprets him in **448**.

happen sooner than the long-term benefit of x, we mistakenly infer that y must be better than x, and so we choose y. Once we correct this error, we will choose x instead.

If this is true, alleged cases of incontinence raise no special difficulty for Socrates, because they do not violate his claim that we always choose what we believe to be better. Hence such cases raise no difficulty for his suggestion that virtue is simply knowledge of what promotes one's own happiness.

435 PLATO, *Meno* 77 B–78 B MENO: It seems to me, then, Socrates, that virtue is, in the words of the poet, 'to rejoice in fine things and to have power'. I say that virtue is this: desiring[15] fine things and being able to supply them. SOCRATES: When you speak of someone 'desiring fine things', do you mean 'desiring good things'?—Certainly.—Then are you assuming that some desire bad things and others desire good things? Don't you think everyone desires good things?—No, I don't.—Do they think the bad things are good, in your view, or do they recognize that they are bad, and still desire them?— Both, I would say.—What? Do you really think anyone recognizes that the bad things are bad, and still desires them?—Yes.—By 'desires' you mean what? Desires to get them?—Of course.—Does he desire them thinking that the bad things benefit the one who gets them, or recognizing that the bad things harm the one who gets them?—Some desire them in the thought that the bad things benefit, and others in the thought that they harm.—Now do you think those who suppose bad things benefit recognize that the bad things are bad?—No, I don't altogether think that.—Isn't it clear, then, that these people who don't know that bad things are bad don't desire bad things, but desire the things they thought were good, though in fact they are bad? And so don't those who don't know that the bad things are bad, but think they are good, obviously desire good things?—For them I suppose that is true.—Now those who, according to you, desire bad things, and think they harm whoever gets them, these people presumably know that they will be harmed by them?—They must.—And don't these people think that whoever is harmed is, in so far as he is injured, miserable?[16]—They must think that too.—And that the miserable are unhappy?—Yes.—Well, does anyone wish to be wretched and unhappy?—I don't think so.—Then no one wishes for bad things; for what else is being wretched than desiring bad things and getting them?—It looks as if you are right, Socrates, and no one wishes for bad things.—Now weren't you just saying that virtue is wishing for good things and having power?—I was.—In what you said, isn't the wish common to everyone? And so, in that respect, surely one person is no better than another?—So it appears.—So if one person is better than another, he must evi-

---

[15] *epithumein:* often translated by 'appetite' and cognates. Cf. **438**.
[16] For 'miserable' (or 'wretched') cf. **500**.

dently be better in respect of power.—Quite right. Then virtue, according to your account, is the power of supplying good things.—Yes, my view is exactly as you now put it.

436 PLATO, *Protagoras* 355 A–357 E[17] [SOCRATES:] You[18] say that often someone recognizes bad things as bad, yet does them, when it is open to him not to do them, because he is led on and distracted by pleasures. Again you say that someone recognizing goods still is unwilling to do them, because of the pleasures of the moment. It will become evident that this is ridiculous, if we[19] stop using all these names together—'pleasant', 'painful', 'good', and 'bad'. Since these things have turned out to be two, let's call them by two names— first of all 'good' and 'bad' and then 'pleasant' and 'painful'. Having settled on this, let's say: someone recognizing that bad things are bad still does them. If someone asks why, we will say it is because he is overcome. 'Overcome by what?', he will ask us. We can no longer say 'by pleasure', because it has been given the name 'good' instead of 'pleasure' So let's answer him and say 'overcome'. 'By what?', he will ask. 'By the good', I suppose we'll say. I'm afraid that if our questioner is insolent, he'll laugh and retort: 'This is a ridiculous thing you describe, if someone does bad things, recognizing they are bad, when he ought not to do them, because he is overcome by goods. Are the goods in you (he will ask) a match for the bad things, or not?' Clearly we'll reply: 'They aren't a match; for if they were, the one we speak of as being overcome by pleasures wouldn't be making an error.' 'And in what way (he may say) do goods fail to be a match for bad things, or bad things for goods? Isn't it by being greater or smaller, more or less, than the other?' We'll have to agree. 'Then in speaking of being overcome you're describing the choosing of greater bad things in exchange for lesser goods.' ...

[356 C][20] Don't the same magnitudes seem greater to the eye from near at hand than they do from a distance? [PROTAGORAS:] They will say so.—Isn't this true of thickness and also of number? And don't sounds of equal loudness seem greater near at hand than at a distance?—They would say so.—Now if our doing well consisted in achieving and choosing greater lengths and avoiding smaller, where would safety in life appear? In the measuring craft, or in the power of appearance? Haven't we seen that the appearance leads us astray and throws us into confusion, so that in our actions and our choices between great and small we are constantly accepting and rejecting the same things, whereas the measuring craft would have unseated this appearance,

---

[17] Continued from **390**. Protagoras is the respondent. Socrates presents it as a dialogue between 'the many' (who take incontinence to be possible) and a 'questioner'.

[18] 'You' are 'the many', the believers in incontinence.

[19] 'We' = Socrates and the many.

[20] Here Socrates is speaking in his own voice and addressing the many. Protagoras replies ('they' refers to the many).

and by revealing the truth would have made our soul undisturbed and stable in the truth, and would have saved our life? Faced with these considerations, would people agree that the measuring craft saves us? ... [357 A] Since our safety in life has turned out to lie in the correct choice of pleasure and pain—more or less, greater or smaller, nearer or more distant—is it not, first of all, measuring, considering relative excess, defect, or equality?—It must be.—Since it measures, it must presumably be a craft and knowledge?—They will agree. ... —[357 D] And you yourselves know that a mistaken action done without knowledge is done by ignorance. And so that is what being overcome by pleasure really is the greatest ignorance.[21]

Rational and non-rational desires

437 In *Republic* iv, Plato returns to questions about the relation of desire and action. His discussion suggests a different treatment of incontinence, and hence a different treatment of virtue, from the Socratic treatment in the *Protagoras*. He argues that some conflicts between desires imply different kinds of desires, distinguished by their different relations to beliefs about good and bad. The different kinds of desires mark different 'parts' or 'kinds' in the soul.

Plato argues (**438**) for the existence of these different parts by identifying the relevant sort of conflict between desires. Suppose I am thirsty and want to drink, but I also refuse to satisfy my desire to drink, because I think it would be unhealthy and hence bad for me to drink. In this case, Plato distinguishes two types of desire:

(1) My desire not to drink rests on my belief about what is good for me on the whole. If I decide, on reflection, that after all it would be good for me to drink, my desire not to drink will be replaced by a desire to drink. Since this desire responds to reasoning about my good, it is a rational desire.

(2) My present desire to drink may not go away after rational reflection; even if I realize that more whisky will make driving dangerous, I may still want it. Since this desire does not respond to reasoning about my good, it is a non-rational desire.

Plato distinguishes rational from non-rational desires, according to their relation to the good, and he assigns them to different parts of the soul. To describe the non-rational part of the soul, he examines our susceptibility to perceptual illusions that persist even when we recognize the illusion (**439**). Plato compares this with our susceptibility to desires that persist even when we recognize it would be better not to satisfy them. In both cases, our non-rational tendency can be counteracted by reason, but it does not lose all its influence thereby.

---

[21] Continued at **390**.

Our non-rational tendencies help to explain our susceptibility, even against our better judgement, to various kinds of appeals to our emotions. Plato mentions the influence of drama that appeals to our emotions to arouse sympathy for people whom we recognize to be evil. Plato's point can easily be understood to apply (for instance) to mass media that appeal to immediate appearances and vivid images to influence beliefs and action. For this reason, Plato is more sceptical than Aristotle about the desirability of our ordinary responses to tragic drama (cf. **402**).

In some places, Plato recognizes two parts of the soul—a rational part that responds to reasoning about the good, and a non-rational part that does not respond to it. In other places, he distinguishes two non-rational parts, the 'spirited' and 'appetitive' parts, each of which can conflict both with the other non-rational part and with the rational part. The spirited part includes anger, resentment, pride, shame, and love of honour. In contrast to basic appetites (hunger, thirst, sexual desire), these are not indifferent to all considerations of good and bad. In contrast to rational desires, they may conflict with rational desires for what is best all things considered. To illustrate this second conflict, Plato describes the anger of Leontius, whose spirited part opposes the appetitive part, and the anger of Odysseus, whose spirited part opposes the rational part (cf. **326**). In Odysseus, anger arouses the desire to take revenge immediately, in conflict with his judgement that it would be better to wait.

The division of the soul into parts with potentially conflicting desires seems to explain incontinence. The explanation rejects Socrates' dissolution of apparent incontinence into mistaken belief about comparative goods and evils. If we have desires that are not responsive to reasoning about the good, it is not surprising that they sometimes move us to action in conflict with our belief about the good.

If Plato accepts this division of desire, he has a reason to deny that virtue is simply a kind of knowledge. To act virtuously, we need not only the right beliefs, but also rightly ordered desires that are not guaranteed by right beliefs. Plato uses the division of desires as the basis for an account of the virtues. Each virtue includes not only right belief, but also the appropriate condition of non-rational desires. To acquire each virtue, we need to have our non-rational desires appropriately trained.

Three of the cardinal virtues fit easily into the division of the soul. When the rational part is properly trained, we have wisdom; when the spirited part is properly trained to follow the rational part, we have bravery; and when the appetitive part is properly trained to follow the rational and the spirited parts, we have temperance. Since we are subject to non-rational desires, the virtues we need for our welfare include not only knowledge of the good, but also the right direction of non-rational desires. Plato's conception of the virtues rejects the assumptions that underlie some of Socrates' arguments.

Plato also discusses the fourth cardinal virtue, justice, as an appropriate ordering of the different parts of the soul. The specific questions that arise about this discussion are best considered in connection with the other-regarding aspects of justice (**468**).

....

438   PLATO, *Republic* 439 A–441 C   [SOCRATES:] ... Won't you place thirst among the things that are what they are by being of something. Presumably, it is thirst—[GLAUCON:] Yes, he said, thirst of drink.—Then if the drink is of a certain kind, so is the thirst; but thirst itself is neither of much nor of little nor of good nor of bad, nor, in sum, of any specific kind of drink. Rather, thirst itself is naturally only of drink itself.—By all means.—The soul of the thirsty person, then, in so far as <it>[22] thirsts, wishes nothing else than to drink, and goes for this and has an impulse towards this.—Obviously.—Then if anything draws the soul back when it is thirsty, it must be something different in it from what thirsts and leads it like a beast to drink. For we say the same thing can't, with the same part[23] of itself and at the same time, act in contrary ways about the same thing.—We must admit that it can't.—Similarly, I think, it would be wrong to say that the hands of an archer at the same time thrust away the bow and draw it near. Instead, we ought to say that the hand that pushes it away is one hand, and the hand that pulls it close is another.—By all means, he said.

—Now are we to say that some people are sometimes thirsty, but unwilling to drink?—Yes indeed, he said; many people and often.—What, then, I said, should we say about them? Shouldn't we say that there is something in the soul that urges them to drink, and something that impedes—something different that masters what urges them on?—I think so.—And doesn't what impedes such actions arise, whenever it arises, from reasoning, whereas the aspects that lead and draw come through affections and diseases?—Apparently.—It's not unreasonable, then, I said, to claim that they are two and different from each other. We'll call the part in the soul by which <it> reasons the rational part, and the part by which <it> loves, hungers, thirsts, and feels the flutter and titillation of other desires, the non-rational and appetitive part, connected with fillings and pleasures.—It's not unreasonable at all, but quite natural, he said, for us to think this.

—Then let's take these two forms to be defined as being in the soul. But what about spirit, by which our spirits are aroused?[24] Is it a third part? Or to which of the other two would it be identical in its nature?—Perhaps, he said, with the second, the appetitive.—But, I said, I once heard a story, which I believe, that Leontius the son of Aglaion, on his way up from the Piraeus under the outer side of the northern wall, realized[25] there were some dead

[22] Either 'the soul' or 'the person' might be the understood subject of 'thirsts' and other verbs.
[23] In many places (where the Greek has just a neuter adjective) 'part' or 'aspect' is supplied.
[24] Or 'by which we feel angry'.
[25] Or 'perceived'.

bodies lying at the place of public execution. At the same time he had an appetite to see them and also deplored it, and turned away. For a time he resisted, and covered his head; but mastered none the less by his appetite, he ran to the corpses with his eyes wide open, and cried, 'Look at that, you miserable eyes! Take your fill of this fine sight!'—I've heard that story too, he said.—Now surely this story, I said, indicates that anger sometimes fights against appetites as one thing against a different thing.—Yes, it does, he said.—And aren't there many other cases where we notice that whenever someone's appetites force him contrary to his reasoning, he reviles himself, and is angry at the part that forces him, and in this conflict, which is like civil conflict in a city, his spirit is an ally of his reason? ... Earlier we thought that the spirited part was some kind of appetitive part, but now we say quite the contrary; for in the conflict of the soul it allies itself with the rational part.— Most certainly.—Then is the spirited part different from the rational part too, or simply a kind of rational part? ... We may appeal to the words of Homer: 'He[26] struck his breast, and reproved his heart'. For here Homer clearly assumes that one thing is attacking another; what has reasoned about the better and worse attacks what is irrationally angry.—Quite true, he said.[27]

439 PLATO, *Republic* 602 C–604 D ... [SOCRATES:] In relation to what part of a human being has imitation the power it has? [GLAUCON:] What sort of thing do you mean?—I mean this: the same magnitude, I presume, viewed from near and from far by sight does not appear equal.—No.—And the same things appear bent and straight to those who view them in water and out, or convex and concave, owing to similar errors of vision about colours, and there is obviously every confusion of this sort in our souls.[28] And so scene painting exploits our natural tendency to be affected in these ways, so that it is nothing less than witchcraft. Jugglery and many other such devices do the same.—True.—And haven't measuring and numbering and weighing proved to be most beneficial helpers against these things, so that what rules in us is not what appears greater or less or more or heavier, but what has reasoned[29] and numbered or even weighed?—Certainly.

—But this surely would be the function of the reasoning part of the soul.—Certainly the function of that part.—And often when this has measured and indicates that some things are larger or that some are smaller than the others or equal, contrary things appear at the same time about the same things.—Yes.—And didn't we say that it is impossible for the same thing at one time to believe contrary things about the same thing?—And we were

---

[26] Odysseus.
[27] Continued at **469**.
[28] Errors of perspective; **436**.
[29] Or 'calculated'.

right to say so.—The part of our soul, then, that believes something against the results of measurement could not be the same as the part that believes in accordance with those results.—Why no. ...

[603 C] ... Imitative poetry, we say, imitates human beings acting under compulsion or voluntarily, and as a result of their actions supposing they have done well or badly, and in all this feeling either grief or joy. Isn't this just what we found?—Just this.—Then does someone agree with himself in all this? Or, just as in the area of sight he was divided, and held within himself contrary beliefs at the same time about the same things, so also in actions isn't he divided and in conflict with himself? ... [604 D] And won't we say that the part of us that leads us to recollect our suffering and to lament, and cannot satisfy itself with those things, is the unreasoning and idle part of us, the ally of cowardice?—Yes, we will say that.

Aristotle: rational and non-rational elements in virtue

440 Aristotle accepts Plato's division of the soul into rational and non-rational parts, and believes that virtue involves both parts of the soul. To show how virtue involves both parts, he claims that it is a 'mean' or 'intermediate' condition between two extremes (**444**). Virtue is intermediate because it excludes some mistaken ways of dealing with non-rational desires.

(1) A lazy reaction to our non-rational impulses leaves them completely uncontrolled, without trying to regulate them by our beliefs about the good.

(2) An over-zealous reaction tries to eliminate them altogether; in Aristotle's view, this reaction rests on the false view that virtue consists in being 'unaffected'.

(3) A less obvious error identifies virtue with control by the rational part over the non-rational part. The self-controlled, 'continent' person avoids the incontinent actions of someone who is moved by appetite contrary to rational desire. In Aristotle's view, continence is better than vice (since one's rational part rejects the vicious outlook and moves one to the right action), but inferior to virtue (since one's non-rational part does not endorse the virtuous outlook).

Hence the correct account of virtue must make it clear that the virtuous person's non-rational desires are not merely subordinate to and controlled by rational desires. They must also be in harmony with rational desires. Such harmony does not result from merely cognitive training (the sort of knowledge that Socrates describes in **436**). It must involve both rational understanding and the appropriate training of one's emotions. Aristotle seeks to describe the appropriate sort of moral education.

Aristotle illustrates his claims about the mean in his accounts of different virtues (**445-6**).

(1) Bravery does not eliminate fears altogether. It modifies and shapes the non-rational part so that our fears are directed towards what deserves to be feared.

(2) Temperance controls and shapes basic biological appetites for food, drink, and sex. It does not eliminate them or stop us enjoying them; it regulates and shapes our enjoyments so that we have them on the right occasions.

(3) A good person ought to be angry about some things (for instance, injustice or wanton cruelty), but it would be inappropriate to lose our temper if there is nothing to be angry about, or when our anger defeats our own ends.

In each case, Aristotle argues that virtuous people are those who control and shape a particular emotional response so that it fits with the other things that we have reason to care about. Virtuous people do not act virtuously with reluctance as a result of struggle against non-rational impulses. They even take pleasure in facing the dangers that brave people have to face, and in avoiding the misguided pleasures that temperate people avoid. This is an important aspect of the difference between virtue and mere continence.

....

441 ARISTOTLE, *Nicomachean Ethics* 1102ᵃ27–1103ᵃ7   One part of the soul is non-rational, while one has reason. For present purposes, it does not matter whether these are distinguished as parts of a body and everything divisible into parts are, or are two only in account, and inseparable by nature, as the convex and the concave are in a surface. ... <Part of the soul> would ... seem to be non-rational, but to share in a way in reason.[30] For in the continent and the incontinent person we praise their reason, i.e. the part of the soul that has reason, because it exhorts them correctly and towards what is best; but they evidently also have in them some other part that is by nature something apart from reason, conflicting and struggling with reason. For just as paralysed parts of a body, when we decide to move them to the right, do the contrary and move off to the left, the same is true of the soul; for incontinent people have impulses in contrary directions. In bodies, admittedly, we see the part go astray, whereas we do not see it in the case of the soul; none the less, presumably, we should suppose that the soul also has something apart from reason, contrary to and countering reason. ... This part also appears, as we said, to share in reason. At any rate, in the continent person it obeys reason; in the temperate and the

---

[30] For these two parts see **408**.

brave person it presumably listens still better to reason, since there it agrees with reason in everything. ... It listens in the way in which we are said to 'listen to reason' from father or friends. ... It is persuaded in some way by reason, as is shown by correction and by every sort of reproof and exhortation. If we ought to say, then, that this part also has reason, the part that has reason will also have two parts: one that, strictly speaking, has reason, by having it within itself, and another that has it by listening to reason as to a father.

The distinction between virtues also reflects this difference. For some virtues are called virtues of thought, other virtues of character; wisdom, comprehension and prudence are called virtues of thought, generosity and temperance virtues of character.

442 ARISTOTLE, *Nicomachean Ethics* 1104^{b}19–26   Every state of soul is naturally related to and concerned with whatever naturally makes it better or worse; and pleasures and pains make people worse, from pursuing and avoiding the wrong ones, at the wrong time, in the wrong ways, or whatever other distinctions of that sort are needed in an account. That is why people actually define the virtues as ways of being unaffected and undisturbed.[31] They are wrong, however, because they speak of being unaffected without qualification, not of being unaffected in the right or wrong way, at the right or wrong time, and the other added qualifications.

443 ARISTOTLE, *Nicomachean Ethics* 1105^{a}17–^{b}12   However, someone might be puzzled about what we mean by saying that to become just we must do just actions and to become temperate we must do temperate actions; for <it may seem> that if we do just or temperate actions, we must thereby be just or temperate, just as we must be grammarians or musicians if we do grammatical or musical actions. But surely this is not so even with the crafts; for it is possible to produce something grammatical by chance or by following someone else's instructions. To be a grammarian, then, we must produce something grammatical, and in the grammarian's way—that is to say, in accordance with one's own grammatical knowledge.[32]

Moreover, what is true of crafts is not true of virtues. For the products of a craft determine by their own character whether they have been produced well; and so it suffices that they are in the right state when they have been produced. But for actions in accord with virtue to be done temperately or justly it does not suffice that they are themselves in the right state; the agent must also be in the right state when he does them. First, he must act with knowledge; second, he must decide on them, and decide on them for themselves;[33] and, third, he must also do them from a firm and stable

[31] Virtue as freedom from affection; cf. **527–8**.
[32] Craft and knowledge; **106**.
[33] Decision (*prohairesis*); **514**.

state.[34] As far as the crafts are concerned, these three conditions do not count, except for the bare knowing. But as far as the virtues are concerned, the knowing counts for nothing, or <rather> for only a little, whereas the other two conditions are very important, indeed all-important, and these other two conditions are achieved by the frequent doing of just and temperate actions. Hence actions are called just or temperate when they are the sort that a just or temperate person would do, but the just and temperate person is not the one who <merely> does these actions, but the one who also does them in the way in which just or temperate people do them. It is right, then, to say that a person comes to be just from doing just actions and temperate from doing temperate actions; for no one has even a prospect of becoming good from failing to do them.

444 ARISTOTLE, *Nicomachean Ethics* 1106ª15–1107ª2 ... Every virtue causes its possessors to be in a good state and to perform their functions well.[35] The virtue of eyes, for instance, makes the eyes and their functioning excellent, because it makes us see well; and similarly, the virtue of a horse makes the horse excellent, and thereby good at galloping, at carrying its rider and at standing steady in the face of the enemy. If this is true in every case, the virtue of a human being will likewise be the state that makes a human being good and makes him perform his function well. We have already said how this will be true, and it will also be evident from our next remarks, if we consider the nature of virtue.

In everything continuous and divisible we can take more, less, and equal, and each of them either in the object itself or relative to us; and the equal is some intermediate between excess and deficiency. By the intermediate in the object I mean what is equidistant from each extremity; this is one and the same for all. But relative to us the intermediate is what is neither superfluous nor deficient; this is not one, and is not the same for all. If, for instance, ten are many and two are few, we take six as intermediate in the object, since it exceeds two and is exceeded by ten by an equal amount, four; this is what is intermediate by numerical proportion. But that is not how we must take the intermediate that is relative to us. For if, for instance, ten pounds of food are a lot for someone to eat, and two pounds a little, it does not follow that the trainer will prescribe six, since this may also be either a little or a lot for the person who is to take it—for Milo the athlete a little, but for the beginner in gymnastics a lot; and the same is true for running and wrestling. In this way every scientific expert avoids excess and deficiency, and seeks and chooses the intermediate—intermediate relative to us, not in the object. This, then, is how each science produces its product well, by focusing on the intermediate

---

[34] Stability of virtue; **107, 506**.
[35] Function; **408, 428**.

and leading the product in that direction. That is why people regularly comment on well-made products that nothing could be added or subtracted; they assume that excess or deficiency ruins a good result while the mean preserves it. Good craftsmen also, we say, focus on the intermediate when they do their work. And since virtue, like nature, is better and more exact than any craft, it will also aim at the intermediate.

By virtue I mean virtue of character; for this deals with feelings and actions, and these admit of excess, deficiency, and the intermediate. We can be afraid, for instance, or be confident, or have appetites, or get angry, or feel pity—in general, have pleasure or pain—both too much and too little, and in both ways not well; but having these feelings at the right times, about the right things, towards the right people, for the right end, and in the right way, is intermediate and best, which is characteristic of virtue ... [1106ᵇ36] Virtue, then, is a state that decides, consisting in a mean, the mean relative to us, which is defined by reference to reason, i.e. to the reason by reference to which the prudent person would define it. It is a mean between two vices, one of excess and one of deficiency.

445 ARISTOTLE, *Nicomachean Ethics* 1115ᵇ7–24   What is frightening is not the same for everyone. We do say, however, that some things are too frightening for a human being to resist; these, then, are frightening for everyone, at least for everyone with any sense. The things that are frightening, but not irresistible for a human being, vary in seriousness and degree, and so do things that inspire confidence. Now the brave person is unperturbed, as far as a human being can be. Hence, though he will fear even the sorts of things that are not irresistible, he will stand firm against them, in the right way, as reason prescribes, for the sake of the fine, since this is the end aimed at by virtue.[36] It is possible to be more or less afraid of these frightening things, and also possible to be afraid of what is not frightening as though it were frightening. The cause of error may be fear of the wrong thing, or in the wrong way, or at the wrong time, or something of that sort; and the same is true for things that inspire confidence. Hence, whoever stands firm against the right things and fears the right things, for the right end, in the right way, and at the right time, and is confident in the same respects, is the brave person;[37] for the brave person's actions and feelings accord with the worth of an action and with what reason prescribes. Every activity aims at actions that accord with the appropriate state of character, and to the brave person bravery is fine; hence the end it aims at is also fine, since each thing is defined by its end. The brave person, then, aims at what is fine in both standing firm and acting in the ways that accord with bravery.

[36] The fine; **449**.
[37] Standing firm; **145**.

446   ARISTOTLE, *Nicomachean Ethics* 1119ª1–20   The intemperate person ... has an appetite for all pleasant things, or rather for the pleasantest of them, and his appetite leads him to choose these at the cost of everything else.[38] That is why he also feels pain both when he fails to get something and when he has an appetite for it, since appetite involves pain; it would seem absurd, though, to suffer pain because of pleasure. People who are deficient in pleasures and enjoy them less than is right are not found very much. For that sort of insensibility is not human; the other animals also discriminate among foods, enjoying some but not others, and if someone finds nothing pleasant, or preferable to anything else, he is far from being human. And the reason he has no name is that he is not found much. The temperate person has an intermediate state in relation to these things. For he takes no pleasure in what most pleases the intemperate person, but he finds it disagreeable; he finds no pleasure at all in the wrong things; and he finds no intense pleasure in any bodily pleasures, suffers no pain at their absence, and has no appetite for them, or only a moderate appetite, not to the wrong degree or at the wrong time or anything else at all of that sort. If something is pleasant and conducive to health or fitness, he will desire this moderately and in the right way; and he will desire in the same way anything else that is pleasant if it is no obstacle to health and fitness, does not deviate from what is fine, and is not beyond his means. For the intemperate person likes these pleasures more than they are worth; the temperate person is different, and likes them as correct reason prescribes.

Weakness of will, desire, and knowledge

447   After describing the virtues of character, Aristotle returns to the problem of incontinence that is raised by Socrates and Plato. Socrates appears to deny the possibility of incontinence, and to explain apparently incontinent behaviour as the result of ignorance of the good (**435–6**). Plato's division of the soul, by contrast, seems to assume that genuine incontinence is possible, and to offer an explanation that does not reduce it to ignorance (**437–9**). Aristotle's account includes both Socratic and Platonic elements. His complex combination of these elements makes his position quite difficult to understand.

At the outset, Aristotle criticizes Socrates for denying the possibility of incontinence. Socrates' mistake (according to Aristotle) lies in treating the allegedly incontinent person's error as simple ignorance about what is better and worse, and hence not as genuine incontinence at all. This criticism of Socrates leads us to expect that Aristotle will agree with Plato's approach. He certainly agrees with Plato to some degree; for he explains incontinence by appeal to rational and non-rational desires.

[38] Intemperance; **392**.

In his own solution, Aristotle appeals again to ignorance, and remarks that part of the Socratic account is correct. He seems to argue that (i) the relevant sort of ignorance is caused by disordered non-rational desires, and (ii) it is not ignorance of general principles (e.g. that we ought not to steal), but of the application of these principles to particular cases (in someone who thinks: 'Perhaps it's all right to take this money; no one will miss it').

Aristotle, therefore, seems to agree with Socrates' view that the cognitive state of the incontinent person must be defective at the moment of incontinent action. He agrees with Plato in believing that non-rational desires are necessary for incontinence; for they cause the incontinent person's ignorance.

448 ARISTOTLE, *Nicomachean Ethics* 1144^{b}35–1147^{b}17   We must now discuss incontinence, softness and self-indulgence, and also continence and resistance ... As in the other cases we must set out the appearances, and first of all go through the puzzles. In this way we must prove the common beliefs about these ways of being affected—ideally, all the common beliefs, but if not all, then most of them, and the most important. For if the objections are solved, and the common beliefs are left, it will be an adequate proof. ... The continent person seems to be the same as one who abides by his rational calculation, and the incontinent person seems to be the same as one who abandons it. The incontinent person knows that his actions are base, but does them because of the way he is affected; the continent person knows that his appetites are base, but because of reason does not follow them. ...

We might be puzzled about the sort of correct supposition someone has when he acts incontinently. First of all, some say he does not act in knowledge. For it would be terrible, Socrates thought, for knowledge to be in someone, but mastered by something else, and dragged around like a slave. For Socrates completely opposed the account of incontinence, in the belief that there is no incontinence; for no one, he thought, acts in the supposition that he is acting against what is best, but we act against what is best only because of ignorance. This argument, then, contradicts things that appear manifestly. If ignorance causes the incontinent person to be affected as he is, then we must investigate what type of ignorance it turns out to be; for it is evident, at any rate, that before he is affected the person who does the incontinent action does not think <he should do it>. ...

[1147^{a}11] We see that having without using knowledge includes different types of having; hence, some people, such as those asleep or mad or drunk, both have knowledge in a way and do not have it. Moreover, this is the condition of those who are intensely affected; for feelings of anger, sexual appetites, and some conditions of this sort clearly disturb the body as well, and even produce fits of madness in some people. Clearly, then, we should say that incontinents have knowledge in a way similar to these people. Saying the words that come from knowledge is no sign; for people affected in these ways even recite demonstrations and verses of Empedocles. Further, those who have just learnt something do not yet know it, though they string the words together; for it must grow into them, and this needs time. Hence we must suppose that those who are acting incontinently say the words in the way that actors do.

Further, we may also look at the cause in the following way, referring to human nature. One belief is universal; the other is about particulars, and because they are particulars perception controls them. And in the cases where these two beliefs result in one belief, it is necessary in the one case[39] for the soul to affirm what has been concluded, and in beliefs about production to act at once on what has been concluded. If, for instance, everything sweet must be tasted, and this—some one particular thing—is sweet, it is necessary for someone who is able and unhindered also to act on this at the same time. Suppose, then, that someone has the universal belief hindering him from tasting; he has the second belief, that everything sweet is pleasant and this is sweet, and this belief is active; and he also has appetite. Hence the belief tells him to avoid this, but appetite leads him on, since it is capable of moving each of the <bodily> parts. The result, then, is that in a way reason and belief make him act incontinently. The belief is contrary to correct reason, but only coincidentally, not in itself. For it is the appetite, not the belief, that is contrary ... And since the last premiss is a belief about something perceptible, and controls action, this must be what the incontinent person lacks when he is being affected. Or <rather> the way he has it is not knowledge of it, but, as we saw, saying the words, as the drunk says the words of Empedocles. Further, since the last term does not seem to be universal, or expressive of knowledge in the same way as the universal term, even the result Socrates was looking for would seem to come about. For the knowledge that is present when someone is affected by incontinence, and that is dragged about because he is affected, is not the sort that seems to be knowledge, strictly speaking, but perceptual knowledge.

[39] i.e. in the case of purely theoretical beliefs.

XII The Good of Others

Morality and justice

449 Plato's and Aristotle's accounts of the virtues explain how happiness includes virtuous action as a part, not simply as a means to some external end. In Aristotle's view, the good for a human being rests on the nature of a human being as a rational agent. The explanation of the virtues through the division of the soul makes it clear how acting on the virtues is exercising rational agency in controlling and modifying non-rational desires.

This account readily fits three of the cardinal virtues: wisdom, bravery, and temperance. It does not so obviously fit justice. For justice introduces an element that is absent from the description of the other virtues; it is especially concerned with the good of others. A common modern use of 'moral' and 'morality' distinguishes principles and standards connected with moral values from those connected with (for instance) prudential, aesthetic, or religious values. We might sometimes say that someone is behaving unwisely and recklessly, but not immorally, if his behaviour harms no one but himself, or that his preferences and tastes are deplorable, but not immoral, if they do not affect his attitude to his obligations to other people. According to this conception of morality, moral requirements (i) are essentially social in their aim and reference; (ii) are independent of the aims and preferences of this or that particular individual; and (iii) impose an obligation that is independent of individual desires and aims.

This description of morality and moral principles, though imprecise, is useful to compare with Greek views. The use of 'moral' and 'morality' just described does not correspond exactly to any distinction explicitly drawn in Greek. This does not mean, however, that Greek moralists do not recognize morality. One may argue that they recognize it in two ways:

(1) Sometimes specific virtues and actions are taken to be 'fine' or 'admirable' (*kalon*, also translated 'beautiful'; **145**, **445**, **455**, **485**, **490**, **508**). Fine actions are taken to benefit others, but they are not taken to be obviously beneficial to the agent; that is a point of dispute.

(2) Justice is taken to be a central virtue; it is essentially concerned with the good of others, and hence with the area of morality.

We have seen (**427**) that one aspect of the functional conception of goodness refers to a person's goodness as a member of a community. This other-directed aspect of virtue is especially clear in justice. To show that both self-directed and other-directed virtue are elements of happiness, we must concentrate on justice.

450 G. J. WARNOCK, *The Object of Morality*,[1] p. 26   Now the general sugges-tion that (guardedly) I wish to put up for consideration is this: that the 'gen-eral object' of morality, appreciation of which may enable us to *understand* the basis of moral evaluation, is to contribute to betterment—or non-deteri-oration—of the human predicament, primarily and essentially by seeking to countervail 'limited sympathies' and their potentially most damaging ef-fects. It is the proper business of morality, and the generic object of moral evaluation ... to expand our sympathies, or, better, to reduce the liability to damage inherent in their natural tendency to be narrowly restricted.

451   ARISTOTLE, *Rhetoric* 1358^{b}38–1359^{a}5   Those who praise or censure someone do not consider whether his acts have been expedient or harmful <to himself>. Indeed, they often make it a ground of actual praise that he has made light of his own interest and done what was fine. They praise Achilles, for instance, because he defended his companion Patroclus, though he knew that he would have to die, though it was open to him to stay alive. For him, such a death was finer, and staying alive was expedient.[2]

Socrates on justice

452 In his defence of his life and character, Socrates claims to be a zealous sup-porter of justice. He asserts the general principle that considerations of what is just and fine take precedence over everything else. Moreover, he claims to have followed this principle in his own actions. He refused to endorse the actions of both the democratic government and of the oligarchy that replaced it, because he believed that the Assembly and the Thirty were bent on an illegal and unjust action (**540**). Similarly, he tells the jury that if he is ordered to give up his philo-sophical inquiries, he will disobey any such order as unjust, because the god re-quires him to engage in philosophy (**453**).

A further question about justice faces him in the *Crito*. Socrates has been found guilty in his trial, but he has the opportunity to escape and so to avoid ex-ecution. In his view, the only relevant question is whether it would be just or un-just to escape. He persuades Crito that in disobeying the law, he would be harming the city because of harm the city has done him, and therefore would be acting unjustly. Since one ought never to act unjustly, Socrates concludes that he must obey the law condemning him to death.

These claims and disputes about justice make it clear why Socrates' 'What is it?' question is often important (**142**); for it is not always clear to everyone what justice requires. In the *Crito* Socrates argues that he would be acting unjustly if

[1] London: Methuen, 1971.
[2] Achilles and Patroclus; **453**.

he violated the laws. In the *Apology*, however, he implies that if he were forbidden by law to engage in philosophy, he would disobey any such law. He also rejects the common view that it is just to return evil for evil; in his view, retaliation is never just. Though Socrates commends himself to his fellow-citizens as a conspicuously just person, and argues from some of their assumptions about justice, he seems to disagree with many of their views about what justice requires.

Even if Socrates persuades us that he is right about what justice requires, he raises a further question for himself. Just actions seem to be identified by reference to the good of the city, rather than the good of the individual. Socrates implies that the obligation to act justly is clear and urgent, independently of his own preferences. How, then, can he reasonably claim that he benefits from being just? This question is especially clear in the *Crito*. Socrates and Crito discuss whether Socrates should obey the law by remaining in prison, or should try to escape. Socrates argues that it is just for him to keep the laws. Hence, in the moral sense of 'should', he should not escape. This conclusion, however, does not seem to imply that Socrates should not escape, in the self-interested sense of 'should'. Crito seems to suggest that Socrates should, from the self-interested point of view, escape, whether or not it is just.

In reply to Crito, Socrates insists that nothing is good for him if it is not also fine and just. He does not defend his conviction about the coincidence of morality and self-interest. In the *Gorgias*, however, he defends this conviction by cross-examining Polus. First Polus takes the apparently reasonable view that some actions are fine and morally praiseworthy, but bad for the agent, and that other actions are shameful and morally blameworthy, but none the less good for the agent. Socrates argues that this attempt to separate the fine from the good is inconsistent with Polus' other convictions.

....

453 PLATO, *Apology* 28 B–30 A But perhaps someone will say, Do you feel no shame Socrates, at having followed a line of action that puts you in danger of the death penalty? I might fairly reply to him: You are mistaken, my friend, if you think that a man who is worth anything ought to waste his time weighing up the prospects of life and death. He has only one thing to consider in performing any action—that is, whether he is acting justly or unjustly, like a good man or a bad one. For, on your account, the sons of gods who were killed at Troy were worthless, and especially Achilles the son of Thetis. He altogether despised the danger of death in comparison with shameful action. When he was eager to kill Hector, his goddess mother spoke to him this way, I think:[3] 'My son, if you avenge the death of your companion Patroclus, you will be killed yourself; for death (as she says) waits for you next after Hector.' But when Achilles heard this, he made light of death and danger, and was

---

[3] Socrates combines paraphrase and amplification with quotation from Homer, *Iliad* xviii. Achilles; **451**.

more afraid of living as a bad man and of not avenging his friend. 'Let me die at once (he says), as soon as I have exacted justice from the one who has done injustice, so that I do not linger here, an object of ridicule, by the beaked ships, a burden on the earth.' Do you suppose he took any thought for death and danger?[4]

The truth of the matter is this, gentlemen. Where a man has once taken up his stand, either because it seems best to him or in obedience to his orders, there I believe he is bound to remain and face the danger, taking no account of death or anything else before dishonour. ... [29B] If I were to claim to be wiser than my neighbour in any respect, it would be in this—that not possessing any real knowledge of what comes after death, I am also conscious that I do not possess it. But I do know that to disobey my superior, whether god or man,[5] is wicked and dishonourable, and so I shall never feel more fear or aversion for something which, for all I know, may really be a blessing, than for those evils which I know to be evils.

Suppose, then, that you ... said to me: 'Socrates, on this occasion we shall disregard Anytus and release you, but only on one condition, that you give up spending your time on your searching and stop your philosophizing. If you are caught still doing the same thing, you will be put to death.' Suppose, then, as I said, that you were to offer to release me on these terms. I would reply: 'Gentlemen, I am your grateful servant and your friend, but I shall obey the god rather than you. As long as I am alive and able to do it, I shall never stop practising philosophy and exhorting you and making things clear to everyone that I meet. I shall go on saying, in my usual way: "My excellent friend, you are an Athenian, and belong to a city which is the greatest and most famous in the world for its wisdom and strength. Aren't you ashamed, then, that you put your mind to the acquisition of all the money, reputation, and honour you can get, but give no attention or thought to understanding and truth, to making your soul as good as possible?" If any of you disputes this and claims to attend to these things, I shall not at once let him go or leave him. No, I will question him and scrutinize him and cross-examine him, and if it seems that he has no virtue, but merely claims to have it, I shall reproach him for attaching the least importance to what is most valuable, and attaching more importance to inferior things.'

454 PLATO, *Crito* 46B–50C SOCRATES: ... not only now but at all times I am the sort of person who listens to nothing in me except the argument that, when I reason about it, seems best to me. And now that I face these circumstances, I can't discard the arguments I used; they seem to me much the same. ... Let's begin, then, by returning to this argument you gave about people's

---

[4] Here Socrates ends the speech he imagines for himself in reply to the imaginary objector.
[5] Obedience to the gods; **380, 582**.

views. Were we right in the past to hold the constant position that some views should be taken seriously, but not others? ... Consider, then; don't you think it is right to hold that one should not esteem all the views people hold, but only some and not others? ... Shouldn't one esteem the good ones, but not the bad? CRITO: Yes. ...

[48B]—Now consider whether this still remains firm, that what one should value most is not living, but living well.—Why, yes.—And that living well is the same thing as living finely and justly?—Yes.—Then in the light of this agreement we must consider whether or not it is just for me to try to get away without an official discharge. ... [48E] Don't we say that one must never willingly do injustice? ... Whatever the popular view is, and whether the alternative is milder or more severe than the present one, doing injustice is still in every way bad and shameful for the person who does it. Is that our view, or not?—Yes, it is.—Then one must not do injustice in any way.—No.—In that case one should not even do injustice in return for suffering it, as most people think one should, since one must not do injustice in any way.—Apparently not.—Tell me another thing, Crito. Ought one to do wrong or not?—Surely not, Socrates.—And tell me: is it just to do wrong to someone in retaliation for wrongdoing, as most people say, or is it not?—No, never.—Because, I suppose, there is no difference between mistreating people and doing injustice to them.—Exactly.—Now be careful, Crito, about answering, so that you don't answer contrary to your belief. For I know that few people believe this, or will believe it. And so, for those who do believe it and those who don't, there is no common deliberation; they must always disdain one another, when they see one another's deliberations. ...

Ought one to fulfil all one's agreements, provided they are just, or break them?—One ought to fulfil them.—Then consider what follows. If we leave this place without first persuading the city, are we or are we not mistreating people, those whom we ought least of all to mistreat? Are we or are we not abiding by our just agreements? ... Suppose that while we were preparing to run away from here—or however one should describe it—the laws and commonwealth[6] of Athens were to confront us and ask: 'Now, Socrates, what are you proposing to do? Don't you intend, in this action that you're undertaking, to destroy us, as far as is up to you, both the laws and the whole city? Or do you think a city can exist and not be turned upside down, if the legal judgements pronounced in it have no force but are nullified and destroyed by private persons?' ... Are we to answer the laws: 'Yes I intend to destroy the laws, because the city treated me unjustly, by passing a mistaken sentence at my trial'? ... Then what if the laws say, 'Were these the terms of our agreement with you, Socrates? Or did you undertake to abide by whatever judgements the city pronounced?'[7]

---

[6] Literally, 'the common'.
[7] More of the speech by the laws; **318**, **542**.

455 PLATO, *Gorgias* 474C–475E[8] SOCRATES: Which of the two do you think is worse, Polus? Doing or suffering injustice? POLUS: I think suffering it is worse.[9]—And is doing or suffering it more shameful? Answer.—Doing it.— And if it's more shameful, isn't it worse?—Certainly not.—I see. It would seem that you don't think the fine is the same as the good, or that the shameful is the same as the bad.—I certainly don't.—What about this? When you call bodies, colours, figures, sounds, or institutions fine, don't you call them fine with reference to something? Don't you say that bodies, for example, are fine in so far as they are useful, relative to whatever they are useful for, or in so far as the sight of them gives pleasure to spectators? Can you say anything apart from this about fineness of bodies?—No, I can't.—And are laws and institutions fine simply because they are useful or pleasant or both?—Yes.—[475 B] If, then, doing injustice is more shameful than suffering it, it must be more painful, and must be more shameful by exceeding in pain, or else it must be more shameful by exceeding in badness, or both. Doesn't that also follow?— Of course.

—First, then, let's see whether doing injustice exceeds suffering it in pain. Do those who do injustice suffer more pain than those who suffer injustice?—No, Socrates; certainly not.—Then doing injustice doesn't exceed in pain?—No.—Then doing injustice will have an excess of badness, and will therefore be worse than suffering injustice?—Clearly.—But haven't you and the many already agreed that doing injustice is more shameful than suffering it?—Yes.—And now it has turned out to be worse?—True.—And would you choose what is worse and more shameful over what is less so? …—I would say no.—Would anyone else?—No, not according to this argument, Socrates.—In that case, Polus, I was right to say that neither you, nor I, nor anyone would choose to do injustice rather than suffer it, since doing injustice is actually worse.—So it appears.

Objections to justice

456 Even if we accept the argument against Polus, we may attack Socrates' claims about justice, by denying that justice is either fine or good. Plato presents three attacks on justice—by Callicles in the *Gorgias*, by Thrasymachus in *Republic* i, and (most elaborately) by Glaucon and Adeimantus in *Republic* ii. These attacks make three apparently different claims about the character of justice:

(1) According to Callicles, other-regarding justice is a conspiracy of the weak against the strong.

[8] Continued from **187**. The words translated 'fine' (*kalon*) and 'shameful' (*aischron*) might also be rendered 'beautiful' and 'ugly' in some contexts.

[9] Polus means that suffering injustice is worse for the sufferer than doing injustice is for the doer.

(2) According to Thrasymachus, it is the advantage of the stronger party over the weaker.

(3) According to Glaucon and Adeimantus, it is an agreement for mutual advantage.

Each of these three claims about justice may appear to conflict with the other two. If justice is a conspiracy of the weak to restrain the strong, how can it also be for the advantage of the stronger against the weaker party. And how can it be either of these if it is mutually advantageous to strong and weak alike?

Callicles uses the contrast between nature and convention to attack other-regarding justice (**458**). In his view, the rules of justice that require respect for the interests of others and prevent him from satisfying his own desires at their expense are simply products of convention. They result from a conspiracy of weak people who fear aggression by strong and resolute people such as himself. These weak people combine for their own advantage, but they also try to deceive superior people into believing that other-regarding justice is really admirable and good. In fact, superior people are really better off if they pursue the satisfaction of their own desires at other people's expense. That is why the other-regarding rules of justice are simply a matter of convention; we have no reason to respect them if we can gain some advantage by violating them. We would have no reason to care about the good of others in our society unless the weak people had formed this general view that other-regarding justice ought to be encouraged. Hence any reason we have for caring about it depends entirely on what the weak people have decided.

According to Thrasymachus, the stronger party in a state enacts rules of justice in its own interest; hence a democracy and an oligarchy have different conceptions of justice (**459**; cf. **559**). In each case, the rules prescribing respect for the interests of others tend to preserve the established regime. If, then, I have other aims apart from preserving the established regime, I have good reasons to violate the rules of justice.

Glaucon suggests that rules of justice are in everyone's interest, in so far as everyone loses by being exposed to aggression by others (**460**). Hence, it is in everyone's interest to accept an agreement establishing rules of justice that prescribe some respect for other people's interests. This account of the origin and basis of rules of justice is quite similar to Hobbes's account, which has influenced one major trend in modern moral and political philosophy. Hobbes derives justice from a social contract intended to limit mutual aggression. For reasons similar to those given by Glaucon, Hobbes argues that it is in everyone's interest to set up a sovereign (or a 'stronger', as Thrasymachus calls it) to enforce rules of justice.

According to this conception of justice, I have a reason to observe rules of justice if someone else has the power to coerce me. If no one has this power, I have no reason not to pursue my own interest. Glaucon illustrates this point by the story of Gyges' ring (cf. **486–7**). Gyges happened to find a ring that made him invisible whenever he liked; he used this to seduce the king's wife, kill the king, and become king himself. Glaucon suggests that most people would behave as Gyges did if they could get away with injustice without bad consequences to themselves. Most people behave this way in ordinary circumstances, since they avoid injustice only if they are likely to be found out and punished. They assume that the observance of rules of justice must rely on superior force.

Thucydides attributes similar assumptions about justice to the Athenians in their discussion with the Melians (**461**). In 416 BC, the island of Melos refused to join the Athenian alliance in the war against Sparta; in return, the Athenians decided to execute the Melian adult males and to enslave the women and children. In a debate with Athenian ambassadors, the Melians argue that the action that the Athenians propose would be an act of unprovoked aggression, and hence unjust. The Athenians reply that expediency is the only appropriate rule in dealings between the strong and the weak. One might argue that they put Callicles' and Glaucon's principles into practice. This dialogue may represent Thucydides' conception of justice, rather than the content of anything the Athenians said at the time. The view that the Athenians' attitude is callous and immoral is not simply a modern objection. A similar objection is expressed in the ancient world by Dionysius of Halicarnassus in his comments on this dialogue (**462**).

A similar conception of justice appears in Xenophon's dialogue between Pericles and Alcibiades (**463**). We might assume that our reason to observe laws and rules of justice is distinct from our purely self-centred reason to submit to threats of force. This assumption about justice is sanctioned by convention (*nomos*) (**125**). Alcibiades argues that it is simply a matter of convention, corresponding to no facts about laws and justice.

These arguments imply that if I understand the nature of justice, and the ways and circumstances in which observance of rules of justice benefits different people, I will also see why I do not have sufficient reason to be a just person. Justice is 'another's good', but not good for me, in cases where I can get away with unjust action. Hobbes also recognizes this objection to his account of justice; he attributes it to a 'fool' (**464**), but he makes a good case for the position of the fool. On closer inspection, therefore, the three attacks on justice have more in common than they initially appear to have. Once we understand Thrasymachus and Glaucon, we see that they agree with some of the main points of Callicles' case against other-regarding justice.

....

457 PLATO, *Republic* 328B–331D SOCRATES: We went with Polemarchus to his house; ... Cephalus the father of Polemarchus was there too. I thought he was quite aged; for I hadn't seen him for a long time. He was sitting on a cushioned chair, and had a garland on his head—for he had been sacrificing in the courtyard ... [330D] I asked him: What do you think is the greatest good you have gained from your wealth? [CEPHALUS:] When I tell you, he said, I'm not likely to persuade many people. For let me tell you, Socrates, that when a man faces the thought that he is going to die, fear and care come into his mind that never occurred to him before. Those stories about Hades, saying that whoever has committed injustice here must pay the just penalty there—once he ridiculed them, but now they torment him with the fear that they may be true, either because of the weakness of age, or because he is now drawing nearer to that other place, and so discerns these things better.[10] He is filled with suspicions and alarms, and he begins to count up and to consider whether he has done injustice to anyone. The one who finds many injustices in his life will often, like a child, start up in his sleep for fear, and he lives with grim forebodings. ... For a decent man, though certainly not for everyone, the great use of wealth is that he does not willingly or unwillingly deceive or defraud others; and so, when he departs to the other world, he is not afraid of still owing offerings to the gods or money to other people. Now to this the possession of wealth contributes greatly. ...—Well said, Cephalus, I replied. But are we to say without qualification that this very thing, justice, is telling the truth and giving back what one has borrowed from anyone? Or is it possible to do these very things sometimes justly and sometimes unjustly? I mean, for example: everyone, I presume, would say that if one were to borrow weapons from a friend in his right mind, and then the lender were to go mad and demand them back, one ought not to give them back and anyone giving them back would not be just—nor would one who was willing to speak nothing but the truth to someone in that state.—You're right, he replied.—Then this is not the definition of justice—to tell the truth and to give back what one has borrowed.

458 PLATO, *Gorgias* 482e–483d[11] CALLICLES: ... For the truth is, Socrates, that you pretend to be engaged in the pursuit of truth, but now you're appealing to the popular vulgarities, which are not fine by nature, but only by convention. For convention and nature are generally contrary to each other, and so if someone is ashamed to say what he thinks, he's forced to contradict himself. You've noticed this clever trick, and so you cheat in your arguments. If someone is arguing by appeal to convention, you slip in a question that rests on an assumption about nature; if he appeals to nature, you resort to convention. That's what you did in this very discussion about doing and suffering injustice; when Polus was speaking of what's shameful by convention, you pursued the argument by appealing to nature. For by nature, suffering injustice is the more shameful, because it's worse; but by convention, doing injustice is more shameful. No real man suffers injustice; it's what happens to a slave, who's better off dead than alive, since he has to suffer injustice and

---

[10] Fear of punishment after death; cf. **584**, **608**.
[11] This follows **455**.

abuse without being able to defend himself or anyone he cares about. It seems to me, however, that the ones who make the laws[12] are the majority who are weak; they make laws and distribute praises and censures with a view to themselves and to their own interests. They try to terrify the stronger people, those who are able to get more. To stop them getting more, they say that taking more is shameful and unjust, and that doing injustice consists in this, trying to have more than others have; for, since they know their own inferiority, I suppose they are satisfied with equality. That's why the attempt to have more than the many is conventionally said to be unjust and shameful, and is called doing injustice, whereas nature herself shows, in my view, that it is just for the better to have more than the worse—in other words, for the stronger to have more than the weaker.[13]

459 PLATO, *Republic* 343B–344A [THRASYMACHUS:] ... You're so far off the mark about the just and justice, and the unjust and injustice, that you don't know that justice and the just are really another's good, namely the advantage of the stronger and the ruler, but one's own harm, for the subject who obeys and serves.[14] Injustice is the contrary; it rules the simpletons who are just, and these subjects do what is for the advantage of the ruler who is the stronger, making him, not themselves, happy by serving him. And this is how you must look at the matter, simpleton Socrates: the just man always comes out with less. First, consider the transactions involved in any joint undertaking of a just and an unjust man; you'll never find that the just man has more than the unjust at the dissolution of the partnership, but that he always has less[15] ... [343E] But to the unjust man all the opposite advantages accrue. I mean, of course, the man ... who has the power to take more on a large scale. Consider this type of man, then, if you want to judge how much more profitable it is for one's own private interest to be unjust than to be just.

460 PLATO, *Republic* 357A–359C [GLAUCON:] ... Socrates, do you want to seem to have persuaded us, or really to persuade us that it's better in every way to be just than to be unjust? [SOCRATES:] Really to persuade, I said, if it were up to me.—Well, then, you aren't doing what you want to. Tell me, do you agree that there is a kind of good that we would choose to possess, not because we aim at its consequences, but because we welcome it for its own sake—for example, enjoyment, and those harmless pleasures that have no later results except continued enjoyment?—I think there is this kind, I said.— And again, a kind that we love both for its own sake and for its consequences, such as understanding, seeing, and being healthy? For these, I presume, we

---

[12] Both 'convention' and 'law' translate *nomos* in this passage. See **125**.
[13] A later stage in Callicles' case against justice; **392**.
[14] Plato's answer to this conception of the ruler; **556**.
[15] Thrasymachus adds further examples of unjust people's being better off (as he conceives it).

welcome because of both.—Yes, I said.—And do you see a third kind of good that includes exercise, being healed when sick, medical treatment, and making money generally? For we would say that all of these are laborious and painful, yet beneficial; we prefer them not for their own sake, but only for the consequent rewards and other benefits.—Yes, I said, I think there is this third kind also. What of it?—In which kind do you place justice? he said.—In my opinion, I said, it belongs to the finest kind, the one which a man who is to be happy must love both for its own sake and for the consequences.—That's not what most people think, he said. They think it belongs to the laborious kind that must be practised for the sake of rewards and reputation, but for its own sake is to be avoided as disagreeable. ...

Come now, ... hear what I have to say, and see if you agree with me. ... For what I want is to hear what each of justice and injustice is—what power each has in and of itself when it is present in the soul, but to dismiss their rewards and consequences. This, then, is what I propose to do; if you agree, I will renew the argument of Thrasymachus. First, I'll say what sort of thing people take justice to be, and how they think it arose. Secondly, I'll say that all who practise justice do so unwillingly, regarding it as something necessary and not as a good. Thirdly, I'll say it's only reasonable to expect them to do this, since, according to them, the life of the unjust person is far better than that of the just person. ...

[358E] By nature, they say, doing injustice is good and suffering it is bad, but the comparative badness in suffering it outweighs the comparative benefit in doing it. And so, when people do injustice to one another and suffer it from one another, and so have a taste of both, those who lack the power to avoid suffering injustice and to choose to do injustice, conclude that it is in their interest to make an agreement with one another neither to do nor to suffer injustice. This is the beginning of legislation and of agreements, and they call what is prescribed by law the lawful and the just. This is the origin and nature of justice; it is a compromise between the best, which is doing injustice with impunity, and the worst, which is suffering injustice without being able to take revenge. Justice, they tell us, being midway between the two, is accepted and approved, not as a good, but as a thing honoured because people are too weak to do injustice. ...

But as to the second point, that those who practise it do so unwillingly and from lack of power to commit injustice, we'll grasp this most easily if we think of something like this: we should allow both the just and the unjust person the freedom to do whatever he wants to, and then follow each of them to see where his appetite will lead him. We'll catch the just person red-handed, in the very act of resorting to the same conduct as the unjust person, in order to get more; for everyone's nature seeks to get more, as a good, though it is forcibly diverted by law to honouring equality. ...[16]

---

[16] Secret injustice; **482**, **584**, **605**. Glaucon continues with the story of Gyges' ring (summarized in **456**).

461 THUCYDIDES V. 89–105   ATHENIANS: For ourselves, we shall not trouble you with fine words. Hence we shall neither claim that we hold our empire justly because we overthrew the Persians, nor claim that we are now attacking you because you have done injustice to us; we shall not make any long speech that would undermine our credibility. In return, we hope that you will not expect us to be persuaded by a plea that you did not join the Spartans, despite being colonists sent out from Sparta, or a plea that you have done no injustice to us. Rather, we hope you will aim at what is feasible, keeping in mind your real views and ours. You know as well as we do that what is just, by a human accounting, is judged from a position of equal compulsion; the strong do what they can and the weak go along with it.[17] ... [104] MELIANS: You may be sure that we are as well aware as you are of how difficult it is to contend against your power and fortune, if it is not on equal terms. Still, we trust in fortune as good as yours from the divine[18]; for we are god-fearing people fighting against unjust <aggressors>, and we trust that what we lack in power will be made up by the alliance of the Spartans, who are bound, if only for very shame, to come to the aid of their own kin. Our confidence, therefore, after all is not so utterly irrational. ATHENIANS: When you speak of divine favour, we may have as much reason as you have to hope for that. For neither our claims nor our conduct are at all contrary to conventional human views about the divine, or to conventional practices among human beings. We suppose about the divine, on the basis of belief, and about human beings, on the basis of clear <knowledge>, that by a necessity of their nature they rule wherever they can.[19] We did not lay down this law; nor are we the first to act on it when made. On the contrary, we found it existing before us, and we shall leave it to exist for ever after us. We simply rely on it, knowing that you and everyone else, if you had the same power as we have, would do what we are doing. And so, as far as the divine goes, we have no reason to fear any disadvantage. But when we come to your belief about the Spartans, which leads you to trust that they will help you because it would be shameful not to, here we congratulate you on your simplicity, but we do not envy you your folly. The Spartans, when their own interests or their country's laws are in question, behave with the highest virtue. Of their behaviour towards other peoples much might be said, but the clearest way to summarize it is to say that of all the people we know they are most conspicuous in regarding what is pleasant to themselves as fine, and what is expedient to themselves as just. And this outlook does not contribute much to the safety that you now unreasonably count on.[20]

[17] See Dionysius' comment, **462**.
[18] *to theion*; cf. **388**.
[19] See Dionysius' comment, **462**.
[20] On injustice in time of war see also **536**.

462   DIONYSIUS OF HALICARNASSUS, *On Thucydides* 39[21]   These words would have been appropriate for barbarian kings to address to Greeks. But for Athenians addressing Greeks whom they had freed from the Persians it was not appropriate to say that justice is <only> for equals in dealings with one another, and that force is for the strong to use in dealings with others. ... [40][22] The conclusion is something like this, that people all find out about the divine on the basis of belief, but judge justice in relation to one another by the common law of nature. This law is that one rules over anyone one can dominate. This view follows from the earlier one, and is unfitting for either Athenians or Greeks to express.

463   XENOPHON, *Memoirs of Socrates* i. 2. 39–46[23]   I venture to affirm that people learn nothing from a teacher with whom they are out of sympathy. Now, all the time that Critias and Alcibiades associated with Socrates they were out of sympathy with him; from the very first they were eager for political prominence. For while they were still with him, they tried most of all to converse with leading politicians. Indeed, it is said that when Alcibiades was under 20 years old, he and his guardian Pericles, the leader of the city, had the following discussion about laws:

[ALCIBIADES:] Tell me, Pericles, he said, can you teach me what a law is? ... For whenever I hear men praised as law-abiding, I think no one can justly be praised for that if he does not know what law is. [PERICLES:] Well, Alcibiades, what you desire isn't difficult[24] to provide, if you want to know what law is. For laws are all the things approved and prescribed by the majority in assembly, declaring what ought and ought not to be done.—Do they suppose one ought to do good or bad things?—Good things, of course, young man, and not bad things.—But if, as happens under an oligarchy, not the majority, but a few meet and prescribe what ought to be done, what are these provisions?—Whatever the controlling element in the city, after deliberation, prescribes as what ought to be done is called law.—If, then, a tyrant[25] controls the city, and prescribes for the citizens what they ought to do, are these things also law?—Yes, whatever a tyrant as ruler prescribes is also called law.—But what are force and lawlessness, Pericles? Isn't that what happens when the stronger compels the weaker to do whatever the stronger thinks fit, not by persuasion, but by force?—I think so, said Pericles.—Then whatever a tyrant compels the citizens to do without persuasion and prescribes for them is lawlessness?—I think so: for I withdraw my previous answer that whatever a tyrant prescribes without persuasion is law.—And when the few prescribe,

---

[21] This comment applies to the text at n. 17.
[22] This comment deals with the text at n. 19.
[23] This passage is generally thought not to have been written by Xenophon.
[24] For the interlocutor's confidence, cf. **181**.
[25] Tyrant: **531–2**.

not by persuading the majority, but by exercising power, are we to call that force or not?—I think everything that one person compels another to do without persuasion, whether by prescription or not, is not law, but force.—It follows then, that if the assembled majority has control over the wealthy people, whatever it prescribes without persuasion is not law, but force?—Alcibiades , said Pericles, at your age, I may tell you, we were also very clever at this sort of thing. Our verbal exercises and sophistical tricks were just like the ones you seem to be practising now.—Ah, Pericles, cried Alcibiades, I wish I'd known you well when you were at your cleverest in these things!

As soon, then, as they thought they had got the better of the politicians, they no longer associated with Socrates. For, apart from their general want of sympathy with him, they were annoyed at being cross-examined about their errors when they came. They went in for political life, which had been their aim in associating with Socrates. But Crito was a true associate of Socrates, and so were Chaerephon, Chaerecrates, Hermogenes, Simmias, Cebes, Phaedondas, and others. These all associated with him not to become leading speakers in the courts or the assembly, but to become fine and good, capable of managing finely their household, friends, city and citizens. None of these, in his youth or old age, either acted badly or was accused of anything.

464 HOBBES, *Leviathan*, ch. 15 The fool hath said in his heart, there is no such thing as justice, and sometimes also with his tongue; seriously alleging, that every man's conversation and contentment being committed to his own care, there could be no reason, why every man ought not to do what he thought conduced thereunto; and therefore also to make or not make; keep or not keep covenants, was not against reason, when it conduced to one's benefit. He does not therein deny that there be covenants; and that they are sometimes broken, sometimes kept; and that such breach of them may be called injustice, and the observance of them justice: but he questioneth, whether injustice, taking away the fear of God, (for the same fool hath said in his heart there is no God,) may not sometimes stand with that reason, which dictateth to every man his own good; and particularly then, when it conduceth to such a benefit, as shall put a man in a condition, to neglect not only the dispraise, and revilings, but also the power of other men.

The questions about justice

465 A common theme in these attacks on justice is captured in this argument:

(1) Justice aims at the good of others.

(2) What benefits others does not always benefit me.

(3) Hence my acting justly does not always benefit me.

(4) I have reason, all things considered, to do only what promotes my own happiness.

(5) Hence I do not always have sufficient reason to act justly.

Each step in this argument is difficult to reject: (1) seems to express a central truth about justice; (2) seems obvious from examples. We might, then, challenge (4); perhaps the attack on justice simply shows that we ought not to defend justice by appeal to self-interest. This reply, however, is not open to Plato, who, like Socrates, believes that one's own happiness is the ultimate end of all rational action (**381**). Apparently, then, Plato must reject either (1) or (2). If he rejects (1), he does not seem to be talking about justice. If he rejects (2), he seems to deny obvious facts; it seems clear, for instance, that sometimes I can gain some advantage for myself at other people's expense by cheating or lying or evading an obligation of justice.

Plato seems to make his task more difficult for himself by insisting that a defence of justice must not appeal purely to its consequences; reference to the good consequences of justice may seem to offer the best prospect of proving that it is worth our while to be just. Plato, however, rejects this defence of justice. He takes Glaucon and Adeimantus to have shown that if we appeal simply to the consequences of justice, we cannot explain why we ought to be just; for the good consequences of justice could be obtained simply by appearing to be just while really being unjust.

Hence, in Plato's view, we must show two things about justice. (i) Justice is always to be chosen for its own sake, irrespective of its consequences. (ii) The just person is always better off and happier than the unjust person, no matter what other benefits the unjust person gains by injustice.

Plato takes the second of these two claims to follow from the first; but we may disagree. Indeed, we may wonder whether the two claims are even consistent. How can he consistently claim both to reject appeals to consequences and to argue that we benefit from being just? Why does the claim about benefit not immediately introduce a reference to consequences? On the other hand, if justice is really to be chosen for its own sake, ought not a genuinely just person to do the just action even when it is against her interest?

....

466 PLATO, *Republic* 367BC[26]   [ADEIMANTUS:] Don't merely show us by argument that justice is better than injustice. Show us also what each of them does, itself because of itself, to the person who has it, in such a way that justice is good and injustice bad. But take away people's opinions about both, as Glaucon urged. For, unless you take away from each the true opinions <that someone is just or unjust> and attach to each the false opinions, we'll say that what you praise is not being just, but seeming just, and what you censure is

---

[26] Adeimantus is addressing Socrates.

not being unjust, but seeming unjust; that you are really urging us to be unjust but conceal it; and that you agree with Thrasymachus that the just is the another's good, the advantage of the stronger, and the unjust is advantageous and profitable to oneself, but disadvantageous to the weaker.

467 H. A. PRICHARD, *Moral Obligation*,[27] p. 208 But if we can manage to consider Plato's endeavour to refute the Sophists[28] with detachment, what strikes us most is not his dissent from their view concerning the comparative profitableness of the actions which men think just and unjust—great, of course, as his dissent is—but the identity of principle underlying the position of both. The Sophists in reaching their conclusion were presupposing that for an action to be really just, it must be advantageous; for it was solely on this ground that they concluded that what we ordinarily think is just is not really just. And what in the end most strikes us is that at no stage in the *Republic* does Plato take the line, or even suggest as a possibility, that the very presupposition of the Sophists' argument is false, and that therefore the question whether some action which men think just will be profitable to the agent has really nothing to do with the question whether it is right … This presupposition, however, as soon as we consider it, strikes us as a paradox. For though we may find ourselves quite unable to state what it is that does render an action a duty, we ordinarily think that, whatever it is, it is not conduciveness to our advantage; and we also think that though an action which is a duty may be advantageous, it need not be so.

Justice as a virtue in the soul

468 In Plato's view, the appearance of conflict between other-regarding justice and self-interest results from false conceptions of justice and of self-interest, which come from a false conception of the self. When we understand what a human soul is like, we will see that we benefit precisely from having a just soul, not only from the consequences of having a just soul.

The account of justice is part of the account of the cardinal virtues that is derived from the division of the soul (**437–9**). Three cardinal virtues—bravery, temperance, and wisdom—are different aspects of a well-ordered soul. They belong to a rationally prudent person; for they ensure that we follow our rational desires for our overall good, and are not distracted by the non-rational desires of the spirited and appetitive parts.

According to Plato, a complete account of the well-ordered soul must ascribe to it not only these three cardinal virtues, but justice as well. To show why

[27] Oxford: Clarendon Press, 1968.
[28] Prichard assumes (disputably) that Thrasymachus, Glaucon, and Adeimantus defend a view widely accepted by sophists (see **8**).

justice is necessary, he considers the structure of the best city. This city is composed of three parts—the ruling class, the military class, and the producing class. Such a city, Plato assumes, is organized for the common good of the whole and of each part; and this organization, to which each part contributes by performing its own function, is justice in the city.[29] Since the soul also has parts that need to be organized for their good and the good of the whole, this order in which each part performs its own function is justice in the soul ('psychic justice'). Life would not be worth living without this justice, any more than it would be worth living without some reasonable degree of bodily health, because without it we could not pursue our own interest.

It is not clear whether Plato takes the other three cardinal virtues to be separable from psychic justice (so that one could, for instance, have bravery without justice), or simply takes justice to be one aspect of every well-ordered soul that that has any of the other three virtues. In any case, he claims that a well-ordered soul, aiming correctly at its own good, must be a just soul.

Does this discussion of psychic justice answer the original question about justice? Glaucon and Adeimantus asked about the justice that is 'another's good', since it seems to be essentially directed to the benefit of others—call this 'ordinary justice'. Could I not have psychic justice without ordinary justice? Suppose I act firmly on my rational plans, unshaken by non-rational impulses, but still form rational plans that require me to cheat other people in my own interest? If I could be a rational cheat of this sort, would I not have psychic justice without ordinary justice? To answer this objection, Plato must explain why this rational cheat really lacks psychic justice. He must show that psychic justice causes us to do actions plausibly regarded as just, and to avoid actions that seem clearly unjust. The injustices that seem to benefit the rational cheat offer unjust gains at other people's expense. But unjust gains appeal to me only if I have overdeveloped irrational impulses: I want lavish and expensive foods, or the unrestricted sexual pleasures that are gained by flattery, force, and deception, or I want to be admired for my wealth and I feel ashamed if I am despised for my poverty. I have these strong desires and act on them because my irrational parts are uncontrolled. If they are rationally controlled, I no longer have these unreasonably demanding desires.

This answer shifts the onus of proof back to the opponents of justice. Their confidence that justice conflicts with one's own interest rests on their view of a person's real interests. Plato maintains that their view is false; once we replace it with a true view, we will see no conflict in principle between being just and pursuing one's own interest.

If Plato is right, his account of the cardinal virtues may reasonably claim to describe moral virtues. We suppose, for instance, that bravery is a moral virtue because the brave person faces dangers not only for his own sake, but also for

---

[29] The organization of the best city; **555–6**. Justice as 'having one's own'; cf. **432**.

the sake of other people. If the virtues recognized by Plato were all purely self-regarding in the sense of being indifferent to the interests of others, we might object that they fail to capture a central aspect of morality. This objection is questionable, however, if Plato's claims about self-interest and the interests of others are correct. While justice is the virtue that makes Plato's concern with morality most obvious, all the four cardinal virtues embody a rational person's concern with morality.

....

469 PLATO, *Republic* 441C–443B [SOCRATES:] And so, I said, … we've fairly agreed that the same kinds, equal in number, are in the city and in the soul of each one of us. [GLAUCON:] That is so.—Then doesn't this also necessarily follow, that a private person is wise in the same way and by the same part[30] as those that were found to make the city wise?—Surely.—And the part and way that made a private person brave also make the city brave, and both the city and the person have all the other aspects of virtue in the same way?—Necessarily.—Just so, then, Glaucon, I presume, we'll say an individual person is just in the same way in which a city was just.—That is also necessary.—But surely we can't have forgotten that the city was just in so far as each of the three parts fulfilled its own function.—I don't think we have forgotten, he said.—We must remember, then, that whenever the parts in each of us fulfil their own functions,[31] this will be a just person who fulfils his own function.—We must indeed remember, he said.—Isn't it proper to the rational part to rule, being wise, and exercising forethought for the whole soul, and proper to the spirited part to be subject to the rational part, and its ally?—Certainly.—… And when these two have been trained and educated to fulfil the functions that are really their own, they will control the appetitive part, which is the largest part of the soul in each of us, with the most insatiable desire for wealth. …

[442E] We might, I said, completely confirm your reply and our own conclusion, if anything in our minds still disputes it, by applying commonplace tests to it.—What are these?—For example, take this city and the man whose birth and training are proper to it, and suppose we had to come to an agreement about whether such a person, once entrusted with a deposit of gold or silver, would embezzle it. Who do you suppose would think that he, rather than a different sort of person, would do this?—No one would think so, he said.—And wouldn't he keep far away from sacrilege, theft, and betrayal of associates in private life or betrayal of the city in public life?—He would.—Moreover, he would never be at all untrustworthy either in keeping his oaths or in other agreements.—How could he be?—And surely adultery, neglect of

[30] On 'part' see **438**n.
[31] 'Fulfil one's function' translates *ta hautou prattein*, literally 'do one's own things', which sometimes might be rendered by 'mind one's own business'.

parents, and slackness towards the gods would be characteristic of anyone rather than such a person.—Quite right, he said.—And isn't the cause of all this the fact that each of the parts within him fulfils its own function in ruling and being ruled?—Yes, exactly that.

470 PLATO, *Republic* 445AB [SOCRATES:] Our remaining task, it seems, is to inquire into this: Does it benefit us to do just actions and practise fine actions and be just, whether or not people believe one is just? Or does it benefit us to do injustice and to be unjust, if one escapes any penalty, and isn't improved by being punished? [GLAUCON:] But Socrates, he said, I think that by this stage our inquiry has become ridiculous. We admit that life is not worth living with our bodily nature ruined, no matter how much food, drink, wealth, and power we may have. But if the very nature of what makes us alive[32] is disordered and corrupted, how can life be worth living, if someone does everything he wants to, and refrains from what will rid him of vice and injustice and produce justice and virtue in him—now that the two have been shown to be as we have described them?[33]

471 PLATO, *Laws* 660E–661B ATHENIAN VISITOR: You[34] compel poets to say that a good man, by being temperate and just, is happy and blessed, no matter whether he is great and mighty or small and feeble, rich or poor. But if a man is unjust, even if he is richer than Midas or Cinyras, he is wretched, and his life is miserable … For the things that most people speak of as goods are not spoken of correctly. For it's said that health is the greatest of goods, beauty comes second, and wealth third. And there are innumerable other things called goods, such as keen sight and hearing, and acute senses generally. Moreover, it's said to be good to be a tyrant and fulfil all one's appetites; indeed, complete blessedness is supposed to be having all these things and at once becoming immortal. But you and I say that all these are the best possessions for just and pious men, but the worst, beginning with health, for unjust men.[35]

Friendship

472 Plato asserts that concern for the good of others promotes the just person's own interest, But he does not say much to connect my interest with the good of others. Aristotle's discussion of friendship argues for a connection.

---

[32] i.e. the soul. See **316**.

[33] In fact Socrates continues with a longer argument in favour of justice and against injustice (books viii–ix; part of the conclusion is quoted at **556**).

[34] The Athenian visitor, a Cretan, and a Spartan are designing an ideal state on the island of Crete.

[35] Cf. **495–7**.

Aristotle distinguishes three kinds of friendship—concerned, respectively, with advantage, pleasure, and goodness. The first two kinds are relatively easy to understand from a purely self-interested point of view. Often we advance our own interests more efficiently if we can rely on help from other people; we might make bargains with them for our mutual advantage. We might also take an interest in other people because we enjoy their company; our concern depends on what we enjoy, not on any concern for the other person herself. The third kind of friendship is different from the other two, since it involves concern for the other person because of herself and for her own sake, not simply as a source of advantage or pleasure. Aristotle argues that this sort of concern for others also promotes one's own good.

He argues that we can see how love of self requires concern for the good of others, once we understand what is meant by speaking of self-love and self-interest. What we think is in our self-interest depends on what we think the self is, and what sorts of desires need to be satisfied in order to achieve its interests. Aristotle argues that a human self is naturally social, so that something is missing from our good if all our concerns are purely self-regarding (**406, 558**).

The argument relies on the general claim that I am better off to the extent that I have a wider range of aims and concerns that I can satisfy. If someone is concerned about very few things, he has very little to take an interest in, and his prospects of well-being are correspondingly reduced. In being concerned about other people, we become interested in aims and activities that would otherwise not interest us, and become capable of activities that would otherwise be beyond us. We do not enjoy playing on a team or in an orchestra very much, unless we care about how well the team or the orchestra as a whole plays. We will not even be able to play in a team or in an orchestra unless we have some concern for the success of these co-operative activities. These examples suggest what Aristotle has in mind in saying that for the virtuous person a friend (of the best sort) is 'another self' (**477**). If we are virtuous, we care about the friend in the way we care about ourselves; we can therefore take an interest that we would not otherwise take in what the friend does. Concern for others does not interfere with our interests, but expands them.

Admittedly, concern for others may sometimes conflict with my other concerns; but this does not show that it is not in my interest. For it is equally true that my interest in running may conflict with my interest in eating and drinking (if I sometimes have to eat and drink less to run better); this does not mean that it is not in my interest to pursue my interest in running. Similarly, if my concern for others expands my interests, then the fact that it may sometimes conflict with some of my other concerns does not show that it is, all things considered, against my interest.

The social nature of human beings is also the basis of justice. Aristotle agrees with Thrasymachus' claim that justice is 'another's good' (**478**). Indeed, he maintains that one form of justice is not a separable virtue, but the whole of virtue in so far as it is practised towards other people. Since virtuous people value the good of other people for the sake of the other people themselves, they also choose virtuous actions for their own sakes. Aristotle describes this attitude to virtuous actions by saying that virtuous people choose them 'because they are fine', or 'for the sake of the fine' (**449**).

....

473 ARISTOTLE, *Nicomachean Ethics* 1155ᵃ1–31 Friendship is a virtue, or involves virtue, and moreover is most necessary for our life; for no one would choose to live without friends even if one had all the other goods. Indeed, rich people and holders of powerful positions, even more than other people, seem to need friends. For how would one benefit from such prosperity if one had no opportunity for beneficence, which is most often displayed, and most highly praised, in relation to friends? And how would one guard and protect prosperity without friends, since it is all the more precarious the greater it is? In poverty also, and in the other misfortunes, people think friends are the only refuge. Moreover, the young need friendship to keep them from error. The old need it to care for them and support the actions that fail because of weakness. And those in their prime need it, to do fine actions; for 'when two go together . . .', they are more capable of understanding and acting. Further, a parent would seem to have a natural friendship for a child, and a child for a parent, not only among human beings but also among birds and most kinds of animals. Members of the same race, and human beings most of all, have a natural friendship for each other; that is why we praise friends of humanity. And in our travels we can see how every human being is akin and beloved to a human being. Moreover, friendship would seem to hold cities together, and legislators would seem to be more concerned about it than about justice; for concord would seem to be similar to friendship and they aim at concord among all, while they try above all to expel civil conflict,³⁶ which is enmity. Further, if people are friends, they have no need of justice, but if they are just they need friendship in addition; and the justice that is most just seems to belong to friendship. Moreover, friendship is not only necessary, but also fine. For we praise lovers of friends, and having many friends seems to be a fine thing.³⁷ Moreover, people think that the same people are good and also friends.

474 ARISTOTLE, *Nicomachean Ethics* 1156ᵃ2–ᵇ12 Friendship has three species, corresponding to the three objects of love. For each object of love has a corresponding type of mutual loving, combined with awareness of it, and those who love each other wish goods to each other in so far as they love each other. Those who love each other for usefulness love the other not in

---

³⁶ Civil conflict (*stasis*); **536**, **552**.
³⁷ Many friends; **384**.

himself, but in so far as they gain some good for themselves from him. The same is true of those who love for pleasure; they like a witty person not because of his character, but because he is pleasant to themselves. ... Hence these friendships are also coincidental, since the beloved is loved not in so far as he is who he is, but in so far as he provides some good or pleasure. And so these sorts of friendships are easily dissolved, when the friends do not remain as they were; for if someone is no longer pleasant or useful, the other stops loving him. ... [1156ᵇ7] But complete friendship is the friendship of good people similar to each other in virtue; for they wish goods in the same way to each other in so far as they are good, and they are good in themselves. Now those who wish goods to their friend for the friend's own sake are friends most of all; for they have this attitude because of the friend himself, not coincidentally. Hence these people's friendship endures as long as they are good; and virtue is enduring.[38]

475 ARISTOTLE, *Nicomachean Ethics* 1168ᵃ28–1169ᵃ15   There is also a puzzle about whether one ought to love oneself or someone else most of all; for those who like themselves most are criticized and denounced as self-lovers, as though this were something shameful. Indeed, the bad person seems to go to every length for his own sake, and all the more the more vicious he is; hence he is accused, for instance, of doing nothing of his own accord. The good person, on the contrary, acts for what is fine, all the more the better he is, and for his friend's sake, disregarding his own good. ... Perhaps, then, it will become clear, if we grasp how those on each side understand self-love.

Those who make self-love a matter for reproach ascribe it to those who award the biggest share in money, honours and bodily pleasures to themselves. For these are the goods desired and eagerly pursued by the many, who assume that they are best; and hence they are also contested. Those who are greedy for these goods gratify their appetites, and in general their feelings[39] and the non-rational part of the soul; and since this is what the many are like, the application of the term 'self-love' is derived from the most frequent kind of self-love, which is bad. This type of self-lover, then, is justifiably reproached. And plainly it is the person who awards himself these goods whom the many normally call a self-lover. For if someone is always eager to excel everyone in doing just or temperate actions, or any other actions in accord with the virtues, and in general always gains for himself what is fine, no one will call him a self-lover or blame him for it.

However, it is this sort of person, more than the other sort, who seems to be a self-lover. At any rate, he awards himself what is finest and best of all, and gratifies the most controlling part of himself, obeying it in everything. And

---

[38] The Stoics on the friendship of virtuous people; **566**.
[39] Or 'passions'. Cf. **526**.

just as a city and every other composite system seems to be above all its most controlling part, the same is true of a human being; hence someone loves himself most if he likes and gratifies this part. ... Hence he most of all is a self-lover, but a different kind from the self-lover who is reproached; he differs from him as much as the life in accord with reason differs from the life in accord with feelings, and as much as the desire for the fine differs from the desire for the advantageous. ... Hence the good person must be a self-lover, since he will both help himself and benefit others by doing fine actions. But the vicious person must not love himself, since he will harm both himself and his neighbours by following his base feelings.

476 ARISTOTLE, *Nicomachean Ethics* 1169^{b}16–1170^{a}7   Surely it is also absurd to make the blessed person solitary. For no one would choose to have all <other> goods and yet be alone, since a human being is political, tending by nature to live together with others. ... [1170^{a}5] The solitary person's life is hard, since it is not easy for him to be continuously active all by himself; but in relation to others and in their company it is easier, and hence his activity will be more continuous.

477 ARISTOTLE, *Nicomachean Ethics* 1170^{b}3–19   Living is choiceworthy, for a good person most of all, since being is good and pleasant for him; for he is pleased to perceive something good in itself together <with his own being>. The excellent person is related to his friend in the same way as he is related to himself, since a friend is another self. Therefore, just as his own being is choiceworthy for him, his friend's being is choiceworthy for him in the same or a similar way. We agreed that someone's own being is choiceworthy because he perceives that he is good, and this sort of perception is pleasant in itself. He must, then, perceive his friend's being together <with his own>, and he will do this when they live together and share conversation and thought. For in the case of human beings what seems to count as living together is this sharing of conversation and thought, not sharing the same pasture, as in the case of grazing animals. If, then, for the blessedly happy person, being is choiceworthy, since it is naturally good and pleasant, and if the being of his friend is closely similar to his own, then his friend will also be choiceworthy. Whatever is choiceworthy for him he must possess, since otherwise he will to this extent lack something. Anyone who is to be happy, then, must have excellent friends.

478 ARISTOTLE, *Nicomachean Ethics* 1129^{b}11–1130^{a}5   Since ... the lawless person is unjust and the lawful person is just, it clearly follows that whatever is lawful is in some way just; for the provisions of legislative science are lawful, and we say that each of them is just. Now in every matter they deal with the laws aim at the benefit of all in common, or of those in control, whose control rests on virtue or on some other such basis. And so in one way what we call just is whatever produces and maintains happiness and its parts for a po-litical association.[40] Now the law instructs us to do the actions of a brave per-son (not to leave the battle-line, for instance, or to flee, or to throw away our weapons), of a temperate person (not to commit adultery or wanton aggres-sion), and of a mild person (not to strike or revile another). Similarly, it re-quires actions in accord with the other virtues, and prohibits actions in accord with the vices. The correctly established law does this correctly, and the less carefully framed one does this worse. This type of justice, then, is complete virtue—not complete virtue without qualification, but complete virtue in relation to another. And this is why justice often seems to be supreme among the virtues, and 'neither the evening star nor the morning star is so marvellous', and the proverb says 'And in justice all virtue is summed up.'

Moreover, justice is complete virtue to the highest degree, because it is the complete exercise of complete virtue. And it is the complete exercise be-cause the person who has justice is able to exercise virtue in relation to an-other, not only in what concerns himself; for many are able to exercise virtue in their own concerns but unable in what relates to another. And hence Bias seems to have been correct in saying that ruling will reveal the man, since a ruler is automatically related to another, and in some association. And for the same reason justice is the only virtue that seems to be another person's good, because it is related to another; for it does what benefits another, either the ruler or the fellow-member of the association.

Epicurus on virtue and justice

479 Plato and Aristotle seek to show that the virtues are parts of happiness, be-cause they believe that we have sufficient reason to be virtuous, and that a vir-tuous person must chose virtuous action for its own sake. In their view, if we cannot prove that virtue is a part of happiness, we cannot prove that virtue re-ally deserves to be chosen for its own sake, and therefore we cannot prove that we have sufficient reason to be virtuous. As Glaucon puts it (**466**), anyone who chooses justice purely for its consequences only appears to be just, and is not re-ally just.

Epicurus rejects this argument. Since he conceives the ultimate good as pleas-ure, understood as the absence of pain and anxiety, any other good can only be instrumentally valuable; it must promote or maintain this condition, or provide pleasant variations in it. He seeks to show, therefore, that we can defend the virtues even if we take a purely instrumental attitude to them; he speaks con-temptuously of those—including Plato, Aristotle, and the Stoics—who regard

[40] Or 'community'. See **557–8**.

the virtues and fine action as valuable in their own right, independently of their yield of pleasure (**481–5**; cf. **387, 407**).

The account of justice offered by Glaucon and Adeimantus provides a test of Epicurus' claims about virtue and happiness. Plato rejects this account on the ground that, if we confine ourselves to defending justice by appeal to its consequences, we cannot defend any stable commitment to justice. In their view, a moderately astute person in a normal society will often face situations where it is reasonable to act unjustly. Epicurus argues that, even if we confine ourselves to the sorts of consequences considered by Glaucon and Adeimantus, we have good reasons for a stable commitment to justice.[41]

Since Epicurus identifies the ultimate good with tranquillity and absence of anxiety, he advises us to regulate our desires so that we do not depend on external conditions; and so Epicureans value the results of temperance. They do not fear the loss of worldly goods, since they do not need many, and so they are not tempted to be cowards. They find mutual aid and pleasure in the society of friends, and so they cultivate friendships. They are not anxious for power or domination over others, since that would be a source of severe anxiety and insecurity.

People with this outlook understand the benefits of mutual aid and physical security. Hence they have every reason to make the sort of agreement that Glaucon and Adeimantus regard as the basis of justice.[42] Contrary to Glaucon and Adeimantus, however, Epicurus believes that the motives that lead Epicureans to welcome justice in society also lead them to obey the rules of justice. Since Epicureans value freedom from anxiety, they want to avoid the risk of detection and punishment—a risk that is the inevitable penalty of injustice, even if it leads to no further penalty. The needs that cause the formation of the state also give the Epicurean hedonist reason to conform to justice.

Admittedly, if we cared as much about wealth, power, and so on as Glaucon and Adeimantus (presenting Thrasymachus' case) assume we do, we would have good reason to violate rules of justice when we could avoid the normal penalty. If, however, we agree with Epicurus about the comparative unimportance of these external advantages, and we regard them as sources of unwelcome anxiety, we will not want to incur the further anxiety that results from unjust action and the fear of punishment.

....

480 EPICURUS = DIOGENES LAERTIUS X. 140   It is not possible to live pleasantly without living prudently, honourably, and justly, or to live prudently, honourably, and justly without living pleasantly ...

481 EPICURUS = DIOGENES LAERTIUS X. 141   Some people wanted to become famous and eminent, supposing that in this way they would gain

---

[41] Epicurean political theory; **564**.
[42] Social contract; **557, 559**.

safety[43] from other people. And so, if such people's life is safe, they have got the good of nature. But if it is not safe, they did not gain the goal they aimed at from the beginning in their desires, according to what is naturally suitable.

482 EPICURUS = DIOGENES LAERTIUS X. 150–1   The justice of nature is a pledge of expediency, neither to harm one another nor to be harmed. Nothing was just or unjust in relation to all those animals that were unable to make agreements about neither harming one another nor being harmed. The same was true of all those nations who were unable or unwilling to make pacts about neither harming one another nor being harmed. Justice was not something in its own right, but it depended on mutual dealings, and it existed wherever an agreement was made about neither harming one another nor being harmed. Injustice is not bad in its own right, but its badness depends on the fear arising from the suspicion that one will not go undetected by those in charge of punishing such actions. If anyone secretly violates what people agreed on to avoid harming one another or being harmed, he cannot be confident that he will escape detection, even if, for the present, he escapes detection ten thousand times. For until his death it will be unclear whether he will continue to escape detection.

483 PLUTARCH, *Against Epicurean Happiness* 1091B   Epicurus says: 'For what produces unexcelled joy is the comparison with the great evil that has been avoided. And this is the nature of the good, if you apply your mind to it correctly, and then stand firm, and do not walk around[44] idly, chattering about the good.'

484 PLUTARCH, *Against Colotes* 1108C   The Epicureans shout that the good is found in the belly, that they would not buy the virtues all in a lump at the price of a penny with a hole in it, if all pleasure was entirely expelled from them.

485 ATHENAEUS, *Sophists of the Dinner-Table* 547A   Again, in his work 'On the End' Epicurus says: 'I spit on the fine and on those who idly admire it, whenever it produces no pleasure.'

486 CICERO, *Duties* iii. 39   And yet on this point certain philosophers who are not at all vicious but who are not very perceptive declare that Plato's story[45] is a mere fiction—as if, indeed, he had defended it either as true or as possible! But the point of the illustration of the ring is this: Suppose that, when you did anything to gain riches or power or mastery, or to satisfy lust, no one were going to know or even to suspect the truth. If, then, your act

[43] Safety; **384**, **417**.
[44] 'Walk around', *peripatein*, may refer to the Peripatetics, followers of Aristotle.
[45] Gyges' ring; **456**, **460**.

were always going to be unknown to gods and to human beings, would you do it? The condition, they say, is impossible. Of course it is.[46] But my question is this: If what they say is impossible were to be possible, what would they do? … For when we ask what they would do if they could escape detection, we are not asking whether they can escape detection. Rather, we are forcing them to answer the crucial question. If they reply that, if they could look forward to avoiding punishment, they would do what was expedient, they admit that they are criminals. If they say they would not do it, they concede that everything shameful is to be avoided because of itself.

487 LACTANTIUS, *Divine Institutions* v. 12. 5–6 = Cicero, *Republic* iii. 27[47] Suppose there are two men, and one is the best of men, outstanding in fairness, justice, and trustworthiness, while the other is distinguished by his extreme wickedness and audacity. Now suppose also that a city is so mistaken that it believes the good man is a wicked, treacherous criminal, and the most wicked man, on the contrary, is a man of outstanding goodness and trustworthiness. Then let us imagine that, in accordance with this belief of all his fellow-citizens, the good man is harassed, attacked, and arrested; his eyes are gouged out, he is sentenced, imprisoned, branded, banished, and reduced to destitution; finally, everyone regards him, completely reasonably, as the most wretched of men. Let the wicked man, on the contrary, be praised, courted, and loved by all; let him be given all sorts of honours, military commands, wealth, and riches from every source; and finally, let all regard him as the best of all men, most worthy of all the best fortune. Now, I ask you, who could be so insane as to doubt which of the two he would rather be?

Difficulties in Epicurus' defence of virtue

488 Epicurus, then, argues that Epicureans will be virtuous because they lack the normal temptations to act badly. It is difficult, however, to accept this account of a virtuous person's motives. A brave person, for instance, faces some apparently significant harm to himself—death or imprisonment, for instance— for the sake of some apparent good that outweighs the harm—the safety of his fellow-citizens, for instance. If we are convinced by Epicurus' arguments, we will not regard the apparent costs of virtuous action as genuine harms; hence, fear of these harms will not prevent us from doing what the brave person does. Still, we will also apparently lack any reason for caring about the cause that the brave person cares about. While we have no reason to fear danger, we have no reason to face it either. The Epicurean's indifference to external conditions will

[46] Text uncertain.
[47] This is part of Carneades' Sceptical argument about justice. Cf. **22**, **292**.

apparently make him indifferent to the goods that should matter to a brave person.

For similar reasons, we may doubt the Epicurean's commitment to justice and friendship. Even if the threat of punishment deters him from all or most unjust actions, he seems to have no positive reason to care about the good of others for its own sake. To care about it for its own sake would be to regard it as a good in itself, not simply a means to some other good; but a hedonist cannot allow this status to any good except pleasure. If the Epicurean is indifferent to the interest of others as a good in itself, he seems to have no reason for doing any good to them, except when it is instrumental to some further benefit to himself, and ultimately instrumental to his own pleasure.

Some Epicureans treat friendship differently from justice. They claim that the wise person will find pleasure in the company of his friend, apart from any further instrumental benefits. It is difficult to see how, on purely Epicurean grounds, such pleasure can be justified. If an Epicurean's happiness essentially consists in (among other things) pleasure taken in his friends, for which no other means to tranquillity can be substituted, then a strictly hedonist conception of happiness must be false. Moreover, friendship seems to bring fears and anxieties—about the welfare of one's friends—that an Epicurean rejects; if we have no such fears and anxieties, we do not seem to have the attitudes that are normally expected of friends.

If, then, we were to work out the consequences of the Epicurean case for the non-instrumental value of friendship, we would apparently find objections to the Epicurean view that every good other than pleasure has only instrumental value. In that case, Epicurus would have to abandon his argument against the Platonic and Aristotelian claim that virtue is to be chosen for its own sake, apart from its further effects on pleasure and pain.

....

489 CICERO, *Ends* ii. 69–71 You will be ashamed of the picture that Cleanthes used to draw so aptly in his lectures. He would instruct his audience to imagine a painting representing pleasure decked as a queen ... The virtues would attend her, as servants who would do nothing, and recognize no duty, except to serve pleasure. They would simply warn her in a whisper ... to avoid any thoughtless action that might offend public opinion, or anything that might lead to pain. ... But Epicurus, you will tell me, ... says that anyone who does not live finely cannot live pleasantly. As if I cared what Epicurus says or denies! I ask this: What is it consistent for someone who places the highest good in pleasure to say? ... Epicurus himself says that the life of gratification is not to be criticized, if these people are not complete fools—that is to say, if they have neither longings nor fears. ... And so, once you Epicureans direct everything by reference to pleasure, you cannot uphold or retain virtue. For a man must not be thought good and just if he refrains from doing injustice for fear of anything bad <for himself>. ... As long as he <avoids injustice because

he> is afraid, he is not just, and assuredly, as soon as he ceases to be afraid, he will not be just ... In this way you Epicureans undoubtedly teach the pretence of justice instead of true and stable justice.

490 CICERO, *Duties* iii. 116–18   The Cyrenaic[48] followers of Aristippus, and the philosophers named after Anniceris, placed all good in pleasure. Virtue, they held, is to be praised only because it produces pleasure. These doctrines are out of fashion nowadays; but Epicurus is in fashion, and he supports and puts forward practically the same views. ... But such advantage—the supreme advantage, in their view—will certainly conflict with the right.[49] First, what role will be left for prudence? The task of finding pleasures from whatever source? What a wretched servitude for virtue, to slave for pleasure. ... And then if someone says that pain is the greatest evil, what role can bravery have, since it is contempt for pains and troubles? Granted, Epicurus often speaks bravely about pain. Still, what matters is not what he says, but what it is consistent to say for one who regards pleasure as the end of goods and pain as the end of evils. The same is true of his many remarks about continence and temperance; 'the stream does not flow freely', as the saying goes. For if he places the highest good in pleasure, how can he praise temperance? For the passions are followers of pleasure, but temperance is their enemy. ... Justice wavers, or rather collapses, and so do all those virtues that are noticed in social life, and in associations between human beings. For goodness, generosity, and courtesy cannot exist, any more than friendship can, if they are not pursued in themselves, but are referred to pleasure or usefulness.

491 CICERO, *Ends* i. 66–9   Some Epicureans say that our friends' pleasures are not to be pursued in themselves, in the way[50] we pursue our own pleasures. ... For since a solitary life without friends is full of dangerous traps and fear, reason herself advises us to form friendships; when we do this, our mind is strengthened, and friendship cannot be separated from the expectation of acquiring pleasures. ... That is why a wise man will have the same feelings for his friend as for himself and will undertake the same labours for the sake of a friend's pleasure as he would undertake for the sake of his own. ... Some Epicureans, however, ... are afraid that if we believe that friendship is to be pursued for the sake of our own pleasure, all of friendship might seem to be crippled. So they say that people first meet, combine, and desire to form associations for the sake of pleasure, but when increasing experience results in intimacy, love flowers to such an extent that, even if no advantage comes from the friendship, the friends themselves are loved because of themselves.

---

[48] Cyrenaics; **22**.
[49] Or 'fine', honestum (= *kalon*). Cf. **449**.
[50] Or perhaps 'to the extent that'.

XIII: Virtue and Happiness

Can a good person be harmed?

492 Plato argues that we are always better off if we choose justice, no matter what the cost, than if we choose injustice, no matter what the benefit. This is the claim expressed in the 'choice of lives' in *Republic* ii (**466**). In his view, virtue is a component of happiness, and not simply an instrumental means to it (cf. **387, 407**). Moreover, it is the dominant component, to be chosen over any combination of other components.

The Stoics present the fullest defence of the claim that virtue is identical to happiness. They argue that we must accept this claim if we properly understand the dominance of virtue in happiness. However surprising their position may seem at first, the Stoics defend it within the context of a comprehensive theory of virtue, goods, and rational action. Their theory as a whole is intended to vindicate their paradoxical claims about virtue. Before we accept or reject individual claims, we should examine them in the context of the whole theory. Much of this chapter, then, will focus on the Stoics; but we must see what other moralists say, and why the Stoics find other accounts of virtue and happiness unsatisfactory.

The Stoics claim to defend Socrates' position. Socrates believes that the just life ('living finely and living justly') is the same as the happy life that benefits the agent himself ('living well': **454**). Nothing could induce him to violate the demands of justice, regardless of the consequences (**453**). He does not expect to suffer severe harms for the sake of acting justly. For he claims that the virtuous person can suffer no harm at all; however badly everything else may seem to go, he never suffers any loss of happiness. If virtue is sufficient for happiness, nothing that happens to just people harms them, if they remain just. A genuine harm would have to deprive them of happiness; but since imprisonment or death cannot make Socrates less virtuous, it cannot deprive him of happiness (**315**).

Socrates' claims about virtue and happiness help to explain why virtue guarantees happiness (cf. **317**). Since virtue alone ensures the correct use of other supposed goods, virtue itself is the only real good. Even if we have health, wealth, security, and the other supposed goods besides virtue, we will use them to harm ourselves, if we are vicious and use them for vicious purposes. Socrates believes both that (i) only the virtuous person uses these supposed goods correctly, so that they benefit her, and that (ii) her correct use of them always results in her happiness. Socrates infers that (iii) virtue guarantees happiness, and the other supposed goods are neither necessary nor sufficient for happiness; hence (iv) virtue is the only realy good. His reasons for believing (ii) and (iii) need careful examination.

493 PLATO, *Gorgias* 470E[1] POLUS: It's clear, Socrates, that you'll say you don't even know that the Great King[2] is happy. SOCRATES: Yes, and I'll be right. For I don't know how far he has advanced in education and justice.—What? Is the whole of happiness in that?—Yes, so I say, Polus. For I say that the fine and good man and woman are happy, and the unjust and bad are wretched.

494 PLATO, *Gorgias* 504E–505B SOCRATES: What's the benefit, Callicles, of giving lots of the most pleasant food or drink, or anything else, to a sick body in wretched condition, since they won't help it one bit more than the opposite treatment would, and indeed, if considered rightly, will help even less? Is that so? CALLICLES: Let it be so.—Yes; for I suppose it's no benefit to someone to live with bodily wretchedness; in that condition you must live wretchedly too. Isn't that so?—Yes. ... —And isn't the same true, my excellent man, for the soul? As long as it's corrupt, by being senseless, intemperate, unjust, and impious, we must restrain it from its appetites, and not allow it to do anything except what will make it better. Do you say so, or not?—I do.—For, I take it, that treatment is better for the soul itself.—Quite.—And by restraining it from satisfying its appetites, don't we temper it?—Yes.—Then being tempered is better for the soul than intemperance, which you just now thought was better.

495 PLATO, *Gorgias* 507A–E SOCRATES:[3] The temperate person would do what is appropriate towards both gods and human beings. For surely he wouldn't be acting temperately if he did what is inappropriate?—This must be so.—Now, by doing what is appropriate towards human beings he would do what is just, and by doing it towards gods, he would do what is pious. And someone who does what is just and pious must be just and pious.—That's true.—Moreover, he must be brave too. For a temperate person does not avoid or pursue anything inappropriate; he will avoid or pursue the things and people, pleasures and pains, he ought to, and will resist and endure where he ought to. And so, Callicles, since the temperate person is just and brave and pious, as we described him, he definitely must be a completely good man; and the good man must do whatever he does well and finely; and the man who does well must be blessed and happy, and the bad man who does badly must be wretched. ... [507E] Such a person could not be befriended by another human being or by a god; for he cannot be a partner, and where there is no partnership, there is no friendship.[4]

---

[1] This follows **187**.

[2] The king of Persia.

[3] Callicles refuses for a while to answer Socrates' questions, and so Socrates both asks the questions and answers on Callicles' behalf.

[4] Partnership (or 'association', *koinônia*); **557**. Friendship; **472–4**.

496 PLATO, *Gorgias* 508 A–E   Either we must refute this argument to show that the happy are made happy by the possession of justice and temperance, and the miserable are made miserable by the possession of vice, or, if this is true, we must consider what the consequences will be. They will be all those I drew before, Callicles, when you asked me whether I really meant them: that anyone ought to accuse himself and his son and his friend if he does any injustice, and that for this purpose he should use his rhetoric. A further consequence is the point that you thought Polus conceded out of shame: that doing injustice is as much worse than suffering injustice as it is more shameful. And still a further consequence is the point that Polus thought Gorgias admitted out of shame: that anyone who is to practise rhetoric correctly must indeed be just and know justice. And now, since this is so, let's proceed to consider whether you are right to reproach me for my inability to help myself or any of my friends or kinsmen, or to save them from the greatest dangers, and for being, like those deprived of civil rights, at the mercy of anyone who feels like boxing my ears (as you so vigorously expressed it), or confiscating my goods or banishing me, or even doing his worst and killing me; in your view, this is the most shameful possible condition to be in. My answer to you has been often repeated already, but it bears repeating once more. I tell you, Callicles, that to be boxed on the ears unjustly, or to have my purse or my body cut open, is not the most shameful thing. No: striking and killing me and mine unjustly is far more shameful and far worse ... for the one who does injustice than for me who suffer injustice.[5]

497 PLATO, *Euthydemus* 281 DE   As for all those things that we said at first were good,[6] the argument does not aim to show that they are, themselves in themselves, good by nature, but rather, it would seem, the truth is this. If ignorance leads them, they are greater evils than their opposites, inasmuch as they are more able to serve the leader which is evil; if intelligence and wisdom lead them, they are greater goods; but, themselves in themselves, neither lot are worth anything at all. ... Then what follows from what has been said? That none of the other things is either good or bad, but of these two wisdom is good and ignorance is bad.

Happiness, virtue, and external goods

498   In the main argument of the *Republic* (books ii–ix) Plato argues only for the claim that virtue is always dominant in happiness. He neither asserts nor defends the stronger claim that virtue alone is sufficient for happiness (**470–1**). He maintains that the first claim does not justify the second.

---

[5] Continued in **178**.
[6] See **383**.

Aristotle argues that virtue is insufficient for happiness, because the 'external' goods not secured by virtue matter for our welfare (**403**). Even if the value of virtue outweighs the value of any combination of other goods, the loss of these other goods still harms us. Hence, just people suffer genuine loss if they are poor, ill, tortured, and so on, even if their justice makes it worthwhile to pay this price.

The life of virtue, therefore, lacks some essential features of happiness, and so is 'incomplete'. The virtuous person who lacks other goods, because he is poor, ill, tortured, and so on, lacks some things that are obviously worth having. This life cannot be happiness, because it is not a life that 'needs nothing added'.

The worthwhile things that can be added to virtue are goods that are not in our control, but subject to good and bad fortune; Aristotle sometimes calls them 'external goods'. They are the goods that are the subject-matter of tragedy (**400–2**), and the loss of them is an appropriate object of pity and fear. Happiness is unstable to the extent that it is subject to fortune. Only one component of it—virtue—is stable.

One might argue that some of Aristotle's claims about virtue count against this conclusion. He claims that virtuous people will never become unhappy (or 'miserable'), because they will never do anything hateful and base. They seem to express his own view that the good is 'our own and difficult to take from us' (**403**). Virtue meets this condition. Hence, we seem to have an argument, on Aristotelian grounds, for taking virtue to constitute happiness all by itself. Aristotle himself does not endorse any such argument, but it helps to show why a Socratic or a Stoic position might appear more plausible than Aristotle's own position.

....

499 ARISTOTLE, *Nicomachean Ethics* 1153[b]14–25[7]   All think the happy life is pleasant and they weave pleasure into happiness—quite reasonably, since no activity is complete if it is impeded, and happiness is something complete. Hence the happy person needs to have goods of the body, external goods, and fortune added, so that he will not be impeded in these ways. Some people actually maintain, on the contrary, that a person is happy when he is tortured on the wheel, or falls into terrible misfortunes, provided he is good. Whether they mean to or not, these people are talking nonsense. And because happiness needs fortune added, some people think good fortune is the same as happiness. But it is not. For when it is excessive, it actually impedes happiness; and then, presumably, it is no longer rightly called *good* fortune, since the limit is defined with reference to happiness.

500 ARISTOTLE, *Nicomachean Ethics* 1100[b]22–35[8]   Many events, however, are subject to fortune, and some are smaller, some greater. Hence, while small

---

[7] With this passage cf. **403**, **511**.
[8] This passage follows **409**.

strokes of good or ill fortune clearly will not influence the good person's life, many great strokes of good fortune will make it more blessed, since in themselves they naturally add adornment to it, and the way he uses them proves to be fine and excellent. Conversely, if they are great misfortunes, they oppress and spoil his blessedness, since they bring sorrows with them and impede many activities. And yet, even in these conditions the fine shines through, whenever someone bears many severe misfortunes with good temper, not because he feels no distress, but because he is noble and magnanimous. And if indeed activities control life, as we said, no blessed person could ever become miserable,[9] since he will never do hateful and base actions.

Epicurus: virtue and self-sufficiency

501 Epicurus agrees with Aristotle's suggestion that happiness must be, as far as possible, stable and in our control, independent of external circumstances. Such a conception of happiness appears in the *Gorgias* (**392**). Socrates suggests that the person who lacks (or 'needs') nothing is happy; he satisfies his desires because he has adapted them to the available resources. Callicles disagrees, claiming that happiness requires not simply complete satisfaction of desires, but the maximum level of satisfaction, requiring expanded desires.

Epicurus uses Socrates' suggestion (whether or not he derives it directly from the *Gorgias*) to explain how virtue is sufficient for happiness. To have the Epicurean virtues is to know what we need to keep ourselves free of pain and anxiety. If we recall past pleasures and avoid any disruptions and anxieties, we remain free of anxiety, and hence we remain happy, whatever our external conditions may be. Epicurus even claims that he remains happy while he suffers severe pains, since they do not disturb his conviction that he has made his life as stable as possible. Since he remembers having lived a secure life free from anxiety, that memory compensates for present pains, and his life remains pleasant rather than painful as a whole.

This argument, then, supports Socrates' claim that the good person cannot be harmed at all. For the virtuous person happiness is stable and assured, if Epicurus is right about the nature of happiness. If, however, our welfare consists partly in our acting a certain way, not merely in feeling a certain way irrespective of what we are doing, Epicurus has not proved that virtue is sufficient for happiness.

....

502 EPICURUS = DIOGENES LAERTIUS X. 130–1[10]   Again, we count self-sufficiency as a great good, not so that we will have only a few things at our disposal,

---

[9] Misery; cf. **435**.
[10] Continued from **415**.

whatever happens, but so that, if we do not possess many, we will find the few sufficient, since we are genuinely persuaded that the people who have the pleasantest enjoyment of luxury are those who need it least, and that everything natural is easy to obtain, whereas what is difficult to obtain is empty. And so plain food brings us pleasure equal to a luxurious diet, once all the pain resulting from need is removed; bread and water produce the highest pleasure when one who needs them takes them. ... And so, when we say pleasure is the end, we do not mean the pleasures of profligates and those that consist in gratification, as is supposed by some who are ignorant, or disagree with us, or take us up wrongly.[11] We mean being without pain in the body and without disturbance in the mind.

503 EPICURUS = DIOGENES LAERTIUS X. 22[12]   I am writing this to you while I pass a blessedly happy day that is also the last day of my life. I am pressed hard by urinary blockages and dysenteric discomforts, unsurpassable in their intensity. But in opposition to all these things stands my soul's enjoyment in recollecting our past discussions.

The Stoics: happiness and nature

504   The Stoics reject Aristotle's view that external goods are necessary for happiness. They recognize, however, that a defence of the sufficiency of virtue for happiness must take account of the apparent plausibility of Aristotle's objections; a convincing argument to show that virtue is sufficient for happiness must also explain why it seems reasonable to value external goods.

The Stoics take the good life for a human being to be a life according to nature, and they argue that the virtuous person lives in accordance with nature. In setting out from nature, they agree with Aristotle, who defends his conception of happiness by appeal to the human function (**407–8**). They also agree with Epicurus in starting from nature, but they reject Epicurus' conclusions. Their position is closer to Aristotle's, though they depart from him on a crucial issue.

According to Epicurus, nature tells us that the good is to be identified with pleasure; he appeals to the behaviour of animals and infants. The Stoics reply that we ought to consider not only the earliest stages of our lives, but also the natural processes of growth and development. Epicurus himself believes that we see the advantages of static pleasures as we grow up and reflect on what we need (**414**). The Stoics claim that this same reflective examination shows us that pleasure is not all we care about.

In the Stoic view, we do not simply value the satisfaction of our impulses; we

---

[11] Or 'dishonestly'.

[12] A fragment of a letter of Epicurus to Idomeneus, written on the last day of his life.

also value the exercise of rational choice in satisfying them. Rational agents organize and arrange the satisfaction of their desires by reason. When they see that the satisfaction of some desires conflicts with the satisfaction of others, practical reason modifies their desires. Once we are used to this instrumental use of reason, we also come to value its exercise for its own sake. Rational choice is not merely instrumentally valuable, as a means to things that we already want. If we were deprived of rational choice, but provided with everything else we want, we would not be better off as a result.

....

505 DIOGENES LAERTIUS vii. 85–6 The Stoics say that an animal's first impulse is to preserve itself, because nature made it congenial to itself from the beginning, as Chrysippus says in Book One of *On Ends*. He says that for every animal the first congenial thing is its own constitution and the consciousness of this. For it is not reasonable to expect that nature would make an animal alienated from itself, or that, having made the animal, nature would make it neither congenial to nor alienated from itself. Therefore, the remaining possibility is to say that nature, having constituted the animal, made it congenial to itself. For in this way it repels harmful things, and allows entry to congenial things. ... [86] And nature ... did not work differently in the case of plants and animals; for it governs the life of plants too, without impulse or perception, and even in us some processes are plant-like. In the case of animals, impulse is added, which they use in the pursuit of congenial things; and so for them it is natural to be governed by what accords with impulse. Rational animals have been given reason as a more complete governor, so that living correctly in accord with reason turns out to be natural for them; for reason supervenes as a craftsman of impulse.

506 CICERO, *Ends* iii. 16–20 The Stoics confirm this doctrine of congeniality by the fact that, before pleasure or pain affects them, infants seek beneficial things and reject contrary things, and this would not happen unless they loved their own constitution and feared death. They could not, however, desire anything unless they were aware of themselves, and thereby loved themselves. From this one ought to understand that the starting-point is derived from self-love. ... [20] The Stoics say that what has value ... is whatever either itself accords with nature or produces what accords with nature, so that it is worthy of selection because it has some weight that deserves to be valued. ... The starting-points, then, are constituted so that things that accord with nature are to be taken for their own sake, and things contrary to nature are, correspondingly, to be rejected. Hence, an animal's first appropriate action[13] ... is to preserve itself in its natural constitution; and then to retain things that accord with nature and to reject things contrary to nature. After this selection

[13] *officium*, also translated 'duty'.

and rejection is discovered, appropriate selection follows; next, constant and appropriate selection; and finally stable selection[14] in agreement with nature. Here for the first time what can truly be called good begins to be present, and we begin to understand it.

507 CICERO, *Ends* iii. 23   [THE STOICS:] It often happens that if someone is introduced to another person, he comes to think more of him than of the one who introduced them. Similarly, then, it is not at all surprising that we are first introduced to wisdom by the natural starting-points, but later we care more about wisdom itself than about the things that brought us to wisdom.

The Stoics: only the fine is good

508 The Stoic argument about the importance of practical reason does not show that happiness is to be identified with acting in accordance with practical reason. Even if the virtues are the various forms of practical reason, virtuous action need not be the whole of happiness.

The Stoics argue that we ought to identify our good with something that is stable and in our control. Aristotle himself recognizes this criterion for happiness; but—from the Stoic point of view—his own conception of happiness does not meet his criterion, since he concludes that happiness is unstable and exposed to fortune. If happiness is to be stable and in our control, we must identify it with the life of virtuous action. Virtuous agents take control of their lives, and guide them by their rational choice; they seek to take the appropriate attitude to their lives, and to express the right sort of character in their actions. It is within their power as rational agents to fulfil this aim, since they can fulfil it no matter what external disasters may overtake them.

This conception of happiness supports Socrates' claim that the good person cannot suffer any harm. The Stoics claim that a person's good consists in rational activity; we achieve this good by bringing our lives under rational control. Since happiness consists in fine and virtuous activity, chosen for its own sake, the Stoics claim that 'only the fine is good'.[15]

509 CICERO, *Stoic Paradoxes* 4   These Stoic views are amazing, and contrary to the opinions of everyone—so that, indeed, the Stoics themselves call them *paradoxa*. And so I wanted to try to see whether they could be brought into the light. ... And I wrote all the more readily in so far as these views that they call *paradoxa* seem to me to be Socratic to the highest degree and by a long way the truest.

[14] Stability; **107**, **443**.
[15] Fine; **449**.

510 CICERO, *Ends* iii. 26–8   Since the goal is to live consistently, and in agreement with nature, it follows necessarily that all sages always live happy, perfect, and fortunate lives, that they are impeded by nothing, prevented by nothing, and in need of nothing. The principle that includes not only the doctrine I am speaking of, but also our life and fortune, is the principle of judging that only what is fine is good. ... The Stoics' arguments have this form: everything good is praiseworthy; but everything praiseworthy is fine; therefore, what is good is fine. ... People usually object to the first of the two premises, on the ground that not everything good is praiseworthy—they concede that what is praiseworthy is fine. But it is quite absurd to claim that something is good but not to be desired, or to be desired but not pleasing, or pleasing but not also to be loved, and so also to be approved of, and thereby also praiseworthy; but what is praiseworthy is fine. In this way it turns out that what is good is also fine.

511 CICERO, *Ends* iii. 42–4   [THE STOICS:] Again, can anything be more certain than that, on the view of those who count pain as bad, the sage cannot be happy when he is being tortured on the rack?[16] By contrast, the view of those who do not count pain as bad firmly proves that the sage retains his happy life in any torments. ... [44] We judge health worthy of a certain value, but we do not count it as a good. Moreover, we take no value to be so great that it outranks virtue. This is not the view of the Peripatetics; they must say that if an action is both fine and without pain, it is more to be desired than the same action with pain.

512 DIOGENES LAERTIUS vii. 127   And the Stoics say that virtue is choiceworthy because of itself. For we are ashamed at what we do badly,[17] as if knowing that only the fine is good.

513 CICERO, *Tusculan Disputations*, v. 80–5   [THE STOICS:] ... The virtues cannot hold together without a happy life, nor a happy life without the virtues. And so they will not allow it to turn back; they will carry it along with them to whatever pain and torment they may be led to. For it is proper to the sage to do nothing he can regret, nothing against his will, to do everything nobly, consistently, soberly, finely, not to anticipate anything as if it were certain to come, not to be astonished at something in such a way that he thinks something unexpected and strange has happened, to refer everything to his own judgement, to stick to his own decisions. And I certainly cannot think what can be happier than this. For the Stoics indeed the conclusion is easy. For they regard the ultimate good as agreeing with nature and living in accord with nature, since this not only belongs to the sage's duty, but also is in his

---

[16] Happiness on the rack; **403**, **499**.
[17] Shame; **431**.

power. And so it follows necessarily that if someone has the highest good in his power, he also has happy life in his power; thus the life of the sage is always happy. ... [85] And besides the Stoics, the Peripatetics' position is clarified. Apart from Theophrastus[18] and any who share his craven fear and abhorrence of pain, the rest of them, at any rate, are allowed to do as they usually do, to exalt the dignity and worthiness of virtue. And when they have raised virtue to the heavens, ... it is easy to trample all else under foot and despise it in comparison with virtue. For if they say that praise must be sought even at the cost of pain, they are not allowed to say that those who attain that praise are not happy ...

514 EPICTETUS, *Discourses* i. 22.1–10 Preconceptions are common to all human beings, and one preconception does not conflict with another. For which of us does not assume that the good is beneficial and choiceworthy, and that we must seek and pursue it in every circumstance? Which of us does not assume that the just is fine and fitting? Then what does the conflict arise from? It arises in the application of preconceptions to particular beings, when one person says 'He has done finely, he is brave', but another says 'Not at all; he's crazy'. Hence arises the conflict of human beings with one another, This is the conflict of Jews, Syrians, Egyptians and Romans, not about whether the holy is always to be honoured above all else and pursued in everything, but about whether this eating of pork is holy or unholy ... [9] What then is it to be educated? It is to learn to apply the natural preconceptions to the particular beings conformably to nature. Further it is to discern that some things that exist are up to us, some not up to us. Up to us are decision,[19] and all actions on decision. Not up to us are the body, the parts of the body, possessions, parents, brothers, children, native land—in short, all our associates.[20]

515 EPICTETUS, *Discourses* iii. 8. 1 As we exercise against sophistical questions, so we should exercise ourselves daily against appearances; for they also propose questions to us. 'So-and-so's son is dead.' Answer: Not a matter for decision; not evil. 'His father left So-and-so without an inheritance. What do you think?' Not a matter for decision; not evil. 'Caesar condemned him.' Not a matter for decision; not evil. 'He was in pain at this.' A matter for decision; evil. 'He has endured it nobly.' A matter for decision; good. And if we habituate ourselves this way, we will progress. For we will never assent to anything except what we are aware of by an apprehending appearance.[21] 'His son is dead. What happened?' His son is dead. 'Nothing else?' Not a thing. 'His ship

---

[18] For some of Theophrastus' other doubts about Aristotelian views see **247**.

[19] Or 'rational choice', *prohairesis*. Cf. **443**.

[20] *koinônoi*. See **472**, **557**.

[21] Apprehending appearance; **291–6**.

was lost. What happened?' His ship was lost. 'He was imprisoned. What happened?' He was imprisoned. That he has fared badly each person adds for himself.

Objections to the Stoic account of happiness

516 If virtue is sufficient for happiness, everything else we regard as good must be, as the Stoics put it 'indifferent', and so neither good nor bad, because such things do not affect happiness. Health turns out to be no better than sickness, and wealth no better than poverty, for ourselves or for other people.

The Stoics might, therefore, appear to be committed, whether they intend it or not, to all these claims:

(1) No external goods and evils are either good or bad for us (since they do not affect our happiness).

(2) If something is neither good nor bad for me, there is no reason for me to prefer its presence over its absence.

(3) Hence there is no reason for me to prefer health (etc.) over sickness (etc.) either for myself or for anyone else.

This conclusion seems absurd, however, because it suggests that the Stoics cannot give any reasonable advice about how we should live our own lives, or about what we should do for other people. What is the point of trying to protect people from physical violence, say, if violence does them no harm? The Stoics seem to have no basis for sharing our ordinary ethical concerns. They cannot agree with Aristotle's claim that the loss of external goods is an appropriate object of pity and fear (**400, 402**); indeed, they seem to have no place for tragedy, pity, and fear, if they recognize no goods and evils other than virtue and vice. They seem to have no basis for the sorts of concern and sympathy with other people that we express in the emotions that seem appropriate to other people's misfortunes.

The Stoics seem to embrace the consequence that their critics regard as absurd. They claim that wise and virtuous people have achieved freedom from emotion (*apatheia*). In their view, emotions (or passions; *pathê*) result from a false opinion about what is good and evil. Since virtuous people regard ordinary misfortunes as indifferents, they have no emotions about them. The Stoics seem to have no motive for sharing ordinary human aims, or for sharing ordinary reactions to success and failure in these aims. But in that case, they do not seem to practise the virtues. For how can we attribute justice or bravery to someone who does not see anything good about the welfare (as we normally conceive it) of other people?

517 CICERO, *For Murena* 61²²   For there was a man of outstanding intellect, Zeno, the followers of whose doctrines are called Stoics. His opinions and precepts are of the following sort. The sage is never moved by favour; he never forgives anyone's offence; no one except a foolish and frivolous person is merciful; a real man is never moved or mollified by pleas; only sages are handsome, however disfigured; only they are rich, however sunk in beggary; only they are kings, however sunk in slavery. We, on the other hand, who are not sages are, in their view, fugitives, exiles, enemies, indeed madmen. All errors are equal; every offence is a shocking crime, and needlessly suffocating a cock is no lighter an offence than suffocating one's father. The sage has no opinions, regrets nothing, makes a mistake in nothing, never changes his mind.

518 EPICTETUS, *Discourses* iii. 24. 1–4   What is contrary to nature for another must not become bad for you. For you are not of a nature to be humiliated with others, or to suffer misfortune with them, but to share good fortune with them. For God made all human beings to be happy, to be serene. Towards this he gave starting-points, making some things a person's own, and some alien to him. Things that can be hindered, or taken away, or compelled are not his own, but the unhindered things are his own. God gave us the nature of good and bad as our own, as was fitting for him who cares for us and watches over us like a father. 'But I have left So-and-so, and he is grieved.' Why then did he think that alien things were his own? When he saw you and was pleased, did he not reflect that you are a mortal and likely to go away? So he pays the penalty for his own folly.

519 EPICTETUS, *Discourses*, iv. 1. 68–71   Then have you nothing in your own power, that is up to you alone, or have you something of this kind? 'I don't know.' Look at it this way, then, and examine it. Can anyone make you assent to something false? 'No one.' Then in the area of assent you are unhindered and unrestrained? 'Granted.' Now then, can anyone compel you to have an impulse to do what you do not want? 'Yes; for when someone threatens me with death or prison, he compels me to have an impulse.' Then if you despise death and prison, do you still listen to him? 'No.' And is it your action, or not yours, to despise death? 'Mine.' Then is it also your action to have an impulse or not? 'Granted, it is mine.'²³

520 CICERO, *Ends* iv. 26   Given that you Stoics start from the same principles as the Peripatetics, how on earth do you manage to conclude that the highest good is living finely, since that is the same as living by virtue, or living

---

²² Cato, a well-known Stoic, has given evidence in court against Lucius Murena. Cicero, Murena's defence counsel, ridicules Cato's Stoicism.

²³ On happiness as 'our own' cf. **403**.

in agreement with nature? And how, and at what point, did you suddenly abandon the body and all those things that accord with nature, but are not in our power, and finally abandon appropriate action itself? I ask, then, how is it that such strong recommendations derived from nature have been suddenly deserted by wisdom?

521 ALEXANDER, *Commentary on the Topics* 211. 9–14 = SVF iii. 62   Thus it would be shown that each of the things called preferred indifferents by the later philosophers[24] is choiceworthy and good. For when each of them is added to virtue it makes the whole more choiceworthy for the virtuous person. For a life in accord with virtue is more choiceworthy if it is combined with health and affluence and good reputation; for choiceworthy things and things to be avoided are judged by the choice and avoidance of the virtuous person.

522 ALEXANDER, *Appendix on the Soul* 163. 14–19   For nature which has given us the soul has also given us the body, and has conciliated[25] us to the completions and the sorts of provisions needful for each of them. And so someone deprived of the completion according to nature of either body or soul would not live in accord with nature either—for what is in accord with nature is understood as what is according to the wish of nature; and if he does not live this way, he does not live happily either.

The Stoics on indifferents

523 According to the Stoics, such criticism rests on misunderstanding. They do not simply reassert the Socratic position rejected by Aristotle. They see that Aristotle's objections to Socrates (**403, 499**) deserve an answer from anyone who believes that virtue is sufficient for happiness.

The key to the Stoic position is the status of preferred and non-preferred indifferents. 'Indifferent' does not mean 'indifferent from every point of view', but simply 'indifferent from the point of view of happiness' (**525**). Some indifferents are preferred and others non-preferred; the preferred ones have value and the non-preferred have disvalue. According to the Stoics, we have good reason to pursue preferred indifferents, and to avoid non-preferred indifferents, to the extent permitted by virtue. Virtuous people select health over sickness, security over danger, and so on, both for themselves and for other people.

The Stoics argue that some indifferents are to be preferred over others because they are more in accordance with nature. Human nature and the proper development of human capacities require these things. If the virtuous person—the Stoics'

---

[24] i.e. the Stoics. Alexander speaks as a follower of Aristotle.

[25] *oikeioun*, cognate with *oikeion*, usually translated 'congenial'.

'sage'—suffers some painful illness, or is impoverished or tortured, he agrees that he has lost something that he has reason to prefer. But he sees that he has lost none of his happiness, and therefore has not been harmed in any way, because he is still virtuous.

This position seeks to reconcile reasonable claims about happiness that might easily appear to conflict:

(1) Happiness is stable and in our control.

(2) Happiness consists in the actions that fit human nature.

(3) It is reasonable to aim at success in the actions that fit human nature.

(4) Success in such actions depends on fortune, and is not in our control.

From Aristotle's point of view, (3) and (4) imply that happiness cannot consist in virtuous action alone. Hence he cannot fully accept (1), since he allows unstable external goods to be components of happiness. The Stoics argue that, once we distinguish genuine goods from preferred indifferents, we can accept (3) and (4), which concern preferred indifferents, while still accepting (1) and (2), which concern goods.

524 CICERO, *Ends* iii. 50–3   Next[26] follows an exposition of the difference between things; for if we said there is no difference, all of life would be thrown into confusion, as it is by Ariston, and no function or task could be found for wisdom, since there would be no distinction at all between things bearing on the conduct of life, and we would not be required to form any preference among them. And so, after it is settled conclusively that only what is fine is good, and that only what is shameful is bad, the Stoics affirm that among those things that do not affect happiness or misery, there is none the less a difference, so that some are to be valued, others the contrary, and others neither … [53] For in fact it was inevitable that intermediate things should include some that either accord with nature or the reverse, and, hence, that these should include some sufficiently valuable things, and, therefore, that some of these should be preferred.

525 DIOGENES LAERTIUS vii. 104–5   Indifferent things are spoken of in two ways. Indifferents of the first kind are those things that do not cooperate towards happiness or unhappiness; this is true of wealth, reputation, health, strength, and similar things. For it is possible to be happy even without these things; good or bad use of them belongs to happiness or unhappiness. Indifferents of the second kind are things that do not move us to impulse or avoidance; this is true of having an odd or even number of hairs on one's head, or extending or retracting one's finger. Indifferents of the first kind are

---

[26] In the account of Stoic doctrine.

not indifferent in the second way; for they move us to impulse and avoidance. This is why some of them are selected and some are deselected, while indifferents of the second kind leave one equally balanced between choosing and avoiding them. Among indifferents ... some are preferred and some dispreferred. The preferred ones are those that have value, and the dispreferred are those that have disvalue. One sort of value is a contribution to the life in agreement, which applies to every good. Another sort is a certain intermediate potential or usefulness, which contributes to the life in accord with nature; in other words, this is the value that life and health supply towards the life in accord with nature.

The Stoics on passions

526 The Stoics' division between goods and indifferents helps to explain their surprising doctrine that Stoic sages are free of passions. Following Socrates, the Stoics identify each of the virtues with a kind of knowledge (cf. **434**); they do not mention any condition of the non-rational part of the soul, because they reject the Platonic and Aristotelian division (cf. **437**). They recognize passions (anger, fear, shame, and so on), but treat them as states of the rational part, not of the spirited or appetitive parts, since they deny the existence of these non-rational parts in human souls.

The Stoics reject the suggestion that passions are irresistible, so that we are not responsible for acting on them. The Platonic and Aristotelian view of passions might appear to support this suggestion.[27] If it is simply the strength of our non-rational desire that determines whether we act continently or incontinently, it does not seem to depend on our rational choice, and therefore it does not seem to be in our control. The Stoics claim, on the contrary, that passions are really mistaken judgements that preferred or non-preferred indifferents are good or evil. Like all judgements, they involve both an appearance and an assent to the appearance; the assent is up to us and voluntary, and we are responsible for it.[28]

Since the Stoics deny that there are any non-rational desires of the sort that Plato and Aristotle recognize, they must explain the choices and actions that seemed to result from non-rational desires. Not every mistaken assent that treats indifferents as goods or evils is a passion; passions are immediate and unreflective assents to appearances of good and evil. I am moved by fear or anger when I thoughtlessly assent to the appearance that imprisonment or torture are really bad, or that it is really good to take revenge for an insult.

The Stoics maintain that their view of passions offers the best way to understand two claims about the passions that may seem to conflict. Plato and Aristotle

---

[27] This is not necessarily a correct interpretation of the Platonic or Aristotelian view.
[28] Assent: **291–6**, **378–80**.

are right, in their view, to claim that (i) acting on passion is in some way opposed to acting on reason, but their explanation fails to show how (ii) we are responsible for acting on passions. The Stoic view explains both features of the passions.

The virtuous person, therefore, according to the Stoics, has no passions. They reject the Aristotelian view that virtue involves well-trained passions (**444**), since they see no place for false estimates of indifferents in a virtuous person. Someone who believes that preferred or non-preferred indifferents are good or evil is not a virtuous person.

Freedom from passion, however, does not imply that the sage is unconcerned about the indifferents that move other people to passions. Virtuous people share some appearances with other people. If they see some immediate threat to their safety, they have a vivid appearance of impending harm. They do not assent to this appearance; but they assent to the appearance of some impending non-preferred indifferent, and their assent normally prompts an effort to avoid the impending threat. The sage's belief that recognized non-moral goods and evils are indifferent does not make her indifferent to them.

....

527 PLUTARCH, *Moral Virtue* 441c–447a   All the Stoics agree that virtue is some condition and power of the leading part of the soul, coming into being because of reason—or rather, that it is itself consistent, secure and unvaried reason. And they believe that the passionate and non-rational part is not distinguished from the rational part by any difference in nature. On the contrary, one and the same part of the soul, the one they call thought and the leading part, is thoroughly changed and altered in passions, and in the changes that come about because of a state or condition, and becomes virtue or vice. It has nothing non-rational in itself, but is called non-rational when it is carried away to something absurd contrary to choosing reason by something excessive in impulse which has become strong and won control. For indeed a passion, in their view, is a corrupt, intemperate reason that has acquired violence and strength from some base and faulty judgement ... [446f] The Stoics say that passion is not something other than reason, nor is there dispute and conflict between the two; rather the single reason turns in both directions, escaping our notice by the suddenness and speed of the change. We do not notice that it is the same part of the soul by which it has appetites and repents, is angry and afraid, is carried away by pleasure towards something shameful, and takes hold of itself again while it is being carried away. For in fact appetites, anger, fear and all such things are corrupt beliefs and judgements, not coming to be in some one part of the soul, but inclinations, concessions, assents, and impulses of the whole leading part, and in general activities liable to change in a short time ...

528 SENECA, *Letters* 116. 1   It has often been asked whether it is better to have moderate passions or no passions. We Stoics expel them, whereas the

Peripatetics temper them. I do not see how any moderate condition of a disease could be healthy or useful. Don't be afraid; I am not depriving you of anything that you do not want to be denied to you.

529 AULUS GELLIUS, *Attic Nights* xix. 1. 17–18 = Epictetus, fr. 9 <The sage turns pale> ... not because any belief in any evil has been accepted, but because of some rapid and unpremeditated movements that outrun the function of mind and reason. Soon, however, that sage does not endorse—that is to say, does not assent to, and does not add his belief to—such appearances, namely these frightening impressions, but he rejects and repudiates them, and nothing in these appearances seems to him to be something to be feared. ... The fool supposes things to be really as harsh and severe as they appeared to him to be when his mind was first struck, and once he has received them, he also endorses them with his assent and adds his belief to them, as though they were rightly to be feared. ... The sage, however, while he is changed in complexion and facial expression for a short time and to a limited degree, does not assent, but at once holds on to the strength of his opinion.

530 EPICTETUS, *Manual* 5 Human beings are disturbed not by things themselves, but by their judgements about things. For instance, death is nothing to be afraid of; if it were, it would have appeared so to Socrates.[29] The judgement that death is something to be afraid of—this is what we ought to be afraid of. And so, whenever we are impeded, or disturbed, or distressed, let us not blame anyone but ourselves—that is to say, our own judgements.

[29] Socrates on death; **317**.

XIV: Political Theory

Disputes over constitutions

531 Greek political thinking begins in the development of Greek political life, and especially in the struggles that resulted in the establishment of different forms of government in different Greek cities.

The Greeks regarded monarchy as the earliest form of government; in Homer both Greek and non-Greek communities are ruled by kings. In Athens the title of 'king' survived in later times as the title of a religious official; in Sparta, the hereditary kings retained an important role as military leaders. The Homeric poems suggest that the kings took advice from other leading families in their community. In the *Iliad*, the leaders of the Greek army at Troy hold deliberative councils, apparently to advise the supreme commander, Agamemnon;[1] they do not seem to make decisions that bind him. The *Odyssey* describes meetings of the assembly of leaders in Ithaca; its procedure is informal, and its role seems to be the offering of advice to the dominant chiefs.

In both the *Iliad* and the *Odyssey*, the common people seem to have no formal political role; though their opinions are mentioned, there is no specific procedure for allowing them to form or to express a collective opinion. But sometimes they are present at mass meetings called to hear the decisions of their rulers.

In different Greek states, the roles of the leading families and of the common people were gradually defined in different ways that resulted in different forms of government. The Spartan constitution established a division of powers between the two hereditary kings, the council of 'elders' of the leading families, and the common people. In Athens, the hereditary kings were replaced by a hereditary aristocracy (from *aristoi*, 'the best people') of the leading families. Later on some states, including Athens, fixed the ruling class by wealth; this was an oligarchy (from *oligoi*, 'the few'). In Athens and in some other Greek states, aristocracy and oligarchy were replaced by a system that gave control to the assembly of all citizens. This system was eventually called democracy (from *dêmos*, 'the people').

An early demand that made an important difference to political life was the demand for government by written laws that would determine the powers of different individual and collective bodies, bind judges in settling disputes and in setting penalties, and bind officials in exercising their powers. Solon's[2] code of laws in Athens (594 BC) divided powers between a council of richer citizens and

---

[1] Agamemnon's speech in **347** is part of one of these councils.
[2] Solon; **388**.

a general assembly of the common people, who also constituted the large jury-courts that heard civil, criminal, and constitutional cases. The later reforms of Cleisthenes (in 510–506 BC) strengthened the role of the popular assembly and courts.

In the fifth and fourth centuries the Athenian democracy gave leading roles to these bodies and officials:

(1) The sovereign Assembly of all the citizens (adult, male, free, and native-born).

(2) The Council had 500 members, 50 chosen by lot from each of the 10 tribes into which the citizen body was divided. The members from each tribe were appointed 'presidents' (*prutaneis*) for one-tenth of the year; they were a standing committee, preparing business for the Assembly and Council. One member each day was chosen (by lot) as 'foreman', who presided over any meeting of the Council or Assembly on his day of office.

(3) A board of nine archons (*archontes*, 'rulers') was chosen by lot for one year of office, to which they were not re-eligible.

(4) A board of ten generals (civil as well as military officials) was chosen by election for one year of office; each general was re-eligible.

(5) The jury-courts (often large, perhaps as many as 1,500 in some cases) were chosen by lot from the citizens.

These are the institutions presupposed in many of the passages quoted below.

Conflicts between advocates of these different systems were sometimes resolved by extra-constitutional means, often involving the rule of a single person not governing in accordance with the established laws. The Greeks called such an extra-constitutional ruler a 'tyrant' (*turannos*; **463**, **544**, **584**). A tyrant might be a partisan of the oligarchic or the democratic side, or he might be a political adventurer taking advantage of instability created by civil conflict.

Herodotus' history describes the wars and other encounters in the 490s and 480s between the Greek states and the Persian empire. A leading theme of the narrative is the character of different forms of government—the Persian hereditary monarchy, the Spartan mixed constitution, and the Athenian democracy—and the contrasting effects of each constitution on the people governed by it. Herodotus highlights this theme through an alleged debate among the leading Persian nobles, about the merits of different forms of government. The speakers present some of the standard arguments used by Greek partisans of different constitutions.

....

532 HERODOTUS iii. 80–1   At the meeting certain speeches were made. Some Greeks do not believe it, but none the less they were made. Otanes urged them to turn things over to the Persian people: 'I think', he said, 'that no one man of us should be sole ruler[3] any more; for that is neither pleasant nor good. ... How can monarchy be well ordered, given that it leaves someone free to do whatever he likes without any scrutiny? Even the best of men raised to this form of rule would be bound to change his habitual outlook. Insolence grows out of his present prosperity, and envy[4] grows in human beings from the beginning. These two bring with them every form of vice; puffed up by insolence and envy, he commits every sort of outrage. ... Contrast this with the rule of the people. First, it has the finest of all names to describe it: equal law.[5] Secondly, the people do none of the things that a monarch does. Office-holders are chosen by lot, and their rule is subject to scrutiny; and all questions are open to public debate.' ...

Megabyxus urged them to entrust things to an oligarchy: 'In so far as Otanes spoke in favour of abolishing tyranny, I agree with him. But he is wrong in asking us to transfer power to the masses. For there is nothing more ignorant or insolent than a useless mob. It would be intolerable to escape the insolence of a king, only to be the victims of the insolence of an undisciplined mass of people. A tyrant at least knows what he is doing, but the people cannot. Indeed how can they, when they have never been taught and do not know what is fine and appropriate? ... Let the people, then, govern Persia's enemies. Instead, let us ourselves choose a group of the best men in the country, and turn over power to them. We ourselves will be among them, and it is only natural for the best men to find the best policy.'

Political struggles

533 Much of Greek political history consists of the struggle between social classes favouring different forms of government. From the point of view of the rich, democracy represented the domination and expropriation of the rich by the poor. From the point of view of the poor, democracy ensured just protection of their interests against the rich. Each side was often willing to call in support from other cities to tip the balance in its favour. Hence the struggles between rich and poor were often prolonged, and sometimes violent.

Athens and Sparta were exceptions (during most of the fifth and fourth centuries) to the general instability of Greek constitutions. The Spartans retained their mixed constitution, with strong oligarchical elements that made them sympathetic towards oligarchies in other Greek cities. The Spartan citizens dominated a much larger class of serfs ('Helots'; unlike most slaves in other Greek states, they were a native Greek people), and the demands of internal security

---

[3] *monarchos.*
[4] *phthonos;* cf. **388**.
[5] *isonomia;* cf. **535–6**.

may help to explain the rigidity of Spartan political and cultural life in the fifth and fourth centuries. Sparta was unusual among Greek cities in its rigid and systematic education and training of children, supervised by the state, and for the prominent social (but not political) place given to women.

In contrast to Sparta, Athens was governed democratically. The Athenian system left an important role for richer citizens as political leaders (often serving as general, as Pericles did for many years), subject to the sovereign power of the popular Assembly. The excerpt from Thucydides' account of Pericles' funeral speech (at the funeral of the Athenians who had died in one year of the war against the Spartans) describes the Athenian democracy as a system that recognizes talent and merit as well as the rights of the majority. While we do not know how far the speech corresponds to anything Pericles actually said, it offers a strong defence of democracy (**534**).

The war between Athens and Sparta (usually called the Peloponnesian War; 431–404 BC) is the subject of Thucydides' history (left unfinished, continued in Xenophon's *History of Greece*). Thucydides often describes the effects of the war on Greek political life. Since the Athenians were recognized as supporters of democracy, and the Spartans as supporters of oligarchy, the rival factions in any city could often count on help from these two powerful cities at war against each other. In Syracuse, the democratic leader Athenagoras criticized those who wanted to bring in an oligarchy with Spartan support (**535**). In Corcyra, help from Athens encouraged the democratic partisans to carry out a violent purge of their political opponents (**536**).

Eventually, the tension between oligarchy and democracy disturbed the political consensus in Athens as well. When Athens lost the war with Sparta (in 404 BC), the democracy was overthrown by disaffected oligarchs, aided by a Spartan army. The rule of the oligarchs, led by the 'Thirty Tyrants', lasted for only two years (403–1) before the restoration of the democracy.

Leaders on both sides of this struggle between the Thirty and the democrats were associates of Socrates and Plato (**9, 139**). Socrates' trial took place in 399 BC, shortly after the restoration of the democracy. These years of instability may (if we believe a letter ascribed to Plato) have affected Plato's attitude to government and political life (**538**).

....

534 THUCYDIDES ii. 37 Our constitution is called a democracy because government belongs to the majority, not to the few. In relation to private disputes, everyone has equal standing before the law. As far as concerns someone's value, in areas where one person excels another, we assign honour, for the public good, not by rotation,[6] but on the basis of excellence.[7] Nor does poverty hold anyone back by the obscurity of his reputation, if he is capable

[6] i.e. by lot (interpretation uncertain).
[7] *aretê*, usually translated 'virtue'.

of doing some good to the city. And just as our political life is free and open, so is our private life in our daily relations with one another. We do not get angry with our neighbour because he does something to please himself, nor do we express displeasure in ways that involve no legal sanctions, but cause distress to others. We are relaxed in our private lives; but in public affairs we keep to the law because of fear, obeying those who are the current rulers, and obeying the laws themselves, especially those laws that are for the protection of victims of injustice, and those unwritten laws whose violation brings acknowledged shame.[8]

535 THUCYDIDES vi. 38. 3–39. 2[9] … Our city is rarely tranquil; it suffers continued factional conflict, and struggles more within itself than against external enemies; sometimes power has been unjustly seized by tyrants or ruling groups. … What is it that you young men really want? Is it to hold office immediately? But that is unlawful; the law was made because you are not yet capable of holding office, not to deny honour to people capable of holding office. Are you unwilling to accept equal law[10] with the many? But how could it be just if people who are equal were not taken to deserve equal treatment? Some people who will say that rule by the people[11] is neither intelligent nor fair,[12] and that the ones with the money are also the best rulers. But I say, first, that 'people'[13] here refers to the whole body of citizens, but 'oligarchy' refers to a part. Next, I say that the rich are best for looking after money, the intelligent are the best advisers, and the many are best at listening to advice, and reaching a judgement. In this all alike—both all together and as distinct classes—have equal shares in a democracy. An oligarchy, by contrast, gives the many their share of dangers, but it not only grabs more of the benefits for itself, but takes and keeps them all. And this is what the rich men and the young men among you are aiming at …

536 THUCYDIDES iii. 81–5 During the seven days that Eurymedon[14] stayed there with his sixty ships, the Corcyreans continued to massacre those of their own citizens whom they considered to be their enemies, on the charge of seeking to overthrow the democracy. Some were killed because of personal feuds, or else by their debtors because of money that was owed. There was death in every form. As usually happens in such situations, people went

---

[8] Shame; **431**.

[9] Athenagoras is speaking at Syracuse after the rumour (later confirmed) of an Athenian invasion had encouraged supporters of oligarchy to speak out against the democratic leaders, who were suspected of pro-Athenian sentiments.

[10] *isonomia;* cf. **532**.

[11] *dēmokratia.*

[12] *ison.* This might also be rendered 'equal'; see **559**.

[13] *dēmos.*

[14] An Athenian general intervening in the civil war in Corcyra.

to every extreme and beyond it. Fathers killed their sons; men were dragged from the temples or even killed in them; some were actually walled up in the temple of Dionysus and died there.

The civil conflict reached this degree of savagery, and it seemed all the worse because it was one of the first that had broken out.[15] Later, practically all the Greek world was disturbed with conflicts in every city; democratic leaders were trying to bring in the Athenians, and oligarchs were trying to bring in the Spartans. ... In the various cities these conflicts were the cause of many disasters of the sort that happen and will always happen as long as human nature is the same, though more and less severe, and varying according to different circumstances and situations. For in times of peace and prosperity, cities and individuals have a better outlook, because they are not compelled to make choices they do not want to make. But war, by depriving them of easy satisfaction of their daily wants, is a violent teacher; it matches most people's passions to their current circumstances. ...

By their justification they changed around the accustomed valuation of names in relation to actions. For unreasoning daring was counted bravery in support of one's party; provident delay was counted fair-seeming cowardice; being temperate was counted a pretext for being cowardly; and understanding every side of a situation was counted as a way of doing nothing about it. Impulsive impetuosity was regarded as characteristically manly, but deliberating without taking risks was regarded as a specious excuse for deserting one's own side. ... The leaders on each side in the cities used the most appealing words. One side championed equal law[16] and citizenship for the many; the other proclaimed a well-ordered aristocracy. But, while supporting the common interest in their words, in fact they turned it into prizes for private gain. They stopped at nothing in struggling for supreme power, and went to the most terrible lengths. ... In the disturbed conditions of life in these circumstances, human nature, already in the habit of committing injustice in violation of law,[17] now overcame law, and gladly showed its uncontrolled passions, its power to overcome justice, and its hostility to every sort of superiority. For they would not have preferred revenge over piety, or gain over the avoidance of injustice, had envy[18] not been so powerful and so destructive.

537 XENOPHON, *History of Greece* ii. 3. 21–3   The Thirty now considered that they were free to do whatever they wanted,[19] and they began to put people to death in great numbers, some because of private enmities, and others

[15] i.e. one of the first during the Peloponnesian War.
[16] *isonomia;* cf. **532**, **535**.
[17] *nomos;* cf. **125**, **149**, **462**.
[18] *phthonos;* cf. **388**.
[19] They had just disarmed the citizens.

for the sake of their money. They also needed money to pay the Spartan garrison; and so they decided that each of them should arrest one of the resident aliens, put him to death, and confiscate his property. They ordered Theramenes also to pick someone and arrest him. Theramenes answered: 'I regard it as shameful for us, who claim to be the best people, to commit worse injustices than the informers did. The informers took money from their victims, but at least left them alive. And are we going to kill people who have done no injustice, simply in order to take their money? Surely this is more unjust in every way.' The Thirty now came to regard Theramenes as an obstacle to their freedom to do what they wanted, and so they began to plot against him.[20]

538 [?PLATO], *Letters* vii. 324B–325C[21]   Many people vilified the democracy ruling at that time, and a revolution occurred. In this revolution ... thirty came to power as supreme rulers of the whole state. Some of these happened to be relatives and acquaintances of mine, who accordingly invited me forthwith to join them, assuming my fitness for the task. It is not surprising that, young as I was, I thought they would lead the city from an unjust life to just practices, and 'manage it', as they put it. And so I was intensely interested to see what would become of it. Of course, I saw in a short time that these men made the democracy look like a golden age in comparison. Among other things, they sent an elderly man, Socrates—a friend of mine whom I would hardly be ashamed to call the most just man of his time—in company with others, against one of the citizens, to fetch him forcibly to be executed.[22] They intended to implicate Socrates in their rule, whether he wished it or not. He refused, and risked any consequences rather than take any part in wicked actions. When I observed all this—and some other similar matters of importance—I withdrew in disgust from the abuses of that time. Not long after that, the Thirty and their whole government fell. ... The restored exiles displayed great moderation. But by some chance some of those in control brought against this associate of mine, Socrates, whom I have mentioned, a most unholy charge, which he least of all men deserved. They put him on trial for impiety, and the people condemned and put to death the man who had refused to take part in the unholy arrest of a friend of the exiles, at a time when they were exiled and suffering misfortunes.

---

[20] Eventually the Thirty put Theramenes to death after a show trial. For Socrates' encounter with them see **540**.

[21] This letter is quite likely to be spurious (as many of the letters ascribed to Plato certainly are). But the author, whoever it is, may be quite well informed, and so may preserve some points of interest about Plato's life (not necessarily about his motives).

[22] This refers to the incident involving Leon; **540**.

Socrates and politics

539 Socrates, Plato, and Aristotle all lived and worked in Athens—Socrates and Plato were Athenian citizens, and Aristotle was a resident alien. Their reflections on politics are all influenced by the Athenian democracy. Socrates has very little to say about other forms of government. Some of Plato's views seem to be influenced by a comparison between Athens and Sparta. Aristotle argues from a still broader acquaintance with different Greek constitutions.

Socrates has no explicit political theory; he does not examine the moral basis of a state, or the basis of legitimate government, or the best constitution. None the less, his discussions have some political significance. In identifying virtue with knowledge, Socrates includes the virtue that makes a person good at deliberating and acting in the common interest of the city. If this political virtue is a craft that can be taught and learnt, then—we might infer—there can be experts in it (**106, 179**). If we could identify political experts who know what is in everyone's interest, should we not entrust government to them?

Measured by this standard, existing constitutions may well seem misguided, since they entrust power to people who seem to lack the specialized craft aiming at the common good. Neither noble birth nor wealth guarantees the right political knowledge; Socrates discovered this by cross-examining the rich, well-born Athenians who were prominent in public life, and finding that they lacked the sort of knowledge that could stand up to his interrogations (**139**). The claims of democracy seem no less questionable, since democratic assemblies give a voice and a vote to everyone, no matter how ignorant or misguided they may be.

Though Socrates' inquiries and arguments implicitly criticize existing constitutions, they do not result in any positive theory. He does not say, for instance, what form of government would be best if political experts could be found, or how experts ought to organize a state. This is not completely surprising, since Socrates does not claim to have acquired the relevant knowledge himself, or to have identified it in anyone else.

Socrates' implicit criticisms of prevailing forms of government do not lead him into rebellion against the Athenian democracy. He resists illegal action, whatever government undertakes it. After the battle of Arginusae, the commanders of the Athenian fleet failed to retrieve the bodies of the Athenian dead. The democratic leaders wanted to try them collectively for this offence (especially repugnant to Athenian religious sentiment). Socrates regarded the collective trial as illegal and unjust, and refused to cooperate. He also refused to cooperate with the Thirty when he was ordered to take part in the illegal arrest of Leon.

Still, Socrates does not seem to be completely neutral between existing forms of government. In the *Crito*, the Laws remind him not only that he has always been a law-abiding citizen, but also that he has preferred Athens and its laws, even over other cities that he describes as well-governed. Neither the Laws nor Socrates make it clear what he found preferable about Athens and Athenian laws.

....

540 PLATO, *Apology* 31C–32E SOCRATES: Perhaps it might seem absurd that I go about in private, giving advice and busying myself with other people's concerns, and do not dare[23] to come forward among you in public to advise the city. I will tell you the reason for this. You have often heard me say in many places that something divine and supernatural[24] comes to me—this is what Meletus is ridiculing in his indictment. It has come to me ever since I was a child, a voice coming to me. Whenever it comes, it forbids me to do what I am about to do, but it never urges me to do anything. This is what opposes my being a politician. It is quite right, as it seems to me. For you can be sure, Athenians, that if I had undertaken politics, I would have perished long ago and benefited neither you nor myself. And don't be offended at my telling you the truth: for the truth is that no one who opposes you or any other mass of people, honestly trying to prevent many injustices and lawless actions in the city, will save his life. If anyone really fights for justice, if he is going to stay alive even for a short time, he must act as a private citizen, not in public affairs.

I can give you clear proofs of this, not words only, but actions, which you esteem more. Listen to what happened to me, so that you will know that fear of death would never make me submit in violation of justice, and that because I did not submit, I would have died at once. I will tell you a story—vulgar perhaps, and commonplace, but nevertheless true. The only office I ever held in the city, Athenians, was that of councillor. My tribe Antiochis held the presidency[25] at the trial of the ten generals who had not taken up the bodies of the dead after the battle of Arginusae; and you proposed to try them all together, which was illegal, as you all thought afterwards. At the time I was the only one of the presidents who opposed you, urging you to do nothing against the laws. I voted against the proposal; and when the orators were ready to impeach me and have me summarily arrested and imprisoned, and you shouted and urged them on, I made up my mind that I ought to run the risk, having law and justice with me, rather than go along with your unjust proposal out of fear of imprisonment and death.

This happened during the democracy. When the oligarchy was in power, the Thirty summoned me and four others to the Rotunda,[26] and ordered us

[23] Or 'do not presume'.

[24] Socrates' sign; **317**, **582**.

[25] The presidents; **531**. Socrates refers to a time when he was one of the presidents (**187** suggests that he was the foreman presiding over the Assembly); he wanted the motion for a collective trial of the generals to be ruled out of order as illegal.

[26] The Rotunda was the building where the presidents met.

to bring Leon the Salaminian from Salamis, so that they could put him to death. This was the sort of order they often gave many people, since they wanted to implicate as many as possible in their crimes.[27] Then once again I showed, not in words only, but in action, that, if it's not too vulgar to say so, I didn't care a scrap about death, and that my whole concern was to avoid doing anything unjust or unholy. For that regime, powerful as it was, did not frighten me into doing anything unjust. When we came out of the Rotunda, the other four went to Salamis and brought Leon, but I went off home. And presumably I would have been put to death for this, if that regime hadn't fallen shortly afterwards. And you will find many witnesses to this. Now do you think I would have lived so many years, if I had engaged in public affairs, and had acted worthily of a good man by always supporting justice, and had made this, as I ought, my primary concern? Far from it, Athenians—neither I nor anyone else.

541 PLATO, *Protagoras* 319B–D[28] [SOCRATES:] Now when we meet in the Assembly, whenever the city has to act on some question about buildings, I notice that the architects are sent for to give advice about the buildings; when it is a question about shipbuilding, the shipbuilders are sent for; and the same applies to everything that the Assembly regards as a subject for learning and teaching. And if anyone else sets out to advise them, and they do not count him as an expert, then, however handsome or wealthy or nobly born he may be, they reject him none the less, with shouts and ridicule, until either they shout him down and he gives up trying to speak, or else the police drag him off or eject him on the orders of the presidents.[29] This is what they do in areas where they think there is a craft. But when they have to take counsel about the government of the city, anyone—builder, metalworker, shoemaker, merchant, or shop-owner, rich or poor, well-born or obscure—stands up to give advice. No one objects, as in the previous cases, that he has never learnt this craft, and has had no teacher, and yet undertakes to give advice. Clearly, this is because they don't think this can be taught.[30]

542 PLATO, *Crito* 52E–53A[31] You had seventy years in which you were free to leave Athens, if you were not satisfied with us, or if the agreements you had made did not seem just to you. But you preferred neither Sparta nor Crete—which you are always saying are well-governed—nor any other Greek or foreign city. You have absented yourself less from the city than the lame or blind or otherwise maimed. So much more than all other Athenians do you care

---

[27] Cf. the story of Theramenes, **537**.

[28] This follows **429**.

[29] The presidents were the *prutaneis*; cf. **531**.

[30] Protagoras replies to Socrates at **430**.

[31] Part of the speech by the laws of Athens to Socrates. Continued at **318**.

for the city and for us the laws—for who would care for a city without caring for its laws?

Plato on existing constitutions

543 The dialogues in which Plato goes beyond the views of the historical Socrates also criticize Athenian democracy.[32] The *Gorgias* attacks democracy for two apparently contrasting vices. On the one hand, it simply translates the desires of the uninformed masses into action, and it makes political leaders into 'flatterers' pandering to current whims and prejudices. On the other hand, it sets up political leaders as tyrants with unlimited power. These leaders have as little understanding of morals and politics as the masses have, but they manipulate the masses through rhetoric and propaganda, until the masses tire of them and depose them. Political leaders such as Pericles can do what they please, as long as they can manipulate popular tastes and preferences. But if the people tire of them, they are discarded in favour of new 'flatterers'.

Plato's objections to democracy are worth comparing with the remarks of two contemporaries of Pericles, Aristophanes and Thucydides. Aristophanes is a comic dramatist, and his picture of Demos as a tyrant surrounded by his flatterers should not be regarded as totally serious political comment, any more than his comments on Socrates should be taken to be accurate or seriously meant.[33] Thucydides rejects the view that a politician such as Pericles was simply a servant of popular whims and prejudices, but he admits that even Pericles depended on popular favour, which sometimes turned against him. Plato presents, in more extreme form, the different sides of democratic politics.

What is wrong with this democratic system? According to Socrates in the *Gorgias*, neither the masses nor the leaders have any idea of genuine human welfare. The *Gorgias* insists that genuine welfare is to be found in the practice of the virtues (**455, 492–6**). Hence Socrates claims that in practising the virtues he practises the genuine 'political craft', which would apply genuine knowledge of the human good to political life; this is the craft that existing political leaders lack.

....

544 ARISTOPHANES, *Knights* 40–8 DEMOSTHENES: The two of us[34] have a master—a boor when he's angry, a bean-chewing peasant, easily irritated, Demos of the Pnyx,[35] a bad-tempered, deaf little old man. At the last new

[32] Plato and Socrates; **17–18**. The *Gorgias* and *Meno* are often supposed to mark a transition between Socratic and Platonic views.

[33] Aristophanes on Socrates; **9, 581**.

[34] Demosthenes and Nicias are Athenian generals, represented as slaves of Demos.

[35] The meeting place of the Athenian Assembly.

moon, he bought a slave, Paphlagon, a tanner,[36] the biggest scoundrel and slanderer. This Paphlagon the tanner recognized the old boy's character, and, cringing before his master, started fawning, toadying, flattering and cheating him. ...

[1112–30] CHORUS: Demos, your rule is truly fine, since all fear you as a tyrant. But you're easily led by the nose. You like being flattered and deceived. You gape in admiration at the orator of the moment; your wits are present, but absent. DEMOS: You're the ones who have no wits under your long hair, when you suppose I've no sense. I intentionally act the fool. For I enjoy getting fed daily, and it's my design to foster one thieving leader at a time. When he is full up, I lift my hand and strike him down. ... [1141–9] Just look at me, how cleverly I encircle them, the ones who think they're so clever and are cheating me. For all the time I'm watching them, seeming to see nothing, while they steal. And then I compel them to spit out whatever they've stolen from me.

545 THUCYDIDES ii. 65. 1–9   In this way Pericles tried to dissolve the Athenians' anger against him, and to divert their thoughts away from their present alarming situation. So far as public policy was concerned, they accepted his arguments; they sent no more delegations to Sparta, and showed increased energy in carrying on the war. As private individuals, however, they were distressed by their sufferings. The people had begun the war with very little, and had now been deprived of even that; the richer classes had lost their fine possessions with their rich and well-equipped houses in the country; worst of all, they were at war instead of being at peace. In fact, they persisted in their anger against Pericles until they had fined him. Not long afterwards, however, they behaved as masses usually do, by re-electing him to the generalship, and entrusting everything to him. By this time people felt their own private sufferings less keenly, and for the needs of the city as a whole they counted Pericles as the one who merited their confidence. Indeed, during the whole period of peacetime when Pericles was leader in the city, he led it with good judgement and guarded it safely, and under him Athens was at its greatest. ... Because of his authority, his intelligence, and his proved incorruptibility, he had the power to keep a firm hand on the people, while leaving them free. It was he who led them rather than they who led him; since he never gained power by any inappropriate means, he did not speak to please them, but because of his reputation he was able to speak against their wishes, and even to anger them, not needing to flatter them. Certainly, when he saw that over-confidence made them insolent, he made them afraid of their dangers; and when they were irrationally afraid, he would restore their confidence. It was becoming a democracy in name, but in reality rule by the first man in the city.

---

[36] He represents Cleon the demagogue in the play.

546 PLATO, *Gorgias* 466A–C[37]   POLUS: Then do you think good orators count[38] as worthless in the city, as flatterers?[39] ... SOCRATES: I think they don't count at all.—What do you mean, they don't count? Don't they have the greatest power in the cities?—No—not if you say that having power is a good to the man with the power?—Well, I say it is.—Then I think the orators have least power of anyone in the city.—What? Aren't they like tyrants? Don't they kill anyone they want to, and expropriate and expel from the cities anyone they think fit?[40]

547 PLATO, *Gorgias* 517B–519A   My friend, I'm not reproaching Pericles, Cimon, Miltiades, and Themistocles any more than you are, as servants of the city. On the contrary; I think they've proved to be better servants than the present people, and better able to supply the city's appetites. But when it comes to redirecting people's appetites, not indulging them, but persuading and forcing them towards what will make the citizens better—here they were practically no better than people now; and that's the only work proper to a good citizen. But ships, walls, dockyards, and many other things—I too agree with you that the previous people were cleverer than the people now at supplying them. ... [518E] You're eulogizing people who feasted the Athenians, indulging their appetites. It's said that they made the city great; but no one notices that it's swelling and festering because of these earlier people. For without justice and temperance they have left the city full of harbours, dockyards, city walls, payments from the allies,[41] and that sort of rubbish.

548 PLATO, *Gorgias* 521DE   I think I am among a few Athenians—not to say the only one—who undertakes the genuine political craft, and practises politics—the only one among people now. In what I say I don't aim at gratifying my hearers; I aim at what is best, not what is pleasantest. ... That's why I won't know what to say in court. ... For I will be judged as a physician might be judged by a jury of children with a cook as prosecutor.[42]

Plato's solutions

549 The *Republic* (from Latin *respublica*, Greek *politeia*, 'constitution') presents a series of bold, extreme, and rather hasty proposals for removing the flaws in existing constitutions. Since Plato believes political knowledge is knowledge of

[37] This follows **179**.

[38] *nomizein*, cognate with *nomos*. Cf. **125**.

[39] Flattery; **179**, **399**.

[40] Socrates goes on to argue that the orators have no real power, because (1) real power must be power to get what we want; (2) everyone wants the good; (3) the orators do not know what the good is (since they have no genuine craft); (4) hence, they cannot get the good; (5) hence they cannot get what they want. The argument for (2) is similar to **435**.

[41] The member cities of the Athenian empire paid tribute to Athens.

[42] The trial of the physician; **179**.

the genuine welfare of the individuals in a community, he believes political knowledge is possible; for the main argument of the *Republic* describes the genuine welfare of individuals in a community. Plato seeks to show that a person's real welfare consists in control, as far as possible, by the rational part of the soul. The rulers of the state ought to be those who have the appropriate order in themselves and know how to produce it in other people.

The end of the *Meno* argues that no contemporary politician has genuine knowledge. Plato speculates about a politician with genuine knowledge, who would be a properly enlightened political leader (**553**). In the *Republic*, Plato describes enlightened leaders, and the sort of city they would design. He recognizes (in the image of the ship, **550**) that actual cities are unprepared to accept the prescriptions of the enlightened expert in politics. The outlook encouraged by prevailing moral and political views is reinforced by the teaching of the sophists, who do not question the basic assumptions of their society (**551**). Since true moral and political knowledge must question popular assumptions, it will not gain popular acceptance. Plato infers that the rulers must put it into practice, and that these rulers must not depend on popular favour.

In giving this account of political knowledge, Plato answers the objection that there is no genuine knowledge that can determine the choice of political goals and values. Since this is a matter for knowledge, there can be experts, and these ought to be the rulers. To suppose that everyone is equally entitled to his own view is to suppose falsely, according to Plato, that we cannot find the right answers to questions about the nature of human welfare. Once we see that we can find the right answers, it seems absurd to give an equal voice to those who cling to the wrong answers.

Plato's political prescriptions rest on these premises:

(1) The account of the virtues as conditions of the tripartite soul is correct; an individual's welfare depends crucially on being controlled by the rational part of the soul, and having the other two parts in harmony with it (**437–9, 468–71**).

(2) The good of the city requires the same order and harmony between the different tendencies in the citizens.

(3) However, this order and harmony cannot consist in rule by the rational part in each person, because some people are naturally incapable of being ruled by the rational part, and are inevitably subject to their spirited or appetitive parts.

(4) Since these people cannot achieve their welfare on their own, they must be ruled by people whose souls are rightly ordered; then they will come as close as they can to having their own souls rightly ordered.

The ideal city, therefore, must be ruled by 'philosopher rulers' who are not subject to the whims and preferences of their unenlightened fellow-citizens. The unenlightened are ruled for their own good, so that they can come as close to virtue as their nature allows.

Most people's political views are warped (according to Plato) not only by intellectual error and incapacity, but also by the outlooks formed by different social classes, occupations, educations, and ways of life. He seeks to remove the bad effects of these distorting influences in the ideal city. The city is divided into classes—producers (including all property-owners, both rich and poor), soldiers, and rulers. All the members of each class receive the education appropriate to their capacities and roles.

The rigid class division of the ideal city shows that Plato does not try to prevent the fragmentation and conflict of actual cities (**552**) by abolishing social distinctions. He seeks to prevent it by educating the ruling class appropriately for its functions, and excluding the sources of disunity among rulers. Individual rulers have no private property, no nuclear families, no distinct upbringings or education to divide them from one another. Both men and women are trained for the ruling class (in contrast with Greek custom); they have sexual relations with other rulers in common, and they hold their children in common. According to Plato, this is the only way to remove the divisions that result from class conflict between the rich and the poor. The extreme unity, as he conceives it, of the ideal city will prevent it from becoming one of the divided cities that provide standing occasions for conflict and instability.

Unity and harmony in the ideal city cannot be secured by the abolition of differences between classes, since most people are incapable of achieving the understanding of the good that the rulers achieve. Most people understand neither the common good nor their own individual goods. If an individual of defective rational understanding is left to rule himself, he will not act in his own interest. Only an enlightened ruler can act in the interest of an individual non-ruler.

Has Plato prescribed a cure that is worse than the disease? The mental distance between the enlightened rulers and the unenlightened masses in the ideal city may seem to be no less serious a division than the division between the rich and the poor in ordinary cities. If his different classes do not share the same common aims, concerns, and interests, how can they constitute a stable community?

Plato answers that the unenlightened people in the ideal city are enlightened enough, if properly brought up and educated, to recognize the qualifications of the rulers. He assumes that if I am a member of the producing class or the military class, I will be able to see that the rulers understand my interest better than I understand it myself. Since I see that they do not enrich themselves by ruling, and indeed have no aims or desires that would be satisfied by oppressing the non-ruling classes, I see that I can trust them to rule in my interest.

550 PLATO, *Republic* 488A–489A Picture a ship-owner, far taller and stronger than all the others on the ship, but a bit deaf, a bit short-sighted, and with similarly limited knowledge of navigation. The seamen are in conflict about piloting the ship; each thinks he should be the pilot, though he has never learnt the craft, and cannot point to anyone as his teacher or to any time when he has learnt it. And, what's more, they claim that it is not even teachable; if anyone says it is teachable, they are ready to tear him to shreds. They are always crowding round the ship-owner, pressing him by any means whatever to turn over control to them. Sometimes, if they fail and others persuade him, they put the others to death or expel them from the ship, and then, after binding and drugging the noble ship-owner with mandragora or intoxication or otherwise, they rule the ship, devour its stores, and with all their eating and drinking they direct the ship's course just as well as you would expect them to do. Besides that, the one they praise as a navigator, a pilot who knows about ships, is the one who is a clever accomplice in schemes to persuade or force the ship-owner to let them rule; anyone of a different sort they blame for being useless. They haven't the least idea of the true pilot—that he must attend to the time of the year, the seasons, the sky, the winds, the stars, and everything that bears on his craft, if he is to be truly fit to rule a ship. As for seizing the helm whether or not others want him to— he does not believe there is any discipline of this that one can acquire together with the pilot's craft. With all this happening on ships, don't you think the true pilot would indeed be called a stargazer,[43] a babbler, a useless fellow, by passengers[44] in ships ordered in this way?

551 PLATO, *Republic* 492A–493D [SOCRATES:] Or do you think, as the many do, that some of the young men are corrupted by sophists,[45] and that some private individuals who are sophists corrupt them, to any extent worth speaking of? Aren't the many who say these things the greatest sophists themselves? Don't they educate people most completely? Don't they form the sorts of characters they want in young people and old, in men and women alike? [ADEIMANTUS:] When do they do that? he asked.—When they meet together and the many take their seats in an assembly, or in a court of law, or a theatre, or a camp, or in any place where they gather, with a great uproar, and they praise some things being said or done, and blame other things, going to excess in either direction, shouting and clapping their hands, so that the echo of the rocks and the place where they are assembled redoubles the volume of the praise or blame. In this situation, what will a young man's heart be like? ... What sort of education that he has been given as an individual will hold firm

---

[43] This recalls a charge against Socrates; **583**.
[44] As opposed to the 'seamen' (i.e. politicians) above.
[45] Sophists; **8**.

for him, without being overwhelmed by such blame or praise and being carried away by the stream that carries him? Won't he agree with the many in what he says are good and bad things? Won't he practise what they practise, and acquire their character?—Yes, Socrates; necessity will compel him. ... — All those money-making private individuals, whom the many call sophists and regard as professional rivals with their craft, really educate people in nothing but the opinion of the many, those they hold in their gatherings; and this is what <the sophists> call wisdom. They are like someone who learns the impulses and appetites of a large and strong beast whom he is feeding— how to approach and touch it, at what times and from what causes it is harder or easier to deal with, what provokes its different sounds, and what sounds uttered by another make him tame or wild. When he has learnt all this by constant attendance over some time, he calls this wisdom, and, setting it up as a craft, proceeds to teach it. But in fact he knows nothing about what is fine or shameful, good or bad, just or unjust, in these opinions and appetites, but applies these terms to things in accordance with the opinions of the great beast. Whatever things the beast likes, he calls these good, and whatever it dislikes he calls bad, but he has no other account of them to give; he calls necessary things just and fine, but he himself has never seen how great is the difference between the nature of the necessary and of the good, nor could he show it to anyone else. Don't you think someone like this would be a remarkable educator?—Indeed, he would.—Then is there any difference between him and the one who thinks wisdom is the discernment of the impulses and pleasures of people at large, in painting or music, or, finally, in politics?

552 PLATO, *Republic* 422D–423A [ADEIMANTUS:] ... If the wealth of all the other cities is gathered into one city, isn't that dangerous for the city that has no wealth? [SOCRATES:] What happy innocence, I said, to suppose that anything other than the sort of city we are establishing deserves to be called a city.—Then what should we call them? he said.—Some greater title, I said, must be applied to the others. For each of them is many cities, not a city ... There are at least two, enemies to each other, the city of the rich and the city of the poor; and in each of these there are many cities. If you deal with each of the other so-called 'cities' as one city, you will go completely wrong, but if you treat it as many, by offering to the one side the property, the power, the very lives, of people on the other side, you will always have few enemies and many allies.

553 PLATO, *Meno* 98D–100B SOCRATES: If virtue was wisdom, then, we thought, it was teachable?[46] MENO: Yes.—And if it was teachable, it was wisdom?—Certainly.—And if there were teachers, it would be teachable, and if

---

[46] Or 'taught'.

there were no teachers, not?—True.—But we agreed that there were no teachers of virtue?—Yes. ... [99B]—And therefore it was not by any wisdom, and not because they were wise, that Themistocles[47] and those others of whom Anytus spoke governed cities. This was why they could not make others like themselves—because they did not rely on knowledge.—That would seem to be so, Socrates.—But if they didn't rely on knowledge, the only alternative is that they relied on right belief in guiding cities, with no more wisdom than diviners and prophets have; for in their inspired moments these also say many things truly, but not because they have knowledge.—So I believe. ... —If, then, our inquiry and discussion were right, virtue is neither natural nor taught, but comes by divine allotment to whomever it comes to, without understanding—unless there were some politician who could make someone else wise in politics. And if there were such a one, he might be said to be among the living what Homer said Teiresias was among the dead: 'he alone has understanding; but the rest are flitting shades'.[48] Here too he will be a reality among shadows, as far as virtue is concerned.—I think you're quite right, Socrates.

554 PLATO, *Republic* 473B–E [SOCRATES:] Next, let me try to seek out and demonstrate the fault in cities that causes their present bad government, and the smallest change that would allow a city to reach this sort of constitution.[49] Best of all would be a change of one thing only, or if not, of two; or at any rate of as few things as possible. [GLAUCON:] Certainly, he replied.—I think, I said, I can show that there might be a reform of a city if only one change were made, which is not a slight or easy change, but still a possible one.—What is it? he asked.— ... Well, I'll say it, even if I'm to be drowned in ridicule and dishonour. Consider what I'm going to say.—Proceed, he said.— I said: Until philosophers are kings in the cities, or those who are now called kings and holders of power genuinely pursue philosophy to the right level, so that political ability[50] and philosophy meet in the same person, and those natures who pursue either in separation from the other are excluded compulsorily—until then, neither cities nor the human race, as I believe, will ever have rest from their evils, and only then will our city become possible and see the light of day. That was the thought, my dear Glaucon, that made me shrink from speaking, since it would go so strongly against common belief; for it is difficult to see that in no other city can anyone be happy, either in private or in public life.[51]

[47] On this Athenian politician cf. **547**.
[48] Plato quotes from the episode in the *Odyssey* excerpted in **301**.
[49] The constitution of the ideal city that has just been described.
[50] Or 'political power'.
[51] Part of the argument to show that philosophers must rule, because only they have the necessary knowledge, is at **213**, **215**, **217–18**.

555 PLATO, *Republic* 462A–C [SOCRATES:] Do we know of any greater evil for a city than whatever tears it apart and makes it many instead of one? Or a greater good than whatever binds it and makes it one?—[GLAUCON:] We do not.—Then doesn't the sharing of pleasure and pain bind, when all the citizens, as far as possible, agree in rejoicing and grieving at the same things coming into being and ceasing to be?—Certainly, he said.—And doesn't the privatization of these things dissolve the city, when some grieve and others rejoice at the same things happening to the city and the people in it?—Of course.—And doesn't that happen for this reason—when people in the city don't agree in saying such words as 'mine' and 'not mine', and similarly with 'alien'?—Precisely so.—And so the city in which the greatest number say 'mine' and 'not mine' of the same things in the same way is best governed.— Best governed by far.

556 PLATO, *Republic* 590C–592B[52] [SOCRATES:] And why do we suppose that menial occupations and manual labour bring reproach? Isn't it when the best part of the soul is naturally weak in someone, so that it cannot rule the beasts in him, but can only serve them, and can learn nothing but the ways of flattering them? [GLAUCON:] So it seems, he said.—Therefore, so that such a person may have a ruler similar to the ruler in the best person, don't we say he ought to be the slave of that best person, the one who has in him the divine part ruling him? And surely this is not because we suppose the slave should be ruled to his own harm, as Thrasymachus supposed in the case of the ruled,[53] but because it is better for everyone to be governed by what is divine and wise, preferably having his own wisdom in him, but, if not, having wisdom imposed from outside, in order that all of us, as far as possible, may be similar and friends, because we are governed by the same thing?—Yes, and we're quite right, he said.—And it's clear that this is the aim of the law, the ally of everyone in the city. And it's the aim of rule over children, not to leave them free until we establish a constitution in them as in the city, and by cultivating the best part in a person, set up in the individual a guardian similar and ruler similar to the one in the city;[54] and then we leave them free.—Yes, he said, that's clear.—In what way, then, Glaucon, and on the basis of what argument, will we say that it benefits someone to act unjustly or intemperately or to do anything else shameful that will make him worse, even if he gets money or some other power?—In no way at all, he said. ... —Anyone with understanding will keep in view the constitution within him, and make sure that no part of him is disturbed either by wealth or by poverty. Governing himself in this way, he will acquire or spend as far as he is able.—Very true.—And he will keep the

[52] This is part of the conclusion of Socrates' defence of the claims he made about justice in **470**.
[53] Thrasymachus; **459**.
[54] Text uncertain.

same aim in view, in willingly accepting and enjoying whatever honours he thinks will make him better, and avoiding those, private or public, that he thinks will destroy his present condition.—Then he won't engage in politics, if that is his concern.—Oh, but indeed he will—in his own city, though presumably not in his native city, unless some divine fortune comes about.—I understand; you mean the city that we described in founding it, the one established in our discourse—for I don't think it's anywhere on earth.—But, I said, presumably a pattern is laid up in heaven,[55] so that anyone who wants to see it can see it, and, while seeing it, can found himself. And it doesn't matter at all whether it is or isn't anywhere; for he will engage in the political activity of this city, and of no other.—That's likely, he said.

Aristotle: the natural basis of the state

|557| Aristotle shares many of Plato's views about the proper aim and function of a political community, but disagrees sharply with Plato's views about the proper way to achieve them. He believes Plato has seriously undervalued one aspect of democracy—the role of individual citizens in determining decisions taken on their behalf by the state. This does not mean, however, that Aristotle agrees with the presuppositions of Greek democracy.

Both Plato's errors and the democrat's errors become clear, in Aristotle's view, only if we set out from a true conception of the role of the city in human happiness. The *Politics* is anticipated in the *Ethics* (**405**); it explains why happiness cannot be achieved by an isolated individual, but requires the specific institutions that constitute a city.

In Aristotle's view, the city is necessary for an individual's happiness because it fulfils human nature; a human being is a 'naturally political animal' (**406, 476**). Aristotle explains this claim in his treatment of friendship. In his view, practical reason is more fully expressed in friendship and cooperative action than in purely self-regarding action. Concern for the common interest of oneself and one's friends establishes a 'community' of interest. The complete community, in which our life as a whole is subject to cooperative deliberation, is a city.

Since cooperative concern for the common interest is to be valued for its own sake, Aristotle rejects the version of a 'social contract' theory put forward by Glaucon and Adeimantus.[56] According to this version, political life is worthwhile because it provides means to ends that we pursue even outside political life: we already want security, and the city provides it. In Aristotle's view, this defence of the state (which he ascribes to Lycophron the sophist) fails to recognize

---

[55] The city in heaven; **572**.

[56] Glaucon and Adeimantus; **460**. Aristotle attributes a somewhat similar view to Lycophron in **559**.

that the state creates and achieves aims that we would not have outside the state. In making us concerned about the common interest, it fulfils our nature.

Aristotle agrees with Plato in regarding the state as a means to securing the virtue and happiness of the citizens. He therefore rejects the view (suggested by Pericles in Thucydides' funeral speech, **534**) that the state ought not to interfere in the private lives of citizens. He agrees with Plato's view that the state ought to intervene in every area of life that promotes the appropriate moral education and moral character.

558 ARISTOTLE, *Politics* 1252^{a}1–1253^{a}39   We see that every city is some sort of association,[57] and that every association is constituted for the sake of some good, since everyone does everything for the sake of what seems good. Clearly, then, while all associations aim at some good, the association that aims most of all at the good—at the good that most of all controls all the other goods—is the one that most of all controls and includes the others; and this is the one called the city, the political association.[58] It is wrong, then, to suppose, as some do, that the politician, the king, the household manager, and the slave-master are the same. People suppose this because they think the difference is not a difference in kind, but only in the number who are ruled, so that the ruler of a few is a master, the ruler of more people is a household manager, and the ruler of still more people is a politician or a king; they assume that a large household is no different from a small city. And all they can say to distinguish a king from a politician is that someone who directs things himself is a king, whereas someone who follows the rules of political science, ruling and being ruled in turn, is a politician. These views are not true. …

If one observes something's growth from the beginning, that is the best way to study this as well as other matters. First, then, those who cannot do without each other necessarily form pairs, as female and male do for reproduction. And they do this not because of any decision, but from the natural impulse that they share with other animals and with plants to leave behind another of the same kind. Ruler and ruled come about by nature because of self-preservation. For the capacity for rational foresight makes one a natural ruler and natural master, while the capacity for bodily labour makes another ruled and a natural slave; that is why the interests of master and slave coincide. … And so from these two associations—between female and male and between slave and master—the first association that results is the household. … The first association formed from a number of households for long-term advantage is a village …

[1252^{b}27] The complete association, formed from a number of villages, is a city. Unlike the others, it has the full degree of practically every sort of

---

[57] *koinônia*; **478, 495**.

[58] Aristotle often alludes to the connection between 'city', *polis*, and the adjective *politikos*.

self-sufficiency; it comes to be for the sake of living, but remains in being for the sake of living well. That is why every city is natural, since the previous associations are natural. For the city is their end, and nature is an end; for we say that the nature of a thing (of a human being, a horse, or a household, for instance) is the character it has when its coming to be is complete. Moreover, what something is for and its end is the best good, and self-sufficiency is both the end and the best good.

It is evident from this, then, that the city exists by nature, and that a human being is by nature a political animal. Anyone without a city because of his nature rather than his fortune is either worthless or superior to a human being. ... It is evident why a human being is more of a political animal than is any bee or any gregarious animal; for nature, we say, does nothing pointlessly, and a human being is the only animal with rational discourse.[59] A voice signifies pleasure and pain, and so the other animals, as well as human beings, have it, since their nature is far enough advanced for them to perceive pleasure and pain and to signify them to one another. But rational discourse is for making clear what is expedient or harmful, and hence what is just or unjust. For this is distinctive[60] of human beings in contrast to the other animals, that they are the only ones with a perception of good and evil, and of just and unjust, and so on; and it is association in these that produces a household and a city. Further, the city is naturally prior to the household and to the individual, since the whole is necessarily prior to the part. For if the whole animal is dead, neither foot nor hand will survive, except homonymously, as if we were speaking of a stone hand—for that is what a dead hand will be like. Now everything is defined by its function and capacity; and so anything that has lost them should not be called the same thing, but a homonymous thing.[61] Clearly, then, the city is both natural and prior to the individual. For if the individual separated from the city is not self-sufficient, his relation to it is similar to that of parts to wholes in other cases; and anyone who is incapable of membership in an association, or who has no need of it because he is self-sufficient, is no part of a city, and so is either a beast or a god.

Everyone has a natural impulse, then, towards this sort of association, and whoever first established it is responsible for the greatest goods. For just as a human being is the best of the animals if he has been completed, he is also the worst of them if he is separated from law and the rule of justice. For injustice is most formidable when it is armed, and a human being naturally grows up armed and equipped for intelligence and virtue, but can most readily use this equipment for ends contrary to them; hence without virtue he is the most unscrupulous and savage of animals, the most excessive in

[59] *logos*; **113** n.
[60] *idion*; **236, 246, 409**.
[61] Homonymy; **252, 257, 336, 407**.

pursuit of sex and food. Justice, however, is political; for the rule of justice is an order in the political association, and justice is the judgement of what is just.

559 ARISTOTLE, *Politics* 1280ᵃ8–1281ᵃ10 First we must understand the received accounts of oligarchy and democracy, and the oligarchic and democratic views of justice; for everyone touches on some sort of justice, but they make only limited progress and do not describe the whole of what is strictly just. For instance, justice seems to be equality, and indeed it is—but for equals, not for everyone. Again, inequality seems to be just; and so it is—but for unequals, not for everyone. But these partisans of each view leave out this point—equality or inequality for whom—and so make bad judgements. The reason is that they are judges in their own case, and most people are practically always bad judges in their own cases. ... Supporters of oligarchy think that if they are unequal in some aspects—wealth, for instance—they are altogether unequal, whereas supporters of democracy think that if they are equal in some aspect—free status, for instance—they are altogether equal. But they fail to mention the most important aspect. For if people combined and associated in order to acquire possessions, someone's share in the city would correspond to his possessions, so that the supporters of oligarchy would seem to have a strong argument; for, they say, if A has contributed one out of 100 minas and B has contributed the other 99, it is not just for A to get the same return as B, either of the original sum or of any later profits. In fact, however, the political association does not aim simply at staying alive, but aims more at a good life. For if it aimed simply at staying alive, slaves and non-human animals would constitute a city, whereas in fact they do not, since they do not participate in happiness or in a life guided by decision.

Nor does the city aim at an alliance, to prevent anyone from doing injustice to anyone, or at exchange and dealings between its members. For if this were the aim, then the Etruscans and the Carthaginians—and any other peoples related by treaty—would all count as citizens of a single city; at any rate, these have made conventions about imports, treaties to prohibit doing injustice, and written articles of alliance. These peoples, however, have no common government, but each has its own. Moreover, neither people is concerned about the character of the citizens of the other city, or about how to remove injustice or any other vice from the other city that is bound by the agreements; each is concerned only to prevent doing injustice to one another. By contrast, those who are concerned with good government consider the virtues and vices of citizens. Hence it is evident that whatever is correctly called a city, not just for the sake of argument, must be concerned with virtue. For otherwise the association turns out to be merely an alliance, differing only in the proximity of its members from the other alliances with more distant members. In that case law turns out to be an agreement and, as

Lycophron the sophist said, a mutual guarantor of just treatment, but unable to make the citizens good and just. ...

Evidently, then, a city is not an association for living in the same place, for preventing the unjust treatment of one member by another, and for exchange. All these are necessary conditions for a city, but their presence does not make a city. Rather, the city is an association for living well for both households and families, aiming at a complete and self-sufficient life (but this requires them to live in the same place and to intermarry). That is why kinship-groups, brotherhoods, religious societies, and pursuits that involve living together have developed in cities; these are the product of friendship, since the decision to live together is friendship. The end of a city, then, is living well, and these pursuits are for the sake of the end. A city is the association of families and villages in a complete and self-sufficient life. This sort of life, as we say, is a happy and fine life; hence we should suppose that a city aims at fine actions, not merely at living together. That is why those who contribute most to this sort of association have a greater share in the city than does someone who is equal or superior in free status or in family, but unequal in a citizen's virtue, and a greater share than do those who excel in wealth but are excelled in virtue. It is evident, then, from what we have said that each of the parties disputing about political systems is describing a part of justice.

Aristotle: criticism of Plato

560 Since the human good requires cooperative deliberation, Aristotle maintains that political rule is essentially different from rule over slaves or over a household (558); the city fulfils our capacity to deliberate in common about our interest, and, to that extent, must be an association of free and equal partners who can take their turn in ruling and being ruled.[62] Aristotle believes Plato misses this fact about political rule. From Aristotle's point of view, Plato's ideal state is not a genuinely political association, since it removes all initiative from most of the citizens.

Since he takes political initiative to be part of citizenship, Aristotle is more sympathetic to democracy than Plato is. He argues that ordinary citizens may have enough collective understanding to make reasonable judgements about many questions affecting their welfare, and that therefore political initiative is not bad for them. His sympathy for democracy is strictly limited, however, since he does not believe that a typical citizen of a Greek democracy has the capacity for deliberation that would make him a suitable participant in political rule.

His own ideal state, therefore, differs sharply both from Plato's ideal and

[62] This may be misleading, if we do not consider Aristotle's own explanation of the relevant sort of freedom and equality; see 559.

from a typical Greek democracy. It differs from Plato, in so far as all citizens—not just a restricted class of philosopher-rulers—take part in ruling. It differs from democracies in so far as it denies political initiative to the poor and to manual workers. In Aristotle's view, such functions should be carried out not by citizens, but by slaves, because such work makes people incapable of the virtue that is needed in a good citizen. Within the citizen body, he demands political freedom, initiative, and a considerable measure of political and social equality.

561   ARISTOTLE, *Politics* 1261ª10–ᵇ9   The proposal in the *Republic* that all <the rulers'> women should be shared raises many objections. In particular, the arguments do not make it apparent why Socrates thinks this legislation is needed. Moreover, the end he prescribes for the city is impossible, taken literally, and he has not explained how else we should take it. I mean his assumption that it is best if all the city is as unified as possible. It is evident, on the contrary, that as the city goes further and further in the direction of unity, it will finally not even be a city. ... A city is composed, not merely of a number of human beings, but of those different in kind—for similar people do not constitute a city. ... This is why reciprocal equality preserves a city, as we said before in the *Ethics*. Even free and equal people presumably need this, since they cannot all rule at the same time, but must rule for a year, or some other fixed length of time. Such an arrangement ensures that they all rule—just as if cobblers and carpenters were to change occupations, and the same people were not cobblers or carpenters all the time. Since the normal practice in the crafts is also better in the political association, it is clearly better if the same people are, if possible, always rulers. But in some circumstances this is not possible, because all are naturally equal, and moreover it is just for all to take part in ruling—whether it is a benefit or a burden. This arrangement—where equals yield office to one another in turn and are similar when they are not holding office—at least imitates the practice of the crafts; some rule and others are ruled, taking turns, as though they had become other people. In the same way, among the rulers themselves, different ones rule in different ruling offices. It is evident, then, from what we have said, that a city is not naturally unified in the way that some claim it is and that the unity alleged to be the greatest good for cities in fact destroys them, whereas a thing's good preserves it.

562   ARISTOTLE, *Politics* 1281ª40–1282ª39   The task of judging who has applied medicine correctly seems to belong to the person who also has the task of applying the medicine and curing the patient from his present illness; and this is the medical expert. And the same is true for the other empirical techniques and for the crafts. And so just as a medical expert should submit his conduct to scrutiny by medical experts, other experts should also be scrutinized by their peers. ... The same puzzle seems to arise about selection as about judging. For selection is also properly a task for those who know the craft; it is the task of geometers, for instance, to select a geometer, and of pilots to select a pilot. ... Hence, on this argument, the masses should not be given control either of selecting rulers or of scrutinizing them.

Presumably, however, this argument is not completely correct. First, it is refuted by our earlier argument, as long as the masses are not too slavish; for though each one individually is a worse judge than one who knows the craft, all combined are better, or no worse. Secondly, the argument is mistaken because in some cases the producer is neither the only judge nor the best judge; this is so whenever laymen also know the products of a craft. It is not only the builder of the house, for instance, who knows it; its user—the householder— is an even better judge. ...

There is another puzzle, however, following this one. For it seems absurd for base people to control issues that are more important than the ones controlled by decent people; but scrutinies and elections to ruling offices are the most important thing, and in some political systems, as we have said, these functions are assigned to the common people, since the assembly controls all of these. And yet participation in the assembly, deliberative council, and jury-court requires only a small property-qualification and no minimum age[63] ... The same solution applies to this puzzle also. For presumably this policy that raises the puzzle is also correct. For the ruler is not the individual juryman or councilman or assemblyman, but the jury-court, the council, and the assembly; each individual councilman, assemblyman, or juryman is a part of the bodies we have mentioned. ... Hence it is just for the masses to control the most important things, since the common people, the council, and the jury-court are all composed of many members.

563 ARISTOTLE, *Politics* 1328^{b}24–1329^{a}34[64] Should everyone share in all these functions, since it is possible for all the same people to be at once farmers, craftsmen, councillors and jurymen? Or should different people be assumed for each of the functions we have listed? Or is it necessary for some to be confined to some people and for others to be shared by everyone? It is not the same in every political system; ... in democracies all share in every function, while in oligarchies the contrary is true. We, however, are investigating the best political system, and this is the one that will result in the greatest happiness for the city; and, as we have said, happiness cannot be separate from virtue. From this it is evident that in a city with the finest system, possessing men who are just without qualification, not merely just in relation to the assumption of this city, the citizens must not live the life of menial workers or tradesmen, since it is ignoble and contrary to virtue; and

---

[63] Aristotle refers to three of the main institutions of the Athenian constitution; see **531**.
[64] Aristotle is describing the constitution of the ideal city.

if they are to be citizens, they must not be farmers, since they need leisure both to develop virtue and for political actions. We have found that a military force and a body that deliberates about what is expedient and judges about what is just are present in the city, and that they, most of all, are evidently parts of the city. Should we, then, assign different functions to different people in this case also, or should we assign both functions to the same people?

The answer to this is also evident, because in one way they should be assigned to the same people, in another way to different people. In so far as each function is appropriate to a different period of life, and one function needs wisdom, the other strength, in this respect they should be assigned to different people. But in so far as it is impossible that people who are able to force and hinder others should accept permanent rule by others, in this respect they must be assigned to the same people, since those who control the arms also control the survival or collapse of the political system. The remaining option, then, is for the political system to assign both of these functions to the same people, but not at the same time of life. Rather, since strength is naturally found in younger people, and wisdom in older people, that would seem to be the just and expedient assignment of functions to each group— for this division corresponds to the worth of each. Moreover, these must also own the possessions, since the citizens must have property, and these are the citizens. For the menial class has no share in the political system, nor has any other class that does not produce virtue. This is clear from our basic assumption. For happiness must involve virtue; and in calling a city happy we must consider all the citizens, not just a part of the city. Moreover, it is also evident that these citizens must own the possessions, since the farmers must be slaves or foreign serfs.

Epicurus

564 Epicurus defends the account of justice put forward by Glaucon and Adeimantus, and prefers it to Plato's account (**479**). Similarly, his conception of the state and its functions is close to the one that Plato and Aristotle reject. Aristotle maintains that the role of political activity in human welfare rules out Lycophron's view that a city simply prevents mutual aggression (**559**). Epicurus, however, believes that Lycophron's account is right. If the good is to be identified with pleasure and freedom from pain, it does not essentially include cooperative activity and deliberation. In Epicurus' view, the role of the state is instrumental; it provides security against attack, starvation, and other sources of distress.

Lucretius supports this conception of the state with a conjectural account of the gradual development of society out of pre-social needs and distresses. As people instinctively noticed the sufferings that resulted from non-social living, and recognized the instrumental benefits of social life, they developed primitive forms of society, which in turn encouraged traits that increased the desire for society. The evolution of society is to be explained neither as a product of divine design (cf. **609**), nor (following Aristotle, **558**) as the expression of the inherently social nature of human beings, but simply as the product of particular responses to insecurity and danger.

Lucretius does not imply that the development of social and political life is unequivocally good. Some parts of his story are notably pessimistic. He points out that social life removes some sources of pain and anxiety, but creates others. He does not claim that, for the Epicurean hedonist, social life is clearly preferable.

565 LUCRETIUS v. 958–1006 They could not consider the common good, and did not know the use of shared practices or laws. Whatever plunder chance had offered to anyone, he grabbed it; for each had learned to stay alive and to prosper on his own impulse, and for himself alone. ... Not much more then than now would mortal generations leave the welcome light of life with lamentation. For then, more often than now, someone would be caught as living prey by wild beasts and be devoured by their teeth, so that he filled woods and mountains and forests with his screams, as he watched his living flesh being buried in a living tomb. ... But at that time many thousands of men were never led into battle, to be killed all on a single day; and the stormy waters of the ocean never dashed ships and men upon the rocks. ... In those days it was the lack of food that brought death to their drooping limbs; but now it is abundance of resources that destroys them. In those days, they would often give themselves poison to drink in their ignorance; but now people use their knowledge to poison others.

Later, after they got themselves huts and skins and fire, and a woman paired with a man went off to a single home ... [65] were learnt, and they saw children produced by them, then for the first time the human race began to soften. For fire saw to it that their chilly limbs were less able to bear cold in the open air; Venus lessened their strength; and the appeals of children easily broke down the self-will of their parents. Then too neighbours began to form friendship with one another, from a longing for an end of doing harm and suffering violence. They begged for mercy to be shown to children and women; with cries and gestures they conveyed in halting expressions that it is fair for all to take pity on the weak. They could not reach harmony on every point, but still many, indeed most, of them faithfully kept their agreements; otherwise the human race would even then have been all destroyed. ...

[65] Some words are missing from the text.

The Stoics

566 The evidence on Stoic political theory is fragmentary, but we can describe some aspects of it, in the light of Stoic ethics and natural philosophy, including theology. The basic principle is the Stoic belief in the supremacy of moral virtue and the indifference (in the technical Stoic sense) of all other supposed goods and evils (**508–13, 523–5**). This basic principle is developed in different directions, resulting in different tendencies in Stoic theory. It is not always clear, from the available evidence, how many of these tendencies are present in an individual Stoic theorist, or how different theorists seek to combine them.

Zeno wrote a *Republic* that criticizes Plato's work on many points, but agrees with Plato's radical criticism of existing cities and institutions. Probably Zeno argues that many of the institutions that people take for granted as essential for a just city and a decent way of life are really indifferent, and need to be examined to see whether they really achieve the appropriate results in specific circumstances. He and Chrysippus may suggest that a city of virtuous people would not need the institutions found in actual states.

A belief in a city of virtuous people may also be defended from the Stoics' treatment of friendship. They develop Aristotle's suggestion that the highest form of friendship is between virtuous people (**474**). In their view, virtuous people are all friends to one another, in so far as they share in a common way of life guided by virtue, whether or not they are citizens in the same state. From this point of view, the community of virtue is a more significant community than the one constituted by the particular political community we are born into; and so virtuous people will treat one another as fellow-citizens, however distant (in ordinary terms) they may be from one another.

This community of virtuous people extends even more broadly than human beings. For God (or the gods) in Stoic theology is also rational, exercising providence for the good of the whole universe. Since virtuous people harmonize their wills with the will of God, they belong to one community extending throughout the universe (**619–23**).

This one community also has one law. The rational principles followed by human beings and God constitute the natural law, a universally valid guide for individual and social life, in the light of which we can examine actual states, to see how far they follow or violate it.

Some of these tendencies in Stoic political theory may lead us to conclude that Stoics are not very interested in political life, as it is ordinarily understood, but abandon it in favour of a search for individual perfection; the purely theoretical community of virtuous people and of a divinely ordered universe may appear to replace the ordinary ties between fellow-citizens.

This conclusion, however, is not justified. The Stoic belief in natural law is a basis for moral criticism and evaluation of existing societies; it seeks to provide some basis for the forms of social life that best suit human nature. The community of the wise and virtuous transcends, but does not replace, attachment to other communities (**568**). This attachment to two communities is a Stoic theme that reappears in Augustine's conception of the 'city of God' (**573**; cf. **623–4**). While Augustine insists that the Christian community is concerned above all with 'heavenly peace', he also maintains that it will be concerned with the 'earthly peace' and welfare of particular human societies.

567 DIOGENES LAERTIUS vii. 32–3 Some, including Cassius the Sceptic and his followers, attack Zeno at length. First, these critics say, he declares at the beginning of his *Republic* that ordinary education is useless. Secondly, he says that all those who are not virtuous are one another's opponents, at war, slaves, foreigners, to one another—parents to children, brothers to brothers, friends to friends. Again, in the *Republic* he sets up virtuous people alone as citizens, friends, kin, and free, so that, in the Stoic view, parents and children are adversaries, since they are not wise. He is said to lay down in the *Republic* that women are to be held in common, and (at line 200) that people should build neither temples nor courthouses nor gymnasia in the cities. About currency he writes thus: 'We should not think we ought to establish currency, either for exchange or for foreign travel.'

568 SENECA, *On Leisure* 4.1 Let us grasp in our minds two commonwealths. One is great and truly common, including both gods and human beings, in which we do not look at this or that corner of the earth, but we measure the boundaries of our city together with the path of the sun. The other is the one we have been enrolled in by the circumstances of our birth. This is the commonwealth of the Athenians or the Carthaginians, or of some other city that belongs to some specific human beings, but not to all human beings.[66]

569 DION CHRYSOSTOM xxxvi. 20 They say a city is a mass of human beings who dwell in the same place, that is governed by law. It is clear thereby that this predicate is proper to none of the so-called cities that are foolish and lawless … For just as the one who lacks the rational part is not a human being either, so also what is not law-abiding is not a city; and if it is foolish and disorderly, it could not be law-abiding.

570 CICERO, *Laws* i. 22–3 What is there—never mind in human beings, but in all of heaven and earth—more divine than reason? And when this has grown and been perfected, it is rightly called wisdom. Since, then, nothing is better than reason, and since it is in human beings and in gods, the first community of human beings and gods is in reason. Now those who share reason also have right reason in common; and since right reason is law, we must suppose that we human beings and the gods are made a community by law. Now those

[66] Loyalty to two cities; **622**.

who have a common law also have a common standard of right; and those who have these things in common must count as members of the same city. This is true all the more if they obey the same commands and ruling powers; and indeed they do obey this heavenly order, divine mind, and supremely powerful god. And so this whole universe must be counted as one common city of gods and human beings.

571 LACTANTIUS, *Divine Institutions* vi. 8. 6–9 = Cicero, *Republic* iii. 33   True law is correct reason agreeing with nature, diffused through everyone, constant, everlasting. It calls to duty by commanding, and deters from wrongdoing by forbidding. It neither commands good people in vain nor moves bad people either by commanding or by forbidding. No alteration to this law is allowed, nor any partial repeal of it, nor can it be completely abolished. Nor can we be released from this law by senate or people, nor should we seek anyone else besides ourselves to explain or interpret it. Nor will it be[67] one law at Rome and another at Athens, or one law now and another later; but one everlasting and immutable law will include all peoples for all time. And God will be the one common master and commander of all—God, who has found and promulgated the law and is its judge. Anyone who does not obey it flees from himself and shuns the nature of a human being, and by this very fact pays the greatest penalties, even if he escapes the other things commonly accounted punishments.

572 CLEMENT, *Miscellanies* iv. 26 = SVF iii. 327   I will pray to the spirit of Christ to wing me to my Jerusalem. For the Stoics also say that heaven is a city, strictly speaking, and that the things here on earth are no longer cities. For a city is something civilized, and a people is a civilized combination, a mass of human beings that is governed by law, as the Church is by the Word, a city on earth impregnable and free from tyranny, a product of the divine will on earth as in heaven … And we know Plato's city, placed as a pattern in heaven.[68]

573 AUGUSTINE, *City of God* xix. 17   And so, while the heavenly city travels as a stranger on earth, it calls citizens out of all peoples, and in all languages gathers together a society of aliens. It is not concerned about what is different in the practices, laws, or institutions that achieve or promote earthly peace. It does not abolish or destroy any of them; indeed it keeps and follows them. For, however different they may be in different nations, they all aim at one and the same end of earthly peace, if it does not hinder the observance by which the one supreme and true God is to be worshipped. And so the heavenly city also in its journey uses earthly peace, and guards and seeks the concord of human wills about whatever bears on the mortal nature of human beings.

[67] Or 'nor will there be'.
[68] Plato; **556**.

XV: Philosophy and Theology

Natural philosophy and theology

574 We have already seen why some of the basic aims and approaches of the Presocratic naturalists conflict with the implications of traditional beliefs in the gods (**33**, **36–8**, **40**, **101**). Traditional beliefs rested on traditional stories, especially those recorded by Homer and Hesiod and the other poets. An attack on the authority of these poets and the stories they told was, not surprisingly, interpreted as an attack on belief in the gods who were the subjects of these stories.

The naturalists also deny that the gods could act in the world in the ways that traditional stories attribute to them. According to traditional belief, natural processes are irregular, always subject to the unpredictable interference of the gods. The belief that Zeus sometimes sends thunderstorms because he is angry conflicts with the naturalist view that natural phenomena can all be explained by laws that refer to such causal forces as heat, cold, condensation, rarefaction, and so on, not to the whims of many different gods engaged in their various quarrels.

Some naturalists recognize these conflicts between their position and the religious tradition. Xenophanes criticizes Homer and Hesiod in general, and specifically attacks their anthropomorphic presentation of the gods as simply powerful human beings with the whims, emotions, and jealousies of Homeric heroes (**575**). When he suggests that Ethiopians must believe in black gods, and that if horses believed in gods, they would believe in equine gods, he ridicules the parochial aspects of the traditional Greek conception (**576–7**).

Heracleitus is even more outspoken in his criticism of traditional belief. He dismisses the claims of Homer and Hesiod, and he denounces the traditional cults, sacrifices, and ceremonies as disgusting. His conception of the universe and its laws has no room for the interference of capricious gods (**352**, **580**).

These criticisms of traditional belief do not imply rejection of belief in gods. Thales is reported to have said that everything is full of gods (**303**). Anaximander describes the Unbounded as 'governing everything', and the opposites as 'paying just retribution' for their mutual aggression (**44**). It is difficult to say more precisely what he means by these expressions suggesting a divine mind and a cosmic ethical order.[1]

Xenophanes' position is clearer. Xenophanes criticizes traditional views not because they express belief in gods, but because they are unworthy of a god; a god should not be represented as having the faults and limitations of a human being. The one god is quite unlike human beings, and directs the universe without effort (**576**, **578**).

[1] Cf. Parmenides' reference to justice in **77**.

Heracleitus recognizes Zeus and the Furies, traditional guardians of justice, as guardians of the natural order, not allowing the sun to overstep its boundaries (**352**). Zeus is not what the narrow outlook of traditional cult takes him to be; he is cosmic wisdom. That is why cosmic wisdom is both willing and unwilling to be called Zeus (**579**). The gods act not by periodic intrusions into the ordinary course of the world, but in the basic structure of natural law itself.

Similarly, the Hippocratic writer denies that the so-called 'sacred' disease has anything especially divine about it, because he believe it is subject to the same sorts of explanations that can be given for other diseases. But he is not expressing disbelief in the divine. When he says that all diseases are divine and all are human, he implies that the natural order is equally a divine order (**36–8**).

The view that the gods are present in the order of natural law and causation is absent from the Atomists. In contrast to the earlier Presocratics we have mentioned, they do not suggest that natural necessity embodies cosmic justice. The gods are entirely outside the natural order, so that they cannot affect the course of natural events.[2]

Since the naturalists reject the traditional picture of the gods, it is not surprising that they are accused of denying the existence of the traditional gods. Aristophanes' parody alleges that naturalist cosmology has expelled Zeus and replaced him with 'Vortex' (or 'Whirl')—some mindless and impersonal force determining the behaviour of the heavenly bodies (**581**). This caricature and distortion of most naturalist positions reflects an understandable reaction.

575 SEXTUS, *Against the Professors* ix. 192–3 = DK 21 B11[3] Different people have different and conflicting views about the gods. Hence, their beliefs cannot all be credible, because they conflict; nor can some, as opposed to others, be credible, because they are all equipollent. This is confirmed by the mythical stories of the theologians and poets; for these are full of every sort of impiety. Hence Xenophanes in his criticism of Homer and Hesiod says: 'Homer and Hesiod ascribed to the gods all the things that among human beings are matters of shame and reproach: theft, adultery, and mutual deception.'

576 CLEMENT, *Miscellanies* v. 14. 109. 1–3 = DK 21 B23, 14, 15 Xenophanes of Colophon, teaching that God is one and incorporeal says: 'There is one god, greatest among gods and human beings, similar to mortals neither in shape nor in thought.' And again: 'But mortals think the gods are born, and have clothes and speech and shape like their own.'[4] And again: 'But if cows or horses or lions had hands, or could draw with their hands and produce the

---

[2] Democritus' view was probably similar to that of Epicurus, **610–11**.
[3] Conflicting appearances; **108**.
[4] Anthropomorphism; **611**.

same works as men, horses would draw the forms of gods similar to horses, and cows would draw gods similar to cows; they would make the gods' bodies similar in shape to those that they themselves have.'

577 CLEMENT, *Miscellanies* vii. 4. 22. 1 = DK 21 B16   The Greeks suppose that the gods have not only human shapes, but also human feelings, just as each race depicts their shapes as similar to themselves; as Xenophanes of Colophon says: 'the Ethiopians make their gods dark and snub-nosed, the Thracians say they are red-haired and grey-eyed.'

578 SIMPLICIUS, *Commentary on the Physics* 22. 26–23. 30 = DK 21 B25   Theophrastus says that Xenophanes of Colophon, the teacher of Parmenides, laid it down that the principle, or all that is, is one, neither finite nor infinite, neither changing nor changeless. ... Xenophanes said that this one and all is god. He shows that god is one from the fact that he is the most powerful of all things; for if there were more than one god, he says, they would all have to possess equal power, but what is the most powerful and best of all things is god. ... He does away with change and changelessness ... What is changeless is what is not; for no other thing goes into what is not, and it does not go into any other thing. But change requires more than one thing; for one thing passes into another. And so, when he says that it remains in the same state and does not change—'Always he remains in the same state, changing not at all, nor is it fitting for him to move now here now there'—he means that it remains not because it has the sort of rest that is opposed to change, but because it has the sort of stability that excludes both change and rest. ... And he says that it thinks of all things, when he writes: 'But far from toil he governs everything with his mind.'

579 CLEMENT, *Miscellanies* v. 14. 115. 1–3 = DK 22 B 32   [HERACLEITUS:] The only wise one is unwilling and willing to be called Zeus.

580 ORIGEN, *Against Celsus* vii. 62 = DK 22 B5   [HERACLEITUS:] They waste their time purifying themselves with blood when they are defiled; it is like someone who steps in mud, and then tries to wash it off with mud. ... And they pray to the statues like people chattering to houses, not knowing who the gods and heroes are.

581 ARISTOPHANES, *Clouds* 365–81   SOCRATES: These clouds are the only gods; all the rest is rubbish. STREPSIADES: But Zeus, by Earth—Olympian Zeus, isn't he a god for you?—What do you mean, Zeus? Stop talking nonsense. There is no Zeus.—What do you mean? Then who rains? Explain that to me first of all.⁵—These clouds do, of course. And I'll teach you this with

---

⁵ Aristotle on rain; **242**.

powerful signs. Come, where have you ever noticed it raining yet without clouds? But Zeus should have rained in a clear sky, while the clouds were out of the way.—By Apollo, you coupled that one nicely with the rest of your argument. To think I used to believe that Zeus was pissing through a sieve! But tell me, who is it who thunders, and makes me tremble at it?—These clouds thunder when they roll around.—You've got a nerve! How does that happen?—Whenever they are full of a lot of water, and necessity makes them move around, hanging in the sky full of water because of necessity, then they bump into one another when they are heavy, and they burst with a bang.—But who is it who compels them by necessity to move? Isn't that Zeus?—Not at all! It's a vortex in the sky.—Vortex? That's something I hadn't heard, that there is no Zeus, but now Vortex has taken over as king.

Socrates

582 Aristophanes' parody of naturalism purports to represent the teaching of Socrates. Socrates himself comments that Aristophanes' picture made people more willing to credit the charges of religious offences that were brought against him many years later.[6] Socrates was accused of not recognizing the gods of the city, of introducing new gods, and of corrupting the young men. One of his associates, Critias, wrote a play in which a character suggests that belief in gods is simply the result of propaganda devised by rulers (**584**).

Socrates denies the religious charges and shows why the charges are unjustified, though not entirely implausible. He believes in the existence of the gods; he believes that Apollo spoke through the Delphic Oracle, and that we are morally required to do what is enjoined on us by the gods.[7] In the *Crito* the Laws tell him that if he disobeys the laws of Athens, he must expect that after his death the divine laws will condemn him for his injustice. These beliefs agree with conventional views. However, some of Socrates' claims and assumptions about the gods are not entirely conventional. In the *Euthyphro* he casts doubt on several aspects of the conventional picture of the gods, derived from Homer and Hesiod. He objects to the view that the gods could quarrel or disagree, or hold different views about what is right and wrong. To cast doubt on such a view is to cast doubt on many of the traditional stories about the gods.

Socrates raises an even broader question about traditional views of the gods. He and Euthyphro agree that the gods must approve of what is pious because it is pious; gods do not make a specific type of behaviour pious simply by commanding or approving of it. We must not conceive the gods as having arbitrary or capricious likes and dislikes; they must approve of what is right and wrong

---

[6] The *Clouds* was performed in 423. The trial of Socrates was in 399.
[7] Obedience to the gods; **453**.

for some other reason than that they approve of it. An unsympathetic critic might conclude that Socrates' gods are not the gods of traditional Greek religion, but his own moralized substitutes for them. This conclusion would be mistaken, but understandable.

The charge that Socrates introduces new supernatural beings might be supported by his references to his 'divine sign' (*daimonion*; **317, 540**). Sometimes he claims to receive instructions from 'the god' instructing him through this sign. He refers to the sign, and hence to divine authority, for many of his most controversial actions. Most important, he takes it as the divine warrant for his life spent in philosophical inquiry.

This appeal to a divine sign may appear to support the charge that Socrates appeals to new gods not recognized by the state. It may also appear to expose him to a charge of inconsistency. Socrates claims to examine himself and others, and to act on the basis of the reason that seems best to him on examination (**454**). Does he not abandon this self-imposed standard if he acts on an appeal to divine authority communicated by his sign?

Socrates' answer to this charge may be inferred from his reaction to the pronouncement by the Delphic Oracle that no one was wiser than Socrates. Though he finds this judgement surprising and difficult to believe, he does not dismiss it as false. Instead, he assumes that the god's utterance needs some interpretation. Examination of other people shows the sense in which the god is right. Socrates has found good reason for believing what the god meant when he 'gave a sign' (as Heracleitus puts it; **139–40**).

....

583   PLATO, *Apology* 18A–19C   First, it is right for me to reply to the first charges and to my first accusers; then I will go to the later ones. For many have accused me to you; they accused me many years ago, and their false charges have continued for many years; and I am more afraid of them than of Anytus and his associates, though these are formidable too. The more formidable accusers are the ones who began when you were children, and kept trying to persuade you with their falsehoods. ... Socrates, they say, is doing injustice, and showing improper curiosity; he inquires into things under the earth and in the heavens, he makes the weaker argument the stronger, and he teaches these same things to others. That is the character of the accusation; for that is what you have seen yourselves in the comedy of Aristophanes; someone called Socrates swings back and forth, claiming to be walking in the air, and talking a great deal of nonsense on questions about which I understand neither much nor little. ... The fact is, Athenians, that I have nothing to do with these things. Very many of those present here can testify to this—all those who have ever heard my conversations.[8] To them I appeal: Tell one another, you who have heard me, whether any of

[8] *dialegesthai*. Perhaps used specifically for Socrates' cross-examinations. See **142**.

you have ever heard me in conversation, either much or little, on matters of this sort.[9]

584 SEXTUS, *Against the Professors* ix. 54–6 And Critias, one of these who held the tyranny at Athens, appears to be one of the atheists, when he says that the ancient lawgivers made up a god as an overseer of correct actions and offences by human beings, so that no one would secretly commit injustice on a neighbour, because of fear of revenge by the gods. What he says is as follows:[10] 'There was a time when the life of human beings was disorderly and bestial and subject to superior strength, and there was no reward for good actions or correction for bad actions. And then human beings, it seems to me, set up laws to correct them, so that justice would become tyrant[11] ... and would hold insolence as a slave. Anyone who committed an offence paid a penalty. But since the laws prevented people by force from committing unjust actions that would be detected, they went on committing them in secret.[12] And so next, it seems to me, some clever and ingenious man first invented fear of the gods for mortals, so that bad people would be afraid even if they were doing or saying or thinking something in secret. For this reason, then, he introduced the divine, saying: "There is a supernatural being flourishing in indestructible life. Through mind, it hears, sees, and understands ... It will hear all that is said among mortals, and will be able to see whatever is done. If in silence you plot some evil action, the gods will find out. ... " With these coils of fear he captured human beings ... and through laws he quelled lawlessness.' ... According to some people, Protagoras of Abdera agrees with these atheists. ... He wrote, in so many words: 'Concerning the gods, I cannot say either whether they are or of what sort they are; for many things prevent me.' On this charge the Athenians condemned him to death, but he escaped and died by shipwreck at sea.[13]

585 DIOGENES LAERTIUS ii. 40 The affidavit in this case against Socrates was as follows—for, according to Favorinus, it is still preserved in the Metroon:[14] 'The following things were alleged and sworn by Meletus son of Meletus of Pitthos, against Socrates son of Sophroniscus of Alopece: Socrates commits injustice by not recognizing the gods whom the city recognizes, but introducing new supernatural beings. He also commits injustice by corrupting the young men. The proposed penalty is death.'

---

[9] Continued in **139**.

[10] This is a speech by Sisyphus in a lost play by Critias (which another source ascribes to Euripides). Probably Sisyphus was punished (in accordance with the traditional story) for his impiety later in the play.

[11] A gap in the text. Tyrants; **531**.

[12] Fear of punishment for injustice; **457**.

[13] Protagoras; **156**.

[14] The Metroon was a temple in Athens that was a depository for official records.

586 PLATO, *Euthyphro* 10A–11E[15] SOCRATES: Consider this: do the gods love the holy because it is holy, or is it holy because they love it? EUTHYPHRO: I don't know what you mean, Socrates.—I'll try to express it more clearly. We speak of something carrying and of something carried, of something leading and something led, of something seeing and something seen. You know that in all such cases one is different from the other, and in what respect they differ?—I think I know.—And isn't what is loved different from what loves?—Certainly.—Now tell me, is what is carried carried because something carries it,[16] or because of something else?—No; because of that.—And the same is true of what is led and of what is seen?—Yes.—And something does not see a thing because it is seen, but, on the contrary, a thing is seen because something sees it. Nor does something lead something because it is led, nor carry something because it is carried, but the contrary is true. ... Equally, then, it is not because something is loved that those who love it love it, but rather it is loved because they love it?—Necessarily.

—Then what do we say about the holy, Euthyphro? Don't all the gods love it, according to your account?—Yes.—Because it is holy, or because of something else?—No, because of this.—Then they love it because it is holy, and it's not the case that it's holy because they love it?—So it would seem.—But it is loved by the gods and beloved of them because they love it?—Of course.— Then the god-beloved is not <the> holy, Euthyphro, nor is the holy <the> god-beloved, but the one is different from the other.—How do you mean, Socrates?—I mean that we agree that the gods love the holy because it is holy, and it is not the case that it is holy because they love it. Isn't that right?— Yes.—Whereas the god-beloved is god-beloved precisely because the gods love it, and it is not the case that they love it because it is god-beloved.— You're right.—But if the god-beloved and the holy were the same, Euthyphro, then, if the holy were loved because it is holy, the gods would also love the god-beloved because it is god-beloved, and if the god-beloved were god-beloved because the gods love it, then the holy would be holy because the gods love it. In fact, however, as you see, quite the contrary is true of them, since they are different. For the god-beloved is such as to be loved because the gods love it, whereas the holy is loved because it is such as to be loved. Indeed, it seems to me, Euthyphro, that when I ask you what the holy is, you don't want to make clear to me what it is,[17] but just tell me something that happens to it, that this is what happens to the holy, that all the gods love it. But what it is because of which this happens to it, you haven't yet said. And so, if you please, don't hide it, but tell me over again from the beginning, what the holy

---

[15] Earlier stages in the argument; **144**, **148**.

[16] The translation tries to convey the main point that Socrates conveys through the use of different parts of the Greek verb.

[17] Literally, 'make clear its being' (essence; *ousia*). On *ousia* see **227** n.

is so that all the gods love it, or whatever else happens to it—for that is not what we will differ about—but tell me eagerly what is the holy and the unholy.

—I really don't know, Socrates, how to express what I have in mind. For somehow or other whatever we put forward, whatever ground we rest it on, it turns round and won't stay where it is.—What you're talking about, Euthyphro, would seem to be the work of my ancestor Daedalus. If I were the one stating and putting forward these things, you would presumably have mocked me, and said that because I'm a descendant of his, my handiwork in my arguments runs away and refuses to stay where it's put. But, as things are, since these are your assumptions, you'll have to find some other joke at my expense; for they certainly, as you yourself allow, refuse to stay still for you.— Well, Socrates, I think what you've said calls for the very same joke. For it isn't me who makes the arguments go round and never stay in the same place. It seems to me that you're the Daedalus; for, as far as it's up to me, they would have stayed still.—Then I seem to be more formidable than that man Daedalus in his craft. For he only made his own products move, whereas I can move other people's products as well as my own. And indeed the most sophisticated aspect of my craft is this, that I am wise against my will. For I would prefer my arguments to stay still and to be immovably stable than to have the wisdom of Daedalus and the wealth of Tantalus thrown in.

Cosmic teleology: Plato

587 In the ostensibly autobiographical sketch in the *Phaedo*, Socrates describes his early interest in natural philosophy (**96**). He believes that human action should be understood as the product of intelligent thought aiming at the good. He is disappointed to find that natural philosophers do not try to explain the universe as a whole in the same way. Anaxagoras came close to the appropriate sort of explanation, because he took mind to be a primary cause; but even he did not notice that it is characteristic of mind to aim at the best result, and so he did not try to understand the cosmos as a product of intelligent design.

This demand for an account of the world relying on cosmic teleological explanation may be influenced by Socrates' moralized conception of the gods. In the *Republic*, Plato insists that the gods must be represented as entirely good and entirely free from vices or imperfections (**590**). Since only human limitations and vices prevent us from diffusing our goodness, the gods, being perfect, must want to diffuse their perfection as widely as possible; hence they must produce a cosmic order that displays their goodness. The Form of the good explains not only human actions and human virtues, but also the nature of the universe and the various processes in it (**214–15**).

This suggestion is developed most elaborately in the *Timaeus* (**591**). The natural world is described as a living organism that has been produced by a divine 'craftsman' or 'Demiurge' (*dêmiourgos*) who was guided by the perfection of the Forms and tried to reproduce it in the material available to him. The goal-directed behaviour of plants and animals and their adaptation to their natural environment display the sort of order that we normally treat as evidence of a designing mind. Plato infers that they have been designed by a divine mind.

Though the Demiurge is good and benevolent, he is not all-powerful. He does not create things from nothing, and he does not choose his raw material. Just as artefacts produced by human craftsmen reflect both the skill of the craftsman and the inherent limitations of the material, the cosmos reflects both the goodness of its designer and the inherent tendencies and limitations of the material he has to work with. Hence the world does not adequately reflect the goodness of its designer.

Plato's division between the divine goodness and the partially recalcitrant matter influences his conception of causation and explanation. As well as recognizing the final cause, ultimately resting on divine design, he recognizes a secondary, 'wandering' cause. This secondary cause sometimes gives us the only available explanation, in cases where the result is explained by the characteristics of the matter, without reference to the goodness of the result (**95–9**).

From this teleological point of view, materialism (of the sort accepted by Atomists) is at most part of the truth. Plato recognizes a place for explanations that refer to material composition and to processes that are neither the result of conscious intention nor goal-directed in any other way. But he believes that non-teleological explanations fail to explain those aspects of the universe that display the order characteristic of design.

Once we recognize that the cosmos as a whole manifests divine intelligence and goodness, we see, in Plato's view, that the gods are also concerned specifically about human well-being. The traditional belief that the gods reward and punish turns out to be partly justified; for though the gods cannot be bribed by gifts and sacrifices,[18] they are concerned about the welfare of human society, and hence they reward justice and punish injustice. In the ideal state described in the *Laws*, Plato makes belief in these gods compulsory; he prescribes re-education or punishment for people who deny the existence of these gods. Plato regards unbelief not simply as an intellectual error, but also as a threat to general acceptance of moral requirements, and hence as a threat to the welfare of the state.

....

588 SIMPLICIUS, *Commentary on the Physics* 156. 13–23 About mind Anaxagoras[19] wrote these things: 'Mind is something infinite and self-controlling, and it has been mixed with no thing, but is alone itself by itself. ...

[18] Contrast Cephalus in **457**.
[19] Anaxagoras; **96**, **242**.

And mind controls all the things, both great and small, that possess soul. And mind controlled the whole revolution, so that it revolved in the beginning.'

589 XENOPHON, *Memoirs of Socrates* i. 4. 2–19   I will first state what I once heard Socrates say about the supernatural in conversation with Little Aristodemus, as he was called. On learning that Aristodemus did not sacrifice or pray or use divination, but ridiculed those who did so, Socrates said: ... 'Take two creatures, and suppose it is unclear what one of them is for, but obvious that the other is for some benefit. Which one, in your judgement, is the product of chance, and which one of intelligence?' 'One would expect the creature that comes into being for some benefit to be the product of intelligence.' 'Then don't you think that whoever made human beings from the beginning made them for some benefit, in giving them their various senses—eyes to see visible objects, ears to hear sounds? And would odours be of any use to us had we not been given nostrils? What perception would we have of sweet and bitter and everything pleasant to the palate if we had no tongue in our mouth to distinguish them? ... When all this is so characteristic of forethought, are you still puzzled about whether they are the products of chance or of intelligence?' 'No, of course not. When I look at them in this way, they look very like the works of some wise and life-loving craftsman.' 'And what about the implanting of the desire to produce children, the mother's desire to care for her children, the children's overriding longing to live and overriding fear of death?' 'Undoubtedly these also look like the contrivances of one who planned the existence of living creatures.' 'Do you think you have any wisdom yourself?' 'Ask me a question, and judge from my answer.' 'Then do you suppose that wisdom is nowhere else to be found, although you know that you have a mere speck of all the earth in your body and a mere drop of all the water, and that of all the other great elements you received, I suppose, just a scrap towards the fashioning of your body? But as for mind, which alone, it seems, is without mass, do you think that you snapped it up[20] by a lucky accident? Do you really think all these huge masses, infinite in number, are in good order because of some unthinking process?' 'Yes; for I don't see the controller, whereas I see the craftsmen of things in this world.' 'But neither do you see your own soul, which controls the body; and so, as far as that argument goes, you might as well say that you do nothing by intelligence, but everything by chance.' Aristodemus said: 'I don't despise the supernatural. On the contrary; I think it is too magnificent to need my service.' 'Then the more magnificent the being that thinks it right to serve you, the more you must honour it.' 'I assure you, that if I believed that the gods took any thought for human beings, I would not neglect them.' 'Then do you suppose they don't think of us? ... Isn't it obvious to you that, in comparison with the

---

[20] This passage is cited in **614**.

other animals, human beings live like gods, since they are naturally superior both in body and in soul? For if they had human intelligence but the body of an ox, they could not do what they wanted; again, having hands but having no reason is of no benefit. After receiving these two most valuable gifts, do you still suppose the gods take no care of you? ... Be well assured, my good friend, that your mind within you deals as it wants to with your body; equally you must recognize that the wisdom in the universe arranges everything as it pleases ... try the gods by serving them, and see whether they will be willing to advise you in matters unclear to human beings. Then you will know that such is the greatness and the nature of the divine that it sees all things and hears all things at the same time, and is present in all places and heedful of all things.' It seemed to me that by saying these things Socrates was making his companions avoid impious, unjust, and shameful actions, not only when other people saw them, but even when they were unobserved, since they thought that nothing they did would ever escape the gods.

590 PLATO, *Republic* 379BC [SOCRATES:] Isn't God good in reality, and mustn't we say so? [ADEIMANTUS:] Certainly.—But further, no good thing is harmful, is it?—I don't think so.—Can what is not harmful harm?—Not at all.—Can what does no harm inflict anything bad?—Not that either.—But can whatever inflicts nothing bad cause anything bad either?—How could it?—Once more, is the good beneficent?—Yes.—It is the cause, then, of welfare?—Then the good is not the cause of all things. It causes things that are in a good condition, but it is not responsible for things in a bad condition.—Quite right, he said.—Neither, then, I said, could God, being good, be the cause of everything, as the many say he is. For human beings he is the cause of few things, but there are many things for which he is not responsible; for good things are far fewer for us than bad things. For the good things we must hold God himself responsible, but for bad things we must seek some other cause, not God.

591 PLATO, *Timaeus* 27E–30B[21] TIMAEUS: First, then, in my judgement, we must make this distinction. What is it that always is and has no becoming, and what is it that is always becoming and never is? The first is grasped by intellect with reason; it is always in the same state. The second is a matter of belief combined with unreasoning sense-perception; it is always becoming and perishing, but never really being. Now everything that becomes must of necessity become from some cause; for without a cause nothing can have any becoming. When the craftsman attends to what is always in the same state, and uses this sort of pattern, so as to produce its character and capacity in his work, everything he produces in this way must necessarily be fine. But when

---

[21] Socrates' brief remarks in reply to Timaeus have been omitted.

he attends to what has come to be, and uses a standard that has come to be, his work cannot be fine.

Was the heaven, then, or the ordered world … always in being without any beginning, or did it come to be from a beginning? It came to be, since it is visible and tangible and has a body, and is therefore sensible, and all sensible things, being grasped by belief with sense-perception, were shown to be things that come to be and have come to be. Now we say that what has come to be must necessarily have come to be from some cause. But the father and producer of all this universe is difficult to find; and even if we found him, we could not describe him to everyone. The question, however, we must ask about the world is this: which of the patterns had the craftsman in view when he made it—the one that is always in the same state, or the one that has come to be? If this world-order is fine and the craftsman is good, clearly he was attending to the eternal pattern; if, however, what cannot be said without blasphemy is true,[22] he attended to one that has come to be. Now it is clear to everyone that he must have attended to the eternal pattern; for the world is the finest of things that have come to be, and he is the best of causes. …

[29D] Let me tell you, then, the reason why the one who constituted coming to be and this whole universe constituted it. He was good, and the good can never have any envy[23] of anything. And being without envy, he wanted all things to be as similar to himself as they could be. … God wanted all things to be good and nothing bad, as far as that was possible. And so, finding the whole visible universe not at rest, but moving with an irregular and disorderly motion, he led it out of disorder into order, considering that this was unconditionally better than the other.

592 PLATO, *Timaeus* 48A   … The coming to be of this world is a mixture of necessity and the constitutive work of mind. Mind ruled necessity by persuading it to bring most things that come to be to the best condition. In this way and on this principle in the beginning, through necessity overcome by wise persuasion, this universe was constituted.

593 PLATO, *Laws* 889A–890A   ATHENIAN VISITOR: It would seem, so they[24] say, that all the greatest and finest things are products of nature and chance, and only the minor things are products of craft … Fire and water, earth and air—so they say—are all by nature and chance, and none is by craft; and their entirely inanimate movements result in the earth, sun, moon, and stars. The elements moved around according to the chance effects of their various capacities. As they happened to come together in some suitable arrangements, … they generated the whole heaven and everything in it …,

---

[22] The goodness of the world; contrast **609**.
[23] *phthonos*, implying the desire for other things to be inferior to oneself. Cf. **350**, **388**.
[24] Atheists, who deny the existence of gods and their concern for human beings.

not, so they say, because of mind, or any god, or craft but ... by nature and chance.

594 PLATO, *Laws* 894E–896C   When we find one thing making a change in a second, the second in turn changing a third, and so on—will there ever, in such a series, be a first source of change? If something is set moving by another thing, how can it ever be the first of the causes of alteration? That would be impossible. But when something that has set itself moving alters a second thing, this second thing still a third, and then thousands and tens of thousands of things are moved, will there be any starting-point for the whole movement of all, other than the change in the motion that initiated itself? ... [895E] Well, then, what is the account of the thing for which 'soul' is the name? Can we find any account besides what we just said, 'the motion that is capable of initiating itself'? ... And so it will be correct, strictly true, and complete to say, as we did, that soul came to be before body, that body is secondary and derivative, and that by nature soul rules and body is ruled.

595 PLATO, *Laws* 899D–900B   We must now win over the one who thinks gods exist, but are not concerned with human matters. My good friend, we will say, as for your belief in gods, some kinship with the divine presumably draws you to honour and to recognize what has a common nature with you. On the other side there are private and public fortunes of bad and unjust people. Though these are really not happy, they are vigorously, though inappropriately, extolled as happy by popular beliefs. These draw you toward impiety, when you hear them incorrectly celebrated in poetry and in all sorts of discourses. ... Because of all this, you are clearly unwilling to blame the gods for the good fortune of bad people, because of your kinship with the gods. Unreasonableness and inability to complain of the gods have brought you to your present condition—to your conviction that though the gods indeed exist, they disdain and disregard human matters.

Aristotle: cosmic teleology

596 Aristotle is influenced by Plato's cosmic teleology, and by Plato's theistic interpretation of it. He disagrees with Plato, however, on some quite central points. He argues that Plato's belief in design is not the only alternative to Atomist materialism.

Aristotle finds final causation primarily in events and processes that benefit a particular organism or a species of organisms (**238–46**). His main arguments for teleological explanation neither presuppose nor defend inter-species teleology. Nor does he ever argue that the world as a whole constitutes a single goal-directed system.

None the less, Aristotle sometimes endorses these broader teleological claims. He treats the world as a single goal-directed order in which the behaviour of one species benefits another species. But he does not infer that this order was produced at any time by a designer. Indeed, he firmly rejects this Platonic inference, since he denies that the world ever began. In his view, the order of nature is unchanging, without beginning or end. He does not ask why the world contains organisms that are susceptible of teleological explanation; he seems to regard this as an ultimate fact not open to further explanation.

597 ARISTOTLE, *Parts of Animals* 696^{b}23–32   Fishes differ in respect of their mouth. Some have it in front, right at the end of the body; others, such as the dolphin and the selachians, have it underneath; that is why they turn on their backs to take food. Nature appears to have done this not only to preserve other animals, because the predators slow down in turning, and the others get away (for all the fishes with the mouth underneath eat other animals), but also to prevent these fishes from giving way too much to their gluttony about food. For if they had been able to get food more easily than they do, they would soon have perished from over-eating.

598 ARISTOTLE, *Politics* 1256^{b}10–26   Nature itself has evidently given possessions, in the sense of the means of life, to all, both when they are first born, and when they are grown up. For some animals bring forth, together with their offspring, enough food to last until they are able to supply themselves. The vermiparous or oviparous animals are an instance of this; and the viviparous animals have up to a certain time a supply of food—called milk—in themselves for their young. In the same way, then, it is clear that one must suppose that, after the birth of animals, plants exist for their sake, and that the other animals exist for the sake of man, the tame for use and food, the wild— most, at any rate, if not all—for food, and to supply clothing and various instruments. Now if nature makes nothing incomplete, and nothing pointlessly, it must necessarily have made all animals for the sake of human beings. And so, from one point of view, the craft of war is by nature an acquisitive craft, since the acquisitive craft includes hunting. It is a craft we ought to use against wild beasts, and against those human beings who, though naturally suited to be ruled, do not want to be ruled; for war of this sort is naturally just.

Aristotle's God

599 Since Aristotle rejects the explanation of natural teleology that takes it to be a temporal product of design, his belief in intra-species and inter-species teleology does not form a premiss of any argument for the existence of a designing god. None the less, he believes that nature as a whole has something divine about it. Nature is not an ordinary agent with specific aims and intentions carried out at particular times. Still, he speaks of nature in personal terms, as trying, succeeding, or failing. It is difficult to say how far Aristotle ascribes some sort of agency to nature.

His argument for the existence of a god rests on the claim that the explanation of motion requires us to recognize a first mover. This first mover cannot itself be moved by something else (since that would lead us into an infinite regress), but must initiate the motion of everything else that is moved. This belief in a first mover implies the acceptance of one part of the traditional belief in gods as causes of natural processes and human actions. Since this first mover needs nothing further to bring its capacity to initiate motion into actuality, it is always in actuality. Since potentiality belongs to matter, and actuality to form, the divine first mover is also pure form, and hence the most perfect substance (**601–2**; cf. **253**). Aristotle's conceptions of nature, motion, and substance combine in his account of the divine substance.

In Aristotle's view, the role of divine substance as first cause does not imply the truth of Plato's claims about design; for he rejects Plato's view about the character of divine activity. While Plato believes that creation is to be expected from perfect gods, Aristotle takes creation to be incompatible with divine perfection. Drawing on another element in traditional views about the gods, he argues that the gods are completely happy, and hence undisturbed, self-sufficient, and unmoved.

....

600 ARISTOTLE, *Physics* 256ᵃ4–259ᵃ13 <Everything that is moved is moved by something.> This is true in two ways: either B moves A not because of B itself, but because of something else C that moves B, or B moves A because of B itself. In the second case this is true either because B is the first thing immediately preceding A, or because B moves A through a number of intermediaries, as when the stick moves the stone, and the stick is moved by the hand, which is moved by the man, who is moved, but not by being moved by some further thing. We say that both the last and the first mover move the object, but the first mover does so to a higher degree. For the first mover moves the last mover, but the last does not move the first. Moreover, without the first mover the last mover will not move the object, but the first will move it without the last; the stick, for instance, will not move the stone unless the man moves the stick. It is necessary, then, for whatever is moved to be moved by some mover, either by a mover that is in turn moved by something else moving it or by a mover that is not moved by something else moving it. And if it is moved by something else moving it, there must be some first mover that is not moved by anything else; and if this is the character of the first mover, no further mover is needed. For it is impossible to have an infinite series of movers each of which moves something and is moved by something else; for there is no first term in an infinite series. If, then, everything that is moved is moved by something, and if the first mover is moved, but not by anything else, it necessarily follows that it is moved by itself ...

[258^{b}10] Since motion must be everlasting and must never fail, there must be some everlasting first mover, one or more than one. The question whether each of the unmoved movers is everlasting is irrelevant to this argument; but it will be clear in the following way that there must be something that is itself unmoved and outside all change, either unqualified or coincidental, but moves something else. Let us suppose, then, if you like, that in the case of some things it is possible for them to be at one time and not to be at another without any coming to be or perishing—for if something has no parts, but it is at one time and is not at another time, perhaps it is necessary for it to be at one time and not to be at another without changing. Let us also suppose that, among the principles that are unmoved but move things, it is possible for some to be at one time and not to be at another time. Still, this is not possible for every principle of that sort; for it is clear that there is something that causes the self-movers to be at one time and not to be at another time. For every self-mover necessarily has some magnitude, if nothing that lacks parts is moved; but from what we have said it is not necessary for every mover to have magnitude.

Hence, the cause of the coming to be of some things and the perishing of other things in a continuous sequence cannot be any of the things that are unmoved but do not always exist; nor can some things be the cause of some parts of the sequence and other things the cause of other parts; for neither any one of them nor all of them together is the cause explaining why the sequence is everlasting and continuous. For the sequence is everlasting and necessary, whereas all these movers are infinitely many and they do not all exist at the same time. It is clear, then, that however many unmoved movers and self-movers perish and are succeeded by others, so that one unmoved mover moves one thing and another moves another, still there is something that embraces them all and is apart from each of them, which is the cause of the existence of some things and of the non-existence of other things, and of the continuity of the change. This is the cause of motion in these other movers, and these are the cause of motion in the other things.

If, then, motion is everlasting, the first mover is also everlasting, if there is just one; and if there are more than one, there are more everlasting movers than one. But we must suppose there is one rather than many, and a finite rather than an infinite number. For in every case where the results of either assumption are the same, we should assume a finite number of causes; for among natural things what is finite and better must exist rather than its opposite if this is possible. And one mover is sufficient, which is first and everlasting among the unmoved things, and the principle of motion for the other things.

601 ARISTOTLE, *Metaphysics* 1072ᵃ9–27   If, then, the same things always exist in a cycle, something must always remain actually operating in the same way. And if there is to be coming to be and perishing, there must be something else that always actually operates, in one way at one time and in another way at another time. This, then, must actually operate in one way because of itself and in another way because of something else, and hence either because of some third mover or because of the first mover. Hence it must be because of the first mover; for otherwise the first mover will cause the motion of both the second and the third. Then surely it is better if the first mover is the cause. For we have seen that it is the cause of what is always the same, and a second mover is the cause of what is different at different times. Clearly both together cause this everlasting succession. Then surely this is also how the motions occur. Why, then, do we need to search for any other principles? Since it is possible for things to be as we have said they are, and since the only alternative is for everything to come to be from night and from all things being together and from what is not,²⁵ this may be taken as the solution of the puzzles.

There is something, then, that is always being moved in a ceaseless motion, and this motion is circular (this is clear not only from argument but also from what actually happens); and so the first heaven is everlasting. Hence there is also some mover. And since whatever both is moved and moves something else is an intermediary, there is a mover that moves something without being moved; this mover is everlasting, substance, and actuality. This is how an object of understanding or desire moves something; it moves it without itself being moved.

602 ARISTOTLE, *Metaphysics* 1072ᵇ13–30   This, then, is the sort of principle on which the heavens and nature depend. Its life has the character that our own life at its best has for a short time. For the primary mover is always in this state of complete actuality, whereas we cannot always be in it; for its actuality is also pleasure (that is why being awake, perceiving, and thinking are pleasantest, while expectations and memories are pleasant because of these).

Understanding in its own right is of what is best in its own right, and the highest degree of understanding is of what is best to the highest degree. And understanding understands itself by sharing the character of the object of understanding; for it becomes an object of understanding by being in contact with and understanding its object, so that understanding and its object are the same. For understanding is what is capable of receiving the object of understanding and the essence, and it is actually understanding when it possesses its object; and so it is this actual understanding and possession rather than the capacity to receive the object that seems to be the divine aspect of

---

²⁵ Various suggestions of the poets and Presocratic philosophers.

understanding, and its actual attention to the object of understanding is pleasantest and best.

If, then, the god is always in the good state that we are in sometimes, that deserves wonder; if he is in a better state, that deserves still more wonder. And that is indeed the state he is in. Further, life belongs to the god. For the actuality of understanding is life, and the god is that actuality; and his actuality in its own right is the best and everlasting life. We say, then, that the god is the best and everlasting living being, so that continuous and everlasting life and duration belong to the god; for that is what the god is.

603 ARISTOTLE, *Metaphysics* 1074ª38–ᵇ14   A tradition has been handed down from the distant past to later generations, that these stars are gods and that the divine embraces the whole of nature. The rest of the tradition is a mythical accretion, added to persuade the many and to use in upholding what is lawful and advantageous;[26] for those who handed it down say that the gods have human form or are similar to other animals, and they add other features following from these and similar to them. But if we separate the first point and consider it alone—that they thought the primary substances were gods—we will regard it as a divine insight, on the assumption that every craft and philosophical discipline has probably often been discovered, as far as people could manage it, and often died out again, and this belief has survived like remains from earlier generations until the present. And so the truth of the ancestral beliefs coming from the earliest times is evident to us only to this extent.

Happiness: becoming like God?

604 Aristotle's conception of the gods and their life also influences his ethics. In his view, the highest fulfilment of a human being's nature as a rational agent is the form of activity that brings us closest to the gods, since these are the most purely rational beings.

In deriving claims abut the human good from the divine nature, Aristotle follows some suggestions by Plato. In some places (especially **605**) Plato urges rational beings to aspire to become like god (or 'like the divine'). In such a condition we are as free as possible of the demands of the body and the other aspects of embodied life, including the demands of other people. By escaping these constraints of our present existence, we come closer to the condition of pure intellects. Since this is the permanent condition of the gods, or of God,[27] we ought to aim at this condition.

---

[26] Political use of belief in gods; **584**.
[27] Plato and Aristotle speak of the divine both in the plural and in the singular.

Aristotle does not connect the life of pure intellect to the life of a disembodied soul. But in other ways his conception of the best life for a human being is similar to Plato's. He sometimes suggests that the highest form of rational activity is 'contemplation' or 'study' (theôria), with no practical aim or application. Since the gods are self-sufficient and need nothing, this is their permanent form of life, and human beings should come as close to it as possible.

What do these claims about pure intellect imply for Plato's and Aristotle's claim that happiness consists in a life that includes the practice of the moral and social virtues for their own sake? Different answers have been suggested.

(1) According to later Platonists, the other-worldly aspect of Plato's ethics is his considered view of the human good. He advocates the moral and social virtues simply as expedients for maintaining ourselves in the world, and as 'purifications' (**327**), freeing us from preoccupation with the needs connected with the body. Similarly, one might take Aristotelian virtues of character to be simply means to secure favourable conditions for contemplation.

(2) The moral and the non-moral conceptions represent two conflicting accounts of the human good. One of them rests on ethical grounds, the other on metaphysical and theological grounds, and they cannot be reconciled (cf. **612**).

(3) They are two alternative conceptions of happiness. The moral conception is intended for people who cannot aspire to the contemplative level. Those who are capable of the contemplative level must leave behind the moral conception.

(4) Plato's and Aristotle's claims about the life of pure intellect are consistent with the composite view of happiness; both intellectual activity and activity guided by the moral virtues are parts of the best life. Both philosophers take intellectual activity to be the most important part, but not the whole, of the best life; while neither explains in detail how we might deal with apparent conflicts between intellectual and moral components of happiness, they do not oppose a purely intellectual to a purely moral conception of happiness.

These different possible interpretations allow us to raise some of the same questions about both Plato and Aristotle. We may not want to give the same answer in each case. It may be relevant, for instance, that Plato and Aristotle draw different conclusions from the self-sufficiency of a god. Aristotle infers that a god has no reason to be interested in the welfare of others. Plato infers that a god will want to diffuse his goodness by creating good things. Trying to become 'like god' may lead to different actions, according to which conception of the god we accept.

605 PLATO, *Theaetetus* 173C–177A SOCRATES: Since this is your wish, I will describe the leaders in philosophy ... First, they have never, from their youth, known their way to the market-place,[28] or the courts, or the council, or any other gathering of the city. They neither see nor hear the laws or decrees of the city written or read out. ... Nor does the philosopher even know that he doesn't know these things. For he does not avoid them for the sake of acquiring a reputation. In fact, only his body resides in the city. His mind regards all these things as trivial and insignificant; it disdains them, and takes flight, ... searching out the whole nature of each thing as a whole, and descending to nothing close at hand. THEODORUS: What do you mean, Socrates?—It's like the story about Thales. He is supposed to have been examining the stars and looking upwards until he fell into a well. Some clever and witty Thracian maid made fun of him, saying he was keen to know about things in the heavens, but he didn't notice things in front of him and at his feet. This joke fits all who spend their time in philosophy. For the philosopher knows nothing about what his next-door neighbour is doing, and scarcely even knows whether he is a human being or some other creature. He inquires to discover what a human being is, and what is proper for such a nature, as distinct from others, to do or to undergo. ...

[176A] Evils, Theodorus, can never pass away; for something must always remain that is opposed to good. Since they cannot settle among the gods, they necessarily haunt mortal nature on this earth.[29] That is why we ought to flee from earth to heaven as quickly as we can. Flight is becoming like God, as far as this is possible; and becoming like him is becoming just, holy, and wise. But it's not easy, my friend, to persuade people that we ought to avoid vice and pursue virtue not simply for the sake of seeming to be good rather than bad, which is the reason most people give[30]—this reason, it seems to me, is simply an old wives' tale. The truth is that God is not unjust in any way or respect, but the most just possible; and the one who is most like him is the one among us who becomes most just. ... There are two patterns set up in reality: one is of the divine and happiest person, and the other is of the godless and wretched. But people do not see that this is the truth, and do not notice that their stupidity and complete folly makes them like one pattern and unlike the other, because of their unjust actions. Their punishment is to live a life that fits the pattern they are coming to resemble.

606 ARISTOTLE, *Nicomachean Ethics* 1177[a]12–1179[a]32[31] If happiness, then, is activity expressing virtue, it is reasonable for it to express the supreme virtue,

---

[28] A place for discussion, not just for buying and selling.

[29] Cf. **607**.

[30] Reasons for being just; **460**.

[31] These excerpts from Aristotle's lengthy discussion of the relation between happiness and theoretical study emphasize the connections that he sees between theoretical study and becoming like the gods.

which will be the virtue of the best thing. If the best is understanding—or whatever else seems to be the natural ruler and leader and to understand what is fine and divine, by being itself either divine or the most divine element in us—complete happiness will be its activity expressing its proper virtue. We have said that this activity is the activity of study. ...

The self-sufficiency[32] we spoke of will be found in study above all. The wise person, the just person and the other virtuous people all need the necessities of life, but when these are adequately supplied the just person also needs other people as partners and recipients of his just actions, and the same is true of the temperate person, the brave person, and each of the others. The wise person, however, is capable, and more capable the wiser he is, of studying even by himself; though he presumably does it better with colleagues, even so he is most self-sufficient.

Besides, study seems to be liked because of itself alone, since it has no result apart from having studied; but from the virtues concerned with action we try to a greater or lesser extent to gain something beyond the action itself. Happiness seems to be found in leisure, since we accept trouble so that we can be at leisure, and fight wars so that we can be at peace. Now the virtues concerned with action have their activities in politics or war, and actions here seem to require trouble. This seems completely true for actions in war, since no one chooses to fight or prepare a war for the sake of fighting—someone would seem to be a complete murderer if he made his friends his enemies so that there could be battles and killings. But the actions of the politician require trouble also. Apart from political activities themselves those actions seek positions of power and honours; or at least they seek happiness for the politician himself and for his fellow-citizens, which is different from the study of political science itself, and clearly is sought on the assumption that it is different. Hence among actions expressing the virtues those in politics and war are pre-eminently fine and great; but they require trouble, aim at some <further> end, and are choiceworthy for something other than themselves. But the activity of understanding seems to be superior in excellence because it is the activity of study, and seems to aim at no end beyond itself and to have its own proper pleasure, which increases the activity. ...

Such a life would be superior to the human level. For someone will live it not in so far as he is a human being, but in so far as he has some divine element in him. And the activity of this divine element is as much superior to the activity expressing the rest of virtue as this element is superior to the compound. Hence if understanding is something divine in comparison with a human being, so also will the life that expresses understanding be divine in comparison with human life. We ought not to follow the proverb-writers, and 'think human, since you are human', or 'think mortal, since you are mor-

---

[32] Self-sufficiency; **406**.

tal'. Rather, as far as we can, we ought to be pro-immortal, and go to all lengths to live a life that expresses our supreme element; for however much this element may lack in bulk, by much more it surpasses everything in power and value. Moreover, each person seems to be his understanding, if he is his controlling and better element; it would be absurd, then, if he were to choose not his own life, but something else's. ...

The life expressing the other kind of virtue[33] is <happiest> in a secondary way, because the activities expressing this virtue are human. For we do just and brave actions, and the other actions expressing the virtues, in relation to other people, by adhering to what is appropriate for each person in contracts, services, all types of actions, and also in feelings; and all these appear to be human conditions. Indeed, some feelings actually seem to arise from the body, and in many ways virtue of character seems to be proper to feelings. Moreover, prudence is joined to virtue of character, and virtue of character with prudence. For the principles of prudence express the virtues of character; and correctness in virtues of character expresses prudence. Since these virtues are also connected to feelings, they are concerned with the compound. Since the virtues of the compound are human virtues, the life and the happiness expressing these virtues are also human. But the virtue of understanding is separated. ... In so far as he is a human being, however, and lives together with a number of other human beings, he chooses to do the actions expressing virtue. Hence he will need these external goods for living a human life.

In another way also it appears that complete happiness is some activity of study. For we traditionally suppose that the gods are most blessed and happy of all; but what sorts of actions ought we to ascribe to them? Just actions? Surely they will appear ridiculous making contracts, returning deposits and so on. Brave actions? Do they face frightening situations and endure dangers because it is fine? Generous actions? Whom will they give to? And surely it would be absurd for them to have currency or anything like that. What would their temperate actions be? Surely it is vulgar praise to say that they do not have base appetites. When we go through them all, anything that concerns actions appears trivial and unworthy of the gods. However, we all traditionally suppose that they are alive and active, since surely they are not asleep like Endymion. Then if someone is alive, and action is excluded, and production even more, what is left but study? Hence the gods' activity that is superior in blessedness will be an activity of study. And so the human activity that is most akin to the gods' activity will most of all have the character of happiness. ...

The person whose activity expresses understanding and who cultivates his understanding would seem to be in the best condition, and most loved by

---

[33] i.e. virtue of character, concerned with action (**444**).

the gods. For if the gods pay some attention to human beings, as they seem to, it would be reasonable for them to take pleasure in what is best and most akin to them, namely understanding, and it would be reasonable for them to benefit in return those who most of all like and honour understanding, on the assumption that these people attend to what is beloved by the gods, and act correctly and finely. Clearly, all this is true of the wise person more than anyone else; hence he is most loved by the gods. And it is likely that this same person will be happiest; hence, by this argument also, the wise person will be happiest.

607 PLOTINUS, *Enneads* i. 2. 1, 7 Since evils are here,[34] and 'necessarily haunt this earth',[35] and the soul wants to escape from evils, we must escape from here. What, then, is the escape? 'Being likened to god', Plato says. And this happens 'if we become just and pious with wisdom',[36] and altogether in virtue. ... It is clear that our good order and our virtues also come from there. Has the intelligible, then, virtues? It is at any rate not reasonable for it to have the virtues called civic: wisdom concerned with the reasoning part, bravery concerned with the spirited part, temperance lying in some sort of agreement and harmony of the appetitive part with reasoning, justice which is each part doing its own work concerning ruling and being ruled.[37] Then it is not the civic virtues, but the greater virtues with the same names that make us like god? ... (7. 20) Perhaps the possessor of the civic virtues will know them, and how much he will get from them, and will act in accordance with some of them as circumstances require. But when he reaches greater principles and different measures, he will act in accordance with these. For instance, he will not make temperance consist in that previous measure, but will altogether separate himself as far as possible, and will not live the human life of the good person that civic virtue demands. He will have left that behind, and chosen another, the life of the gods; for he becomes similar to them, not to good human beings.

Epicurus on cosmic teleology

608 Epicurus maintains one of the positions attacked by Plato in the *Laws*; he holds that the gods exist, but are not concerned with the world or with human beings. He has two main reasons for denying any cosmic activity to the gods:

---

[34] Plotinus, following Plato, often uses 'here' and 'there' for sensible and intelligible reality.
[35] Quoted from **605**.
[36] See **327**.
[37] Justice; **469**.

(1) In his view, unhappiness comes from fear of death, which we fear because of the threat of punishments after death.[38] If we believe in gods who care about the world, we cannot dismiss the possibility that they reward and punish; and so belief in such gods is a source of fear and anxiety.

(2) Belief in cosmic teleology requires us to recognize explanations that do not refer simply to atoms and their motions. In particular organisms, final causes require the reality of form, as Aristotle conceives it. In the cosmos as a whole, they require some goal-direction on a larger scale, in conflict with the Epicurean belief that the world as a whole is itself simply the product of purposeless movements of atoms.

To undermine belief in any sort of teleology, Epicurus accumulates evidence of imperfections in the world. These are flaws that we would not expect if the world were ordered by final causes. Theophrastus notices some of these limits on the scope of teleological explanation (**247**). Indeed, Plato and Aristotle already acknowledge them; Plato gives an important explanatory role to the 'wandering cause' of the *Timaeus*, and Aristotle attributes a similar role to the material cause (**99, 244–5, 591–2**).

Epicurus also intends his catalogue of imperfections to undermine belief in cosmic teleology and in divine providence. He argues that adverse conditions of life (hunger, disease, natural disasters) would not exist if the world were the product of an intelligent and benevolent designer. Since our world is so unsuitable in many ways for animal and human life, it cannot have been made by a designer, unless the designer was malevolent or incompetent.

Though Epicurus takes these arguments from imperfection to undermine belief in gods who care about the world, he does not reject belief in gods altogether. He takes the existence of gods to be secured by our experience in dreams, visions, and so on. This empirical evidence is supposed to show that the gods have human form, and that they have perfect happiness. Epicurus, however, drawing on Aristotle and opposing Plato, believes that divine perfection and happiness exclude concern for the world. Hence the gods do not guide the world, and do not make moral demands of us; but they provide ideals. The gods have the perfect happiness that the Epicurean ought to aim at.

....

609 LUCRETIUS v. 195–234 Even if I did not know what the primary elements of the world are, I would still be confident enough to affirm from the very character of the heavens, and to show from many other things, that the nature of the world was by no means made for us by the gods—so great is the flaw that disfigures it. First, out of all that the sky's wide expanse covers, mountains and beast-infested forests have captured a greedy share. It is occupied by rocks, vast swamps, and sea, which keeps the coastlines of the lands

---

[38] Cephalus on fear of death; **457**.

far apart. ... And why do the seasons bring diseases with them? Why is un-
timely death all around?

610   EPICURUS = DIOGENES LAERTIUS X. 123   ... Regard god as an animal
who is free from destruction and blessed, as the generally held conception indicates. And do not ascribe to god anything alien to his freedom from destruction or inconsistent with his blessedness. ... For gods do exist, since we
have clear knowledge of them. But the sort that the many recognize do not
exist. ... Since the gods are congenial to their own virtues, and regard anything different as uncongenial, they always welcome human beings who are
like themselves.

611   CICERO, *Nature of the Gods* i. 46–54   [The Epicurean view:] It is partly
nature and partly reason that instructs us about the shape of the gods. From
nature all of us, of all races, gather no other appearance of the gods than a
human shape; for what other shape ever confronts anyone either waking or
sleeping? But so that not everything will be derived from the primary conceptions, reason itself reveals the same thing. For it seems suitable for the
most excellent nature, excellent either because it is blessed or because it is
everlasting, to also be the most beautiful; and what configuration of limbs, or
arrangements of features, or shape, or appearance can be more beautiful
than the human?[39] ... [52] We will be entitled to call this god blessed.

But you Stoics make god a complete drudge. For if god is the world itself,
what can be less tranquil than revolving around the heaven's axis at amazing
speed, without any pause at all? ... [53] For the same person[40] who taught us the
other things also taught us that the world was produced by nature and that
there was no need for any artisan. What you say cannot be produced without
divine wisdom is in fact so easy that nature has produced, is producing, and will
produce, an unlimited number of worlds. Since you do not see how nature can
produce them without some sort of mind, you resort to god, as tragedians do,[41]
when you cannot bring the play to a satisfactory conclusion. ... [54] And so you
have laid on our necks an everlasting master for us to fear day and night; for
who would not fear an inquisitive and busy god who foresees everything, considers and notices everything, and supposes that everything concerns him?

Stoicism: nature and the world order

612   Plato's account of the world treats it as an artefact, designed and produced
by a craftsman who is external to it. Against Plato, Aristotle argues that final

---

[39] Anthropomorphism; **576–7**.

[40] i.e. Epicurus.

[41] In the deus ex machina, the god who sometimes appears above the stage at the end of a Greek
play, to decree a happy ending.

causation is possible without design; he rejects the suggestion that organisms are artefacts and that the world containing them is one large artefact. The Stoic conception of the cosmos combines elements of the Platonic and the Aristotelian views.

The Stoics agree with Plato in regarding the cosmos as a product of intelligent design, but they agree with Aristotle in claiming that final causation does not require an external designer. Instead of thinking of the world as an artefact, they treat it as a rational animal. They argue that it displays the sorts of self-regulation, selection of suitable means to beneficial ends, and so on, that we find in a particular human being, and they infer that the cosmos is also a rational animal, a system of which particular rational and non-rational animals are subsystems. The nature and proper goals of these subsystems are determined by their role in the larger system of which they are parts, just as the nature and proper goals of organs are determined by their place in the larger organism.

According to this organic conception of the cosmos, a cosmic god does not exist outside the world, but is a part of it. Following a suggestion in Plato's *Timaeus*, they attribute a soul to the cosmos as a whole; unlike Plato, they do not clearly recognize a god apart from the world soul. Hence they identify God with the cosmic soul animating the cosmic organism. Since they identify soul with pneuma (**342**), they identify god with the pneuma in the world. This is the immanent rationality in the world order.

The Stoics believe that this conception of God counts as acceptance of the traditional gods. Hence they speak of Zeus as the cosmic pneuma, and treat the other traditional gods as aspects of the world order. In some ways, their claim to be speaking of the traditional gods seems far-fetched. The Stoics reject the Epicurean view that the gods must be conceived anthropomorphically, since they do not suppose that they have human shape. Nor do they ascribe to the gods the impulses and passions of human beings. When they speak, as Homer does, of the will of Zeus, they do not refer to the impulses of an extremely powerful being with human passions and concerns. The will of Zeus is identified with fate, the deterministic order of natural processes (**372–4, 617**).

This does not mean, however, that the Stoics treat talk of god as simply a way of speaking of natural law. In saying that the order of nature is a divine order they are not simply saying that it is law-governed and regular. They are also claiming that it is a providential order. They expect us to see that the processes in the world display the direction that we would expect from a benevolent agent concerned with the good of the whole and of its parts. On this point, they can reasonably claim to be speaking of the gods, rather than replacing them with something quite alien to traditional belief.

A Stoic must therefore answer Epicurus' arguments for the imperfection of the world, since they seem to threaten belief in providence and in a benevolent god. The Stoic may reasonably answer that our understanding of the providential order is more limited than the point of view of cosmic reason. We cannot expect to see the point of everything in the cosmos; some features of it that may be unwelcome or inconvenient from our point of view may none the less be part of an order that can be seen to be good from some larger point of view. Hence these apparent imperfections cannot be taken to conflict with a providential order in the mind of a benevolent god.

This answer is sometimes legitimate, but it may sometimes endanger the Stoic position. If the goodness of the divine order is entirely inscrutable to us, we no longer have any clear reason for believing in it. The Stoics must claim, therefore, that the Epicurean arguments for imperfection are exaggerated, and that the essential goodness of the cosmic order is clear enough to justify belief in the providence immanent in nature.

....

613   PHILO, *Special Laws* i. 32–5 = SVF ii. 1010   In investigations about God the mind of the genuine philosopher is puzzled about these most important questions. First, about whether the divine exists—for the sake of those who have practised atheism, the worst of vices. Second, about what it is in its essence.[42] The first of these does not take much effort to see, whereas the second is not only difficult, but perhaps impossible; still, both must be considered.

Invariably the products are by nature ways of recognizing the craftsman. For who looked at statues or paintings and did not at once think of the sculptor or painter? Who saw clothes or ships or houses and did not get a conception of the weaver or shipwright or housebuilder? If someone comes into a well-governed city, where constitutional matters are well ordered, surely he will infer that this city is overseen by good rulers? Then suppose someone arrives in this true Megalopolis, the universe, and sees hill and plain full of animals and plants, rivers from natural springs and winter rain, the ebbs and flows of seas, the right mixture of air, the cycles of the annual seasons, the sun and moon leading in days and nights, and the movements and processions of the moving and fixed bodies and the whole heaven. If he sees all this, is it not likely, or rather necessary, for him to acquire a conception of the one who is father, producer, and, moreover, leader? For no work of a craft comes to be all by itself; and the universe displays the highest degree of craft and knowledge, as the product of a craftsman who is in every way good and complete in knowledge of production. In this way we have acquired a conception of the existence of God.

614   CICERO, *Nature of the Gods* ii. 16–19   [CHRYSIPPUS:] If there is something in the nature of things that the human mind, reason, strength, and capacity could not produce, certainly what produces it is better than human beings. But the celestial things and all those with an everlasting order cannot be

---

[42] *ousia*; **227** n.

produced by human beings; and so what produces them is better than human beings. And what would you call that rather than god? ... [18] And even from the existence of human intelligence we must infer the existence of some mind that is keener than the human mind and is divine. For from where did human beings 'snap up'—as Socrates put it in Xenophon[43]—the intelligence they have? If anyone asks where we get the moisture and the heat diffused throughout the body, and the earthy density of the flesh, and finally the soul breathing within us—it is plain that we acquire one from earth, one from moisture, one from fire, and one from the air that we take in by breathing. But the thing that surpasses all of these—reason, I mean, or, if you prefer to say it in several words, mind, intelligence, thought, wisdom—where did we find it, where did we take it from? Or is the universe to contain all the other things and not this one that is of most value? But certainly nothing there is is finer or more beautiful than the universe; and not only is there nothing better, but something better cannot even be thought. And if nothing better than reason and wisdom exists, we must allow these to be present in the thing we concede to be best. Such an agreement, conspiracy, connection, and affinity of things—who will not be forced by it to agree with everything I have said? Could the earth flower at one time and then in turn be bare, or could the approach and departure of the sun at midsummer and midwinter be noticed from so many things changing themselves, or could the tides in seas and narrows be moved by the rising and setting of the moon, or could the different courses of the stars be maintained by one turning of the whole sky? These processes involving all the parts of the universe in harmony simply could not happen, unless they were held together by one divine and all-pervading spirit.

615 CICERO, *Nature of the Gods* ii. 22   Chrysippus argued for his position by one of his frequent methods, using a comparison, as follows: 'If flutes playing tunes grew on an olive tree, surely you would have no doubt that some knowledge of flute-playing was present in the olive tree? What if plane trees produced well-tuned lutes? Clearly, you would suppose in the same way that the musical craft was present in the plane trees. Why, then, is the world not judged to be alive and wise, given that from itself it produces living and wise offspring?'[44]

616 DIOGENES LAERTIUS vii. 148–9   By 'nature' the Stoics mean sometimes the nature that holds together the world, sometimes the nature that gives birth to the things on earth. Nature is a state moved from itself, producing and holding together its offspring in accordance with seminal principles, at

---

[43] Xenophon; quoted from **589**.
[44] Cosmos as alive; **264**.

definite times, producing effects similar to their sources. They say that nature aims both at advantage and pleasure, as is clear from the work of human craftsmen.

617 PLUTARCH, *Stoic Contradictions* 1049f–1050b   In his first book *On Nature* Chrysippus says: 'Since the government of the whole proceeds in this way, it is necessary, in accordance with this government, that we are in whatever condition we are in, whether we are ill contrary to our particular nature, or maimed, or have become grammarians or musicians.' And again, a little later: 'In accordance with this account we will say similar things about our virtues and our vices, and in general about crafts and the lack of them, as I said.' And a little later, removing all ambiguity: 'For it is impossible for any particular thing, even the smallest, to come to be except in accordance with the common nature and its account.' That common nature and the common account of nature are fate and providence and Zeus—even the Antipodes have heard this, since the Stoics keep harping on it; and they say that Homer was right to say 'The plan of Zeus was being fulfilled',[45] since he was referring to fate and the nature of the whole, the nature according to which everything is administered.

618 VIRGIL, *Aeneid* vi. 724–32   First, internal breath sustains the heavens, the earth, the flowing expanses of the sea, the shining globe of the moon, and the sun, the Titan's child; mind activates the whole mass, mixed throughout its frame, and blends itself into the huge body. From this source come the race of human beings and of beasts, the lives of flying birds, and the strange creatures that the ocean brings forth below its shining surface. All have their strength from fire, and their seeds have a heavenly origin, in so far as the impeding bodies do not slow them down, or the earthly frame and mortal limbs dull the fire's strength.

Cosmology, ethics, and politics

619 The Stoics' belief in immanent, universal providence is relevant to their moral and political theory. Aristotle describes the relation of an individual human being to a city by comparing it to the relation of an organ to the whole organism (**558**). The Stoics exploit this comparison. They argue that individuals are fellow-citizens (*politai*) in the cosmos, which is the city (*polis*) ruled by god. This is the basis of their cosmopolitan outlook.

In ethics, the cosmopolitan point of view throws a new light on Stoic claims about virtue and happiness. If we practise the virtues, and thereby achieve

[45] Homer; **346–8**.

happiness (as the Stoics understand it; **508–15**), we also harmonize our aims with universal providence. The practical reason that vindicates the life of bravery, justice, and temperance is also our share of the universal reason, which prescribes these same virtues for the good of the whole cosmos.

These claims about the agreement between the moral point of view and the point of view of universal providence raise some questions:

(1) How can we be sure that virtuous action always promotes the plan of providence? Why should providence not sometimes require morally objectionable means to its ends?

(2) How can we be sure that promoting the plan of providence will always promote our individual good? Why not suppose that cosmic order requires the sacrifice of some individuals' good for the greater good of the whole?

(3) Vicious people and vicious actions also promote the plan of providence, since everything that happens is part of the providential order. Must we not, then, advise at least some people to be vicious, for the sake of universal providence?

The Stoics answer the first two questions by appealing to the identity and harmony of individual and cosmic reason. The same cosmic reason is the source of our moral convictions and of our insight into the plan of providence. It would not be cosmic reason if it gave us conflicting guidance from these two sources.

They answer the third question by arguing that it rests on a misunderstanding of the relation between fate, providence, and responsibility. The divine mind foresees the vicious actions and choices that will happen as part of universal providence. But since it foresees that some people will freely choose to act viciously, the fact that these actions are part of the providential order does not alter the fact that agents ought not to do these actions and are rightly condemned for doing them.

In political theory, the Stoics argue once again that our moral convictions harmonize with our understanding of the order of the universe. As we develop, we expand our interests and plans; we extend our concern beyond ourselves to the welfare of others. At first our concern may extend only to our immediate family and friends; but we discover that this limitation of our concern is arbitrary, and that it ought to extend to our fellow-citizens.

So far, the Stoic position can be defended by appeal to Aristotle's arguments about friendship and citizenship (**474, 566**). The Stoics, however, take these arguments to a conclusion that would have surprised Aristotle; they argue that limitation of concern to fellow-citizens (as ordinarily understood) is arbitrary; once we recognize the humanity that we share with other human beings, we cannot refuse to extend our concern to all of them. In extending this concern, we agree with the conclusion of Stoic arguments about cosmic providence; for these arguments show us that we really are fellow-citizens with other human beings. We are all parts of a single cosmic system, and the well-being of each one depends on the proper connection to the whole. This theological cosmopolitanism has some striking parallels in St Paul's letters, whether or not Paul is directly influenced by Stoic views.

620 MARCUS AURELIUS, iii. 11. 1–3   To the aids that have been mentioned let us add this one. Make a definition or sketch of the thing that appears to you and confronts you, so that you can see distinctly the thing itself, what sort of thing it is in its essence,[46] bare and complete in itself; and tell yourself its appropriate name, and the names of the things that compose it, into which it will be resolved. For nothing helps towards a broader view as much as the ability to examine methodically and truly every object that confronts you in life, and always to look at things so that at the same time you form a conception of what kind of universe this is; what use everything has in it; what everything is worth, in relation to the whole and in relation to a human being, who is a citizen of the highest city, of which all other cities are like households; what each thing is, what it is composed of, how long this thing now producing an appearance for me naturally lasts, and what virtue I need in relation to it, such as gentleness, bravery, truthfulness, trustworthiness, simplicity, self-sufficiency, and the rest. And so, in each case, we must say: This comes from God; this accords with the texture and spinning of fate, and this sort of coincidence and chance; this is from a compatriot, kinsman, and associate, though one who does not know what accords with his nature. But I know; that is why I treat him with goodwill and justice, in accordance with the natural law of association.

621 MARCUS AURELIUS iv. 3. 2–4   What makes you discontented? Human vice? Then go over the argument for the conclusion that rational animals are for the sake of one another, that patience is a part of justice, and that people commit errors involuntarily. Then consider how many already, after mutual enmity, suspicion, hatred, and fighting, have been laid out dead, and reduced to ashes; and be quiet at last. But perhaps you are dissatisfied with the part of the universe that has been assigned to you. Then recall this disjunction: either providence or atoms. Remember how many arguments demonstrate that the cosmos is a kind of city. ... [4] If our intellectual part is common, the reason that makes us rational beings is also common. If this is so, the reason that prescribes to us what to do and what not to do is also common. If this is so, law[47] is also common. If this is so, we

[46] *ousia*; **227** n.
[47] Or 'the law'.

are fellow-citizens. If this is so, we share in one citizen body. If this is so, the world is a sort of city. For what other common citizen body is there that anyone will say the whole human race shares in? And this common city is the source of our own intellectual and rational faculty and law-abiding capacity; or what else is their source?

622 EPICTETUS, *Discourses* ii. 5. 24–9 What, then, does it mean to say that some external things are in accordance with nature or contrary to nature? It is as though we were detached <individuals>. For I'll say that for the foot it is in accordance with nature to be clean; but if you take it as a foot, not as a detached thing, it will be fitting for it both to step into the mud and to tread on thorns, and sometimes to be cut off for the sake of the whole body—otherwise it is no longer a foot.[48] We should think in the same way about ourselves also. What are you? A human being. If you consider yourself as detached from others, it is in accordance with nature to live to old age, to be rich, to be healthy. But if you consider yourself as a human being and a part of a certain whole, for the sake of that whole it is fitting for you at one time to be sick, at another time to make a voyage and run risks, at another time to be without resources, and, in some cases, to die prematurely. Why then do you complain? Don't you know that, just as a detached foot is no longer a foot, so you are no longer a human being if you are detached? For what is a human being? A part of a city—of that first city composed of gods and of human beings, and then of the city said to be nearest to the first, a small image of the universal city.[49] 'Then must I be brought to trial?', you ask. Well, should someone else have a fever, someone else sail on the sea, another die, and another be condemned? For it is impossible in such a body, in this universe that surrounds us, among so many living together, for such things not to happen, some to one and others to others. It is your function then, to step forward and to say what you ought to say, to arrange these things as it falls to you.

623 MARCUS AURELIUS iv. 23 Everything that fits you, cosmos, fits me too. Nothing that is at the right time for you is too early or too late for me. Everything that your seasons bring, nature, is fruit for me; everything comes from you, is in you, and goes to you. He[50] says 'Dear city of Cecrops'; and surely we will say 'Dear city of Zeus'.

624 PAUL, Galatians 3: 26 ... in Christ Jesus you are all sons of God through faith. ... There is neither Jew or Greek, slave or free, male and female; for you are all one <person> in Christ Jesus.

---

[48] The individual as part; **558**.
[49] Two cities; **568**.
[50] Aristophanes.

625 EPHESIANS[51] 2: 13   But now in Christ Jesus you who once were far away have come to be near in the blood of Christ. For he himself is our peace, since in his flesh he has made both groups into one and has broken down the dividing wall of hostility.

626 COLOSSIANS 3: 11   ... There is no longer Greek and Jew, circumcised and uncircumcised, barbarian, Scythian, slave and free; but Christ is all and in all.

627 PHILIPPIANS 3: 20   For our commonwealth is in the heavens, and from it we also expect a saviour, the Lord Jesus Christ.

[51] The authorship of Ephesians and Colossians is disputed.

Further Reading

This list is simply intended to give the reader some suggestions to get started. Many of the works listed below include bibliographies. Translations of most of the Greek and Latin texts excerpted in this volume may be found in volumes of the Loeb Classical Library (with facing Greek or Latin; texts and translations of varying quality). Some other translations are listed below.

Abbreviations:
[T]   translation
[C]   commentary or explanatory notes
[B]   includes extensive bibliography
[E]   collection of essays by several authors
[I]   introductory, especially suitable for beginners

REFERENCE

The most convenient general work of reference:

HORNBLOWER, S. and SPAWFORTH, S. (eds.), *The Oxford Classical Dictionary*, 3rd edn., Oxford, 1997.

A shorter work with a more literary emphasis:

HOWATSON, M. C. (ed.), *The Oxford Companion to Classical Literature*, 2nd edn., Oxford, 1989.

A large encyclopaedia covering philosophy and its history:

Routledge Encyclopaedia of Philosophy, 10 vols., London, 1998.

HISTORY

A readable general history, including literature, philosophy, and religion:

[I] BOARDMAN, J., GRIFFIN, J., and MURRAY, O. (eds.), *The Oxford History of the Classical World*, Oxford, 1986.

A multi-volume history of the Greek and Roman world:

The Cambridge Ancient History, 2nd edn., Cambridge, 1970– .

Shorter periods:

[I] BURY, J. B., and MEIGGS, R., *A History of Greece*, London, 1975.
[I] POWELL, C. A., *Athens and Sparta*, London, 1988.
EHRENBERG, V., *From Solon to Socrates*, London, 1973.
HORNBLOWER, S., *The Greek World*, 479–323 BC, London, 1983.
STOCKTON, D. L., *The Classical Athenian Democracy*, Oxford, 1990.
WALBANK, F. W., *The Hellenistic World*, London, 1981.
SCULLARD, H. H., *From the Gracchi to Nero*, 2nd edn., London, 1970.

LITERATURE

Individual authors:

[T] Homer, *Iliad*, tr. R. Lattimore, Chicago, 1951.

[T] Homer, *Odyssey*, tr. R. Lattimore, Chicago, 1967.

[T] Hesiod, *Works and Days and Theogony*, tr. M. L. West, Oxford, 1988.

[T] *Complete Greek Tragedies*, ed. D. Grene and R. Lattimore, 4 vols., Chicago, 1959.

[T] Herodotus, *History*, tr. D. Grene, Chicago, 1987.

[T] Thucydides, tr. R. Crawley, London, 1876.

[TC] Aristophanes, tr. A. H. Sommerstein, 9 vols., Warminster, 1980–94 (Greek and English).

General histories:

EASTERLING, P. E., and KNOX, B. M. W. (eds.), *Cambridge History of Classical Literature: Greek Literature*, Cambridge, 1985.

KENNEY, E. J. (ed.), *Cambridge History of Classical Literature: Latin Literature*, Cambridge, 1982.

LESKY, A., *History of Greek Literature*, New York, 1968.

Some books on specific topics:

LLOYD-JONES, H., *The Justice of Zeus*, 2nd edn., Berkeley, Calif., 1983.

GRIFFIN, J., *Homer on Life and Death*, Oxford, 1980.

GOULD, J., *Herodotus*, London, 1989.

HORNBLOWER, S., *Thucydides*, London, 1987.

TAPLIN, O., *Greek Tragedy in Action*, London, 1978.

MacDOWELL, D. M., *Aristophanes and Athens*, Oxford, 1995.

PHILOSOPHY: GENERAL

Short surveys:

[I] IRWIN, T. H., *Classical Thought*, Oxford, 1989.

[I] LLOYD, G. E. R., *Early Greek Science*, London, 1970.

[I] ——*Greek Science after Aristotle*, London, 1973.

Books covering several periods of ancient philosophy:

GUTHRIE, W. K. C., *A History of Greek Philosophy*, 6 vols., Cambridge, 1962–81.

LLOYD, G. E. R., *Methods and Problems in Greek Science*, Cambridge, 1991.

[EB] EVERSON, S. (ed.), *Companions to Ancient Thought*, Cambridge, vol. 1: *Epistemology*, (1990); vol. 2: *Psychology* (1991); vol. 3: *Language* (1994); vol. 4: *Ethics* (1998).

FREDE, M., *Essays on Ancient Philosophy*, Oxford, 1987.

OWEN, G. E. L., *Logic, Science, and Dialectic*, London, 1986.

VLASTOS, G., *Studies in Greek Philosophy*, 2 vols., Princeton, 1995.

PHILOSOPHY BEFORE SOCRATES

Collections of sources:

DIELS, H., and KRANZ, W. (eds.), *Die Fragmente der Vorsokratiker*, 10th edn., Berlin, 1952. (Greek and German.)

[TC] KIRK, G. S., RAVEN, J. E., and SCHOFIELD, M., *The Presocratic Philosophers*, 2nd edn., Cambridge, 1983.

[T] *Early Greek Philosophy*, tr. J. Barnes, Harmondsworth, 1987.

[TC] McKIRAHAN, R., *Philosophy Before Socrates*, Indianapolis, 1994.

[T] SPRAGUE, R. K. (ed.), *The Older Sophists*, Columbia, SC, 1972.

[T] *Early Greek Political Thought from Homer to the Sophists*, tr. P. Woodruff and M. Gagarin, Cambridge, 1995.

[T] *Hippocratic Writings*, ed. G. E. R. Lloyd, Harmondsworth, 1978.

Volumes on individual Presocratics in the Toronto series (Toronto: University of Toronto Press) include translations and notes:

[TC] Xenophanes, tr. J. H. Lesher (1992).

[TC] Parmenides, tr. D. Gallop (1984).

[TC] Heracleitus, tr. T. M. Robinson (1987).

[TC] Empedocles, tr. B. Inwood (1992).

[TC] Democritus, tr. C. C. W. Taylor (forthcoming).

Books on the Presocratics:

[I] HUSSEY, E. L., *The Presocratics*, London, 1972.

BARNES, J., *The Presocratics*, 2 vols., London, 1979.

FURLEY, D. J., *The Greek Cosmologists*, vol. 1, Cambridge, 1987.

[EB] MOURELATOS, A. P. D. (ed.), *The Presocratics*, 2nd edn., Princeton, 1993.

[E] FURLEY, D. J., and ALLEN, R. E. (eds.), *Studies in Presocratic Philosophy*, 2 vols., London, 1970.

SOCRATES AND PLATO

A complete translation:

[T] Plato, *Complete Works*, ed. J. M. Cooper, Indianapolis, 1997.

Volumes in the Clarendon Plato series (Oxford: OUP) include translations and notes:

[TC] *Protagoras*, tr. C. C. W. Taylor, 2nd edn., 1991.

[TC] *Gorgias*, tr. T. H. Irwin, 1979.

[TC] *Phaedo*, tr. D. Gallop, 2nd edn., 1986.

[TC] *Theaetetus*, tr. J. H. McDowell, 1973.

[TC] *Philebus*, tr. J. C. B. Gosling, 1975.

Some other translations of individual dialogues including useful notes:

[TC] CORNFORD, F. M., *Plato's Cosmology*, London, 1937 (*Timaeus*).

[T] *Laws*, tr. T. J. Saunders, Harmondsworth, 1970.

[TC] *Republic*, tr. P. Shorey, 2 vols., London, 1930–5 (Greek and English).

Books on several aspects of Plato:

[IEB] KRAUT, R. (ed.), *Cambridge Companion to Plato*, Cambridge, 1992.

[E] BENSON, H. H. (ed.), *Essays on the Philosophy of Socrates*, Oxford, 1992.

[EB] FINE, G. (ed.), *Plato (Oxford Readings in Philosophy)*, 2 vols., Oxford, forthcoming.

[I] TAYLOR, C. C. W., *Socrates*, Oxford, 1998.

VLASTOS, G., *Platonic Studies*, 2nd edn., Princeton, 1981.

——Socrates: Ironist and Moral Philosopher, Ithaca, 1991.
——Socratic Studies, Cambridge, 1993.

Studies of individual dialogues:

[I] ANNAS, J., *An Introduction to Plato's Republic*, Oxford, 1981.
BOSTOCK, D., *Plato's Phaedo*, Oxford, 1986.
BURNYEAT, M. F., *Plato: Theaetetus*, Indianapolis, 1990.

Books on particular topics:

[I] VLASTOS, G., *Plato's Universe*, Seattle, 1975.
IRWIN, T. H., *Plato's Ethics*, Oxford, 1995.
WHITE, N. P., *Plato on Knowledge and Reality*, Indianapolis, 1976.

ARISTOTLE

A complete translation:

[T] *Complete Works of Aristotle*, ed. J. Barnes, 2 vols., Princeton, 1984.

A selection:

[TC] *Aristotle: Selections*, tr. T. H. Irwin and G. Fine, Indianapolis, 1995.

Volumes in the Clarendon Aristotle Series (Oxford) contain translation and full notes. They include:

[TC] *Categories and De Interpretatione*, tr. J. L. Ackrill (1963).
[TC] *Posterior Analytics*, tr. J. Barnes, 2nd edn., 1993.
[TC] *Physics I–II*, tr. W. Charlton, 1970.
[TC] *De Generatione et Corruptione*, tr. C. J. F. Williams, 1982.
[TC] *De Partibus Animalium i*, tr. D. M. Balme, 1972.
[TC] *Physics III–IV*, tr. E. L. Hussey, 1983.
[TC] *Metaphysics IV, V, VI*, tr. C. A. Kirwan, 2nd edn., 1993.
[TC] *Metaphysics VII–VIII*, tr. D. Bostock, 1994.
[TC] *De Anima II–III*, tr. D. W. Hamlyn, 2nd edn., 1993.
[TC] *Politics I–II*, tr. T. J. Saunders, 1995.
[TC] *Politics VII–VIII*, tr. R. Kraut, 1997.

Commentaries or notes on individual works:

[C] *Metaphysics*, ed. W. D. Ross, 2 vols., Oxford, 1924.
[TC] *Nicomachean Ethics*, tr. T. H. Irwin, Indianapolis, 1985.
[TC] *Poetics*, tr. R. Janko, Indianapolis, 1987.

Books on several aspects of Aristotle's philosophy:

[I] ACKRILL, J. L., *Aristotle the Philosopher*, Oxford, 1981.
[I] BARNES, J., *Aristotle*, Oxford, 1982.
ROSS, W. D., *Aristotle*, London, 1923 (summary and description of Aristotle's works).
[EB] BARNES, J., SCHOFIELD, M., SORABJI, R. (eds.), *Articles on Aristotle*, 4 vols., London, 1975–9.
LEAR, J., *Aristotle: The Desire to Understand*, Cambridge, 1988.
IRWIN, T. H. *Aristotle's First Principles*, Oxford, 1988.

Metaphysics, natural philosophy, philosophy of mind:

[E] JUDSON, L. (ed.), *Aristotle's Physics*, Oxford, 1991.

[E] GOTTHELF, A., and LENNOX, J. (eds.), *Philosophical Essays on Aristotle's Biology*, Cambridge, 1987.

[I] WITT, C. *Substance and Essence in Aristotle*, Ithaca, 1989.

FURTH, M., *Substance, Form, and Psyche*. Cambridge, 1988.

WATERLOW, S., *Nature, Change, and Agency*, Oxford, 1982.

SORABJI, R., *Necessity, Cause, and Blame*, London, 1980.

[E] NUSSBAUM, M. C., and RORTY, A. O. (eds.), *Essays on Aristotle's De Anima*, Oxford, 1992.

Ethics and politics:

HARDIE, W. F. R., *Aristotle's Ethical Theory*, 2nd edn., Oxford, 1980.

BROADIE, S. W., *Ethics with Aristotle*, Oxford, 1991.

KRAUT, R., *Aristotle on the Human Good*, Princeton, 1989.

[E] RORTY, A. O. (ed.), *Essays on Aristotle's Ethics*, Berkeley, Calif., 1980; similar volumes on the *Poetics* (Princeton, 1992) and *Rhetoric* (Berkeley, Calif., 1996).

[E] KEYT, D., and MILLER, F. D., (eds.), *A Companion to Aristotle's Politics*, Oxford, 1991.

Aristotle and his commentators in antiquity:

[E] SORABJI, R. (ed.), *Aristotle Transformed*, London, 1990.

PHILOSOPHY AFTER ARISTOTLE

Collections of sources:

[TC] LONG, A. A., and SEDLEY, D. N., *The Hellenistic Philosophers*, Cambridge, 1987.

[T] *Hellenistic Philosophy: Introductory Readings*, tr. B. Inwood and L.P. Gerson, 2nd edn., Indianapolis, 1998.

Individual works:

[TC] Theophrastus, *Metaphysics*, tr. W. D. Ross and F. H. Fobes, Oxford, 1929 (Greek and English).

[T] Sextus Empiricus, tr. R. G. Bury, 4 vols., London, 1933–46 (Greek and English).

[TC] Sextus Empiricus, *Outlines of Scepticism*, tr. J. Annas and J. Barnes, Cambridge, 1994.

[TC] MATES, B., *The Skeptic Way*, Oxford, 1996.

[TC] Cicero, *On Stoic Good and Evil (De Finibus III and Paradoxa Stoicorum)*, tr. M. R. Wright , Warminster, 1991 (Latin and English).

[TC] Cicero, *On Fate*, and Boethius, *Consolation of Philosophy*, tr. R. W. Sharples, Warminister, 1991 (Latin and English).

[TC] Alexander of Aphrodisias, *On Fate*, tr. R. W. Sharples, London, 1983 (Greek and English).

[TC] Alcinous, *The Handbook of Platonism*, tr. J. M. Dillon, Oxford, 1993.

General:

[I] LONG, A. A., *Hellenistic Philosophy*, London, 1974.

[I] SHARPLES, R. W., *Stoics, Epicureans, and Sceptics*, London, 1996.

[E] GRIFFIN, M., and BARNES, J. (eds.), *Philosophia Togata I: Essays on Philosophy and Roman Society*, Oxford, 1989.

[E] GRIFFIN, M., and BARNES, J. (eds.), *Philosophia Togata II: Plato and Aristotle at Rome*. Oxford, 1997.

DILLON, J. M., *The Middle Platonists*, London, 1977.

Knowledge and nature:

[I] ANNAS, J., and BARNES, J., *The Modes of Scepticism*, Cambridge, 1985.

[EB] *Doubt and Dogmatism*, ed. M. Schofield, M. Burnyeat, and J. Barnes, Oxford, 1980 (on epistemology).

STRIKER, G., *Essays on Hellenistic Epistemology and Ethics*, Cambridge, 1996.

MATES, B., *Stoic Logic*, 2nd edn., Berkeley Calif., 1963.

[E] *Science and Speculation*, ed. J. Barnes *et al.*, Cambridge, Calif., 1982 (on natural philosophy).

[E] FREDE, M., BURNYEAT, M. F., and BARNES, J., *The Original Sceptics*, Indianapolis, 1997.

HANKINSON, R. J., *The Sceptics*, London, 1995.

Mind:

ANNAS, J., *Hellenistic Philosophy of Mind*. Berkeley, Calif., 1992.

[E] *Passions and Perception*, ed. J. Brunschwig and M. Nussbaum, Cambridge, 1993.

Moral and political theory:

ANNAS, J., *The Morality of Happiness*, Oxford, 1993.

[E] *The Norms of Nature*, ed. M. Schofield and G. Striker, Cambridge, 1986.

Schofield, M., *The Stoic Idea of the City*, Cambridge, 1991.

Source Acknowledgements

RICHARD BOYD, 'Materialism without reductionism', in N. J. Block (ed.), *Readings in Philosophical Psychology* (Cambridge, MA: Harvard University Press, 1980), reprinted by permission of the author.

F. M. CORNFORD, *Plato's Theory of Knowledge* (London: Routledge, 1935), reprinted by permission of Routledge.

D. J. FURLEY, *Two Studies in the Greek Atomists* (Princeton: Princeton University Press, 1967), reprinted by permission of Princeton University Press.

JONATHAN LEAR, *Aristotle: the Desire to Understand* (Cambridge: Cambridge University Press, 1988), reprinted by permission of Cambridge University Press.

G. E. L. OWEN, 'The place of the *Timaeus* in Plato's Dialogues', in R. E. Allen (ed.), *Studies in Plato's Metaphysics*, p. 323, reprinted from *Classical Quarterly* 3 (1953), reprinted by permission of Routledge.

H. A. PRICHARD, *Moral Obligation* (Oxford: Clarendon Press, 1968), reprinted by permission of Oxford University Press.

GREGORY VLASTOS, *Plato's Universe* (Seattle: University of Washington Press, 1975), reprinted by permission of the University of Washington Press.

G. J. WARNOCK, *The Object of Morality* (London: Methuen and Co., 1971), reprinted by permission of Routledge.

BERNARD WILLIAMS, *Morality* (Cambridge: Cambridge University Press, 1976), reprinted by permission of Cambridge University Press.

LUDWIG WITTGENSTEIN, *The Blue and Brown Books* (Oxford: Blackwell, 1958), reprinted by permission of Blackwell Publishers.

Index of Authors and Texts

The references are to the continuous numerical sequence of sections throughout the book, and not to page numbers.

PLOTINUS, AD 204–70. The leading philosopher of later Platonism, founder of 'Neoplatonism'

PLUTARCH, AD 46–after 120. He wrote pairs of 'parallel lives' (each comparing a Greek with a Roman) and a long series of philosophical essays, from a Platonist standpoint

Against Colotes = *Adversus Colotem*, an attack on Colotes the Epicurean, arguing that Epicurean anti-Sceptical arguments are ineffective, and that Epicureanism itself leads to Scepticism

Camillus

Common Conceptions = *De Communibus Notitiis*, arguing that the Stoics violate 'common (i.e. widely accepted) conceptions', even though they claim to argue from them

On the Decay of the Oracles = *De Defectu Oraculorum*

The E at Delphi

Exile

Stoic Contradictions = *De Stoicorum Repugnantiis*, arging that some of the central Stoic doctrines conflict

Superstition

Moral Virtue

Against Epicurean Happiness = *Non Posse Suaviter Vivere Secundum Epicurum*

Table Talk = *Quaestiones Conviviales*

Sulla

Theseus

POSEIDONIUS, c.135–c.50 BC. Stoic. He criticizes and modifies the views of some earlier Stoics, especially with reference to Plato and Aristotle

PROCLUS, AD c.410–485. Neoplatonist, author of commentaries on Plato, as well as of original philosophical works

General Index

The entries refer to numbered sections, not to pages.
Many entries on topics (e.g., cause, virtue) should be consulted together with the entries for the major philosophers under these topics.
If an entry refers to a section of comment, it will normally be useful to consult the texts following that section.